BILINGUAL
VISUAL
DICTIONARY

London, New York, Melbourne, Munich, Delhi

Senior Editor Angela Wilkes
Project Art Editor Katie Eke
Production Editor Luca Frassinetti
Production Controller Linda Dare
Managing Art Editor Lee Griffiths
Managing Editor Stephanie Farrrow

Designed for Dorling Kindersley by WaltonCreative.com
Art Editor Colin Walton, assisted by Tracy Musson
Designers Peter Radcliffe, Earl Neish, Ann Cannings
Picture Research Marissa Keating

Language content for Dorling Kindersley by
g-and-w PUBLISHING
Managed by Jane Wightwick
Translation by Kazumi Honda
Layout by Mark Wightwick
Editing by Cheryl Hutty

First published in Great Britain in 2011 by
Dorling Kindersley Limited,
80 Strand, London WC2R 0RL
Penguin Group (UK)

10 9 8 7 6 5 4
011 – 179043 – May/2011

A CIP catalogue record for this book is available from
the British Library

ISBN 978 1 4053 5984 9

Printed and bound in China by L. Rex Printing Co. Ltd.

Discover more at
www.dk.com

目次 mokuji
contents

42

健康
kenkō
health

146

外食
gaishoku
eating out

252

娯楽
goraku
leisure

この辞典について
kono jiten nitsuite
about the dictionary

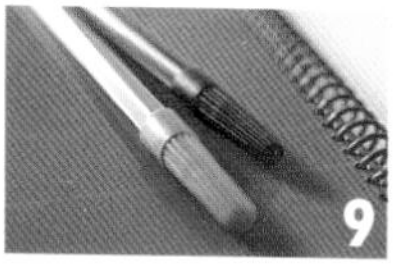

9
この辞典の使い方
kono jiten no tsukaikata
how to use this book

10
人
hito
people

28
外観
gaikan
appearance

56
家庭
katei
home

92
職務
shokumu
services

102
買い物
kaimono
shopping

116
食べ物
tabemono
food

160
学習
gakushū
study

170
仕事
shigoto
work

192
交通
kōtsū
transport

218
スポーツ
supōtsu
sports

278
環境
kankyō
environment

302
参考資料
sankō shiryō
reference

324
索引
sakuin
index

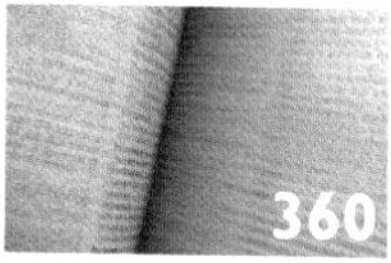

360
謝辞
shaji
acknowledgments

人 hito • people

身体 karada I body	12
顔 kao I face	14
手 te I hand	15
足 ashi I foot	15
筋肉 kinniku I muscles	16
骨格 kokkaku I skeleton	17
内蔵 naizō internal organs	18
生殖器 seishokuki reproductive organs	20
家族 kazoku I family	22
人間関係 ningen kankei relationships	24
感情 kanjō I emotions	25
人生 jinsei I life events	26

外観 gaikan • appearance

子供服 kodomo fuku children's clothing	30
男性服 dansei fuku men's clothing	32
女性服 josei fuku women's clothing	34
装身具 sōshingu I accessories	36
髪 kami I hair	38
美容 biyō I beauty	40

健康 kenkō • health

病気 byōki I illness	44
医者 isha I doctor	45
怪我 kega I injury	46
応急手当 ōkyū teate I first aid	47
病院 byōin I hospital	48
歯医者 haisha I dentist	50
眼鏡店 megane-ten I optician	51
妊娠 ninshin I pregnancy	52
出産 shussan I childbirth	53
代替療法 daitai ryōhō alternative therapy	54

家庭 katei • home

住宅 jūtaku I house	58
住宅内設備 jūtaku-nai setsubi internal systems	60
居間 ima I living room	62
ダイニングルーム dainingu rūmu dining room	64
台所 daidokoro I kitchen	66
調理用具 chōri yōgu kitchenware	68
寝室 shinshitsu I bedroom	70
浴室 yokushitsu I bathroom	72
子供部屋 kodomobeya I nursery	74
ユティリティルーム yutiriti rūmu utility room	76
作業場 sagyōba I workshop	78
道具箱 dōgubako toolbox	80
内装工事 naisō kōji I decorating	82
庭 niwa I garden	84
庭の植物 niwa no shokubutsu garden plants	86
園芸用品 engei yōhin garden tools	88
園芸 engei I gardening	90

職務 shokumu • services

緊急サービス kinkyū sābisu emergency services	94
銀行 ginkō I bank	96
コミュニケーション komyunikēshon communications	98
ホテル hoteru I hotel	100

買い物 kaimono • shopping

ショッピングセンター shoppingu sentā I shopping centre	104
デパート depāto department store	105
スーパーマーケット sūpāmāketto supermarket	106
薬局 yakkyoku I chemist	108
花屋 hanaya I florist	110
新聞販売店 shimbun hambaiten newsagent	112
菓子屋 kashiya confectioner	113
その他の店 sonota no mise other shops	114

食べ物 tabemono • food

肉 niku I meat	118
魚 sakana I fish	120
野菜 yasai I vegetables	122
果物 kudamono I fruit	126
穀類と豆類 kokurui to mamerui grains and pulses	130
ハーブと香辛料 hābu to kōshinryō I herbs and spices	132
瓶詰め食品 binzume shokuhin bottled foods	134
乳製品 nyūseihin dairy produce	136
パンと小麦粉 pan to komugiko breads and flours	138
ケーキとデザート kēki to dezāto cakes and desserts	140
デリカテッセン derikatessen delicatessen	142
飲物 nomimono I drinks	144

外食 gaishoku • eating out

カフェ kafe I café	148
バー bā I bar	150
レストラン resutoran I restaurant	152
ファーストフード fāsuto fūdo fast food	154
朝食 chōshoku I breakfast	156
食事 shokuji I dinner	158

学習 gakushū • study

学校 gakkō I school 162
数学 sūgaku I maths 164
科学 kagaku I science 166
大学 daigaku college 168

仕事 shigoto • work

事務所 jimusho I office 172
コンピュータ kompyūta computer 176
報道 hōdō I media 178
法律 hōritsu I law 180
農場 nōjō I farm 182
建設 kensetsu I construction 186
職業 shokugyō I occupations 188

交通 kōtsū • transport

道路 dōro I roads 194
バス basu I bus 196
自動車 jidōsha I car 198
オートバイ ōtobai motorbike 204
自転車 jitensha I bicycle 206
列車 ressha I train 208
航空機 kōkūki I aircraft 210
空港 kūkō I airport 212
船 fune I ship 214
港湾 kōwan I port 216

スポーツ supōtsu • sports

アメリカンフットボール amerikan futtobōru American football 220
ラグビー ragubī I rugby 221
サッカー sakkā I soccer 222
ホッケー hokkē I hockey 224
クリケット kuriketto I cricket 225

バスケットボール basukettobōru basketball 226
野球 yakyū I baseball 228
テニス tenisu I tennis 230
ゴルフ gorufu I golf 232
陸上競技 rikujō kyōgi athletics 234
格闘技 kakutōgi combat sports 236
水泳 suiei I swimming 238
セーリング sēringu I sailing 240
乗馬 jōba I horse riding 242
釣り tsuri I fishing 244
スキー sukī I skiing 246
他のスポーツ ta no supōtsu other sports 248
フィットネス fittonesu I fitness 250

娯楽 goraku • leisure

劇場 gekijō I theatre 254
オーケストラ ōkesutora orchestra 256
コンサート konsāto I concert 258
観光 kankō I sightseeing 260
野外活動 yagai katsudō outdoor activities 262
海辺 umibe I beach 264
キャンプ kyampu I camping 266
娯楽家電 goraku kaden home entertainment 268
写真 shashin photography 270
ゲーム gēmu I games 272
美術と工芸 bijutsu to kōgei arts and crafts 274

環境 kankyō • environment

宇宙空間 uchūkūkan I space 280
地球 chikyū I Earth 282
地勢 chisei I landscape 284
気象 kishō I weather 286

岩石 ganseki I rocks 288
鉱石 kōseki I minerals 289
動物 dōbutsu I animals 290
植物 shokubutsu I plants 296
市街 shigai I town 298
建築 kenchiku I architecture 300

参考資料 sankō shiryō • reference

時間 jikan I time 304
カレンダー karendā I calendar 306
数字 sūji I numbers 308
計量 keiryō weights and measures 310
世界地図 sekai chizu world map 312
不変化詞と反義語 fuhenkashi to hangigo I particles and antonyms 320
便利な表現 benri na hyōgen useful phrases 322

この辞典について

情報の理解と記憶に視覚的資料が効果的なことは、既に実証されています。その原理に従って図版を主体に作成された本和英ビジュアル辞典は、広範な分野の実用的現代用語を収録しています。

内容はテーマ別に分けられ、レストラン、ジム、家庭や職場から、動物界や宇宙に至るまで、日常社会のほとんどの分野が詳細に網羅されています。さらに会話と語彙の拡大に役立てられるよう、関連用語や便利な言い回しも付け加えられています。

実用的で使いやすく、見ておもしろい本辞典は、日本語に関心のある方に欠かせない参考資料です。

表記法について
本辞典には、日本で一般に使われている漢字仮名まじり表記が使用されています。魚の名前など、漢字でも仮名でも表記できる言葉は、発音ガイドとして載せたローマ字から仮名の綴りが分かるため、漢字の方を使うようにしました。

発音ガイドには、日本語の学習者なら大抵知っているローマ字が使われています。ローマ字の表記法にはいくつかありますが、本書ではもっとも発音しやすいと思われる方法を選びました。なお、長音は母音の上に長音記号をつけて表記しています。

単語はすべて、次のように漢字・仮名、ローマ字、英語の順で掲載されています。

昼食　　　　　旅券
chūshoku　　　ryoken
lunch　　　　**passport**

動詞は英語の後に (v) をつけて示しています。

収穫する shūkaku suru | **harvest (v)**

辞典の後ろには和英別の索引があり、ローマ字または英語で引きたい言葉を調べ、該当する図が載っているページを探すことができます。漢字・仮名の書き方を調べる場合は、先ずローマ字または英語の索引を調べ、該当するページをご覧ください。

about the dictionary

The use of pictures is proven to aid understanding and the retention of information. Working on this principle, this highly-illustrated English–Japanese bilingual dictionary presents a large range of useful current vocabulary.

The dictionary is divided thematically and covers most aspects of the everyday world in detail, from the restaurant to the gym, the home to the workplace, outer space to the animal kingdom. You will also find additional words and phrases for conversational use and for extending your vocabulary.

This is an essential reference tool for anyone interested in languages – practical, stimulating, and easy-to-use.

A few things to note

The three different writing systems of the Japanese script (*Kanji, Katakana* and *Hiragana*) are employed in the dictionary following common usage. However, where alternative usages exist for individual items of vocabulary (for example animals), we have usually chosen to use Kanji since the pronunciation that follows will indicate the Katakana or Hiragana spellings.

The pronunciation included for the Japanese is shown in *Romaji*, the romanization system familiar to most learners of Japanese (see Pronunciation tips).

The entries are always presented in the same order – Japanese, Romaji, English:

昼食　　　　　旅券
chūshoku　　　ryoken
lunch　　　　**passport**

Verbs are indicated by a **(v)** after the English, for example:

収穫する shūkaku suru | **harvest (v)**

Each language also has its own index at the back of the book. Here you can look up a word in either English or Romaji and be referred to the page number(s) where it appears. To reference the Japanese characters, look up a word in the Romaji or English index and then go to the page indicated.

Pronunciation tips
The pronunciation in the dictionary is shown in the Romaji system. There are some variations possible in Romaji, but we have tried to use the most user-friendly transcription.

Many of the letters used in Romaji can be pronounced as they would in English, but some require special explanation:

r	Never rolled; pronounced with the tip of the tongue against the gum of the upper front teeth
f	Pronounced more with the lips and less with the teeth than its English equivalent
w	A semi-vowel pronounced with slack lips
ts	As in "pits"
	ei As in "pay" or "rein"
n/m	The Japanese characters ん and ン are generally pronounced "n" as in さん san, but this changes to "m" before the sounds "b" or "p", e.g. コンピュータ kompyūta.

Japanese vowels are pronounced short similar to the English "pat/pet/pit/pot/put". However, they can also be lengthened. This is shown in the Japanese script by a dash (ー) and in the Romaji by a macron (flat line) over the vowel (ū). Lengthened vowels should have the sound sustained for approximately twice the amount of time.

In general, Japanese words do not have a particular stress, or emphasis. Each syllable is stressed roughly equally. Take care also to pronounce the syllables separately; there are no 'silent' letters. For example, カフェ kafe is pronounced "ka-fay" rather than "kayf".

この辞典の使い方

how to use this book

仕事や趣味、海外旅行の準備で初めて日本語を習う方でも、あるいは既に日本語を知っていて語彙を伸ばしたい方でも、本書は大切な学習ツールとして様々な方法で使うことができます。

　初心者の方は、同源語（外来語など異なる言語で語源が共通する言葉）や派生語（同一言語で語源が共通する言葉）に注目すると語彙の習得に便利です。また、こうした学習によって、異なる言語が互いに影響しあっていることも分かってくるでしょう。たとえば日本語には英語圏から流入した食物関連の言葉が多くありますが、一方、日本から英語圏へ流出した技術や大衆文化に関する言葉も多くあります。

実用的な学習方法
• 自宅、職場、学校や大学の構内を歩いているとき、辞典の該当するページを見てみましょう。そして辞典を閉じ、周りを見回して、名前をいえるものがいくつあるか見てみましょう。
• 単語カードを作り、表に英語、裏に漢字や仮名、ローマ字で日本語を書きましょう。単語カードは常に持ち歩き、頻繁に自分でテストしてみましょう。一回テストが終わったら、次のテストの前にカードを入れ替えましょう。
• 特定のページに載っている単語をできるだけたくさん使い、短い物語、手紙、会話文などを書いてみましょう。これは語彙を記憶し、書き方を覚えるのに役立ちます。長い文章を書いてみたい場合は、一つの文に単語を2〜3語使ってみましょう。
• 視覚的記憶に強い方は、紙に図を描くか写し、辞典を閉じて、図の下に単語を書いてみましょう。
• 自信がついてきたら、ローマ字索引から単語を選択し、該当ページの図を見る前に、その意味を覚えているかどうかチェックしましょう。

Whether you are learning a new language for business, pleasure, or in preparation for a holiday abroad, or are hoping to extend your vocabulary in an already familiar language, this dictionary is a valuable learning tool which you can use in a number of different ways.

　When learning a new language, look out for cognates (words that are alike in different languages) and derivations (words that share a common root in a particular language). You can also see where the languages have influenced each other. For example, English has imported some terms for food from Japanese but, in turn, has exported many terms used in technology and popular culture.

Practical learning activities

• As you move about your home, workplace, or college, try looking at the pages which cover that setting. You could then close the book, look around you and see how many of the objects and features you can name.
• Make flashcards for yourself with English on one side and Japanese/Romaji on the other side. Carry the cards with you and test yourself frequently, making sure you shuffle them between each test.
• Challenge yourself to write a story, letter, or dialogue using as many of the terms on a particular page as possible. This will help you retain the vocabulary and remember the spelling. If you want to build up to writing a longer text, start with sentences incorporating 2–3 words.
• If you have a very visual memory, try drawing or tracing items from the book onto a piece of paper, then close the book and fill in the words below the picture.
• Once you are more confident, pick out words in the foreign language index and see if you know what they mean before turning to the relevant page to check if you were right.

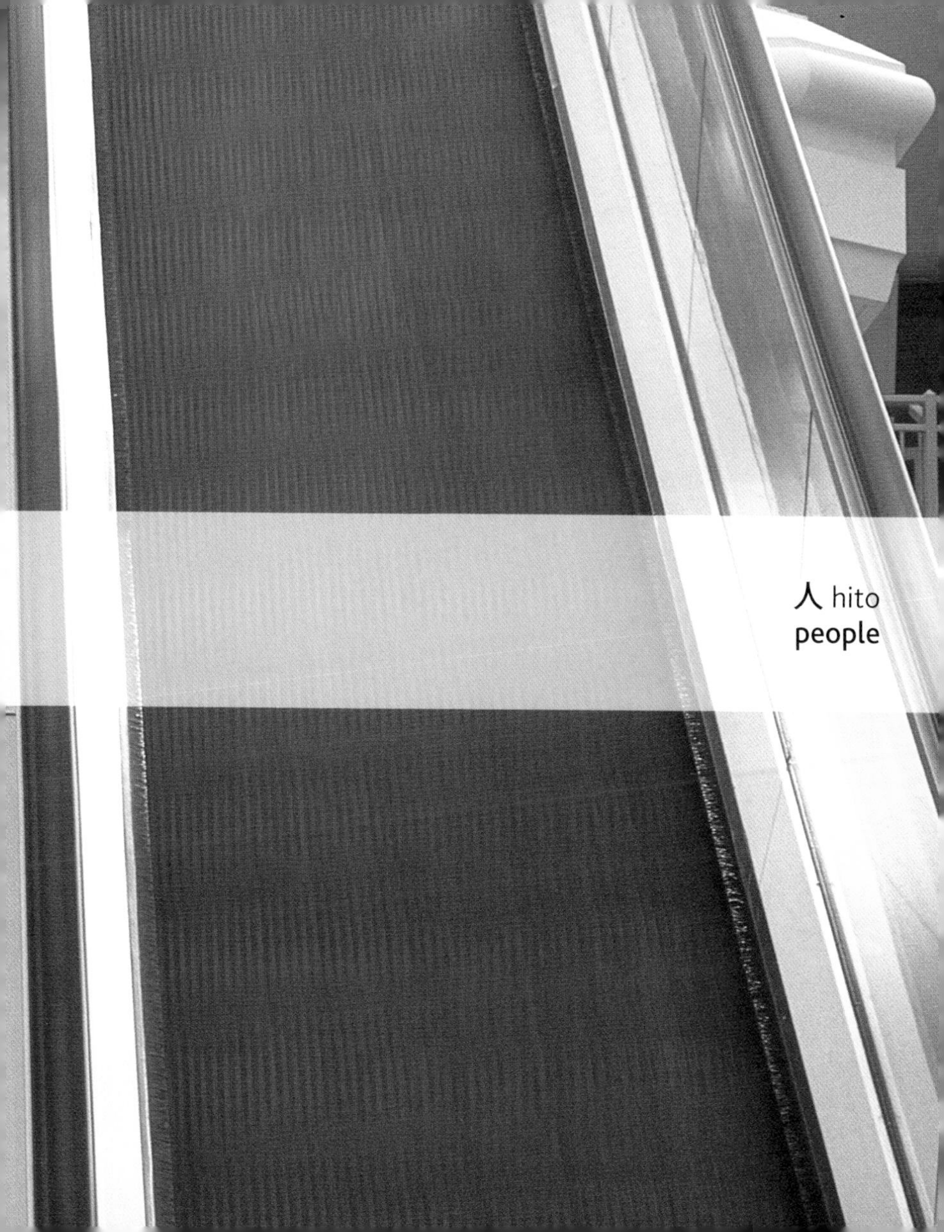

人 hito
people

身体 karada • body

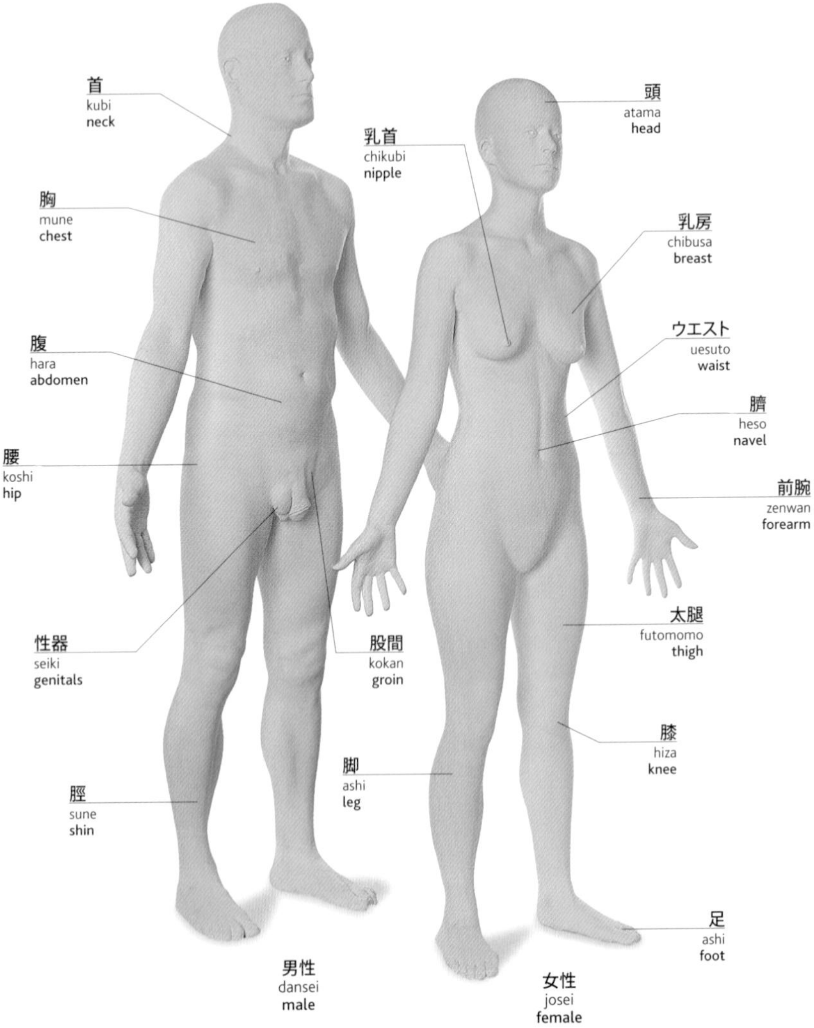

首
kubi
neck

乳首
chikubi
nipple

頭
atama
head

胸
mune
chest

乳房
chibusa
breast

ウエスト
uesuto
waist

腹
hara
abdomen

臍
heso
navel

腰
koshi
hip

前腕
zenwan
forearm

太腿
futomomo
thigh

性器
seiki
genitals

股間
kokan
groin

膝
hiza
knee

脛
sune
shin

脚
ashi
leg

足
ashi
foot

男性
dansei
male

女性
josei
female

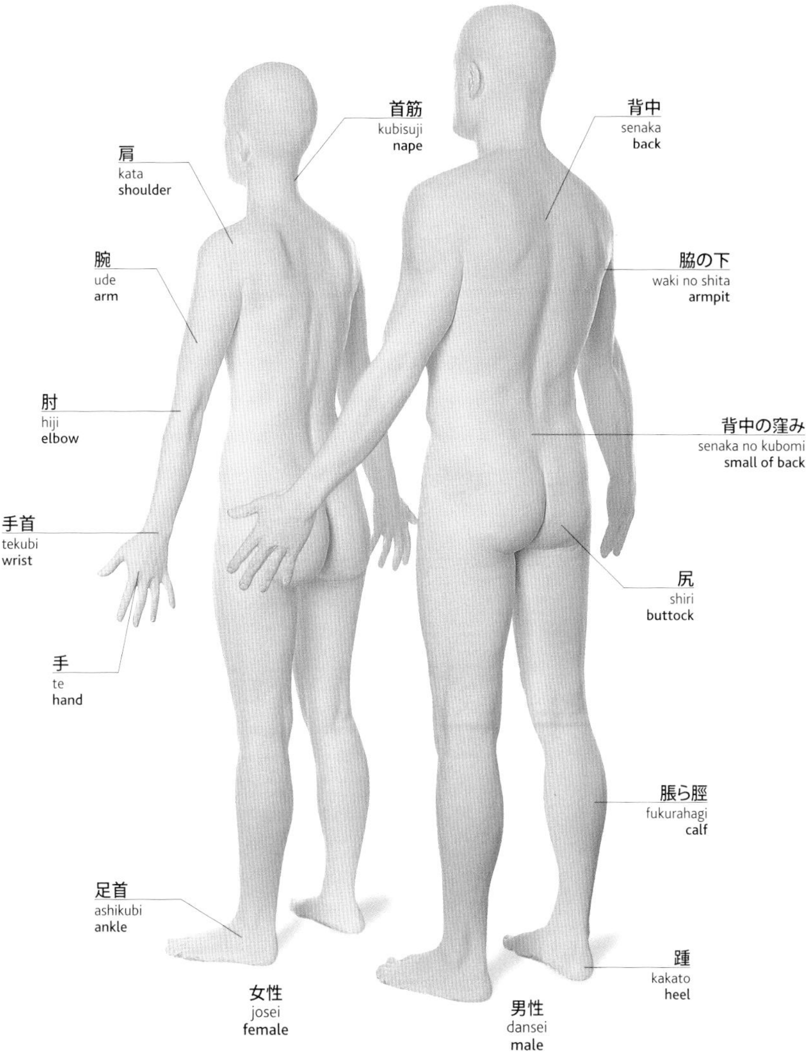

首筋
kubisuji
nape

背中
senaka
back

肩
kata
shoulder

腕
ude
arm

脇の下
waki no shita
armpit

肘
hiji
elbow

背中の窪み
senaka no kubomi
small of back

手首
tekubi
wrist

尻
shiri
buttock

手
te
hand

脹ら脛
fukurahagi
calf

足首
ashikubi
ankle

踵
kakato
heel

女性
josei
female

男性
dansei
male

顔 kao • face

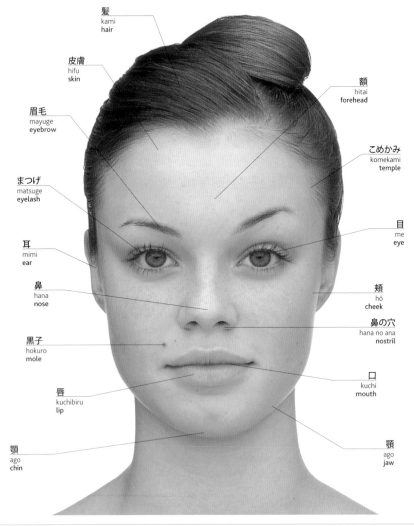

髪
kami
hair

皮膚
hifu
skin

眉毛
mayuge
eyebrow

まつげ
matsuge
eyelash

耳
mimi
ear

鼻
hana
nose

黒子
hokuro
mole

唇
kuchibiru
lip

顎
ago
chin

額
hitai
forehead

こめかみ
komekami
temple

目
me
eye

頬
hō
cheek

鼻の穴
hana no ana
nostril

口
kuchi
mouth

顎
ago
jaw

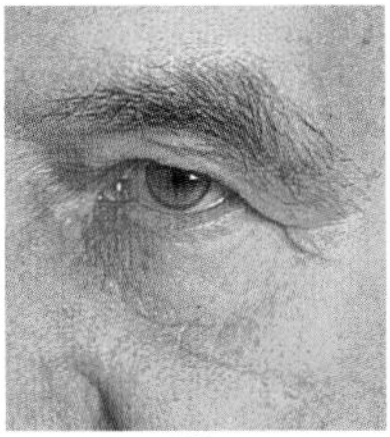

皺
shiwa
wrinkle

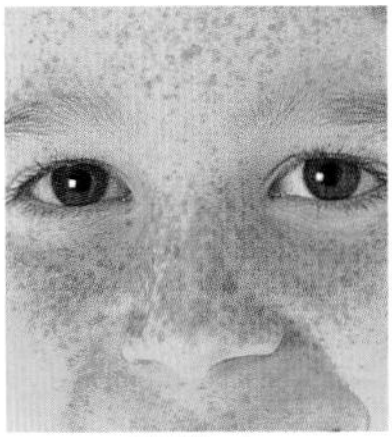

そばかす
sobakasu
freckle

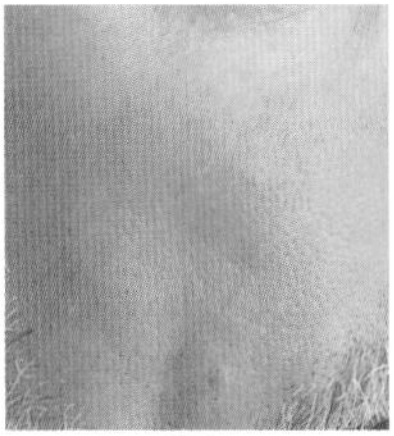

毛穴
keana
pore

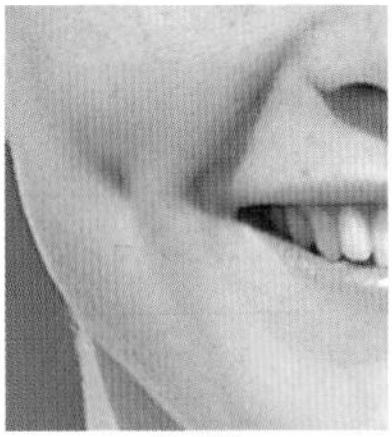

えくぼ
ekubo
dimple

手 te • hand

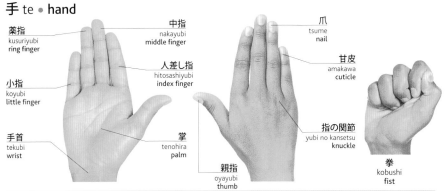

薬指
kusuriyubi
ring finger

中指
nakayubi
middle finger

爪
tsume
nail

小指
koyubi
little finger

人差し指
hitosashiyubi
index finger

甘皮
amakawa
cuticle

手首
tekubi
wrist

掌
tenohira
palm

指の関節
yubi no kansetsu
knuckle

親指
oyayubi
thumb

拳
kobushi
fist

足 ashi • foot

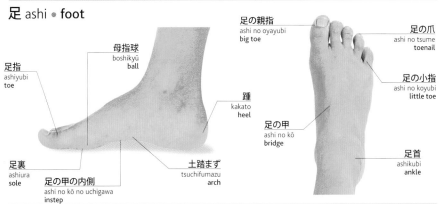

母指球
boshikyū
ball

足の親指
ashi no oyayubi
big toe

足の爪
ashi no tsume
toenail

足指
ashiyubi
toe

踵
kakato
heel

足の小指
ashi no koyubi
little toe

足の甲
ashi no kō
bridge

足裏
ashiura
sole

足の甲の内側
ashi no kō no uchigawa
instep

土踏まず
tsuchifumazu
arch

足首
ashikubi
ankle

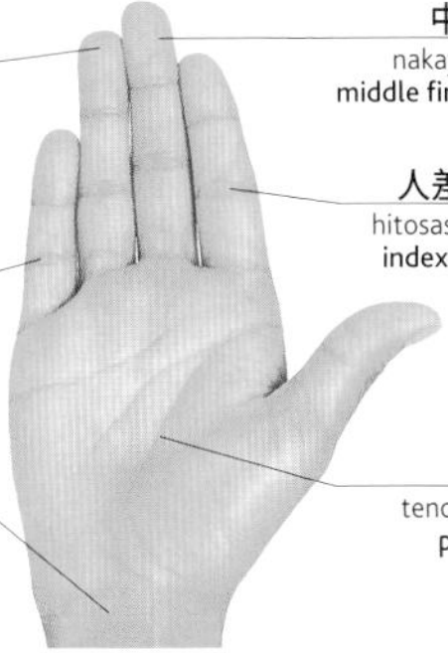

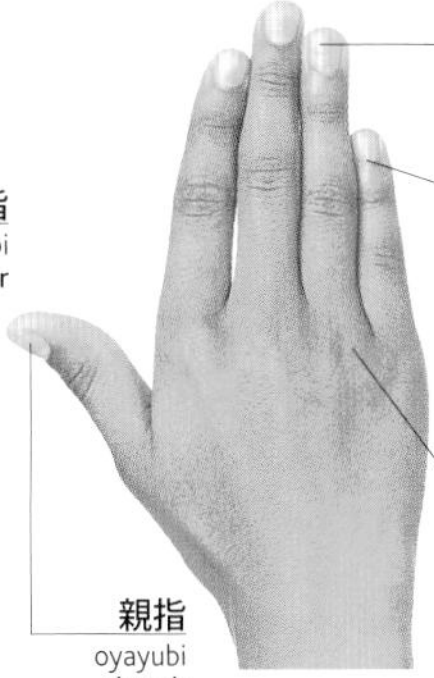

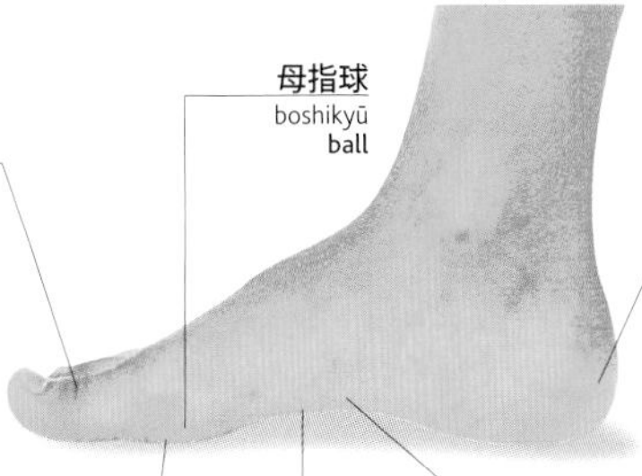

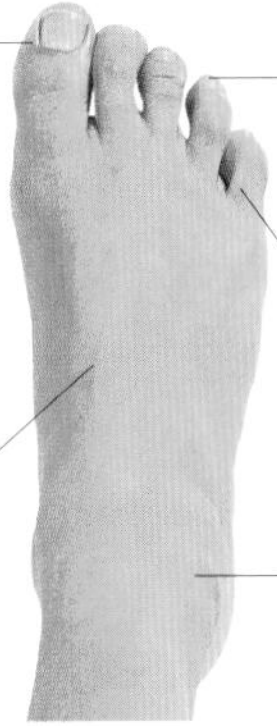

筋肉 kinniku • muscles

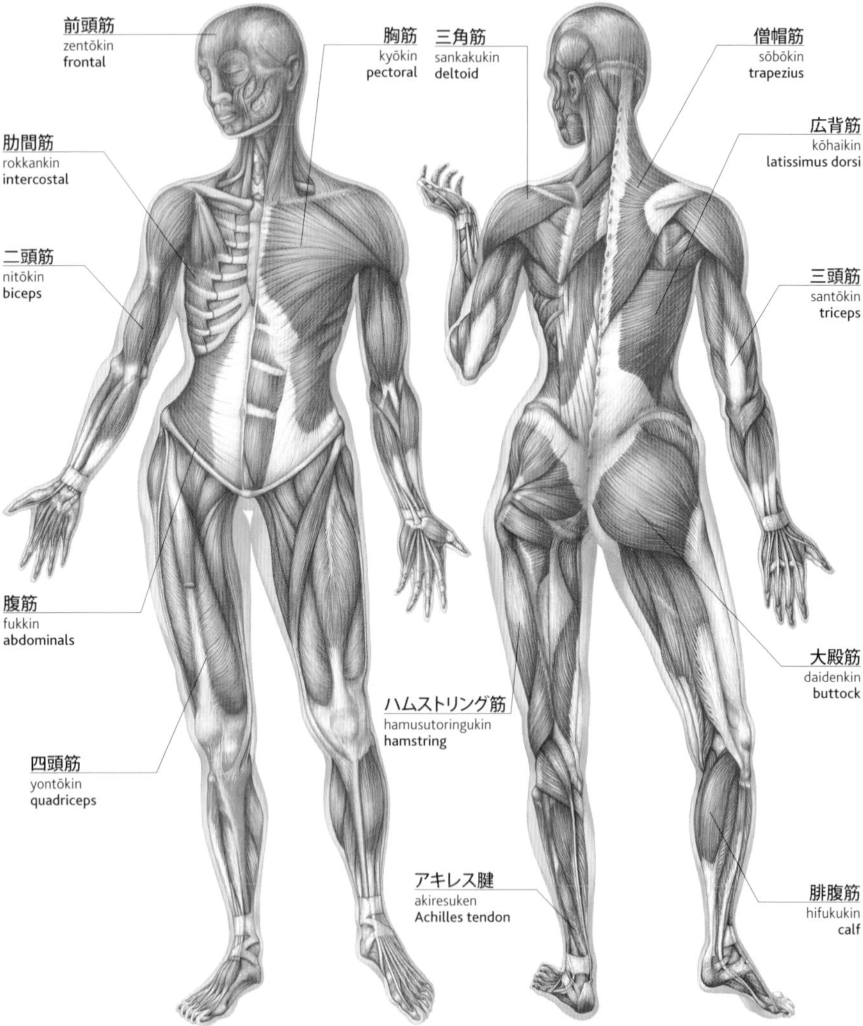

前頭筋
zentōkin
frontal

胸筋
kyōkin
pectoral

三角筋
sankakukin
deltoid

僧帽筋
sōbōkin
trapezius

肋間筋
rokkankin
intercostal

広背筋
kōhaikin
latissimus dorsi

二頭筋
nitōkin
biceps

三頭筋
santōkin
triceps

腹筋
fukkin
abdominals

大殿筋
daidenkin
buttock

四頭筋
yontōkin
quadriceps

ハムストリング筋
hamusutoringukin
hamstring

アキレス腱
akiresuken
Achilles tendon

腓腹筋
hifukukin
calf

骨格 kokkaku • skeleton

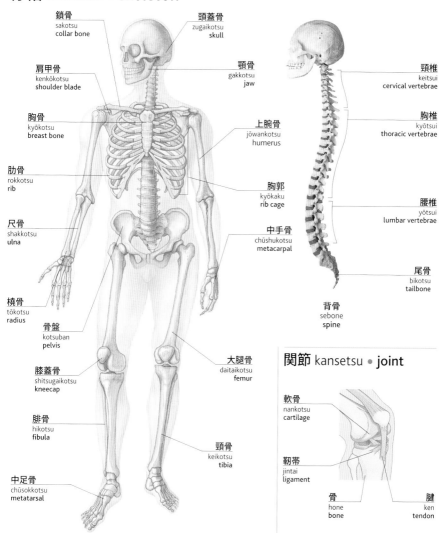

鎖骨
sakotsu
collar bone

頭蓋骨
zugaikotsu
skull

肩甲骨
kenkōkotsu
shoulder blade

顎骨
gakkotsu
jaw

胸骨
kyōkotsu
breast bone

上腕骨
jōwankotsu
humerus

肋骨
rokkotsu
rib

胸郭
kyōkaku
rib cage

尺骨
shakkotsu
ulna

中手骨
chūshukotsu
metacarpal

橈骨
tōkotsu
radius

骨盤
kotsuban
pelvis

膝蓋骨
shitsugaikotsu
kneecap

大腿骨
daitaikotsu
femur

腓骨
hikotsu
fibula

脛骨
keikotsu
tibia

中足骨
chūsokkotsu
metatarsal

頸椎
keitsui
cervical vertebrae

胸椎
kyōtsui
thoracic vertebrae

腰椎
yōtsui
lumbar vertebrae

尾骨
bikotsu
tailbone

背骨
sebone
spine

関節 kansetsu • joint

軟骨
nankotsu
cartilage

靭帯
jintai
ligament

骨
hone
bone

腱
ken
tendon

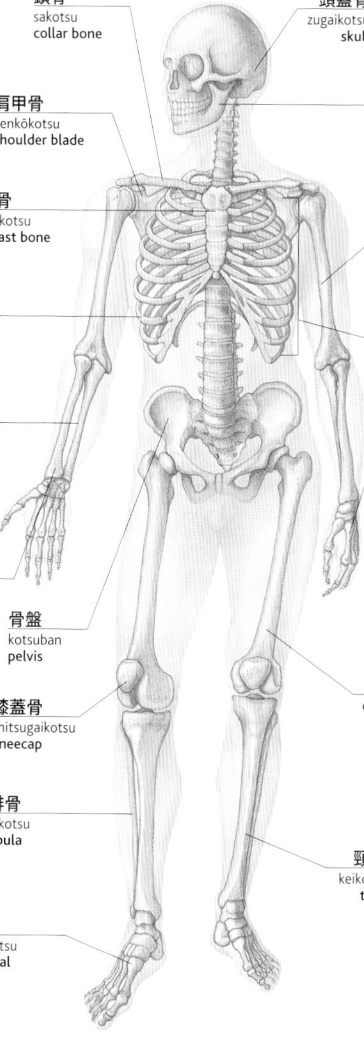

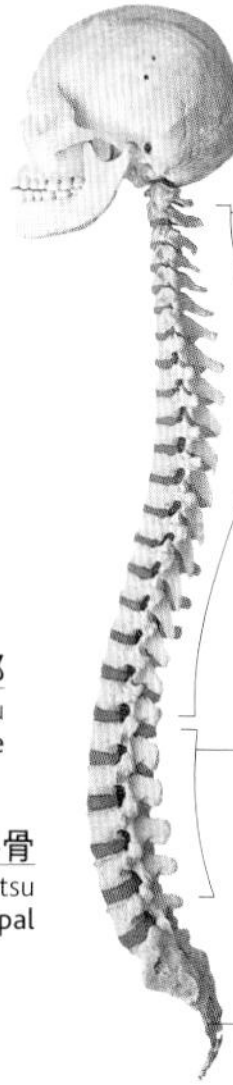

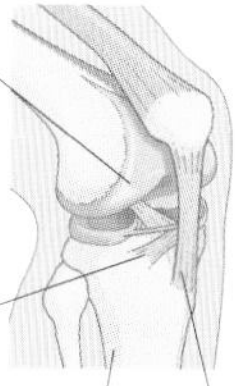

内蔵 naizō • internal organs

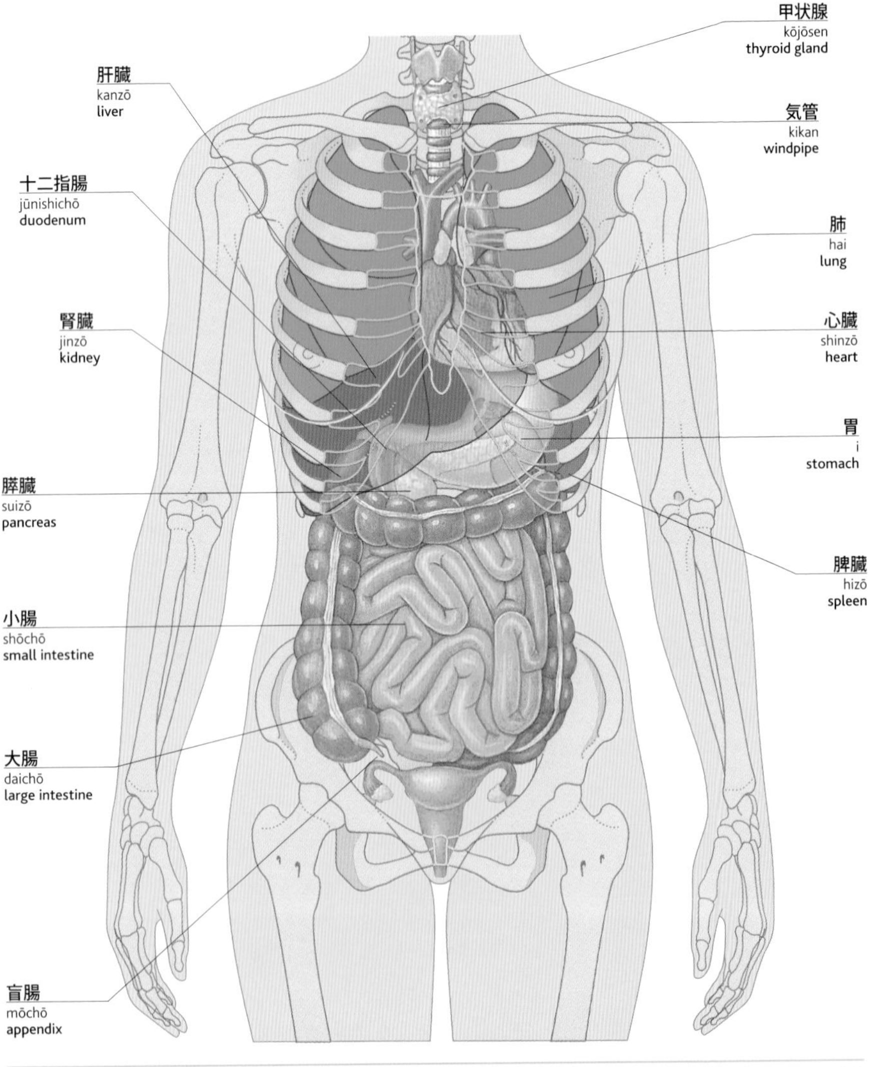

甲状腺
kōjōsen
thyroid gland

肝臓
kanzō
liver

気管
kikan
windpipe

十二指腸
jūnishichō
duodenum

肺
hai
lung

腎臓
jinzō
kidney

心臓
shinzō
heart

胃
i
stomach

膵臓
suizō
pancreas

脾臓
hizō
spleen

小腸
shōchō
small intestine

大腸
daichō
large intestine

盲腸
mōchō
appendix

頭 atama • head

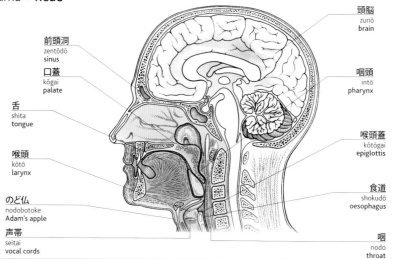

頭脳
zunō
brain

前頭洞
zentōdō
sinus

口蓋
kōgai
palate

咽頭
intō
pharynx

舌
shita
tongue

喉頭蓋
kōtōgai
epiglottis

喉頭
kōtō
larynx

食道
shokudō
oesophagus

のど仏
nodobotoke
Adam's apple

声帯
seitai
vocal cords

咽
nodo
throat

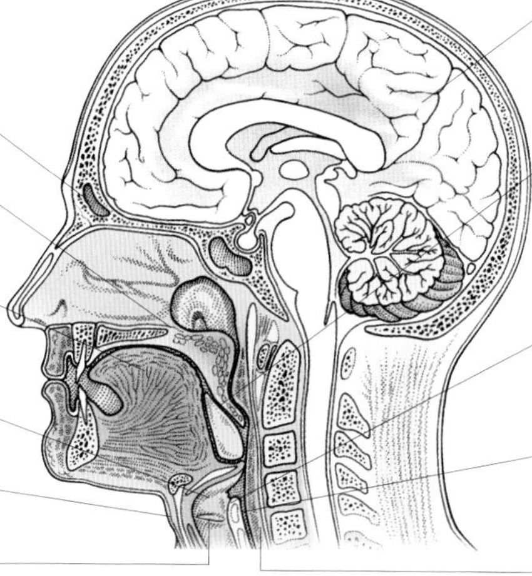

人体系統 jintai keitō • body systems

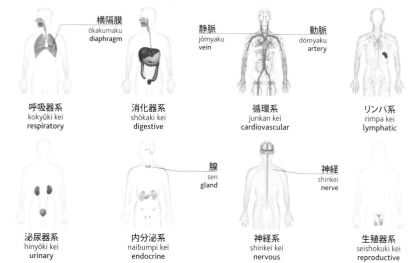

横隔膜
ōkakumaku
diaphragm

静脈
jōmyaku
vein

動脈
dōmyaku
artery

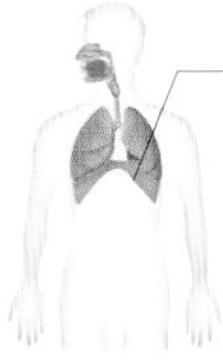

呼吸器系
kokyūki kei
respiratory

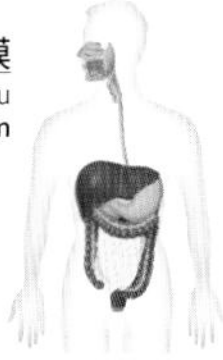

消化器系
shōkaki kei
digestive

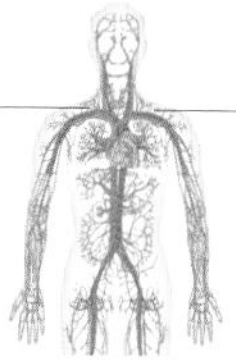

循環系
junkan kei
cardiovascular

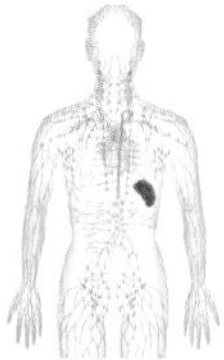

リンパ系
rimpa kei
lymphatic

腺
sen
gland

神経
shinkei
nerve

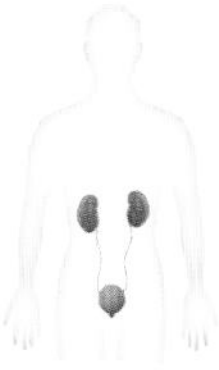

泌尿器系
hinyōki kei
urinary

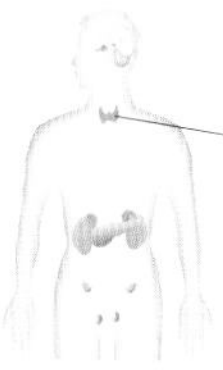

内分泌系
naibumpi kei
endocrine

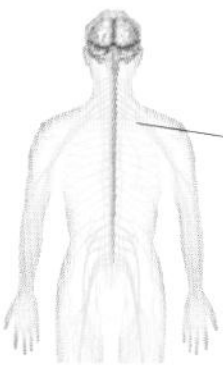

神経系
shinkei kei
nervous

生殖器系
seishokuki kei
reproductive

生殖器 seishokuki • reproductive organs

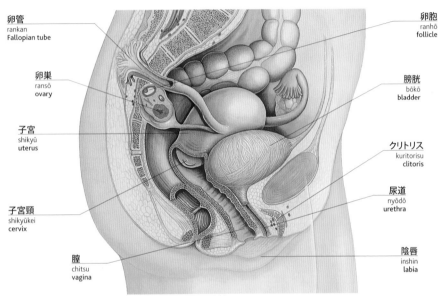

卵管
rankan
Fallopian tube

卵巣
ransō
ovary

子宮
shikyū
uterus

子宮頸
shikyūkei
cervix

膣
chitsu
vagina

卵胞
ranhō
follicle

膀胱
bōkō
bladder

クリトリス
kuritorisu
clitoris

尿道
nyōdō
urethra

陰唇
inshin
labia

女性 josei | female

生殖 seishoku • reproduction

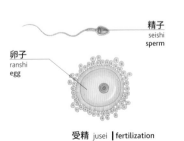

精子
seishi
sperm

卵子
ranshi
egg

受精 jusei | fertilization

関連用語 kanrenyōgo • vocabulary

ホルモン
horumon
hormone

排卵
hairan
ovulation

不妊症
funinshō
infertile

不能症
funōshō
impotent

妊娠する
ninshin suru
conceive

性交
seikō
intercourse

妊娠できる
ninshin dekiru
fertile

月経
gekkei
menstruation

性感染症
sei kansenshō
sexually transmitted disease

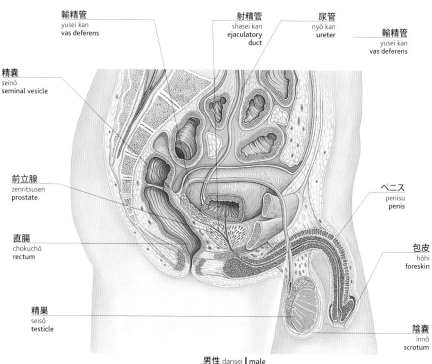

輪精管
yusei kan
vas deferens

射精管
shasei kan
ejaculatory duct

尿管
nyō kan
ureter

輪精管
yusei kan
vas deferens

精囊
seinō
seminal vesicle

前立腺
zenritsusen
prostate

直腸
chokuchō
rectum

精巣
seisō
testicle

ペニス
penisu
penis

包皮
hōhi
foreskin

陰囊
innō
scrotum

男性 dansei | male

避妊 hinin • contraception

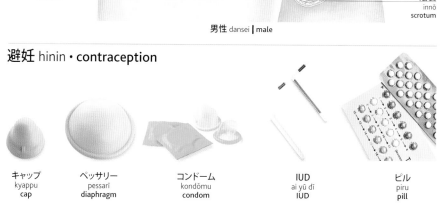

キャップ
kyappu
cap

ペッサリー
pessarī
diaphragm

コンドーム
kondōmu
condom

IUD
ai yū dī
IUD

ビル
piru
pill

家族 kazoku • family

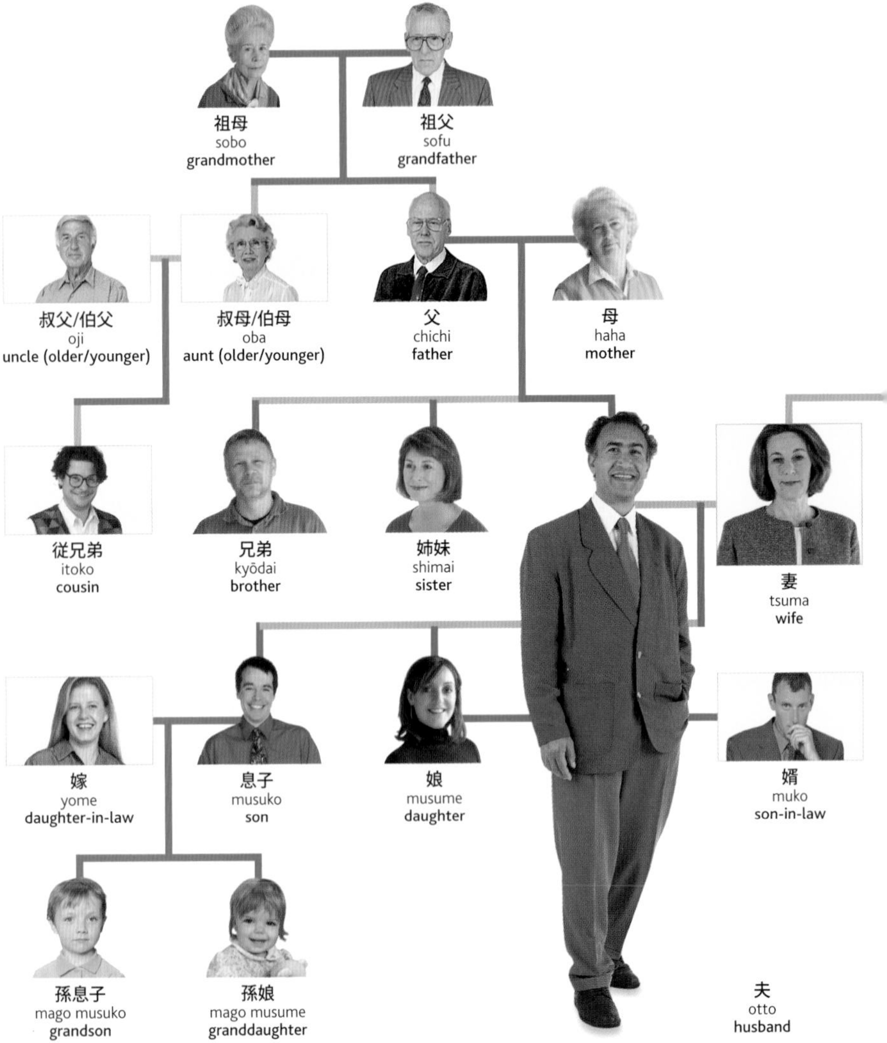

祖母
sobo
grandmother

祖父
sofu
grandfather

叔父/伯父
oji
uncle (older/younger)

叔母/伯母
oba
aunt (older/younger)

父
chichi
father

母
haha
mother

従兄弟
itoko
cousin

兄弟
kyōdai
brother

姉妹
shimai
sister

妻
tsuma
wife

嫁
yome
daughter-in-law

息子
musuko
son

娘
musume
daughter

婿
muko
son-in-law

孫息子
mago musuko
grandson

孫娘
mago musume
granddaughter

夫
otto
husband

関連用語 kanrenyōgo • vocabulary

親類 shinrui relatives	両親 ryōshin parents	孫 mago grandchildren	継母 mama haha stepmother	継息子 mama musuko stepson	配偶者 haigūsha partner
世代 sedai generation	子供 kodomo children	祖父母 sofubo grandparents	継父 mama chichi stepfather	継娘 mama musume stepdaughter	双子 futago twins

義母
gibo
mother-in-law

義父
gifu
father-in-law

義兄弟
gikyōdai
brother-in-law

義理の姉妹
giri no shimai
sister-in-law

姪
mei
niece

甥
oi
nephew

敬称 keishō • titles

さん
san
Mrs

さん
san
Mr

ちゃん
chan
Miss/Master

成長段階 seichō dankai • stages

乳児
nyūji
baby

子供
kodomo
child

男の子
otoko no ko
boy

女の子
onna no ko
girl

ティーンエージャー
tīn'ējā
teenager

大人
otona
adult

男性
dansei
man

女性
josei
woman

人間関係 ningen kankei · relationships

マネージャー
manējā
manager

アシスタント
ashisutanto
assistant

ビジネス・パートナー
bijinesu pātonā
business partner

雇用主
koyōnushi
employer

従業員
jūgyōin
employee

同僚
dōryō
colleague

オフィス ofisu | office

隣人
rinjin
neighbour

友人
yūjin
friend

知人
chijin
acquaintance

ペンパル
pemparu
penfriend

ボーイフレンド
bōifurendo
boyfriend

ガールフレンド
gārufurendo
girlfriend

婚約者
kon'yakusha
fiancé

婚約者
kon'yakusha
fiancée

カップル kappuru | couple

婚約中のカップル kon'yaku-chū no kappuru | engaged couple

感情 kanjō • emotions

微笑
bishō
smile

嬉しい
ureshī
happy

悲しい
kanashī
sad

興奮する
kōfun suru
excited

飽きる
akiru
bored

驚く
odoroku
surprised

怖がる
kowagaru
scared

しか目面
shikame-zura
frown

怒る
okoru
angry

混乱する
konran suru
confused

心配する
shimpai suru
worried

不安
fuan
nervous

誇る
hokoru
proud

自信
jishin
confident

恥ずかしい
hazukashī
embarrassed

はにかむ
hanikamu
shy

関連用語 kanrenyōgo • vocabulary

狼狽する rōbai suru upset	笑う warau laugh (v)	溜息をつく tameiki o tsuku sigh (v)	怒鳴る donaru shout (v)
衝撃を受ける shōgeki o ukeru shocked	泣く naku cry (v)	気絶する kizetsu suru faint (v)	欠伸する akubi suru yawn (v)

人生 jinsei • life events

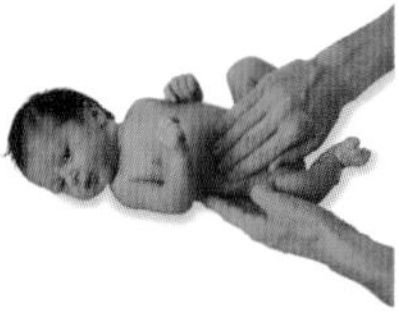

生まれる
umareru
be born (v)

入学する
nyūgaku suru
start school (v)

友達になる
tomodachi ni naru
make friends (v)

卒業する
sotsugyō suru
graduate (v)

就職する
shūshoku suru
get a job (v)

恋愛する
ren'ai suru
fall in love (v)

結婚する
kekkon suru
get married (v)

出産する
shussan suru
have a baby (v)

結婚式 kekkonshiki | wedding

離婚
rikon
divorce

葬式
sōshiki
funeral

関連用語 kanrenyōgo • vocabulary

洗礼
senrei
christening

記念日
kinembi
anniversary

移民する
imin suru
emigrate (v)

退職する
taishoku suru
retire (v)

死ぬ
shinu
die (v)

遺言状を書く
yuigonjō o kaku
make a will (v)

出生証明書
shussei shōmeisho
birth certificate

結婚披露宴
kekkon hirōen
wedding reception

ハネムーン
hanemūn
honeymoon

バルミツバー
barumitsubā
bar mitzvah

お祝い oiwai • celebrations

誕生パーティー
tanjō pātī
birthday party

カード
kādo
card

プレゼント
purezento
present

誕生日
tanjōbi
birthday

クリスマス
kurisumasu
Christmas

祭り matsuri • festivals

過越祭
sugikoshimatsuri
Passover

正月
shōgatsu
New Year

カーニバル
kānibaru
carnival

行列
gyōretsu
procession

ラマダーン
ramadān
Ramadan

リボン
ribon
ribbon

感謝祭
kanshasai
Thanksgiving

復活祭
fukkatsusai
Easter

ハロウィーン
harowīn
Halloween

ディワーリ
diwāri
Diwali

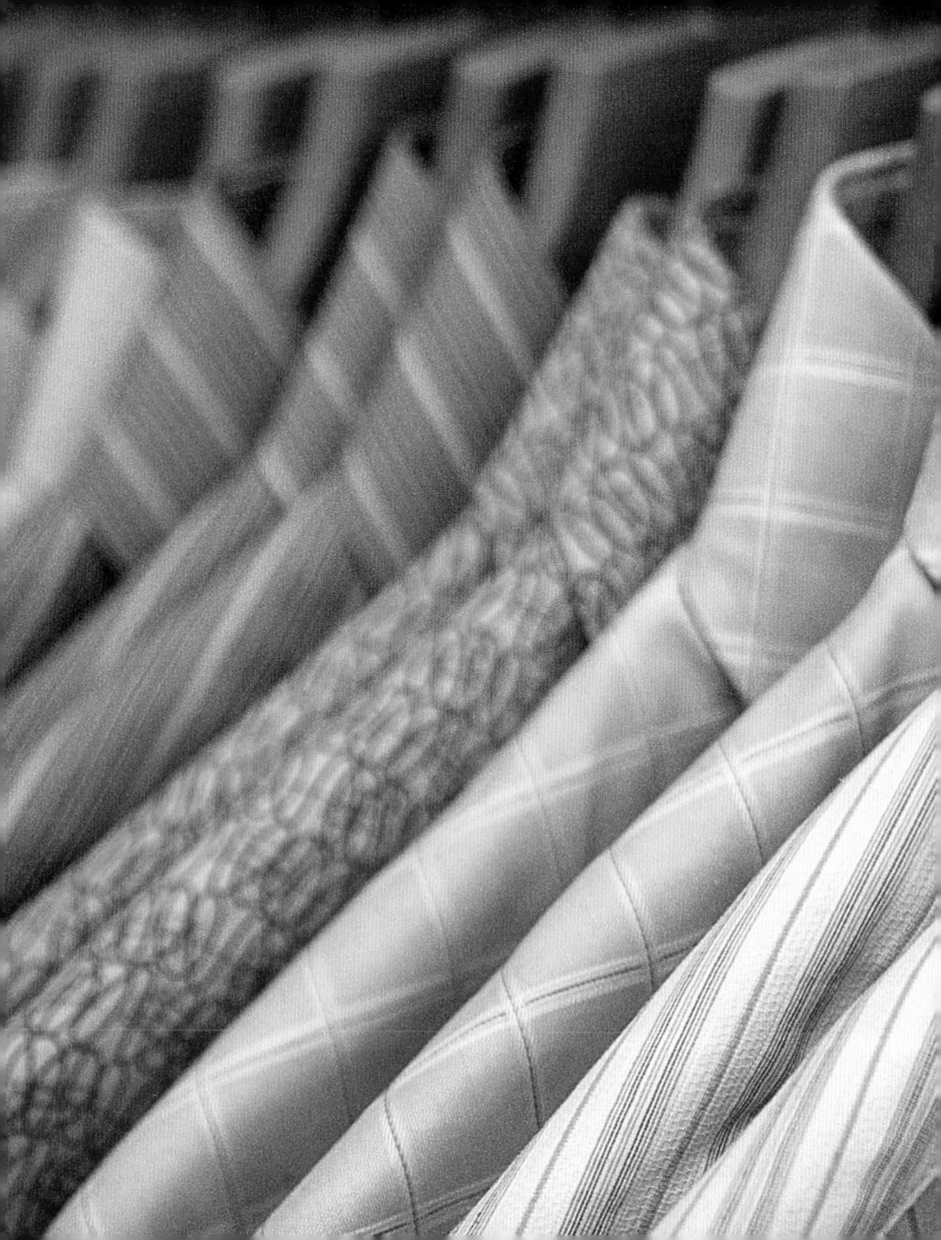

外観 gaikan
appearance

子供服 kodomo fuku • children's clothing

赤ちゃん akachan • baby

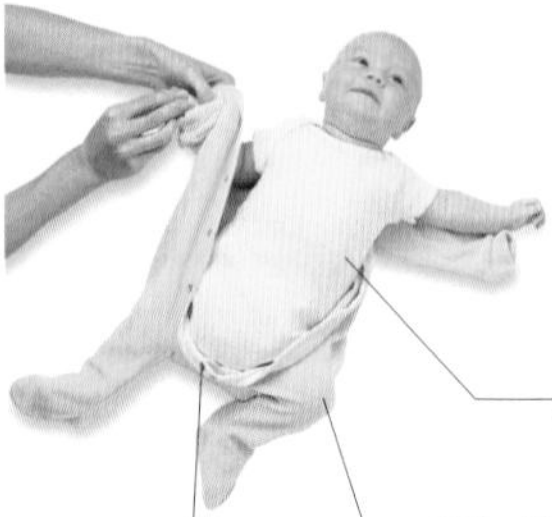

スノースーツ
sunōsūtsu
snowsuit

肌着
hadagi
vest

ベビーグロー
bebīgurō
babygro

スナップ
sunappu
popper

スリープスーツ
surīpusūtsu
sleepsuit

ロンパース
rompāsu
romper suit

よだれ掛け
yodarekake
bib

ミトン
miton
mittens

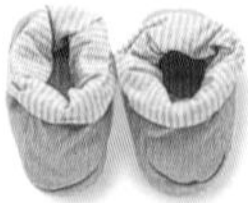

ブーティ
būti
booties

おむつ
omutsu
terry nappy

紙おむつ
kami omutsu
disposable nappy

おむつカバー
omutsu kabā
plastic pants

幼児 yōji • toddler

日よけ帽
hiyokebō
sunhat

エプロン
epuron
apron

オーバーオール
ōbāōru
dungarees

半ズボン
hanzubon
shorts

Tシャツ
tīshatsu
t-shirt

スカート
sukāto
skirt

子供 kodomo • child

ワンピース
wampīsu
dress

フード
fūdo
hood

ジーパン
jīpan
jeans

サンダル
sandaru
sandals

夏
natsu
summer

レインコート
reinkōto
raincoat

リュックサック
ryukkusakku
backpack

トグルボタン
togurubotan
toggle

秋
aki
autumn

ダッフルコート
daffurukōto
duffel coat

マフラー
mafurā
scarf

アノラック
anorakku
anorak

長靴
nagagutsu
wellington boots

冬
fuyu
winter

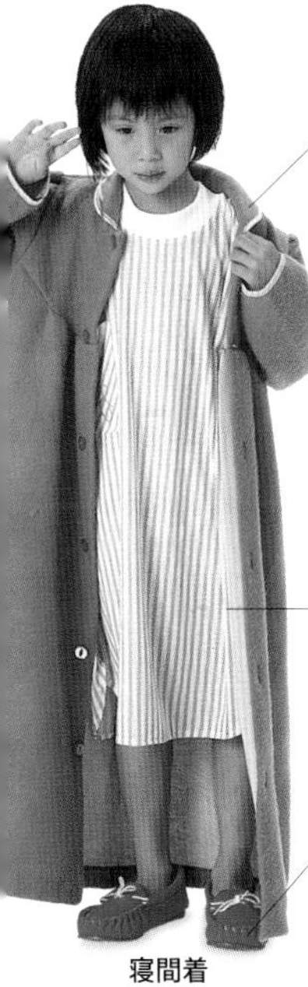

ナイトガウン
naitogaun
dressing gown

ロゴ
rogo
logo

スニーカー
sunīkā
trainers

ネグリジェ
negurije
nightie

スリッパ
surippa
slippers

寝間着
nemaki
nightwear

サッカー着
sakkā-gi
football strip

トラックスーツ
torakkusūtsu
tracksuit

レギンス
reginsu
leggings

関連用語 kanrenyōgo • vocabulary

天然繊維
tennen sen'i
natural fibre

合成繊維
gōsei sen'i
synthetic fibre

洗濯機で洗えますか。
sentakki de araemasuka?
Is it machine washable?

2歳児に着れますか。
nisai-ji ni kiremasuka?
Will this fit a two-year-old?

男性服 dansei fuku • men's clothing

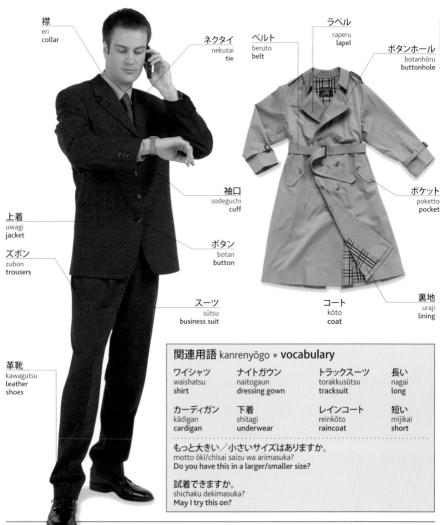

襟
eri
collar

ネクタイ
nekutai
tie

ベルト
beruto
belt

ラベル
raperu
lapel

ボタンホール
botanhōru
buttonhole

袖口
sodeguchi
cuff

ポケット
poketto
pocket

上着
uwagi
jacket

ズボン
zubon
trousers

ボタン
botan
button

スーツ
sūtsu
business suit

コート
kōto
coat

裏地
uraji
lining

革靴
kawagutsu
leather
shoes

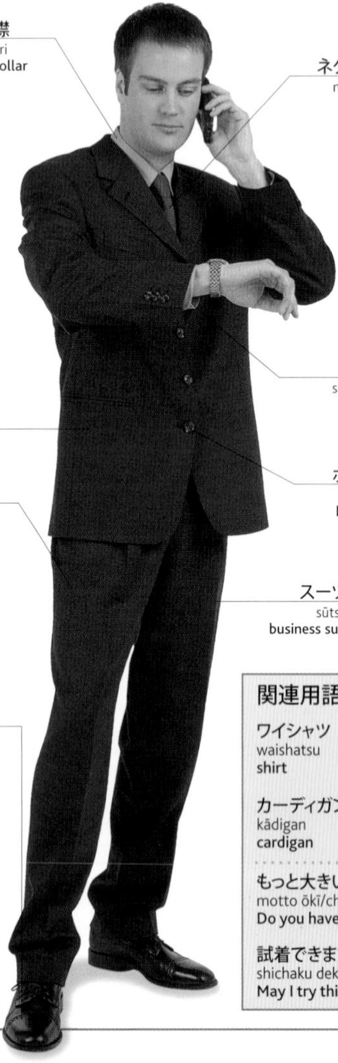

関連用語 kanrenyōgo • vocabulary

ワイシャツ waishatsu shirt	ナイトガウン naitogaun dressing gown	トラックスーツ torakkusūtsu tracksuit	長い nagai long
カーディガン kādigan cardigan	下着 shitagi underwear	レインコート reinkōto raincoat	短い mijikai short

もっと大きい／小さいサイズはありますか。
motto ōkī/chīsai saizu wa arimasuka?
Do you have this in a larger/smaller size?

試着できますか。
shichaku dekimasuka?
May I try this on?

ブレザー
burezā
blazer

スポーツジャケット
supōtsu jaketto
sports jacket

ベスト
besuto
waistcoat

Vネック
buinekku
v-neck

丸首
marukubi
round neck

Tシャツ
tīshatsu
t-shirt

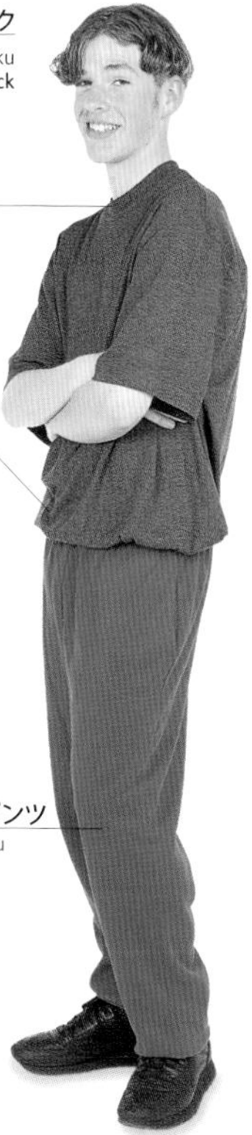

アノラック
anorakku
anorak

トレーナー
torēnā
sweatshirt

ウインドブレーカー
uindoburēkā
windcheater

スエットパンツ
suettopantsu
sweatpants

セーター
sētā
sweater

パジャマ
pajama
pyjamas

肌着
hadagi
vest

カジュアルウェア
kajuaruwea
casual wear

短パン
tampan
shorts

ブリーフ
burīfu
briefs

ボクサーショーツ
bokusāshōtsu
boxer shorts

靴下
kutsushita
socks

女性服 josei fuku • women's clothing

ネックライン
nekkurain
neckline

ジャケット
jaketto
jacket

縫い目
nuime
seam

袖
sode
sleeve

くるぶし丈
kurubushi-take
ankle-length

スカート
sukāto
skirt

裾
suso
hem

膝丈
hiza-take
knee-length

パンスト
pansuto
tights

靴
kutsu
shoes

ストラップレス
sutorappuresu
strapless

ノースリーブ
nōsurību
sleeveless

イブニングドレス
ibuningudoresu
evening dress

ワンピース
wampīsu
dress

ブラウス
burausu
blouse

スラックス
surakkusu
trousers

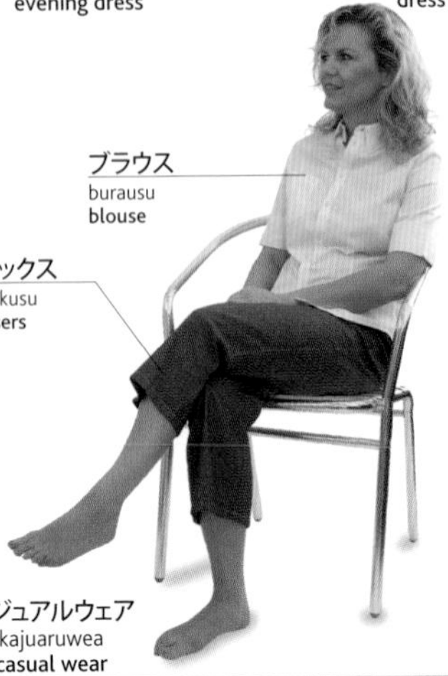

カジュアルウェア
kajuaruwea
casual wear

ランジェリー ranjerī • lingerie

結婚式 kekkonshiki • wedding

ストラップ
sutorappu
strap

ナイトガウン
naitogaun
negligée

スリップ
surippu
slip

キャミソール
kyamisōru
camisole

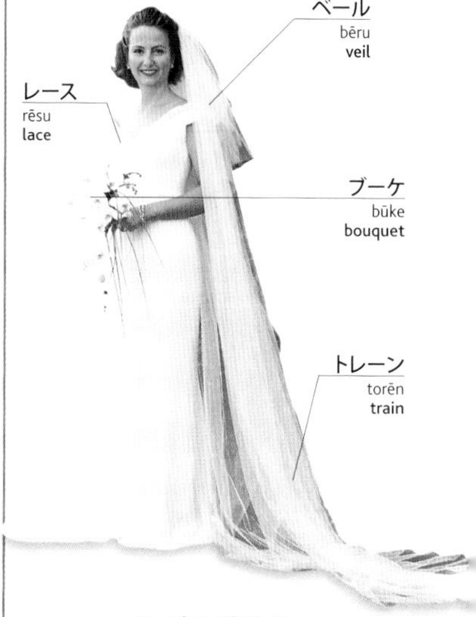

ベール
bēru
veil

レース
rēsu
lace

ブーケ
būke
bouquet

トレーン
torēn
train

ガーター
gātā
suspenders

バスク
basuku
basque

ストッキング
sutokkingu
stockings

パンスト
pansuto
tights

ウェディングドレス
wedingudoresu
wedding dress

ベスト
besuto
vest

ブラジャー
burajā
bra

パンティ
panti
knickers

ネグリジェ
negurije
nightdress

関連用語 kanrenyōgo • vocabulary

コルセット korusetto **corset**	**テーラード** tērādo **tailored**
ガーター gātā **garter**	**ホールターネック** hōrutā nekku **halter neck**
ショルダーパッド shorudāpaddo **shoulder pad**	**ワイヤーカップ** waiyā kappu **underwired**
ウエストバンド uesutobando **waistband**	**スポーツ用ブラジャー** supōtsu-yō burajā **sports bra**
着物 kimono **kimono**	

装身具 sōshingu • accessories

バックル
bakkuru
buckle

柄
e
handle

野球帽
yakyūbō
cap

帽子
bōshi
hat

スカーフ
sukāfu
scarf

ベルト
beruto
belt

先端
sentan
tip

ハンカチ
hankachi
handkerchief

蝶ネクタイ
chōnekutai
bow tie

ネクタイピン
nekutaipin
tie-pin

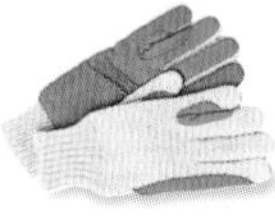

手袋
tebukuro
gloves

傘
kasa
umbrella

アクセサリー akusesarī • jewellery

真珠の首飾
shinju no kubikaz
string of pea

ペンダント
pendanto
pendant

ブローチ
burōchi
brooch

カフスボタン
kafusubotan
cufflink

リンク
rinku
link

クラスプ
kurasupu
clasp

イヤリング
iyaringu
earring

指輪
yubiwa
ring

宝石
hōseki
stone

ネックレス
nekkuresu
necklace

腕時計
udedokei
watch

ブレスレット
buresuretto
bracelet

チェーン
chēn
chain

宝石箱 hōseki-bako | jewellery box

バッグ baggu • bags

札入れ
satsuire
wallet

財布
saifu
purse

ショルダーバッグ
shorudābaggu
shoulder bag

留め金
tomegane
fastening

ストラップ
sutorappu
shoulder strap

取っ手
totte
handles

旅行鞄
ryokōkaban
holdall

ブリーフケース
burīfukēsu
briefcase

ハンドバッグ
handobaggu
handbag

リュックサック
ryukkusakku
backpack

靴 kutsu • shoes

靴紐穴
kutsuhimo ana
eyelet

靴紐
kutsuhimo
lace

ベロ
bero
tongue

底
:suzoko
e

踵
kakato
heel

編上靴
amiagegutsu
lace-up

ハイキングブーツ
haikingu būtsu
walking boot

スニーカー
sunīkā
trainer

革靴
kawagutsu
leather shoe

ゴム草履
gomuzōri
flip-flop

ハイヒール
haihīru
high heel shoe

プラットフォームシューズ
purattofōmu shūzu
platform shoe

サンダル
sandaru
sandal

スリッポン
surippon
slip-on

短靴
tangutsu
brogue

髪 kami • hair

櫛
kushi
comb

櫛で梳く
kushi de suku
comb (v)

ヘアブラシ
heaburashi
brush

ブラシをかける
burashi o kakeru | **brush (v)**

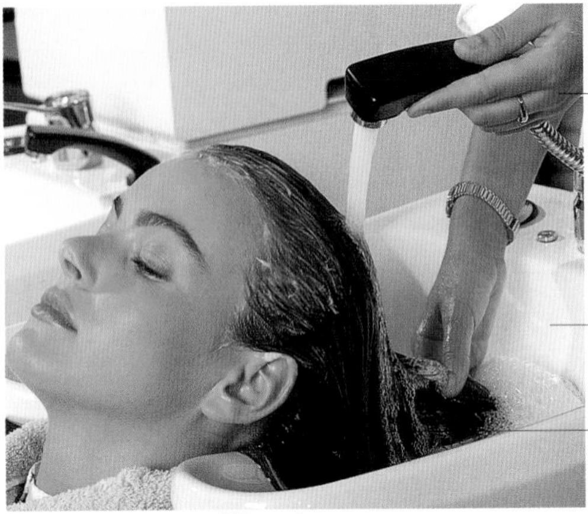

髪結い
kamiyui
hairdresser

シャンプー台
shampū dai
sink

客
kyaku
client

洗う arau | **wash (v)**

ガウン
gaun
robe

濯ぐ
yusugu
rinse (v)

カットする
katto suru
cut (v)

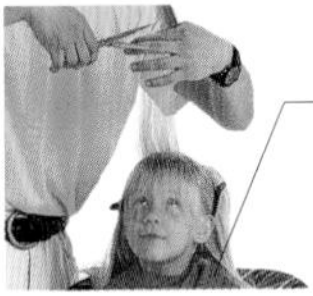

ブローする
burō suru
blow dry (v)

セットする
setto suru
set (v)

備品 bihin • accessories

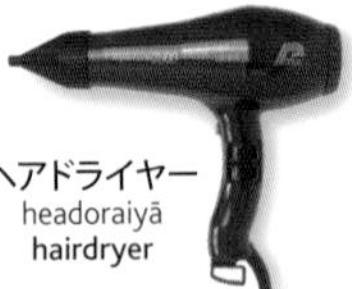

ヘアドライヤー
headoraiyā
hairdryer

シャンプー
shampū
shampoo

コンディショナー
kondishonā
conditioner

ジェル
jeru
gel

ヘアスプレー
heasupurē
hairspray

カールアイロン
kāru airon
curling tongs

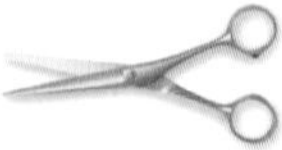

鋏
hasami
scissors

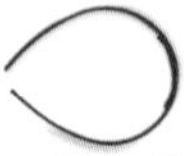

ヘアバンド
heabando
hairband

カーラー
kārā
curler

ヘアピン
heapin
hairpin

髪型 kamigata • **styles**

リボン
ribon
ribbon

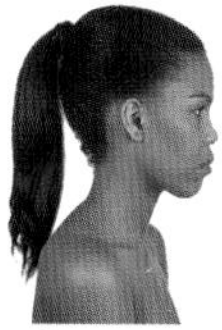

ポニーテール
ponītēru
ponytail

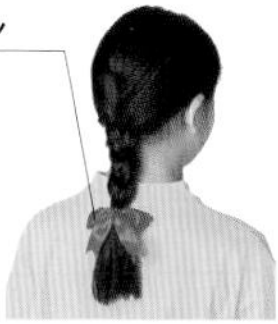

三つ編み
mitsuami
plait

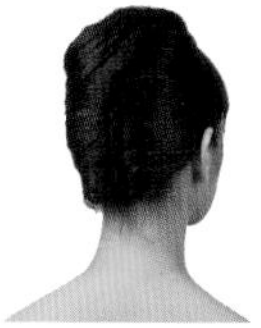

フレンチプリーツ
furenchi purītsu
french pleat

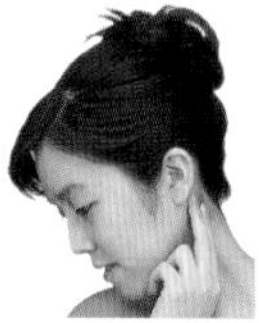

お団子
odango
bun

お下げ
osage
pigtails

ボブ
bobu
bob

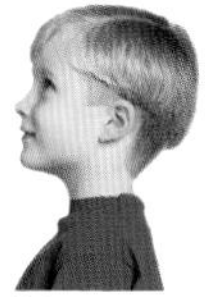

坊ちゃん刈り
botchangari
crop

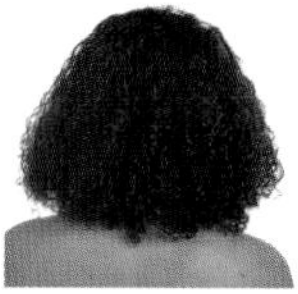

カール
kāru
curly

パーマ
pāma
perm

ストレート
sutorēto
straight

毛根
mōkon
roots

ハイライト
hairaito
highlights

はげ頭
hageatama
bald

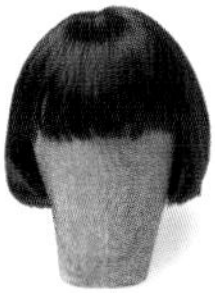

髪
katsura
wig

関連用語 kanrenyōgo • **vocabulary**

整髪する	脂質
seihatsu suru	abura shitsu
trim (v)	**greasy**
ストレートにする	乾燥質
sutorēto ni suru	kansō shitsu
straighten (v)	**dry**
床屋	普通
tokoya	futsū
barber	**normal**
フケ	頭皮
fuke	tōhi
dandruff	**scalp**
枝毛	ヘアタイ
edage	heatai
split ends	**hairtie**

ヘアカラー hea karā • **colours**

ブロンド
burondo
blonde

ブルネット
burunetto
brunette

赤茶色
akachairo
auburn

赤毛
akage
ginger

黒髪
kurokami
black

グレー
gurē
grey

ホワイト
howaito
white

染髪
sempatsu
dyed

美容 biyō ● beauty

ヘアカラー
heakarā
hair dye

アイシャドー
aishadō
eye shadow

マスカラ
masukara
mascara

アイライナー
airainā
eyeliner

頬紅
hōbeni
blusher

ファンデーション
fandēshon
foundation

口紅
kuchibeni
lipstick

メーキャップ mēkyappu ● make-up

アイブロウペンシル
aiburow penshiru
eyebrow pencil

アイブロウブラシ
aiburow burashi
eyebrow brush

毛抜き
kenuki
tweezers

リップグロス
rippu gurosu
lip gloss

リップブラシ
rippu burashi
lip brush

リップライナー
rippu rainā
lip liner

ブラシ
burashi
brush

コンシーラー
konshīrā
concealer

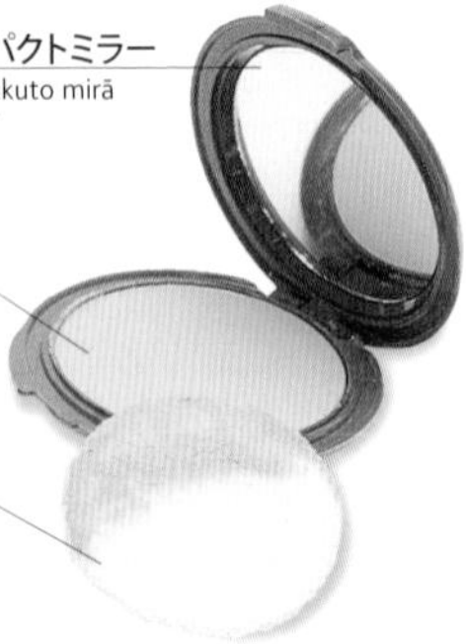

コンパクトミラー
kompakuto mirā
mirror

白粉
oshiroi
face powder

パフ
pafu
powder puff

コンパクト kompakuto | compact

エステ esute · beauty treatments

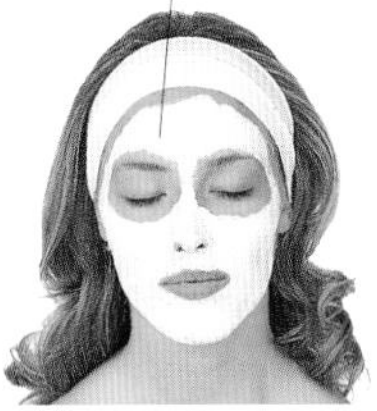

フェースパック
fēsu pakku
face pack

サンベッド
sambeddo
sunbed

フェーシャル
fēsharu
facial

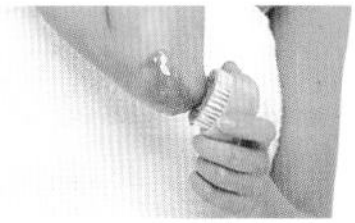

角質除去する
kakushitsu jokyo suru
exfoliate (v)

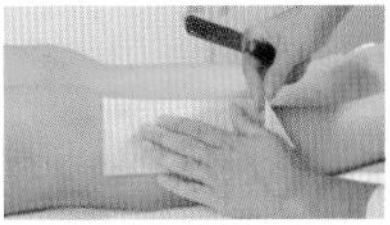

ワックス
wakkusu
wax

ペディキュア
pedikyua
pedicure

化粧品 keshōhin · toiletries

クレンザー
kurenzā
cleanser

化粧水
keshōsui
toner

乳液
nyūeki
moisturizer

セルフタンニング・クリーム
serufu tanningu kurīmu
self-tanning cream

香水
kōsui
perfume

オードトワレ
ōdotoware
eau de toilette

マニキュア manikyua · manicure

除光液
jokō eki
nail varnish remover

爪やすり
tsume yasuri
nail file

マニキュア
manikyua
nail varnish

爪切り鋏
tsumekiri-basami
nail scissors

爪切り
tsumekiri
nail clippers

関連用語 kanrenyōgo · vocabulary

肌の色 hada no iro **complexion**	脂肌 abura hada **oily**	日焼け hiyake **tan**
色白 irojiro **fair**	敏感肌 binkan hada **sensitive**	入れ墨 irezumi **tattoo**
色黒 iroguro **dark**	低刺激性 tei-shigeki sei **hypoallergenic**	皺取り shiwa tori **anti-wrinkle**
乾燥肌 kansō hada **dry**	色合い iroai **shade**	コットンボール kotton bōru **cotton balls**

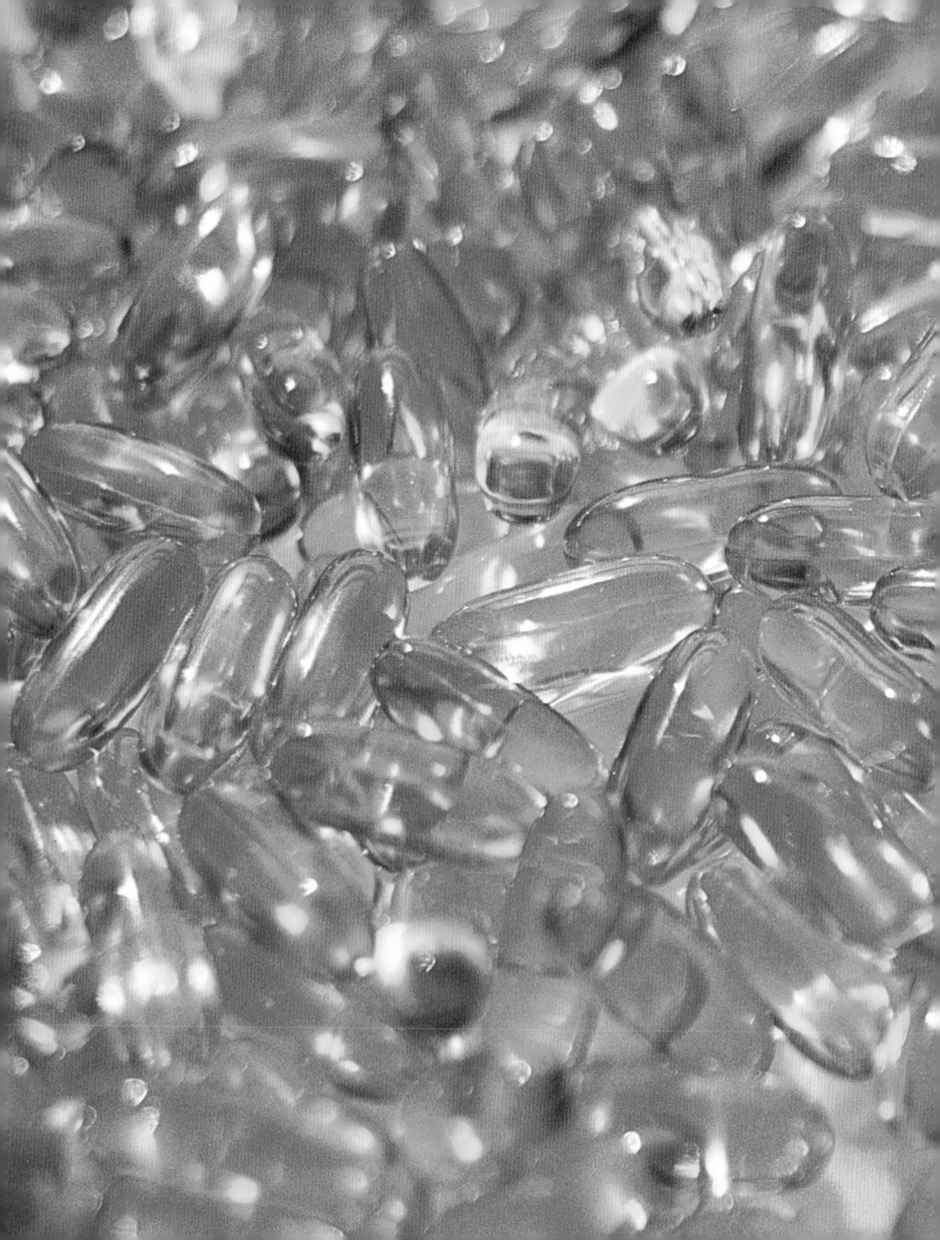

健康 kenkō
health

病気 byōki · **illness**

熱 netsu | fever

頭痛
zutsū
headache

鼻血
hanaji
nosebleed

咳
seki
cough

くしゃみ
kushami
sneeze

風邪
kaze
cold

インフルエンザ
infuruenza
flu

吸入器
kyūnyūki
inhaler

喘息
zensoku
asthma

腹痛
fukutsū
cramps

吐き気
hakike
nausea

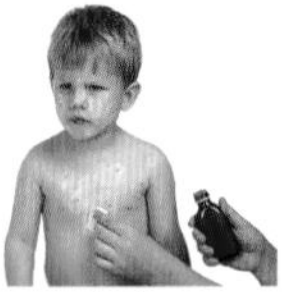

水痘
suitō
chickenpox

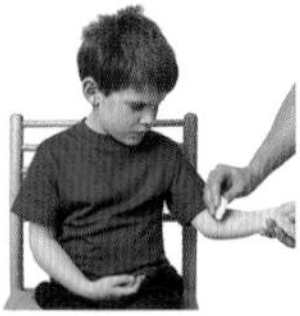

発疹
hosshin
rash

関連用語 kanrenyōgo · vocabulary

脳卒中 nōsotchū stroke	糖尿病 tōnyōbyō diabetes	アトピー性皮膚炎 atopīsei hifuen eczema	悪寒 okan chill	吐く haku vomit (v)	下痢 geri diarrhoea
血圧 ketsuatsu blood pressure	アレルギー arerugī allergy	感染 kansen infection	胃痛 itsū stomach ache	癲癇 tenkan epilepsy	麻疹 hashika measles
心臓発作 shinzōhossa heart attack	花粉症 kafunshō hayfever	ウイルス uirusu virus	失神する shisshin suru faint (v)	片頭痛 henzutsū migraine	おたふく風邪 otafukukaze mumps

医者 isha · doctor
診察 shinsatsu · consultation

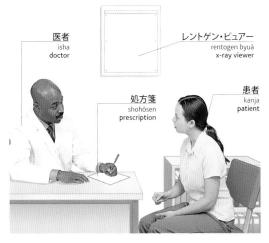

医者
isha
doctor

レントゲン・ビュアー
rentogen byuā
x-ray viewer

処方箋
shohōsen
prescription

患者
kanja
patient

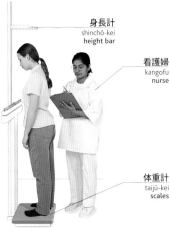

身長計
shinchō-kei
height bar

看護婦
kangofu
nurse

体重計
taijū-kei
scales

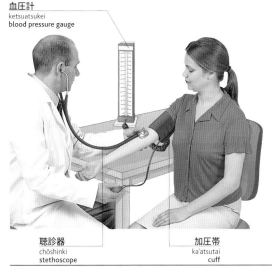

血圧計
ketsuatsukei
blood pressure gauge

聴診器
chōshinki
stethoscope

加圧帯
ka'atsutai
cuff

関連用語 kanrenyōgo
· vocabulary

予約
yoyaku
appointment

予防接種
yobō-sesshu
inoculation

診療室
shinryō-shitsu
surgery

体温計
taionkei
thermometer

待合室
machiai-shitsu
waiting room

診察
shinsatsu
medical
examination

医者に行かなければなりません。
isha ni ikanakereba narimasen.
I need to see a doctor.

ここが痛い。
koko ga itai.
It hurts here.

怪我 kega • injury

捻挫 nenza | sprain

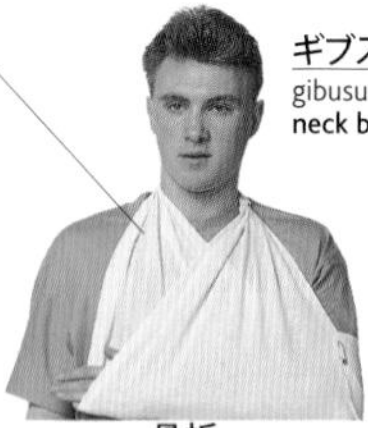

三角布
sankakufu
sling

骨折
kossetsu
fracture

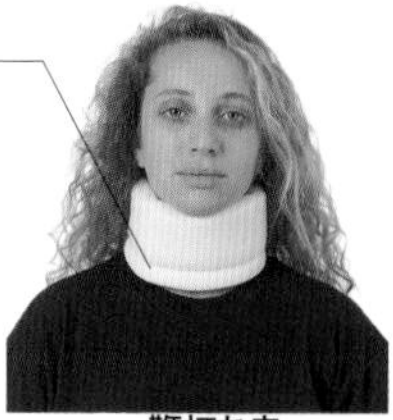

ギブス
gibusu
neck brace

鞭打ち症
muchiuchishō
whiplash

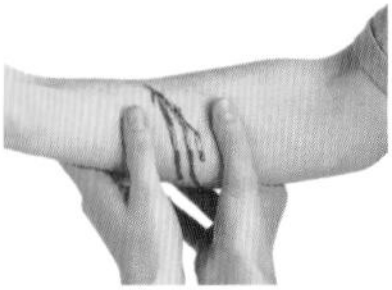

切り傷
kirikizu
cut

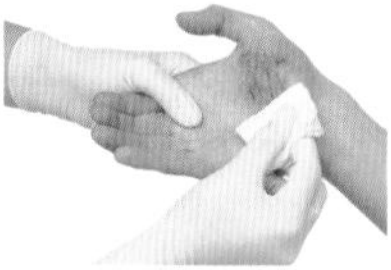

擦り傷
surikizu
graze

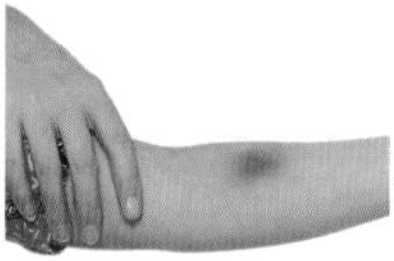

痣
aza
bruise

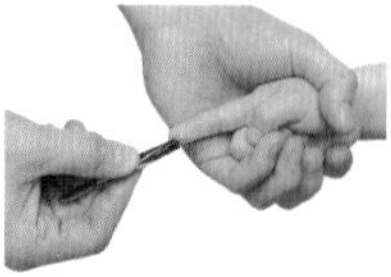

刺
toge
splinter

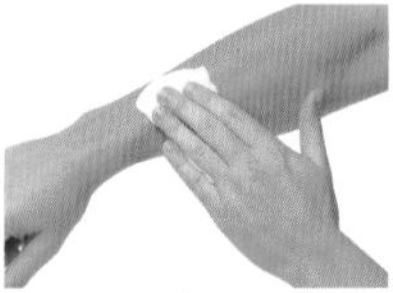

日焼け
hiyake
sunburn

火傷
yakedo
burn

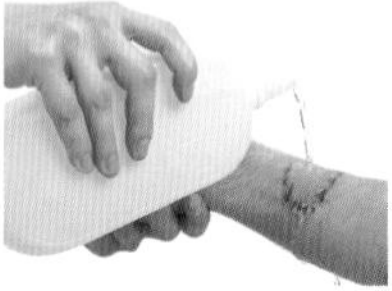

かみ傷
kamikizu
bite

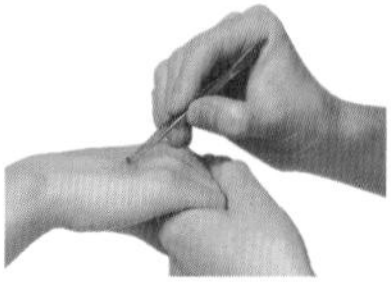

虫刺され
mushi-sasare
sting

関連用語 kanrenyōgo • vocabulary

事故
jiko
accident

緊急事態
kinkyūjitai
emergency

傷
kizu
wound

出血
shukketsu
haemorrhage

水ぶくれ
mizubukure
blister

脳しんとう
nōshintō
concussion

中毒
chūdoku
poisoning

感電
kanden
electric shock

頭部外傷
tōbu gaishō
head injury

大丈夫でしょうか。
daijōbu deshōka?
Will he/she be all right?

どこが痛みますか。
doko ga itamimasuka?
Where does it hurt?

救急車を呼んでください。
kyūkyūsha o yonde kudasai.
Please call an ambulance.

応急手当 ōkyū teate • **first aid**

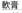

軟膏
nankō
ointment

バンドエード
bandoēdo
plaster

安全ピン
anzempin
safety pin

包帯
hōtai
bandage

痛み止め
itami-dome
painkillers

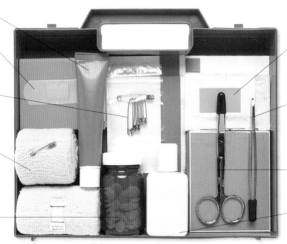

消毒ワイプ
shōdoku waipu
antiseptic wipe

ピンセット
pinsetto
tweezers

鋏
hasami
scissors

消毒液
shōdoku eki
antiseptic

救急箱 kyūkyūbako | **first aid box**

ガーゼ
gāze
gauze

手当
teate
dressing

副木 fukuboku | **splint**

絆創膏
bansōkō
adhesive tape

救急蘇生
kyūkyū sosei
resuscitation

関連用語 kanrenyōgo • **vocabulary**

ショック shokku **shock**	脈拍 myakuhaku **pulse**	窒息する chissoku suru **choke (v)**	助けてください。 tasukete kudasai. **Please help.**
意識不明 ishikifumei **unconscious**	呼吸 kokyū **breathing**	殺菌 sakkin **sterile**	応急手当のやり方を知っていますか。 ōkyū teate no yarikata o shitte imasuka? **Do you know first aid?**

病院 byōin • hospital

外科医
geka-i
surgeon

看護婦
kangofu
nurse

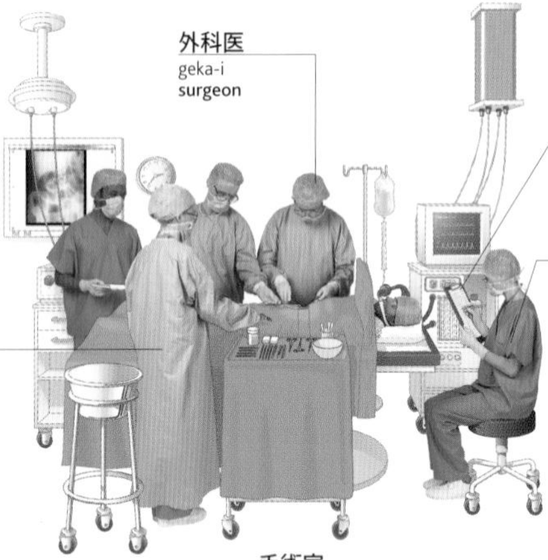

手術室
shujutsu-shitsu
operating theatre

カルテ
karute
chart

麻酔士
masui-shi
anaesthetist

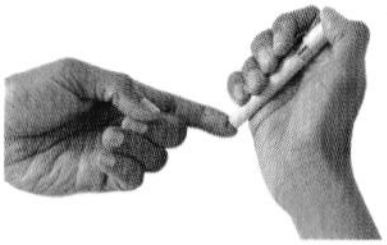

血液検査
ketsueki kensa
blood test

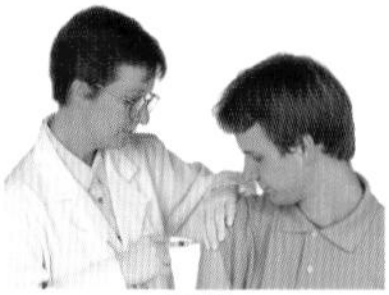

注射
chūsha
injection

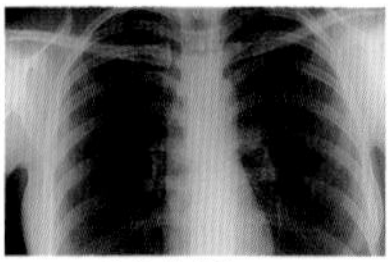

レントゲン
rentogen
x-ray

スキャン
sukyan
scan

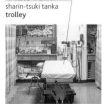

車輪付き担架
sharin-tsuki tanka
trolley

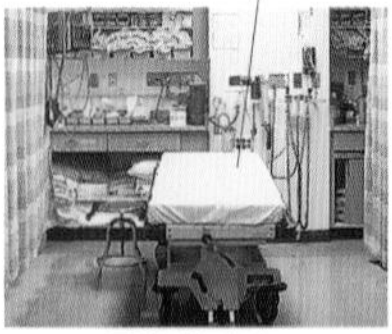

緊急治療室
kinkyū chiryō-shitsu
emergency room

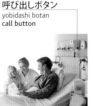

呼び出しボタン
yobidashi botan
call button

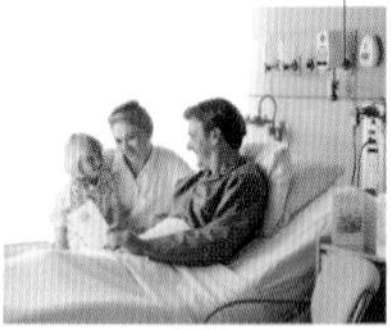

病室
byōshitsu
ward

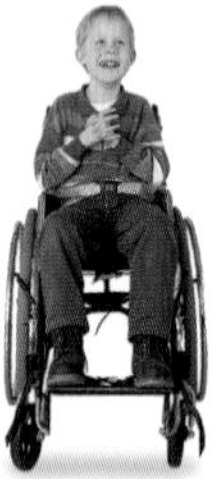

車椅子
kurumaisu
wheelchair

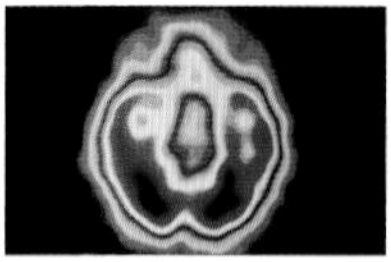

関連用語 kanrenyōgo • vocabulary

手術 shujutsu **operation**	**退院** tai'in **discharged**	**面会時間** menkai jikan **visiting hours**	**小児病棟** shōni byōtō **children's ward**	**集中治療室** shūchū chiryō-shitsu **intensive care unit**
入院 nyūin **admitted**	**診療所** shinryōjo **clinic**	**産科病棟** sanka byōtō **maternity ward**	**個室** koshitsu **private room**	**外来患者** gairaikanja **outpatient**

医療部門 iryō bumon ● departments

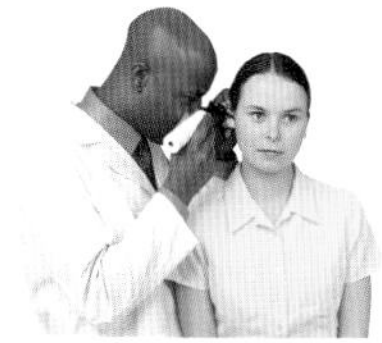

耳鼻咽喉科
jibi'inkō-ka
ENT

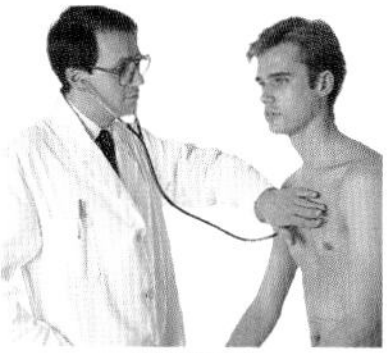

心臓病科
shinzōbyō-ka
cardiology

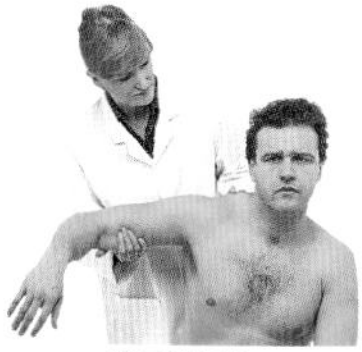

整形外科
seikeige-ka
orthopedics

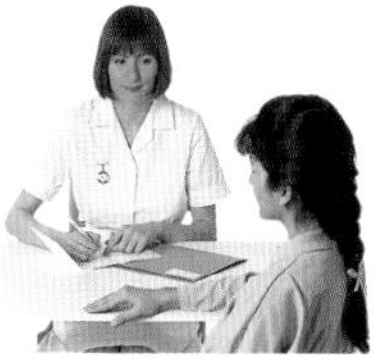

婦人科
fujin-ka
gynaecology

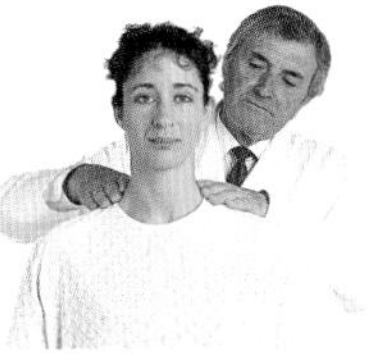

理学療法科
rigakuryōhō-ka
physiotherapy

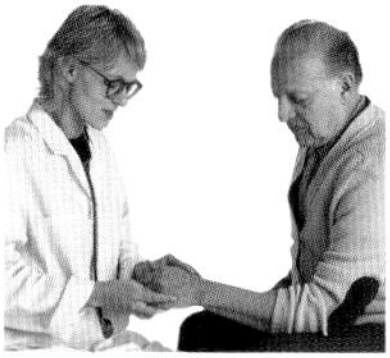

皮膚科
hifu-ka
dermatology

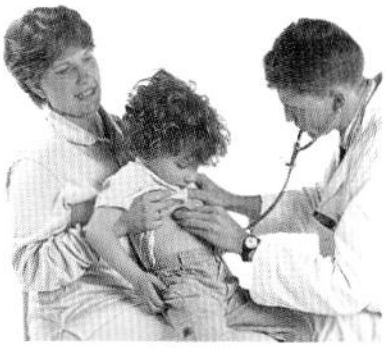

小児科
shōni-ka
paediatrics

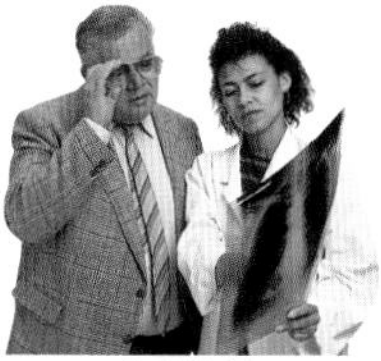

放射線科
hōshasen-ka
radiology

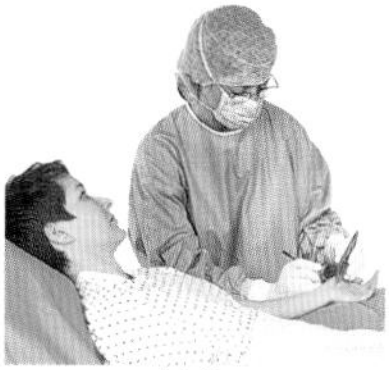

外科
geka
surgery

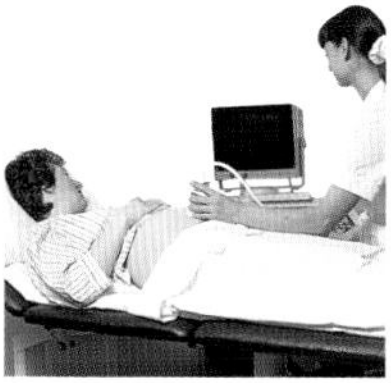

産科
sanka
maternity

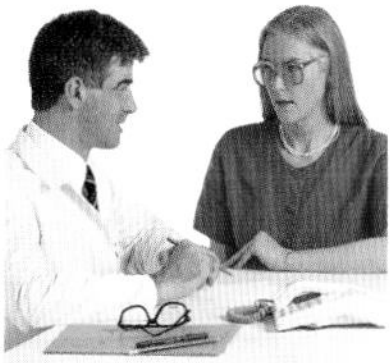

精神科
seishin-ka
psychiatry

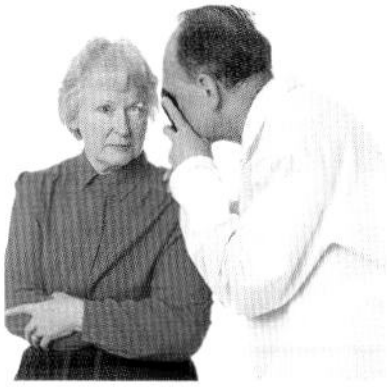

眼科
ganka
ophthalmology

関連用語 kanrenyōgo ● vocabulary

神経科 shinkei-ka neurology	**泌尿器科** hinyōki-ka urology	**内分泌科** naibumpi-ka endocrinology	**病理科** byōri-ka pathology	**結果** kekka result
癌科 gan-ka oncology	**形成外科** keisei-geka plastic surgery	**照会** shōkai referral	**検査** kensa test	**専門医** senmon'i consultant

歯医者 haisha · dentist

歯 ha · tooth

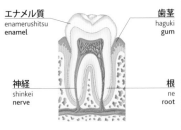

エナメル質
enamerushitsu
enamel

歯茎
haguki
gum

神経
shinkei
nerve

根
ne
root

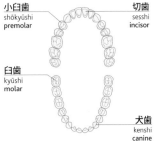

小臼歯
shōkyūshi
premolar

切歯
sesshi
incisor

臼歯
kyūshi
molar

犬歯
kenshi
canine

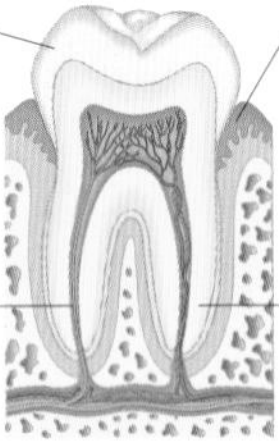

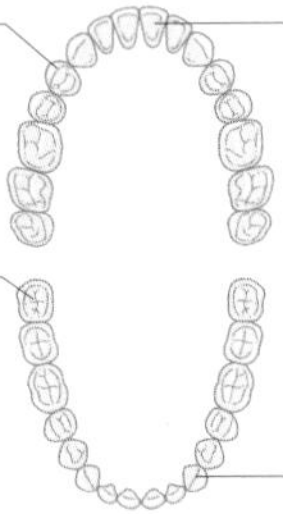

関連用語 kanrenyōgo · vocabulary

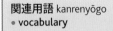

歯痛
haita
toothache

ドリル
doriru
drill

歯垢
shikō
plaque

デンタルフロス
dentaru furosu
dental floss

虫歯
mushiba
decay

抜歯
basshi
extraction

詰め物
tsumemono
filling

歯冠
shikan
crown

歯科検診 shika kenshin · check-up

反射鏡
hanshakyō
reflector

探針
tanshin
probe

エプロン
epuron
apron

うがい台
ugai dai
basin

歯科ユニット
shika yunitto
dentist's chair

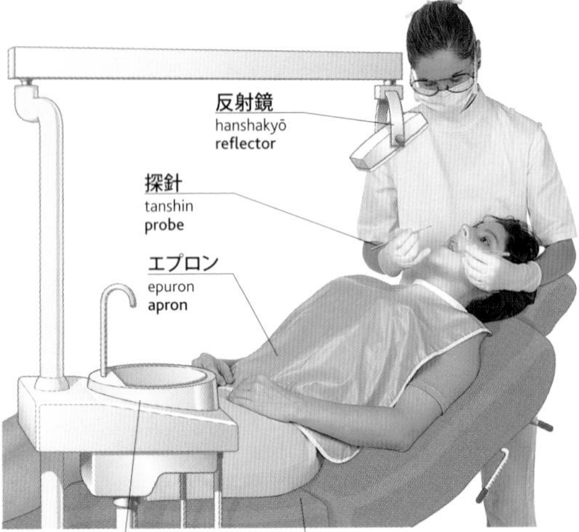

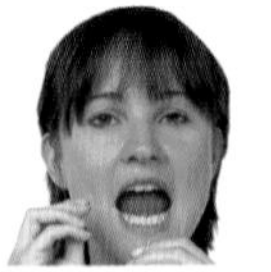

デンタルフロスで掃除する
dentaru furosu de sōji suru
floss (v)

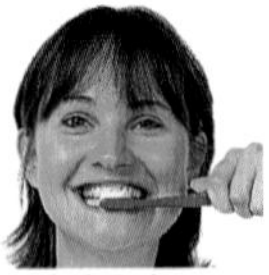

歯磨きする
hamigaki suru
brush (v)

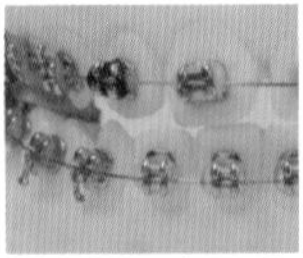

歯列矯正ブリッジ
shiretsu kyōsei burijji
brace

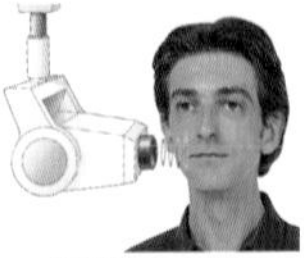

歯科レントゲン
shika rentogen
dental x-ray

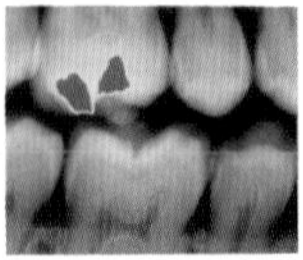

レントゲン写真
rentogen shashin
x-ray film

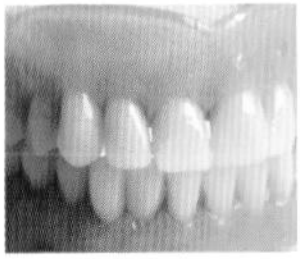

入れ歯
ireba
dentures

眼鏡店 megane-ten • optician

ケース
kēsu
case

レンズ
renzu
lens

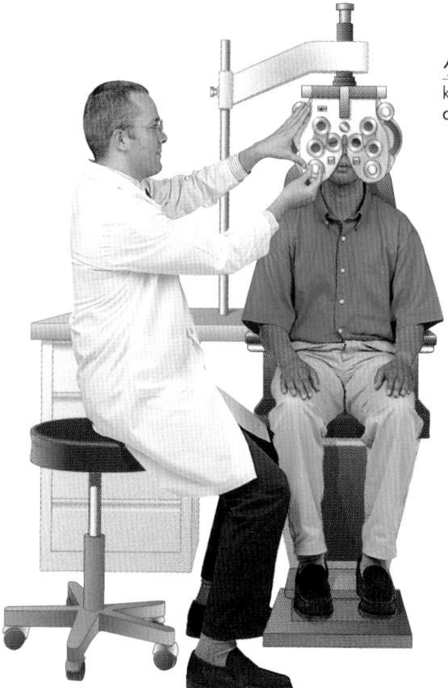

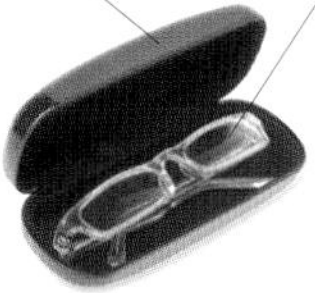

フレーム
furēmu
frame

眼鏡
megane
glasses

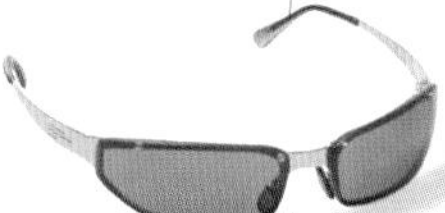

サングラス
sangurasu
sunglasses

洗浄液
senjō eki
cleaning fluid

消毒液
shōdoku eki
disinfectant solution

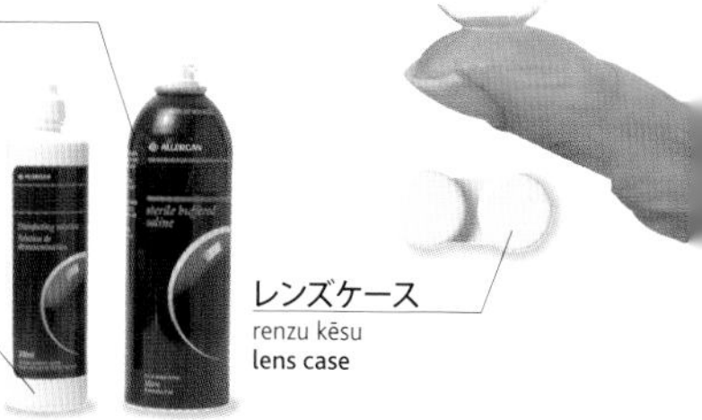

レンズケース
renzu kēsu
lens case

視力検査 shiryoku kensa | eye test

コンタクトレンズ kontakutorenzu | contact lenses

目 me • eye

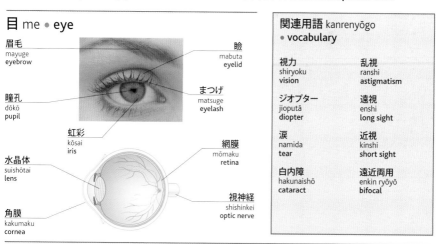

眉毛
mayuge
eyebrow

瞼
mabuta
eyelid

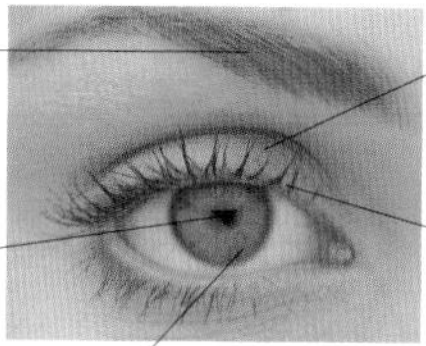

まつげ
matsuge
eyelash

瞳孔
dōkō
pupil

虹彩
kōsai
iris

網膜
mōmaku
retina

水晶体
suishōtai
lens

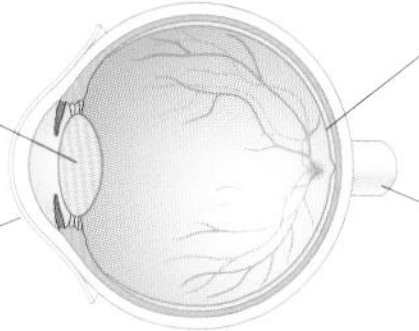

視神経
shishinkei
optic nerve

角膜
kakumaku
cornea

関連用語 kanrenyōgo • vocabulary

視力 shiryoku vision	乱視 ranshi astigmatism
ジオプター jioputā diopter	遠視 enshi long sight
涙 namida tear	近視 kinshi short sight
白内障 hakunaishō cataract	遠近両用 enkin ryōyō bifocal

妊娠 ninshin · **pregnancy**

看護婦
kangofu
nurse

妊娠テスト
ninshin tesuto
pregnancy test

スキャン
sukyan
scan

へその緒
hesono'o
umbilical cord

胎盤
taiban
placenta

頸部
keibu
cervix

子宮
shikyū
uterus

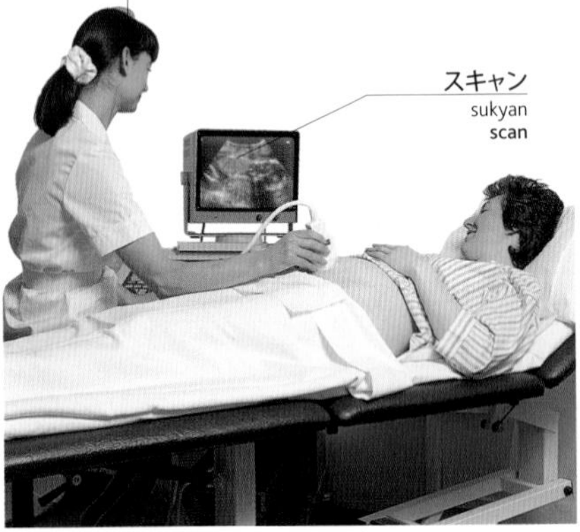

超音波（検査）chōompa (kensa) | ultrasound (test)

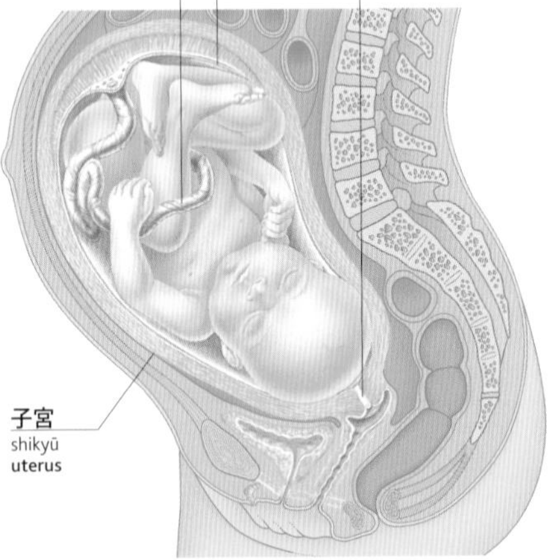

胎児 taiji | foetus

関連用語 kanrenyōgo · **vocabulary**

排卵 hairan **ovulation**	出産前 shussan mae **antenatal**	陣痛 jintsū **contraction**	子宮頸部拡張 shikyū keibu kakuchō **dilation**	分娩 bumben **delivery**	逆子 sakago **breech**
受胎 jutai **conception**	胚 hai **embryo**	破水する hasui suru **break waters (v)**	硬膜外麻酔 kōmaku-gai masui **epidural**	誕生 tanjō **birth**	未熟児 mijukuji **premature**
妊娠 ninshin **pregnant**	子宮 shikyū **womb**	羊水 yōsui **amniotic fluid**	会陰切開 kai'in sekkai **episiotomy**	流産 ryūzan **miscarriage**	婦人科医 fujinka-i **gynaecologist**
妊娠している ninshin shiteiru **expectant**	三半期 sanhanki **trimester**	羊水穿刺 yōsui senshi **amniocentesis**	帝王切開 teiō sekkai **caesarean section**	縫合 hōgō **stitches**	産科医 sanka-i **obstetrician**

出産 shussan • childbirth

点滴
tenteki
drip

助産婦
josampu
midwife

モニター
monitā
monitor

カテーテル
katēteru
catheter

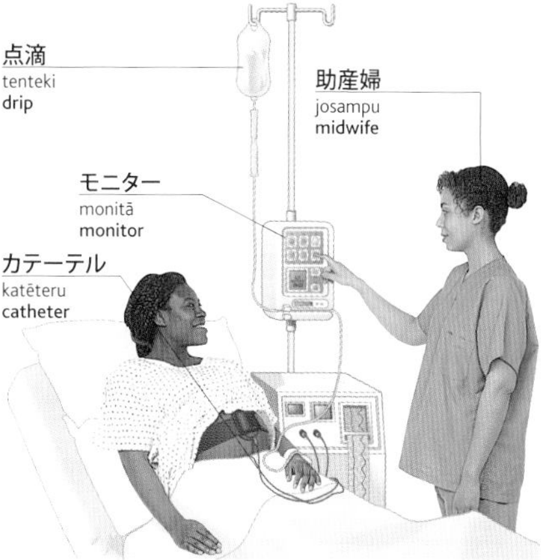

陣痛促進する jintsū sokushin suru | induce labour (v)

鉗子
kanshi
forceps

真空カップ
shinkū kappu
ventouse cup

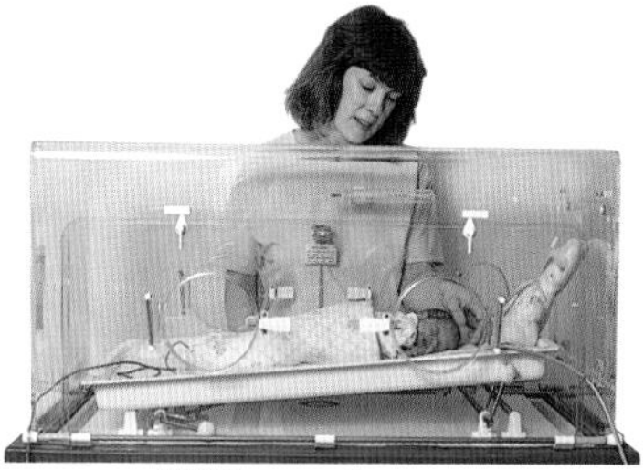

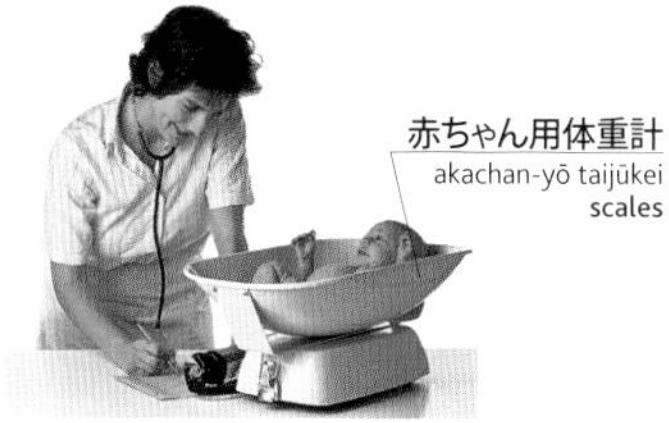

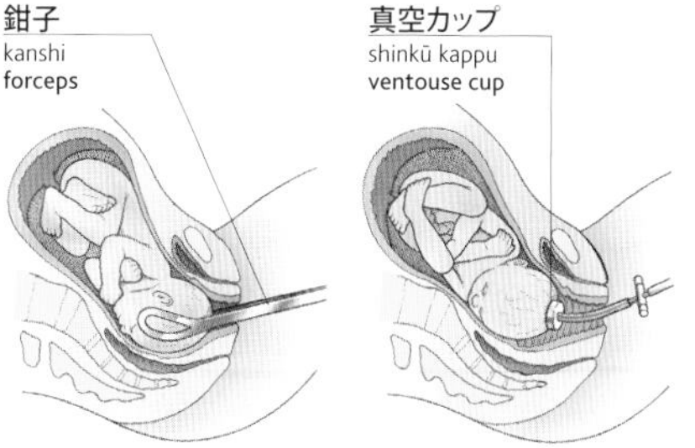

介助分娩
kaijo bumben
assisted delivery

識別バンド
shikibetsu bando
identity tag

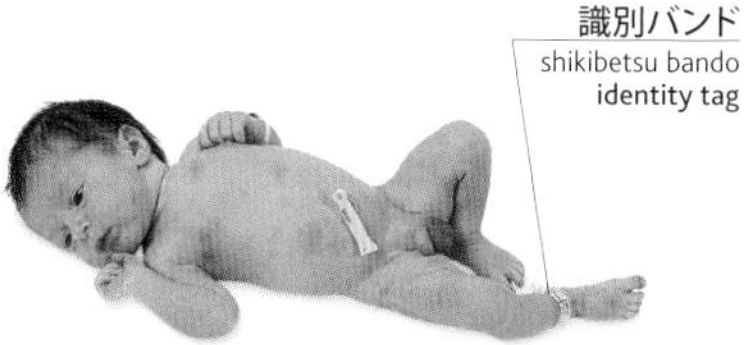

新生児 shinseiji | newborn baby

保育器 hoikuki | incubator

赤ちゃん用体重計
akachan-yō taijūkei
scales

出生時体重 shussei-ji taijū | birth weight

授乳 junyū • nursing

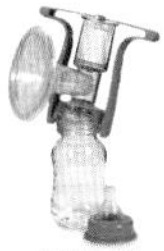

搾乳機
sakunyū-ki
breast pump

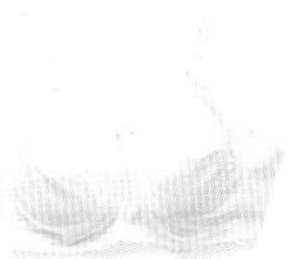

授乳ブラジャー
junyū burajā
nursing bra

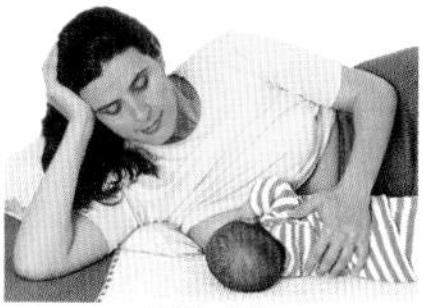

授乳する
junyū suru
breastfeed (v)

パッド
paddo
pads

代替療法 daitai ryōhō ● alternative therapy

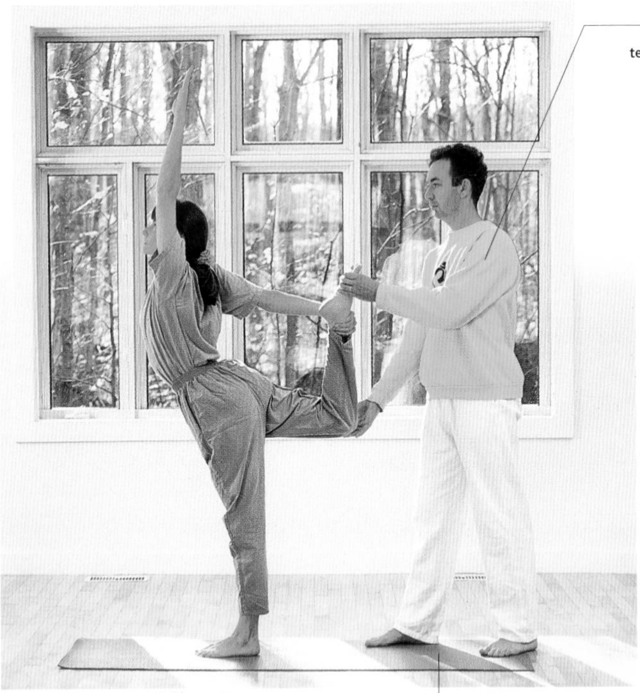

先生
sensei
teacher

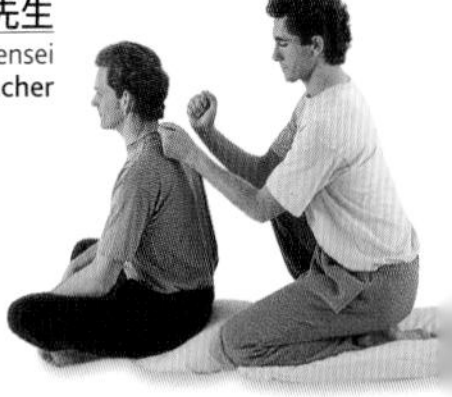

マッサージ
massāji
massage

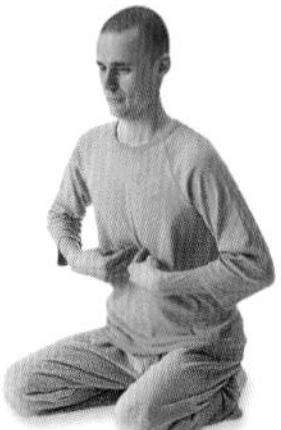

指圧
shiatsu
shiatsu

ヨガ yoga | yoga

マット
matto
mat

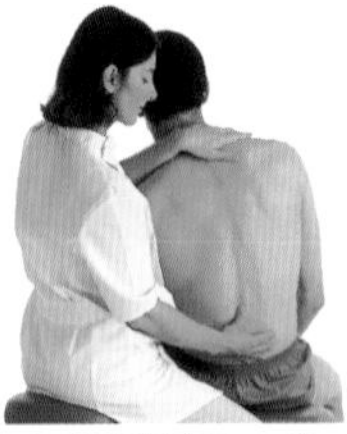

カイロプラクティック
kairopurakutikku
chiropractic

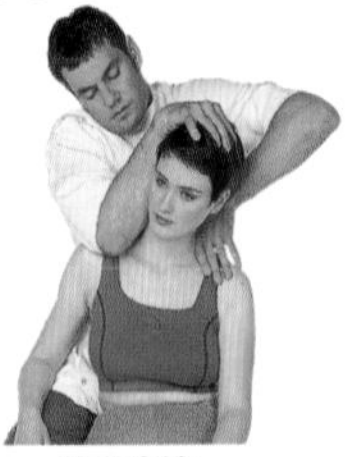

整骨療法
seikotsu ryōhō
osteopathy

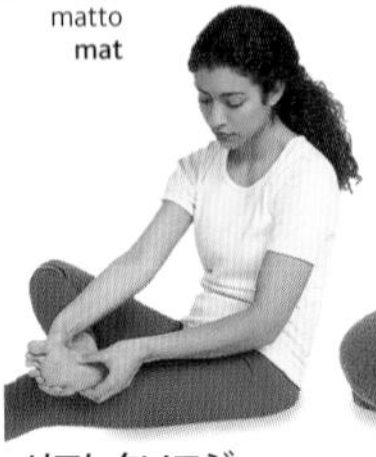

リフレクソロジー
rifurekusorojī
reflexology

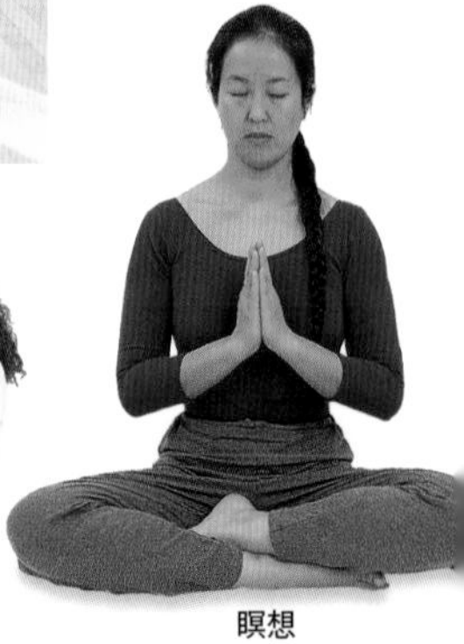

瞑想
meisō
meditation

カウンセラー
kaunserā
counsellor

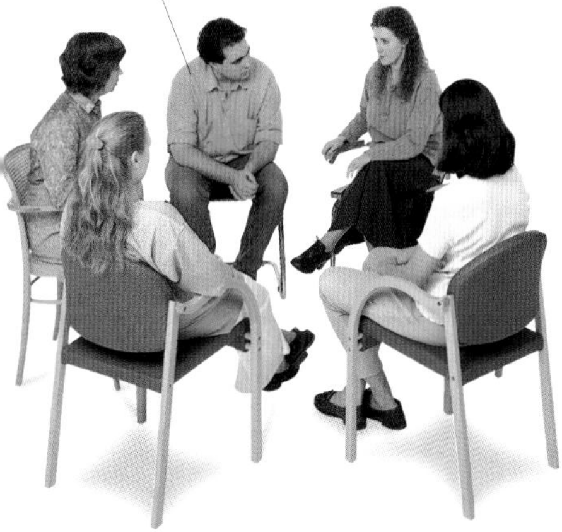

グループ療法
gurūpu ryōhō
group therapy

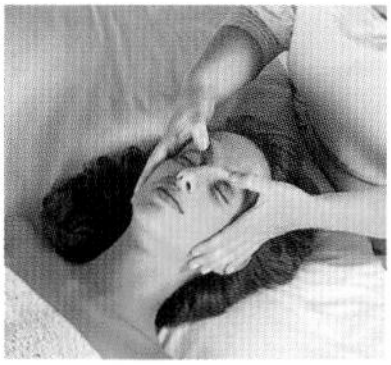

レイキ療法
reiki ryōhō
reiki

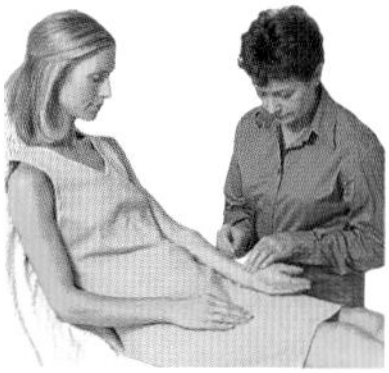

鍼療法
hari ryōhō
acupuncture

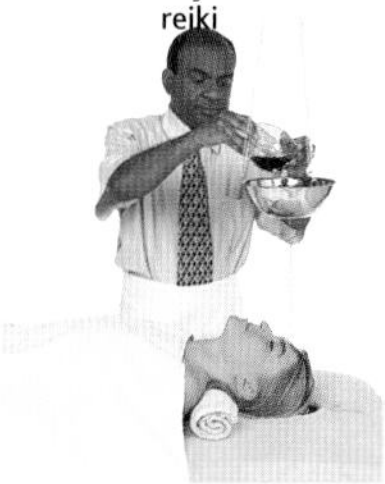

アユルヴェーダ
ayuruvēda
ayurveda

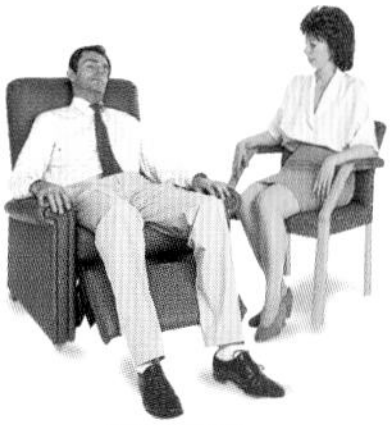

催眠療法
saimin ryōhō
hypnotherapy

精油
seiyu
essential oils

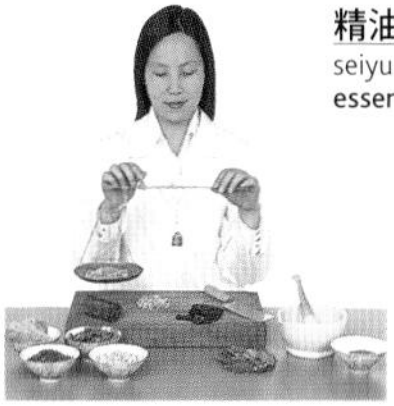

本草学
honsō-gaku
herbalism

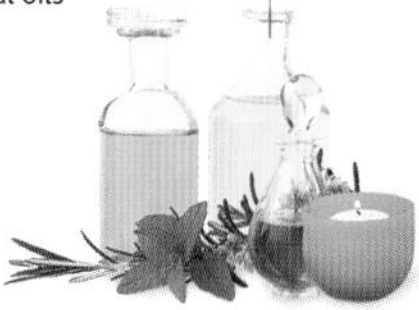

アロマテラピー
aromaterapī
aromatherapy

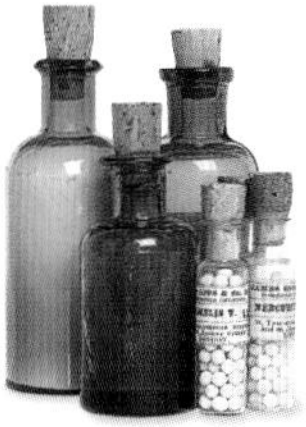

ホメオパシー
homeopashī
homeopathy

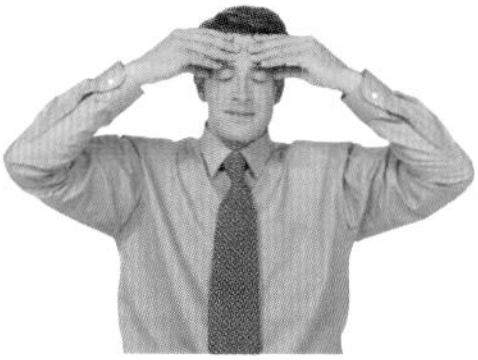

指圧療法
shiatsu ryōhō
acupressure therapy

療法士
ryōhōshi
therapist

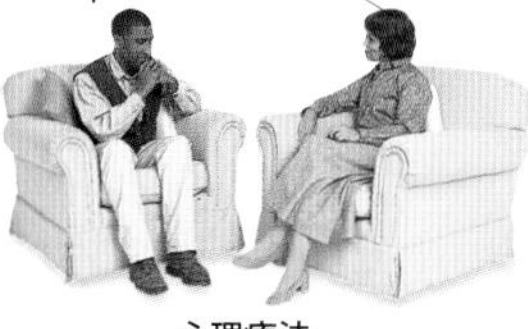

心理療法
shinri ryōhō
psychotherapy

関連用語 kanrenyōgo • vocabulary

サプリメント sapurimento **supplement**	自然療法 shizen ryōhō **naturopathy**	リラクセーション rirakusēshon **relaxation**	薬草 yakusō **herb**
水治療法 suichi ryōhō **hydrotherapy**	風水 fūsui **feng shui**	ストレス sutoresu **stress**	水晶療法 suishō ryōhō **crystal healing**

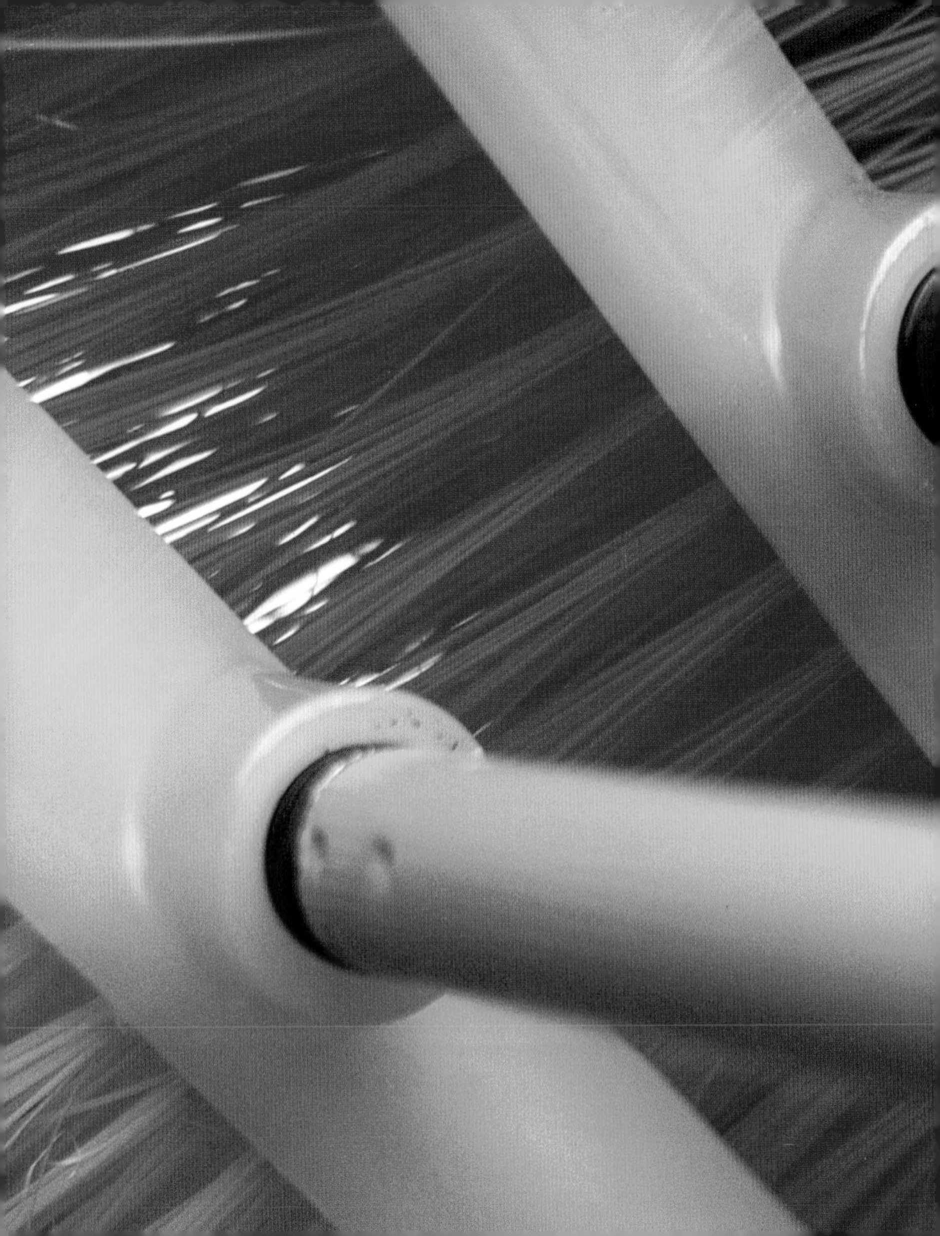

家庭 katei
home

住宅 jūtaku • house

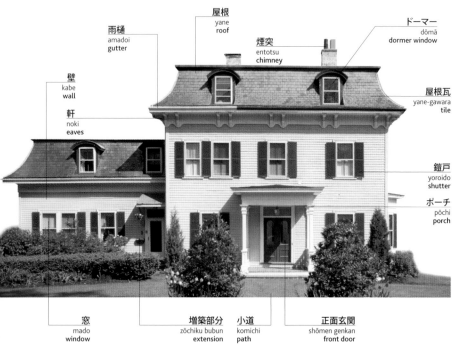

屋根
yane
roof

雨樋
amadoi
gutter

煙突
entotsu
chimney

ドーマー
dōmā
dormer window

壁
kabe
wall

軒
noki
eaves

屋根瓦
yane-gawara
tile

鎧戸
yoroido
shutter

ポーチ
pōchi
porch

窓
mado
window

増築部分
zōchiku bubun
extension

小道
komichi
path

正面玄関
shōmen genkan
front door

関連用語 kanrenyōgo • vocabulary

一戸建て ikkodate **detached**	借家人 shakuyanin **tenant**	車庫 shako **garage**	郵便受け yūbin'uke **letterbox**	防犯ベル bōhan beru **burglar alarm**	貸す kasu **rent (v)**
セミデタッチ semidetatchi **semidetached**	平屋 hiraya **bungalow**	屋根裏部屋 yaneura-beya **attic**	玄関灯 genkan-tō **porch light**	中庭 nakaniwa **courtyard**	家賃 yachin **rent**
タウンハウス taunhausu **townhouse**	地下室 chikashitsu **basement**	部屋 heya **room**	大家 ōya **landlord**	床 yuka **floor**	テラス terasu **terraced**

入口 iriguchi • entrance

マンション
manshon • flat

手摺
tesuri
hand rail

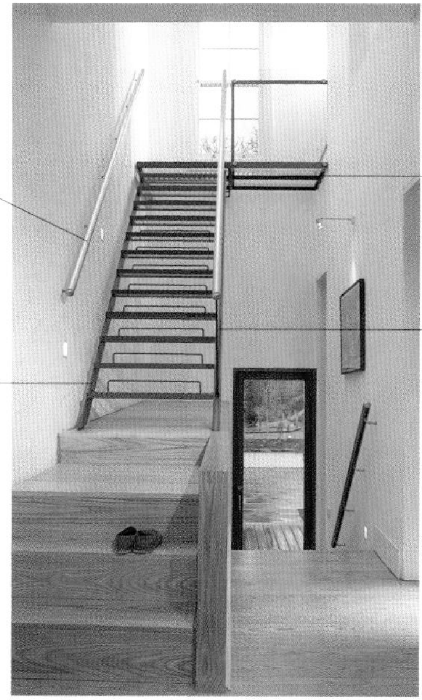

踊り場
odoriba
landing

階段の手摺
kaidan no tesuri
banister

階段
kaidan
staircase

玄関
genkan
hallway

ベランダ
beranda
balcony

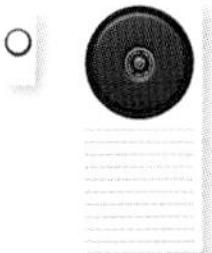

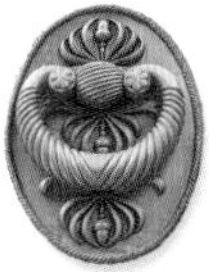

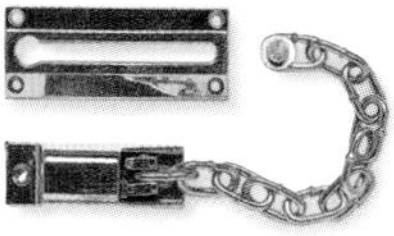

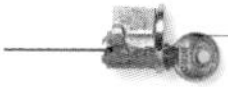

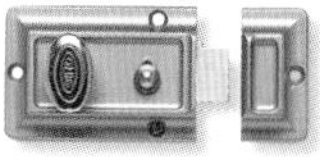

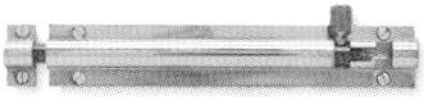

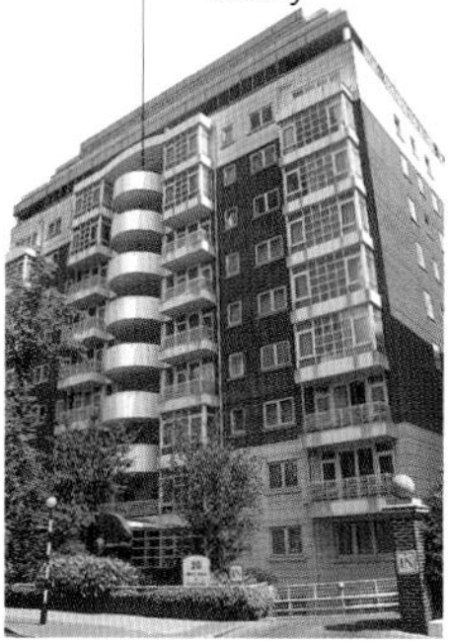

マンション棟
manshon-tō
block of flats

インターホン
intāhon
intercom

呼び鈴
yobirin
doorbell

玄関マット
genkan matto
doormat

ドアノッカー
doanokkā
door knocker

ドアチェーン
doachēn
door chain

鍵
kagi
key

錠
jō
lock

閂
kannuki
bolt

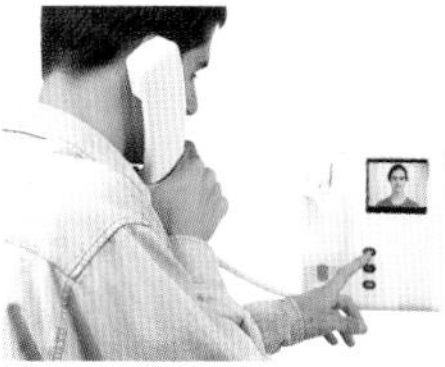

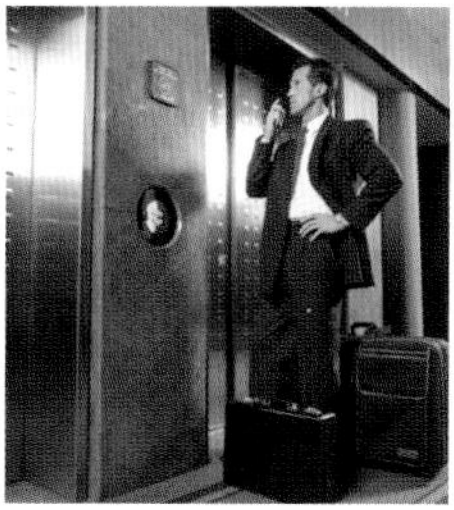

エレベーター
erebētā
lift

住宅内設備 jūtaku-nai setsubi • **internal systems**

羽
hane
blade

扇風機
sempūki
fan

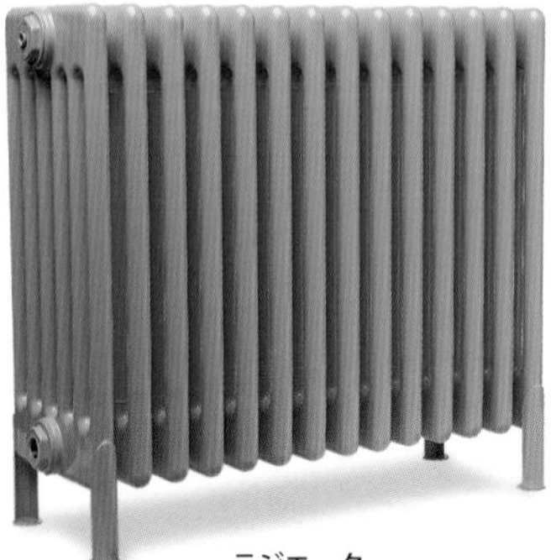

ラジエーター
rajiētā
radiator

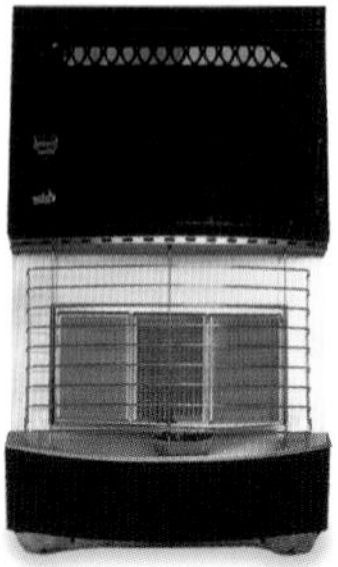

ヒーター
hītā
heater

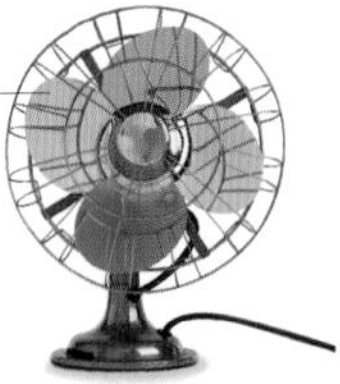

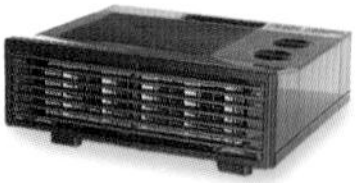

ファンヒーター
fanhītā
convector heater

電気設備 denki setsubi • **electricity**

フィラメント
firamento
filament

接地ピン
setchi pin
earthing

バヨネット式
bayonetto-shiki
bayonet fitting

ピン
pin
pin

マイナス
mainasu
neutral

プラス
purasu
live

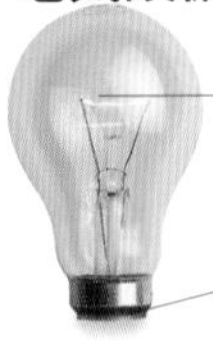

電球 denkyū | light bulb

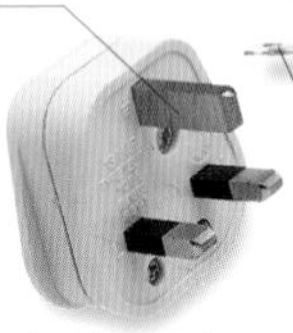

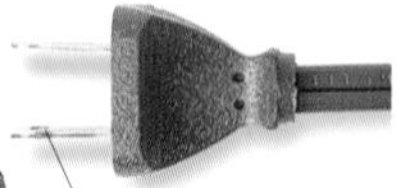

プラグ puragu | plug

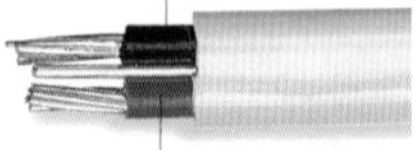

電線 densen | wires

関連用語 kanrenyōgo • **vocabulary**

電圧 den'atsu **voltage**	ヒューズ hyūzu **fuse**	コンセント konsento **socket**	直流連流 chokuryū denryū **direct current**	停電 teiden **power cut**
アンペア ampea **amp**	ヒューズボックス hyūzu bokkusu **fuse box**	スイッチ suitchi **switch**	変圧器 hen'atsuki **transformer**	電源 dengen **mains supply**
電力 denryoku **power**	発電機 hatsudenki **generator**	交流電流 kōryū denryū **alternating current**	電力量計 denryokuryō-kei **electricity meter**	

配管設備 haikan setsubi • plumbing

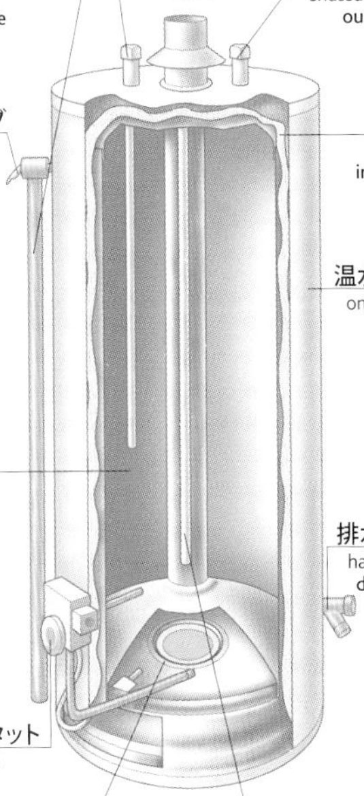

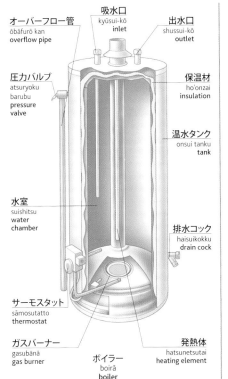

オーバーフロー管
ōbāfurō kan
overflow pipe

吸水口
kyūsui-kō
inlet

出水口
shussui-kō
outlet

圧力バルブ
atsuryoku barubu
pressure valve

保温材
ho'onzai
insulation

温水タンク
onsui tanku
tank

水室
suishitsu
water chamber

排水コック
haisuikokku
drain cock

サーモスタット
sāmosutatto
thermostat

ガスバーナー
gasubānā
gas burner

ボイラー
boirā
boiler

発熱体
hatsunetsutai
heating element

流し台 nagashidai • sink

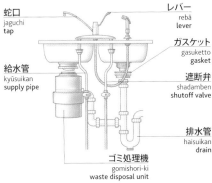

蛇口
jaguchi
tap

レバー
rebā
lever

ガスケット
gasuketto
gasket

給水管
kyūsuikan
supply pipe

遮断弁
shadamben
shutoff valve

排水管
haisuikan
drain

ゴミ処理機
gomishori-ki
waste disposal unit

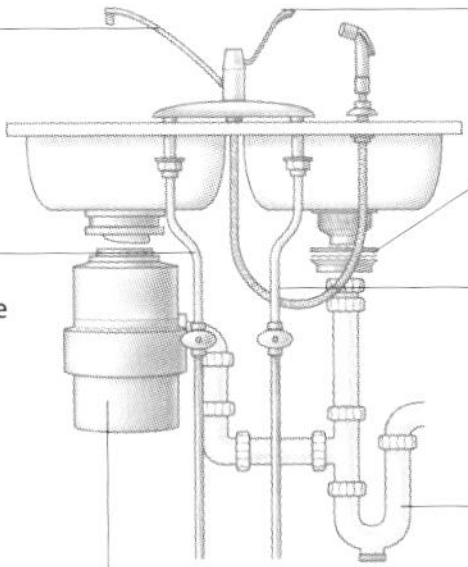

トイレ toire • water closet

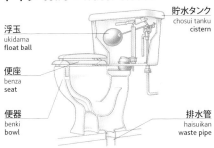

貯水タンク
chosui tanku
cistern

浮玉
ukidama
float ball

便座
benza
seat

便器
benki
bowl

排水管
haisuikan
waste pipe

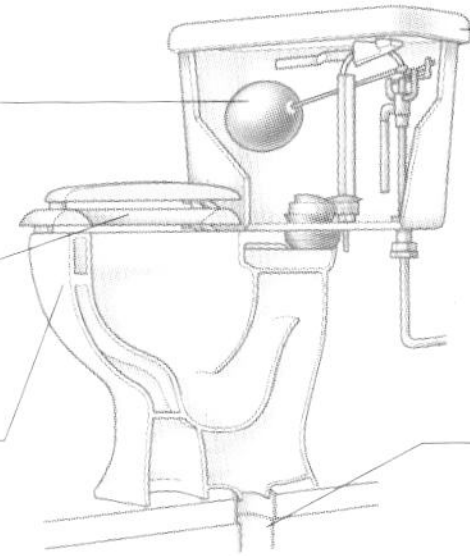

ゴミ処理 gomishori • waste disposal

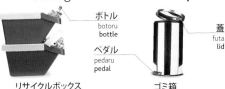

ボトル
botoru
bottle

ペダル
pedaru
pedal

蓋
futa
lid

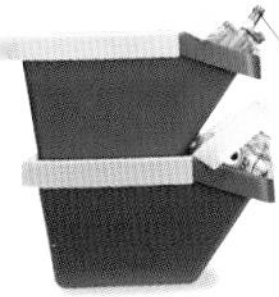

リサイクルボックス
risaikuru bokkusu
recycling bin

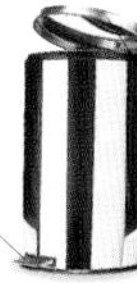

ゴミ箱
gomibako
rubbish bin

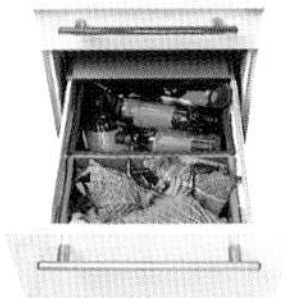

分別ユニット
bumbetsu yunitto
sorting unit

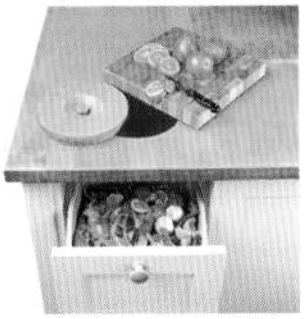

有機ゴミ
yūki gomi
organic waste

居間 ima · living room

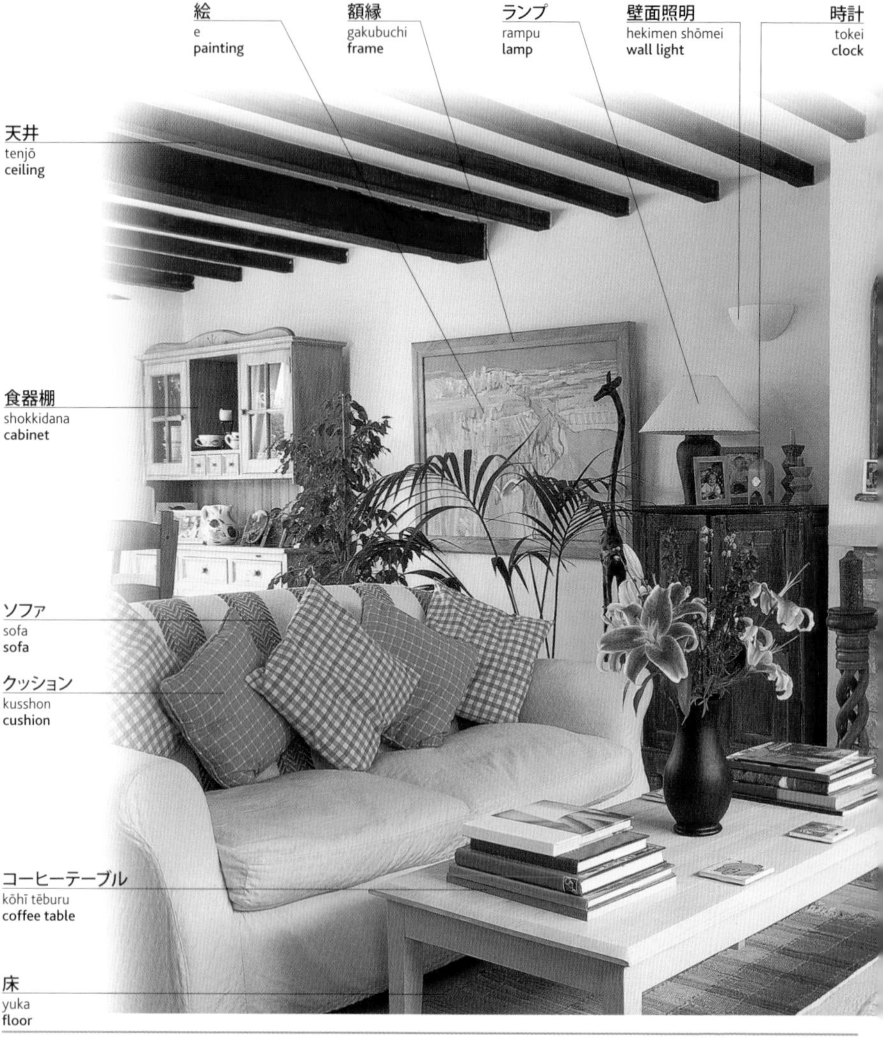

絵
e
painting

額縁
gakubuchi
frame

ランプ
rampu
lamp

壁面照明
hekimen shōmei
wall light

時計
tokei
clock

天井
tenjō
ceiling

食器棚
shokkidana
cabinet

ソファ
sofa
sofa

クッション
kusshon
cushion

コーヒーテーブル
kōhī tēburu
coffee table

床
yuka
floor

鏡
kagami
mirror

花瓶
kabin
vase

マントルピース
mantorupīsu
mantelpiece

暖炉
danro
fireplace

ファイヤースクリーン
faiyā sukurīn
screen

蝋燭
rōsoku
candle

本棚
hondana
bookshelf

ソファベッド
sofa beddo
sofabed

絨毯
jūtan
rug

カーテン
kāten
curtain

メッシュカーテン
messhu kāten
net curtain

ベネシャンブラインド
beneshan buraindo
venetian blind

ロールスクリーン
rōru sukurīn
roller blind

モールディング
mōrudingu
moulding

アームチェア
āmuchea
armchair

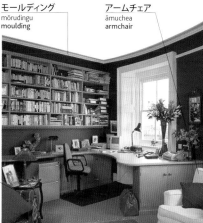

書斎 shosai | study

ダイニングルーム dainingu rūmu • **dining room**

胡椒
koshō
pepper

塩
shio
salt

テーブル
tēburu
table

食器
shokki
crockery

椅子
isu
chair

背もたれ
semotare
back

座面
zamen
seat

脚
ashi
leg

関連用語 kanrenyōgo • **vocabulary**

給仕する kyūji suru **serve (v)**	朝食 chōshoku **breakfast**	満腹 mampuku **full**	箸 hashi **chopsticks**	おかわりできますか。 okawari dekimasuka? **Can I have some more, please?**
食べる taberu **eat (v)**	昼食 chūshoku **lunch**	一人分 hitoribun **one portion**	ご飯茶碗 gohan-jawan **rice bowl**	もう結構です。 mō kekkō desu. **I've had enough, thank you.**
空腹 kūfuku **hungry**	夕食 yūshoku **dinner**	食事 shokuji **meal**	茶碗 chawan **(Japanese) tea cup**	美味しかったです。 oishikatta desu. **That was delicious.**
テーブルクロス tēburukurosu **tablecloth**	ランチョンマット ranchon matto **place mat**	客 kyaku **guest**	座布団 zabuton **(Japanese) floor cushion**	

食器類 shokki rui · crockery and cutlery

マグカップ
magu kappu
mug

コーヒーカップ
kōhīkappu
coffee cup

ティーカップ
tīkappu
teacup

ティースプーン
tīsupūn
teaspoon

皿
sara
plate

ボウル
bōru
bowl

カフェプレス
kafe puresu
cafetière

ティーポット
tīpotto
teapot

水差し
mizusashi
jug

エッグカップ
eggu kappu
egg cup

ワイングラス
waingurasu
wine glass

タンブラー
tamburā
tumbler

コップ類
koppu rui
glassware

ナプキンリング
napukin ringu
napkin ring

小皿
kozara
side plate

大皿
ōzara
dinner plate

スープ皿
sūpuzara
soup bowl

スープスプーン
sūpusupūn
soup spoon

ナプキン
napukin
napkin

フォーク
fōku
fork

テーブル・セッティング
tēburu settingu
place setting

スプーン
supūn
spoon

ナイフ
naifu
knife

台所 daidokoro · **kitchen**

棚
tana
shelves

水はね防止板
mizuhane bōshi-ban
splashback

蛇口
jaguchi
tap

流し
nagashi
sink

引き出し
hikidashi
drawer

換気扇
kankisen
extractor

セラミックコンロ
seramikku konro
ceramic hob

調理台
chōridai
worktop

オーブン
ōbun
oven

戸棚
todana
cabinet

電気器具 denki kigu · **appliances**

電子レンジ
denshirenji
microwave oven

ミキシングボウル
mikishingubōru
mixing bowl

蓋
futa
lid

ブレード
burēdo
blade

電気やかん
denki yakan
kettle

トースター
tōsutā
toaster

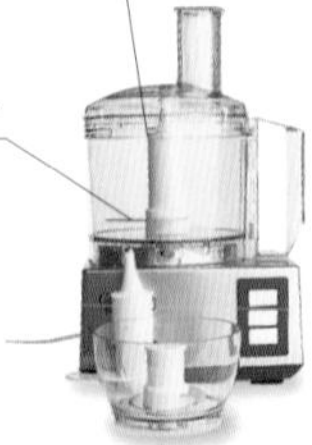

フードプロセッサー
fūdopurosessā
food processor

ミキサー
mikisā
blender

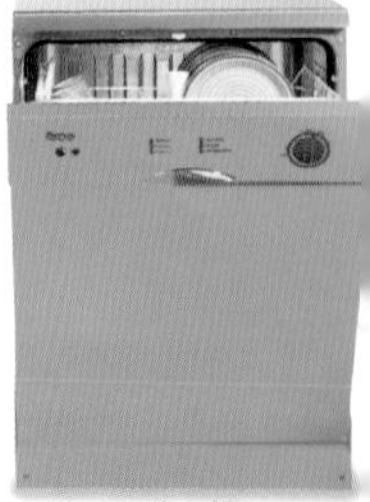

皿洗い機
sara'arai-ki
dishwasher

製氷室
seihyōshitsu
ice maker

冷蔵庫
reizōko
refrigerator

棚
tana
shelf

冷凍庫
reitōko
freezer

野菜室
yasai-shitsu
crisper

冷凍冷蔵庫 reitōreizōko | fridge-freezer

関連用語 kanrenyōgo • vocabulary

水切り台
mizukiridai
draining board

ガスレンジ
gasurenji
burner

コンロ
konro
hob

ゴミ箱
gomibako
rubbish bin

冷凍する
reitō suru
freeze (v)

解凍する
kaitō suru
defrost (v)

蒸す
musu
steam (v)

炒める
itameru
sauté (v)

調理 chōri • cooking

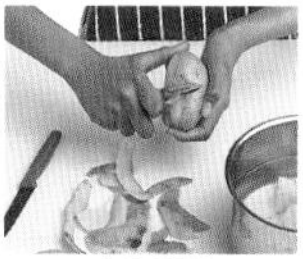

皮を剥く
kawa o muku
peel (v)

切る
kiru
slice (v)

すり下ろす
suriorosu
grate (v)

注ぐ
sosogu
pour (v)

混ぜる
mazeru
mix (v)

泡立てる
awadateru
whisk (v)

茹でる
yuderu
boil (v)

揚げる
ageru
fry (v)

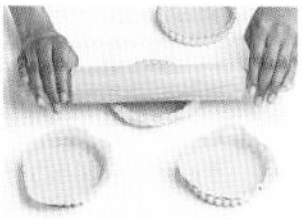

巻く
maku
roll (v)

かき回す
kakimawasu
stir (v)

煮込む
nikomu
simmer (v)

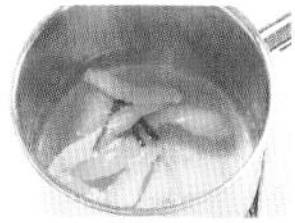

（沸騰前の温度で）茹でる
(futtō mae no ondo de) yuderu
poach (v)

（オーブンで）焼く
(ōbun de) yaku
bake (v)

ローストする
rōsuto suru
roast (v)

焼く
yaku
grill (v)

調理用具 chōri yōgu • kitchenware

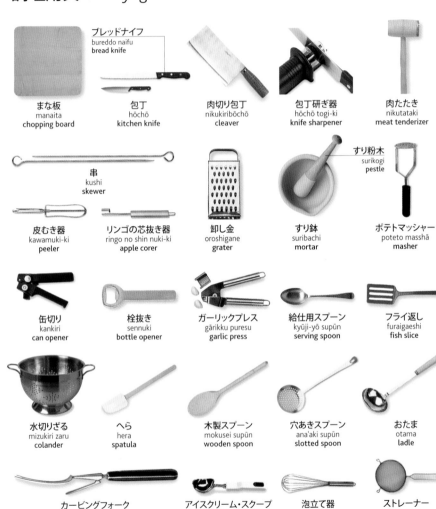

まな板
manaita
chopping board

ブレッドナイフ
bureddo naifu
bread knife

包丁
hōchō
kitchen knife

肉切り包丁
nikukiribōchō
cleaver

包丁研ぎ器
hōchō togi-ki
knife sharpener

肉たたき
nikutataki
meat tenderizer

串
kushi
skewer

皮むき器
kawamuki-ki
peeler

リンゴの芯抜き器
ringo no shin nuki-ki
apple corer

卸し金
oroshigane
grater

すり鉢
suribachi
mortar

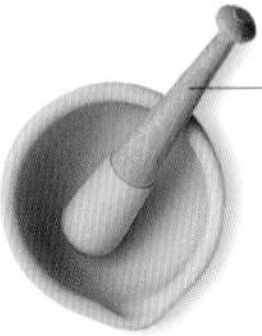

すり粉木
surikogi
pestle

ポテトマッシャー
poteto masshā
masher

缶切り
kankiri
can opener

栓抜き
sennuki
bottle opener

ガーリックプレス
gārikku puresu
garlic press

給仕用スプーン
kyūji-yō supūn
serving spoon

フライ返し
furaigaeshi
fish slice

水切りざる
mizukiri zaru
colander

へら
hera
spatula

木製スプーン
mokusei supūn
wooden spoon

穴あきスプーン
ana'aki supūn
slotted spoon

おたま
otama
ladle

カービングフォーク
kābingu fōku
carving fork

アイスクリーム・スクープ
aisukurīmu sukūpu
scoop

泡立て器
awadateki
whisk

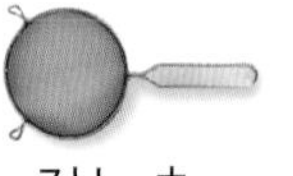

ストレーナー
sutorēnā
sieve

蓋
futa
lid

テフロン加工
tefuron kakō
non-stick

フライパン
furaipan
frying pan

片手鍋
katate nabe
saucepan

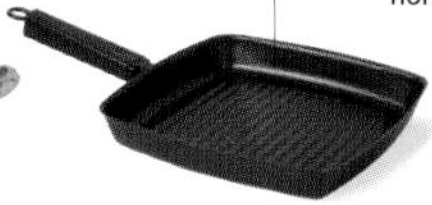

グリルパン
gurirupan
grill pan

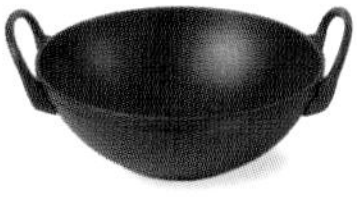

中華鍋
chūka nabe
wok

土鍋
donabe
earthenware dish

ガラス製
garasusei
glass

耐熱性
tainetsusei
ovenproof

ミキシングボウル
mikishingu bōru
mixing bowl

ココット
kokotto
soufflé dish

グラタン皿
guratan-zara
gratin dish

ラミキン
ramikin
ramekin

キャセロール鍋
kyaserōru nabe
casserole dish

ケーキ作り kēki-zukuri • baking cakes

秤
hakari
scales

計量ジャグ
keiryō jagu
measuring jug

ケーキ焼き型
kēki yaki-gata
cake tin

パイ焼き皿
pai yaki-zara
pie tin

タルト型
taruto-gata
flan tin

刷毛 hake
pastry brush

のし棒 noshibō
rolling pin

絞り袋 shibori bukuro
piping bag

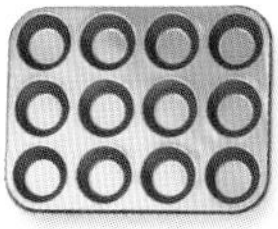

マフィン型
mafin-gata
muffin tray

ベーキングトレイ
bēkingu torei
baking tray

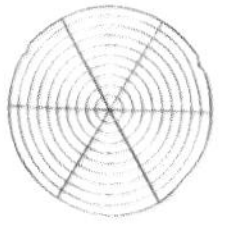

クーリングラック
kūringu rakku
cooling rack

オーブンミット
ōbunmitto
oven glove

エプロン
epuron
apron

寝室 shinshitsu • **bedroom**

洋服ダンス
yōfukudansu
wardrobe

ベッドサイドランプ
beddosaido rampu
bedside lamp

ヘッドボード
heddobōdo
headboard

ベッドサイドテーブル
beddosaido tēburu
bedside table

タンス
tansu
chest of drawers

引き出し
hikidashi
drawer

ベッド
beddo
bed

マットレス
mattoresu
mattress

ベッドカバー
beddokabā
bedspread

枕
makura
pillow

湯たんぽ
yutampo
hot-water bottle

時計付きラジオ
tokei-tsuki rajio
clock radio

目覚まし時計
mezamashi-dokei
alarm clock

ティッシュの箱
tisshu no hako
box of tissues

ハンガー
hangâ
coat hanger

ベッド beddo • bed

鏡
kagami
mirror

化粧台
keshōdai
dressing table

床
yuka
floor

枕カバー
makurakabā
pillowcase

シーツ
shītsu
sheet

ベッドスカート
beddo sukāto
valance

羽布団
hanebuton
duvet

キルト
kiruto
quilt

毛布
mōfu
blanket

関連用語 kanrenyōgo • vocabulary

シングルベッド shinguru beddo **single bed**	フットボード futtobōdo **footboard**	不眠症 fuminshō **insomnia**	目覚める mezameru **wake up (v)**	目覚ましをかける mezamashi o kakeru **set the alarm (v)**
ダブルベッド daburu beddo **double bed**	スプリング supuringu **spring**	床につく toko ni tsuku **go to bed (v)**	起きる okiru **get up (v)**	鼾をかく ibiki o kaku **snore (v)**
布団 futon **futon**	カーペット kāpetto **carpet**	寝る neru **go to sleep (v)**	ベッドメーキングする beddomēkingu suru **make the bed (v)**	電気毛布 denkimōfu **electric blanket**

浴室 yokushitsu • bathroom

タオル掛け
taorukake
towel rail

シャワードア
shawā doa
shower door

冷水タップ
reisui tappu
cold tap

温水タップ
onsui tappu
hot tap

シャワーヘッド
shawāheddo
shower head

流し台
nagashidai
washbasin

シャワー
shawā
shower

栓
sen
plug

排水口
haisuikō
drain

便座
benza
toilet seat

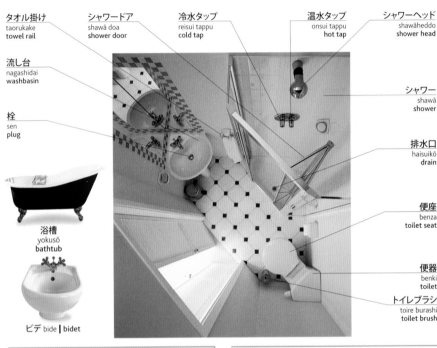

浴槽
yokusō
bathtub

便器
benki
toilet

トイレブラシ
toire burashi
toilet brush

ビデ bide | bidet

関連用語 kanrenyōgo • vocabulary

浴室用キャビネット
yokushitsu-yō kyabinetto
medicine cabinet

バスマット
basu matto
bath mat

トイレットペーパー
toiretto pēpā
toilet roll

シャワーカーテン
shawā kāten
shower curtain

シャワーを浴びる
shawā o abiru
take a shower (v)

風呂に入る
furo ni hairu
take a bath (v)

歯の手入れ ha no teire • dental hygiene

歯ブラシ
haburashi
toothbrush

歯磨き粉
hamigakiko
toothpaste

デンタルフロス
dentaru furosu
dental floss

マウスウォッシュ
mausu wosshu
mouthwash

ヘチマ
hechima
loofah

スポンジ
suponji
sponge

軽石
karuishi
pumice stone

背中洗いブラシ
senaka arai burashi
back brush

デオドラント
deodoranto
deodorant

石鹸皿
sekken-zara
soap dish

石鹸
sekken
soap

シャワージェル
shawā jeru
shower gel

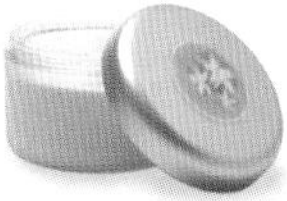

フェースクリーム
fēsu kurīmu
face cream

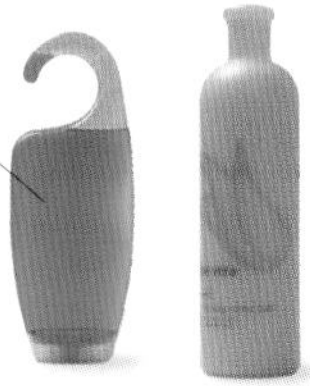

バブルバス
baburu basu
bubble bath

ハンドタオル
hando taoru
hand towel

バスタオル
basu taoru
bath towel

タオル
taoru
towels

ボディローション
bodi rōshon
body lotion

タルカムパウダー
tarukamu paudā
talcum powder

バスローブ
basurōbu
bathrobe

髭剃り higesori ● **shaving**

電気剃刀
denki kamisori
electric razor

髭剃りクリーム
higesori kurīmu
shaving foam

使い捨てカミソリ
tsukaisute kamisori
disposable razor

カミソリの刃
kamisori no ha
razor blade

アフターシェーブ
afutāshēbu
aftershave

子供部屋 kodomobeya • **nursery**

ベビーケア bebī kea • **baby care**

オムツかぶれクリーム
omutsu kabure kurīmu
nappy rash cream

スポンジ
suponji
sponge

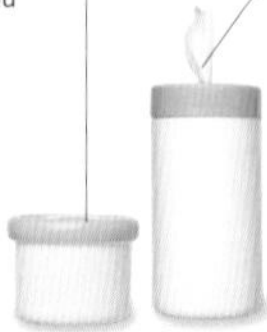

おしり拭き
oshiri fuki
wet wipe

ベビーバス
bebī basu
baby bath

おまる
omaru
potty

おむつ替えシート
omutsu kae shīto
changing mat

睡眠 suimin • **sleeping**

モビール
mobīru
mobile

シーツ
shītsu
sheet

毛布
mōfu
blanket

柵
saku
bars

フリース
furīsu
fleece

ベッドバンパー
beddo bampā
bumper

寝具
shingu
bedding

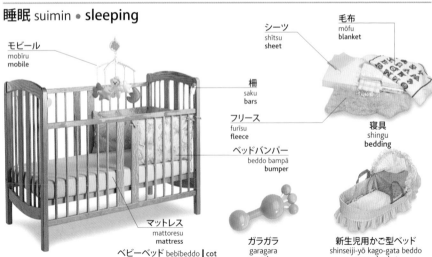

マットレス
mattoresu
mattress

ベビーベッド bebībeddo | **cot**

ガラガラ
garagara
rattle

新生児用かご型ベッド
shinseiji-yō kago-gata beddo
moses basket

遊び asobi • playing

人形
ningyō
doll

縫いぐるみ
nuigurumi
soft toy

ドールハウス
dōru hausu
doll's house

子供の家
kodomo no ie
playhouse

安全用品
anzen yōhin
• safety

戸棚ロック
todana rokku
child lock

ベビーモニター
bebī monitā
baby monitor

テディベア
tedibea
teddy bear

おもちゃ
omocha
toy

おもちゃ籠
omocha kago
toy basket

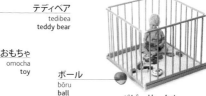

ボール
bōru
ball

ベビーサークル
bebīsākuru
playpen

ベビーゲート
bebī gēto
stair gate

食事 shokuji
• eating

ハイチェア
haichea
high chair

乳首
chikubi
teat

ベビー用マグカップ
bebī-yō magu kappu
drinking cup

哺乳瓶
honyūbin
bottle

外出 gaishutsu • going out

ベビーカー
bebīkā
pushchair

キャリーコット
kyarīkotto
carrycot

乳母車
ubaguruma
pram

フード
fūdo
hood

おむつ
omutsu
nappy

おむつ替えバッグ
omutsu kae baggu
changing bag

ベビースリング
bebī suringu
baby sling

ユティリティルーム yutiriti rūmu • utility room

洗濯 sentaku • laundry

汚れ物
yogoremono
dirty washing

洗濯物
sentakumono
clean clothes

洗濯物入れ
sentakumono ire
laundry basket

洗濯機
sentakki
washing machine

洗濯乾燥機
sentaku kansōki
washer-dryer

乾燥機
kansōki
tumble dryer

洗濯かご
sentakukago
linen basket

物干用ロープ
monohoshi-yō rōpu
clothes line

アイロン
airon
iron

洗濯バサミ
sentaku-basami
clothes peg

乾かす
kawakasu
dry (v)

アイロン台 airondai | **ironing board**

関連用語 kanrenyōgo • vocabulary

（汚れ物を洗濯機に）入れる
(yogoremono o sentakki ni) ireru
load (v)

濯ぐ
susugu
rinse (v)

脱水する
dassui suru
spin (v)

脱水機
dassuiki
spin dryer

アイロンをかける
airon o kakeru
iron (v)

柔軟仕上げ剤
jūnan shiagezai
fabric conditioner

この洗濯機は、どうやって使うのですか。
kono sentakki wa dōyatte tsukaunodesuka?
How do I operate the washing machine?

色物／白系の設定は何ですか。
iromono/shirokei no settei wa nandesuka?
What is the setting for coloureds/whites?

掃除道具 sōji dōgu · cleaning equipment

吸い込みホース
suikomi hōsu
suction hose

ブラシ
burashi
brush

ちりとり
chiritori
dustpan

漂白剤
hyōhakuzai
bleach

粉末洗剤
funmatsu senzai
powder

バケツ
baketsu
bucket

液体洗剤
ekitai senzai
liquid

ダスター
dasutā
duster

掃除機
sōjiki
vacuum cleaner

モップ
moppu
mop

洗剤
senzai
detergent

艶出し剤
tsuyadashizai
polish

掃除 sōji · activities

擦る
kosuru
clean (v)

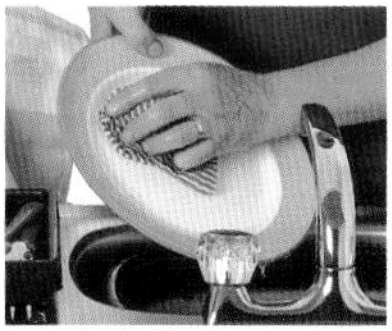

洗う
arau
wash (v)

拭く
fuku
wipe (v)

ゴシゴシ洗う
goshigoshi arau
scrub (v)

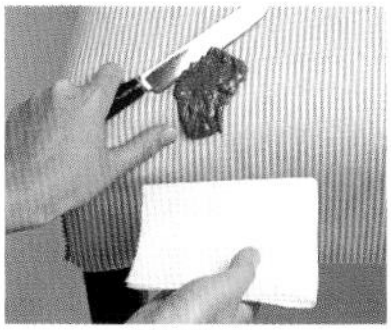

擦り取る
kosuritoru
scrape (v)

箒
hōki
broom

掃く
haku
sweep (v)

埃を払う
hokori o harau
dust (v)

磨く
migaku
polish (v)

作業場 sagyōba ● workshop

チャック
chakku
chuck

ドリルビット
doriru bitto
drill bit

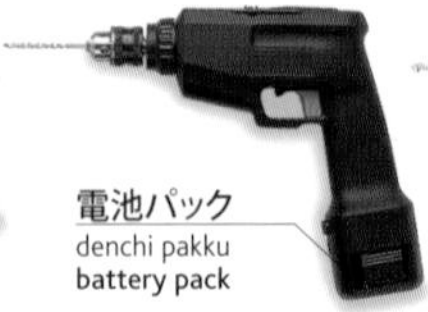

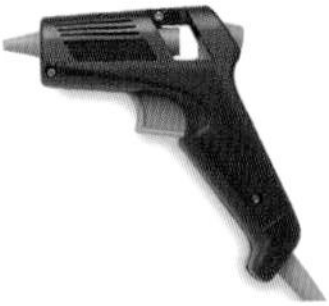

電池パック
denchi pakku
battery pack

ジグソー
jigusō
jigsaw

充電式ドリル
jūden-shiki doriru
rechargeable drill

電気ドリル
denki doriru
electric drill

グルーガン
gurū gan
glue gun

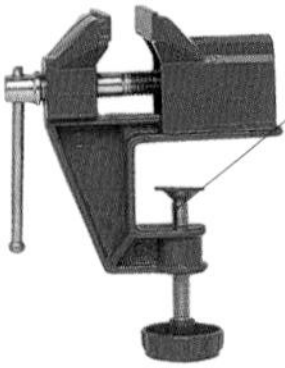

クランプ
kurampu
clamp

鋸刃
nokogiri-ba
blade

万力
manriki
vice

サンダー
sandā
sander

丸鋸
marunoko
circular saw

作業台
sagyōdai
workbench

木工用接着剤
mokkō-yō setchakuzai
wood glue

ルーター
rūtā
router

鉋屑
kannakuzu
wood shavings

工具棚
kōgu-dana
tool rack

ハンドドリル
hando doriru
bit brace

延長コード
enchō kōdo
extension lead

テクニック tekunikku • techniques

切る
kiru
cut (v)

（鋸で）切る
(nokogiri de) kiru
saw (v)

穴をあける
ana o akeru
drill (v)

（金槌で）打つ
(kanazuchi de) utsu
hammer (v)

鉋をかける kanna o kakeru
plane (v)

旋盤加工する
sembankakō suru | turn (v)

半田
handa
solder

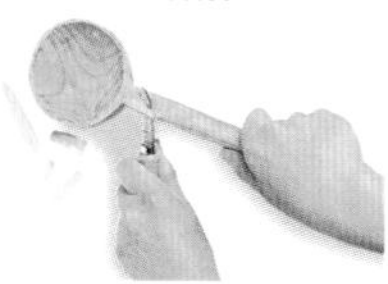

削る kezuru | carve (v)

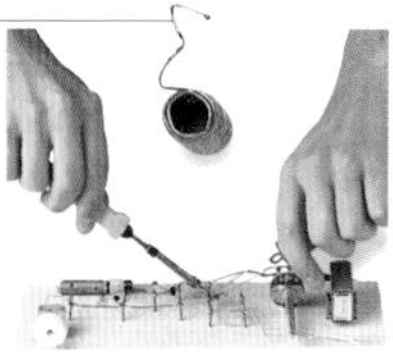

半田付けする
handazuke suru | solder (v)

材料 zairyō • materials

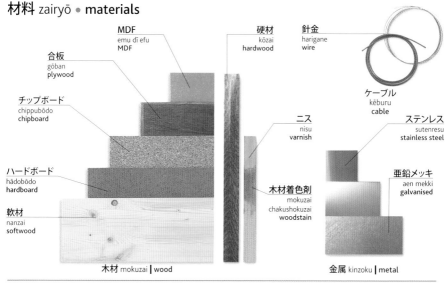

MDF
emu dī efu
MDF

硬材
kōzai
hardwood

針金
harigane
wire

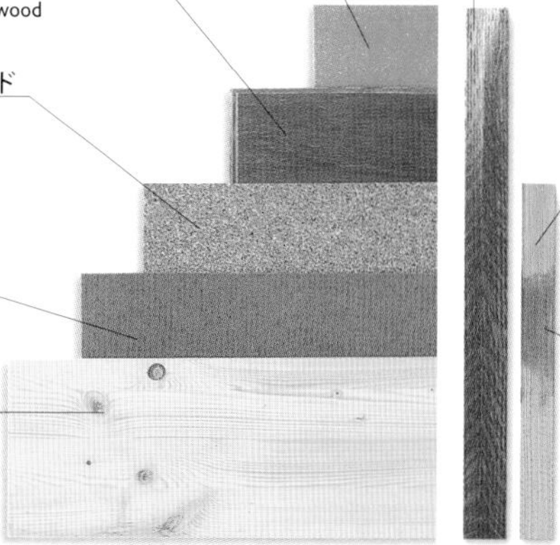

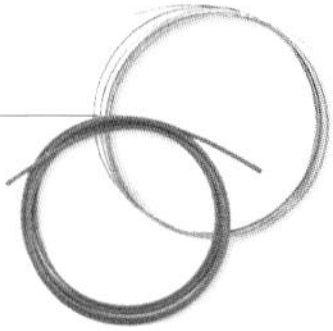

合板
gōban
plywood

ケーブル
kēburu
cable

チップボード
chippubōdo
chipboard

ニス
nisu
varnish

ステンレス
sutenresu
stainless steel

ハードボード
hādobōdo
hardboard

木材着色剤
mokuzai
chakushokuzai
woodstain

亜鉛メッキ
aen mekki
galvanised

軟材
nanzai
softwood

木材 mokuzai | wood

金属 kinzoku | metal

道具箱 dōgubako • toolbox

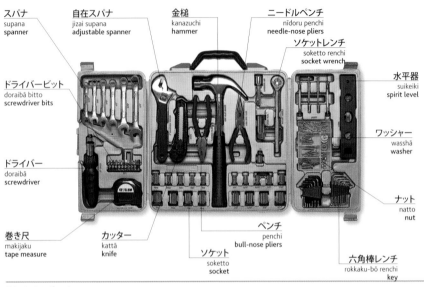

スパナ
supana
spanner

自在スパナ
jizai supana
adjustable spanner

金槌
kanazuchi
hammer

ニードルペンチ
nīdoru penchi
needle-nose pliers

ソケットレンチ
soketto renchi
socket wrench

水平器
suikeiki
spirit level

ドライバービット
doraibā bitto
screwdriver bits

ワッシャー
wasshā
washer

ドライバー
doraibā
screwdriver

ナット
natto
nut

巻き尺
makijaku
tape measure

カッター
kattā
knife

ペンチ
penchi
bull-nose pliers

ソケット
soketto
socket

六角棒レンチ
rokkaku-bō renchi
key

ドリルビット doriru bitto • drill bits

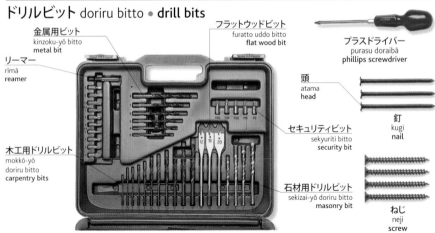

金属用ビット
kinzoku-yō bitto
metal bit

フラットウッドビット
furatto uddo bitto
flat wood bit

プラスドライバー
purasu doraibā
phillips screwdriver

リーマー
rīmā
reamer

頭
atama
head

セキュリティビット
sekyuriti bitto
security bit

釘
kugi
nail

木工用ドリルビット
mokkō-yō
doriru bitto
carpentry bits

石材用ドリルビット
sekizai-yō doriru bitto
masonry bit

ねじ
neji
screw

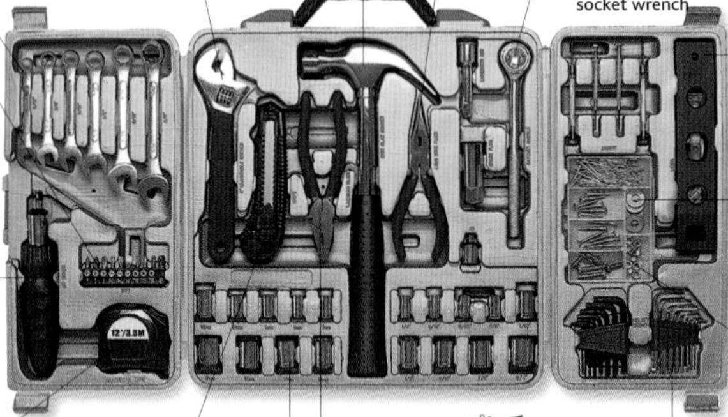

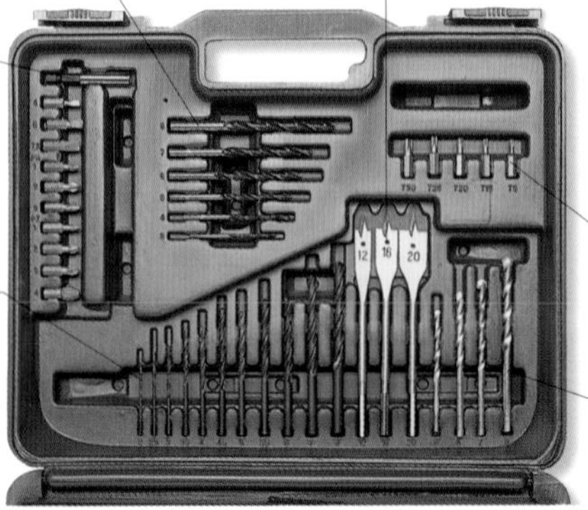

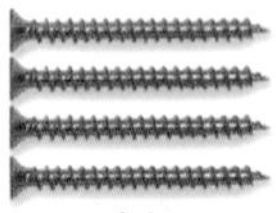

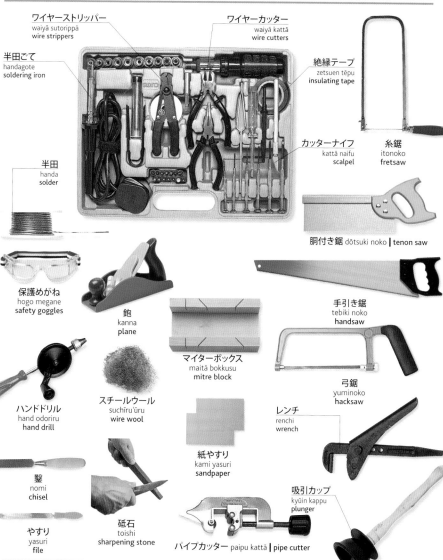

ワイヤーストリッパー
waiyā sutorippā
wire strippers

ワイヤーカッター
waiyā kattā
wire cutters

半田ごて
handagote
soldering iron

絶縁テープ
zetsuen tēpu
insulating tape

半田
handa
solder

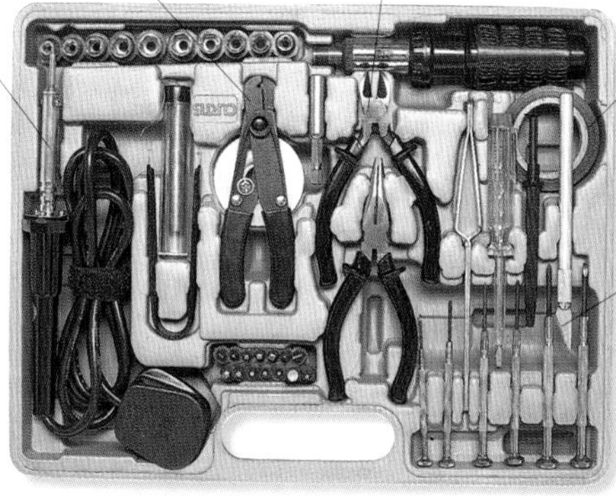

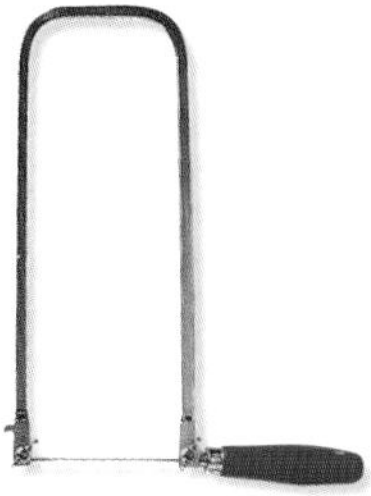

カッターナイフ
kattā naifu
scalpel

糸鋸
itonoko
fretsaw

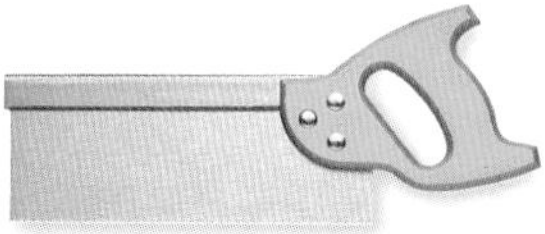

胴付き鋸 dōtsuki noko | tenon saw

保護めがね
hogo megane
safety goggles

鉋
kanna
plane

手引き鋸
tebiki noko
handsaw

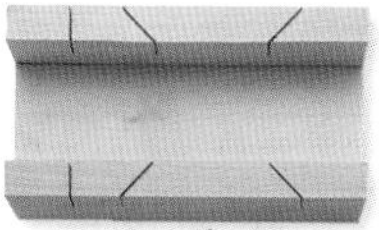

マイターボックス
maitā bokkusu
mitre block

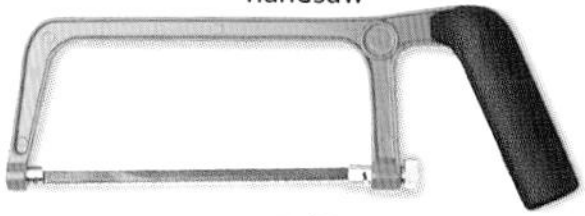

ハンドドリル
hand odoriru
hand drill

スチールウール
suchīru'ūru
wire wool

弓鋸
yuminoko
hacksaw

レンチ
renchi
wrench

鑿
nomi
chisel

紙やすり
kami yasuri
sandpaper

吸引カップ
kyūin kappu
plunger

やすり
yasuri
file

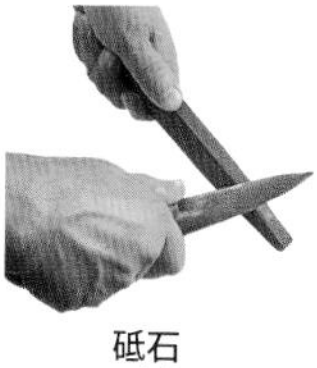

砥石
toishi
sharpening stone

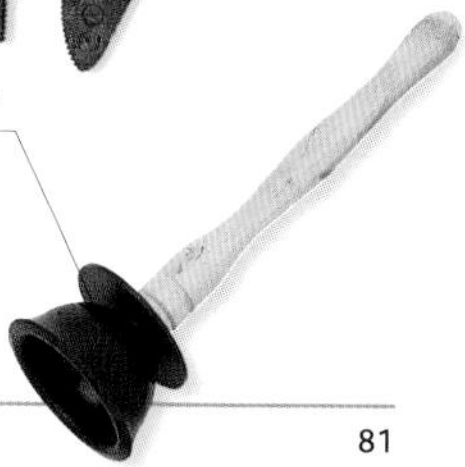

パイプカッター paipu kattā | pipe cutter

内装工事 naisō kōji • decorating

鋏
hasami
scissors

クラフトナイフ
kurafuto naifu
craft knife

下げ振り
sagefuri
plumb line

スクレーパー
sukurēpā
scraper

内装工事職人
naisō kōji shokunin
decorator

壁紙
kabegami
wallpaper

脚立
kyatatsu
stepladder

壁紙刷毛
kabegami-bake
wallpaper brush

糊付け台
nori-zuke dai
pasting table

糊刷毛
noribake
pasting brush

壁紙用糊
kabegami-yō nori
wallpaper paste

バケツ
baketsu
bucket

壁紙を張り替える kabegami o harikaeru | **wallpaper (v)**

剥がす hagasu | **strip (v)**

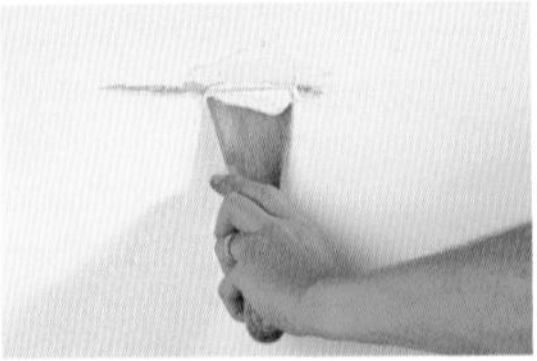

埋める umeru | **fill (v)**

研磨する kenma suru | **sand (v)**

漆喰を塗る shikkui o nuru | **plaster (v)**

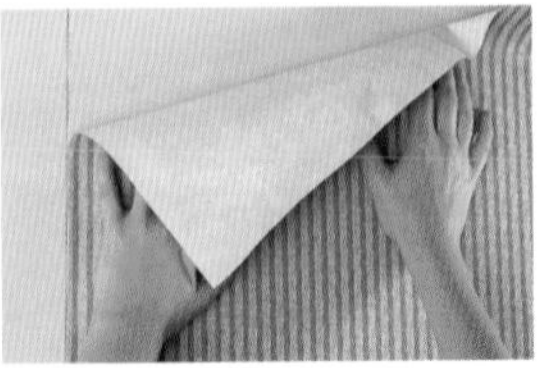

壁紙を貼る kabegami o haru | **hang (v)**

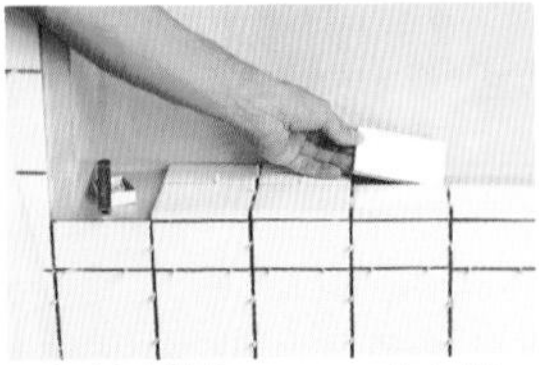

タイルを貼る tairu o haru | **tile (v)**

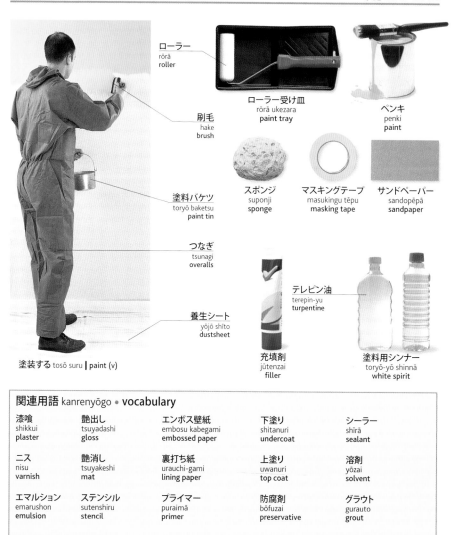

ローラー
rôrā
roller

ローラー受け皿
rôrā ukezara
paint tray

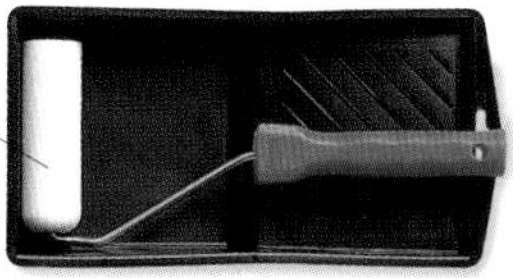

ペンキ
penki
paint

刷毛
hake
brush

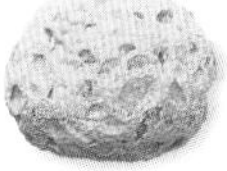

スポンジ
suponji
sponge

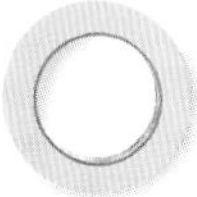

マスキングテープ
masukingu têpu
masking tape

サンドペーパー
sandopêpā
sandpaper

塗料バケツ
toryō baketsu
paint tin

つなぎ
tsunagi
overalls

テレビン油
terepin-yu
turpentine

養生シート
yōjō shīto
dustsheet

充填剤
jūtenzai
filler

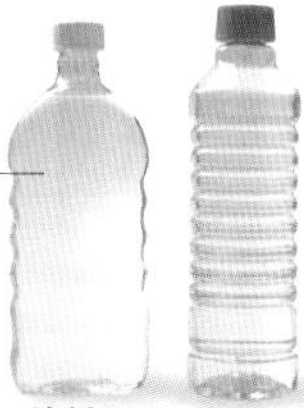

塗料用シンナー
toryō-yō shinnā
white spirit

塗装する tosō suru **|** paint (v)

関連用語 kanrenyōgo • vocabulary

漆喰 shikkui **plaster**	艶出し tsuyadashi **gloss**	エンボス壁紙 embosu kabegami **embossed paper**	下塗り shitanuri **undercoat**	シーラー shīrā **sealant**
ニス nisu **varnish**	艶消し tsuyakeshi **mat**	裏打ち紙 urauchi-gami **lining paper**	上塗り uwanuri **top coat**	溶剤 yōzai **solvent**
エマルション emarushon **emulsion**	ステンシル sutenshiru **stencil**	プライマー puraimā **primer**	防腐剤 bōfuzai **preservative**	グラウト gurauto **grout**

庭 niwa • **garden**

庭の様式 niwa no yōshiki • **garden styles**

庭のアクセント
niwa no akusento
• **garden features**

テラスガーデン terasu gāden | patio garden

フォーマルな庭園 fōmaru-na teien | formal garden

コテージガーデン
kotēji gāden
cottage garden

ハーブ園
hābu-en
herb garden

屋上庭園
okujō teien
roof garden

石庭
sekitei
rock garden

中庭 nakaniwa | courtyard

ウォーターガーデン
wōtā gāden
water garden

ハンギングバスケット
hangingu basuketto
hanging basket

トレリス torerisu | trellis

パーゴラ
pāgora
pergola

敷石
shiki'ishi
paving

小道
komichi
path

堆肥積み
taihi-zumi
compost heap

門
mon
gate

花壇
kadan
flowerbed

芝生
shibafu
lawn

池
ike
pond

垣根
kakine
hedge

アーチ
āchi
arch

家庭菜園
katei saien
vegetable garden

ハーブのボーダー花壇
hābu no bōdā kadan
herbaceous border

納屋
naya
shed

温室
onshitsu
greenhouse

柵
saku
fence

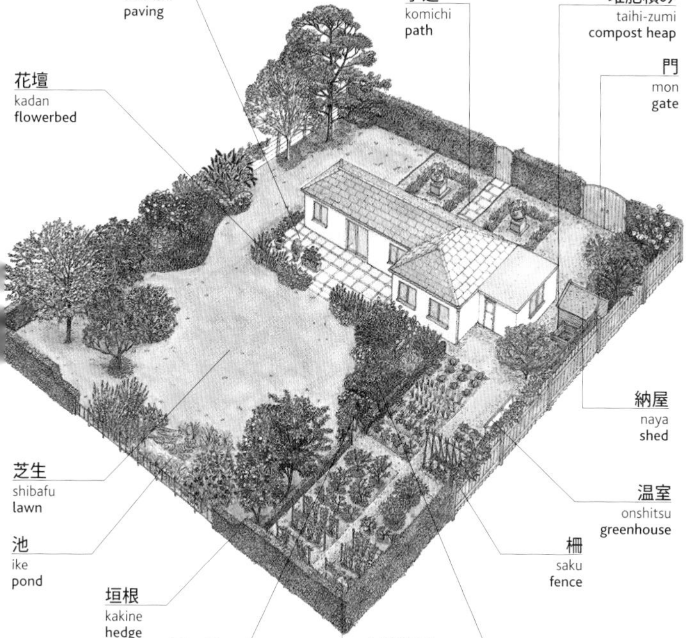

土壌 dojō
● soil

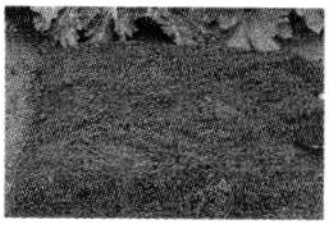

表土
hyōdo
topsoil

砂土
sunatsuchi
sand

石灰質土壌
sekkai-shitsu dojō
chalk

沈泥
chindei
silt

粘土
nendo
clay

デッキ
dekki
decking

噴水 funsui | fountain

庭の植物 niwa no shokubutsu • **garden plants**

植物の種類 shokubutsu no shurui • **types of plants**

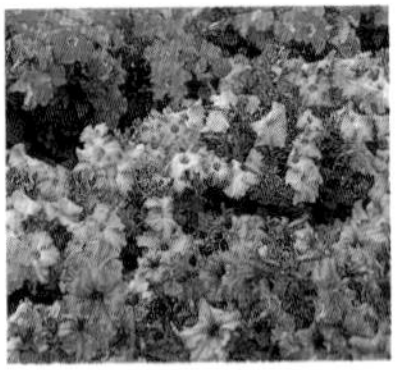

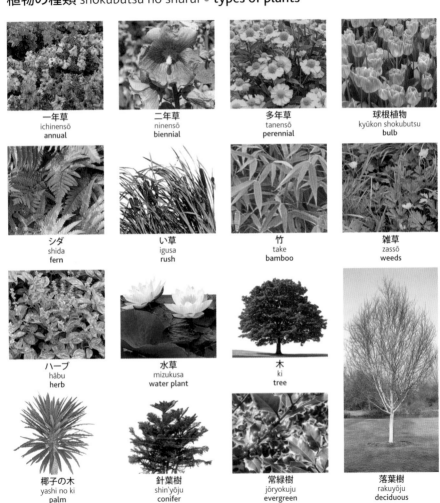

一年草
ichinensō
annual

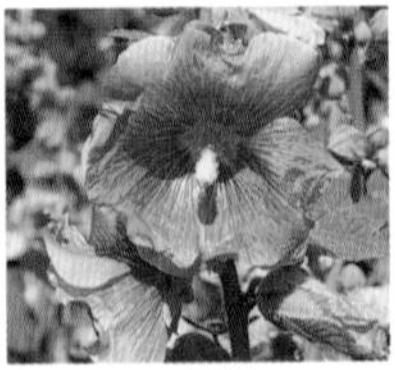

二年草
ninensō
biennial

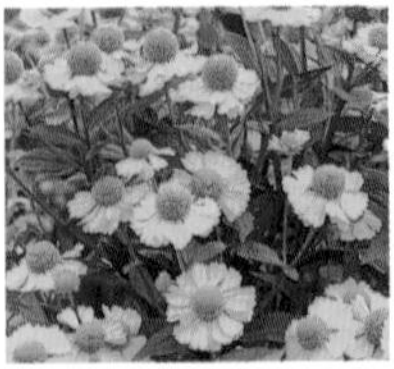

多年草
tanensō
perennial

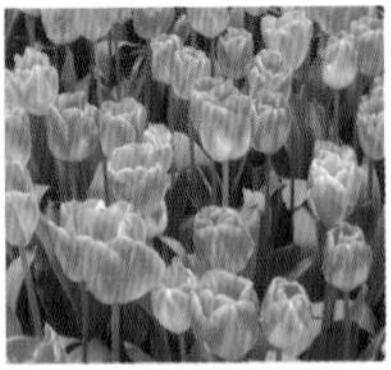

球根植物
kyūkon shokubutsu
bulb

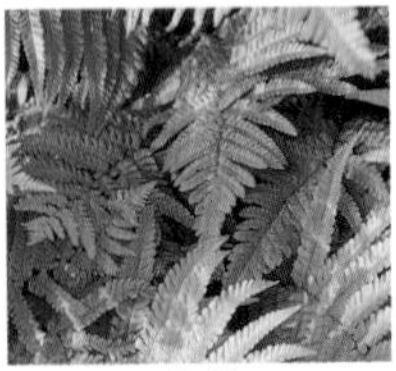

シダ
shida
fern

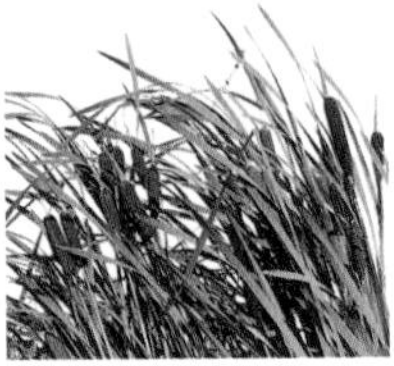

い草
igusa
rush

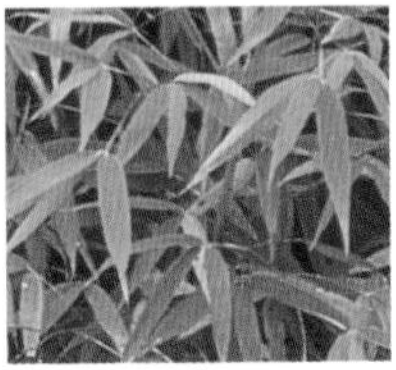

竹
take
bamboo

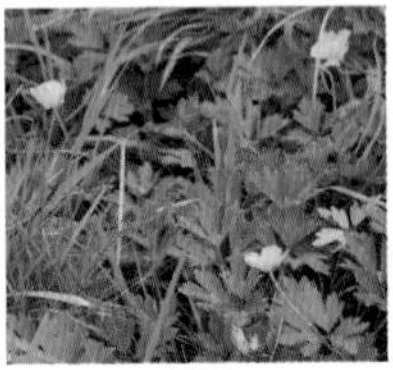

雑草
zassō
weeds

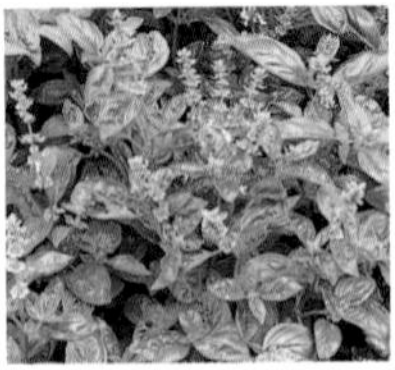

ハーブ
hābu
herb

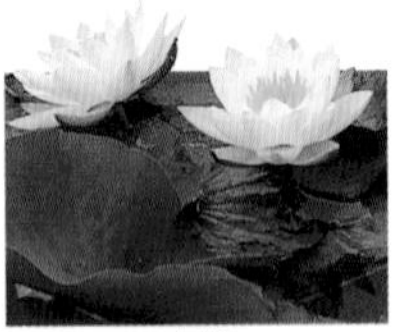

水草
mizukusa
water plant

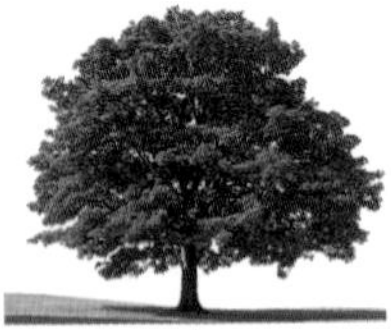

木
ki
tree

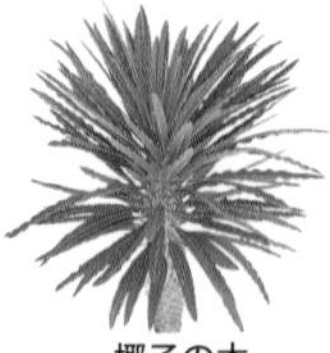

椰子の木
yashi no ki
palm

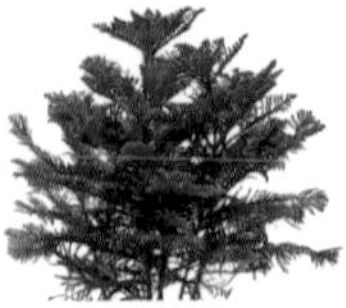

針葉樹
shin'yōju
conifer

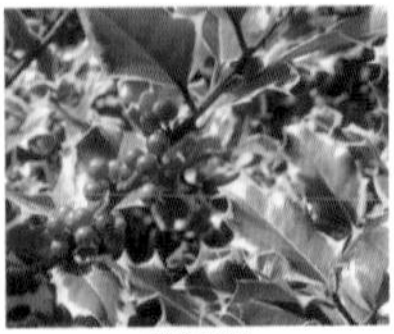

常緑樹
jōryokuju
evergreen

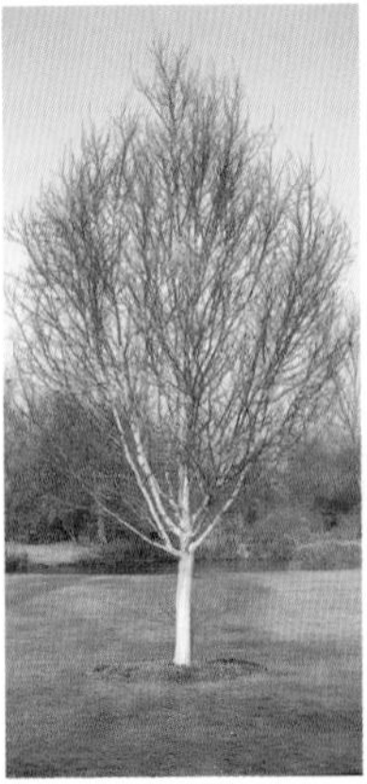

落葉樹
rakuyōju
deciduous

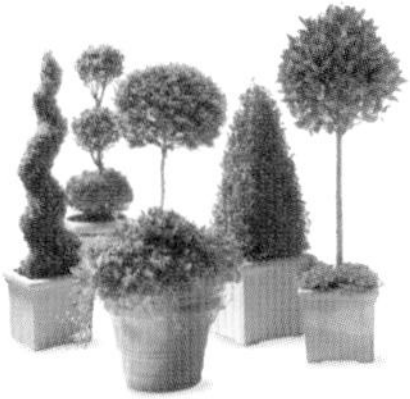

トピアリー
topiarī
topiary

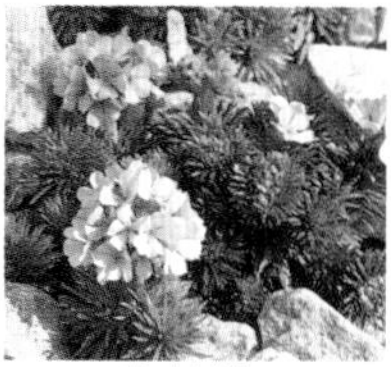

高山植物
kōzan shokubutsu
alpine

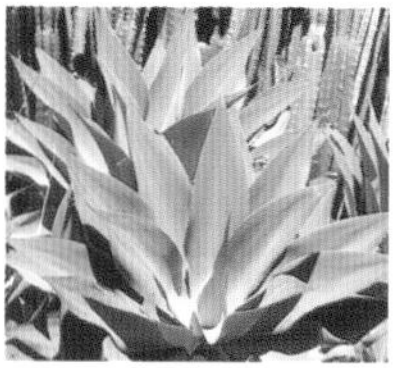

多肉植物
taniku shokubutsu
succulent

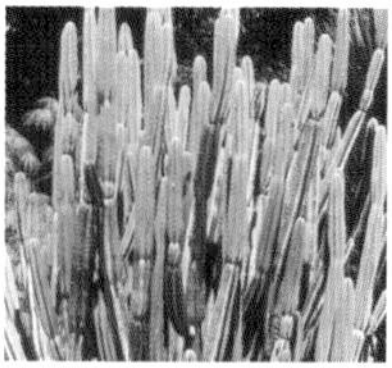

サボテン
saboten
cactus

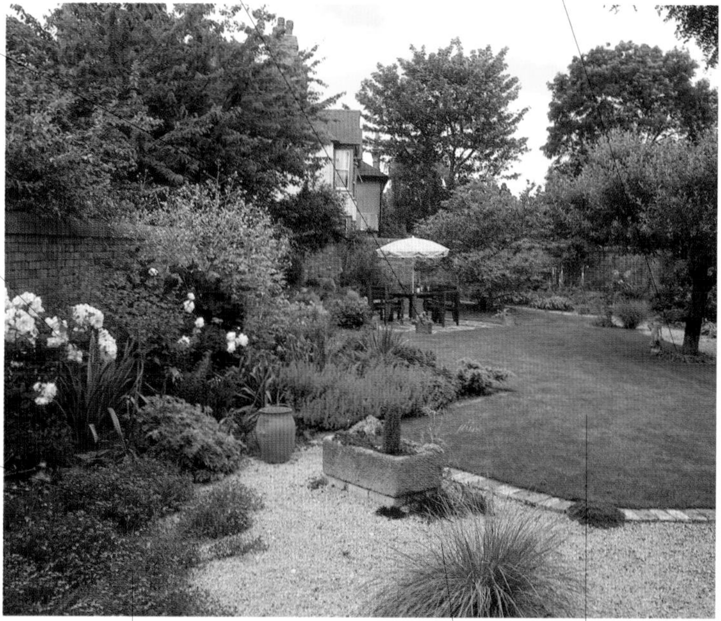

植木
ueki
potted plant

陰性植物
insei shokubutsu
shade plant

蔓性植物
tsurusei shokubutsu
climber

顕花性低木
kenkasei teiboku
flowering shrub

グランドカバー
gurando kabā
ground cover

匍匐植物
hofuku shokubutsu
creeper

観葉植物
kan'yō
shokubutsu
ornamental

草
kusa
grass

園芸用品 engei yōhin • garden tools

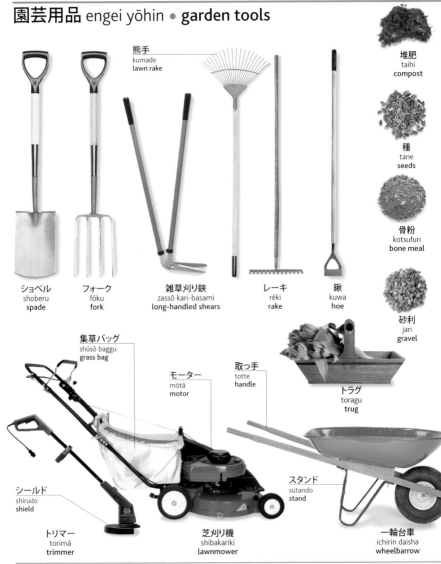

堆肥
taihi
compost

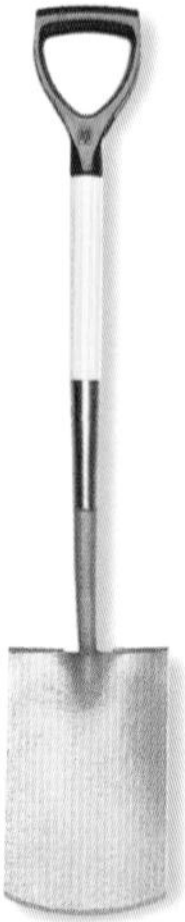

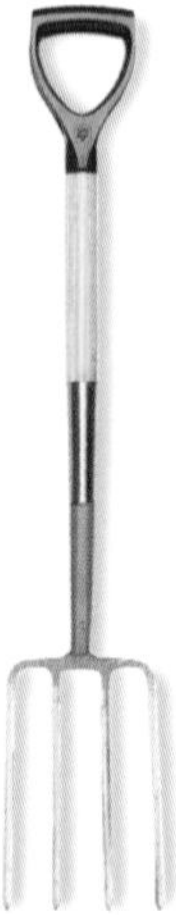

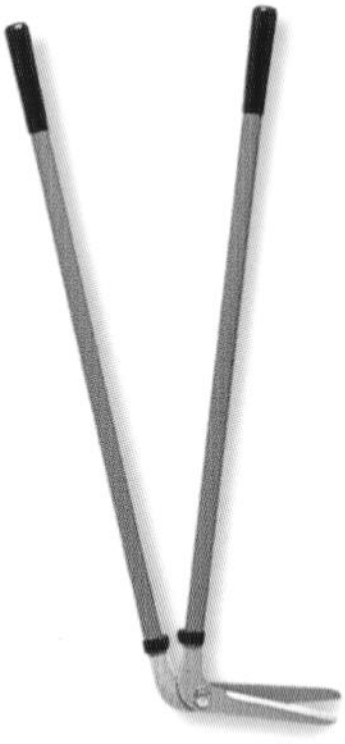

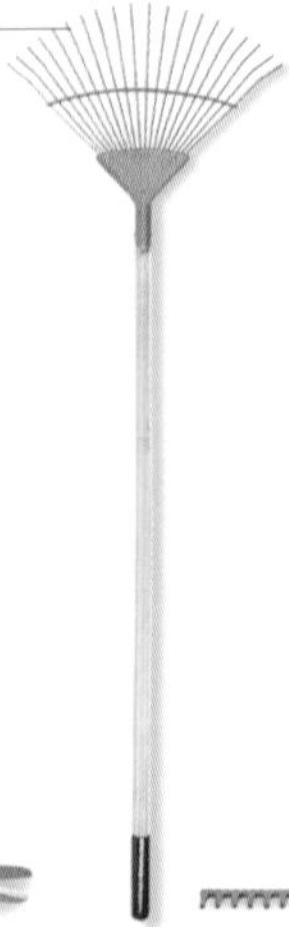

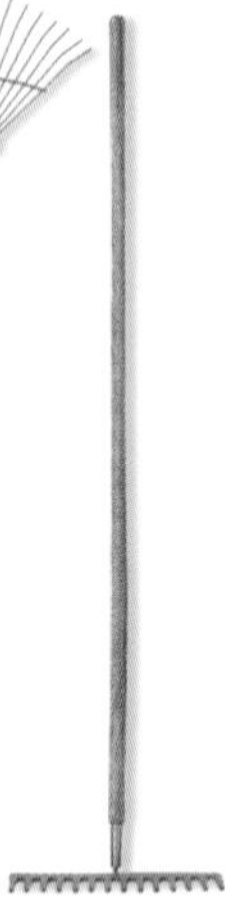

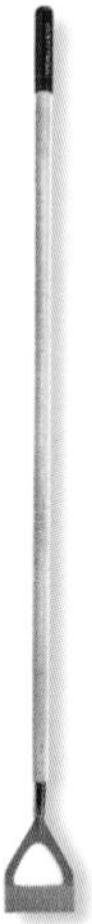

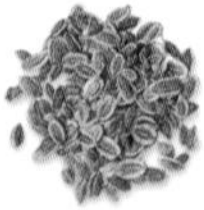

種
tane
seeds

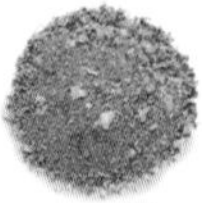

骨粉
kotsufun
bone meal

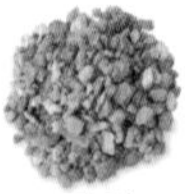

砂利
jari
gravel

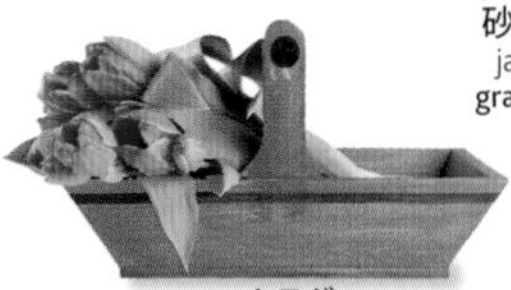

ショベル
shoberu
spade

フォーク
fōku
fork

熊手
kumade
lawn rake

雑草刈り鋏
zassō kari-basami
long-handled shears

レーキ
rēki
rake

鍬
kuwa
hoe

集草バッグ
shūsō baggu
grass bag

モーター
mōtā
motor

取っ手
totte
handle

トラグ
toragu
trug

シールド
shīrudo
shield

トリマー
torimā
trimmer

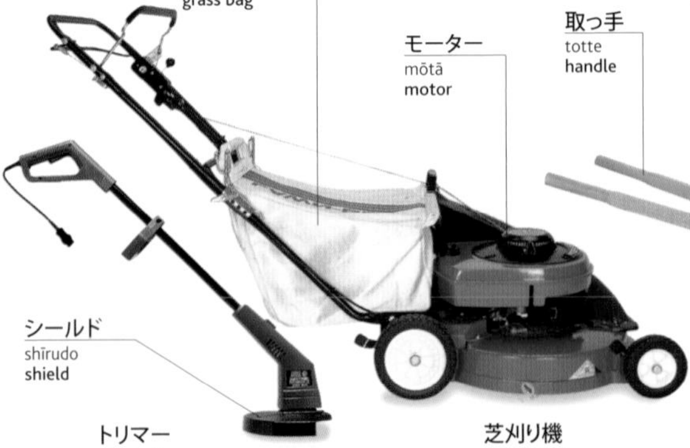

芝刈り機
shibakariki
lawnmower

スタンド
sutando
stand

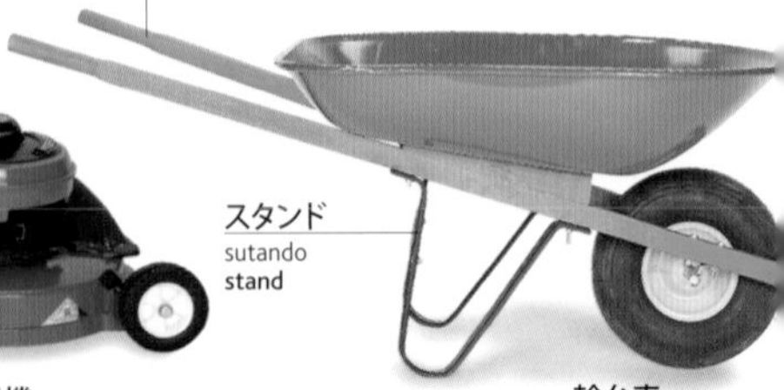

一輪台車
ichirin daisha
wheelbarrow

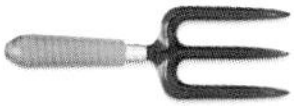

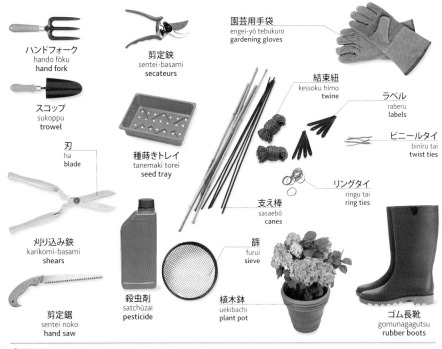

ハンドフォーク
hando fōku
hand fork

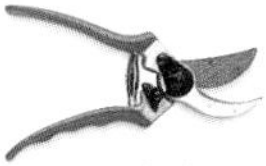

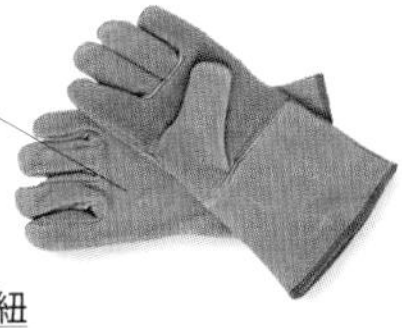

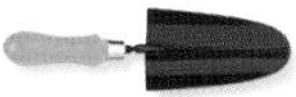

スコップ
sukoppu
trowel

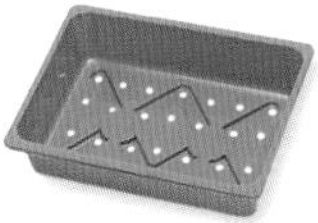

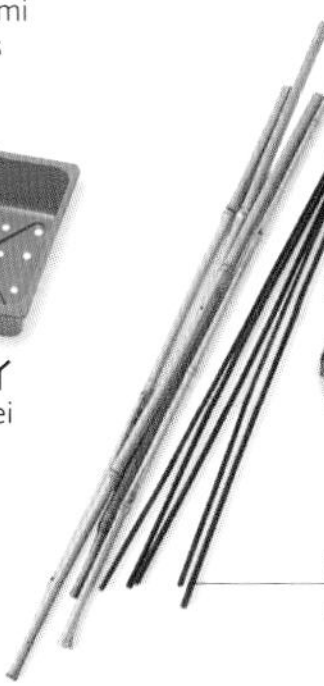

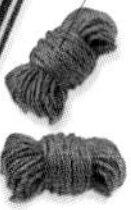

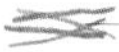

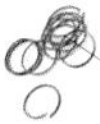

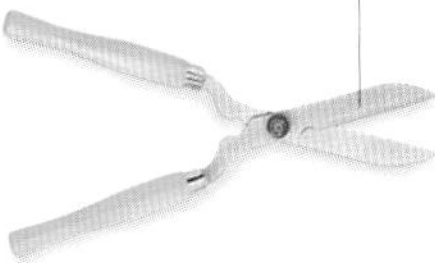

刃
ha
blade

刈り込み鋏
karikomi-basami
shears

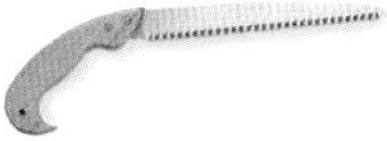

剪定鋸
sentei noko
hand saw

剪定鋏
sentei-basami
secateurs

種蒔きトレイ
tanemaki torei
seed tray

殺虫剤
satchūzai
pesticide

園芸用手袋
engei-yō tebukuro
gardening gloves

結束紐
kessoku himo
twine

ラベル
raberu
labels

ビニールタイ
binīru tai
twist ties

リングタイ
ringu tai
ring ties

支え棒
sasaebō
canes

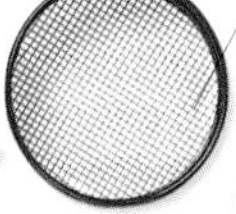

篩
furui
sieve

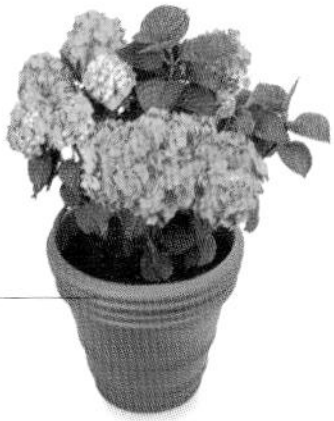

植木鉢
uekibachi
plant pot

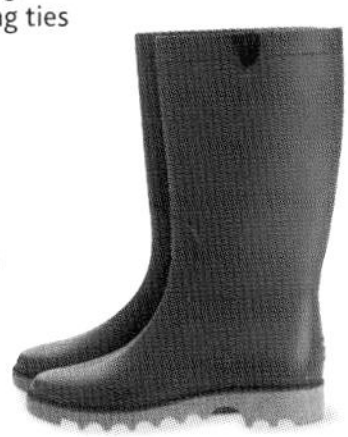

ゴム長靴
gomunagagutsu
rubber boots

水やり mizuyari • watering

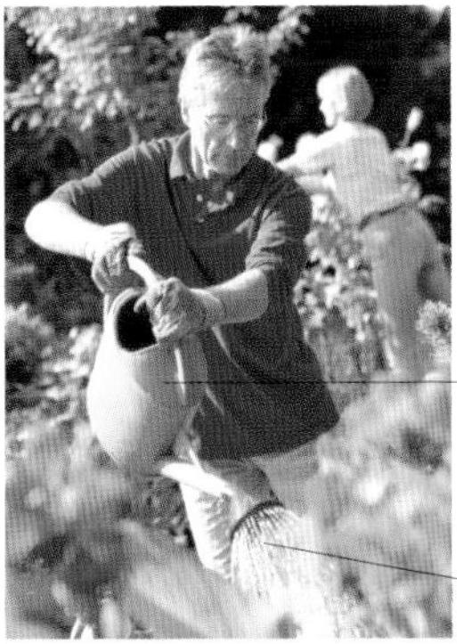

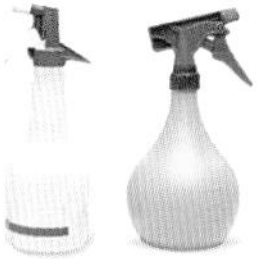

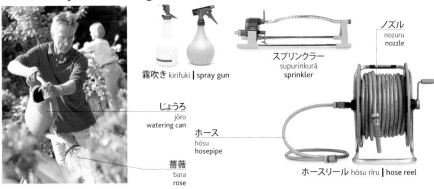

霧吹き kirifuki | spray gun

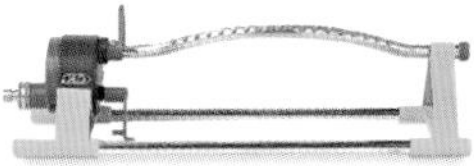

スプリンクラー
supurinkurā
sprinkler

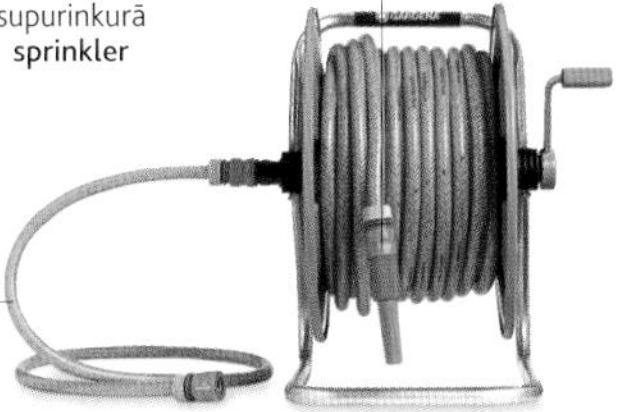

ノズル
nozuru
nozzle

じょうろ
jōro
watering can

ホース
hōsu
hosepipe

薔薇
bara
rose

ホースリール hōsu rīru | hose reel

園芸 engei • **gardening**

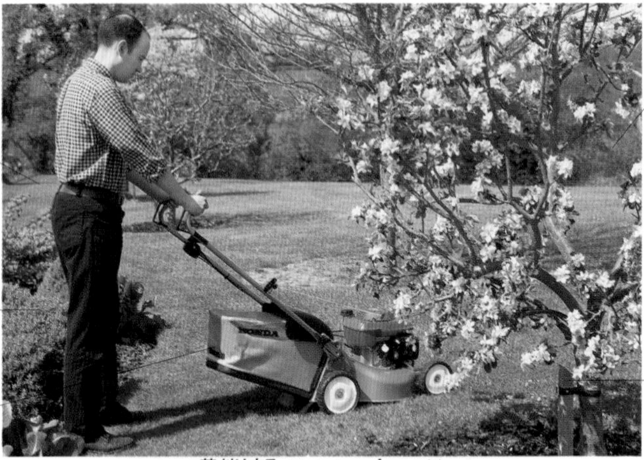

垣根
kakine
hedge

芝生
shibafu
lawn

花壇
kadan
flowerbed

芝刈り機
shibakariki
lawnmower

杭
kui
stake

芝刈りする shibakari suru | mow (v)

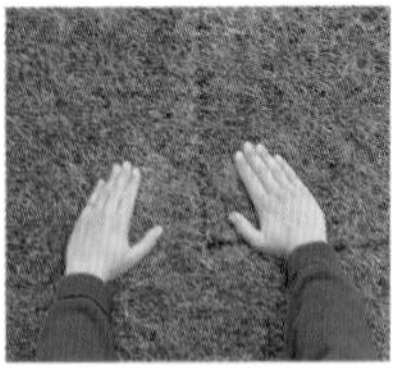

芝で覆う
shiba de ōu
turf (v)

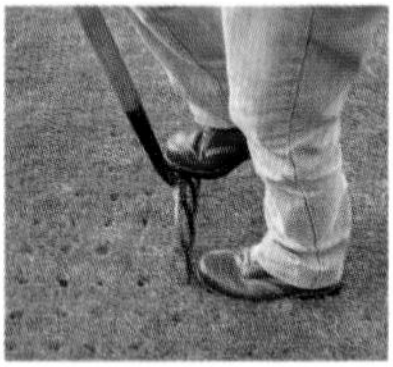

刺す
sasu
spike (v)

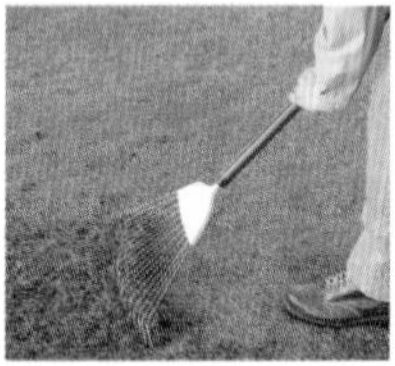

掃く
haku
rake (v)

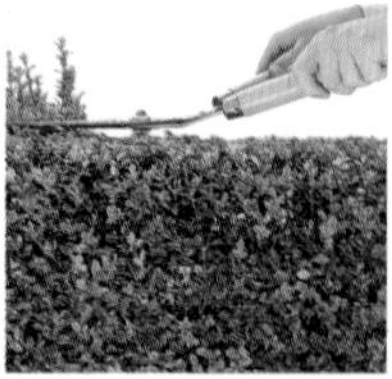

刈り込む
karikomu
trim (v)

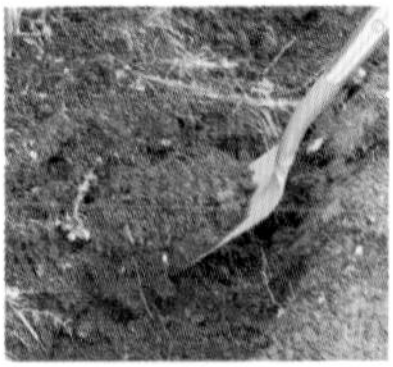

掘る
horu
dig (v)

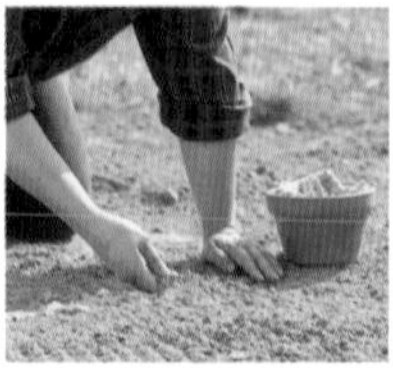

種を植える
tane o ueru
sow (v)

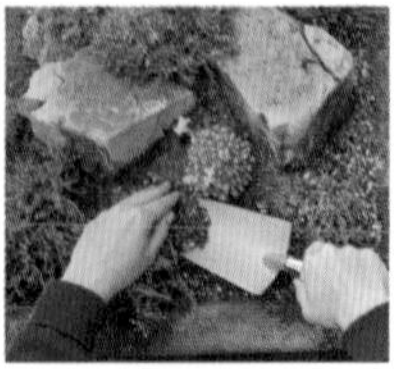

追肥する
tsuihi suru
top dress (v)

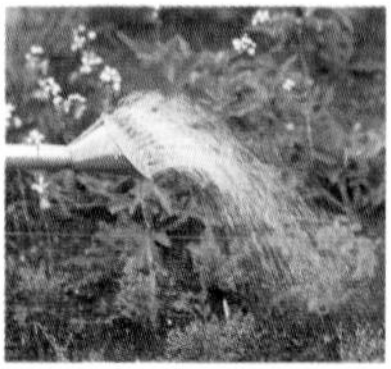

水をやる
mizu o yaru
water (v)

支え棒
sasaebō
cane

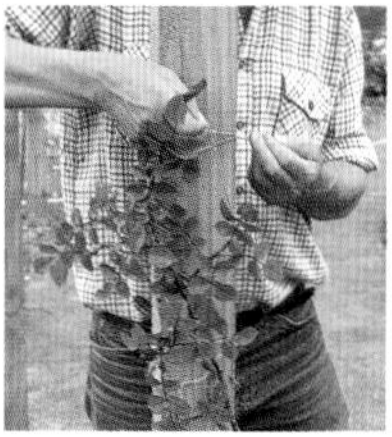

整枝する
seishi suru
train (v)

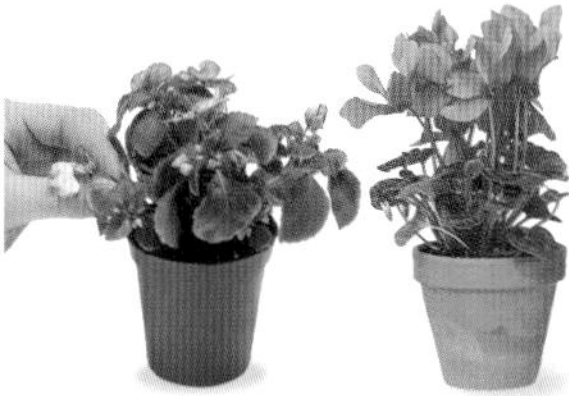

（終わった花を）摘み取る
(owatta hana o) tsumitoru
deadhead (v)

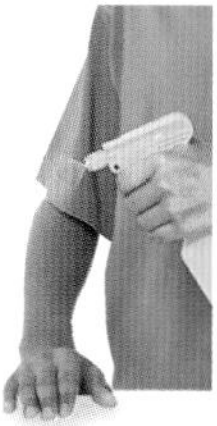

噴霧する
funmu suru
spray (v)

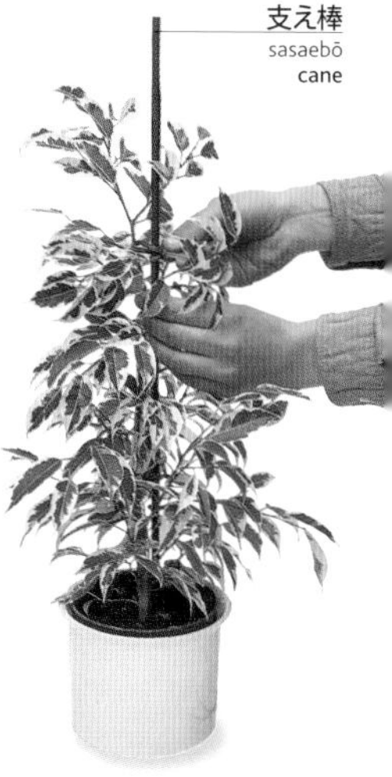

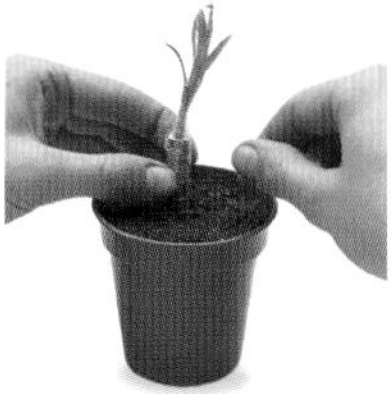

接ぎ木する
tsugiki suru
graft (v)

切り枝
kirieda
cutting

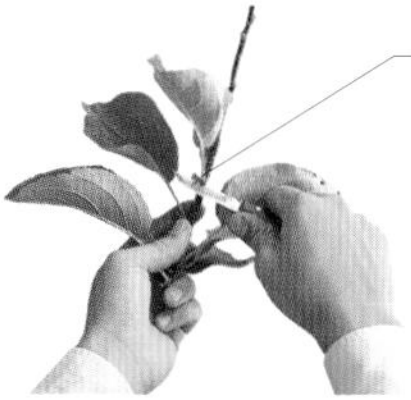

枝分けする
edawake suru
propagate (v)

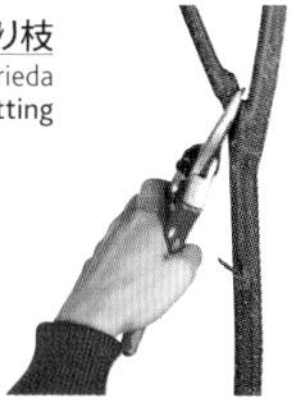

剪定する
sentei suru
prune (v)

（支えに）繋ぐ
(sasae ni) tsunagu
stake (v)

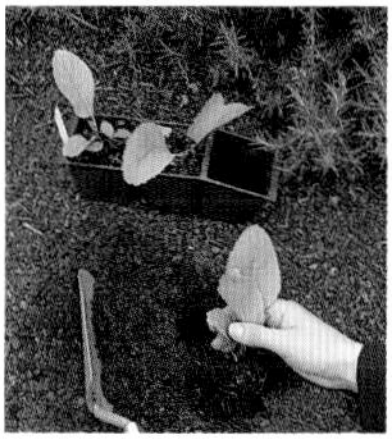

植え替える
ue-kaeru
transplant (v)

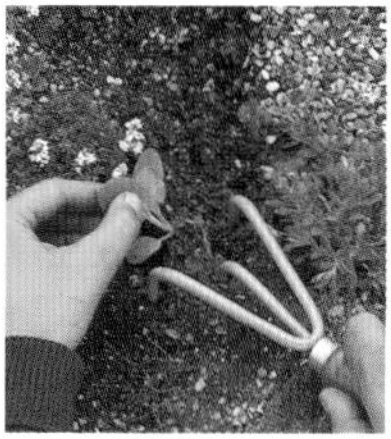

除草する
josō suru
weed (v)

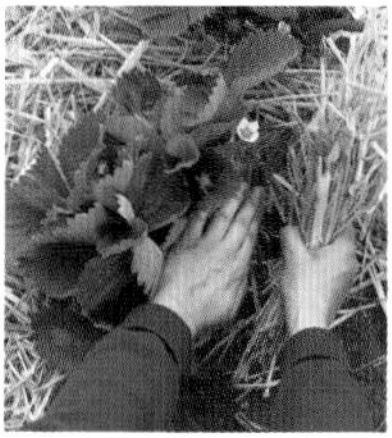

根覆いする
neōi suru
mulch (v)

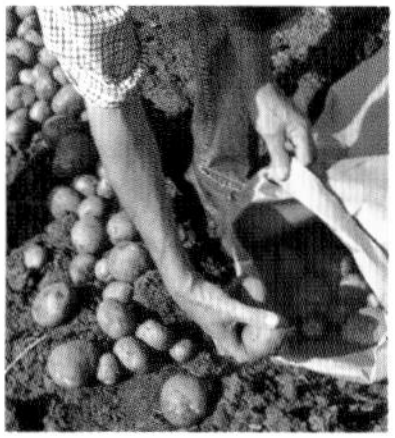

収穫する
shūkaku suru
harvest (v)

関連用語 kanrenyōgo • **vocabulary**

栽培する saibai suru **cultivate (v)**	造園する zōen suru **landscape (v)**	肥料をやる hiryō o yaru **fertilize (v)**	篩にかける furui ni kakeru **sieve (v)**	有機 yūki **organic**	苗 nae **seedling**	心土 shindo **subsoil**
手入れする teire suru **tend (v)**	（大きな鉢に）植え替える (ōkina hachi ni) ue-kaeru **pot up (v)**	摘む tsumu **pick (v)**	空気に曝す kūki ni sarasu **aerate (v)**	排水 haisui **drainage**	肥料 hiryō **fertilizer**	除草剤 josōzai **weedkiller**

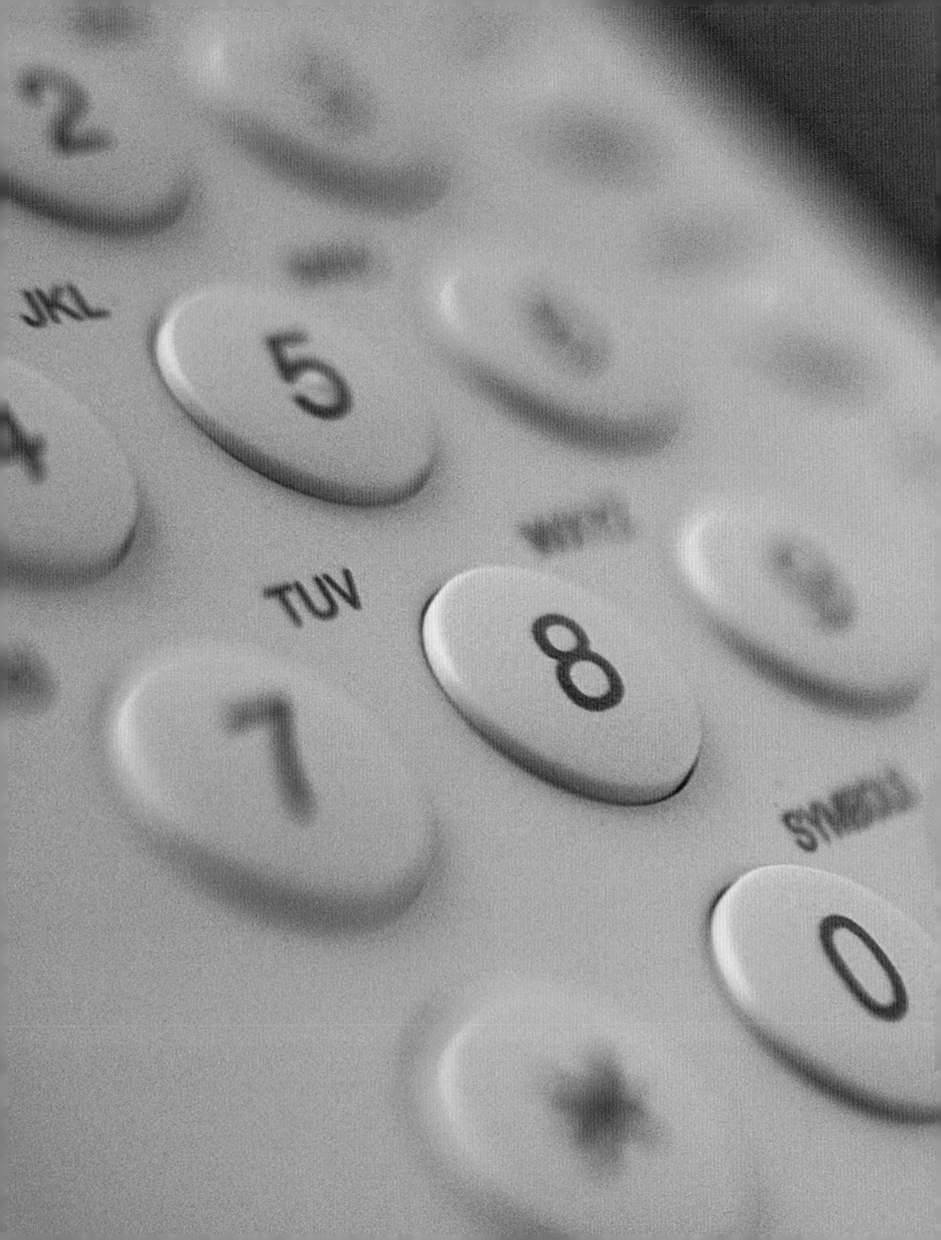

職務 shokumu
services

緊急サービス kinkyū sābisu • emergency services

救急車 kyūkyūsha • ambulance

救急車 kyūkyūsha | ambulance

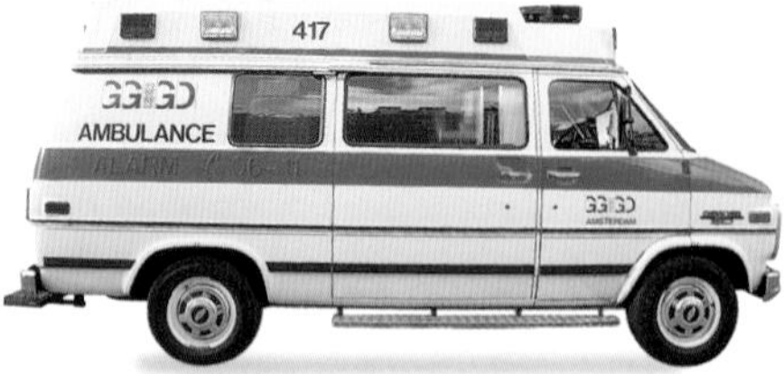

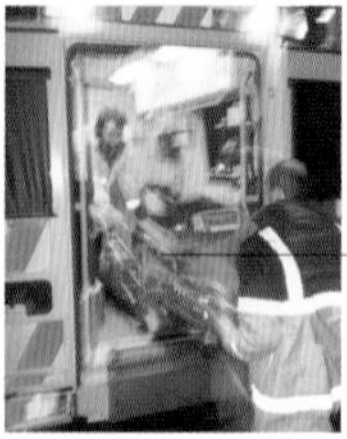

担架
tanka
stretcher

救急医療隊員 kyūkyū iryō tai'in
paramedic

警察 keisatsu • police

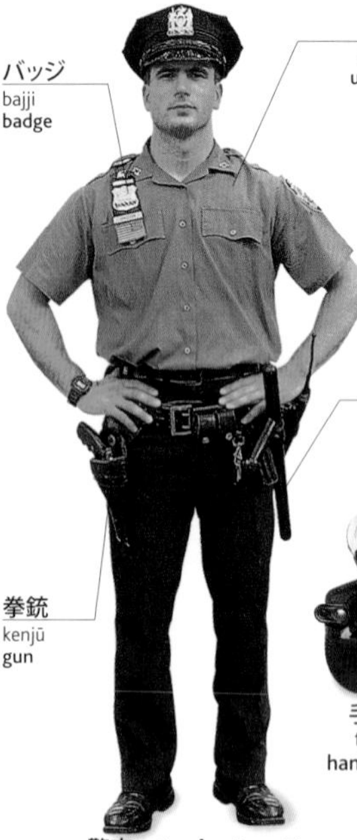

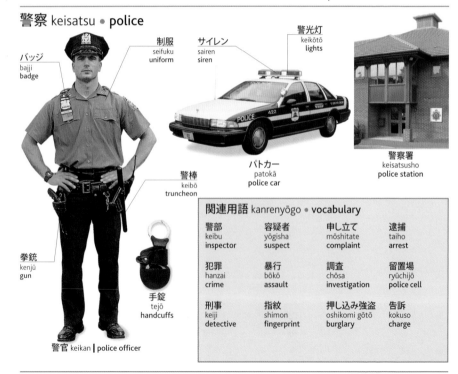

バッジ
bajji
badge

制服
seifuku
uniform

サイレン
sairen
siren

警光灯
keikōtō
lights

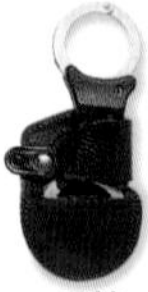

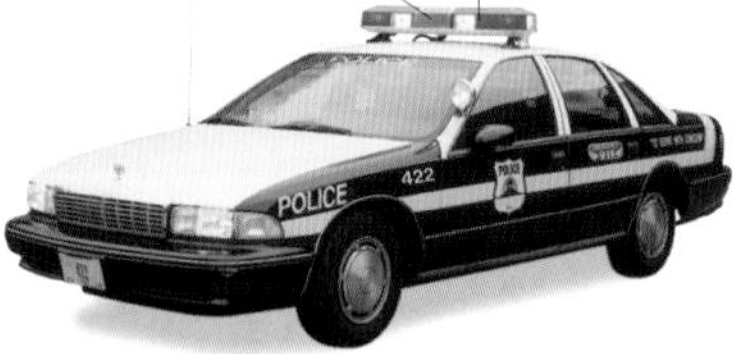

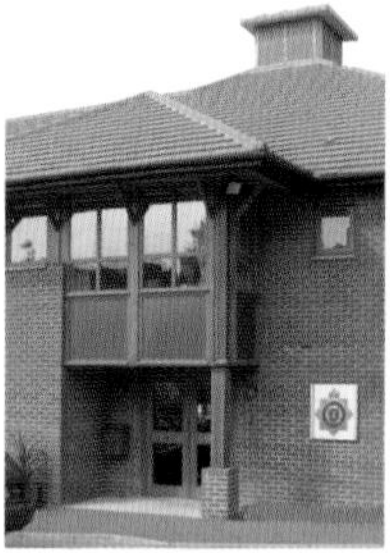

警察署
keisatsusho
police station

警棒
keibō
truncheon

パトカー
patokā
police car

拳銃
kenjū
gun

手錠
tejō
handcuffs

警官 keikan | police officer

関連用語 kanrenyōgo • vocabulary

警部 keibu inspector	容疑者 yōgisha suspect	申し立て mōshitate complaint	逮捕 taiho arrest
犯罪 hanzai crime	暴行 bōkō assault	調査 chōsa investigation	留置場 ryūchijō police cell
刑事 keiji detective	指紋 shimon fingerprint	押し込み強盗 oshikomi gōtō burglary	告訴 kokuso charge

消防隊 shōbōtai • fire brigade

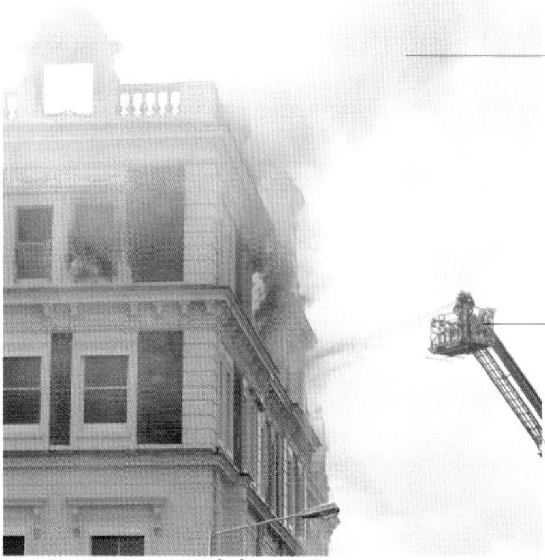

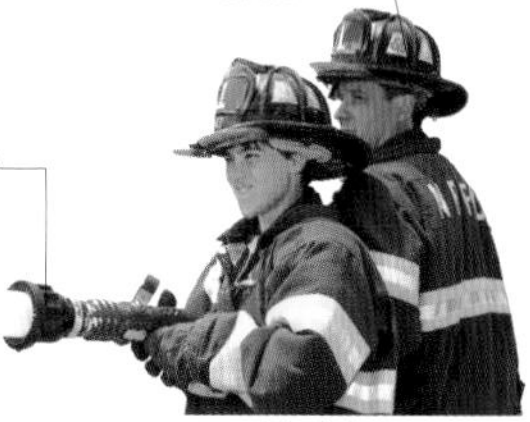

ヘルメット
herumetto
helmet

煙
kemuri
smoke

ホース
hōsu
hose

消防士
shōbōshi
fire fighters

バスケット
basuketto
cradle

水ジェット
mizu jetto
water jet

運転台
untendai
cab

腕
ude
boom

梯子
hashigo
ladder

火事 kaji | fire

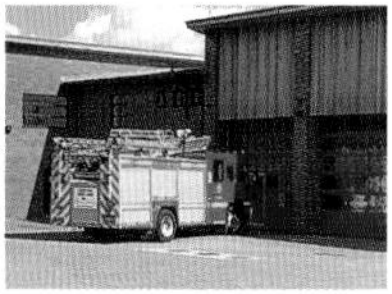

消防署
shōbōsho
fire station

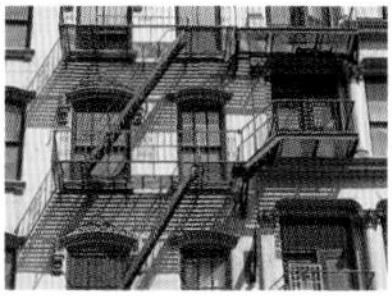

非常階段
hijō kaidan
fire escape

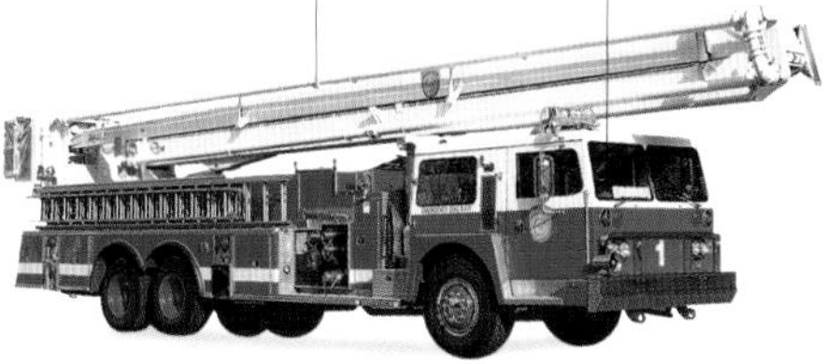

消防車
shōbōsha
fire engine

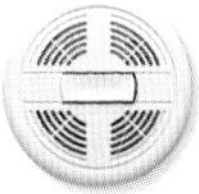

煙報知器
kemuri hōchiki
smoke alarm

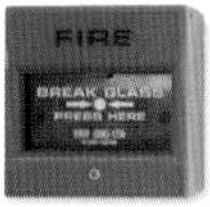

火災警報機
kasai keihōki
fire alarm

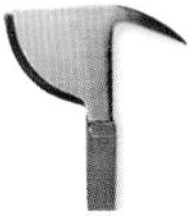

防災斧
bōsai ono
axe

消化器
shōkaki
fire extinguisher

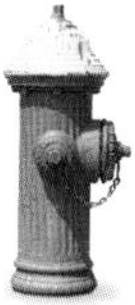

消火栓
shōkasen
hydrant

警察／消防車／救急車が必要です。
keisatsu/shōbōsha/kyūkyūsha ga hitsuyō desu.
I need the police/fire brigade/ambulance.

…で火が出ています。
… de hi ga dete imasu.
There's a fire at…

事故がありました。
jiko ga arimashita.
There's been an accident.

警察を呼んでください。
keisatsu o yonde kudasai!
Call the police!

銀行 ginkō · bank

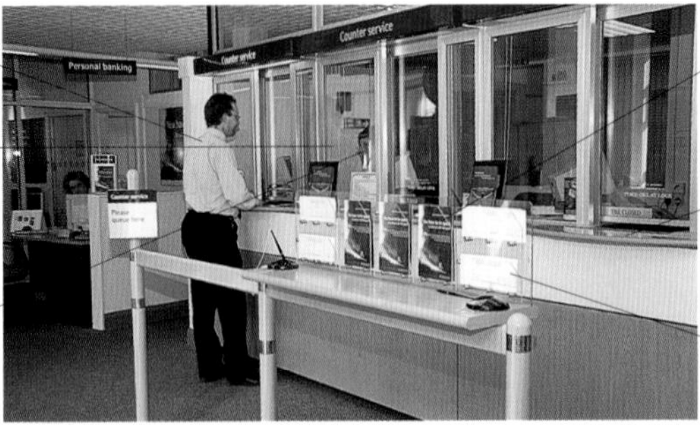

客
kyaku
customer

窓口
madoguchi
window

出納係
suitō-gakari
cashier

リーフレット
rīfuretto
leaflets

カウンター
kauntā
counter

入金書
nyūkin-sho
paying-in slips

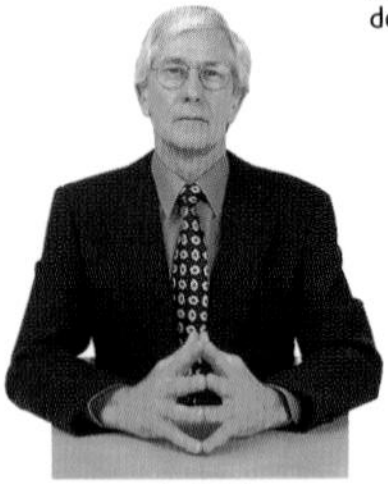

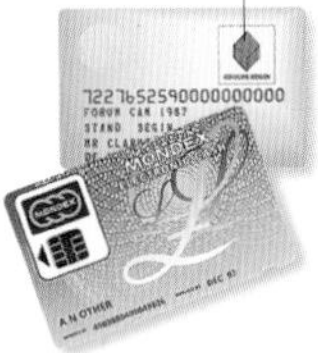

デビットカード
debitto kādo
debit card

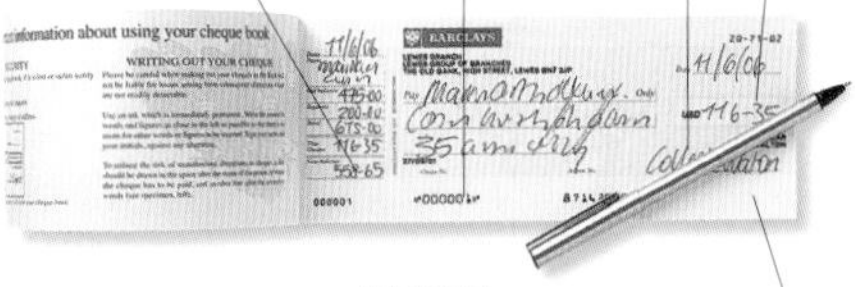

半券
hanken
stub

口座番号
kōza bangō
account number

署名
shomei
signature

金額
kingaku
amount

支店長
shitenchō
bank manager

クレジットカード
kurejitto kādo
credit card

小切手帳
kogitte-chō
chequebook

小切手
kogitte
cheque

関連用語 kanrenyōgo · vocabulary

貯金 chokin **savings**	住宅ローン jūtaku rōn **mortgage**	支払い shiharai **payment**	入金する nyūkin suru **pay in (v)**	当座預金口座 tōzayokin kōza **current account**
税 zei **tax**	超過引き出し chōka hikidashi **overdraft**	自動引き落とし jidō hikiotoshi **direct debit**	銀行手数料 ginkō tesūryō **bank charge**	普通預金口座 futsūyokin kōza **savings account**
ローン rōn **loan**	金利 kinri **interest rate**	出金依頼書 shukkin irai-sho **withdrawal slip**	銀行振込 ginkō furikomi **bank transfer**	暗証番号 anshō bangō **pin number**

硬貨
kōka
coin

紙幣
shihei
note

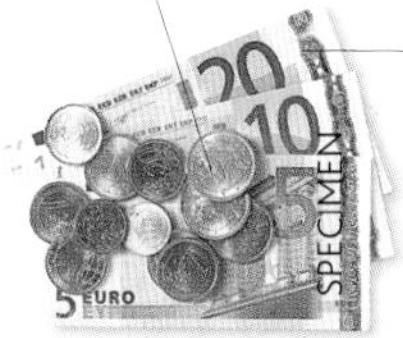

金銭 kinsen | money

画面
gamen
screen

キーパッド
kīpaddo
key pad

カード挿入口
kādo sōnyū-guchi
card slot

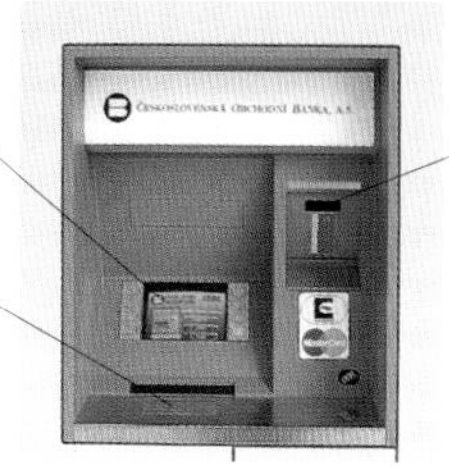

ATM ē tī emu | cash machine

外貨 gaika • foreign currency

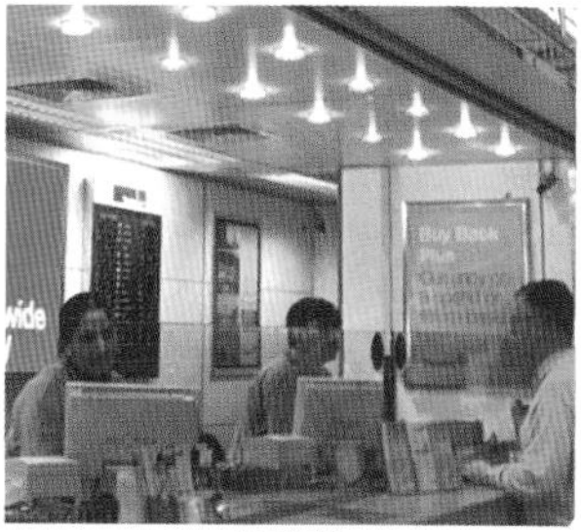

両替所
ryōgaejo
bureau de change

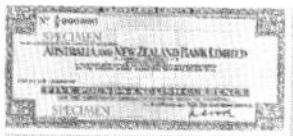

旅行小切手
ryokō kogitte
traveller's cheque

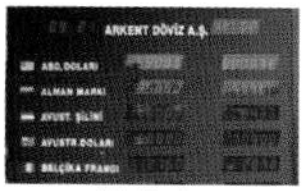

換算率
kansan ritsu
exchange rate

金融 kin'yū • finance

株価
kabuka
share price

ブローカー
burōkā
stockbroker

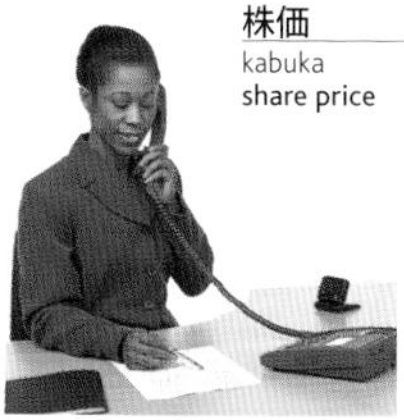

金融アドバイザー
kin'yū adobaizā
financial advisor

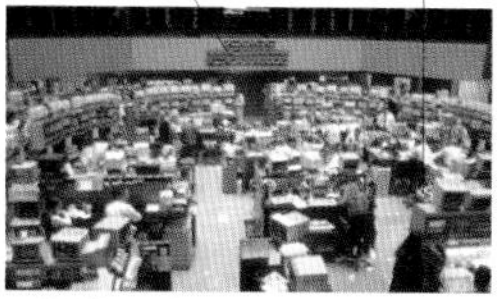

証券取引所 shōken torihiki-jo
stock exchange

関連用語 kanrenyōgo • vocabulary

換金する
kankin suru
cash (v)

株
kabu
shares

額面金額
gakumen kingaku
denomination

配当
haitō
dividends

手数料
tesūryō
commission

会計士
kaikeishi
accountant

投資
tōshi
investment

ポートフォリオ
pōtoforio
portfolio

株式
kabushiki
stocks

エクイティ
ekuiti
equity

これを両替できますか。
kore o ryōgae dekimasuka?
Can I change this please?

今日の換算率は何ですか。
kyō no kansan ritsu wa nandesuka?
What's today's exchange rate?

コミュニケーション komyunikēshon • communications

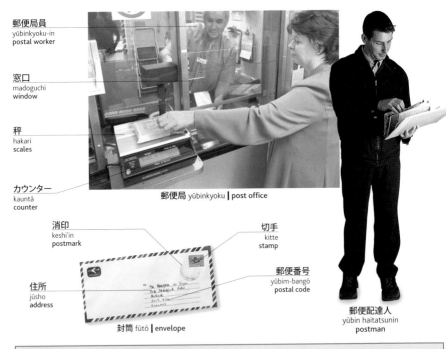

郵便局員
yūbinkyoku-in
postal worker

窓口
madoguchi
window

秤
hakari
scales

カウンター
kauntā
counter

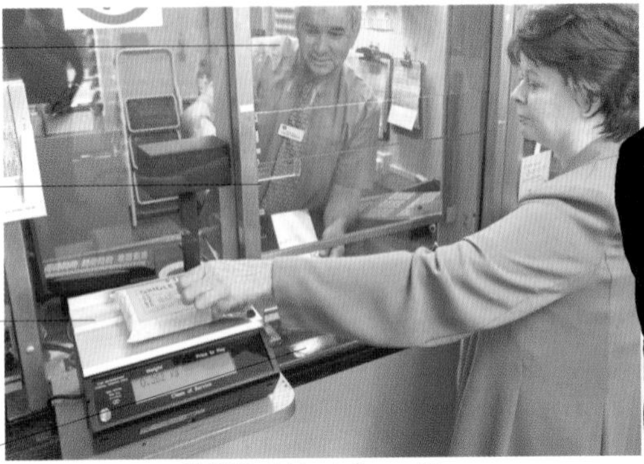

郵便局 yūbinkyoku | post office

消印
keshi'in
postmark

切手
kitte
stamp

住所
jūsho
address

郵便番号
yūbim-bangō
postal code

封筒 fūtō | envelope

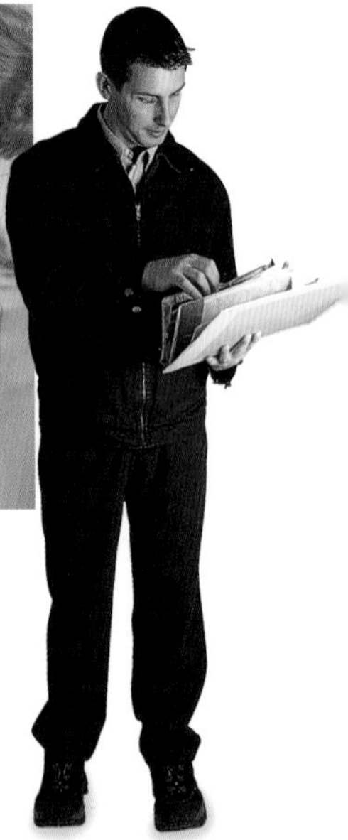

郵便配達人
yūbin haitatsunin
postman

関連用語 kanrenyōgo • vocabulary

手紙
tegami
letter

差出人住所
sashidashinin jūsho
return address

配達
haitatsu
delivery

壊れ物
kowaremono
fragile

折曲厳禁
orimage genkin
do not bend (v)

航空便
kōkūbin
by airmail

署名
shomei
signature

郵便為替
yūbin kawase
postal order

郵便袋
yūbim-bukuro
mailbag

こちらが上
kochira ga ue
this way up

書留郵便
kakitome yūbin
registered post

集荷
shūka
collection

郵送料
yūsō-ryō
postage

電報
dempō
telegram

ファクス
fakusu
fax

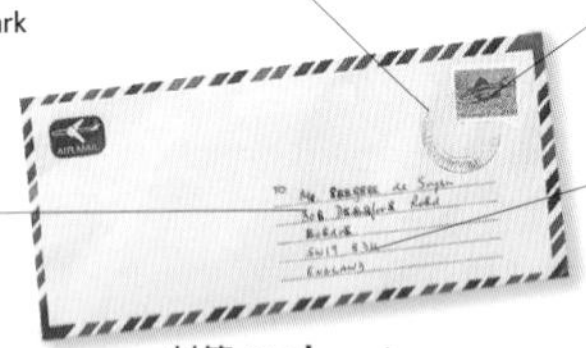

郵便ポスト
yūbin posuto
postbox

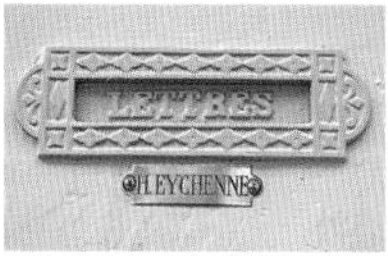

郵便受け
yūbin-uke
letterbox

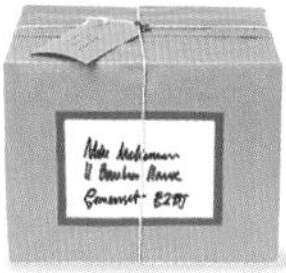

小包
kozutsumi
parcel

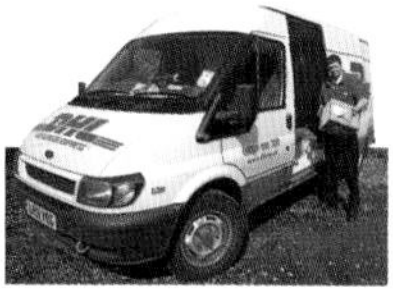

宅配
takuhai
courier

電話 denwa • telephone

受話器
juwaki
handset

ベース
bēsu
base station

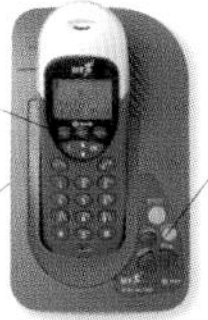

留守番電話
rusuban denwa
answering machine

コードレス電話
kōdoresu denwa
cordless phone

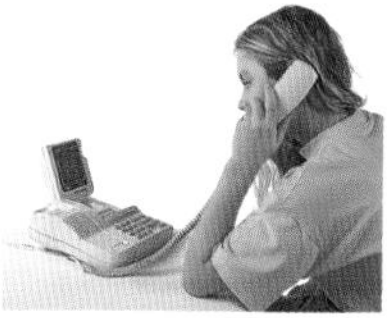

ビデオ電話
bideo denwa
video phone

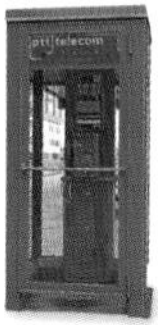

公衆電話ボックス
kōshū-denwa bokkusu
telephone box

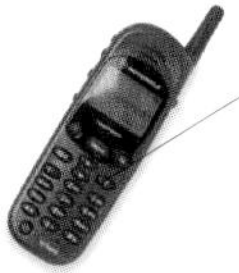

キーパッド
kīpaddo
keypad

受話器
juwaki
receiver

おつり
otsuri
coin return

携帯電話
keitai denwa
mobile phone

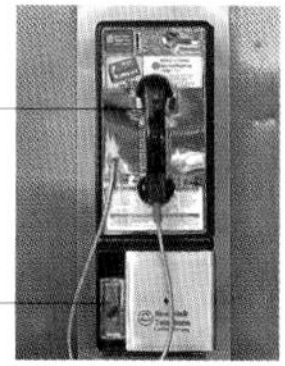

硬貨式公衆電話
kōka-shiki kōshū-denwa
coin phone

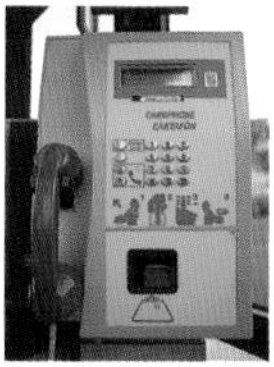

カード式公衆電話
kādo-shiki kōshū-denwa
card phone

関連用語 kanrenyōgo • vocabulary

番号案内 bangō annai directory enquiries	電話に出る denwa ni deru answer (v)	交換手 kōkanshu operator	…の電話番号を教えてください。 … no denwa bangō o oshiete kudasai. Please give me the number for…
コレクトコール korekuto kōru reverse charge call	携帯メール keitai mēru text message	通話中 tsūwa-chū engaged/busy	…の局番は何ですか。 … no kyokuban wa nandesuka? What is the dialling code for…?
電話する denwa suru dial (v)	音声メッセージ onsei messēji voice message	不通 futsū disconnected	

ホテル hoteru ● hotel

ロビー robī ● lobby

メッセージ
messēji
messages

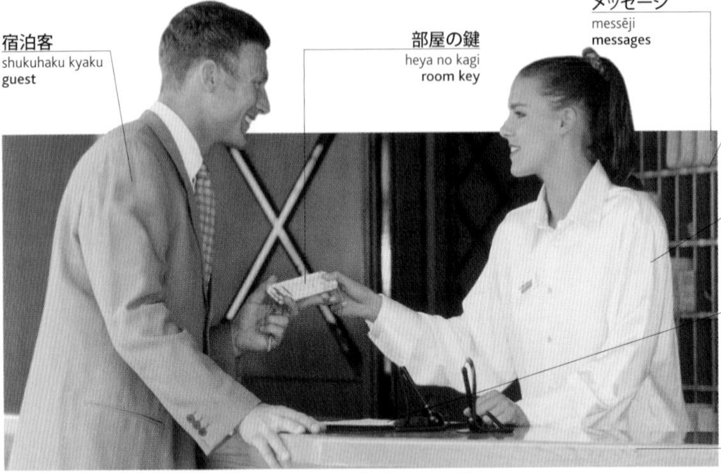

宿泊客
shukuhaku kyaku
guest

部屋の鍵
heya no kagi
room key

分類棚
bunrui-dana
pigeonhole

フロント係
furonto-gakari
receptionist

宿泊者名簿
shukuhaku-
sha meibo
register

カウンター
kauntā
counter

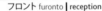

フロント furonto | reception

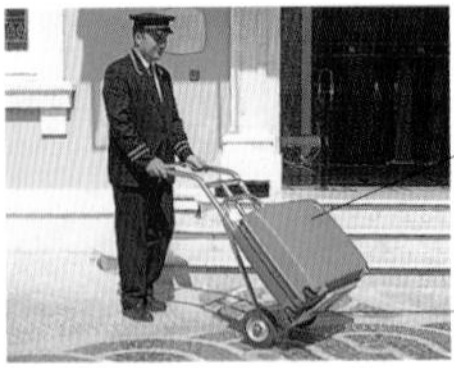

荷物
nimotsu
luggage

カート
kāto
trolley

ポーター pōtā | porter

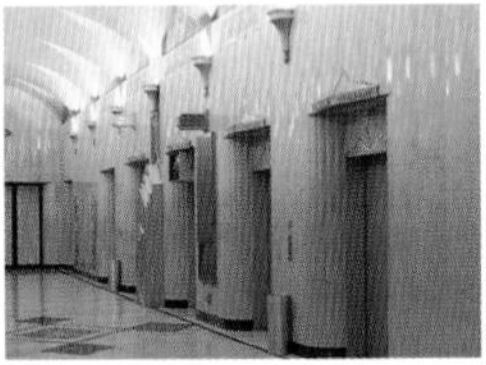

エレベーター erebētā | lift

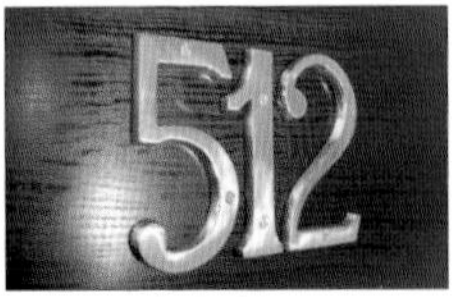

部屋番号
heya bangō
room number

客室 kyakushitsu ● rooms

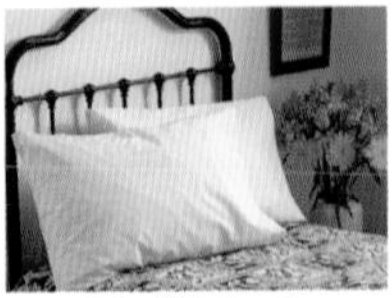

シングルルーム
shinguru rūmu
single room

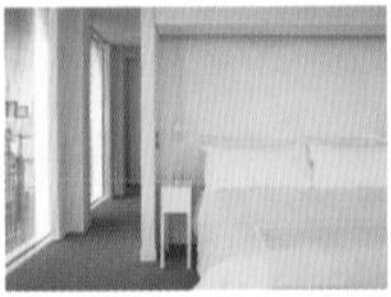

ダブルルーム
daburu rūmu
double room

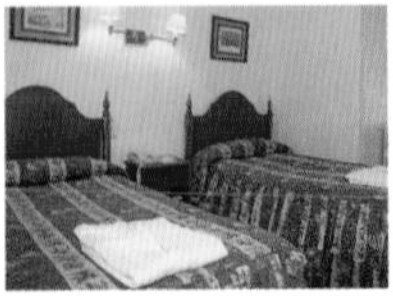

ツインルーム
tsuin rūmu
twin room

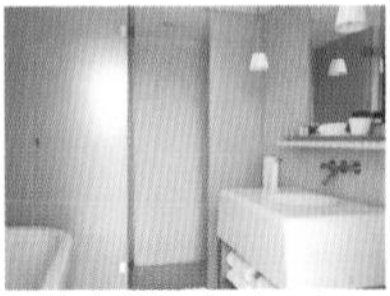

客室付きバスルーム
kyakushitsu-zuki basurūmu
private bathroom

職務 shokumu・services

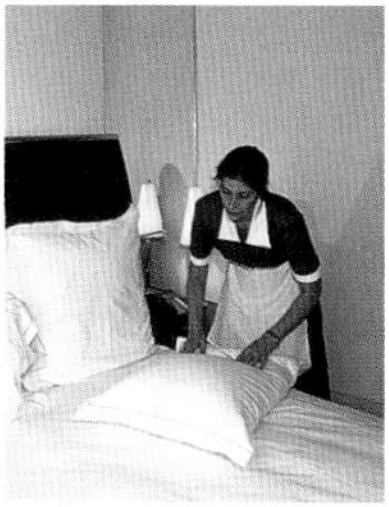
朝食トレイ
chōshoku torei
breakfast tray

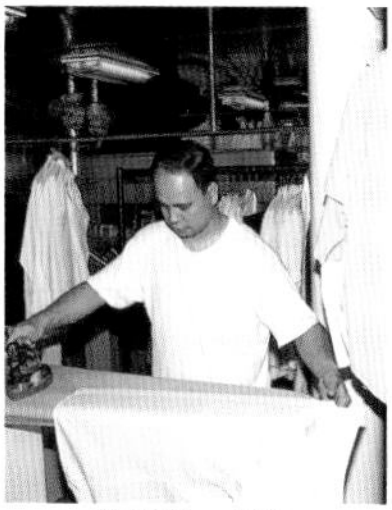
掃除サービス
sōji sābisu
maid service

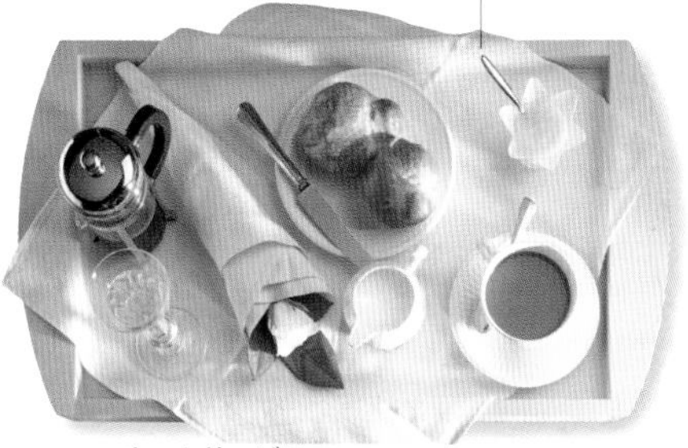
洗濯サービス
sentaku sābisu
laundry service

ルームサービス rūmu sābisu | room service

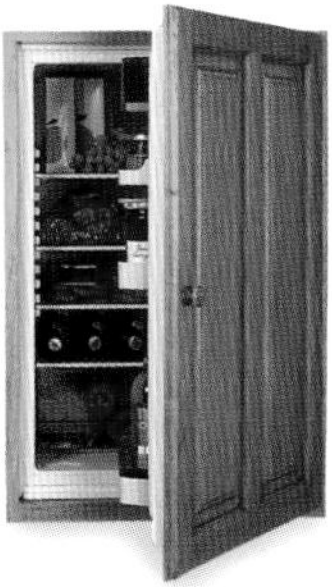
ミニバー
minibā
mini bar

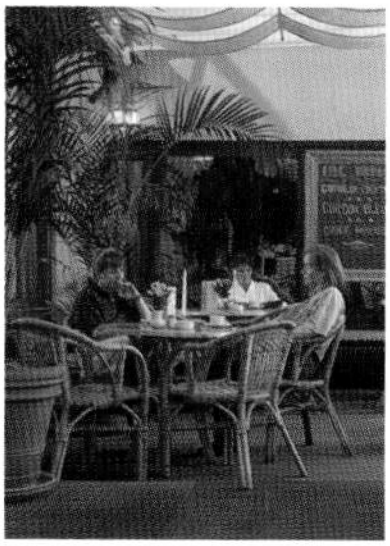
レストラン
restoran
restaurant

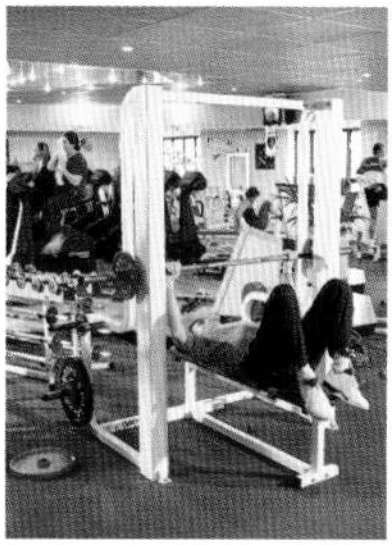
ジム
jimu
gym

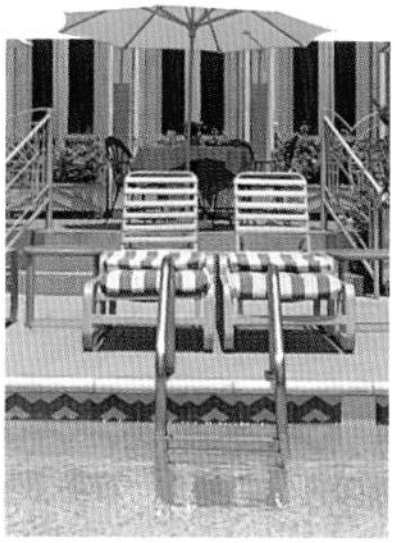
プール
pūru
swimming pool

関連用語 kanrenyōgo・vocabulary

朝食付き
chōshoku-tsuki
bed and breakfast

3食付き
sanshoku-tsuki
full board

2食付き
nishoku-tsuki
half board

空室はありますか。
kūshitsu wa arimasuka?
Do you have any vacancies?

予約してあります。
yoyaku shite arimasu.
I have a reservation.

シングルルームをお願いします。
shinguru rūmu o onegai shimasu.
I'd like a single room.

3泊お願いします。
sampaku onegai shimasu.
I'd like a room for three nights.

一泊いくらですか。
ippaku ikura desuka?
What is the charge per night?

チェックアウトは何時ですか。
chekkuauto wa nanji desuka?
When do I have to vacate the room?

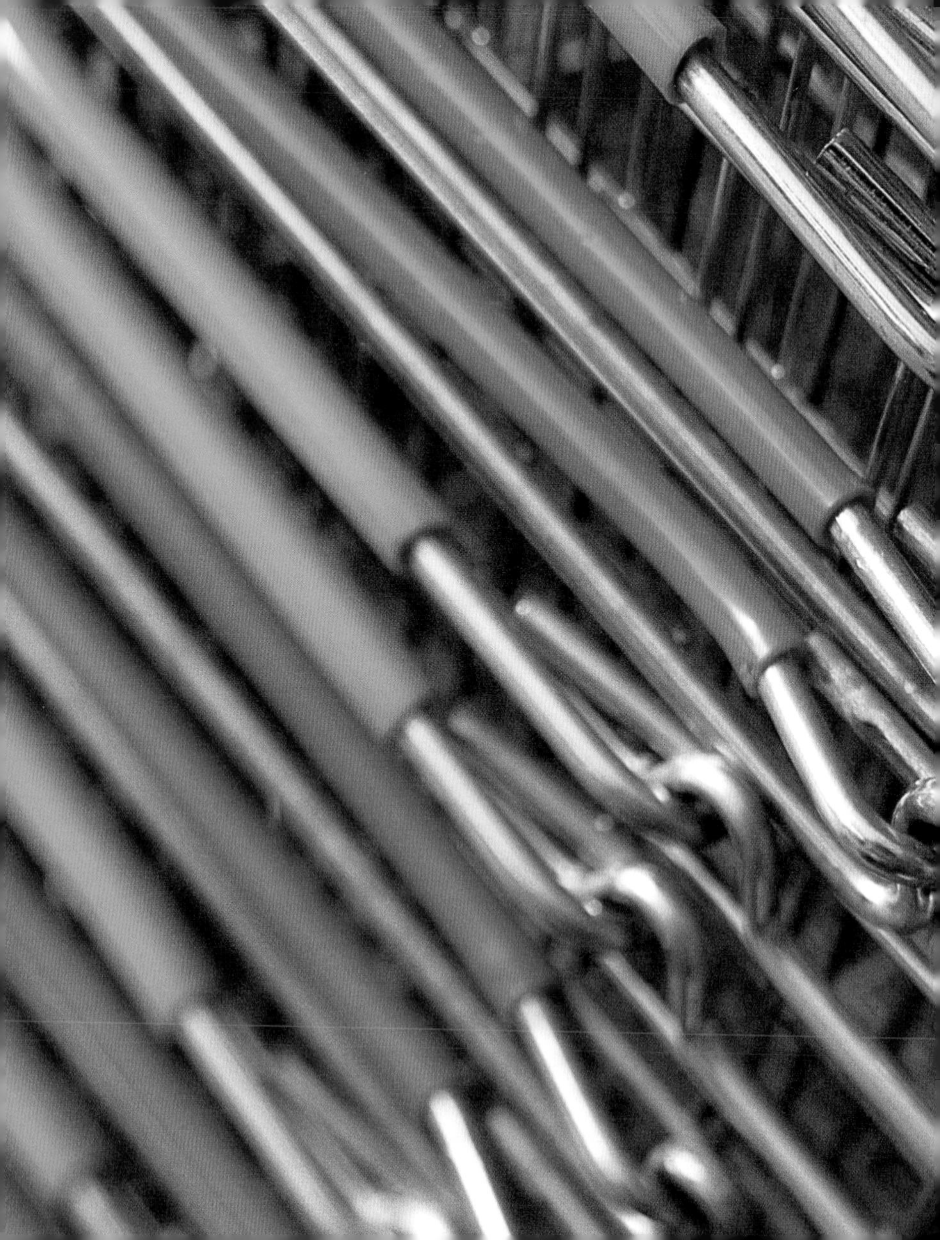

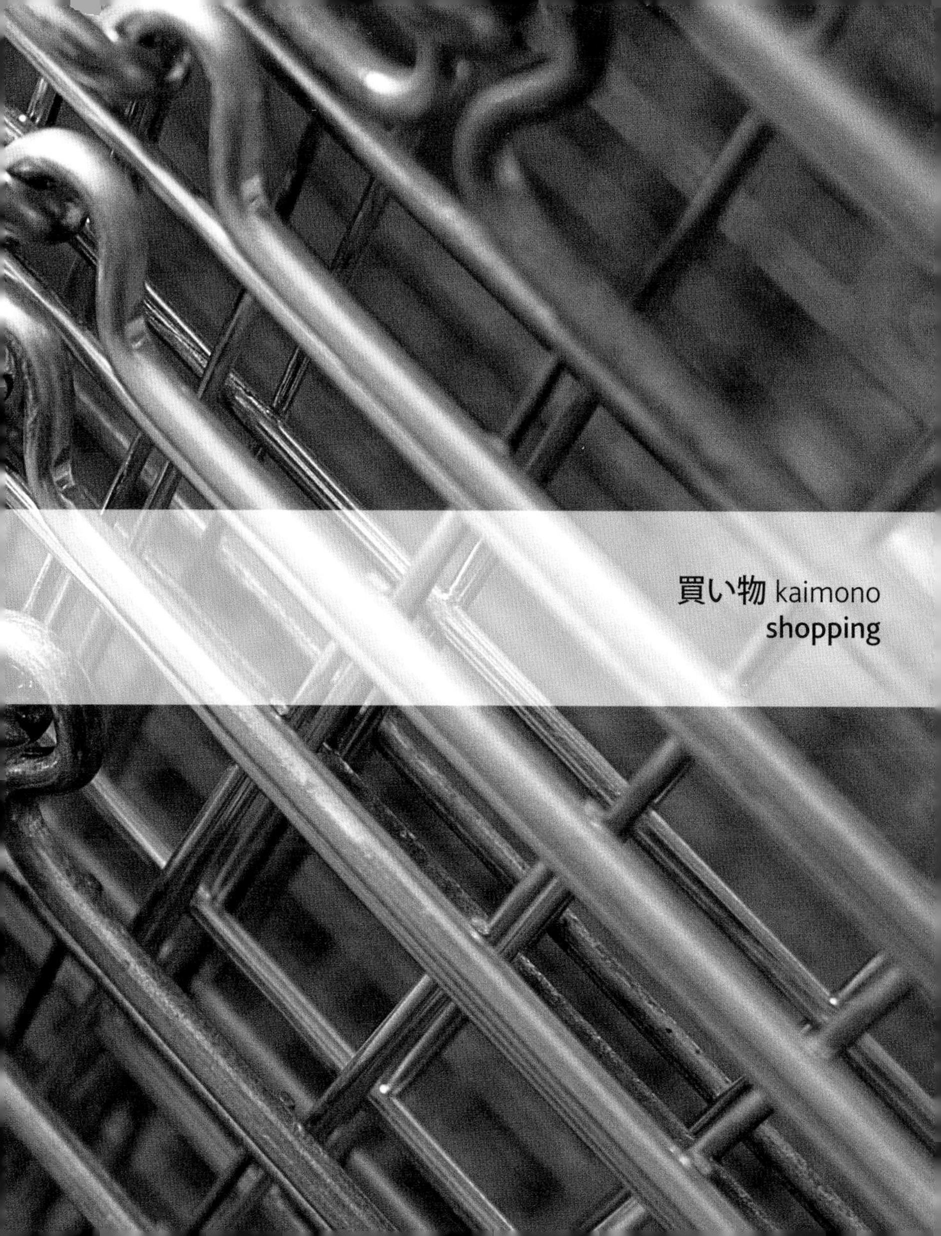

買い物 kaimono
shopping

ショッピングセンター shoppingu sentā ● **shopping centre**

アトリウム
atoriumu
atrium

看板
kamban
sign

エレベーター
erebētā
lift

3階
sangai
second floor

2階
nikai
first floor

エスカレーター
esukarētā
escalator

1階
ikkai
ground floor

客
kyaku
customer

関連用語 kanrenyōgo ● **vocabulary**

子供用品売場
kodomo yōhin uriba
children's department

鞄売場
kaban uriba
luggage department

靴売場
kutsu uriba
shoe department

売場案内
uriba annai
store directory

店員
ten'in
sales assistant

カスタマーサービス
kasutamā sābisu
customer services

試着室
shichaku shitsu
changing rooms

ベビールーム
bebī rūmu
baby changing facilities

お手洗い
o-tearai
toilets

これは、いくらですか。
kore wa ikura desuka?
How much is this?

これを交換できますか。
kore o kōkan dekimasuka?
May I exchange this?

デパート depāto • department store

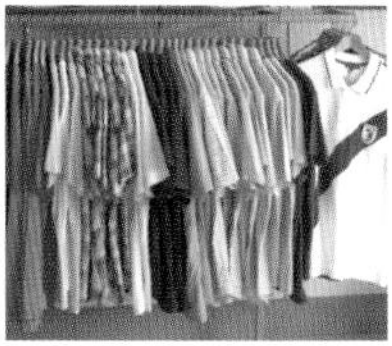

紳士服
shinshi fuku
men's wear

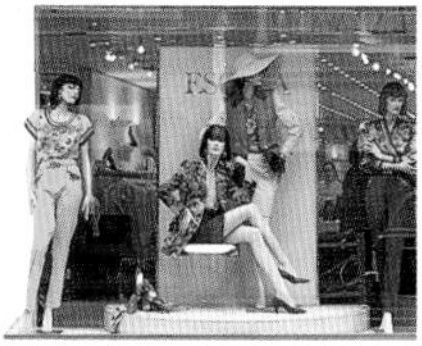

婦人服
fujin fuku
women's wear

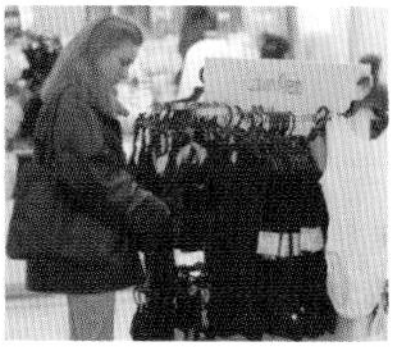

ランジェリー
ranjerī
lingerie

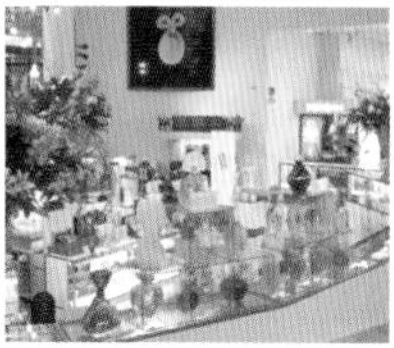

香水売場
kōsui uriba
perfumery

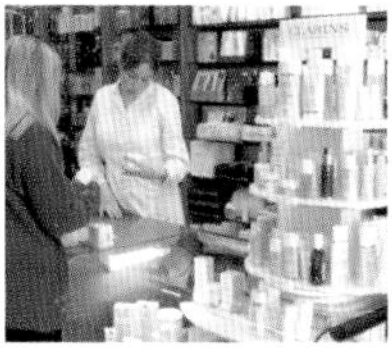

化粧品
keshōhin
beauty

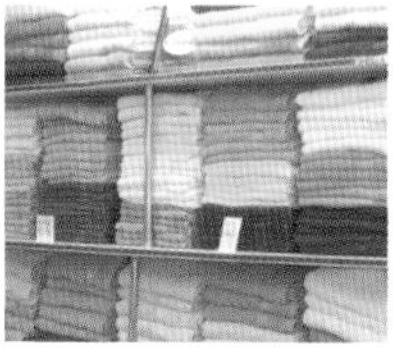

寝具・タオル類
shingu taoru rui
linen

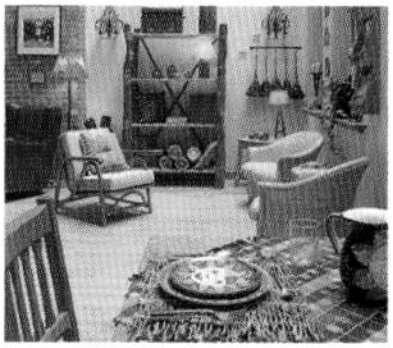

家具
kagu
home furnishings

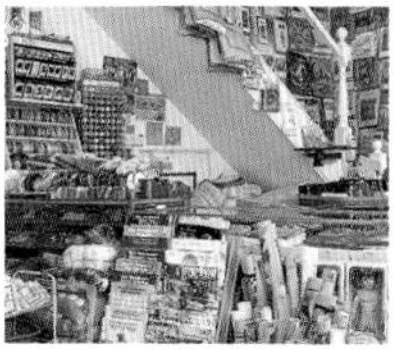

小間物
komamono
haberdashery

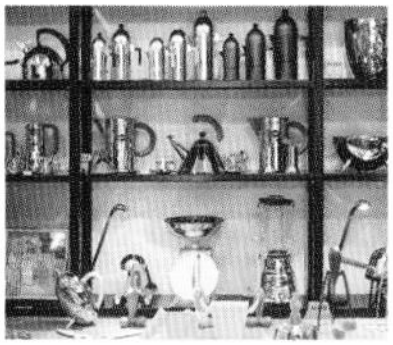

台所用品
daidokoro yōhin
kitchenware

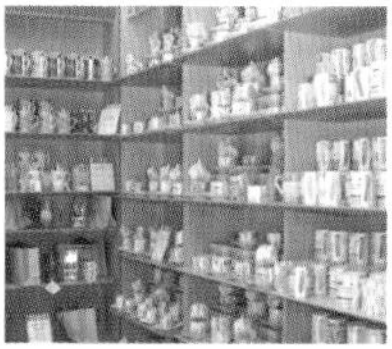

陶磁器
tōjiki
china

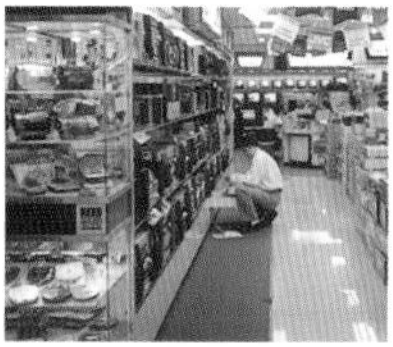

電気製品
denki seihin
electrical goods

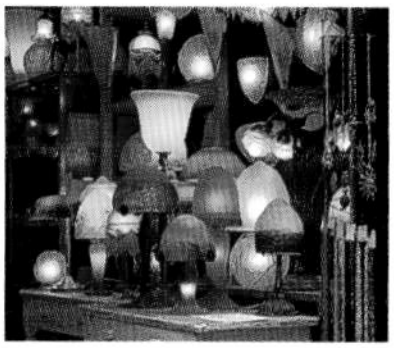

照明器具
shōmei kigu
lighting

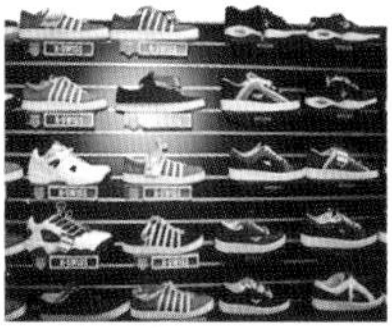

スポーツ用品
supōtsu yōhin
sports

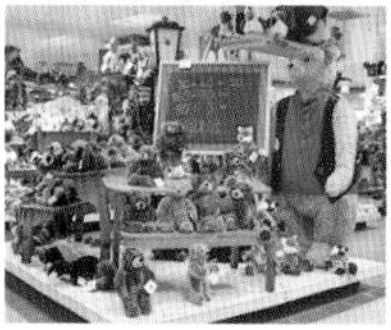

玩具
omocha
toys

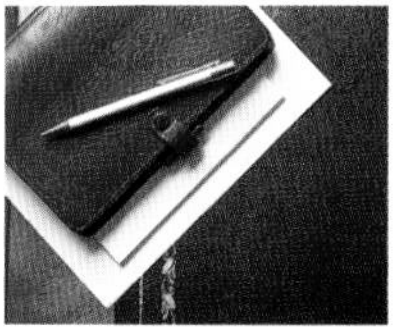

文房具
bumbōgu
stationery

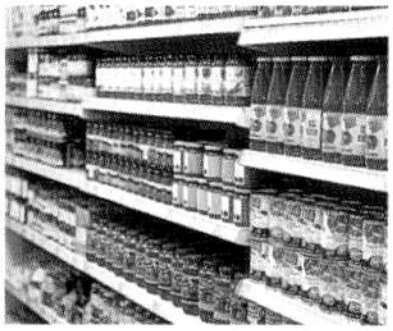

食品売場
shokuhin uriba
food hall

スーパーマーケット sūpāmāketto • supermarket

ベルトコンベア
beruto kombea
conveyer belt

レジ係
reji-gakari
cashier

特売品
tokubaihin
offers

通路
tsūro
aisle

棚
tana
shelf

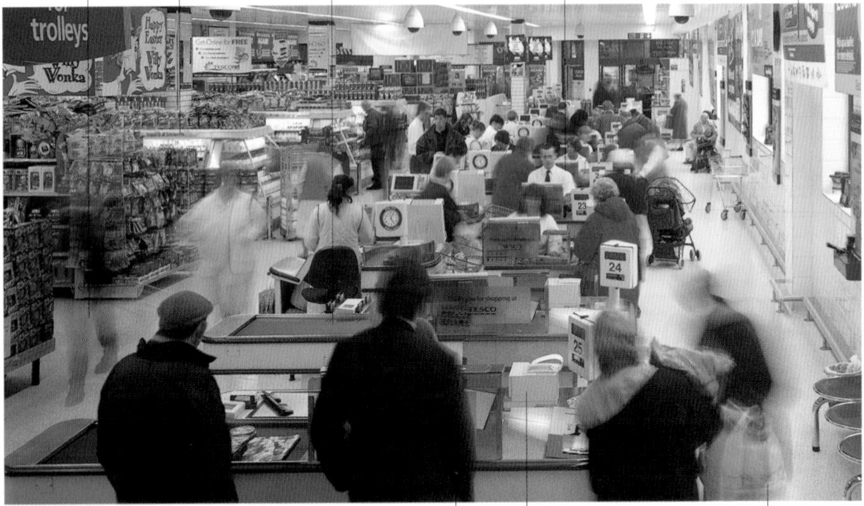

チェックアウト chekkuauto | **checkout**

客
kyaku
customer

レジ
reji
till

買い物袋
kaimono-bukuro
shopping bag

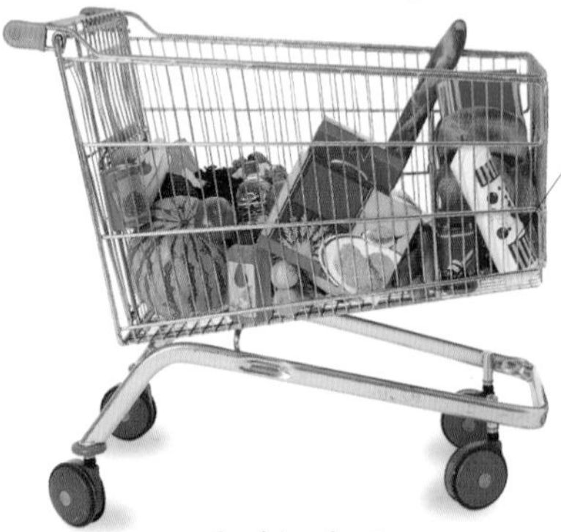

食料品
shokuryōhin
groceries

取っ手
totte
handle

バーコード
bākōdo
bar code

カート kāto | **trolley**

籠 kago | **basket**

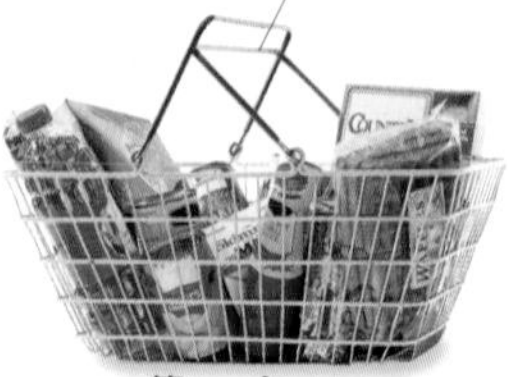

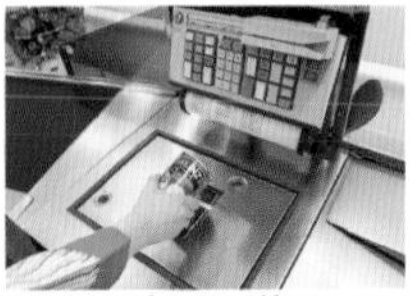

バーコード読み取り装置 bākōdo
yomitori sōchi | **scanner**

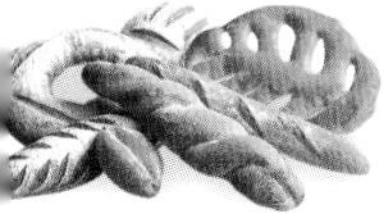

パン類
pan rui
bakery

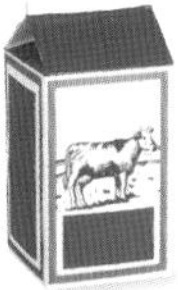

乳製品
nyūseihin
dairy

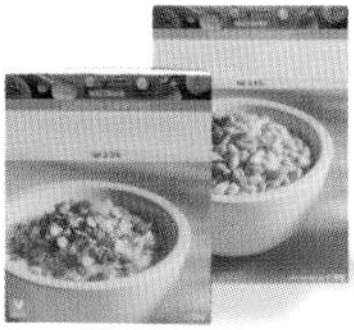

シリアル食品
shiriaru shokuhin
breakfast cereals

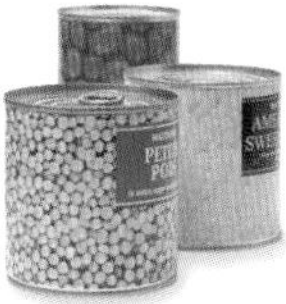

缶詰
kanzume
tinned food

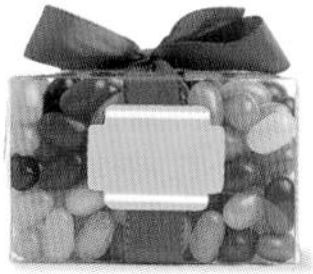

菓子類
kashi rui
confectionery

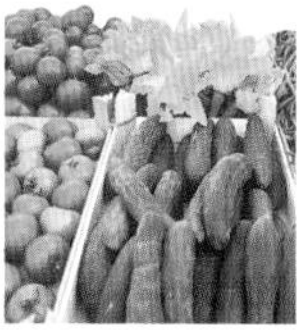

野菜
yasai
vegetables

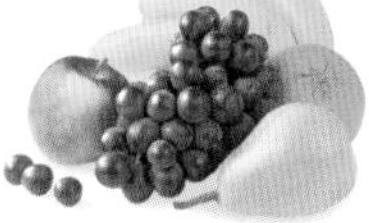

果物
kudamono
fruit

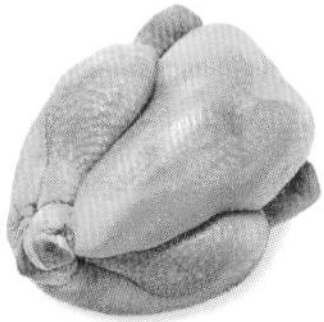

肉
niku
meat and poultry

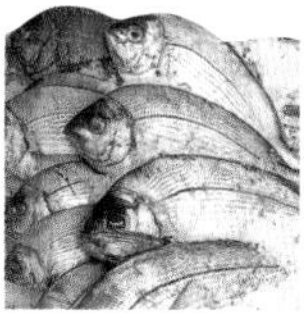

魚
sakana
fish

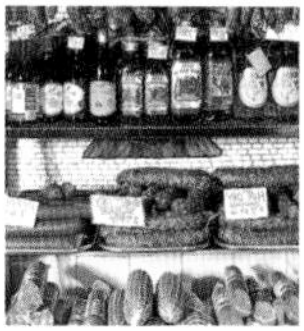

デリカテッセン
derikatessen
deli

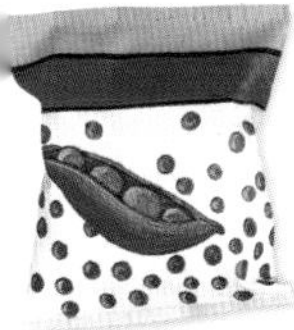

冷凍食品
reitō shokuhin
frozen food

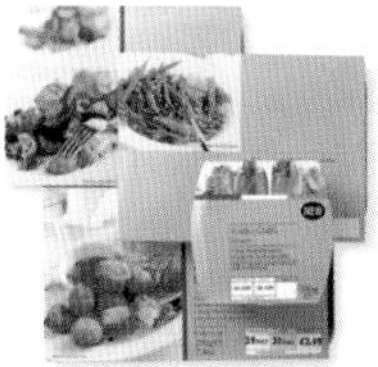

インスタント食品
insutanto shokuhin
convenience food

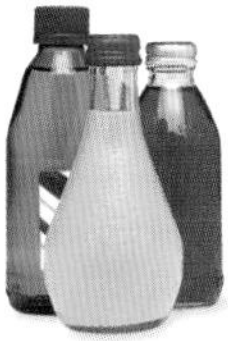

飲物
nomimono
drinks

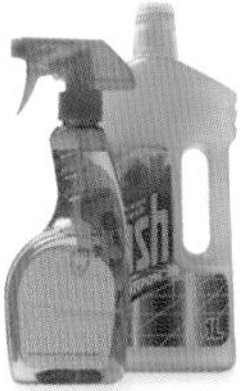

家庭用品
katei yōhin
household products

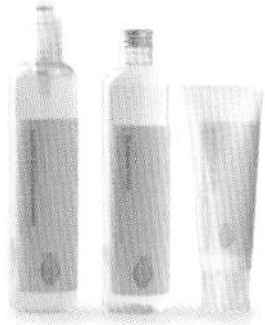

化粧品
keshōhin
toiletries

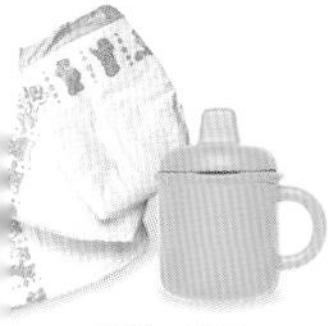

ベビー用品
bebī yōhin
baby products

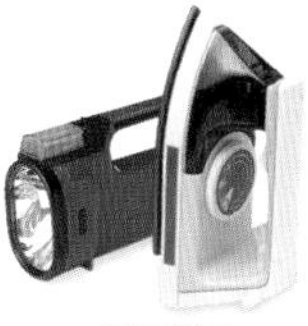

電気製品
denki seihin
electrical goods

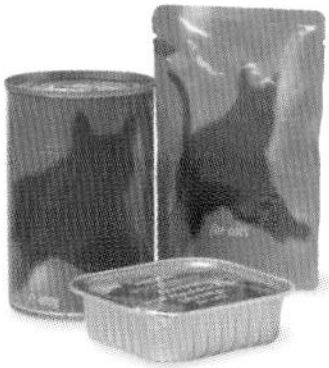

ペットフード
petto fūdo
pet food

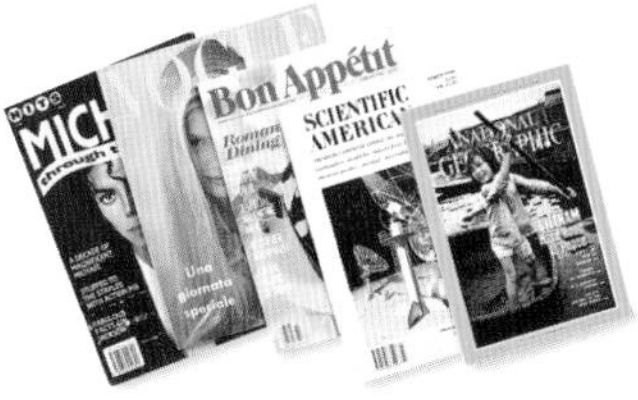

雑誌 zasshi | magazines

薬局 yakkyoku ● chemist

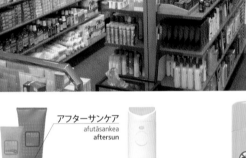

歯磨き用品
hamigaki yōhin
dental care

生理用品
seiri yōhin
**feminine
hygiene**

デオドラント
deodoranto
deodorants

ビタミン剤
bitamin-zai
vitamins

調剤室
chōzai shitsu
dispensary

薬剤師
yakuzaishi
pharmacist

咳止め
sekidome
cough medicine

薬草剤
yakusō-zai
herbal remedies

スキンケア
sukinkea
skincare

アフターサンケア
afutāsankea
aftersun

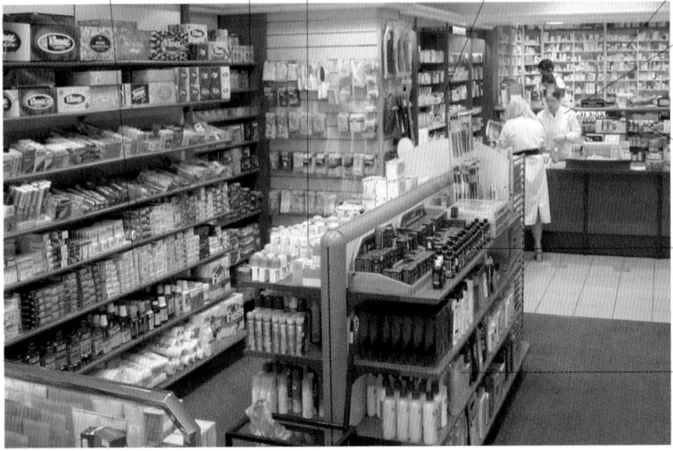

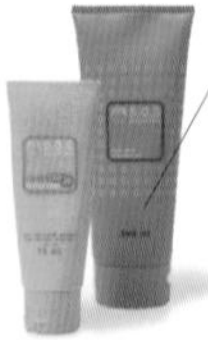

サンスクリーン
sansukurīn
sunscreen

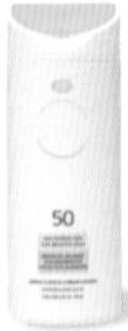

日焼け止め
hiyakedome
sunblock

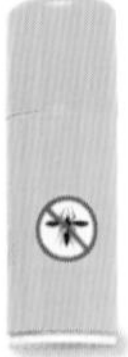

虫除け
mushiyoke
insect repellent

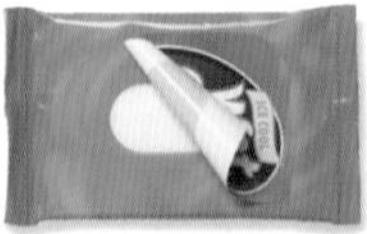

ウェットティッシュ
wetto tisshu
wet wipe

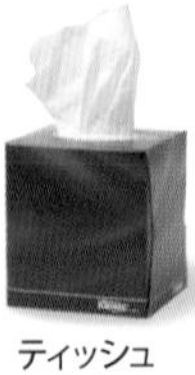

ティッシュ
tisshu
tissue

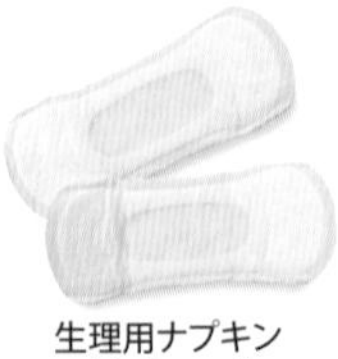

生理用ナプキン
seiri-yō napukin
sanitary towel

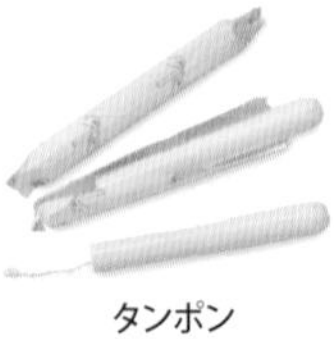

タンポン
tampon
tampon

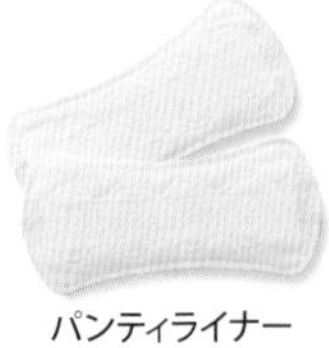

パンティライナー
panti rainā
panty liner

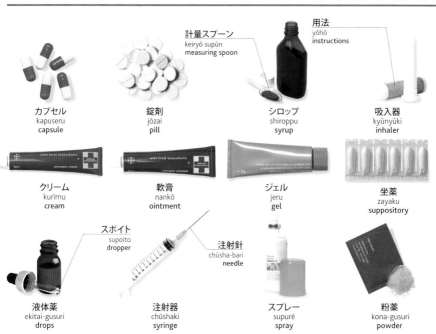

計量スプーン
keiryō supūn
measuring spoon

用法
yōhō
instructions

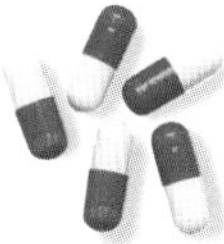

カプセル
kapuseru
capsule

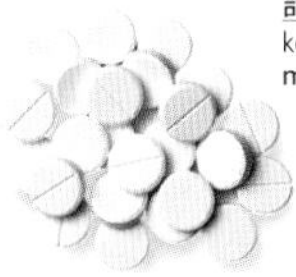

錠剤
jōzai
pill

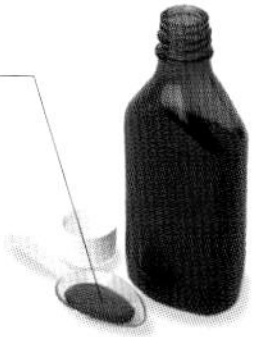

シロップ
shiroppu
syrup

吸入器
kyūnyūki
inhaler

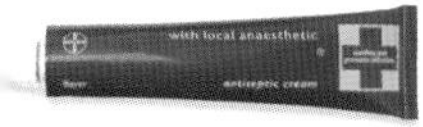

クリーム
kurīmu
cream

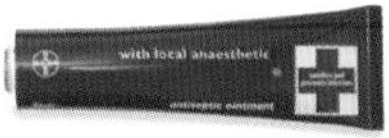

軟膏
nankō
ointment

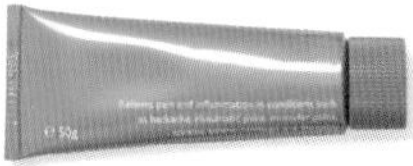

ジェル
jeru
gel

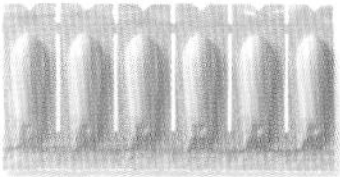

坐薬
zayaku
suppository

スポイト
supoito
dropper

注射針
chūsha-bari
needle

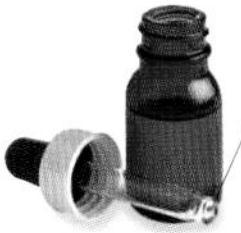

液体薬
ekitai-gusuri
drops

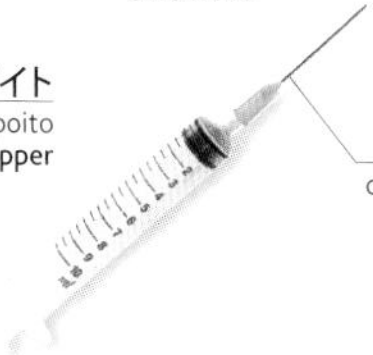

注射器
chūshaki
syringe

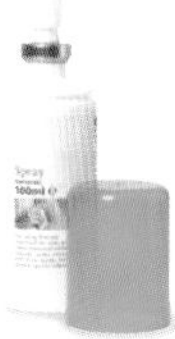

スプレー
supurē
spray

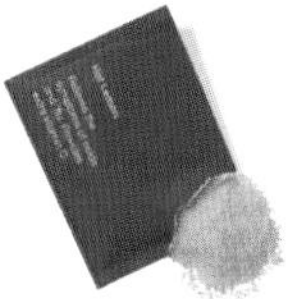

粉薬
kona-gusuri
powder

関連用語 kanrenyōgo • vocabulary

鉄分 tetsubun iron	**インスリン** insurin insulin	**使い捨て** tsukaisute disposable	**医薬品** iyakuhin medicine	**痛み止め** itamidome painkiller
カルシウム karushiumu calcium	**副作用** fukusayō side-effects	**水溶性** suiyōsei soluble	**下剤** gezai laxative	**鎮静剤** chinsei-zai sedative
マグネシウム maguneshiumu magnesium	**使用期限** shiyō kigen expiry date	**用量** yōryō dosage	**下痢** geri diarrhoea	**睡眠薬** suimin'yaku sleeping pill
マルチビタミン maruchi bitamin multivitamins	**酔い止め** yoidome travel sickness pills	**投薬** tōyaku medication	**のど飴** nodo ame throat lozenge	**抗炎症剤** kōenshō-zai anti-inflammatory

花屋 hanaya • florist

花
hana
flowers

グラジオラス
gurajiorasu
gladiolus

菖蒲
ayame
iris

百合
yuri
lily

ひな菊
hinagiku
daisy

アカシア
akashia
acacia

菊
kiku
chrysanthemum

カーネーション
kānēshon
carnation

かすみ草
kasumisō
gypsophila

植木
ueki
pot plant

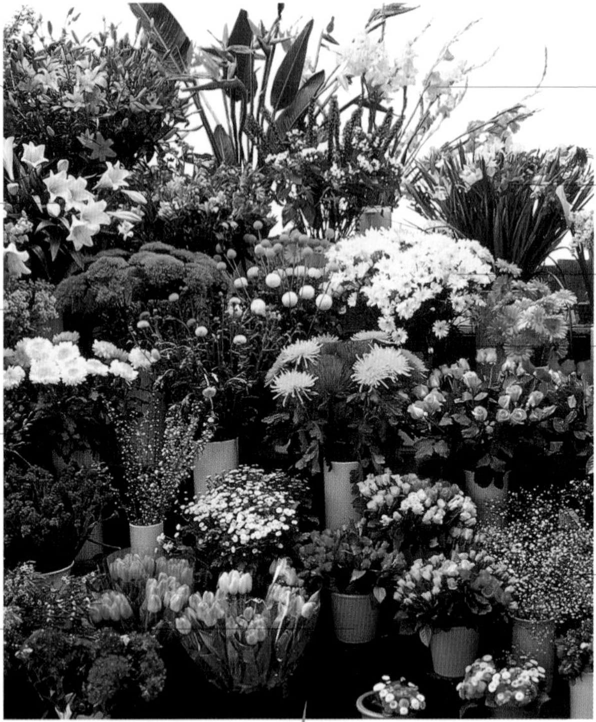

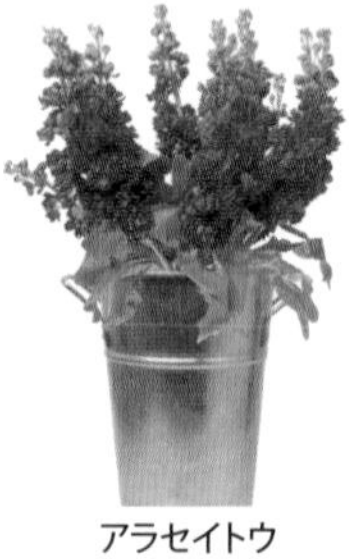

アラセイトウ
araseitō
stocks

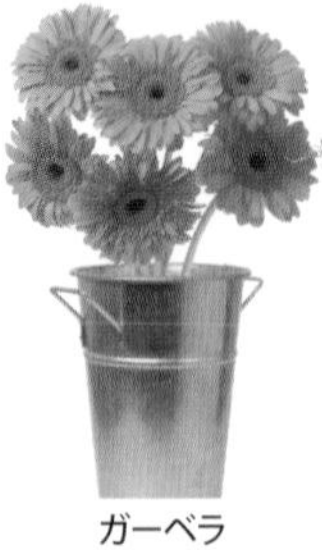

ガーベラ
gābera
gerbera

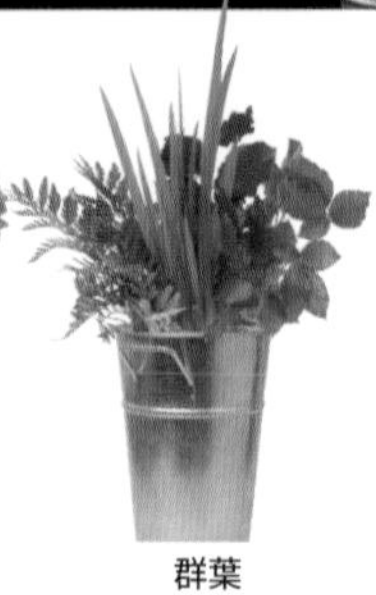

群葉
gun'yō
foliage

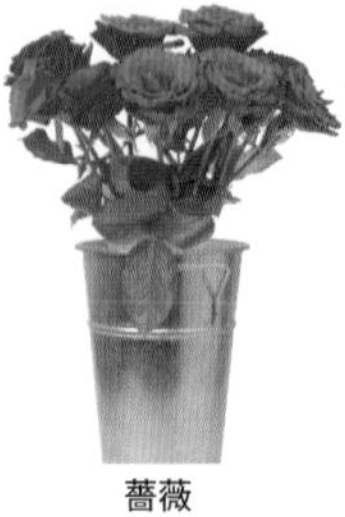

薔薇
bara
rose

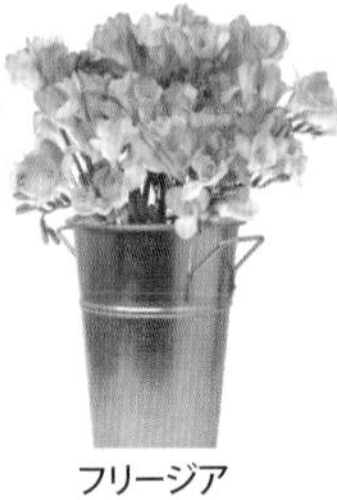

フリージア
furījia
freesia

花瓶
kabin
vase

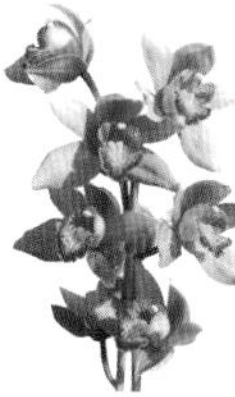

蘭
ran
orchid

牡丹
botan
peony

花束
hanataba
bunch

茎
kuki
stem

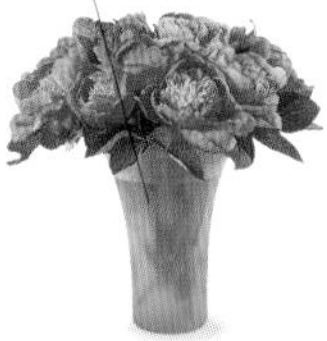

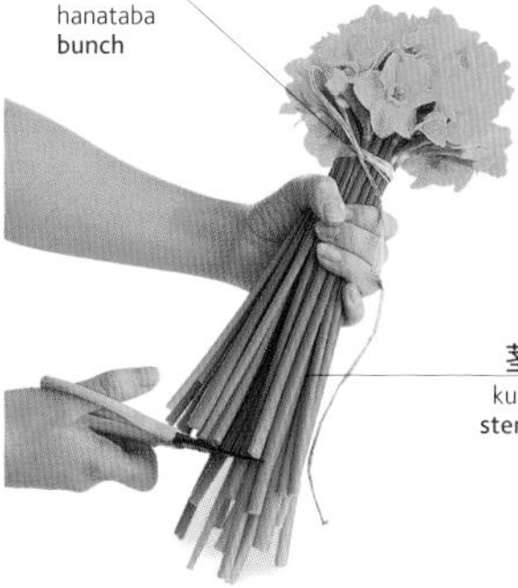

水仙
suisen
daffodil

蕾
tsubomi
bud

包装紙
hōsō-shi
wrapping

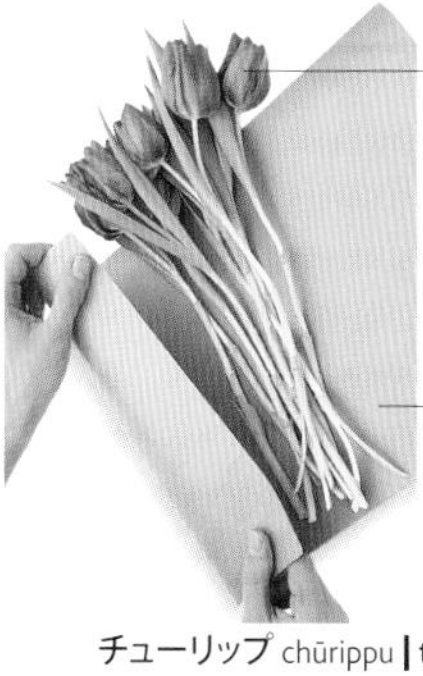

チューリップ chūrippu | tulip

アレンジメント arenjimento • arrangements

リボン
ribon
ribbon

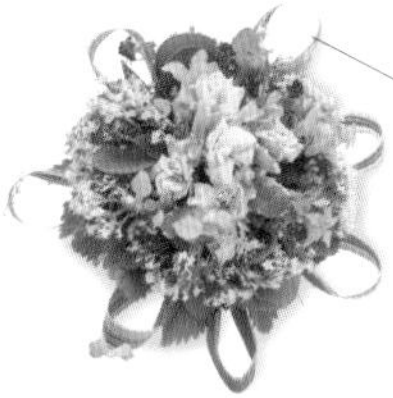

ブーケ
būke
bouquet

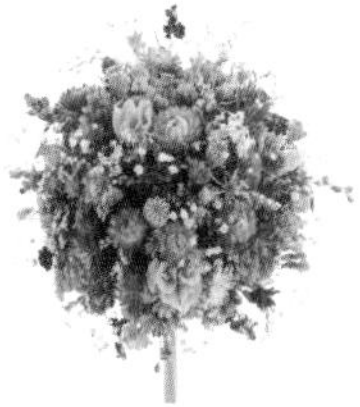

ドライフラワー
dorai furawā
dried flowers

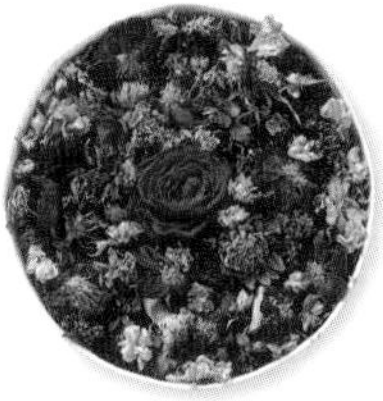

ポプリ popuri | pot-pourri

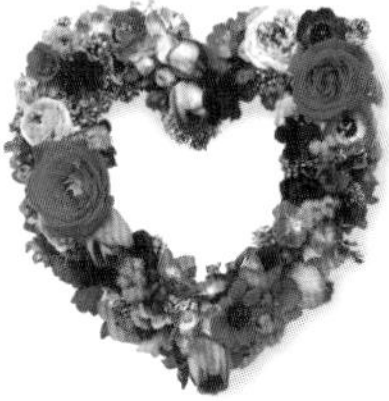

花輪 hanawa | wreath

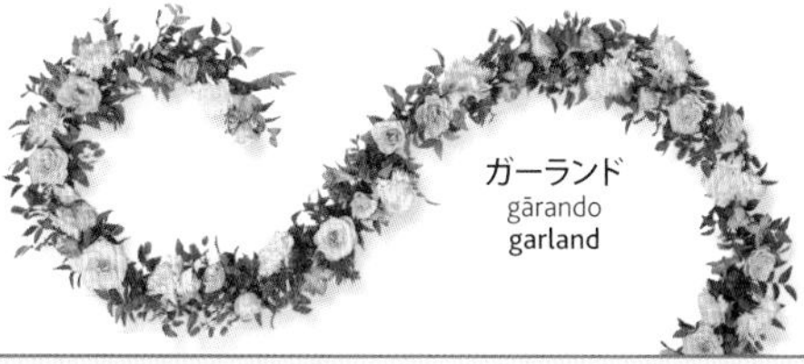

ガーランド
gārando
garland

メッセージを付けてください。
messēji o tsukete kudasai?
Can I attach a message?

包んでください。
tsutsunde kudasai?
Can I have them wrapped?

...に送っていただけますか。
... ni okutte itadakemasuka?
Can you send them to…?

何日ぐらい保ちますか。
nannichi gurai tamochimasuka?
How long will these last?

香りがしますか。
kaori ga shimasuka?
Are they fragrant?

...の花束をください。
… no hanataba o kudasai?
Can I have a bunch of… please?

新聞販売店 shimbun hambaiten ● **newsagent**

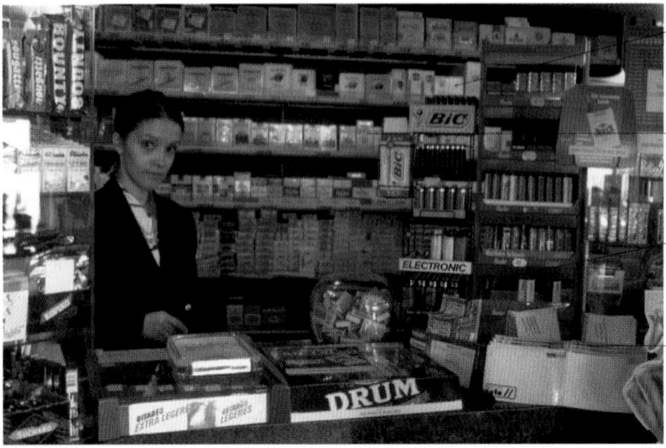

煙草
tabako
cigarettes

煙草一箱
tabako hitohako
packet of cigarettes

マッチ
matchi
matches

宝くじ
takarakuji
lottery tickets

切手
kitte
stamps

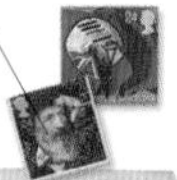

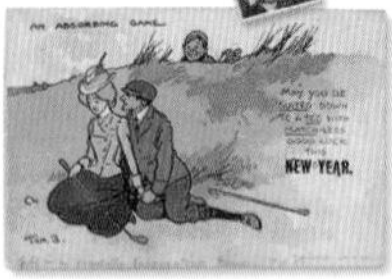

絵葉書
ehagaki
postcard

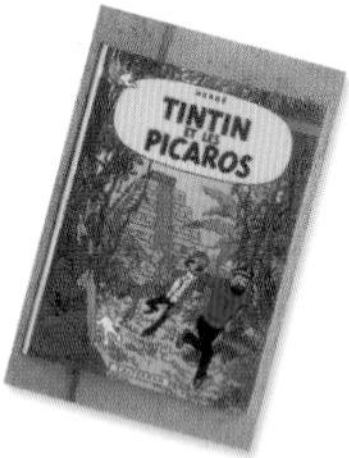

漫画本
manga-bon
comic

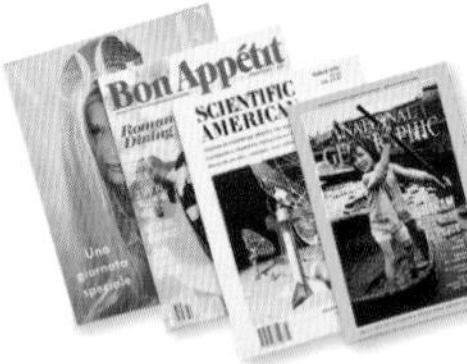

雑誌
zasshi
magazine

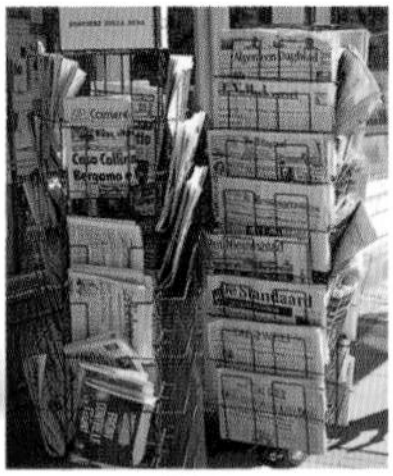

新聞
shimbun
newspaper

喫煙 kitsuen ● **smoking**

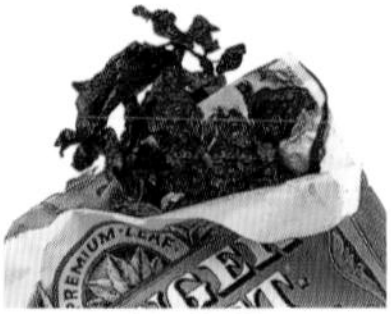

刻み煙草
kizami tabako
tobacco

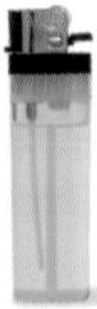

ライター
raitā
lighter

ステム
sutemu
stem

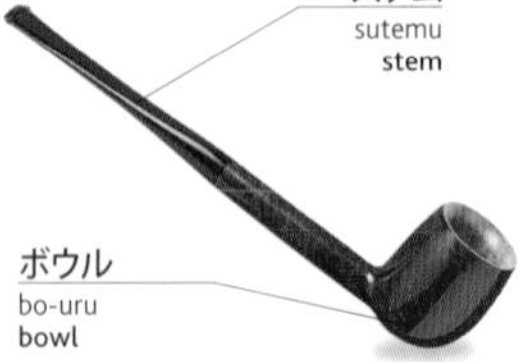

ボウル
bo-uru
bowl

パイプ
paipu
pipe

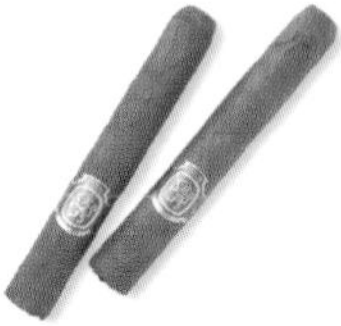

葉巻
hamaki
cigar

菓子屋 kashiya • confectioner

箱詰めチョコレート
hakozume chokorēto
box of chocolates

チョコバー
chokobā
snack bar

ポテトチップス
poteto chippusu
crisps

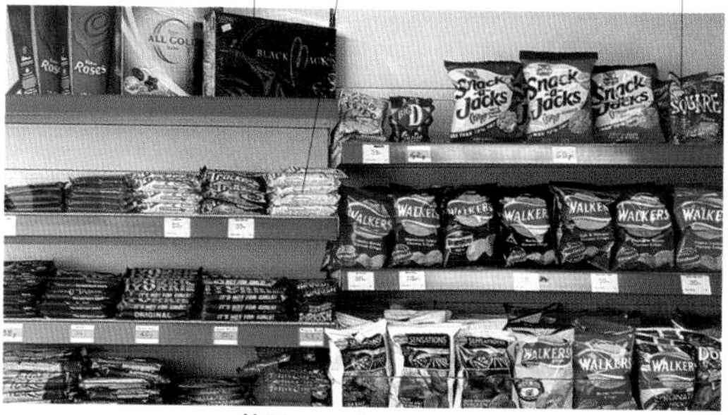

飴屋 ameya | sweet shop

関連用語 kanrenyōgo • vocabulary

ミルクチョコレート
miruku chokorēto
milk chocolate

キャラメル
kyarameru
caramel

スイートチョコレート
suīto chokorēto
plain chocolate

トラッフル
toraffuru
truffle

ホワイトチョコレート
howaito chokorēto
white chocolate

クッキー
kukkī
biscuit

ピックンミックス
pikkunmikkusu
pick and mix

飴
ame
boiled sweets

菓子 kashi • confectionery

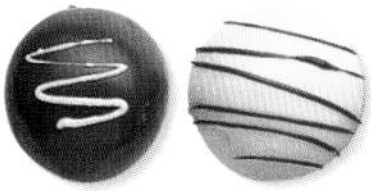

チョコレート
chokorēto
chocolate

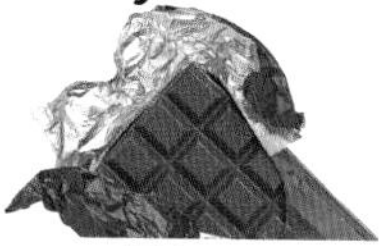

板チョコ
itachoko
chocolate bar

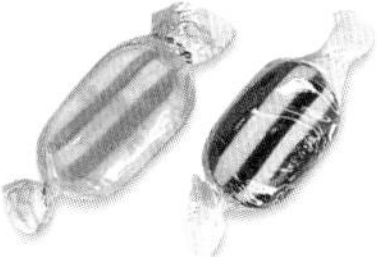

飴
ame
sweets

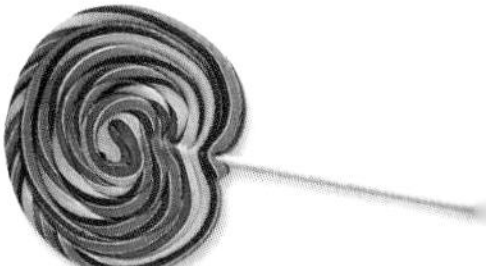

棒付きキャンディー
bō-tsuki kyandī
lollipop

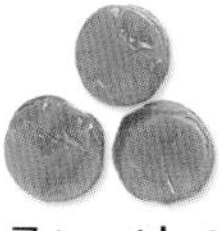

トフィー tofī | toffee

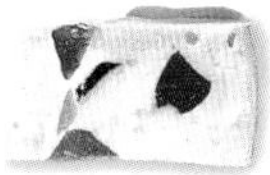

ヌガー
nugā | nougat

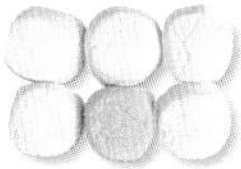

マシュマロ
mashumaro
marshmallow

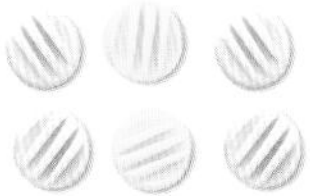

ハッカ飴
hakka ame
mint

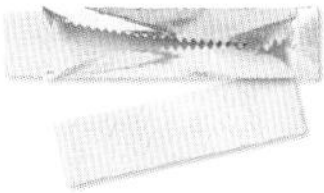

ガム
gamu
chewing gum

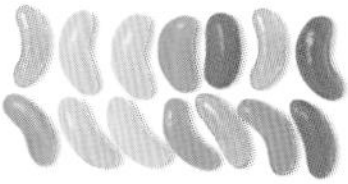

ゼリービーンズ
zeribīnzu
jellybean

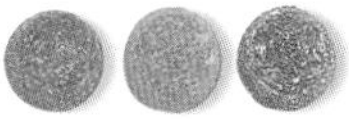

フルーツガム
furūtsu gamu
fruit gum

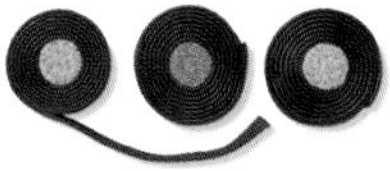

甘草飴
kanzō ame
liquorice

その他の店 sonota no mise • other shops

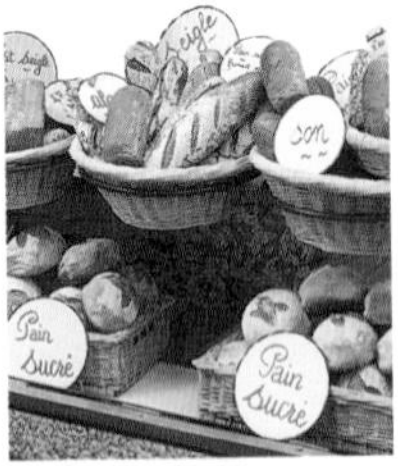

パン屋
pan'ya
baker's

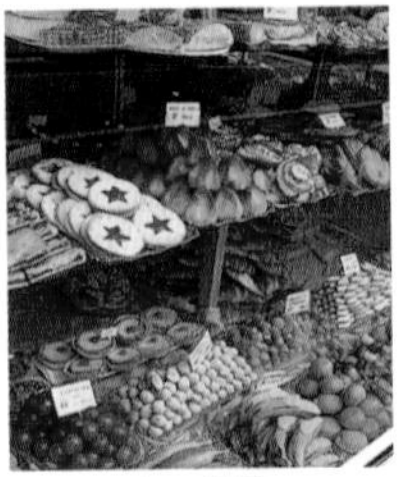

ケーキ屋
kēkiya
cake shop

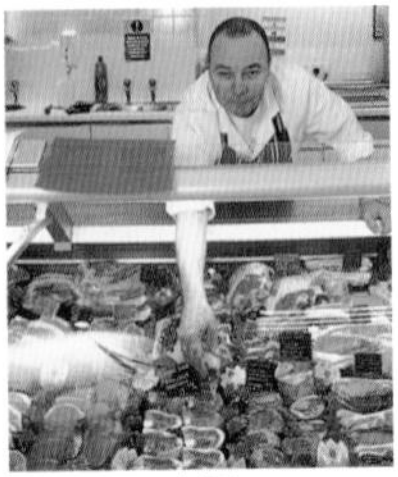

肉屋
nikuya
butcher's

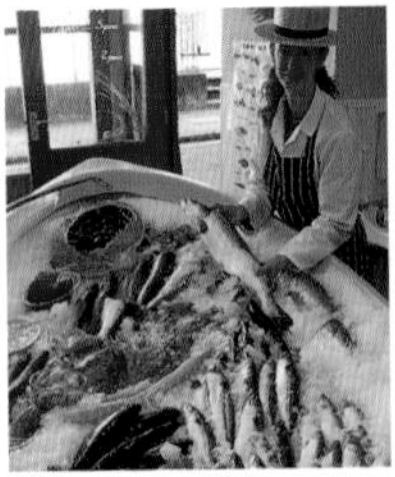

魚屋
sakanaya
fishmonger's

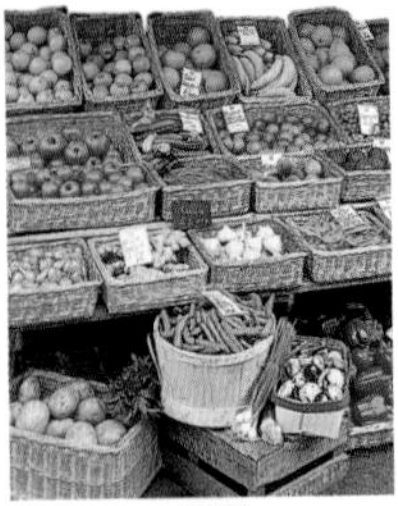

八百屋
yaoya
greengrocer's

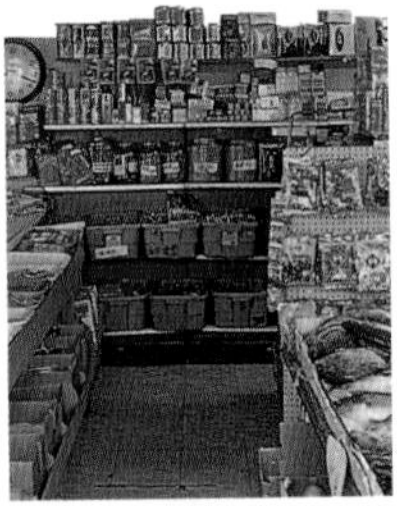

食料品店
shokuryōhin-ten
grocer's

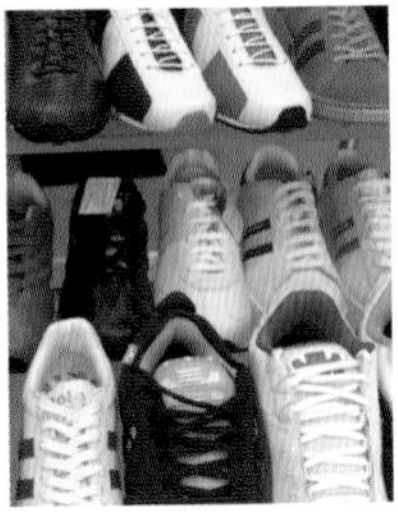

靴屋
kutsuya
shoe shop

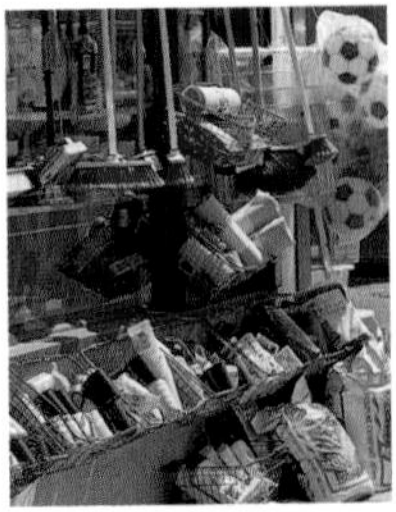

金物屋
kanamonoya
hardware shop

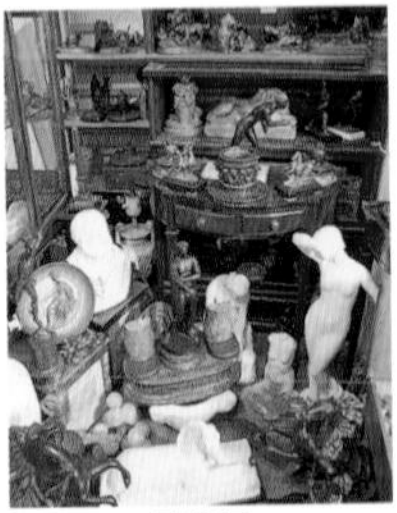

骨董屋
kottōya
antiques shop

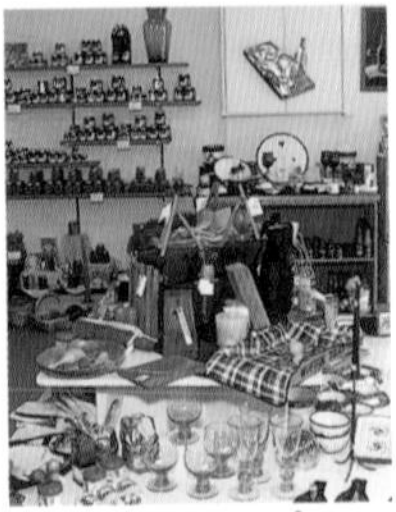

ギフトショップ
gifuto shoppu
gift shop

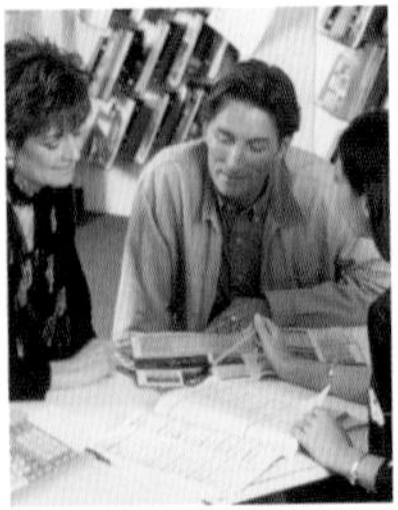

旅行代理店
ryokō dairiten
travel agent's

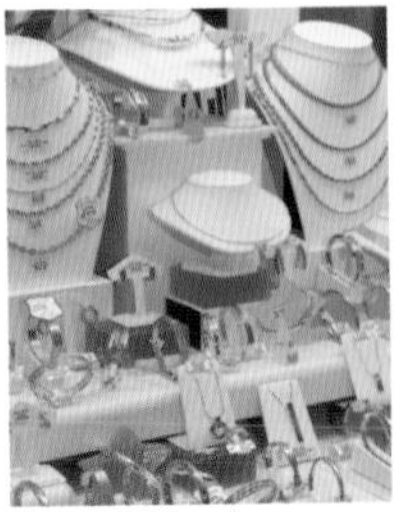

宝石店
hōseki-ten
jeweller's

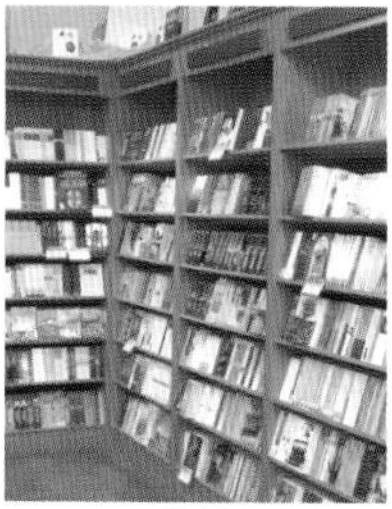

本屋
hon'ya
book shop

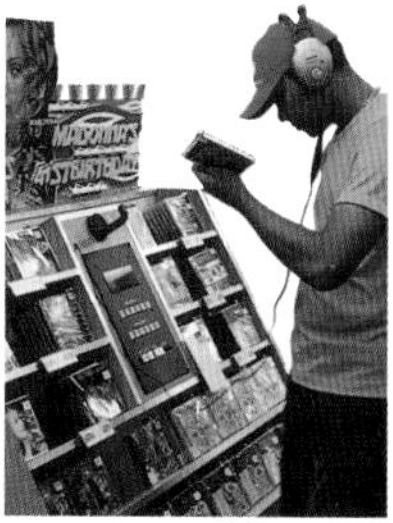

レコード店
rekōdo-ten
record shop

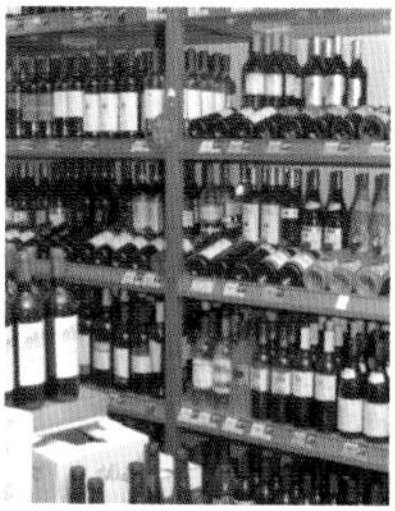

酒屋
sakaya
off licence

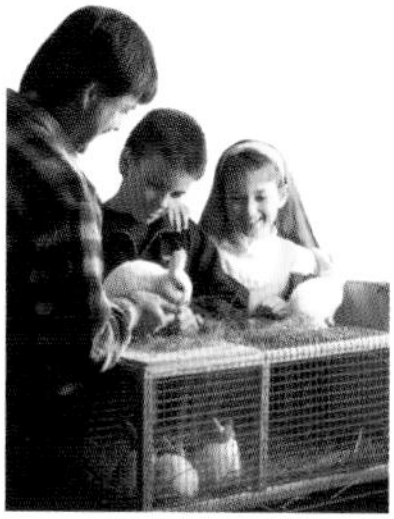

ペットショップ
petto shoppu
pet shop

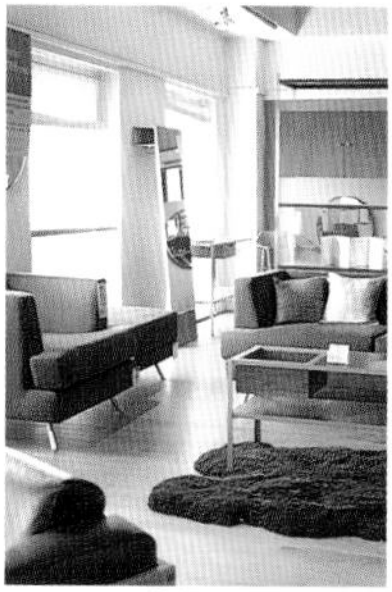

家具屋
kaguya
furniture shop

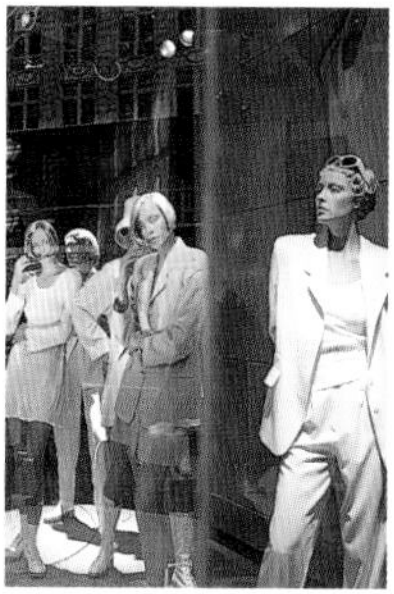

ブティック
butikku
boutique

関連用語 kanrenyōgo • vocabulary

不動産屋
fudōsan-ya
estate agent's

園芸センター
engei sentā
garden centre

クリーニング屋
kurīningu-ya
dry cleaner's

コインランドリー
koin randorī
launderette

カメラ屋
kamera-ya
camera shop

健康食品店
kenkō shokuhin-ten
health food shop

画材屋
gazai-ya
art shop

中古販売店
chūko hambai-ten
second-hand shop

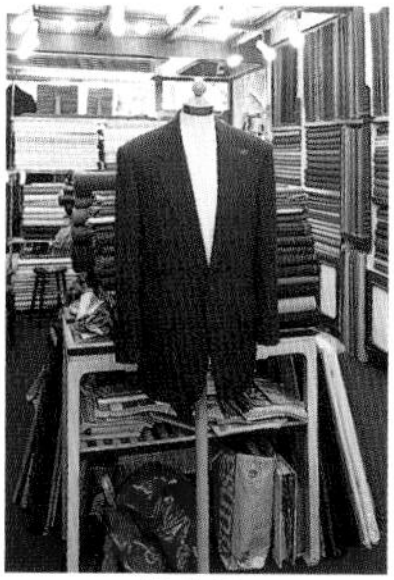

仕立屋
shitateya
tailor's

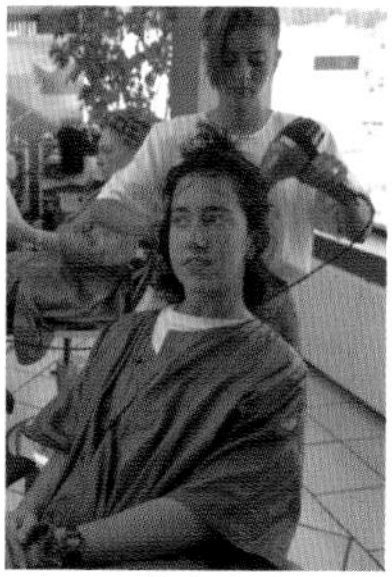

美容院
biyōin
hairdresser's

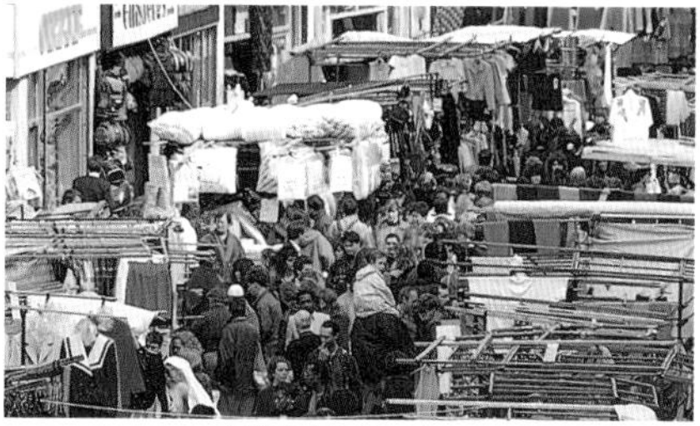

市場 ichiba | market

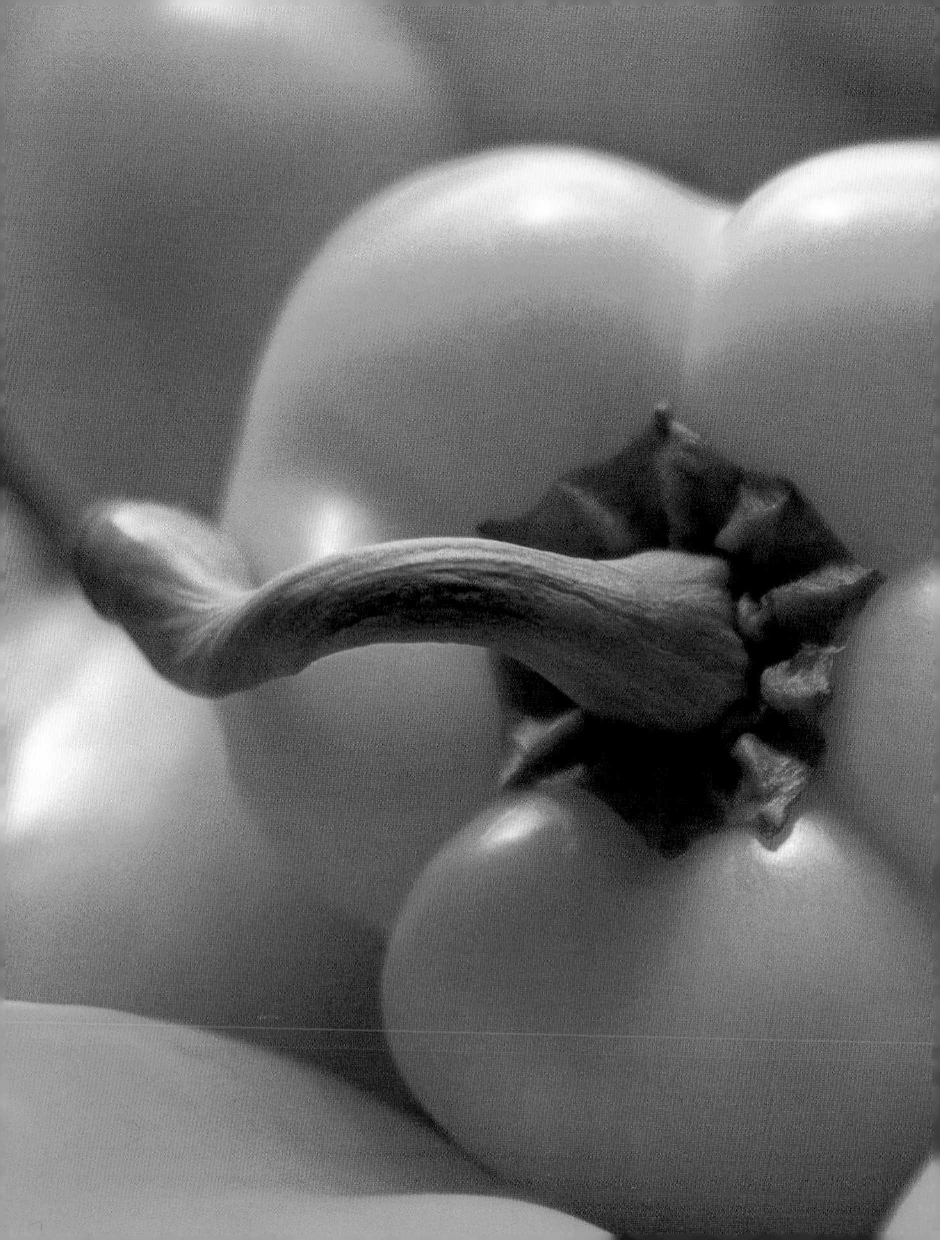

食べ物 tabemono
food

肉 niku • meat

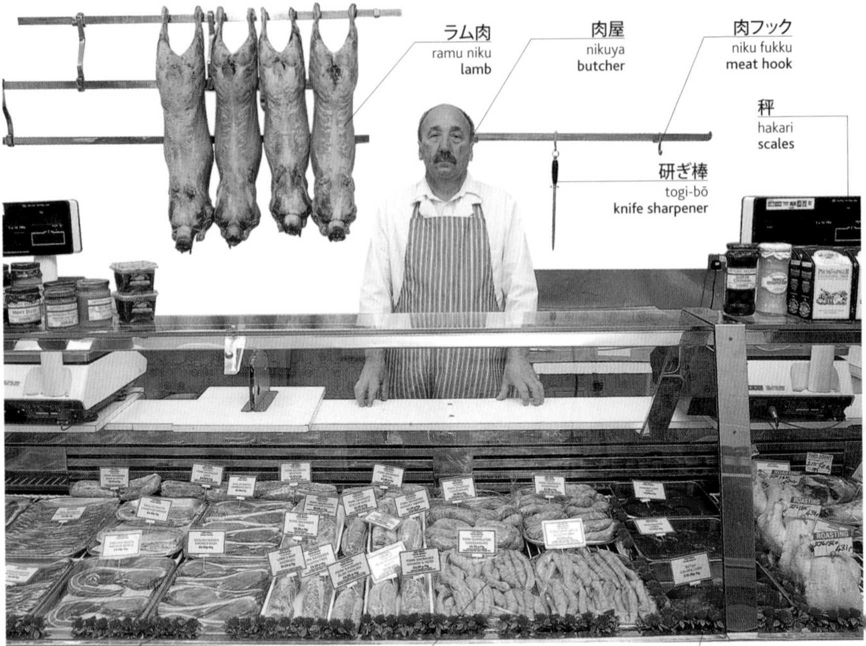

ラム肉
ramu niku
lamb

肉屋
nikuya
butcher

肉フック
niku fukku
meat hook

秤
hakari
scales

研ぎ棒
togi-bō
knife sharpener

ベーコン
bēkon
bacon

ソーセージ
sōsēji
sausages

レバー
rebā
liver

関連用語 kanrenyōgo • vocabulary

豚肉 butaniku **pork**	鹿肉 shika niku **venison**	内蔵 naizō **offal**	放し飼いの hanashigai no **free range**	調理済み肉 chōri-zumi niku **cooked meat**
牛肉 gyūniku **beef**	ウサギ肉 usagi niku **rabbit**	保存処理 hozon shori **cured**	有機性 yūki-sei **organic**	白身肉 shiromi niku **white meat**
子牛肉 ko-ushi niku **veal**	タン tan **tongue**	薫製 kunsei **smoked**	低脂肪肉 teishibō niku **lean meat**	赤身肉 akami niku **red meat**

切り身 kirimi • cuts

薄切り
usugiri
slice

（ベーコンの）薄切り
(bēkon no) usugiri
rasher

挽肉
hikiniku
mince

ヒレ肉
hire niku
fillet

ランプステーキ
rampusutēki | rump steak

ハム
hamu
ham

皮
kawa
rind

脂身
aburami
fat

骨
hone
bone

腎臓
jinzō
kidney

サーロインステーキ
sāroinsutēki
sirloin steak

あばら肉
abaraniku
rib

チョップ
choppu
chop

かたまり肉
katamari niku
joint

心臓
shinzō
heart

鳥肉 toriniku • poultry

皮
kawa
skin

胸肉
muneniku
breast

もも肉
momoniku
thigh

手羽肉
tebaniku
wing

猟鳥
ryōchō
game

下拵えした鶏
shitagoshirae shita tori
dressed chicken

足
ashi
leg

雉 kiji | pheasant

鶉 uzura | quail

七面鳥
shichimenchō
turkey

鶏 tori | chicken

鴨 kamo | duck

鵞鳥 gachō | goose

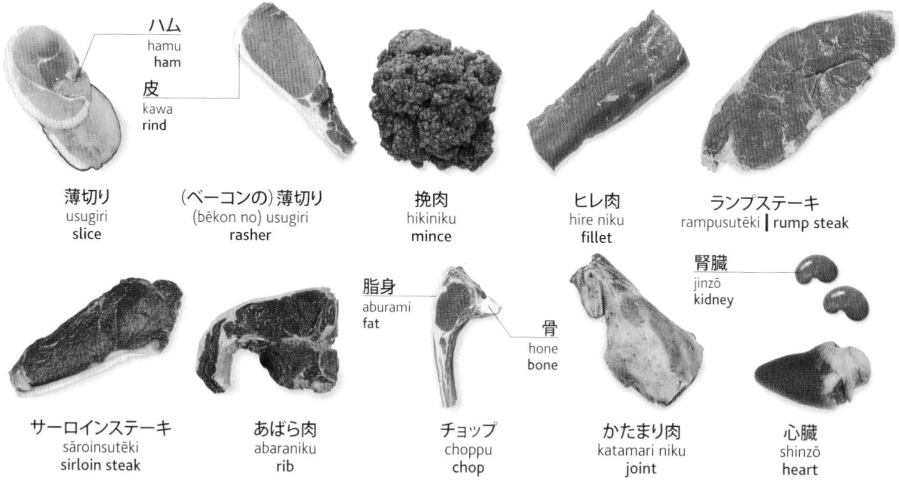

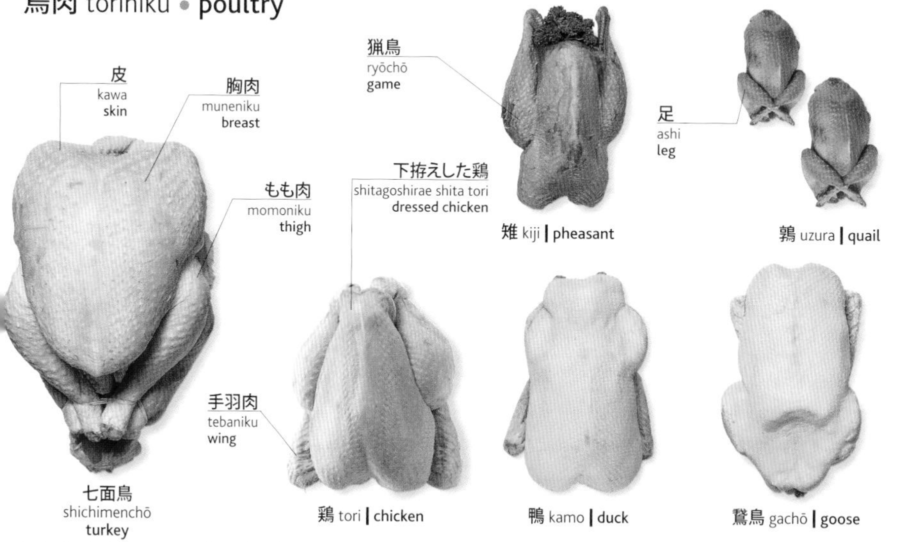

魚 sakana • fish

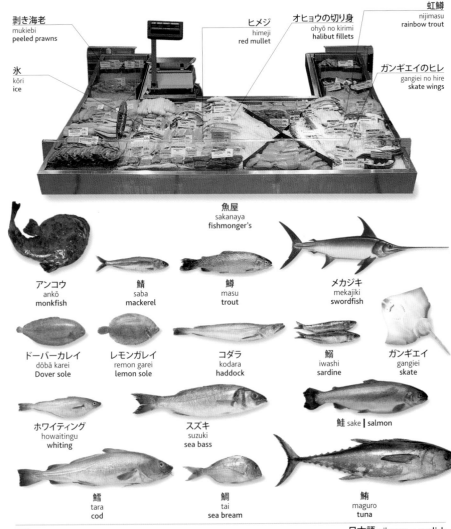

虹鱒
nijimasu
rainbow trout

剥き海老
mukiebi
peeled prawns

ヒメジ
himeji
red mullet

オヒョウの切り身
ohyō no kirimi
halibut fillets

ガンギエイのヒレ
gangiei no hire
skate wings

氷
kōri
ice

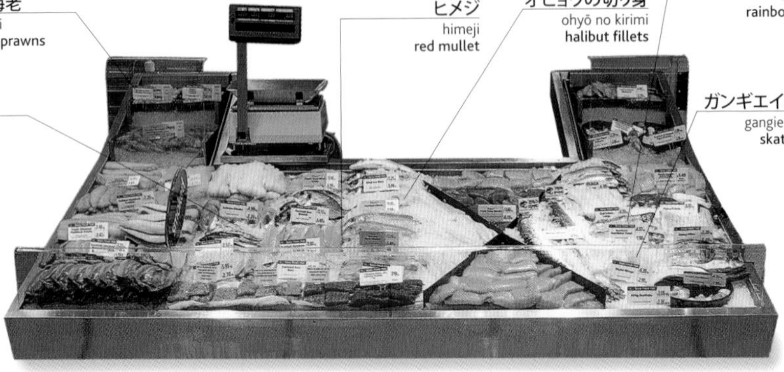

魚屋
sakanaya
fishmonger's

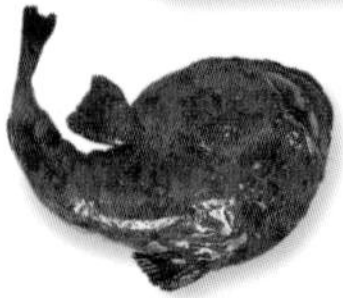

アンコウ
ankō
monkfish

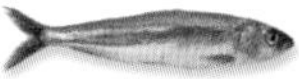

鯖
saba
mackerel

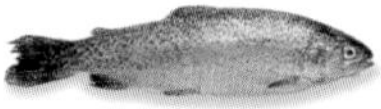

鱒
masu
trout

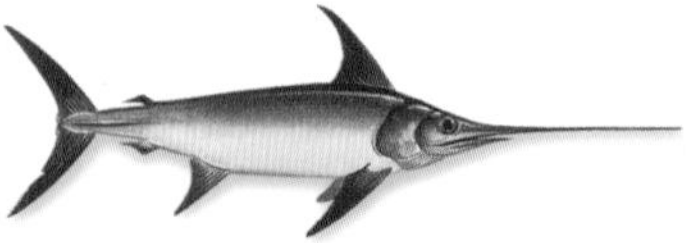

メカジキ
mekajiki
swordfish

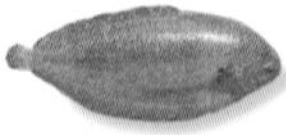

ドーバーカレイ
dōbā karei
Dover sole

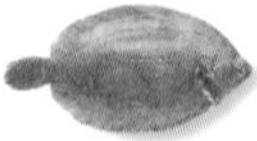

レモンガレイ
remon garei
lemon sole

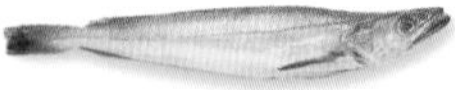

コダラ
kodara
haddock

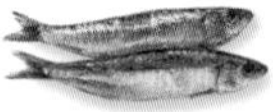

鰯
iwashi
sardine

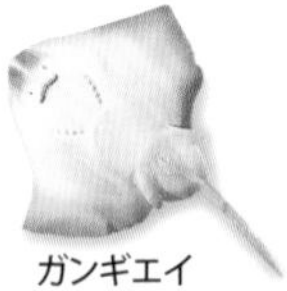

ガンギエイ
gangiei
skate

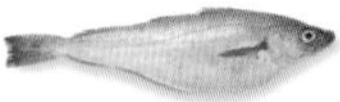

ホワイティング
howaitingu
whiting

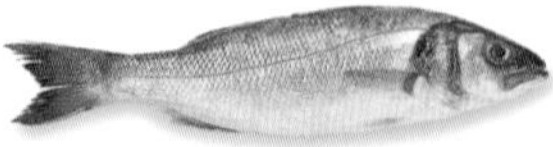

スズキ
suzuki
sea bass

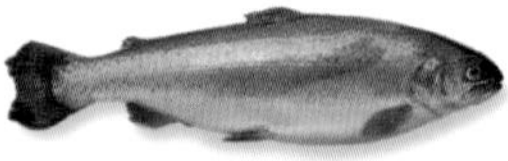

鮭 sake | salmon

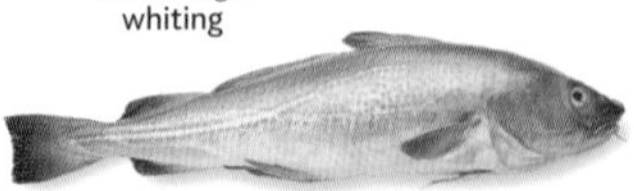

鱈
tara
cod

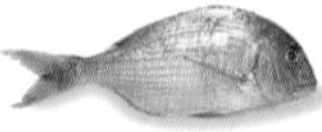

鯛
tai
sea bream

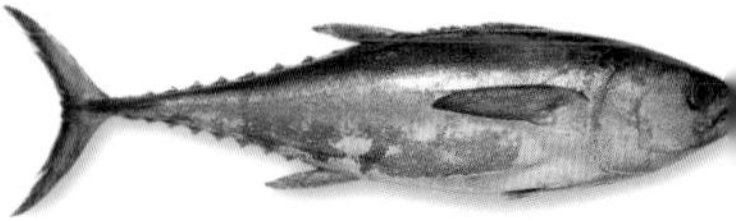

鮪
maguro
tuna

海産物 kaisambutsu · **seafood**

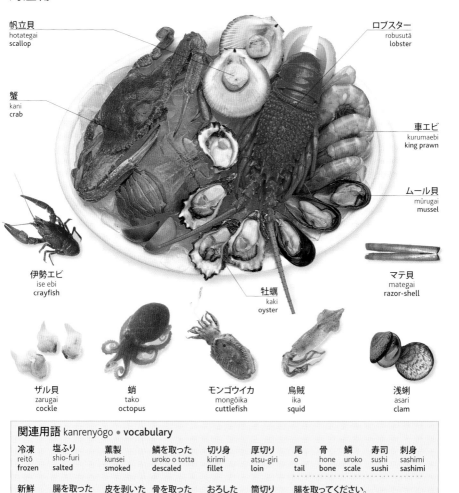

帆立貝
hotategai
scallop

ロブスター
robusutā
lobster

蟹
kani
crab

車エビ
kurumaebi
king prawn

ムール貝
mūrugai
mussel

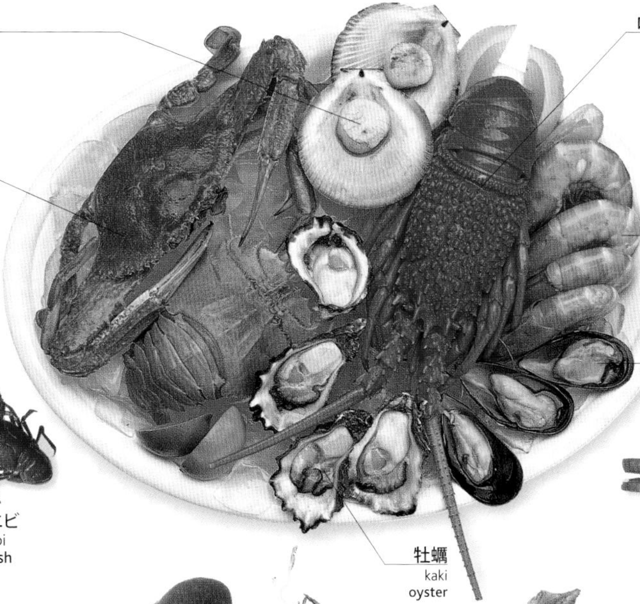

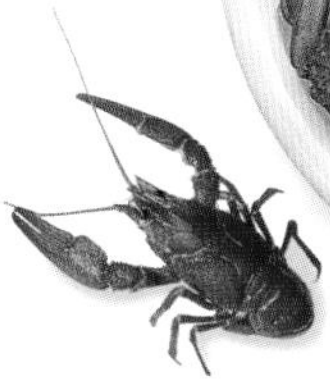

伊勢エビ
ise ebi
crayfish

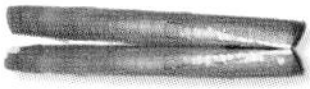

マテ貝
mategai
razor-shell

牡蠣
kaki
oyster

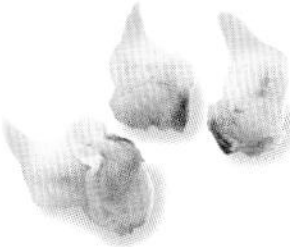

ザル貝
zarugai
cockle

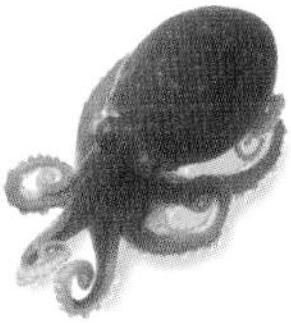

蛸
tako
octopus

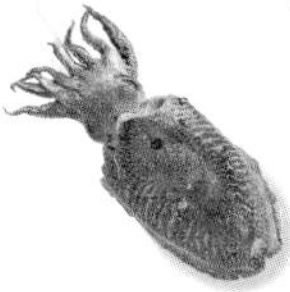

モンゴウイカ
mongōika
cuttlefish

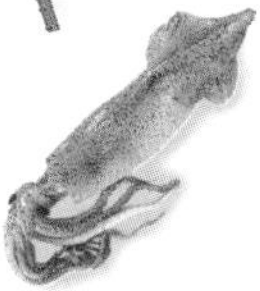

烏賊
ika
squid

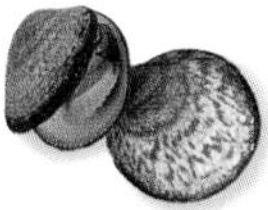

浅蜊
asari
clam

関連用語 kanrenyōgo · **vocabulary**

冷凍	塩ふり	薫製	鱗を取った	切り身	厚切り	尾	骨	鱗	寿司	刺身
reitō	shio-furi	kunsei	uroko o totta	kirimi	atsu-giri	o	hone	uroko	sushi	sashimi
frozen	**salted**	**smoked**	**descaled**	**fillet**	**loin**	**tail**	**bone**	**scale**	**sushi**	**sashimi**

新鮮	腸を取った	皮を剥いた	骨を取った	おろした	筒切り	腸を取ってください。
shinsen	wata o totta	kawa o muita	hone o totta	oroshita	tsutsugiri	wata o totte kudasai?
fresh	**cleaned**	**skinned**	**boned**	**filleted**	**steak**	**Will you clean it for me?**

野菜1 yasai ● vegetables 1

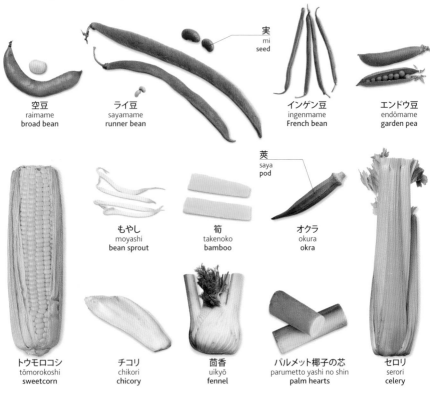

実
mi
seed

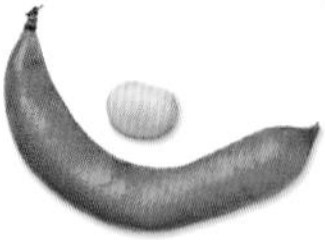

空豆
raimame
broad bean

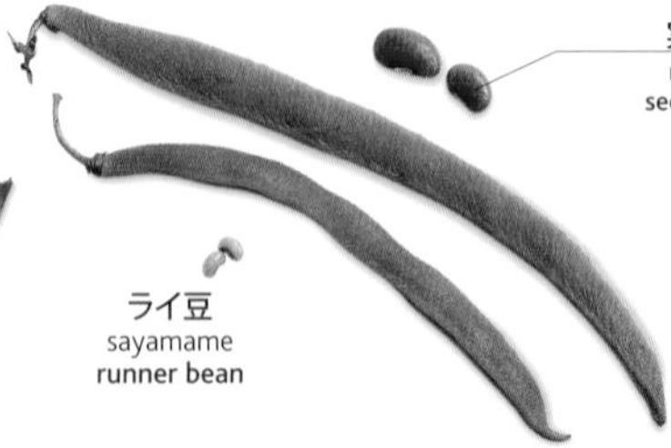

ライ豆
sayamame
runner bean

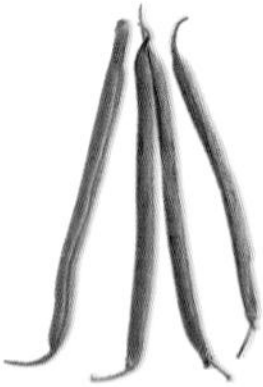

インゲン豆
ingenmame
French bean

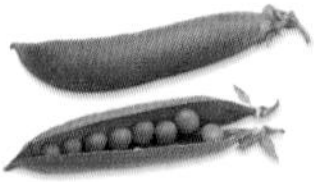

エンドウ豆
endōmame
garden pea

莢
saya
pod

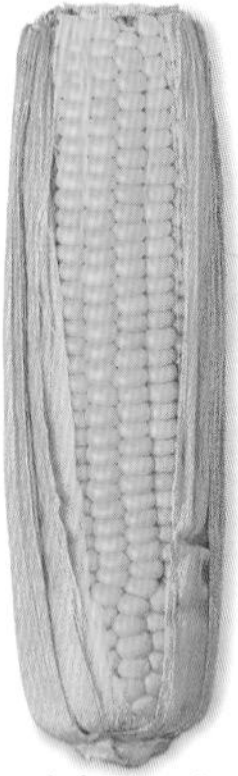

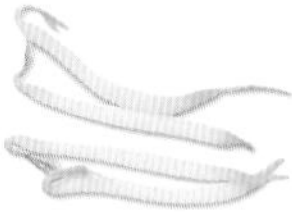

もやし
moyashi
bean sprout

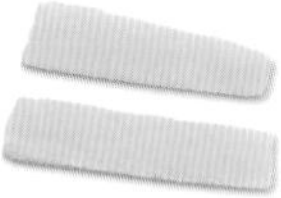

筍
takenoko
bamboo

オクラ
okura
okra

トウモロコシ
tōmorokoshi
sweetcorn

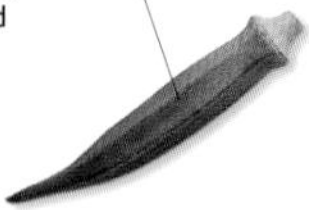

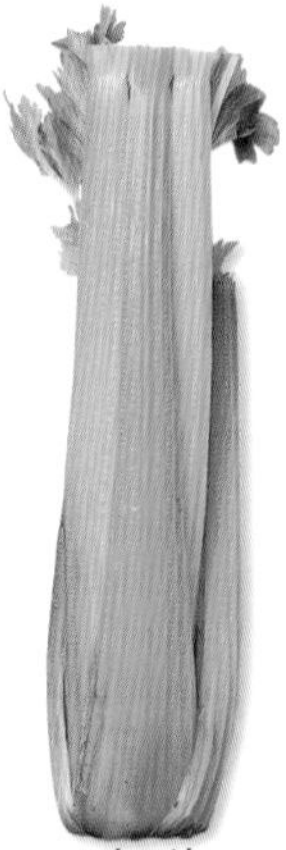

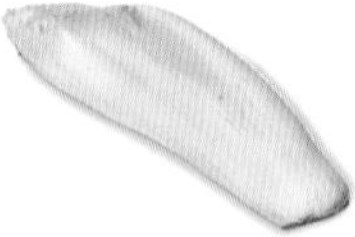

チコリ
chikori
chicory

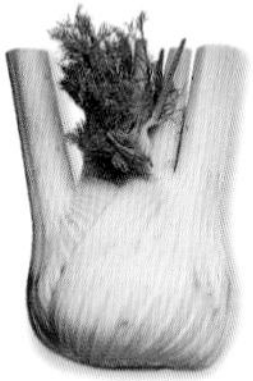

茴香
uikyō
fennel

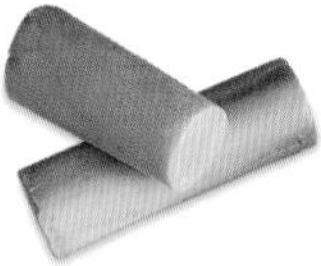

パルメット椰子の芯
parumetto yashi no shin
palm hearts

セロリ
serori
celery

関連用語 kanrenyōgo ● vocabulary

白菜
hakusai
Chinese leaves

茎
kuki
stalk

種
tane
kernel

芯
shin
heart

有機野菜はありますか。
yūki yasai wa arimasuka?
Do you sell organic vegetables?

葉
ha
leaf

房
fusa
floret

先端
sentan
tip

有機（栽培）
yūki (saibai)
organic

これは地元産ですか。
kore wa jimoto-san desuka?
Are these grown locally?

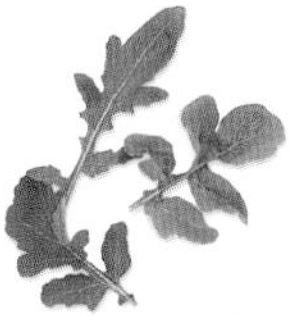

ロケットサラダ
rokettosarada
rocket

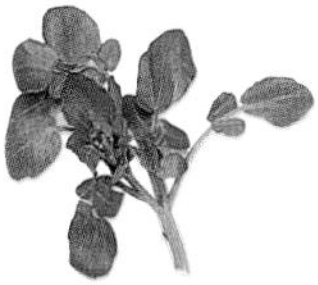

クレソン
kureson
watercress

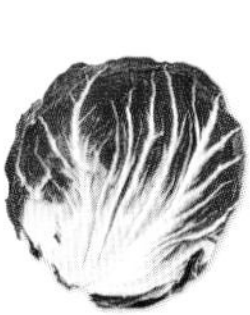

赤チコリ
aka chikori
radicchio

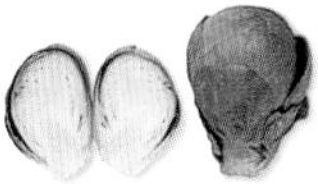

芽キャベツ
mekyabetsu
Brussels sprouts

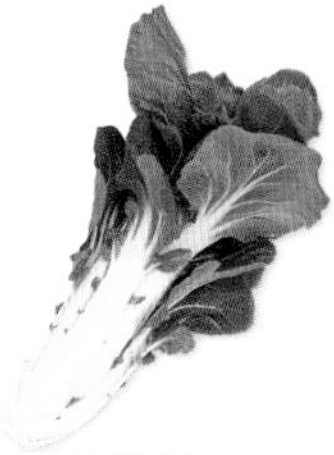

フダンソウ
fudansō
Swiss chard

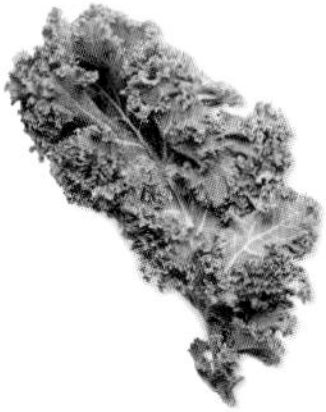

ケール
kēru
kale

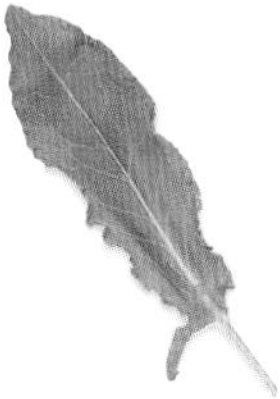

ギシギシ
gishigishi
sorrel

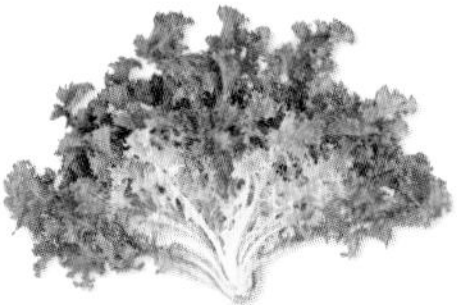

エンダイブ
endaibu
endive

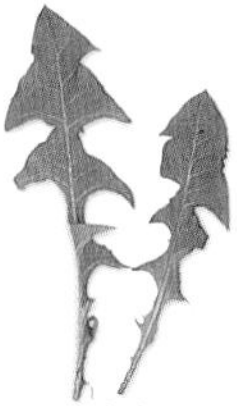

タンポポ
tampopo
dandelion

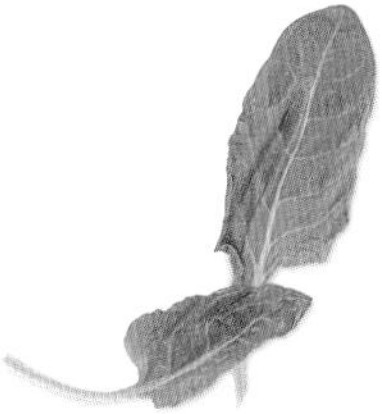

ホウレン草
hōrensō
spinach

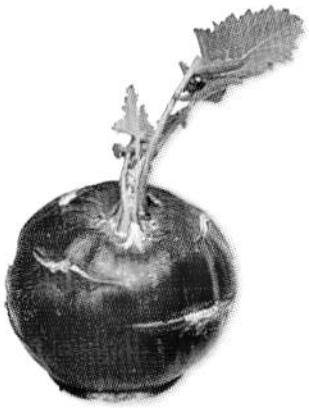

コールラビ
kōrurabi
kohlrabi

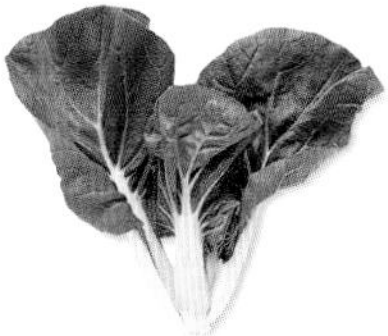

チンゲン菜
chingensai
pak-choi

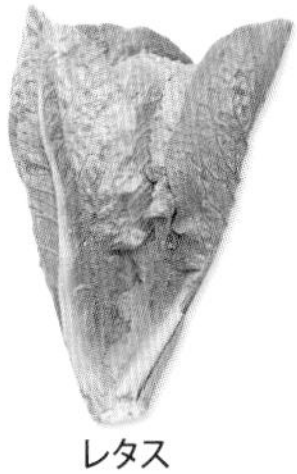

レタス
retasu
lettuce

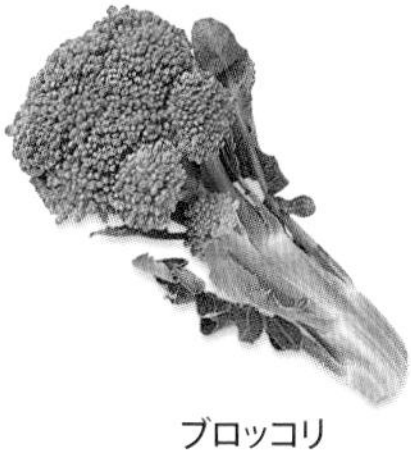

ブロッコリ
burokkori
broccoli

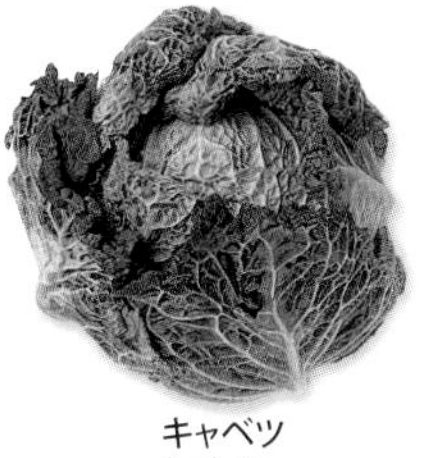

キャベツ
kyabetsu
cabbage

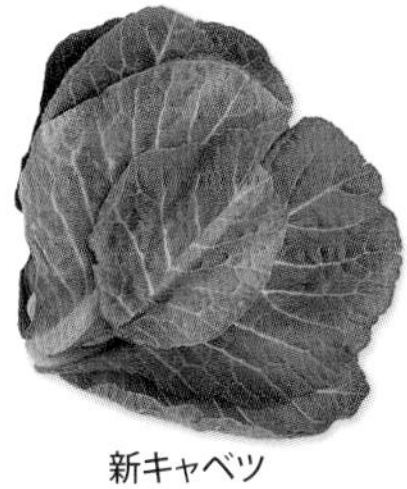

新キャベツ
shin kyabetsu
spring greens

野菜2 yasai • vegetables 2

アーティチョーク
ātichōku
artichoke

ラディッシュ
radisshu
radish

カリフラワー
karifurawā
cauliflower

カブ
kabu
turnip

ジャガイモ
jagaimo
potato

洋葱
tamanegi
onion

ピーマン
pīman
pepper

赤唐辛子
aka tōgarashi
chilli

ナタウリ
natauri
marrow

関連用語 kanrenyōgo • vocabulary

プチトマト puchi tomato **cherry tomato**	タロ芋 taroimo **taro root**	冷凍 reitō **frozen**	苦い nigai **bitter**
人参 ninjin **carrot**	菱の実 hishi no mi **water chestnut**	生 nama **raw**	硬い katai **firm**
新ジャガ shinjaga **new potato**	椎茸 shītake **shitake mushrooms**	辛い karai **hot (spicy)**	果肉 kaniku **flesh**
セロリアック seroriakku **celeriac**	わさび wasabi **Japanese horseradish**	甘い amai **sweet**	根 ne **root**

ジャガイモを1キロください。
jagaimo o ichi kiro kudasai.
One kilo of potatoes, please.

1キロいくらですか。
ichi kiro ikura desuka?
What's the price per kilo?

あれは何と言いますか。
are wa nan to īmasuka?
What are those called?

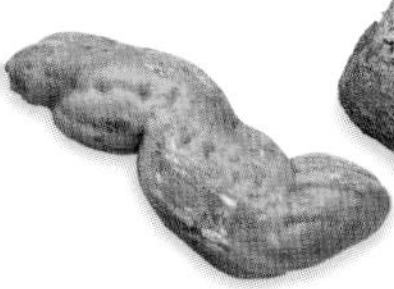

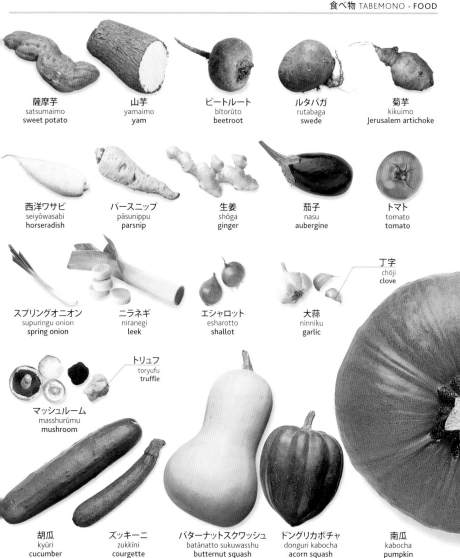

薩摩芋
satsumaimo
sweet potato

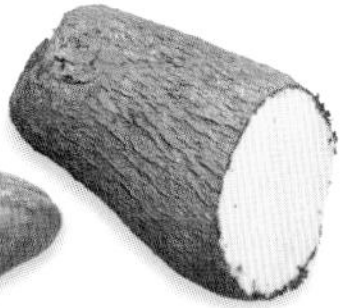

山芋
yamaimo
yam

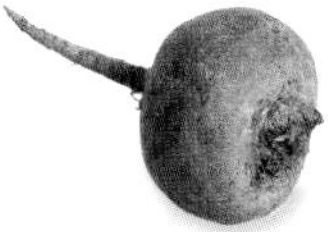

ビートルート
bītorūto
beetroot

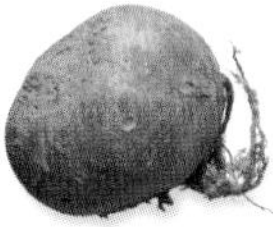

ルタバガ
rutabaga
swede

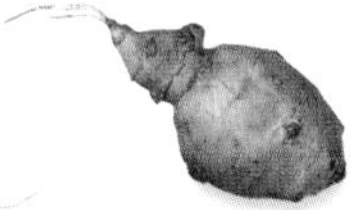

菊芋
kikuimo
Jerusalem artichoke

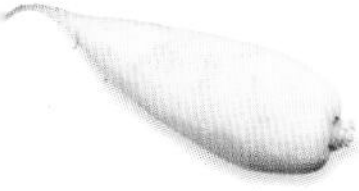

西洋ワサビ
seiyōwasabi
horseradish

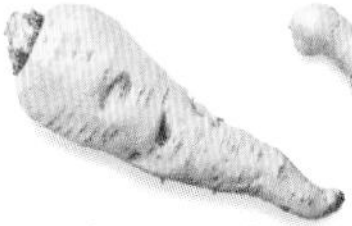

パースニップ
pāsunippu
parsnip

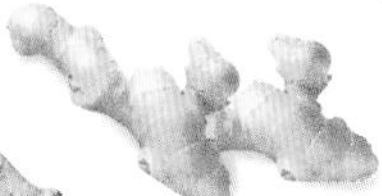

生姜
shōga
ginger

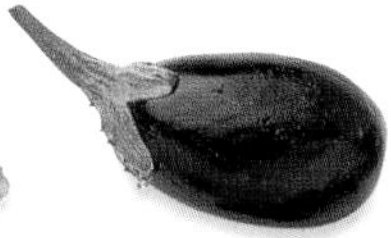

茄子
nasu
aubergine

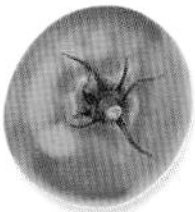

トマト
tomato
tomato

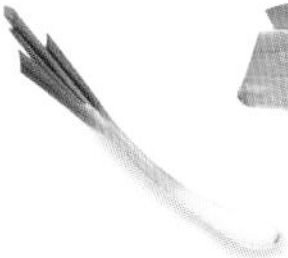

スプリングオニオン
supuringu onion
spring onion

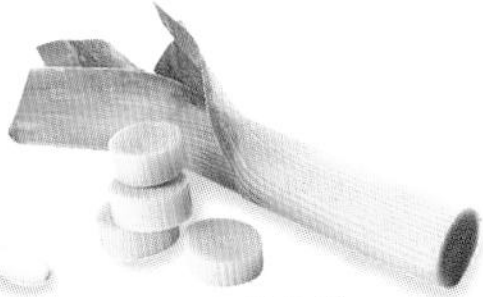

ニラネギ
niranegi
leek

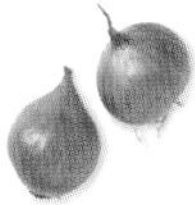

エシャロット
esharotto
shallot

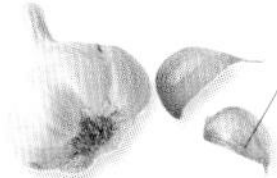

大蒜
ninniku
garlic

丁字
chōji
clove

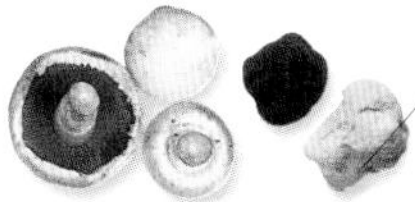

トリュフ
toryufu
truffle

マッシュルーム
masshurūmu
mushroom

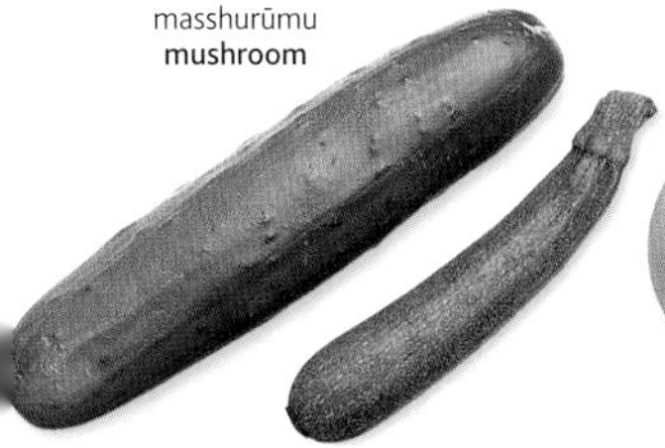

胡瓜
kyūri
cucumber

ズッキーニ
zukkīni
courgette

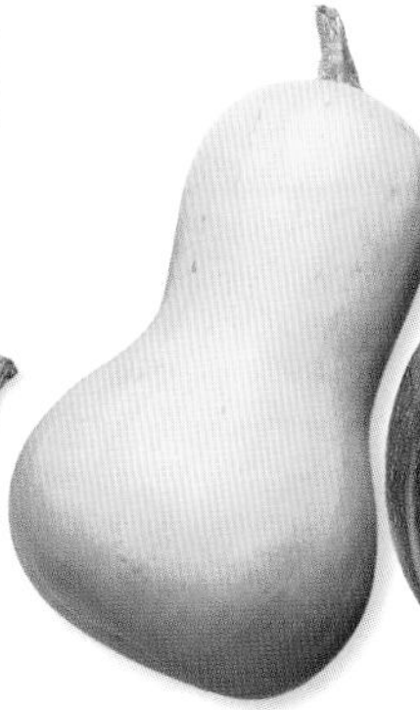

バターナットスクワッシュ
batānatto sukuwasshu
butternut squash

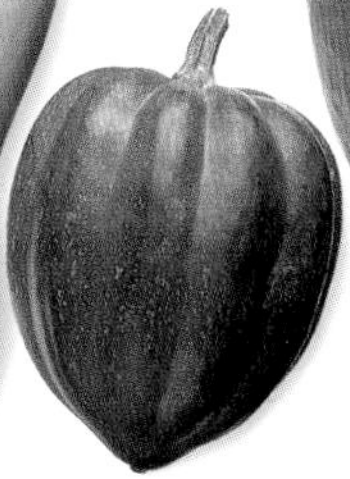

ドングリカボチャ
donguri kabocha
acorn squash

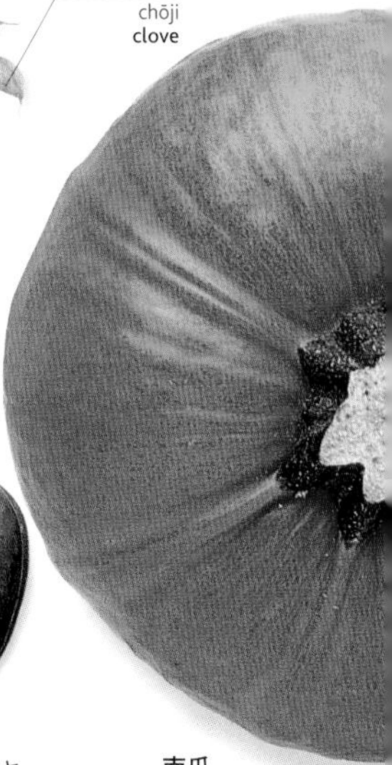

南瓜
kabocha
pumpkin

果物1 kudamono • fruit 1

柑橘類 kankitsu rui
• citrus fruit

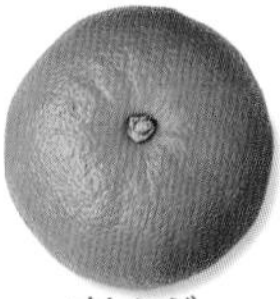

オレンジ
orenji
orange

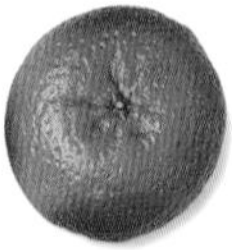

クレメンティン
kurementin
clementine

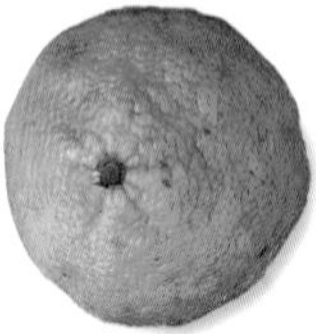

アグリフルーツ
agurifurūtsu
ugli fruit

筋
suji
pith

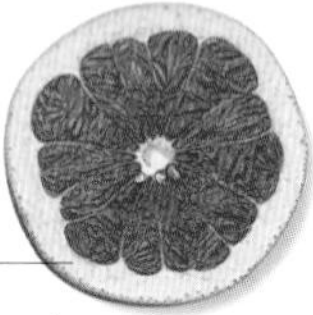

グレープフルーツ
gurēpufurūtsu
grapefruit

房
fusa
segment

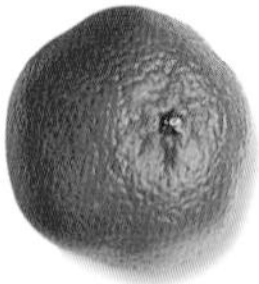

タンジェリン
tanjerin
tangerine

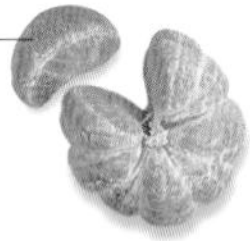

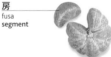

薩摩みかん
satsuma mikan
satsuma

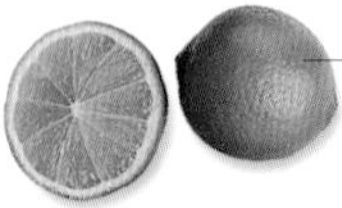

皮
kawa
zest

ライム
raimu
lime

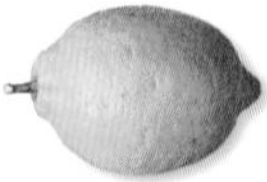

レモン
remon
lemon

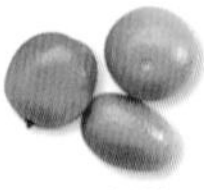

金柑
kinkan
kumquat

石果 sekika
• stoned fruit

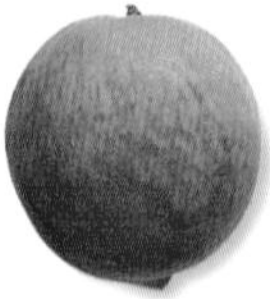

桃
momo
peach

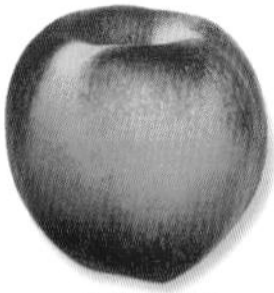

ネクタリン
nekutarin
nectarine

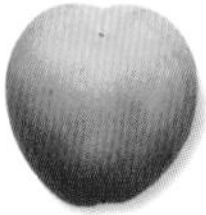

杏
anzu
apricot

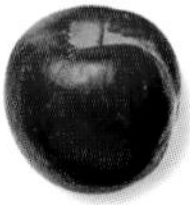

プラム
puramu
plum

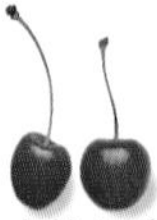

さくらんぼ
sakurambo
cherry

洋梨
yōnashi
pear

林檎
ringo
apple

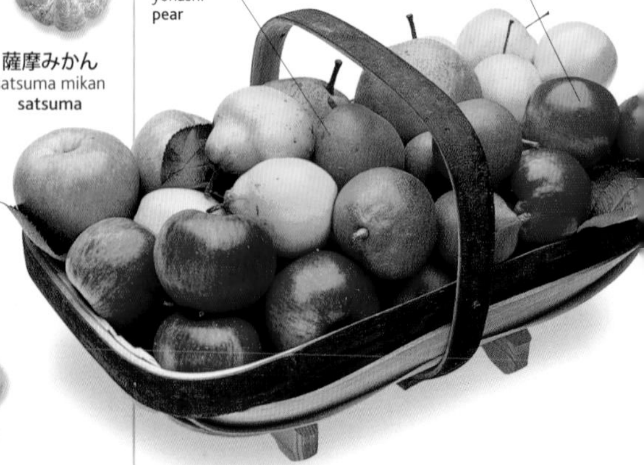

果物籠 kudamono kago | basket of fruit

液果とメロン ekika to meron • berries and melons

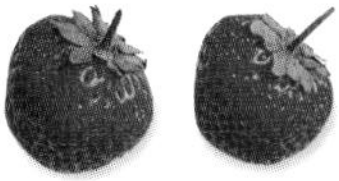

苺
ichigo
strawberry

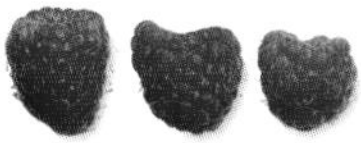

ラズベリー
razuberī
raspberry

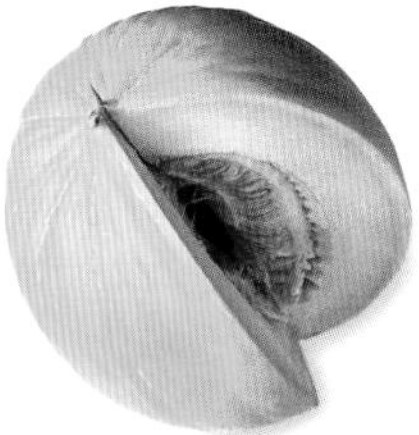

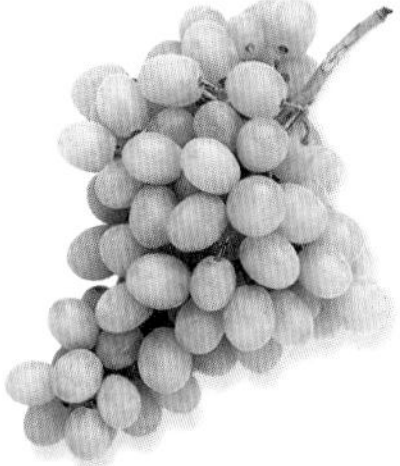

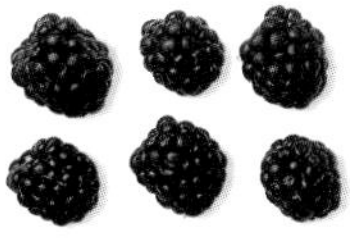

ブラックベリー
burakkuberī
blackberry

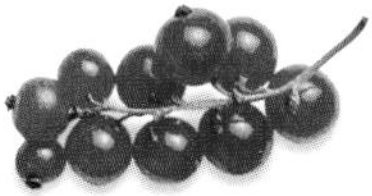

レッドカラント
reddokaranto
redcurrant

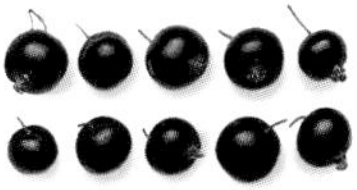

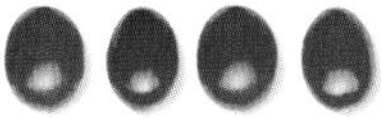

クランベリー
kuranberī
cranberry

ブラックカラント
burakkukaranto
blackcurrant

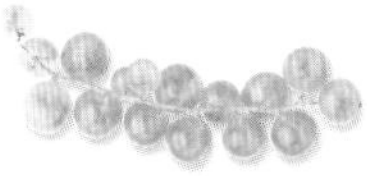

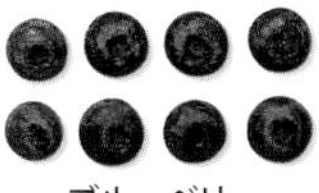

ブルーベリー
burūberī
blueberry

ホワイトカラント
howaitokaranto
white currant

メロン
meron
melon

葡萄
budō
grapes

皮
kawa
rind

種
tane
seed

果肉
kaniku
flesh

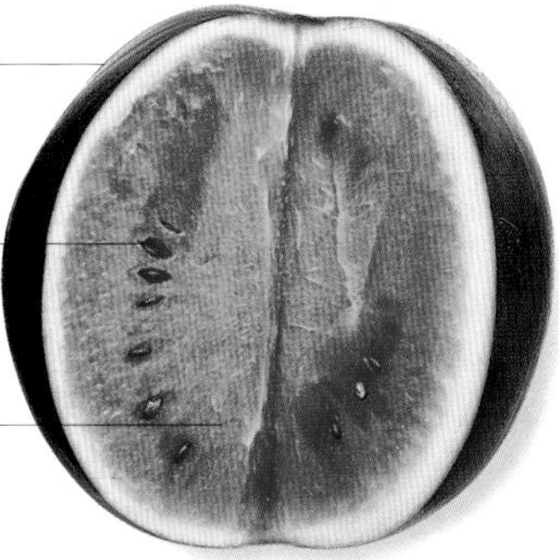

西瓜
suika
watermelon

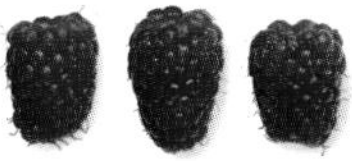

ローガンベリー
rōganberī
loganberry

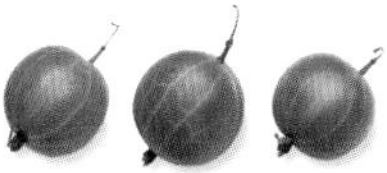

グーズベリー
gūzuberī
gooseberry

関連用語 kanrenyōgo • vocabulary

ダイオウ daiō **rhubarb**	酸っぱい suppai **sour**	パリッとした parittoshita **crisp**	果汁 kajū **juice**	熟していますか。 jukushite imasuka? **Are they ripe?**
繊維 sen'i **fibre**	新鮮 shinsen **fresh**	腐った kusatta **rotten**	芯 shin **core**	試食できますか。 shishoku dekimasuka? **Can I try one?**
甘い amai **sweet**	みずみずしい mizumizushī **juicy**	(柔らかい)果肉 (yawarakai) kaniku **pulp**	種なし tanenashi **seedless**	何日ぐらい保ちますか。 nannichi gurai tamochimasuka? **How long will they keep?**

果物2 kudamono 2 • fruit 2

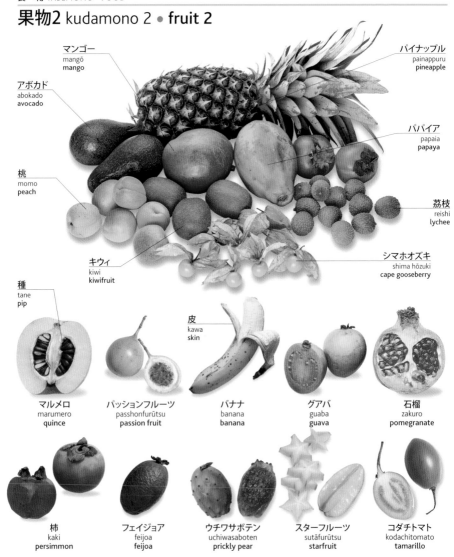

マンゴー
mangō
mango

パイナップル
painappuru
pineapple

アボカド
abokado
avocado

パパイア
papaia
papaya

桃
momo
peach

荔枝
reishi
lychee

キウィ
kiwi
kiwifruit

シマホオズキ
shima hōzuki
cape gooseberry

種
tane
pip

皮
kawa
skin

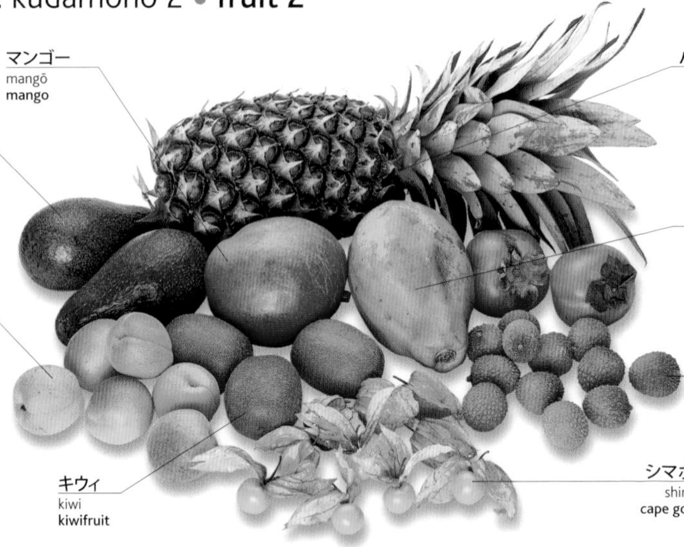

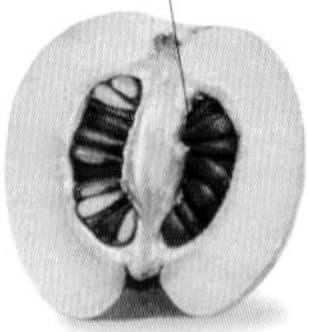

マルメロ
marumero
quince

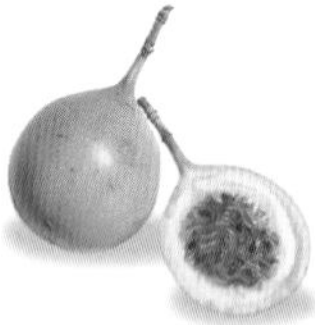

パッションフルーツ
passhonfurūtsu
passion fruit

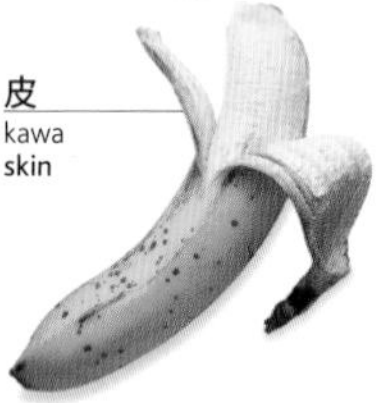

バナナ
banana
banana

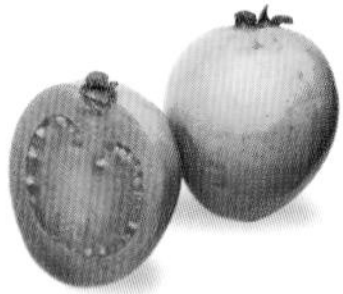

グアバ
guaba
guava

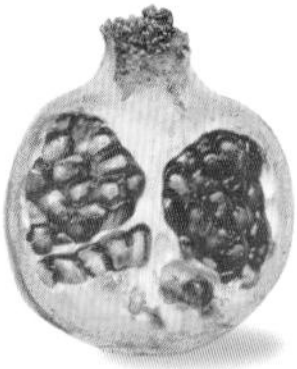

石榴
zakuro
pomegranate

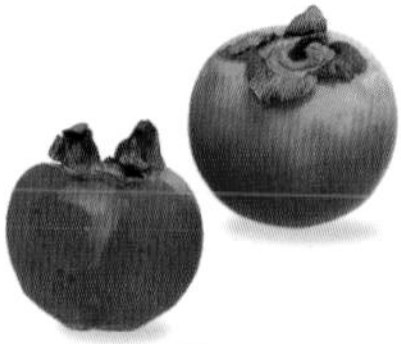

柿
kaki
persimmon

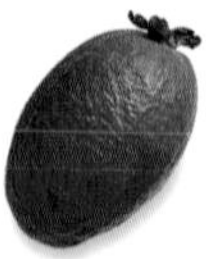

フェイジョア
feijoa
feijoa

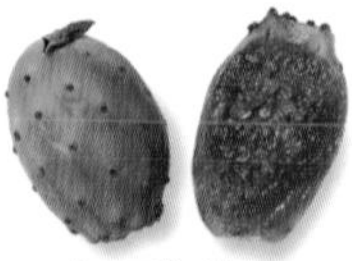

ウチワサボテン
uchiwasaboten
prickly pear

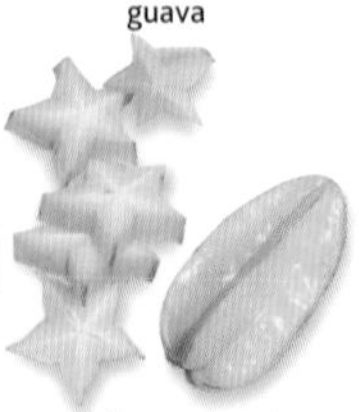

スターフルーツ
sutāfurūtsu
starfruit

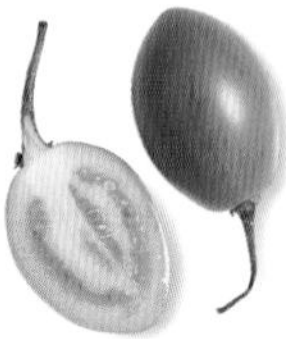

コダチトマト
kodachitomato
tamarillo

ナッツとドライフルーツ nattsu to doraifurūtsu・**nuts and dried fruit**

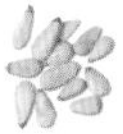

松の実
matsu no mi
pine nut

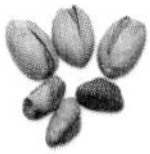

ピスタチオ
pisutachio
pistachio

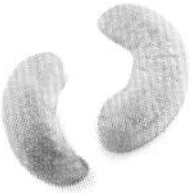

カシューナッツ
kashūnattsu
cashew nut

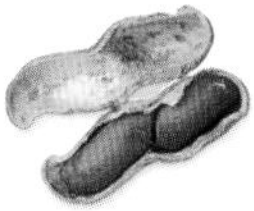

ピーナッツ
pīnattsu
peanut

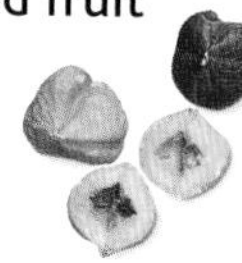

ヘーゼルナッツ
hēzerunattsu
hazelnut

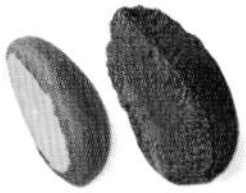

ブラジルナッツ
burajirunattsu
brazil nut

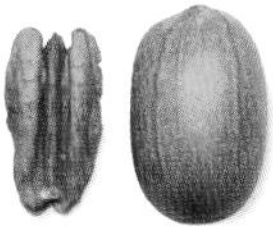

ピーカンナッツ
pīkannattsu
pecan

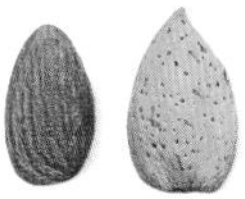

アーモンド
āmondo
almond

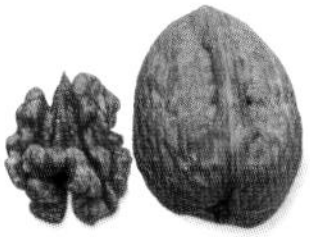

胡桃
kurumi
walnut

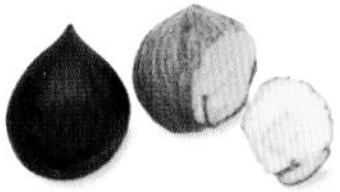

栗
kuri
chestnut

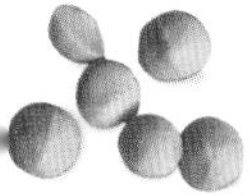

マカデミアナッツ
makademianattsu
macadamia

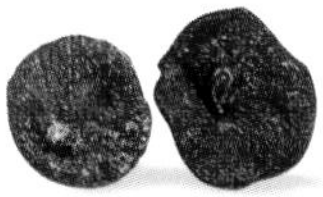

無花果
ichijiku
fig

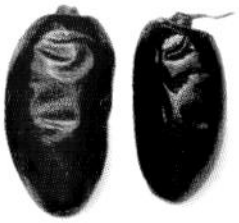

棗
natsume
date

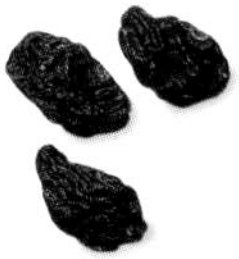

李
sumomo
prune

殻
kara
shell

果肉
kaniku
flesh

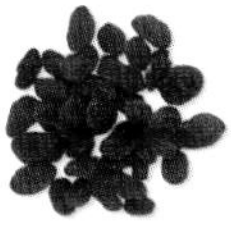

サルタナレーズン
sarutana rēzun
sultana

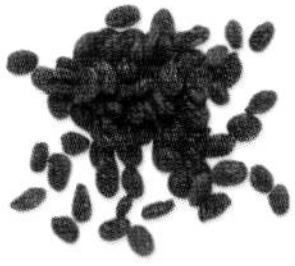

干し葡萄
hoshibudō
raisin

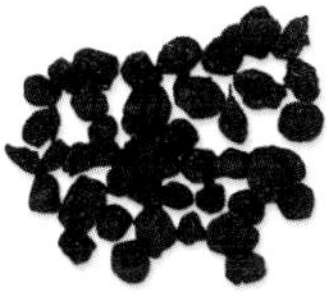

カラント
karanto
currant

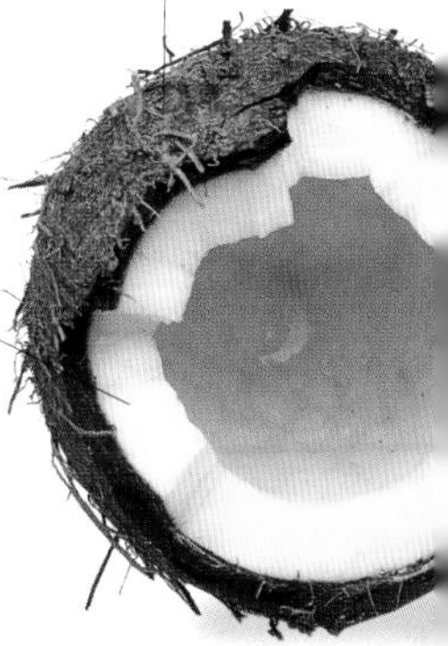

ココナッツ
kokonattsu
coconut

関連用語 kanrenyōgo・**vocabulary**

青い aoi **green**	硬い katai **hard**	仁 nin **kernel**	塩 shio **salted**	煎った itta **roasted**	殻を剥いた kara o muita **shelled**	砂糖漬け果物 satōzuke kudamono **candied fruit**
完熟 kanjuku **ripe**	柔らかい yawarakai **soft**	乾燥 kansō **desiccated**	生 nama **raw**	季節もの kisetsu mono **seasonal**	丸ごと marugoto **whole**	熱帯果実 nettai kajitsu **tropical fruit**

穀類と豆類 kokurui to mamerui • grains and pulses

穀類 kokurui • grains

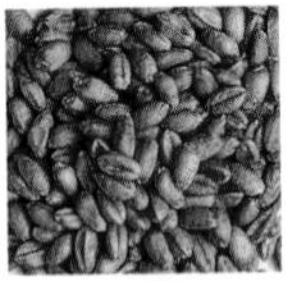

小麦
komugi
wheat

からす麦
karasumugi
oats

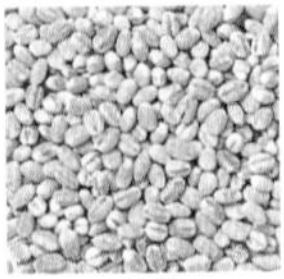

大麦
ōmugi
barley

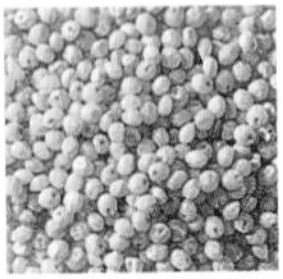

キビ
kibi
millet

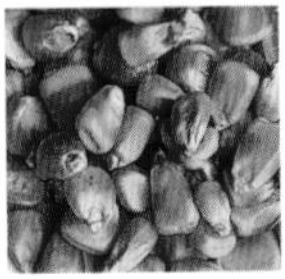

トウモロコシ
tōmorokoshi
corn

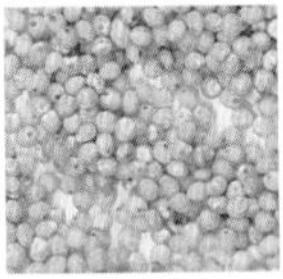

キノア
kinoa
quinoa

関連用語 kanrenyōgo • vocabulary

種 tane seed	香りのある kaori no aru fragranced	スピードクック supīdo kukku easy cook
殻 kara husk	シリアル食品 shiriaru shokuhin cereal	長粒 chōryū long-grain
穀粒 kokuryū kernel	全粒 zenryū wholegrain	短粒 tanryū short-grain
乾燥 kansō dry	（水に）漬ける (mizu ni) tsukeru soak (v)	
新しい atarashī fresh		

米 kome • rice

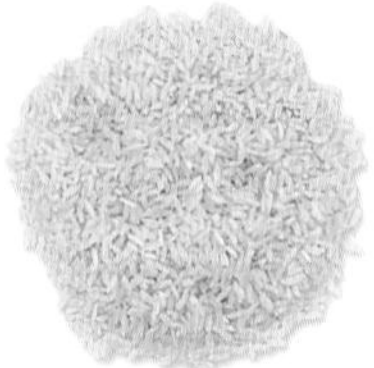

白米
hakumai
white rice

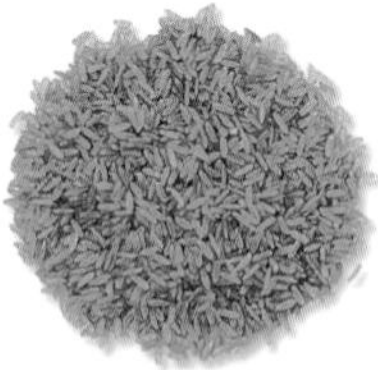

玄米
genmai
brown rice

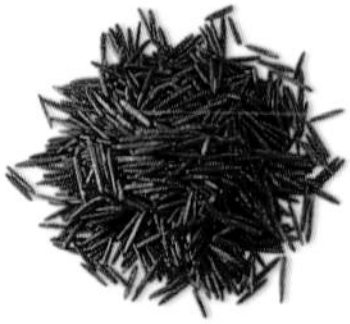

野生米
yasei mai
wild rice

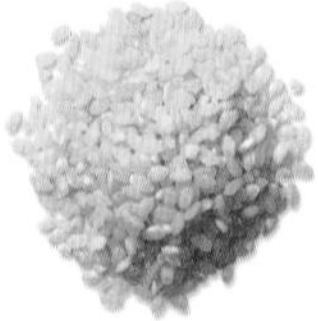

プディングライス
pudingu raisu
pudding rice

加工穀物 kakō kokumotsu • processed grains

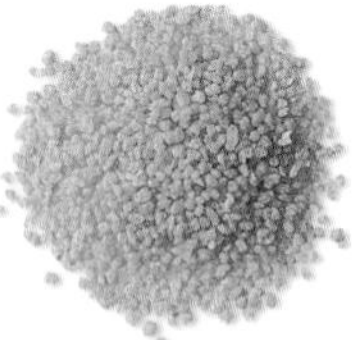

クスクス
kusukusu
couscous

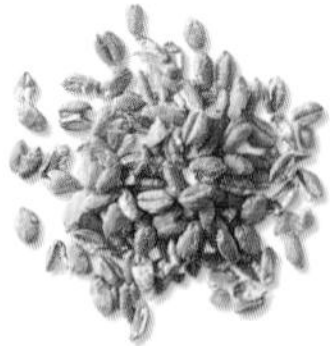

粗挽き麦
arabiki mugi
cracked wheat

セモリナ
semorina
semolina

麬
fusuma
bran

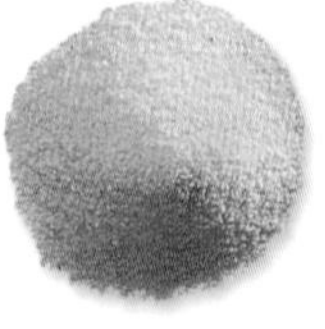

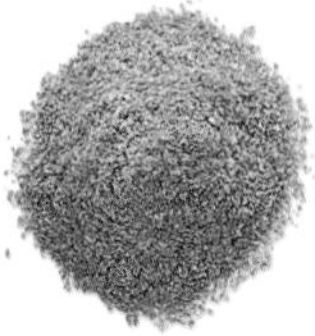

豆類 mamerui • beans and peas

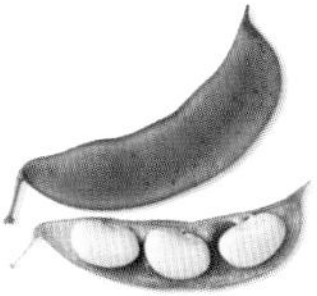

ライ豆
raimame
butter beans

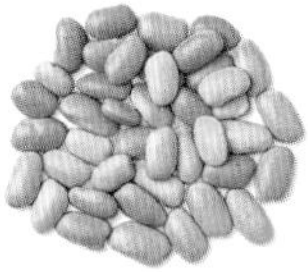

いんげん豆
ingenmame
haricot beans

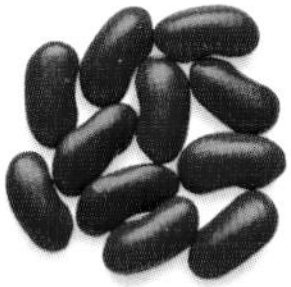

金時豆
kintoki mame
red kidney beans

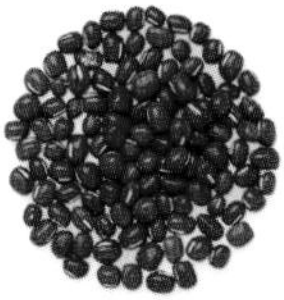

小豆
azuki
aduki beans

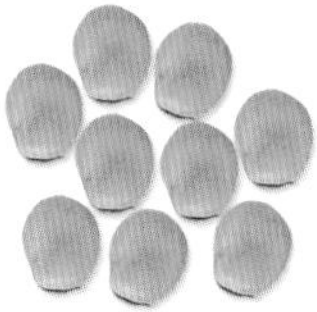

空豆
soramame
broad beans

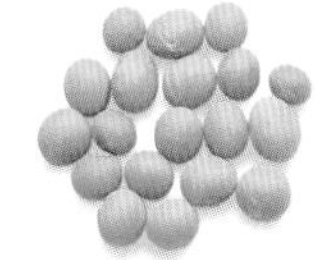

大豆
daizu
soya beans

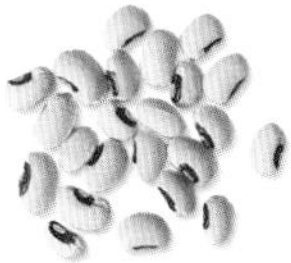

黒目豆
kurome mame
black-eyed beans

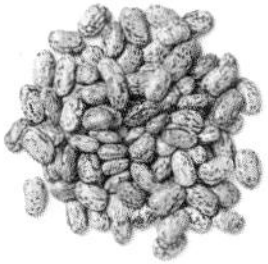

鶉豆
uzura mame
pinto beans

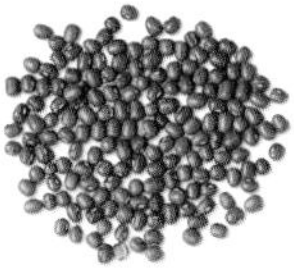

緑豆
ryokutō
mung beans

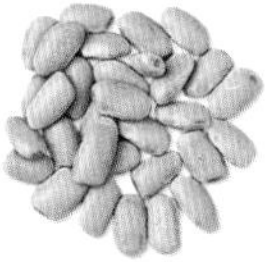

フラジョレ豆
furajore mame
flageolet beans

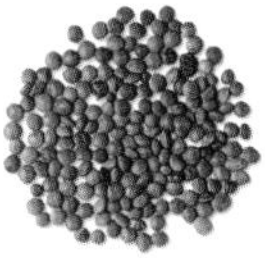

レンズ豆
renzumame
brown lentils

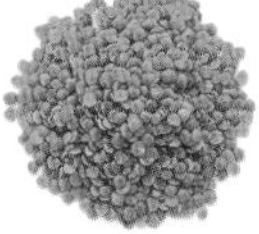

赤レンティル
aka rentiru
red lentils

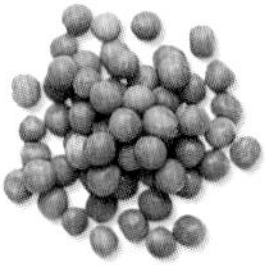

グリンピース
gurin pīsu
green peas

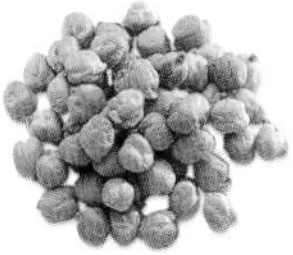

雛豆
hiyoko mame
chickpeas

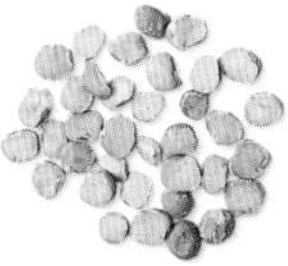

スプリットピー
supuritto pī
split peas

種 tane • seeds

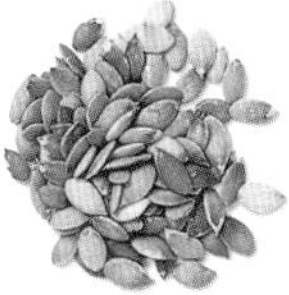

南瓜の種
kabocha no tane
pumpkin seed

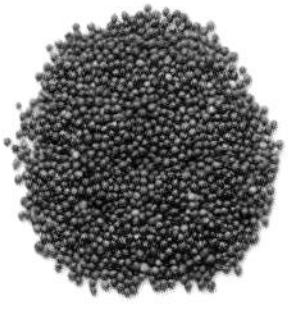

辛子の種
karashi no tane
mustard seed

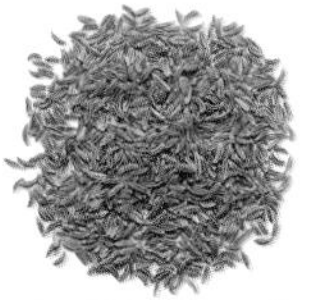

キャラウェイシード
kyarawei shīdo
caraway

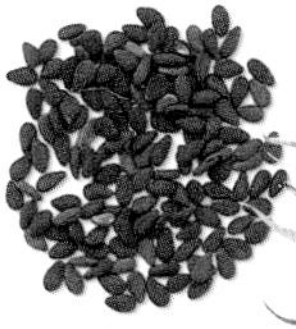

胡麻
goma
sesame seed

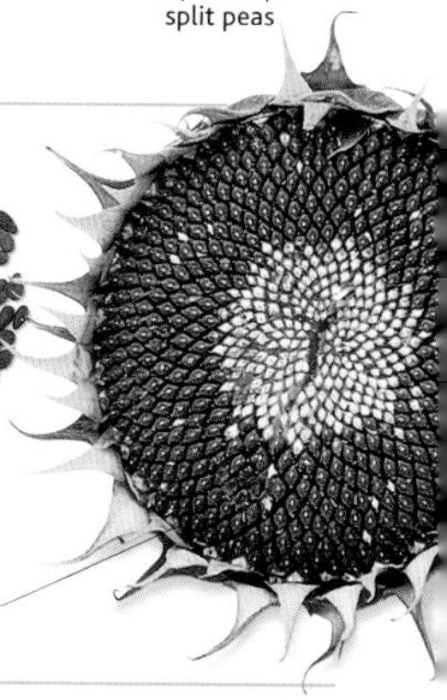

向日葵の種
himawari no tane
sunflower seed

ハーブと香辛料 hābu to kōshinryō • herbs and spices

香辛料 kōshinryō • spices

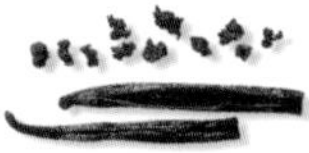

バニラ banira | vanilla

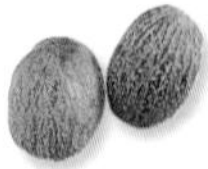

ナツメッグ
natsumeggu
nutmeg

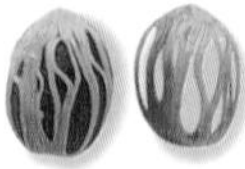

メース
mēsu
mace

ウコン
ukon
turmeric

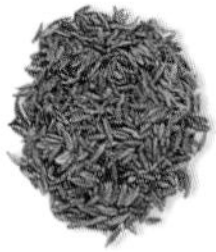

クミン
kumin
cumin

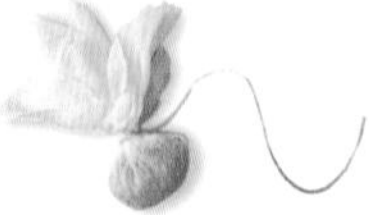

ブーケガルニ
būkegaruni
bouquet garni

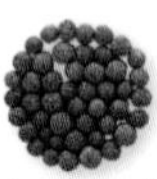

オールスパイス
ōrusupaisu
allspice

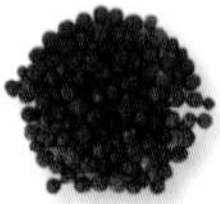

胡椒の実
koshō no mi
peppercorn

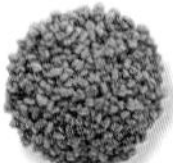

フェヌグリーク
fenugurīku
fenugreek

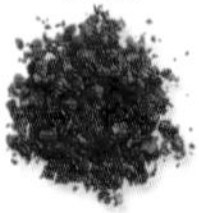

唐辛子
tōgarashi
chilli

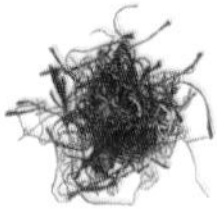

サフラン
safuran
saffron

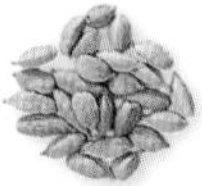

カルダモン
karudamon
cardamom

カレー粉
karēko
curry powder

丸ごと
marugoto
whole

つぶした
tsubushita
crushed

パウダー
paudā
ground

パプリカ
papurika
paprika

フレーク
furēku
flakes

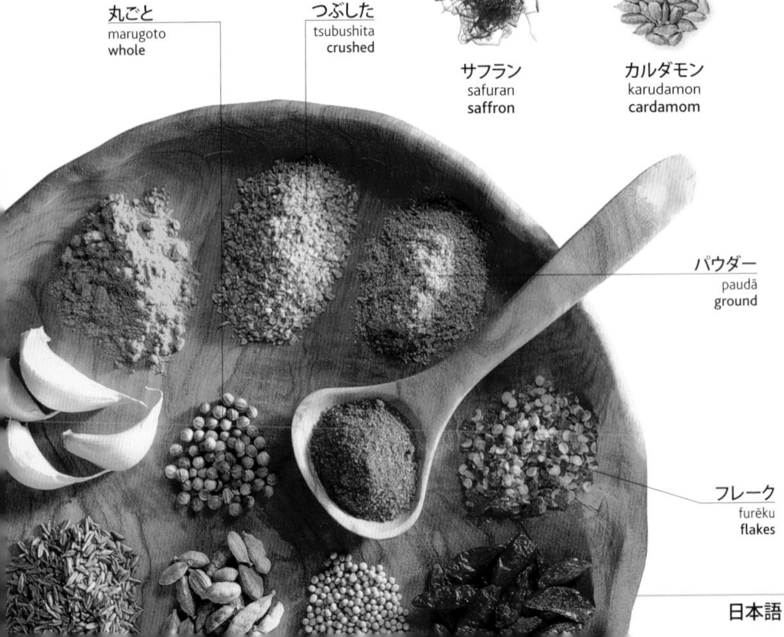

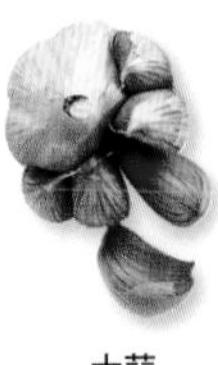

大蒜
ninniku
garlic

ハーブ hābu • herbs

スティック
sutikku
sticks

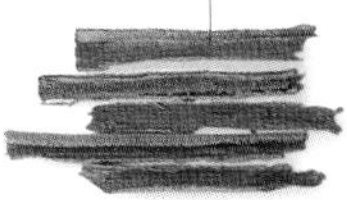

シナモン
shinamon
cinnamon

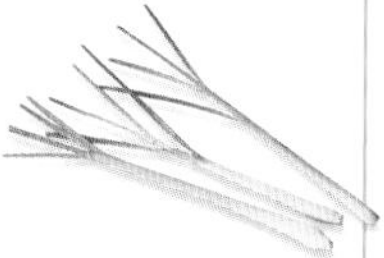

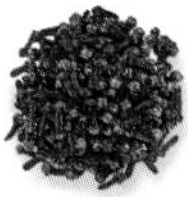

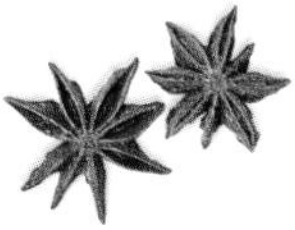

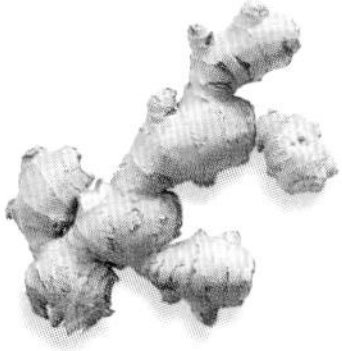

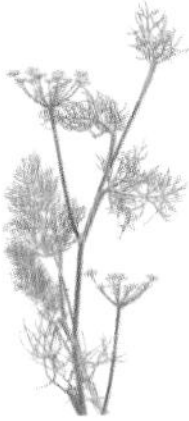

茴香
uikyō
fennel

茴香の種
uikyō no tane
fennel seeds

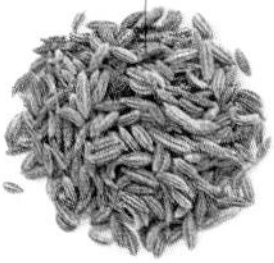

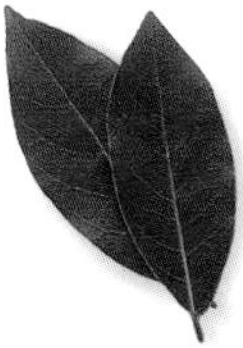

ローリエ
rōrie
bay leaf

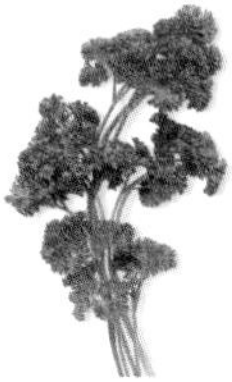

パセリ
paseri
parsley

レモングラス
remongurasu
lemon grass

クローブ
kurōbu
cloves

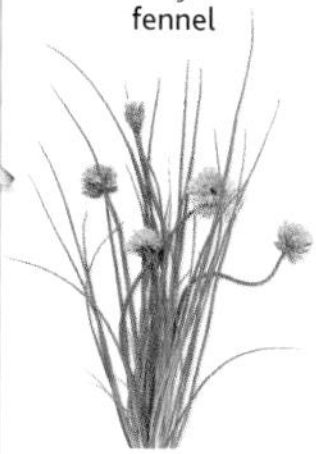

朝葱
asatsuki
chives

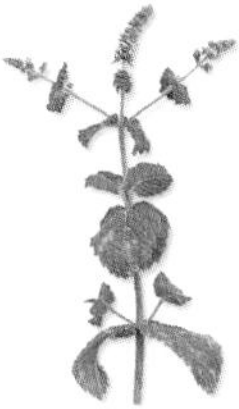

ハッカ
hakka
mint

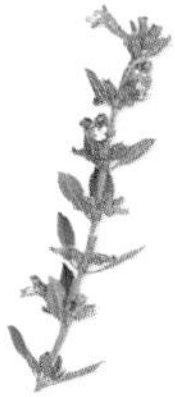

タイム
taimu
thyme

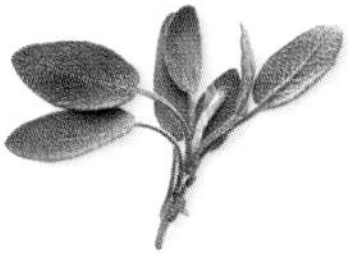

セージ
sēji
sage

大茴香
daiuikyō
star anise

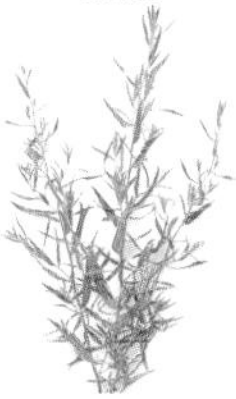

タラゴン
taragon
tarragon

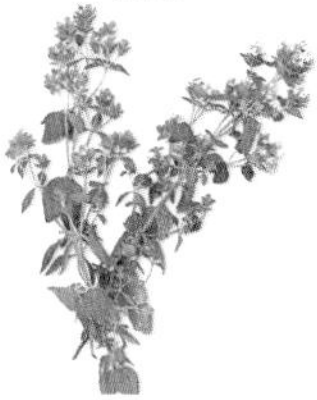

マジョラム
majoramu
marjoram

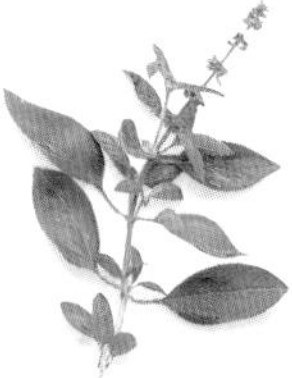

バジリコ
bajiriko
basil

生姜
shōga
ginger

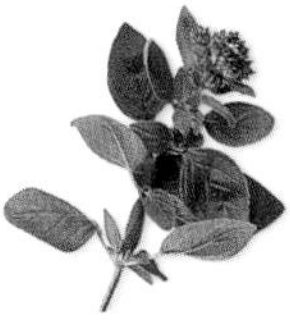

オレガノ
oregano
oregano

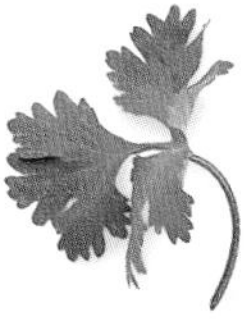

コリアンダー
koriandā
coriander

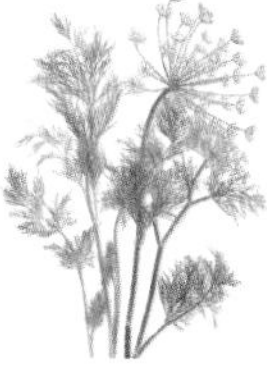

ディル
diru
dill

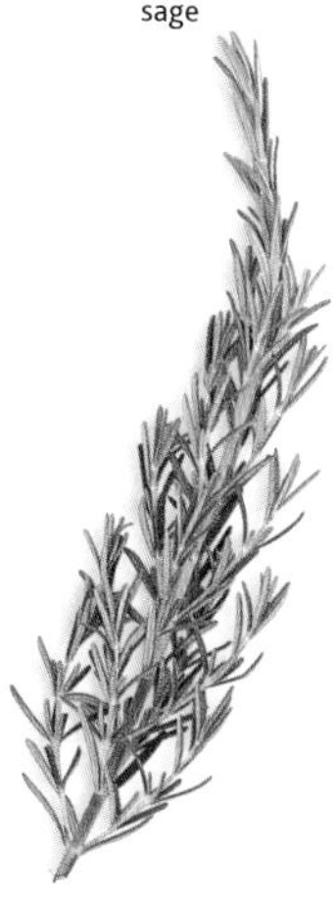

ローズマリー
rōzumarī
rosemary

瓶詰め食品 binzume shokuhin • bottled foods

コルク栓
koruku sen
cork

向日葵油
himawari abura
sunflower oil

胡桃油
kurumia bura
walnut oil

葡萄油
budō abura
grapeseed oil

アーモンドオイル
āmondo oiru
almond oil

胡麻油
goma'abura
sesame seed
oil

ヘーゼルナッツオイル
hēzerunattsu oiru
hazelnut oil

オリーブ油
orībuyu
olive oil

ハーブ
hābu
herbs

香味油
kōmi abura
flavoured oil

食用油
shokuyō abura
oils

甘味スプレッド kanmi supureddo • sweet spreads

瓶
bin
jar

ハニカム
hanikamu
honeycomb

クリーム蜂蜜
kurīmu hachimitsu
set honey

レモンカード
remon kādo
lemon curd

ラズベリージャム
razuberī jamu
raspberry jam

マーマレード
māmarēdo
marmalade

透明蜂蜜
tōmei hachimitsu
clear honey

メープルシロップ
mēpuru shiroppu
maple syrup

薬味とスプレッド yakumi to supureddo
• condiments and spreads

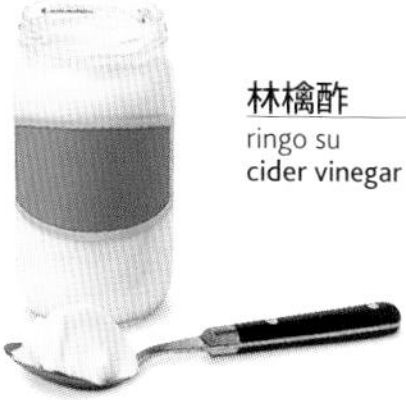

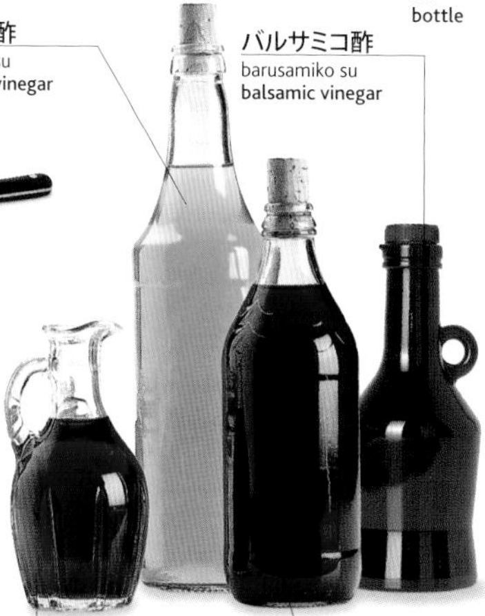

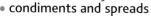

林檎酢
ringo su
cider vinegar

バルサミコ酢
barusamiko su
balsamic vinegar

瓶
bin
bottle

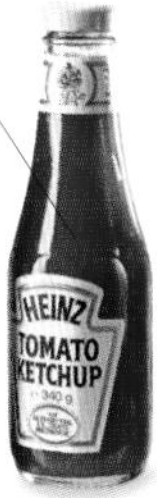

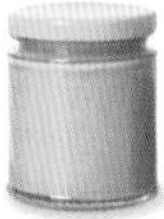

イングリッシュマスタード
ingurisshu masutādo
English mustard

マヨネーズ
mayonēzu
mayonnaise

ケチャップ
kechappu
ketchup

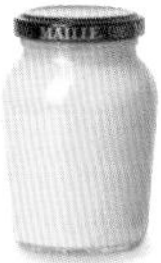

ディジョンマスタード
dijon masutādo
French mustard

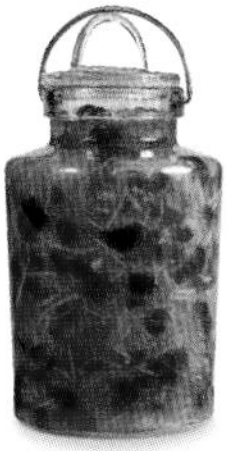

チャツネ
chatsune
chutney

モルト酢
moruto su
malt vinegar

ワイン酢
wain su
wine vinegar

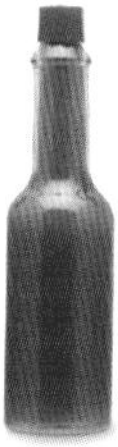

ソース
sōsu
sauce

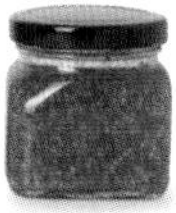

粒マスタード
tsubu masutādo
wholegrain mustard

酢
su
vinegar

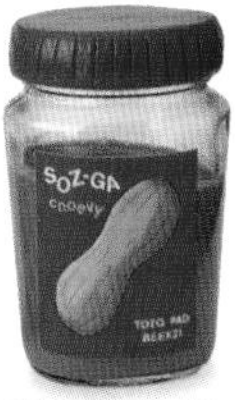

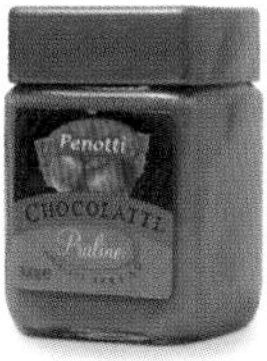

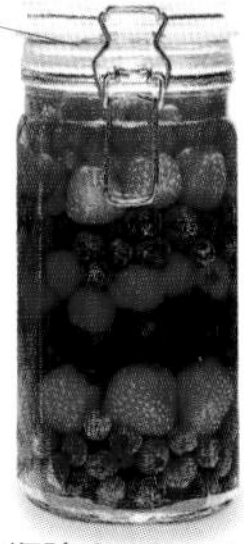

密封瓶
mippū bin
sealed jar

ピーナッツバター
pīnattsubatā
peanut butter

チョコレートスプレッド
chokorēto supureddo
chocolate spread

瓶詰めフルーツ
binzume furūtsu
preserved fruit

関連用語 kanrenyōgo
• vocabulary

コーン油
kōn yu
corn oil

落花生油
rakkasei yu
groundnut oil

サラダ油
sarada yu
vegetable oil

菜種油
natane abura
rapeseed oil

コールドプレス油
kōrudopuresu yu
cold-pressed oil

醤油
shōyu
soy sauce

米酢
komezu
rice vinegar

乳製品 nyūseihin • dairy produce

チーズ chīzu • cheese

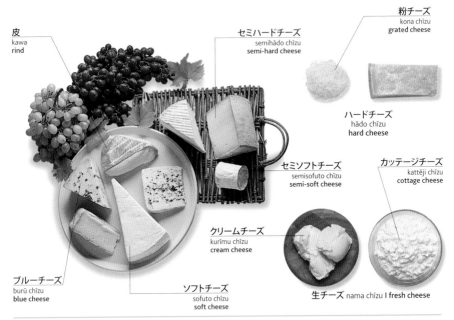

粉チーズ
kona chīzu
grated cheese

皮
kawa
rind

セミハードチーズ
semihādo chīzu
semi-hard cheese

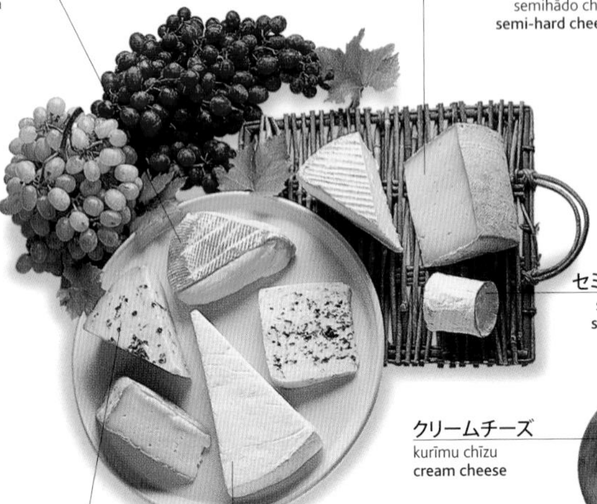

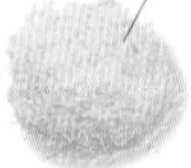

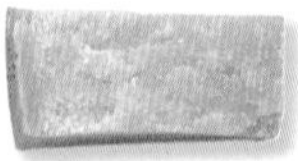

ハードチーズ
hādo chīzu
hard cheese

セミソフトチーズ
semisofuto chīzu
semi-soft cheese

カッテージチーズ
kattēji chīzu
cottage cheese

クリームチーズ
kurīmu chīzu
cream cheese

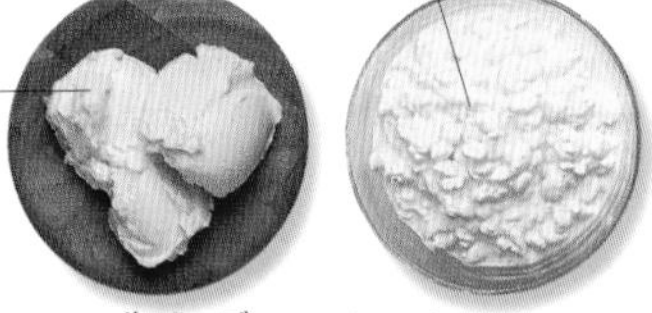

ブルーチーズ
burū chīzu
blue cheese

ソフトチーズ
sofuto chīzu
soft cheese

生チーズ nama chīzu I fresh cheese

ミルク miruku • milk

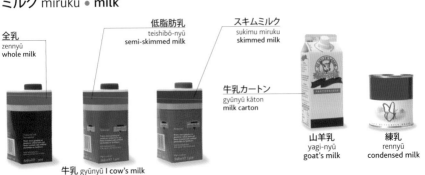

全乳
zennyū
whole milk

低脂肪乳
teishibō-nyū
semi-skimmed milk

スキムミルク
sukimu miruku
skimmed milk

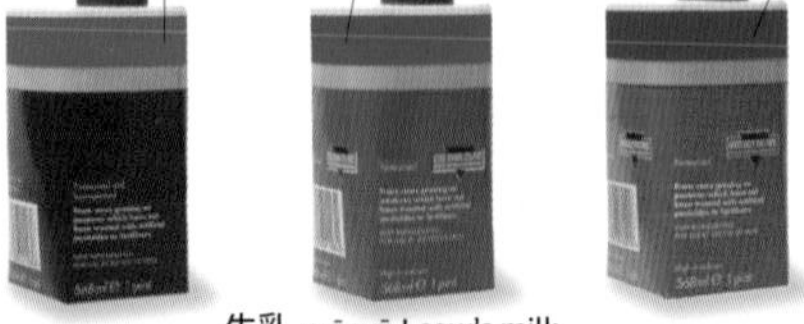

牛乳カートン
gyūnyū kāton
milk carton

牛乳 gyūnyū I cow's milk

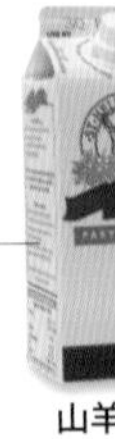

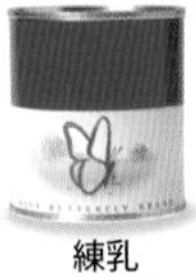

山羊乳
yagi-nyū
goat's milk

練乳
rennyū
condensed milk

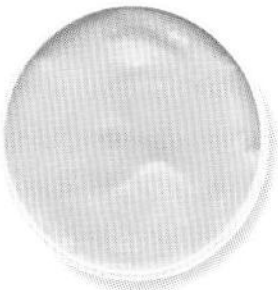

バター
batā
butter

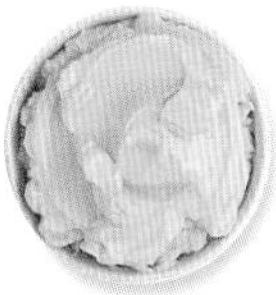

マーガリン
māgarin
margarine

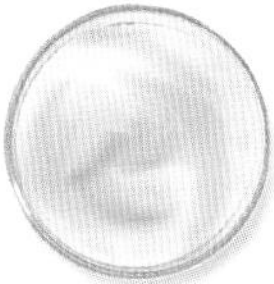

生クリーム
nama kuriīmu
cream

シングルクリーム
shinguru kurīmu
single cream

ダブルクリーム
daburu kurīmu
double cream

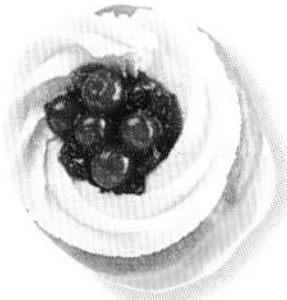

ホイップクリーム
hoippu kurīmu
whipped cream

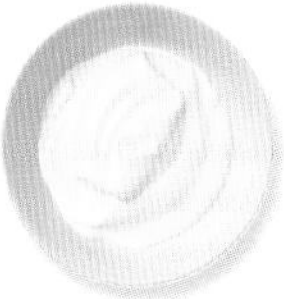

サワークリーム
sawā kurīmu
sour cream

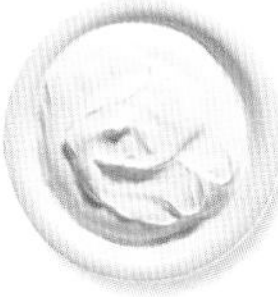

ヨーグルト
yōguruto
yoghurt

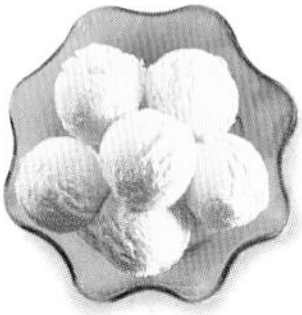

アイスクリーム
aisukurīmu
ice-cream

卵 tamago・eggs

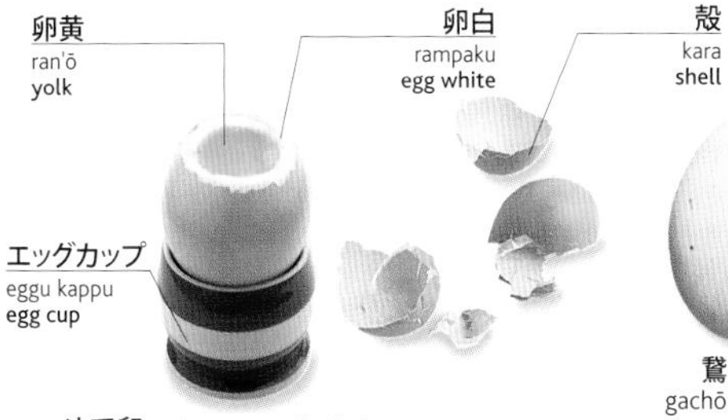

卵黄
ran'ō
yolk

卵白
rampaku
egg white

殻
kara
shell

エッグカップ
eggu kappu
egg cup

ゆで卵 yudetamago I boiled egg

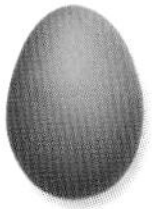

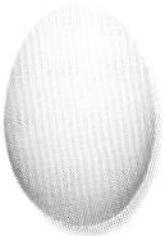

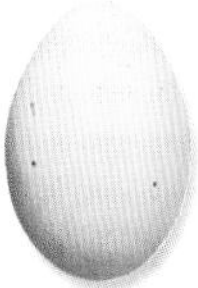

鵞鳥の卵
gachō no tamago
goose egg

鶏卵
keiran
hen's egg

家鴨の卵
ahiru no tamago
duck egg

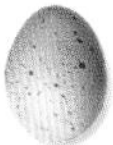

鶉卵
uzura tamago
quail egg

関連用語 kanrenyōgo・vocabulary

低温殺菌 teionsakkin **pasteurized**	ミルクセーキ mirukusēki **milkshake**	塩入り shio-iri **salted**	羊乳 yōnyū **sheep's milk**	乳糖 nyūtō **lactose**	ホモジナイズ homojinaizu **homogenised**
低温殺菌していない teionsakkin shiteinai **unpasteurized**	フローズンヨーグルト furōzun yōguruto **frozen yoghurt**	無塩 muen **unsalted**	バターミルク batāmiruku **buttermilk**	無脂肪 mu-shibō **fat free**	粉乳 funnyū **powdered milk**

パンと小麦粉 pan to komugiko • **breads and flours**

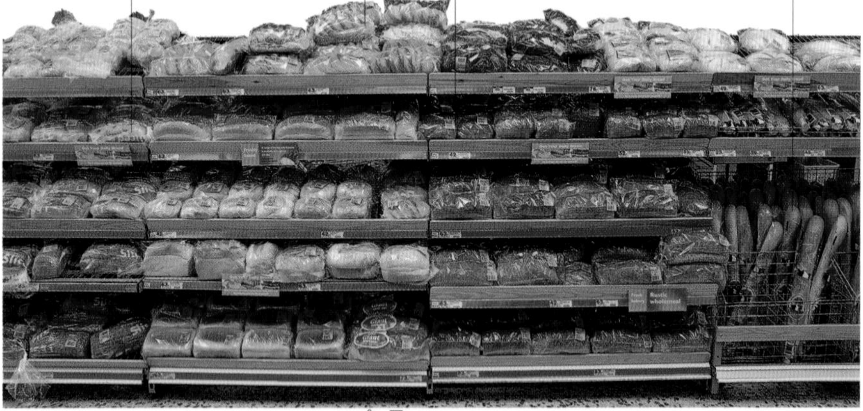

スライス食パン
suraisu shokupan
sliced bread

ケシの実
keshi no mi
poppy seeds

ライ麦パン
raimugi pan
rye bread

バゲット
bagetto
baguette

パン屋 pan'ya I bakery

パン作り pan-zukuri • **making bread**

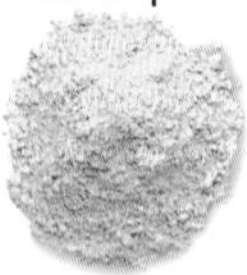

白小麦粉
shiro komugiko
white flour

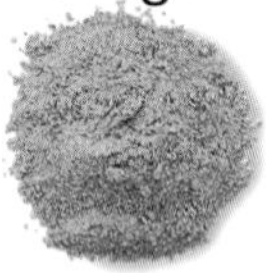

黒小麦粉
kuro komugiko
brown flour

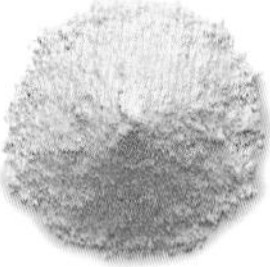

全粒粉
zenryū-fun
wholemeal flour

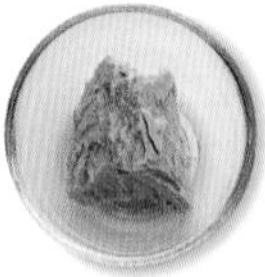

酵母
kōbo
yeast

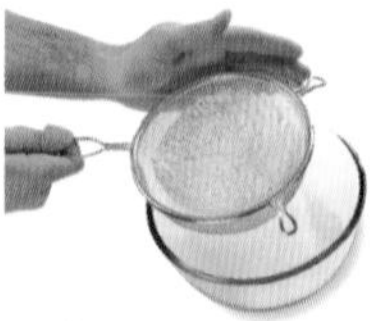

篩にかける furui ni kakeru
sift (v)

混ぜる mazeru I mix (v)

パン生地
pan kiji
dough

こねる koneru I knead (v)

焼く yaku I bake (v)

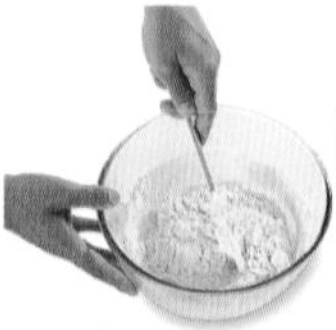

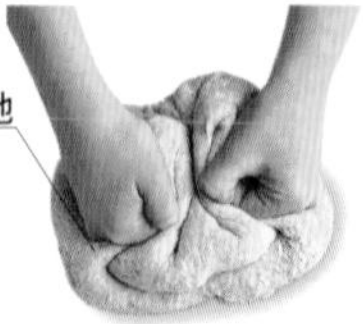

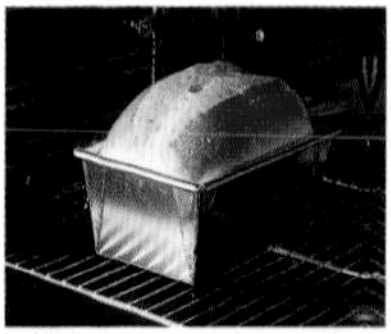

耳
mimi
crust

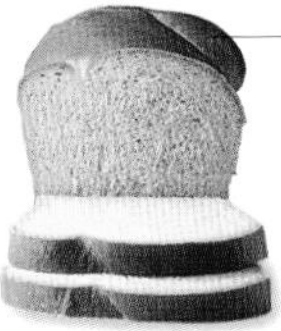

白パン
shiro pan
white bread

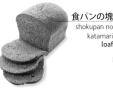

食パンの塊
shokupan no
katamari
loaf

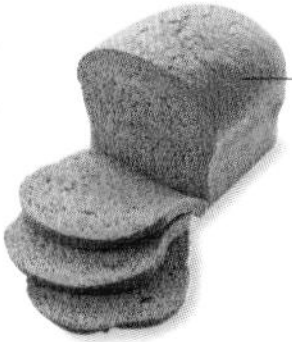

黒パン
kuro pan
brown bread

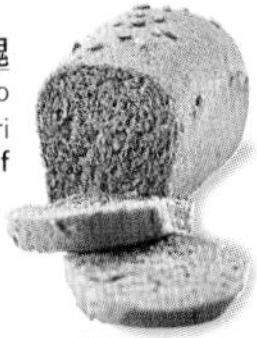

全粒パン
zenryū pan
wholemeal bread

スライス
suraisu
slice

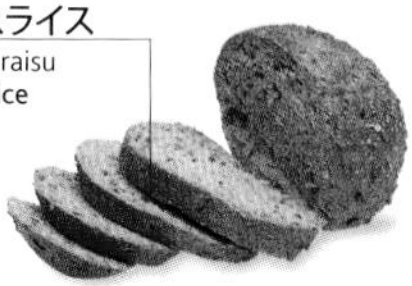

グラナリブレッド
guranari bureddo
granary bread

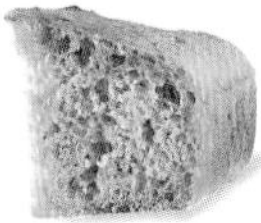

とうもろこしパン
tōmorokoshi pan
corn bread

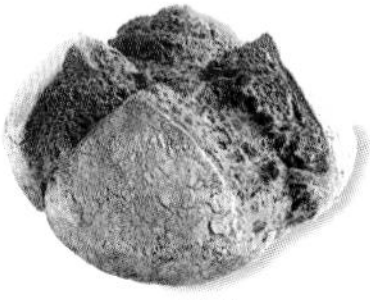

ソーダパン
sōda pan
soda bread

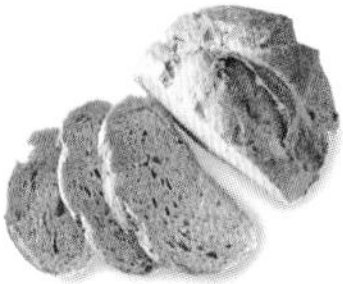

サワードウブレッド
sawādo-u bureddo
sourdough bread

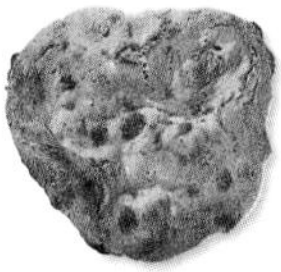

フラットブレッド
furattobureddo
flatbread

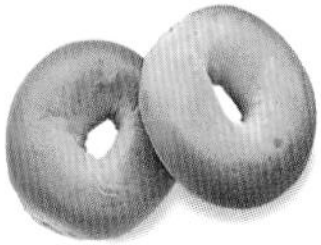

ベーグル
bēguru
bagel

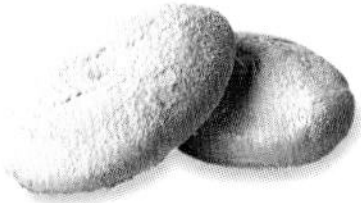

バップ
bappu **| bap**

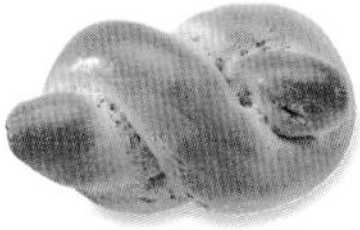

ロールパン
rōrupan **| roll**

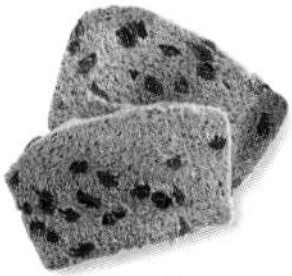

フルーツパン
furūtsu pan
fruit bread

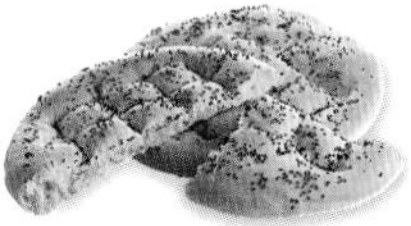

種入りパン
tane-iri pan
seeded bread

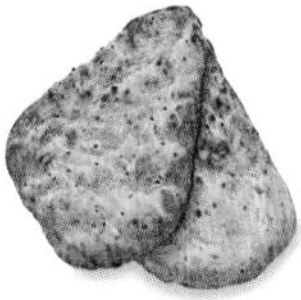

ナン
nan
naan bread

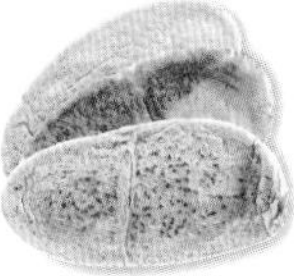

ピタパン
pita pan
pitta bread

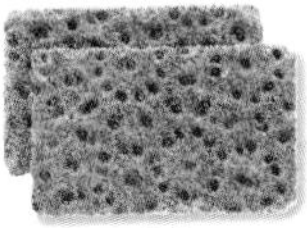

クリスプブレッド
kurisupu bureddo
crispbread

関連用語 kanrenyōgo • vocabulary

強力粉 kyōrikiko **strong flour**	膨れる fukureru **rise (v)**	発酵させる hakkō saseru **prove (v)**	パン粉 panko **breadcrumbs**	スライサー suraisā **slicer**
膨らし粉入り小麦粉 fukurashiko-iri komugiko **self-raising flour**	薄力粉 hakurikiko **plain flour**	グレーズを塗る gurēzu o nuru **glaze (v)**	波形 namigata **flute**	パン職人 pan shokunin **baker**

ケーキとデザート kēki to dezāto ● cakes and desserts

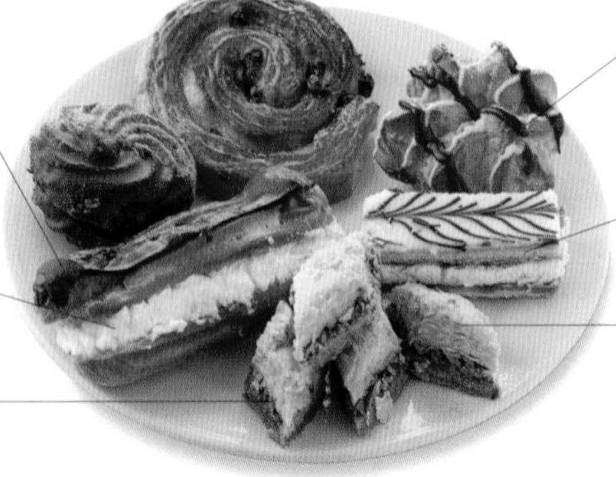

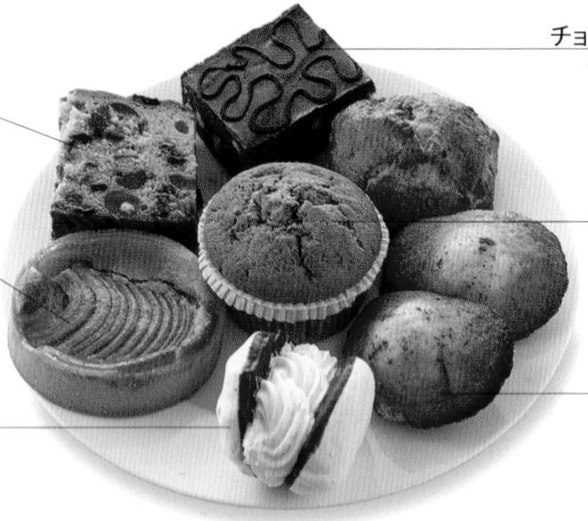

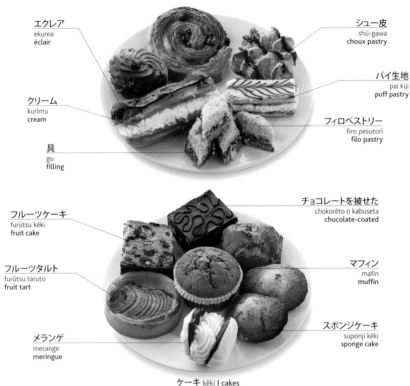

エクレア
ekurea
éclair

シュー皮
shū-gawa
choux pastry

パイ生地
pai kiji
puff pastry

クリーム
kurīmu
cream

フィロペストリー
firo pesutorī
filo pastry

具
gu
filling

フルーツケーキ
furūtsu kēki
fruit cake

チョコレートを被せた
chokorēto o kabuseta
chocolate-coated

フルーツタルト
furūtsu taruto
fruit tart

マフィン
mafin
muffin

スポンジケーキ
suponji kēki
sponge cake

メランゲ
merange
meringue

ケーキ kēki I cakes

関連用語 kanrenyōgo ● vocabulary

カスタードクリーム kasutādo kurīmu crème pâtissière	丸い小型パン marui kogata pan bun	ペストリー pesutorī pastry	ライスプディング raisu pudingu rice pudding	一切れください。 hitokire kudasai? May I have a slice please?
チョコレートケーキ chokorēto kēki chocolate cake	カスタード kasutādo custard	一切れ hitokire one slice	お祝い oiwai celebration	

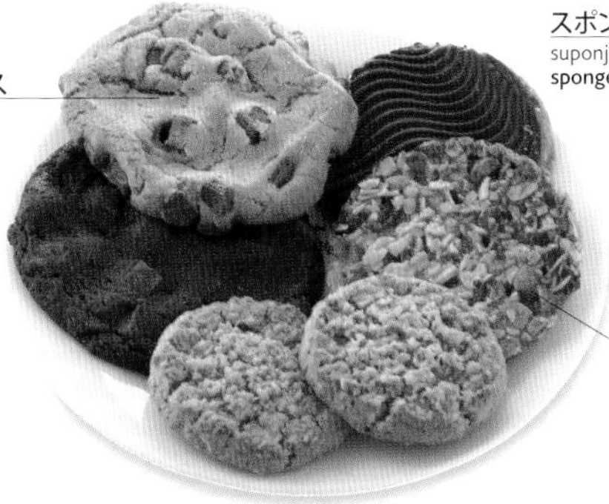

チョコレートチップス
chokorēto chippusu
chocolate chip

スポンジフィンガー
suponji fingā
sponge fingers

フロレンティン
furorentin
florentine

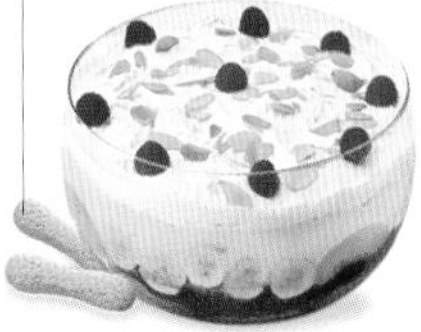

トライフル
toraifuru
trifle

ビスケット bisuketto I biscuits

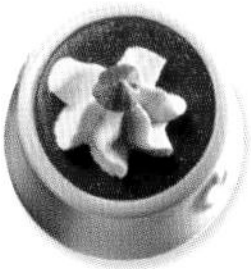

ムース
mūsu
mousse

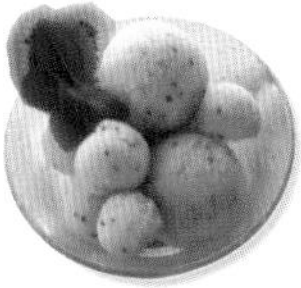

シャーベット
shābetto
sorbet

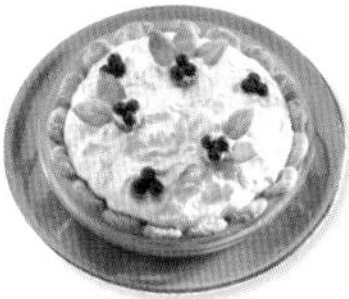

クリームパイ
kurīmu pai
cream pie

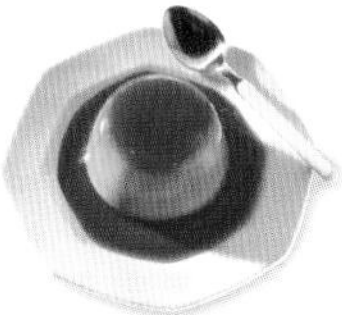

プリン
purin
crème caramel

お祝い用ケーキ oiwai-yō kēki • celebration cakes

最上段
saijōdan
top tier

リボン
ribon
ribbon

下段
gedan
bottom tier

アイシング
aishingu
icing

マジパン
majipan
marzipan

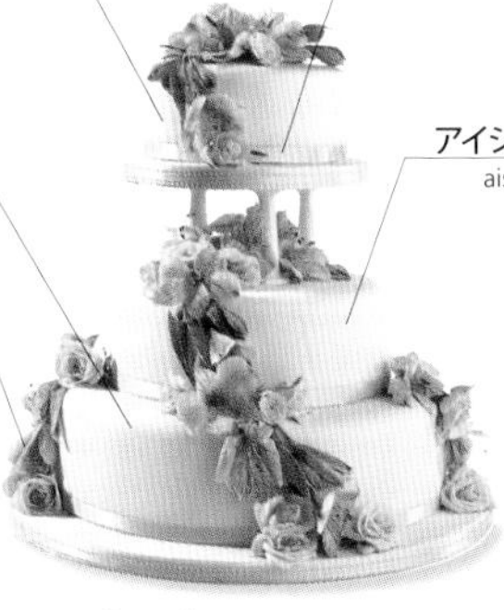

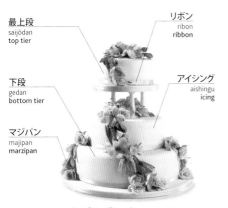

ウェディングケーキ wedingu kēki
wedding cake

飾り
kazari
decoration

誕生日ケーキの蝋燭
tanjōbi kēki no rōsoku
birthday candles

吹き消す
fukikesu
blow out (v)

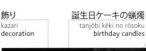

誕生日ケーキ tanjōbi kēki I birthday cake

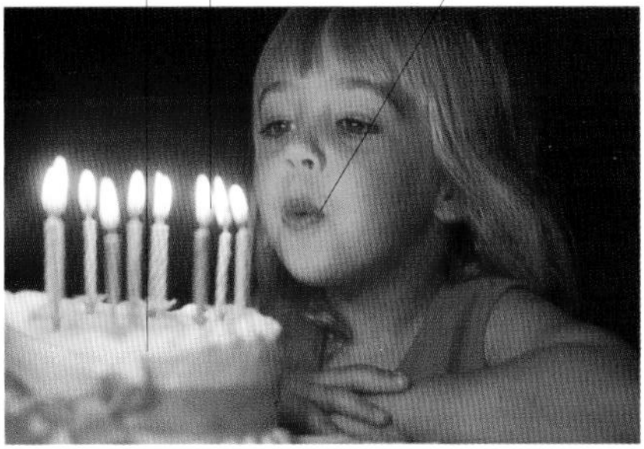

デリカテッセン derikatessen • **delicatessen**

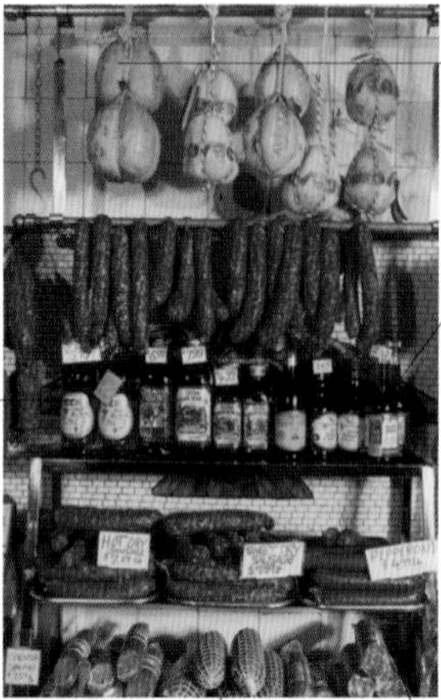

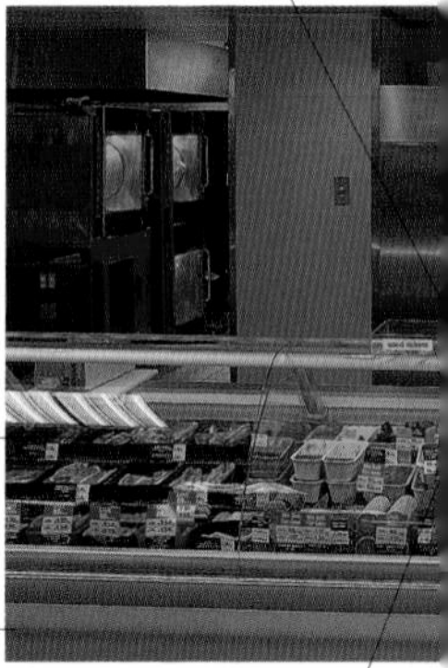

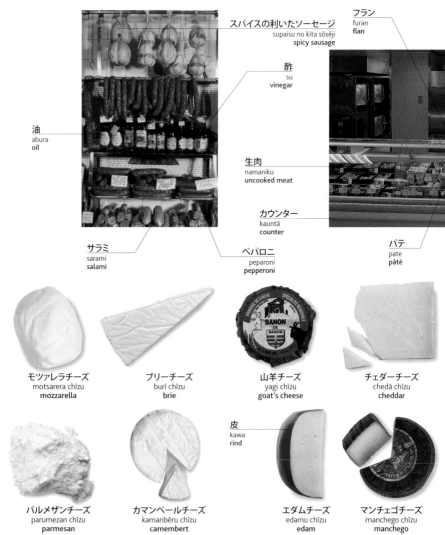

スパイスの利いたソーセージ
supaisu no kīta sōsēji
spicy sausage

フラン
furan
flan

酢
su
vinegar

油
abura
oil

生肉
namaniku
uncooked meat

カウンター
kauntā
counter

パテ
pate
pâté

サラミ
sarami
salami

ペパロニ
peparoni
pepperoni

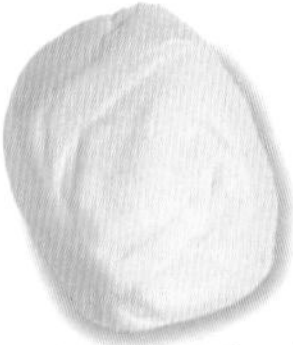

モツァレラチーズ
motsarera chīzu
mozzarella

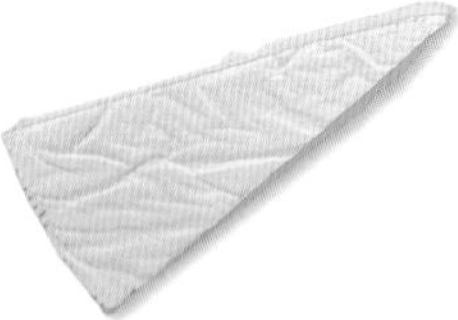

ブリーチーズ
burī chīzu
brie

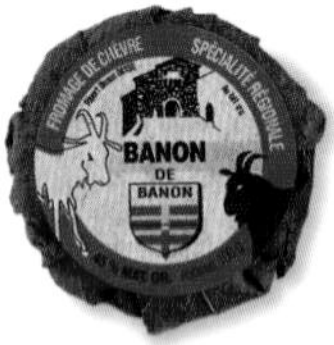

山羊チーズ
yagi chīzu
goat's cheese

チェダーチーズ
chedā chīzu
cheddar

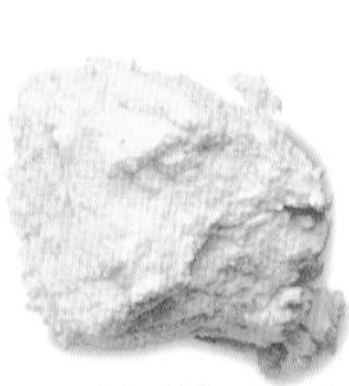

パルメザンチーズ
parumezan chīzu
parmesan

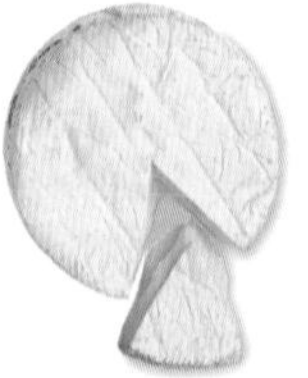

カマンベールチーズ
kamanbēru chīzu
camembert

皮
kawa
rind

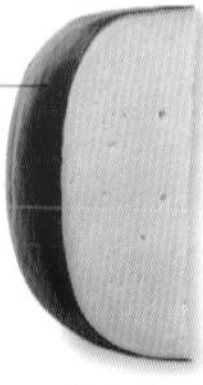

エダムチーズ
edamu chīzu
edam

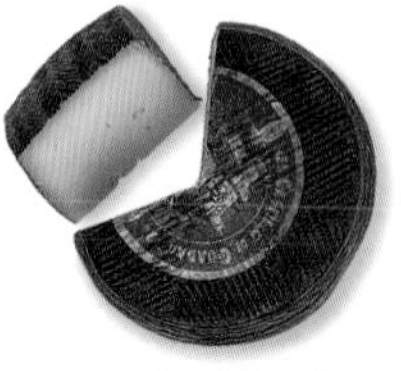

マンチェゴチーズ
manchego chīzu
manchego

パイ
pai
pies

黒オリーブ
kuro orību
black olive

唐辛子
tōgarashi
chilli pepper

ソース
sōsu
sauce

ロールパン
rōrupan
bread roll

調理肉
chōri niku
cooked meat

緑オリーブ
midori orību
green olive

サンドイッチ売場 sandoitchi uriba | sandwich counter

ハム
hamu
ham

魚の薫製
sakana no kunsei
smoked fish

ケーパー
kēpā
capers

チョリソ
choriso
chorizo

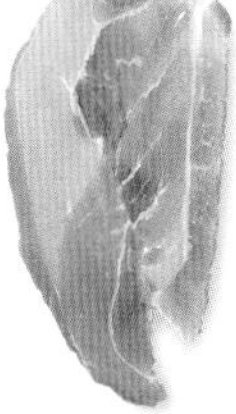

プロシュット
puroshutto
prosciutto

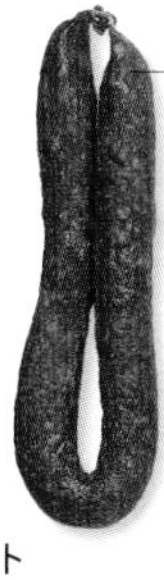

スタッフドオリーブ
sutaffudo orību
stuffed olive

関連用語 kanrenyōgo • vocabulary

油漬け abura-zuke in oil	マリネ marine marinated	薫製 kunsei smoked
塩水漬け shiomizu-zuke in brine	塩漬け shiozuke salted	保存処理 hozon shori cured

番号札を取ってください。
bangō fuda o totte kudasai.
Take a number please.

それを試食できますか。
sore o shishoku dekimasuka?
Can I try some of that please?

それを6切れください。
sore o rokkire kudasai.
Six slices of that, please.

飲物 nomimono • drinks

水 mizu • water

容器入り飲料水
yōki-iri inryōsui
bottled water

発泡
happō
sparkling

水道水
suidōsui
tap water

スティル
sutiru
still

トニックウォーター
tonikku wōtā
tonic water

ミネラルウォーター mineraru wōtā
mineral water

ソーダ水
sōdasui
soda water

暖かい飲物 atatakai nomimono • hot drinks

ティーバッグ
tī baggu
teabag

リーフティー
rīfu tī
loose leaf tea

紅茶
kōcha
tea

コーヒー豆
kōhī-mame
beans

コーヒー粉
kōhī-fun
ground coffee

コーヒー
kōhī
coffee

ホットココア
hotto kokoa
hot chocolate

麦芽飲料
bakuga inryō
malted drink

ソフトドリンク sofuto dorinku • soft drinks

ストロー
sutorō
straw

トマトジュース
tomato jūsu
tomato juice

グレープジュース
gurēpu jūsu
grape juice

レモネード
remonēdo
lemonade

オレンジエード
orenjiēdo
orangeade

コーラ
kōra
cola

アルコール飲料 arukōru inryō • alcoholic drinks

ジン
jin | gin

ビール
bīru
beer

缶
kan
can

林檎酒
ringoshu
cider

ビター
bitā
bitter

黒ビール
kurobīru
stout

ウォッカ
wokka | vodka

ウイスキー uisukī | whisky

ラム酒
ramushu
rum

ブランデー
burandē
brandy

ポートワイン
pōtowain
port

シェリー
sherī
sherry

辛口
karakuchi
dry

カンパリ
kampari
campari

ロゼ（ワイン）
roze (wain)
rosé (wine)

白（ワイン）
shiro (wain)
white (wine)

赤（ワイン）
aka (wain)
red (wine)

リキュール
rikyūru
liqueur

テキーラ
tekīra
tequila

シャンパン
shampan
champagne

ワイン wain | wine

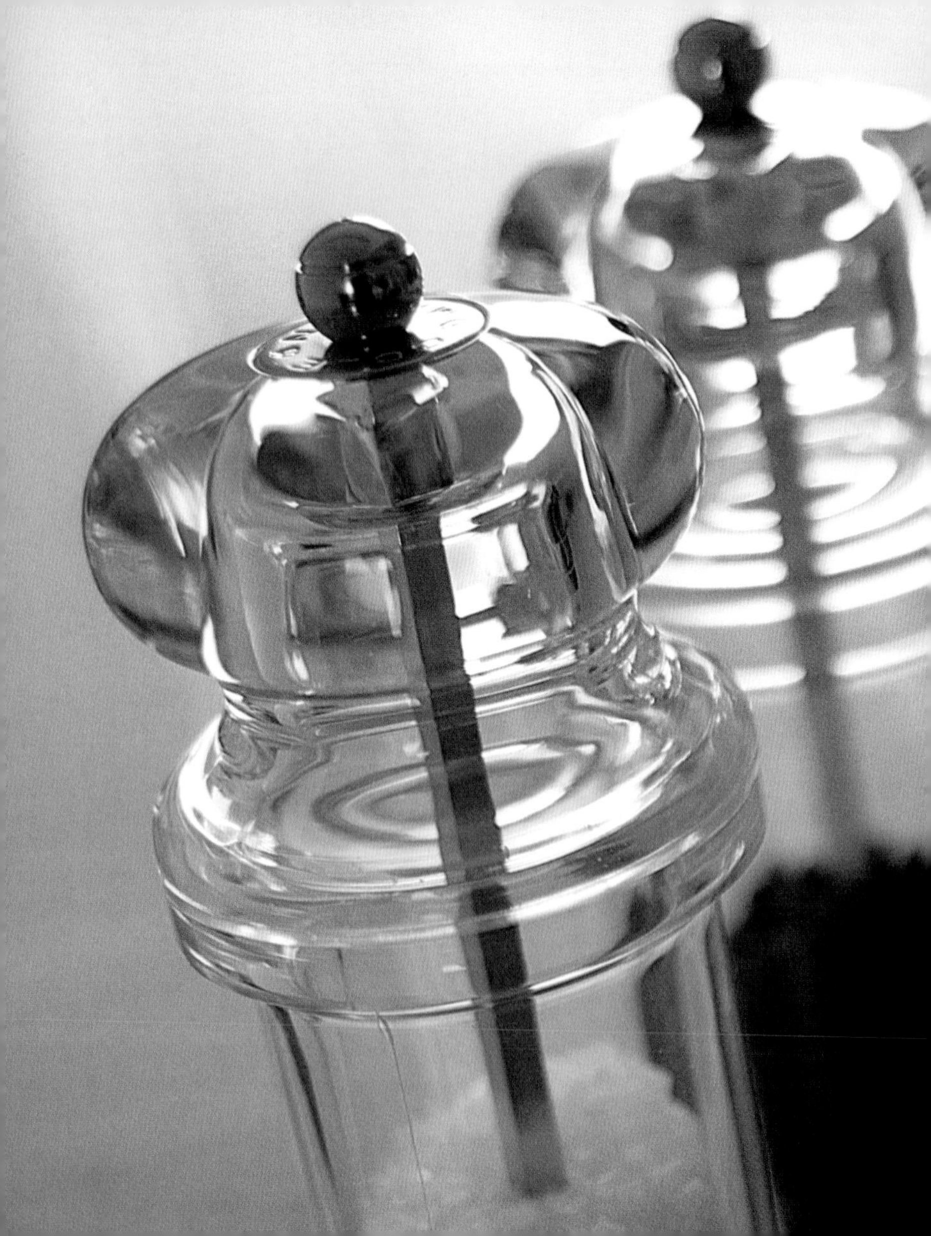

外食 gaishoku
eating out

カフェ kafe • café

パラソル
parasoru
umbrella

オーニング
ōningu
awning

メニュー
menyū
menu

テラスカフェ
terasu kafe
terrace café

ウェイター
weitā
waiter

コーヒーメーカー
kōhī mēkā
coffee machine

テーブル
tēburu
table

路上カフェ rojō kafe | **pavement café**

スナックバー sunakku bā | **snack bar**

コーヒー kōhī • coffee

ミルクコーヒー
miruku kōhī
white coffee

ブラックコーヒー
burak kukōhī
black coffee

ココアパウダー
kokoa paudā
cocoa powder

泡
awa
froth

フィルターコーヒー
firutā kōhī
filter coffee

エスプレッソ
esupuresso
espresso

カプチーノ
kapuchīno
cappuccino

アイスコーヒー
aisu kōhī
iced coffee

紅茶 kōcha • tea

ハーブ茶
hābu cha
herbal tea

カモミール茶
kamomīru cha
camomile tea

緑茶
ryokucha
green tea

ミルクティー
miruku tī
tea with milk

紅茶
kōcha
black tea

レモンティー
remon tī
tea with lemon

ミントティー
minto tī
mint tea

アイスティー
aisu tī
iced tea

ジュースとミルクセーキ jūsu to mirukusēki • juices and milkshakes

チョコレートミルクセーキ
chokorēto mirukusēki
chocolate milkshake

苺のミルクセーキ
ichigo no mirukusēki
strawberry milkshake

オレンジジュース
orenji jūsu
orange juice

林檎ジュース
ringo jūsu
apple juice

パイナップルジュース
painappuru jūsu
pineapple juice

トマトジュース
tomato jūsu
tomato juice

コーヒーミルクセーキ
kōhī mirukusēki
coffee milkshake

食べ物 tabemono • food

スクープ
sukūpu
scoop

黒パン
kuro pan
brown bread

トーストサンド
tōsuto-sando
toasted sandwich

サラダ
sarada
salad

アイスクリーム
aisukurīmu
ice cream

ペストリー
pesutorī
pastry

バー bā • bar

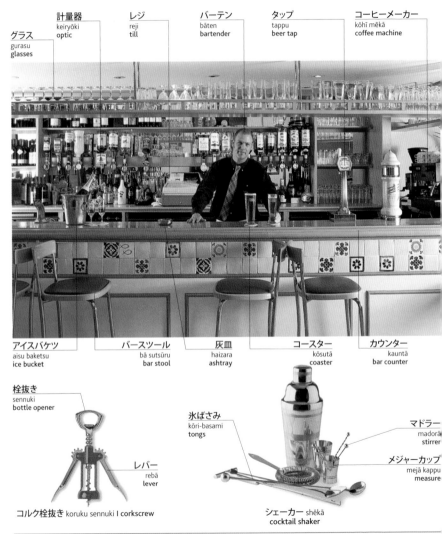

グラス
gurasu
glasses

計量器
keiryōki
optic

レジ
reji
till

バーテン
bāten
bartender

タップ
tappu
beer tap

コーヒーメーカー
kōhī mēkā
coffee machine

アイスバケツ
aisu baketsu
ice bucket

バースツール
bā sutsūru
bar stool

灰皿
haizara
ashtray

コースター
kōsutā
coaster

カウンター
kauntā
bar counter

栓抜き
sennuki
bottle opener

レバー
rebā
lever

コルク栓抜き koruku sennuki I corkscrew

氷ばさみ
kōri-basami
tongs

マドラー
madorā
stirrer

メジャーカップ
mejā kappu
measure

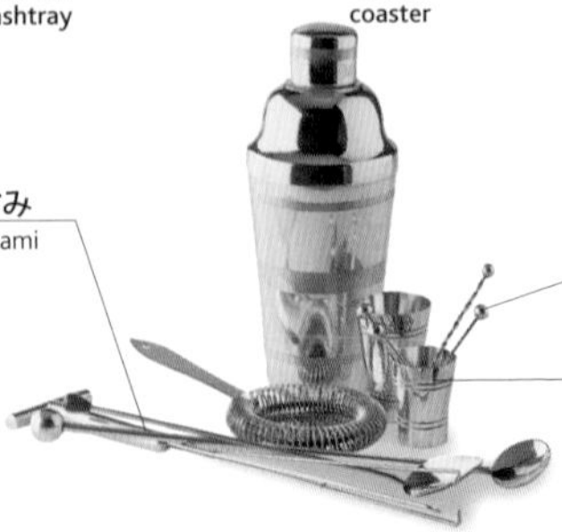

シェーカー shēkā
cocktail shaker

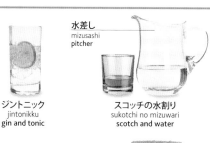

水差し
mizusashi
pitcher

角氷
kaku-gōri
ice cube

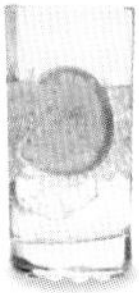

ジントニック
jintonikku
gin and tonic

スコッチの水割り
sukotchi no mizuwari
scotch and water

キューバリブレ
kyūba ribure
rum and coke

スクリュードライバー
sukuryū doraibā
vodka and orange

マティーニ
matīni
martini

カクテル
kakuteru
cocktail

ワイン
wain
wine

ビール bīru I beer

シングル
shinguru
single

ダブル
daburu
double

氷とレモン
kōri to remon
ice and lemon

ワンショット
wanshotto
a shot

分量
bunryō
measure

氷無し
kōri nashi
without ice

氷入り
kōri-iri
with ice

お摘み o-tsumami • bar snacks

カシューナッツ
kashūnattsu
cashew nuts

ピーナッツ
pīnattsu
peanuts

アーモンド
āmondo
almonds

ポテトチップス poteto chippusu
crisps

ナッツ nattsu I nuts

オリーブ orību I olives

レストラン resutoran • restaurant

禁煙席
kin'en seki
non-smoking
section

ナプキン
napukin
napkin

コミシェフ
komi shefu
commis chef

テーブルセッティング
tēburu settingu
table setting

シェフ
shefu
chef

グラス
gurasu
glass

トレイ
torei
tray

キッチン kitchin | kitchen

ウェイター weitā | waiter

関連用語 kanrenyōgo • vocabulary

ワインリスト wain risuto wine list	デザートワゴン dezāto wagon sweet trolley	領収書 ryōshūsho receipt	サービス料抜き sābisu-ryō nuki service not included	喫煙席 kitsuen seki smoking section	胡椒 koshō pepper
酒 sake rice wine	値段 nedan price	チップ chippu tip	ビュッフェ byuffe buffet	客 kyaku customer	座卓 zataku (low Japanese) table
アラカルト arakaruto à la carte	会計 kaikei bill	サービス料込み sābisu-ryō komi service included	お薦め料理 o-susume ryōri specials	塩 shio salt	座布団 zabuton (Japanese) cushion

メニュー
menyū
menu

お子様メニュー
okosama menyū
child's meal

注文する chūmon suru | order (v)

支払う shiharau | pay (v)

コース料理 kōsu ryōri • courses

食前酒
shokuzenshu
aperitif

前菜
zensai
starter

スープ
sūpu
soup

主菜
shusai
main course

サイドオーダー
saido ōdā
side order

フォーク
fōku
fork

コーヒースプーン
kōhī supūn
coffee spoon

デザート dezāto
dessert

コーヒー kōhī | coffee

2人分の席をお願いします。
futari-bun no seki o onegaishimasu.
A table for two please.

メニュー/ワインリストを見せてください。
menyū/wainrisuto o misete kudasai?
Can I see the menu/winelist please?

セットメニューはありますか。
setto menyū wa arimasuka?
Is there a fixed price menu?

ベジタリアン料理はありますか。
bejitarian ryōri wa arimasuka?
Do you have any vegetarian dishes?

会計/領収書をお願いします。
o-kaikei/ryōshūsho o onegaishimasu?
Could I have the bill/a receipt please?

会計は別々にお願いします。
kaikei wa betsubetsu ni onegaishimasu?
Can we pay separately?

お手洗いはどこですか。
o-tearai wa doko desuka?
Where are the toilets, please?

ファーストフード fāsuto fūdo ● fast food

ストロー
sutorō
straw

ハンバーガー
hambāgā
burger

ソフトドリンク
sofuto dorinku
soft drink

フライドポテト
furaido poteto
french fries

ペーパーナプキン
pēpā napukin
paper napkin

トレイ
torei
tray

バーガーミール bāgā mīru | burger meal

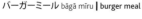

ピザ
piza
pizza

価格表
kakaku hyō
price list

缶飲料
kan inryō
canned drink

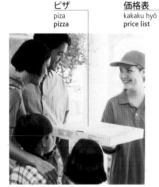

宅配 takuhai | home delivery

露店 roten | street stall

関連用語 kanrenyōgo ● vocabulary

ピザ屋
piza-ya
pizza parlour

ハンバーガー屋
hambāgā-ya
burger bar

メニュー
menyū
menu

店内飲食
tennai inshoku
eat-in

持ち帰り
mochikaeri
take-away

温め直す
atatamenaosu
reheat (v)

ケチャップ
ketchappu
tomato sauce

おにぎり
onigiri
rice ball

弁当
bentō
lunch box

それを持ち帰りにしてください。
sore o mochikaeri ni shite kudasai?
Can I have that to go please?

出前はできますか。
demae wa dekimasuka?
Do you deliver?

バンズ
banzu
bun

マスタード
masutādo
mustard

ソーセージ
sōsēji
sausage

ハンバーガー
hambāgā
hamburger

チキンバーガー
chikin bāgā
chicken burger

ベジバーガー
beji bāgā
veggie burger

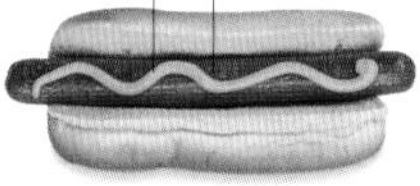

ホットドッグ hotto doggu
hot dog

具
gu
filling

サンドイッチ
sandoitchi
sandwich

クラブサンド
kurabu-sando
club sandwich

オープンサンド
ōpun-sando
open sandwich

ラップサンド
rappu-sando
wrap

ソース
sōsu
sauce

塩味
shioaji
savoury

甘い
amai
sweet

トッピング
toppingu
topping

ケバブ
kebabu
kebab

チキンナゲット
chikin nagetto
chicken nuggets

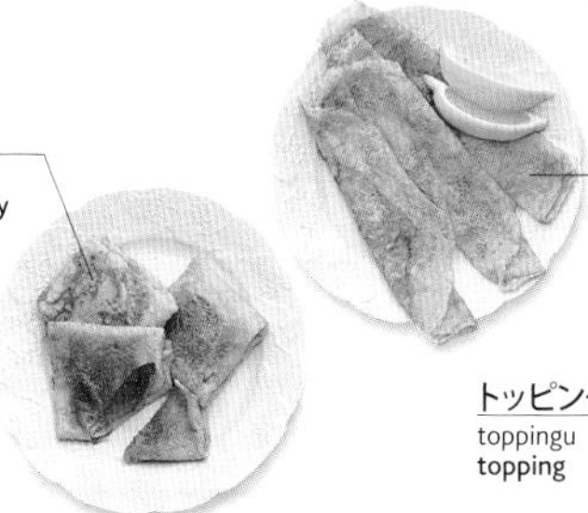

クレープ kurēpu | crêpes

フィッシュ＆チップス
fisshu ando chippusu
fish and chips

スペアリブ
supea ribu
ribs

フライドチキン
furaido chikin
fried chicken

ピザ
piza
pizza

朝食 chōshoku • breakfast

牛乳
gyūnyū
milk

シリアル
shiriaru
cereal

ジャム
jamu
jam

ドライフルーツ
dorai furūtsu
dried fruit

ハム
hamu
ham

チーズ
chīzu
cheese

クリスプブレッド
kurisupu bureddo
crispbread

朝食ビュッフェ
chōshoku byuffe
breakfast buffet

マーマレード
māmarēdo
marmalade

パテ
pate
pâté

バター
batā
butter

果物ジュース
kudamono jūsu
fruit juice

コーヒー
kōhī
coffee

ホットココア
hotto kokoa
hot chocolate

クロワッサン
kurowassan
croissant

紅茶
kōcha
tea

朝食のテーブル chōshoku no tēburu | breakfast table

飲物 nomimono | drinks

トマト
tomato
tomato

ブラックプディング
burakku pudingu
black pudding

トースト
tōsuto
toast

ソーセージ
sōsēji
sausage

目玉焼き
medamayaki
fried egg

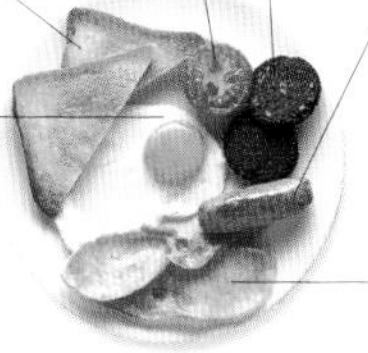

ベーコン
bēkon
bacon

イングリッシュ・ブレックファースト
ingurisshu burekkufāsuto
English breakfast

ブリオッシュ
buriosshu
brioche

パン
pan
bread

黄身
kimi
yolk

薫製ニシン
kunsei nishin
kippers

フレンチトースト
furenchi tōsuto
french toast

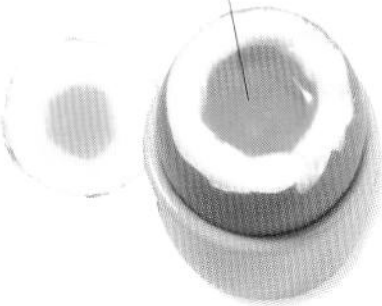

ゆで卵
yudetamago
boiled egg

スクランブルエッグ
sukuramburu eggu
scrambled eggs

クリーム
kurīmu
cream

フルーツヨーグルト
furūtsu yōguruto
fruit yoghurt

パンケーキ
pankēki
pancakes

ワッフル
waffuru
waffles

ポリッジ
porijji
porridge

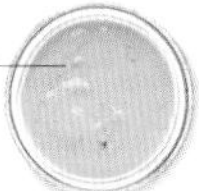

フルーツサラダ
furūtsu sarada
fruit salad

食事 shokuji • dinner

スープ sūpu | soup

コンソメ konsome | broth

シチュー shichū | stew

カレー karē | curry

ロースト rōsuto | roast

ミートパイ mītopai | pie

スフレ sufure | soufflé

ケバブ kebabu | kebab

ミートボール mītobōru
meatballs

オムレツ omuretsu
omelette

焼きそば yaki shoba
fried noodles

麺
men
noodles

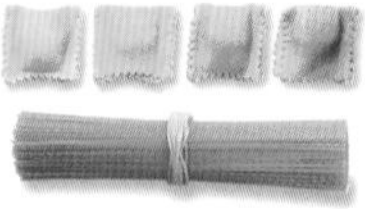

パスタ pasuta
pasta

ご飯 gohan | rice

ミックスサラダ mikkusu sarada
mixed salad

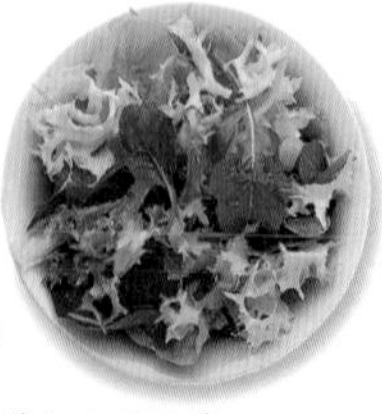

グリーンサラダ gurīn sarada
green salad

サラダドレッシング sarada
doresshingu | dressing

調理方法 chōri hōhō • techniques

詰め物 tsumemono
stuffed

煮込んだ nikonda | **in sauce**

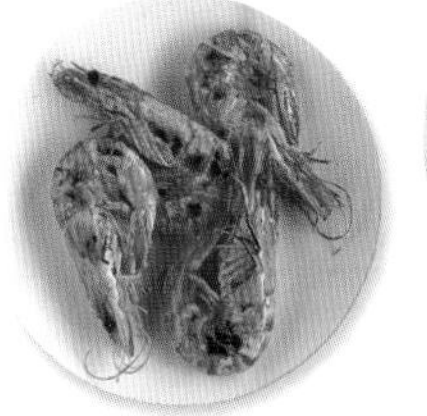

（グリルで）焼いた
(guriru de) yaita | **grilled**

マリネ marine | **marinated**

（沸騰前の温度で）茹でた (futtō
mae no ondo de) yudeta | **poached**

つぶした tsubushita
mashed

（オーブンで）焼いた
(ōbun de) yaita | **baked**

（フライパンで）焼いた
(furaipan de) yaita | **pan-fried**

炒めた itameta | **fried**

ピクルス pikurusu | **pickled**

薫製 kunsei | **smoked**

揚げた ageta | **deep-fried**

シロップ漬け shiroppu-zuke
in syrup

ドレッシングをかけた
doresshingu o kaketa | **dressed**

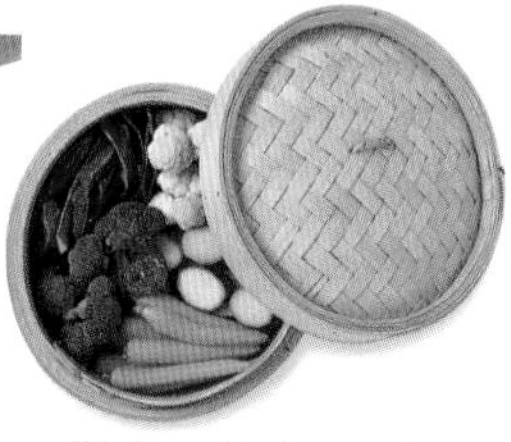

蒸した mushita | **steamed**

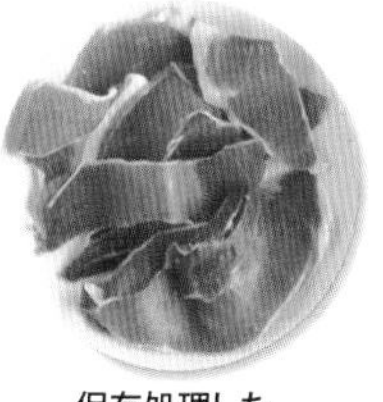

保存処理した
hozon shori shita | **cured**

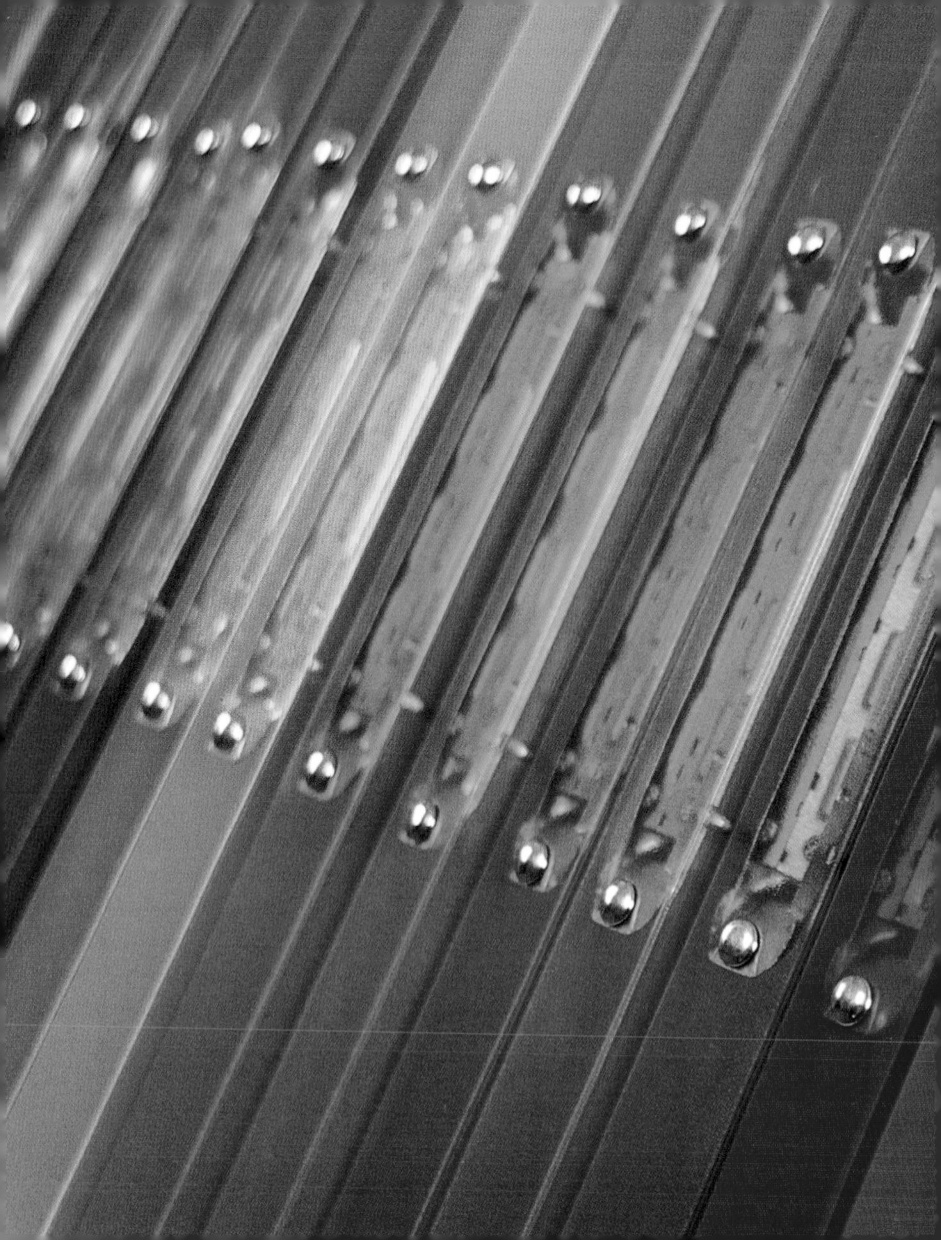

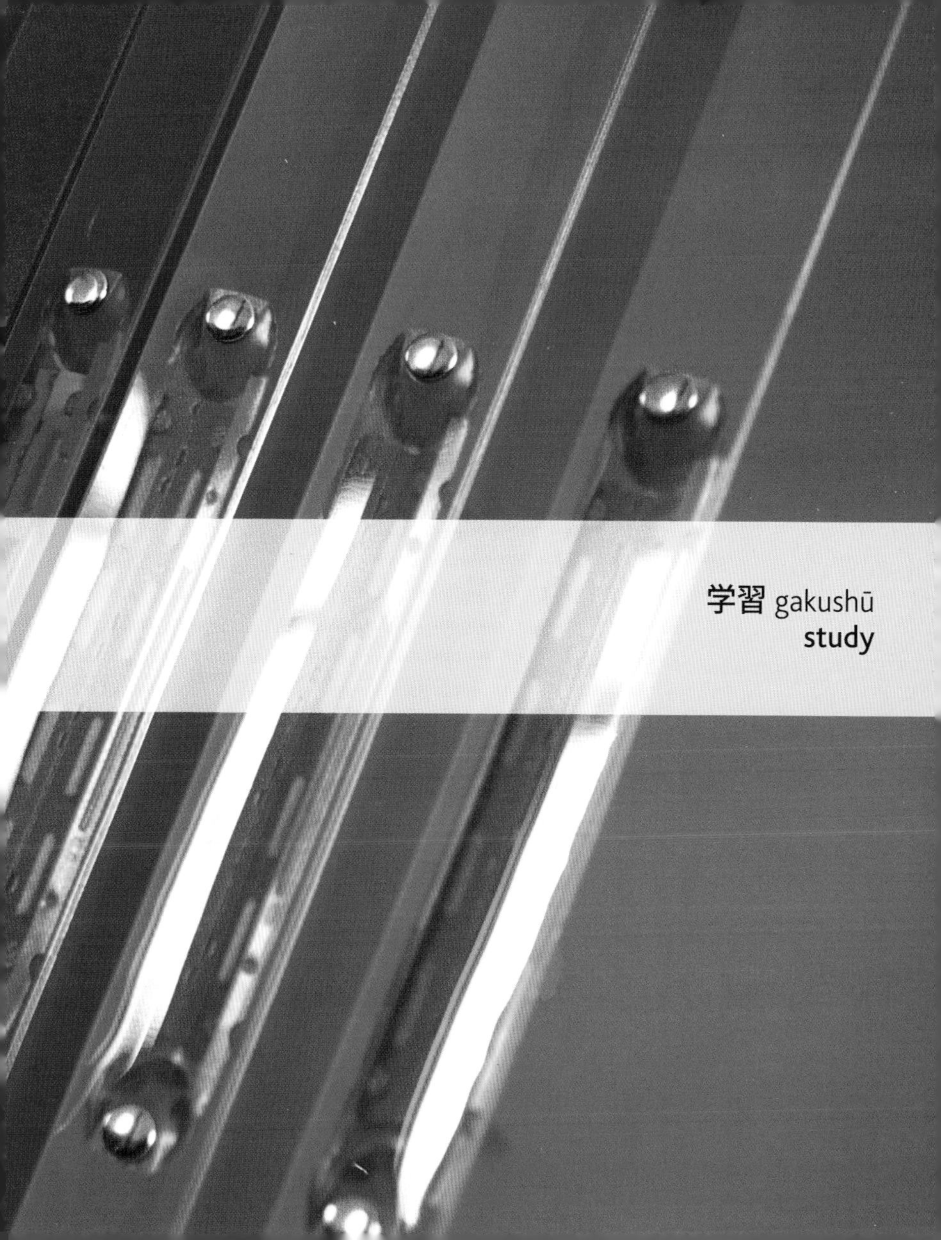

学習 gakushū
study

学校 gakkō • school

先生
sensei
teacher

黒板
kokuban
blackboard

男子生徒 danshi seito
schoolboy

生徒
seito
pupil

学校の制服
gakkō no seifuku
school uniform

机
tsukue
desk

通学鞄
tsūgaku kaban
school bag

チョーク
chōku
chalk

教室 kyōshitsu | classroom

女子生徒
joshi seito
schoolgirl

関連用語 kanrenyōgo • vocabulary

歴史 rekishi **history**	科学 kagaku **science**	物理 butsuri **physics**
外国語 gaikokugo **languages**	美術 bijutsu **art**	化学 kagaku **chemistry**
文学 bungaku **literature**	音楽 ongaku **music**	生物 seibutsu **biology**
地理 chiri **geography**	数学 sūgaku **maths**	体育 tai'iku **physical education**

学業 gakugyō • activities

読む yomu | **read (v)**

書く kaku | **write (v)**

綴る tsuzuru | **spell (v)**

描く egaku | **draw (v)**

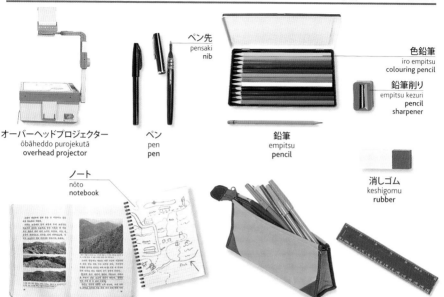

ペン先
pensaki
nib

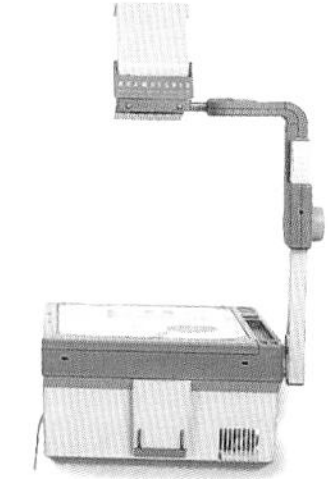

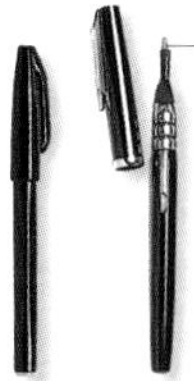

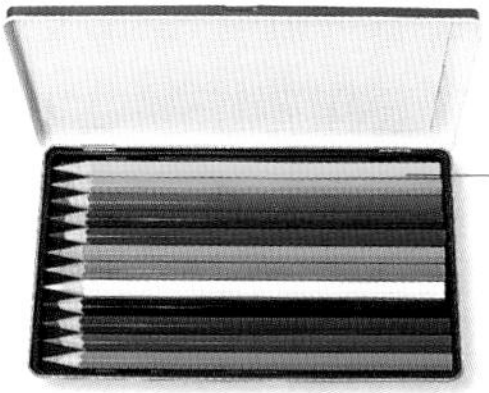

色鉛筆
iro empitsu
colouring pencil

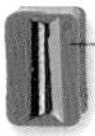

鉛筆削り
empitsu kezuri
pencil
sharpener

オーバーヘッドプロジェクター
ōbāheddo purojekutā
overhead projector

ペン
pen
pen

鉛筆
empitsu
pencil

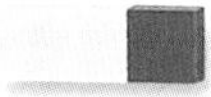

消しゴム
keshigomu
rubber

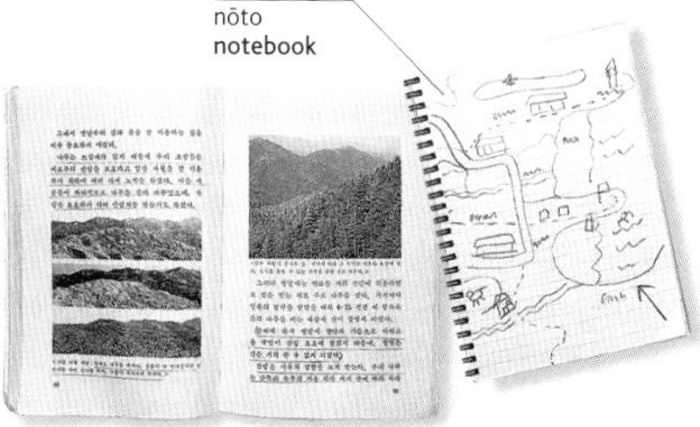

ノート
nōto
notebook

教科書 kyōkasho | textbook

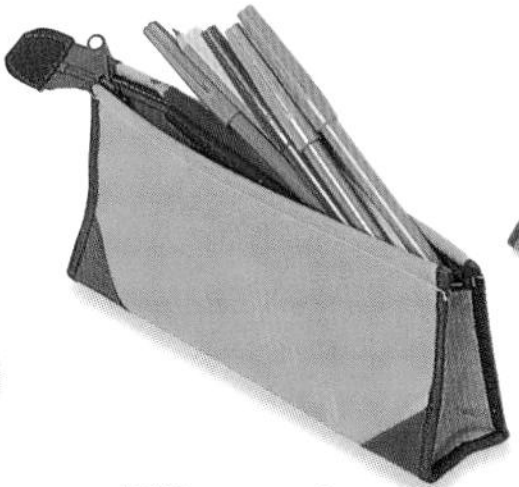

筆箱 fudebako | pencil case

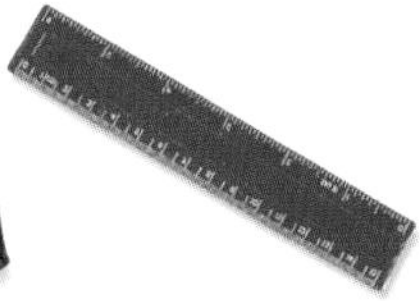

定規 jōgi | ruler

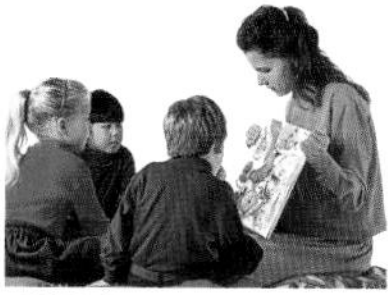

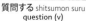

質問する shitsumon suru
question (v)

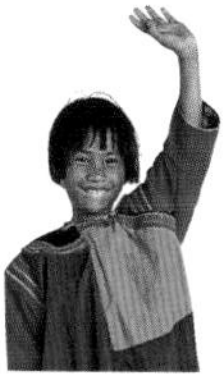

答える kotaeru | answer (v)

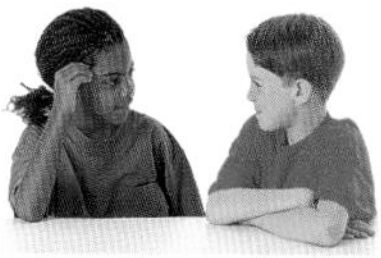

話し合う hanashiau | discuss (v)

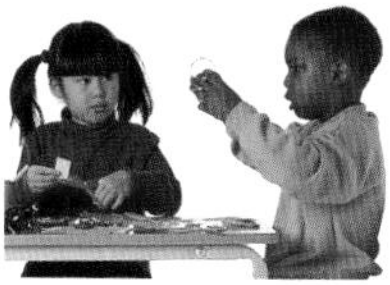

学ぶ manabu | learn (v)

関連用語 kanrenyōgo • vocabulary

校長先生 kōchō sensei head teacher	答え kotae answer	成績 seiseki grade
授業 jugyō lesson	宿題 shukudai homework	学年 gakunen year
質問 shitsumon question	試験 shiken examination	辞書 jisho dictionary
ノートを取る nōto o toru take notes (v)	作文 sakubun essay	百科事典 hyakkajiten encyclopedia

数学 sūgaku • maths

平面図形 heimenzukei • shapes

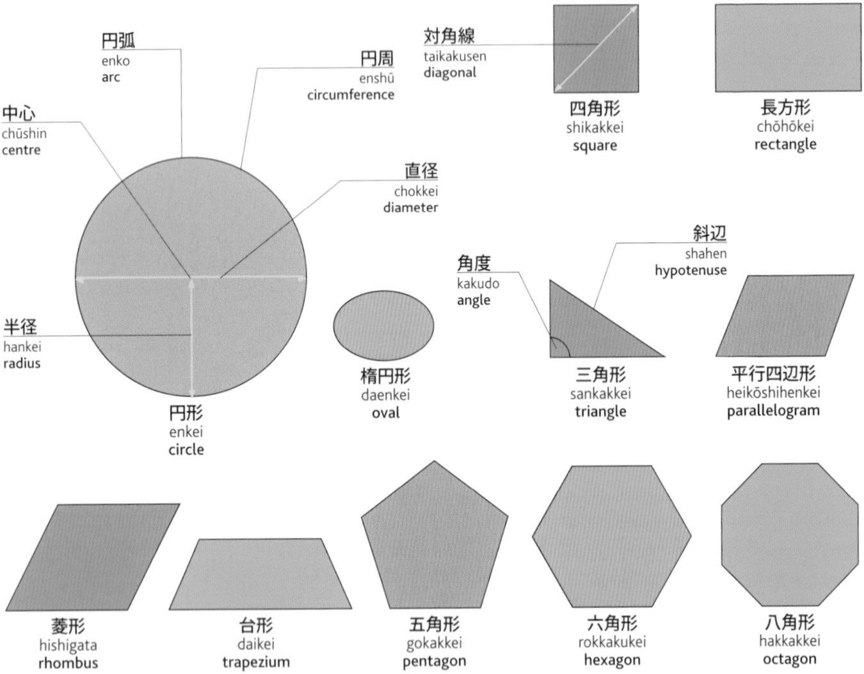

円弧
enko
arc

円周
enshū
circumference

対角線
taikakusen
diagonal

四角形
shikakkei
square

長方形
chōhōkei
rectangle

中心
chūshin
centre

直径
chokkei
diameter

半径
hankei
radius

楕円形
daenkei
oval

斜辺
shahen
hypotenuse

角度
kakudo
angle

三角形
sankakkei
triangle

平行四辺形
heikōshihenkei
parallelogram

円形
enkei
circle

菱形
hishigata
rhombus

台形
daikei
trapezium

五角形
gokakkei
pentagon

六角形
rokkakukei
hexagon

八角形
hakkakkei
octagon

立体図形 rittaizukei • solids

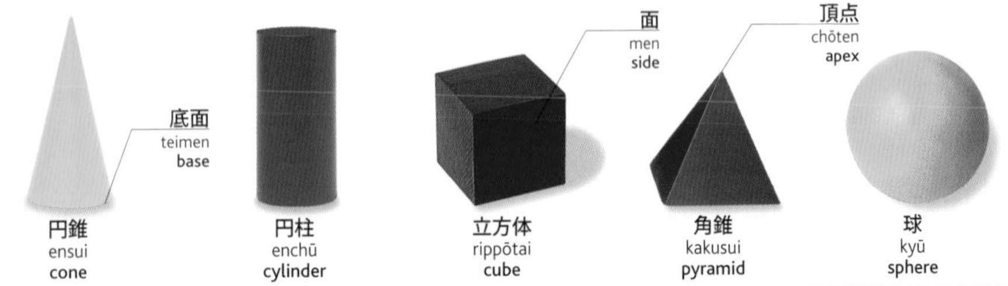

面
men
side

頂点
chōten
apex

底面
teimen
base

円錐
ensui
cone

円柱
enchū
cylinder

立方体
rippōtai
cube

角錐
kakusui
pyramid

球
kyū
sphere

線 sen • lines

直線	平行線	垂直線	曲線
chokusen	heikōsen	suichokusen	kyokusen
straight	**parallel**	**perpendicular**	**curved**

測定 sokutei • **measurements**

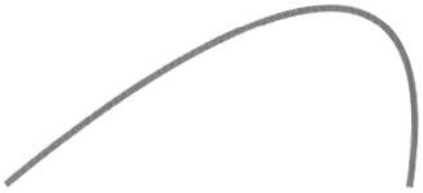

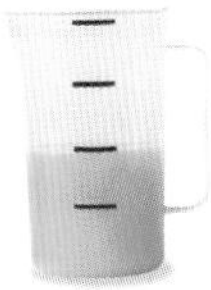

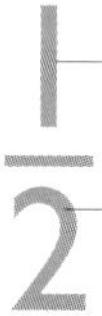

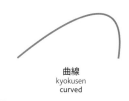

分子
bunshi
numerator

分母
bumbo
denominator

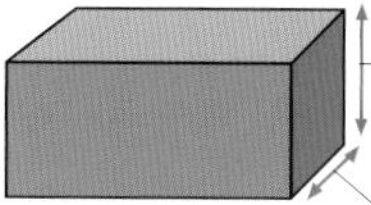

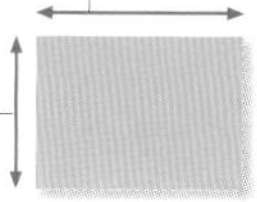

幅
haba
width

長さ
nagasa
length

高さ
takasa
height

奥行き
okuyuki
depth

体積	分数	寸法	面積
taiseki	bunsū	sumpō	menseki
volume	**fraction**	**dimensions**	**area**

数学用品 sūgaku yōhin • **equipment**

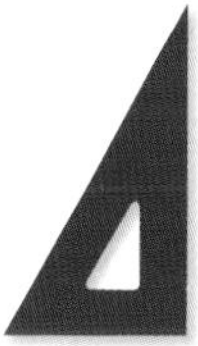

三角定規	分度器	定規	コンパス	電卓
sankakujōgi	bundoki	jōgi	kompasu	dentaku
set square	**protractor**	**ruler**	**compass**	**calculator**

関連用語 kanrenyōgo • **vocabulary**

幾何学	プラス	掛ける	イコール	足す	掛ける	数式
kikagaku	purasu	kakeru	ikōru	tasu	kakeru	sūshiki
geometry	**plus**	**times**	**equals**	**add (v)**	**multiply (v)**	**equation**

算数	マイナス	割る	数える	引く	割る	百分率
sansū	mainasu	waru	kazoeru	hiku	waru	hyakubunritsu
arithmetic	**minus**	**divided by**	**count (v)**	**subtract (v)**	**divide (v)**	**percentage**

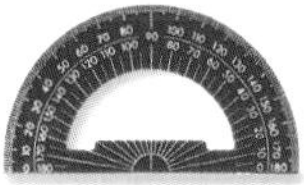

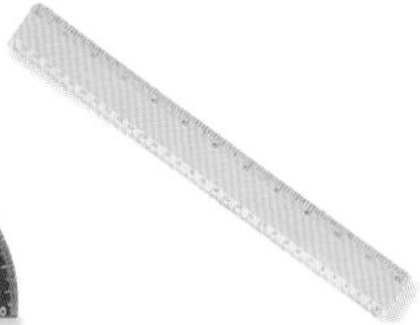

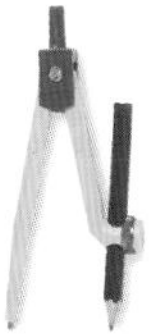

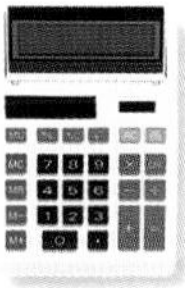

科学 kagaku • science

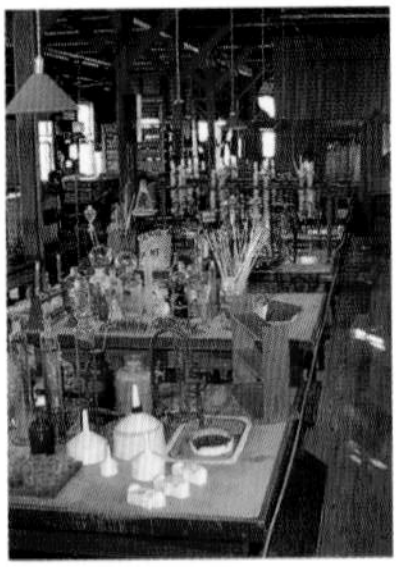

実験室
jikken shitsu
laboratory

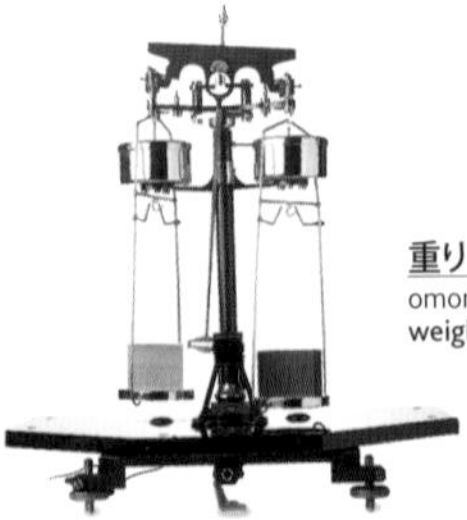

天秤
tembin
scales

重り
omori
weight

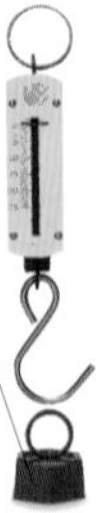

バネ秤
banebakari
spring balance

坩堝
rutsubo
crucible

ブンゼンバーナー
bunsen bānā
bunsen burner

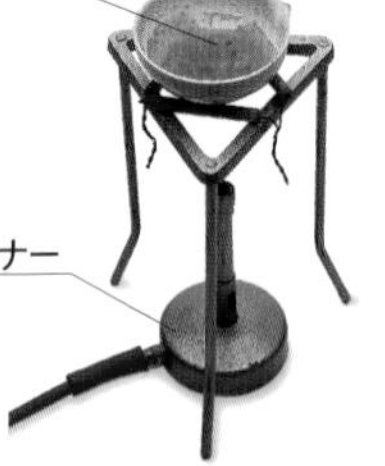

三脚
sankyaku
tripod

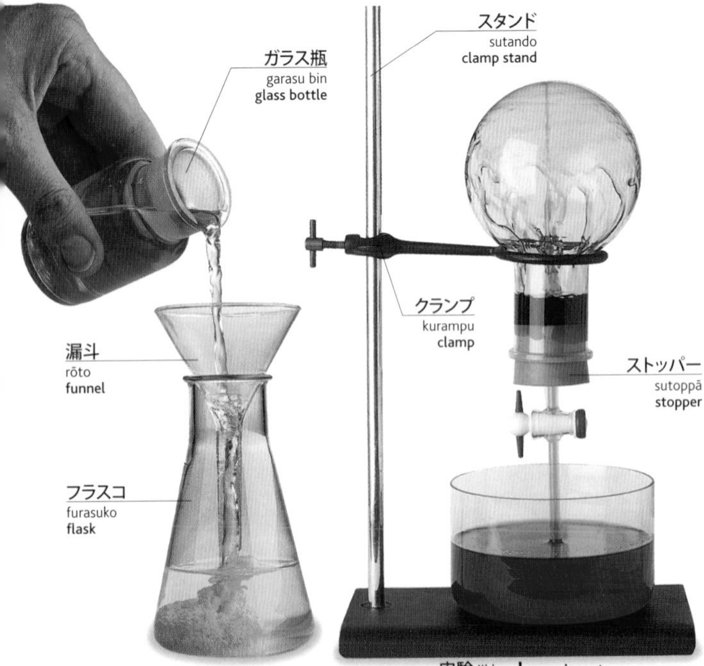

ガラス瓶
garasu bin
glass bottle

スタンド
sutando
clamp stand

試験管
shikenkan
test tube

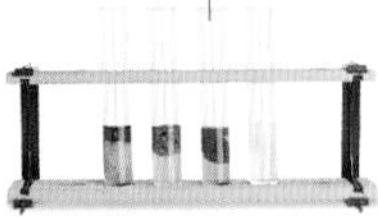

試験管立て
shikenkan-tate
rack

クランプ
kurampu
clamp

ストッパー
sutoppā
stopper

タイマー
taimā
timer

漏斗
rōto
funnel

フラスコ
furasuko
flask

シャーレー
shārē
petri dish

実験 jikken | **experiment**

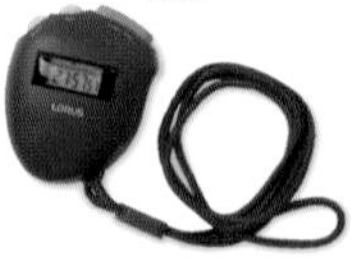

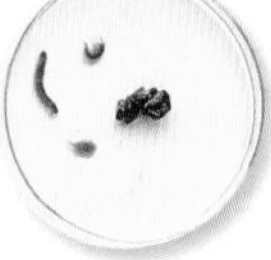

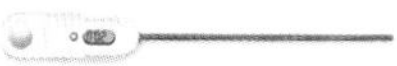

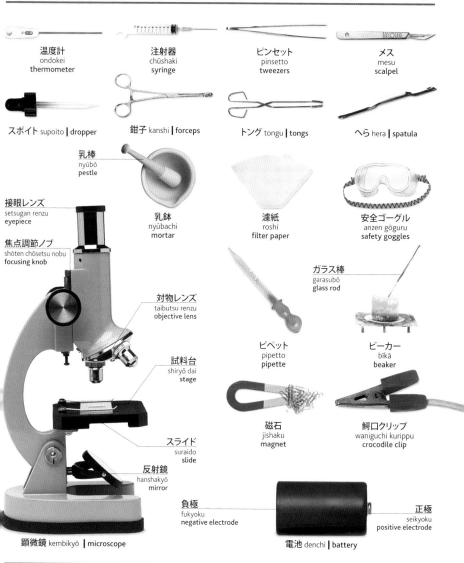

温度計
ondokei
thermometer

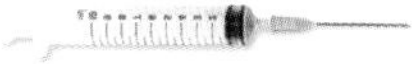

注射器
chūshaki
syringe

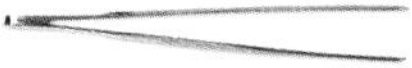

ピンセット
pinsetto
tweezers

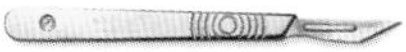

メス
mesu
scalpel

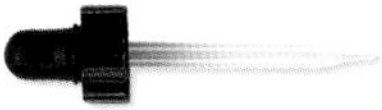

スポイト supoito | dropper

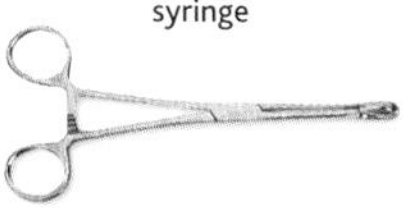

鉗子 kanshi | forceps

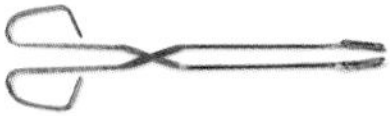

トング tongu | tongs

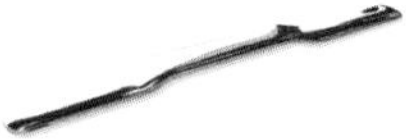

へら hera | spatula

乳棒
nyūbō
pestle

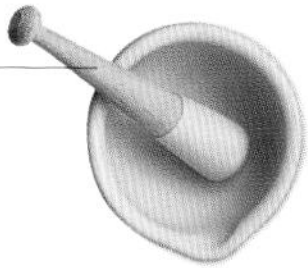

乳鉢
nyūbachi
mortar

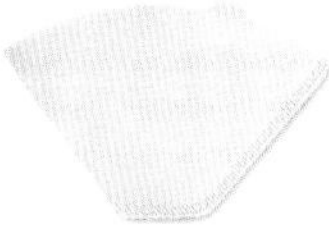

濾紙
roshi
filter paper

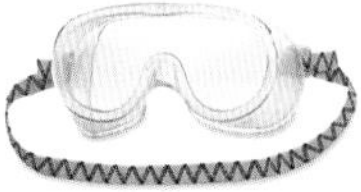

安全ゴーグル
anzen gōguru
safety goggles

接眼レンズ
setsugan renzu
eyepiece

焦点調節ノブ
shōten chōsetsu nobu
focusing knob

対物レンズ
taibutsu renzu
objective lens

試料台
shiryō dai
stage

スライド
suraido
slide

反射鏡
hanshakyō
mirror

ガラス棒
garasubō
glass rod

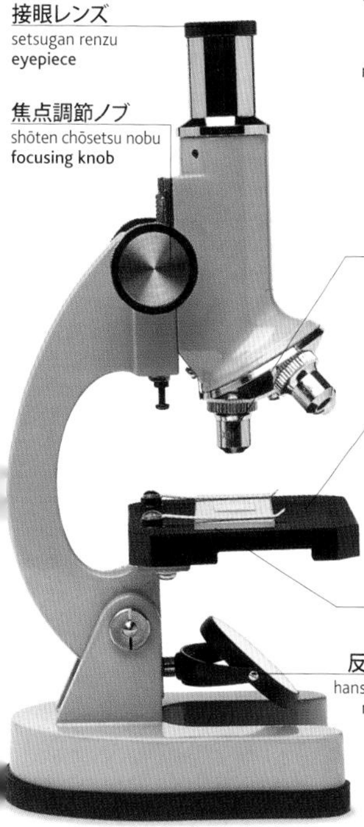

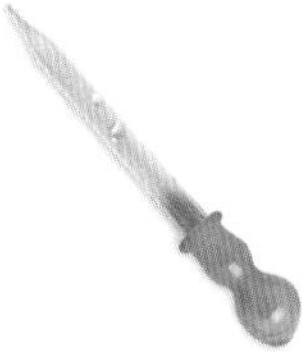

ピペット
pipetto
pipette

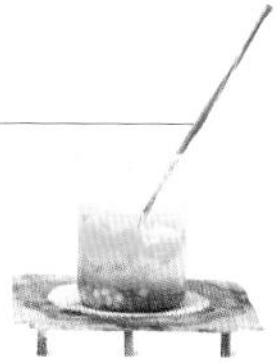

ビーカー
bīkā
beaker

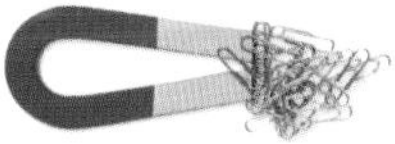

磁石
jishaku
magnet

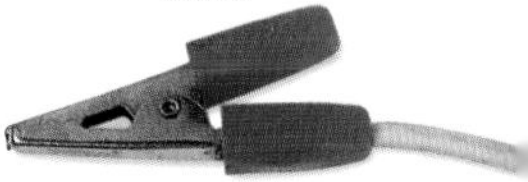

鰐口クリップ
waniguchi kurippu
crocodile clip

顕微鏡 kembikyō | microscope

負極
fukyoku
negative electrode

正極
seikyoku
positive electrode

電池 denchi | battery

大学 daigaku・college

スポーツフィールド
supōtsu fīrudo
sports field

入学事務局
nyūgaku
jimukyoku
admissions

学生食堂
gakusei shokudō
refectory

学生寮
gakusei ryō
**hall of
residence**

医療センター
iryō sentā
health centre

図書目録
tosho mokuroku
catalogue

キャンパス kyampasu | campus

司書
shisho
librarian

関連用語 kanrenyōgo・vocabulary

図書カード tosho kādo **library card**	問い合わせ toiawase **enquiries**	借出し karidashi **loan**
閲覧室 etsuran shitsu **reading room**	借りる kariru **borrow (v)**	本 hon **book**
読書リスト dokusho risuto **reading list**	予約する yoyaku suru **reserve (v)**	題名 daimei **title**
返却日 henkyaku-bi **return date**	延長する enchō suru **renew (v)**	通路 tsūro **aisle**

貸出カウンター
kashidashi kauntā
loans desk

書架
shoka
bookshelf

定期刊行物
teiki kankōbutsu
periodical

雑誌
zasshi
journal

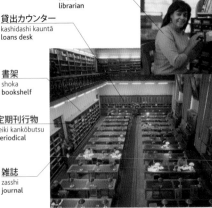

図書館 toshokan | library

大学生 daigakusei undergraduate

講師 kōshi lecturer

卒業生 sotsugyōsei graduate

ローブ rōbu robe

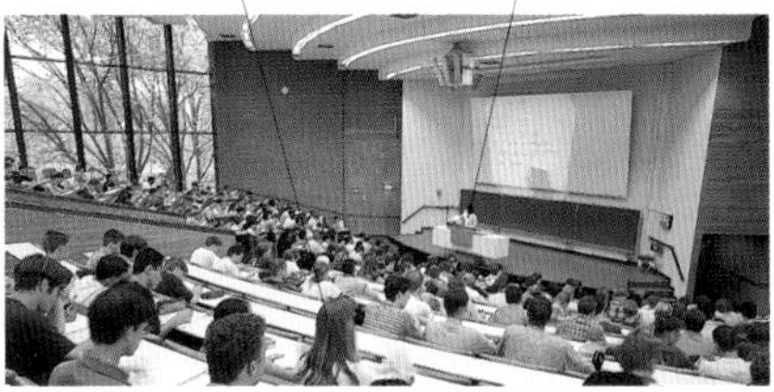

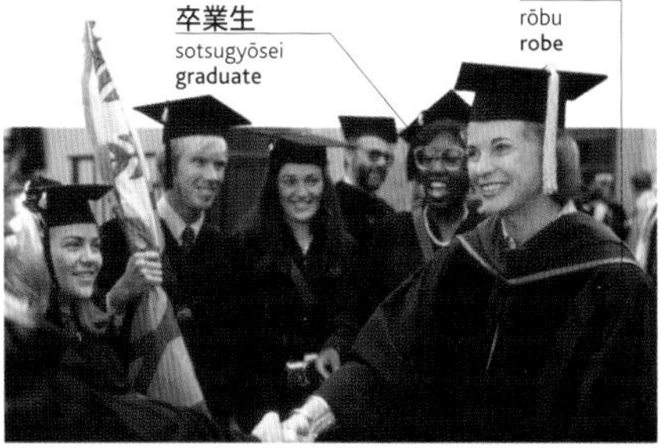

講堂 kōdō | lecture theatre

卒業式 sotsugyō-shiki | graduation ceremony

専門学校 senmongakkō • **schools**

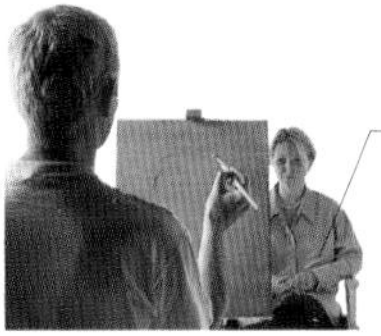

モデル moderu model

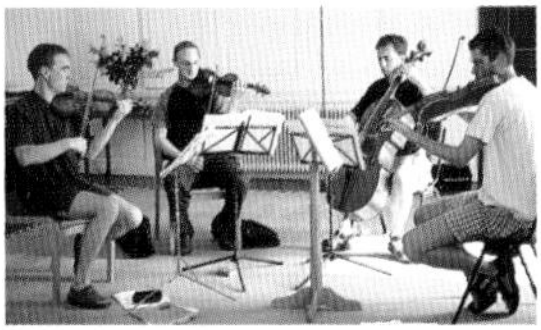

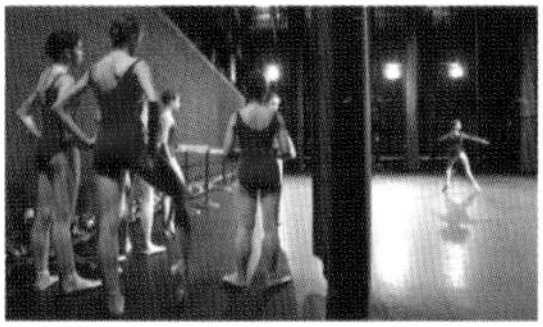

美術大学 bijutsu daigaku art college

音楽学校 ongaku gakkō music school

舞踊学院 buyō gakuin dance academy

関連用語 kanrenyōgo • **vocabulary**

奨学金 shōgakuhin scholarship	**研究** kenkyū research	**学位論文** gakui-rombun dissertation	**医学** igaku medicine	**哲学** tetsugaku philosophy
卒業証書 sotsugyō-shōsho diploma	**修士号** shūshi gō masters	**学部** gakubu department	**動物学** dōbutsugaku zoology	**文学** bungaku literature
学位 gakui degree	**博士号** hakase gō doctorate	**法学** hōgaku law	**物理学** butsurigaku physics	**美術史** bijutsushi history of art
大学院 daigakuin postgraduate	**卒業論文** sotsugyō-rombun thesis	**工学** kōgaku engineering	**政治学** seijigaku politics	**経済学** keizaigaku economics

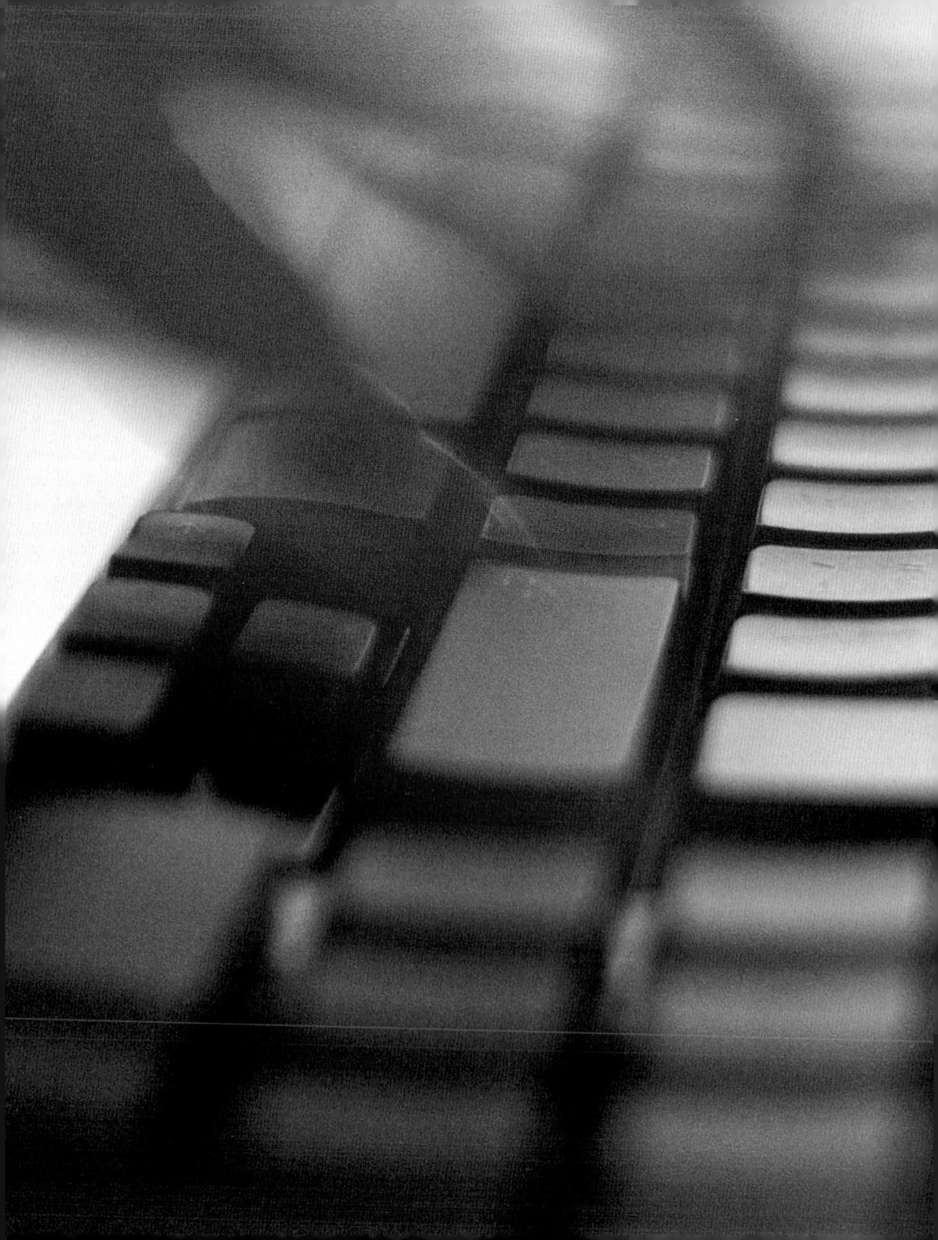

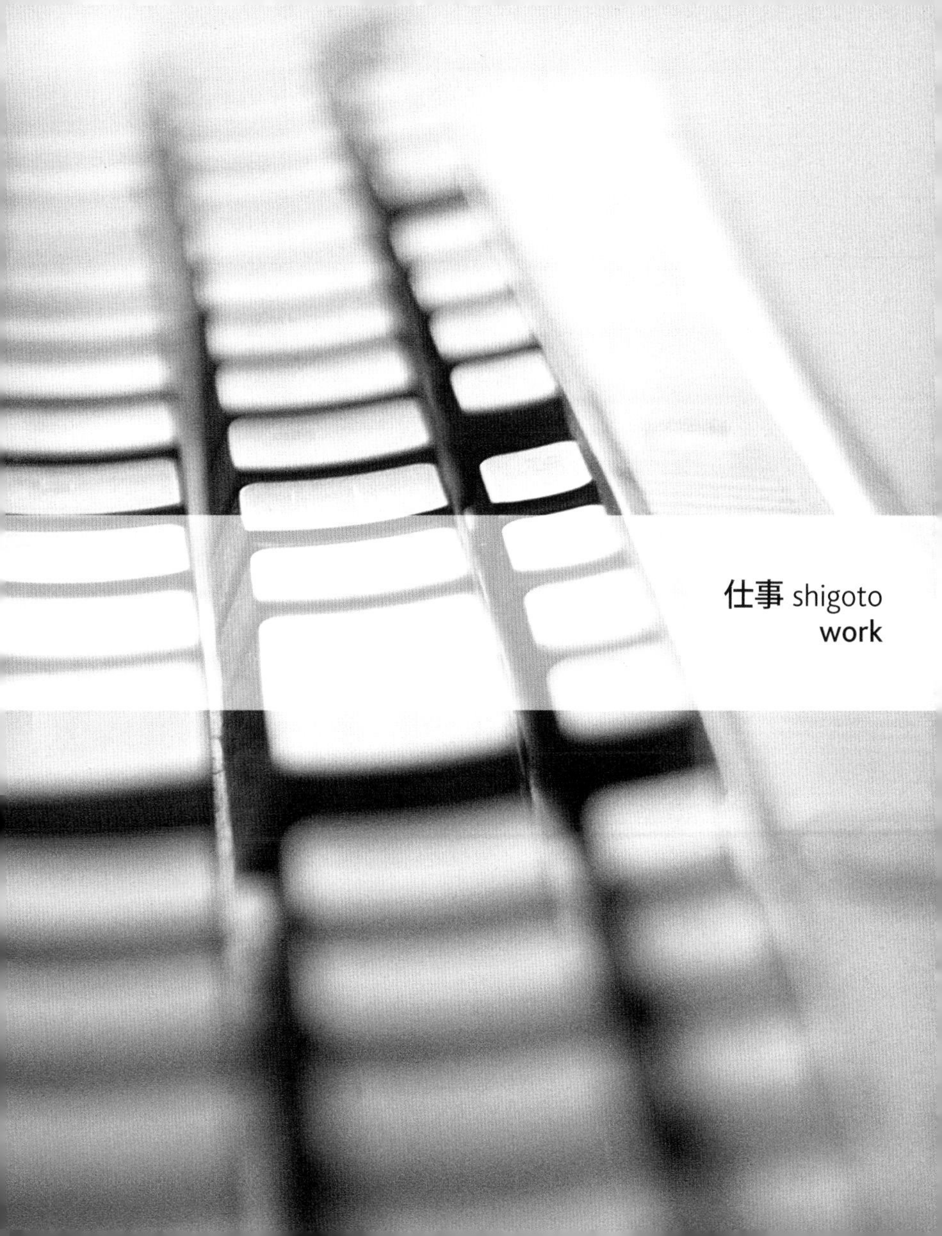

仕事 shigoto
work

事務所1 jimusho • office 1
事務所 jimusho • office

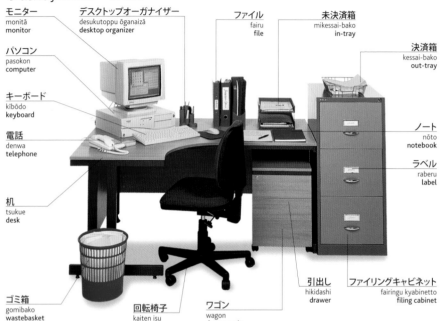

モニター
monitā
monitor

デスクトップオーガナイザー
desukutoppu ōganaizā
desktop organizer

ファイル
fairu
file

未決済箱
mikessai-bako
in-tray

決済箱
kessai-bako
out-tray

パソコン
pasokon
computer

キーボード
kībōdo
keyboard

電話
denwa
telephone

ノート
nōto
notebook

ラベル
raberu
label

机
tsukue
desk

ゴミ箱
gomibako
wastebasket

回転椅子
kaiten isu
swivel chair

ワゴン
wagon
drawer unit

引出し
hikidashi
drawer

ファイリングキャビネット
fairingu kyabinetto
filing cabinet

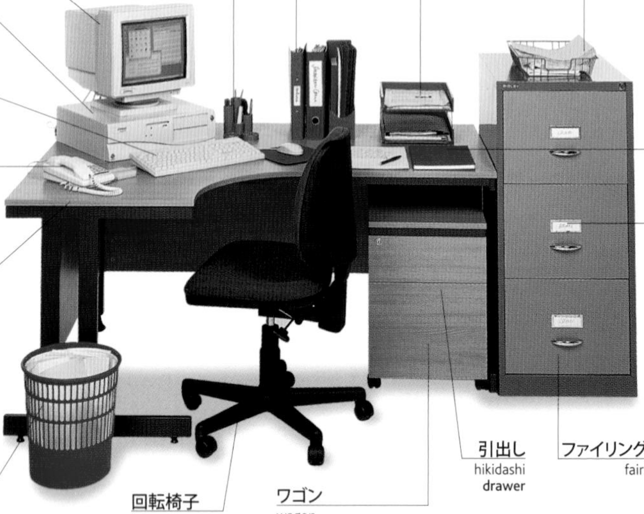

事務機器 jimu kiki • office equipment

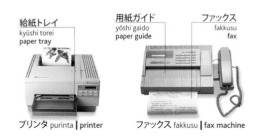

給紙トレイ
kyūshi torei
paper tray

用紙ガイド
yōshi gaido
paper guide

ファックス
fakkusu
fax

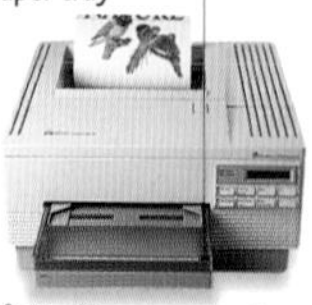

プリンタ purinta | **printer**

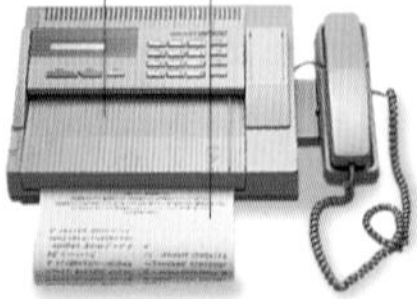

ファックス fakkusu | **fax machine**

関連用語 kanrenyōgo • vocabulary

印刷する
insatsu suru
print (v)

拡大する
kakudai suru
enlarge (v)

複写する
fukusha suru
copy (v)

縮小する
shukushō suru
reduce (v)

コピーを取らなければなりません。
kopī o toranakereba narimasen.
I need to make some copies.

事務用品 jimu yōhin • office supplies

レターヘッド
retāheddo
letterhead

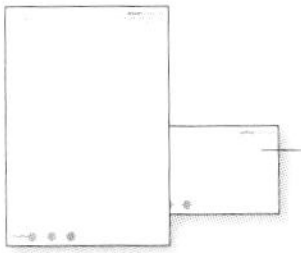

謹呈スリップ
kintei surippu
compliments slip

封筒
fūtō
envelope

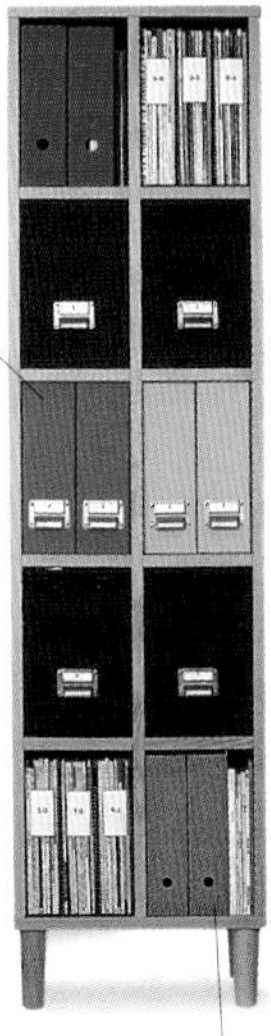

箱型ファイル
hako-gata fairu
box file

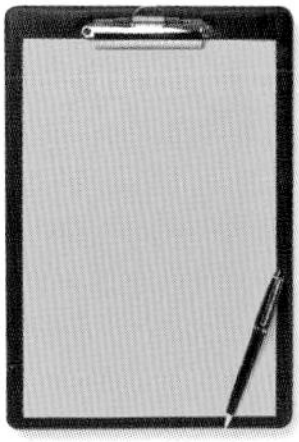

クリップボード
kurippubōdo
clipboard

ノート
nōto
note pad

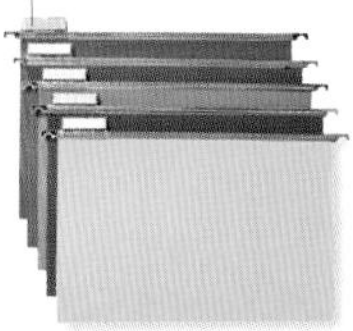

インデックス
indekkusu
tab

吊り下げ式フォルダー
tsurisage-shiki forudā
hanging file

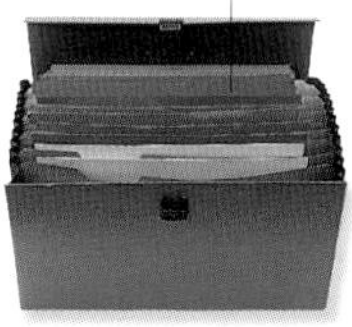

仕切りカード
shikiri kādo
divider

ドキュメントファイル
dokyumento fairu
concertina file

レバーアーチ式ファイル
rebā'āchi-shiki fairu
lever arch file

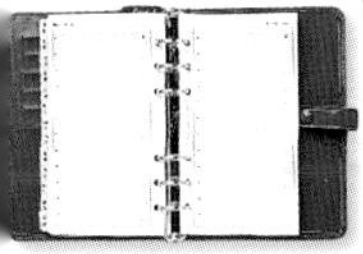

システム手帳
shisutemu techō
personal organizer

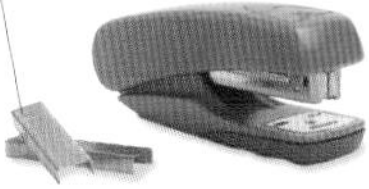

(ホチキスの)針
(hochikisu no) shin
staples

ホチキス
hochikisu
stapler

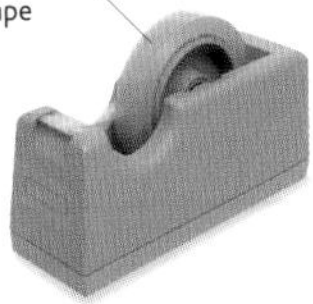

セロテープ
serotēpu
sticky tape

テープカッター
tēpu kattā
tape dispenser

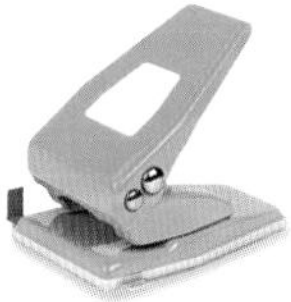

穴あけパンチ
ana'ake panchi
hole punch

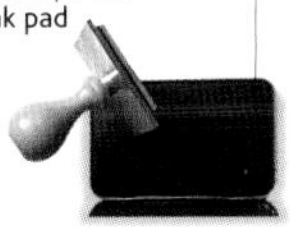

スタンプ台
sutampu dai
ink pad

ゴム印
gomuin
rubber stamp

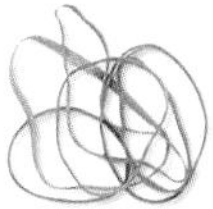

輪ゴム
wagomu
rubber band

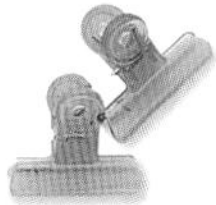

目玉クリップ
medama kurippu
bulldog clip

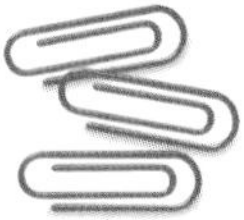

ゼムクリップ
zemu kurippu
paper clip

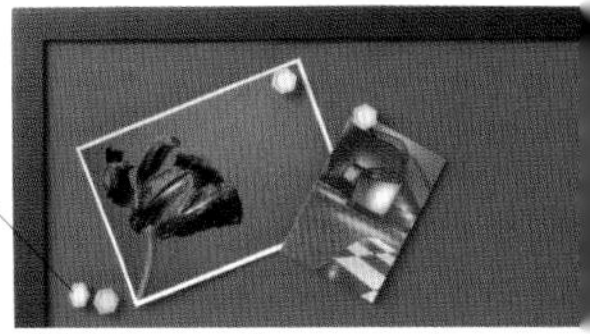

画鋲
gabyō
drawing pin

掲示板 keijiban | notice board

事務所2 jimusho ● office 2

フリップチャート
furippu chāto
flipchart

イーゼル
īzeru
easel

マネージャー
manējā
manager

提案書
teian sho
proposal

報告書
hōkokusho
report

幹部
kambu
executive

議事録
gijiroku
minutes

会議 kaigi | meeting

関連用語 kanrenyōgo ● vocabulary

会議室 kaigi shitsu **meeting room**	**出席する** shusseki suru **attend (v)**
議題 gidai **agenda**	**議長を務める** gichō o tsutomeru **chair (v)**

会議は何時ですか。
kaigi wa nanji desuka?
What time is the meeting?

営業時間は何時から何時までですか。
eigyōjikan wa nanji kara nanji made desuka?
What are your office hours?

プレゼンター
purezentā
speaker

プロジェクター
purojekutā
projector

プレゼンテーション purezentēshon | presentation

ビジネス bijinesu • **business**

ノートパソコン
nōtopasokon
laptop

メモ
memo
notes

ビジネスマン
bijinesuman
businessman

ビジネスウーマン
bijimesu'ūman
businesswoman

ビジネスランチ bijinesu ranchi | business lunch

出張 shutchō | business trip

取引先
torihikisaki
client

予定
yotei
appointment

電子手帳
denshitechō
palmtop

手帳 techō | diary

社長
shachō
managing
director

商取引 shōtorihiki | business deal

関連用語 kanrenyōgo • **vocabulary**

会社
kaisha
company

従業員
jūgyōin
staff

経理部
keiri bu
accounts department

法務部
hōmu bu
legal department

本社
honsha
head office

給料
kyūryō
salary

市場開発部
shijōkaihatsu bu
marketing department

顧客サービス部
kokyaku sābisu bu
customer service department

支社
shisha
branch

従業員名簿
jūgyōin meibo
payroll

営業部
eigyō bu
sales department

人事部
jinji bu
personnel department

コンピュータ kompyūta ● **computer**

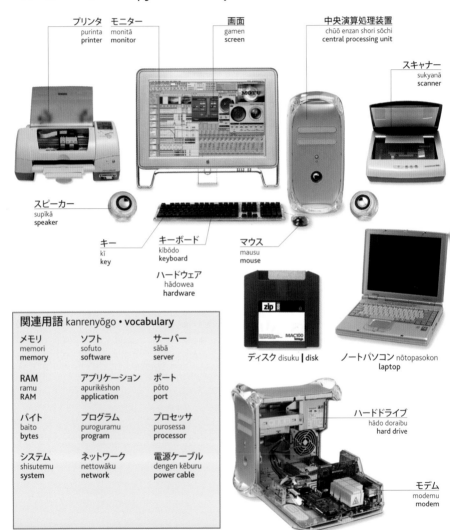

プリンタ
purinta
printer

モニター
monitā
monitor

画面
gamen
screen

中央演算処理装置
chūō enzan shori sōchi
central processing unit

スキャナー
sukyanā
scanner

スピーカー
supīkā
speaker

キー
kī
key

キーボード
kībōdo
keyboard

マウス
mausu
mouse

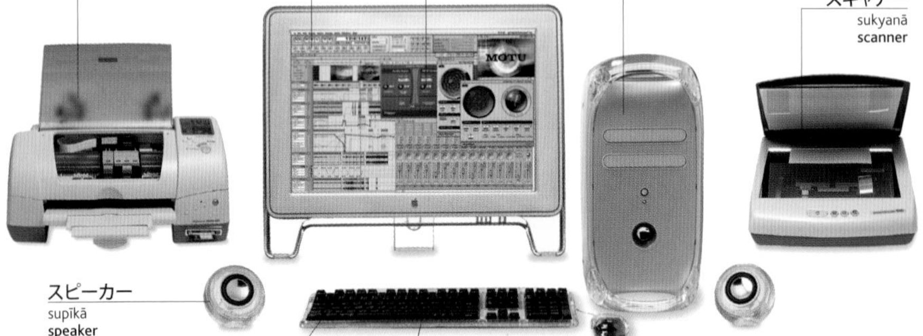

ハードウェア
hādowea
hardware

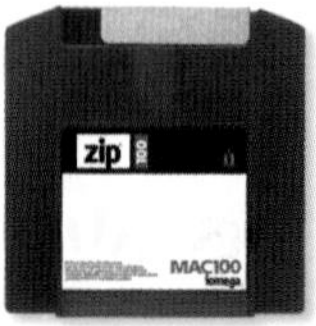

ディスク disuku | disk

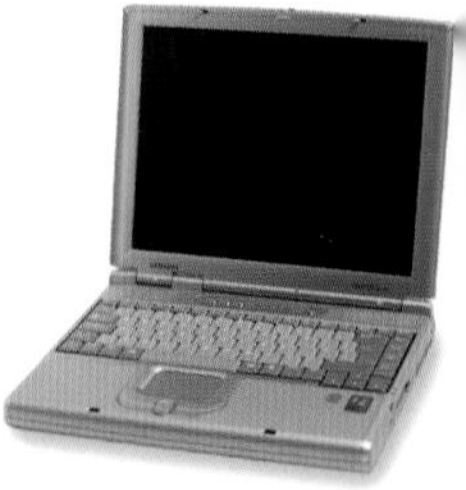

ノートパソコン nōtopasokon
laptop

ハードドライブ
hādo doraibu
hard drive

モデム
modemu
modem

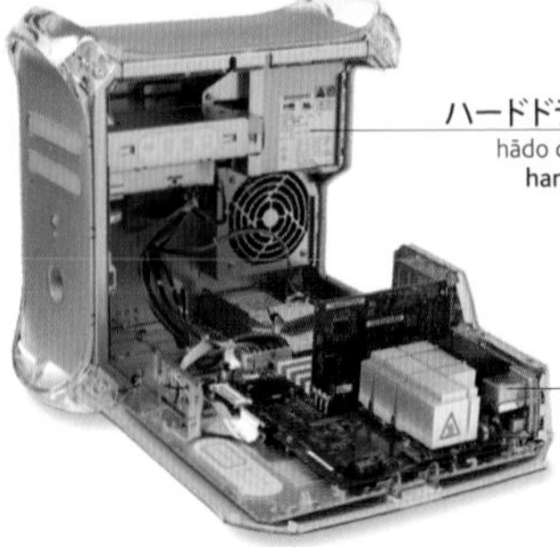

関連用語 kanrenyōgo ● **vocabulary**

メモリ memori **memory**	ソフト sofuto **software**	サーバー sābā **server**
RAM ramu **RAM**	アプリケーション apurikēshon **application**	ポート pōto **port**
バイト baito **bytes**	プログラム puroguramu **program**	プロセッサ purosessa **processor**
システム shisutemu **system**	ネットワーク nettowāku **network**	電源ケーブル dengen kēburu **power cable**

デスクトップ desukutoppu · desktop

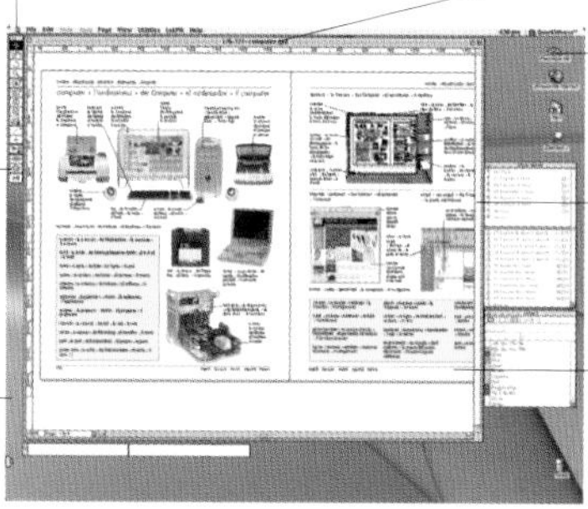

メニューバー
menyūbā
menubar

フォント
fonto
font

アイコン
aikon
icon

ツールバー
tsūrubā
toolbar

スクロールバー
sukurōrubā
scrollbar

壁紙
kabegami
wallpaper

ウィンドウ
windo-u
window

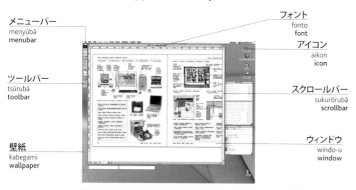

ファイル
fairu
file

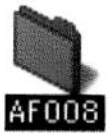

フォルダ
foruda
folder

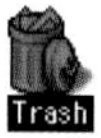

ごみ箱
gomibako
trash

インターネット intānetto · internet

電子メール denshimēru · email

ブラウザ
burauza
browser

受信箱
jushin-bako
inbox

ウェブサイト
webusaito
website

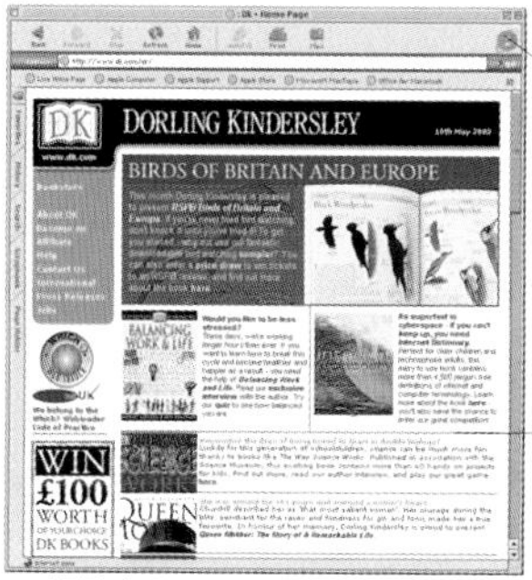

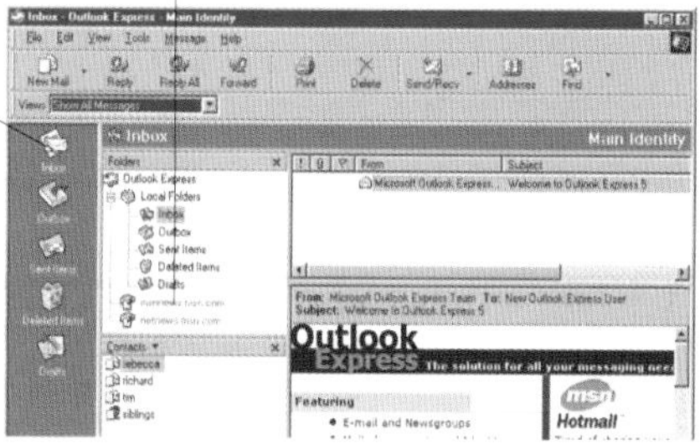

メールアドレス
mēru adoresu
email address

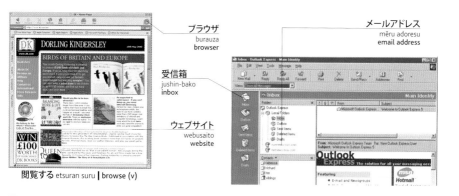

閲覧する etsuran suru | browse (v)

関連用語 kanrenyōgo · vocabulary

接続する setsuzoku suru **connect (v)**	サービスプロバイダ sābisu purobaida **service provider**	ログオンする roguon suru **log on (v)**	ダウンロードする daunrōdo suru **download (v)**	送信する sōshin suru **send (v)**	保存する hozon suru **save (v)**
インストールする insutōru suru **install (v)**	メールアカウント mēru akaunto **email account**	オンライン onrain **online**	添付書類 tempu shorui **attachment**	受信する jushin suru **receive (v)**	検索する kensaku suru **search (v)**

報道 hōdō • media

テレビスタジオ terebi sutajio • television studio

司会者
shikai-sha
presenter

照明
shōmei
light

セット
setto
set

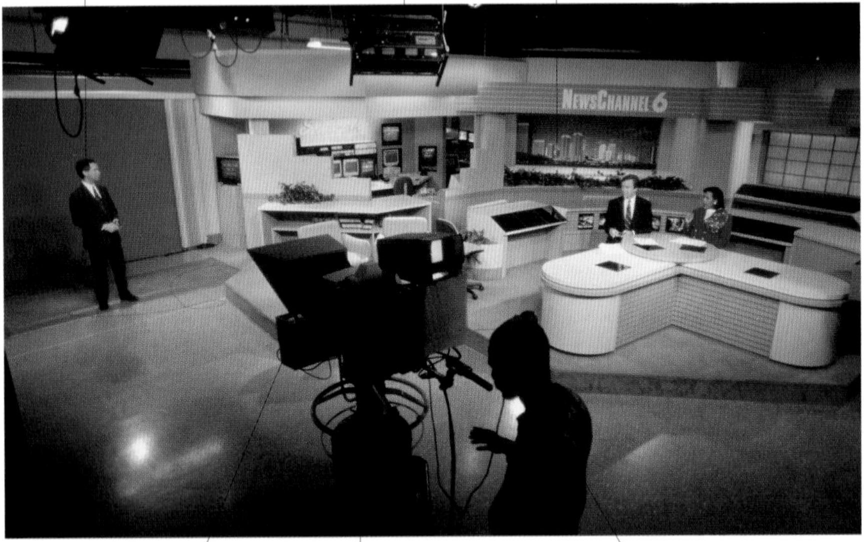

カメラ
kamera
camera

カメラ台
kamera dai
camera crane

カメラマン
kameraman
cameraman

関連用語 kanrenyōgo • vocabulary

チャンネル channeru channel	ニュース nyūsu news	新聞 shimbun press	連続ドラマ renzoku dorama soap	アニメ anime cartoon	ライブ raibu live
番組制作 bangumi seisaku programming	ドキュメンタリー dokyumentarī documentary	シリーズ番組 shirīzu bangumi television series	ゲーム番組 gēmu bangumi game show	録画 rokuga prerecorded	放送する hōsō suru broadcast (v)

（仕事 SHIGOTO • WORK）

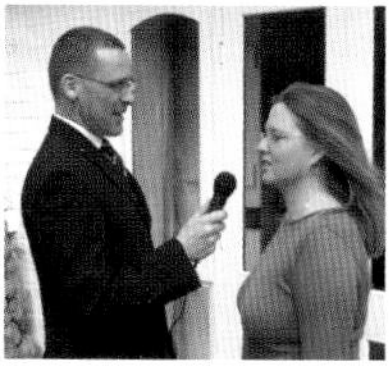

インタビュアー intabyuā
interviewer

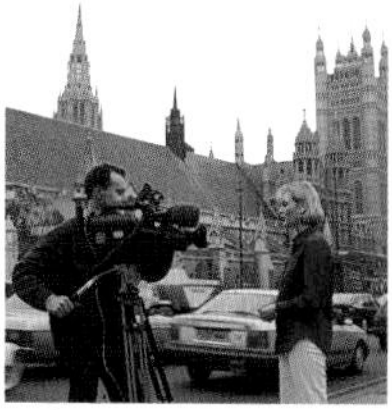

レポーター repōtā | reporter

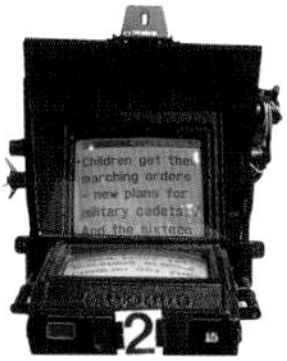

テロップ teroppu | autocue

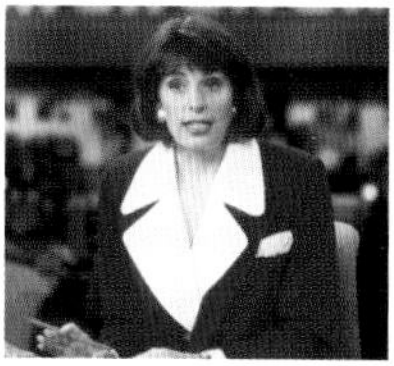

ニュースキャスター
nyūsukyasutā | newsreader

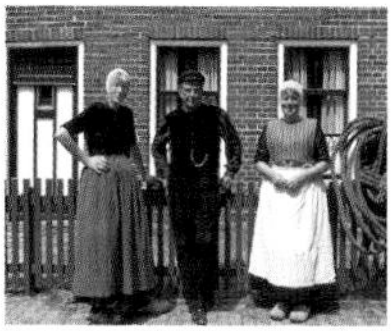

俳優 haiyū | actors

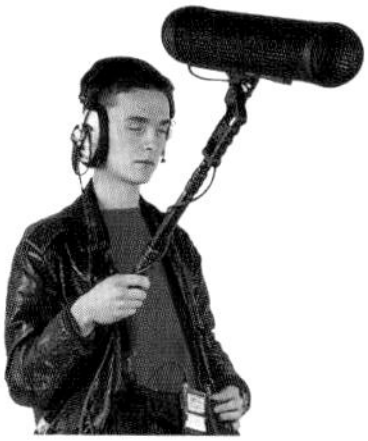

ブームマイク būmumaiku
sound boom

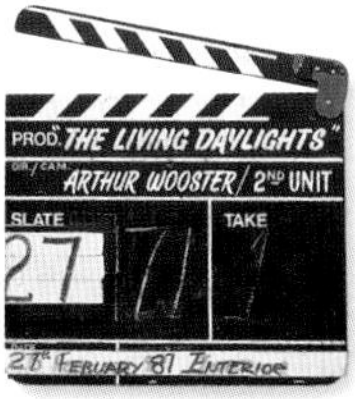

カチンコ kachinko
clapper board

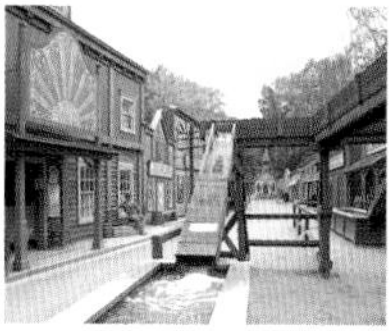

映画のセット eiga no setto
film set

ラジオ rajio • radio

調整卓
chōsei taku
mixing desk

マイク
maiku
microphone

サウンドエンジニア
saundo enjinia
sound technician

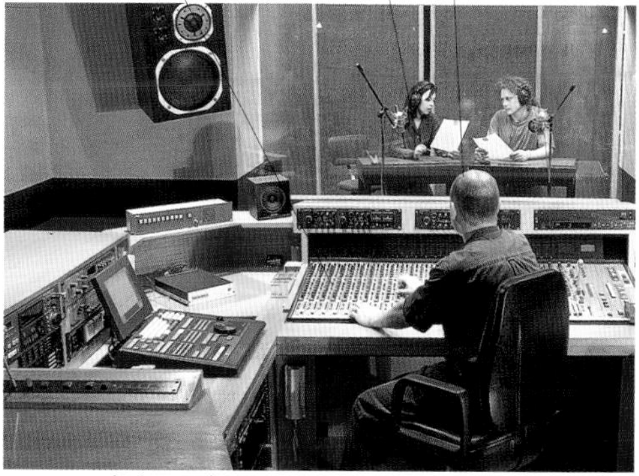

録音スタジオ rokuon sutajio | recording studio

関連用語 kanrenyōgo • vocabulary

ラジオ局
rajio kyoku
radio station

放送
hōsō
broadcast

波長
hachō
wavelength

長波
chōha
long wave

短波
tampa
short wave

中波
chūha
medium wave

周波数
shūhasū
frequency

音量
onryō
volume

合わせる
awaseru
tune (v)

ディスクジョッキー
disuku jokkī
DJ

法律 hōritsu • law

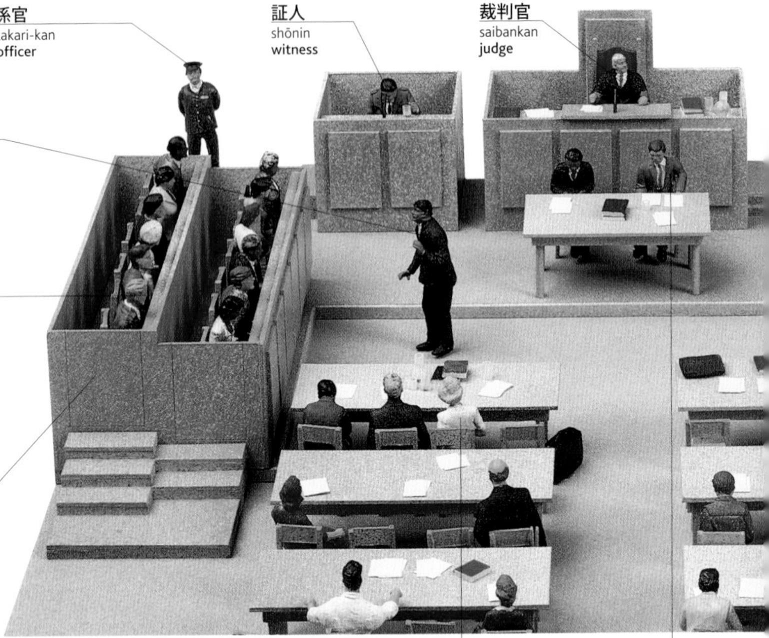

法廷係官
hōtei kakari-kan
court officer

証人
shōnin
witness

裁判官
saibankan
judge

弁護士
bengoshi
lawyer

陪審員
baishin'in
jury

陪審員席
baishin'in seki
jury box

法廷 hōtei | courtroom

起訴側
kiso-gawa
prosecution

裁判所職員
saibansho shokuin
court official

関連用語 kanrenyōgo • vocabulary

法律事務所 hōritsu jimusho lawyer's office	**呼出し状** yobidashijō summons	**命令** meirei writ	**訴訟案件** soshō anken court case
法律相談 hōritsu sōdan legal advice	**陳述書** chinjutsu-sho statement	**公判日** kōhan-bi court date	**罪状** zaijō charge
クライアント kuraianto client	**令状** reijō warrant	**罪状認否** zaijōnimpi plea	**被疑者** higisha accused

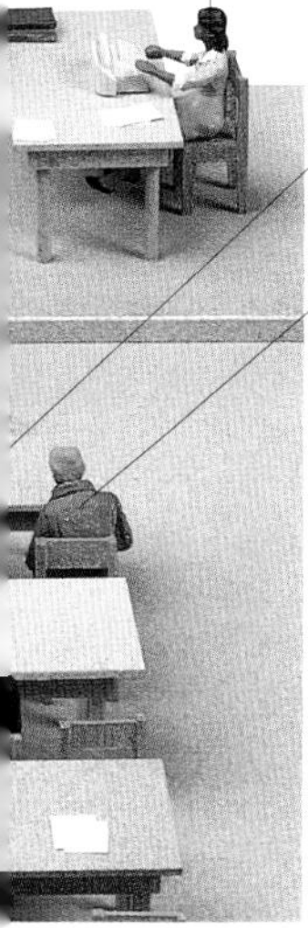

速記者
sokki-sha
stenographer

容疑者
yōgisha
suspect

被告人
hikokunin
defendant

被告側
hikoku-gawa
defence

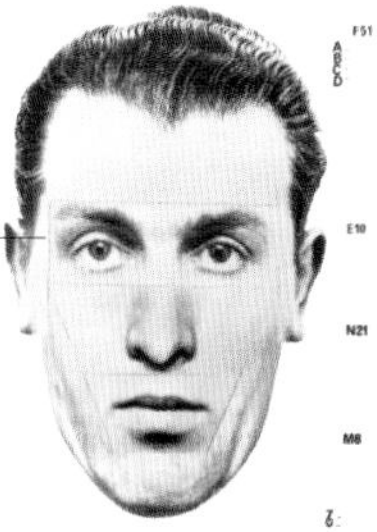

モンタージュ写真 montāju
shashin | photofit

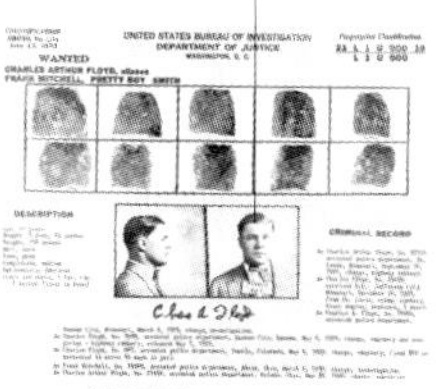

犯罪者
hanzai-sha
criminal

犯罪歴 hanzai-reki
criminal record

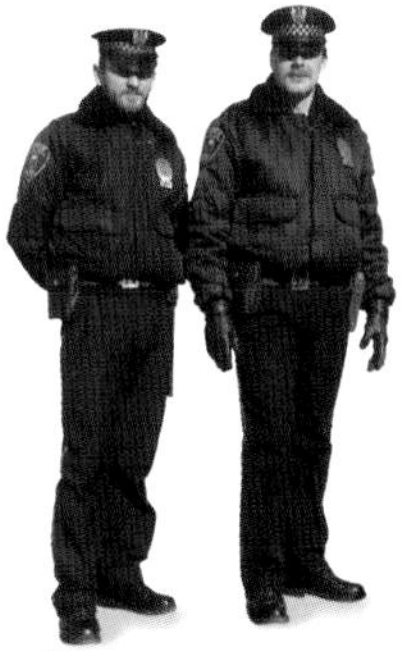

看守 kanshu | prison guard

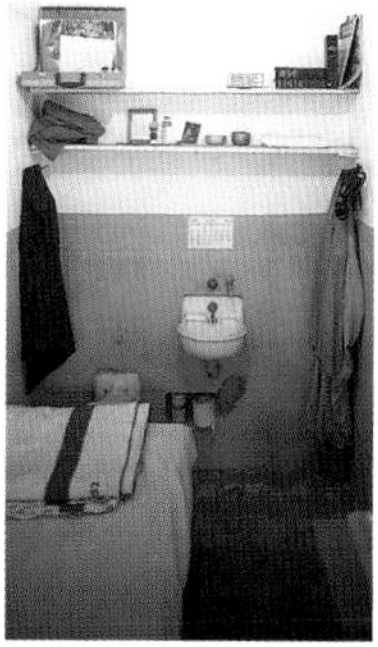

監房 kambō | cell

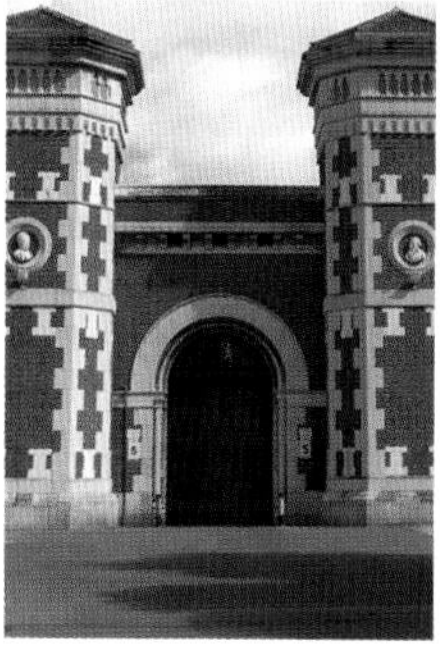

刑務所 keimusho | prison

関連用語 kanrenyōgo • vocabulary

証拠 shōko **evidence**	有罪 yūzai **guilty**	保釈金 hoshakukin **bail**	弁護士に会わせてください。 bengoshi ni awasete kudasai **I want to see a lawyer.**
判決 hanketsu **verdict**	無罪 muzai **acquitted**	上訴 jōso **appeal**	裁判所はどこですか。 saibansho wa doko desuka? **Where is the courthouse?**
無実 mujitsu **innocent**	刑罰 keibatsu **sentence**	仮釈放 karishakuhō **parole**	保釈金を払えますか。 hoshakukin o haraemasuka? **Can I post bail?**

農場1 nōjō ● farm 1

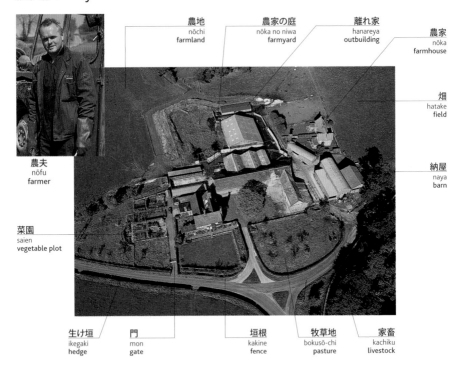

農地
nōchi
farmland

農家の庭
nōka no niwa
farmyard

離れ家
hanareya
outbuilding

農家
nōka
farmhouse

畑
hatake
field

農夫
nōfu
farmer

納屋
naya
barn

菜園
saien
vegetable plot

生け垣
ikegaki
hedge

門
mon
gate

垣根
kakine
fence

牧草地
bokusō-chi
pasture

家畜
kachiku
livestock

耕運機
kō'unki
cultivator

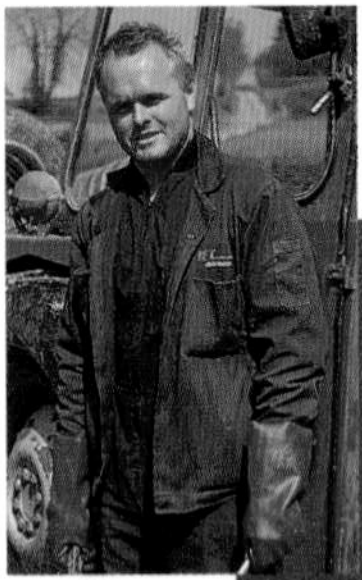

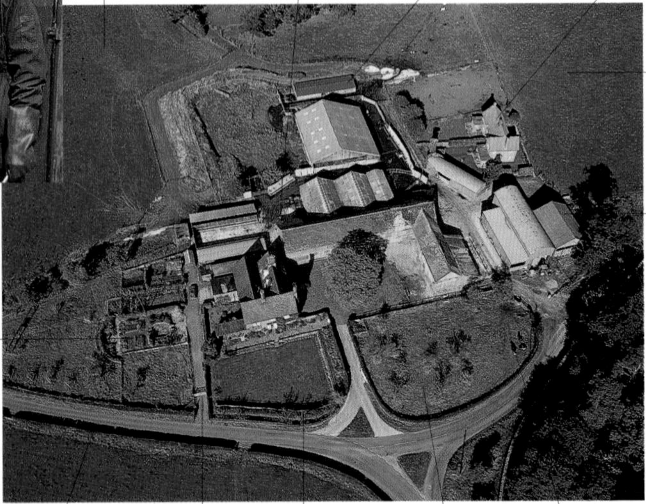

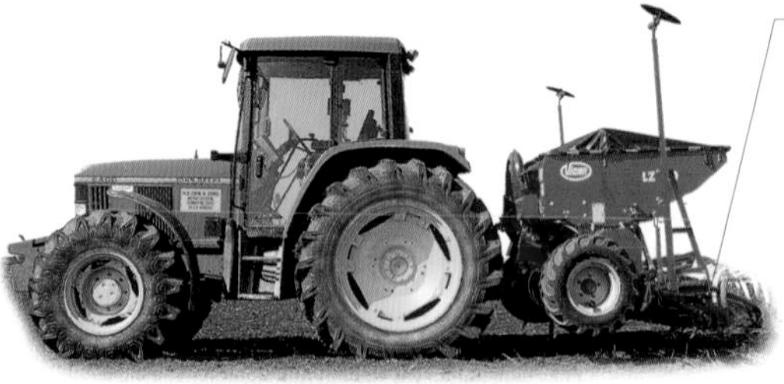

トラクター torakutā | tractor

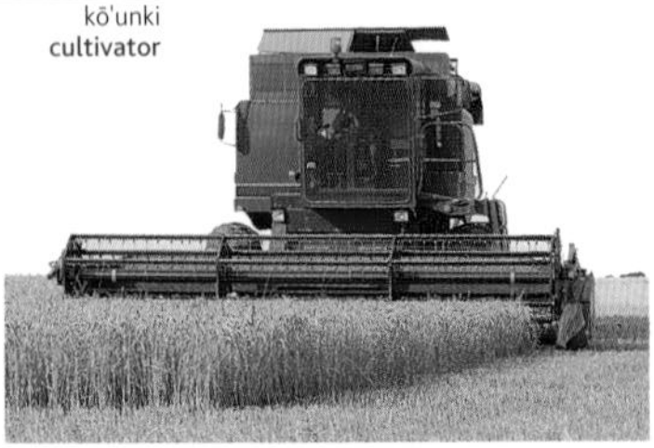

コンバイン kombain | combine harvester

農場の種類 nōjō no shurui • types of farm

作物
sakumotsu
crop

羊の群れ
hitsuji no mure
flock

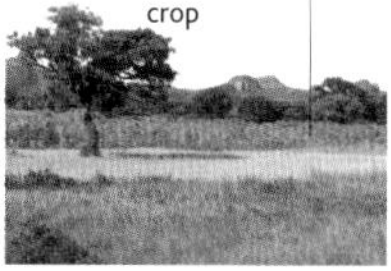

耕作農場
kōsaku nōjō
arable farm

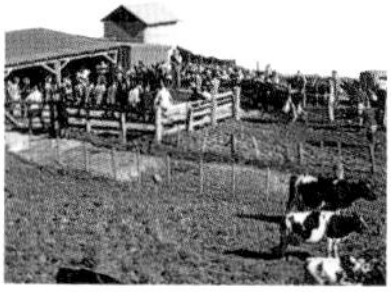

酪農場
rakunōjō
dairy farm

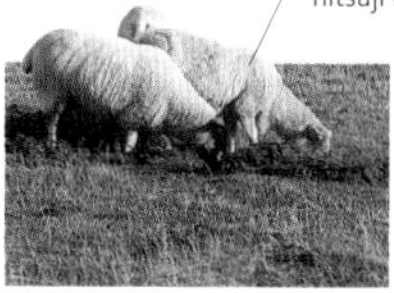

牧羊農場
bokuyō nōjō
sheep farm

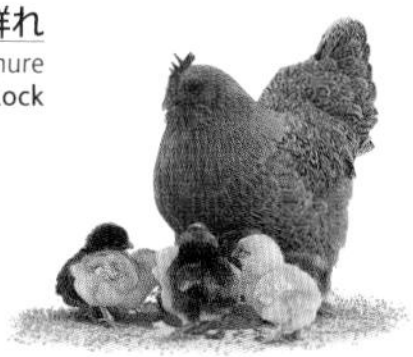

養鶏場 yōkeijō
poultry farm

葡萄の木
budō no ki
vine

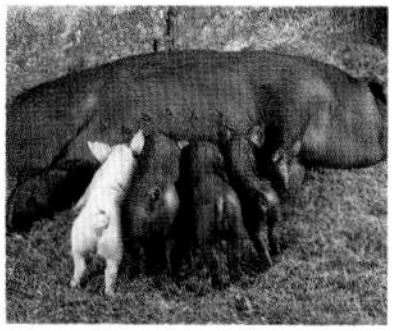

養豚場
yōtonjō
pig farm

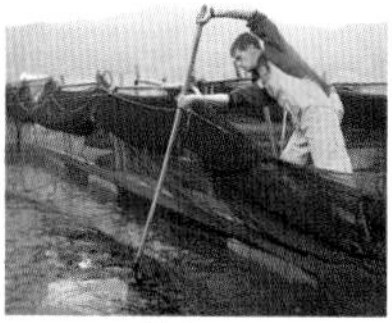

養魚場
yōgyojō
fish farm

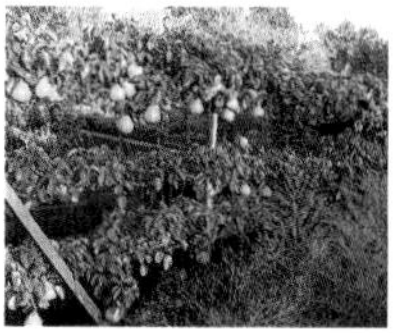

果樹園
kajuen
fruit farm

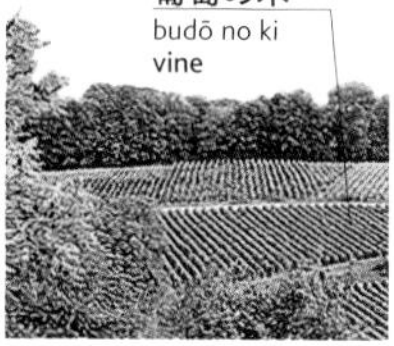

葡萄園
budōen
vineyard

業務 gyōmu • actions

畝
aze
furrow

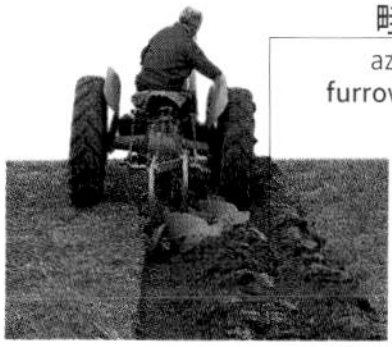

耕す
tagayasu
plough (v)

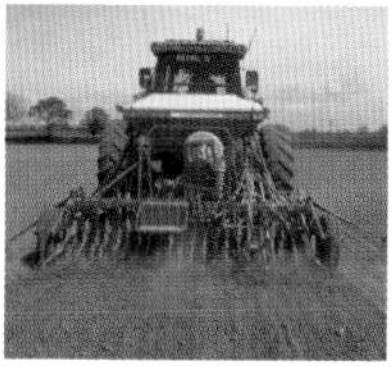

種を蒔く
tane o maku
sow (v)

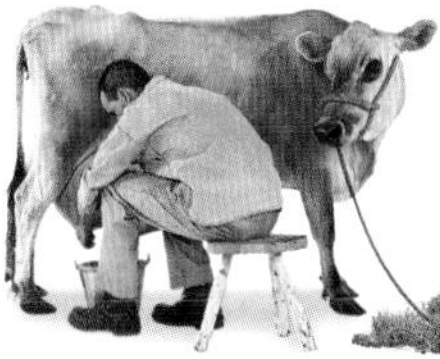

乳を搾る
chichi o shiboru
milk (v)

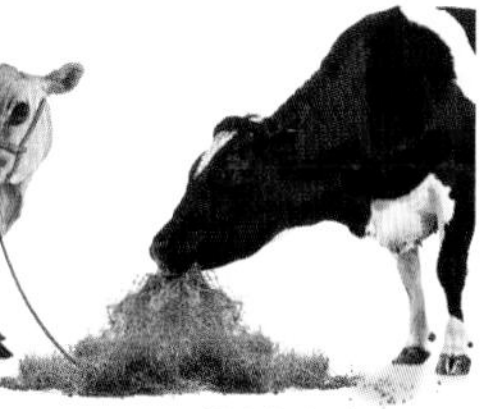

餌を与える
esa o ataeru
feed (v)

関連用語 kanrenyōgo • vocabulary

除草剤 josōzai herbicide	群れ mure herd	かいば桶 kaibaoke trough
殺虫剤 satchūzai pesticide	サイロ sairo silo	植える ueru plant (v)

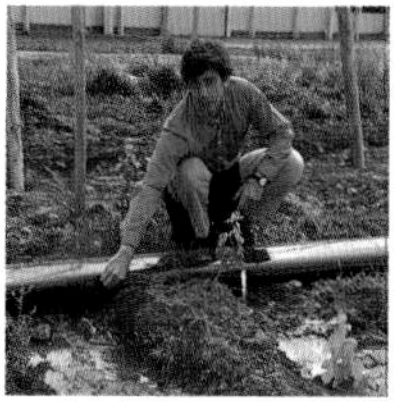

水を引く mizu o hiku
water (v)

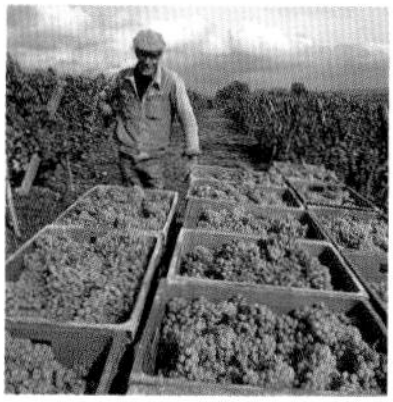

刈り入れる kari'ireru
harvest (v)

農場2 nōjō ● farm 2

作物 sakumotsu ● crops

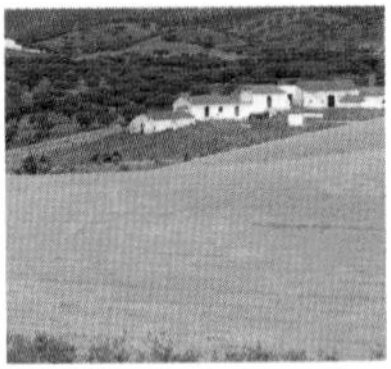

小麦
komugi
wheat

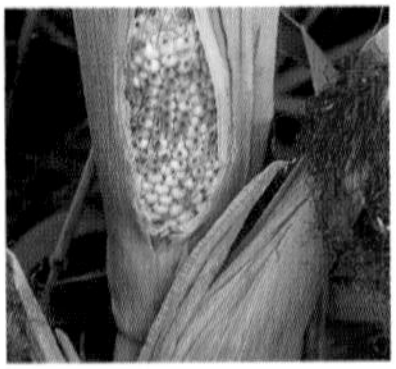

トウモロコシ
tōmorokoshi
corn

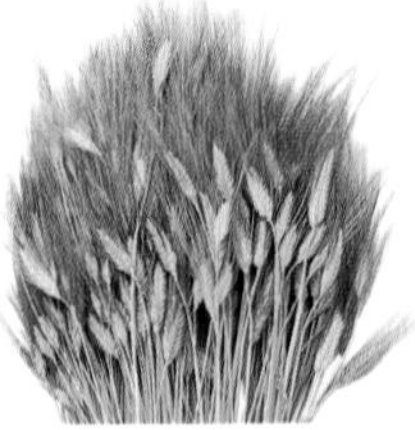

大麦
ōmugi
barley

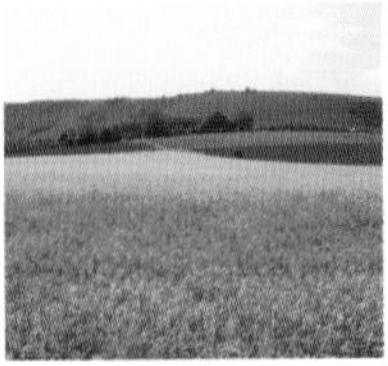

菜種
natane
rapeseed

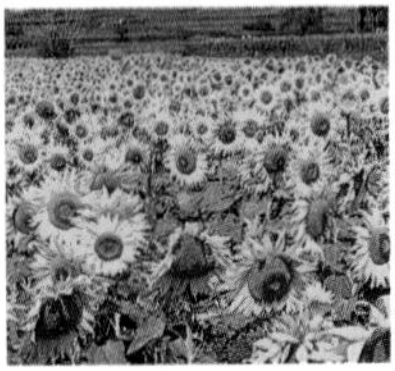

向日葵
himawari
sunflower

俵
tawara
bale

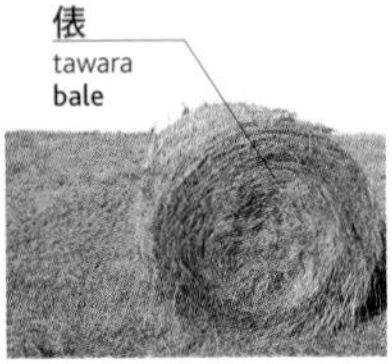

干し草
hoshikusa
hay

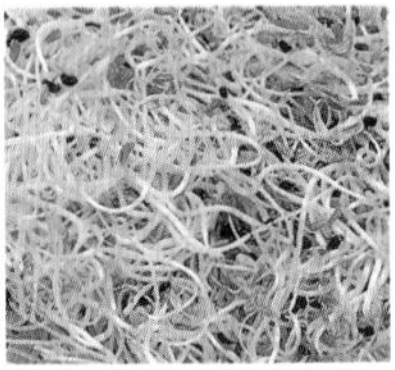

アルファルファ
arufarufa
alfalfa

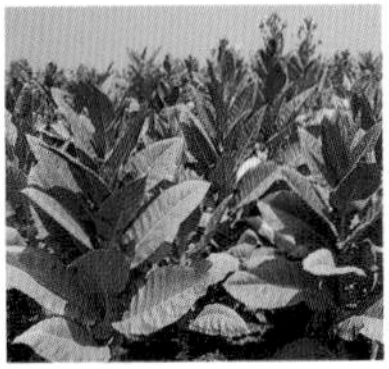

煙草
tabako
tobacco

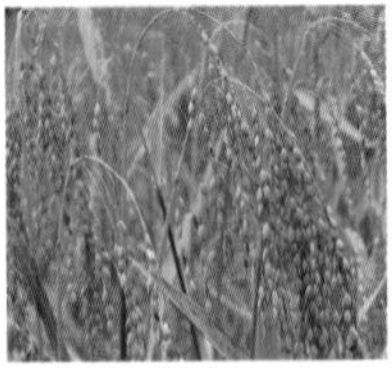

米
kome
rice

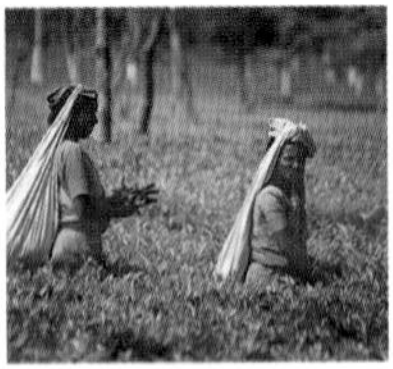

茶
cha
tea

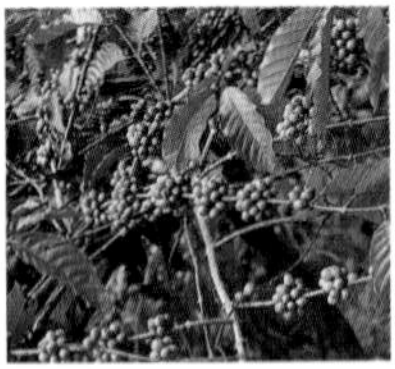

コーヒー
kōhī
coffee

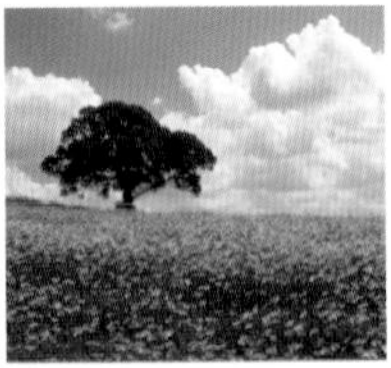

亜麻
ama
flax

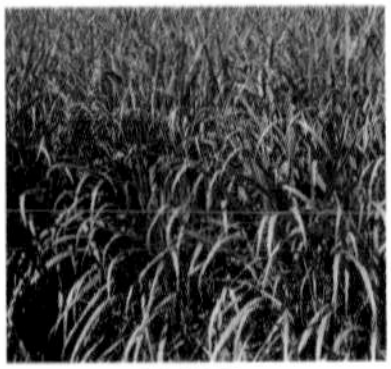

砂糖黍
satōkibi
sugarcane

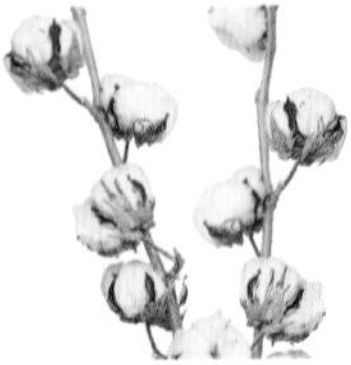

綿花
menka
cotton

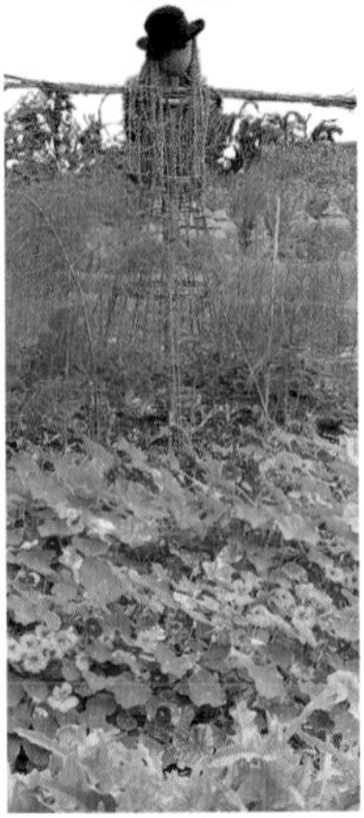

かかし
kakashi
scarecrow

家畜 kachiku • livestock

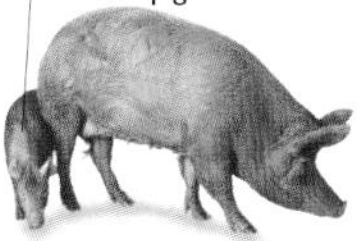

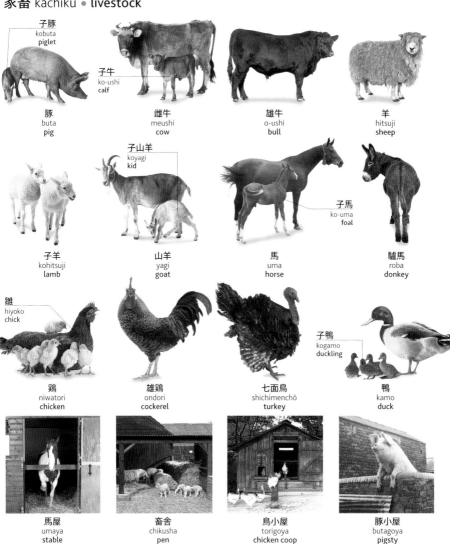

子豚
kobuta
piglet

豚
buta
pig

子牛
ko-ushi
calf

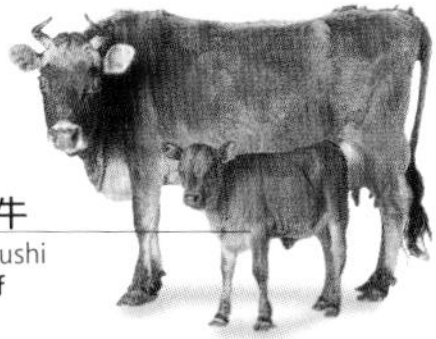

雌牛
meushi
cow

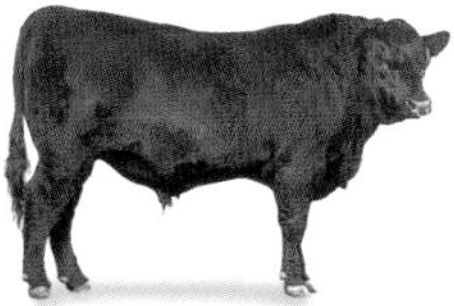

雄牛
o-ushi
bull

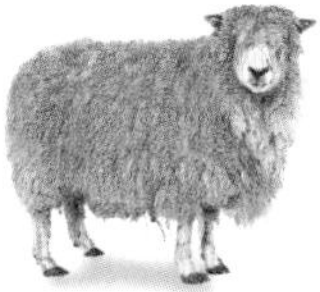

羊
hitsuji
sheep

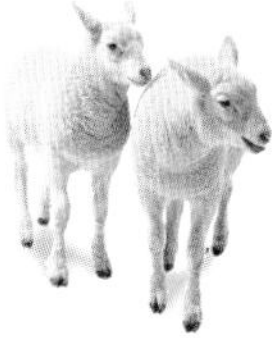

子羊
kohitsuji
lamb

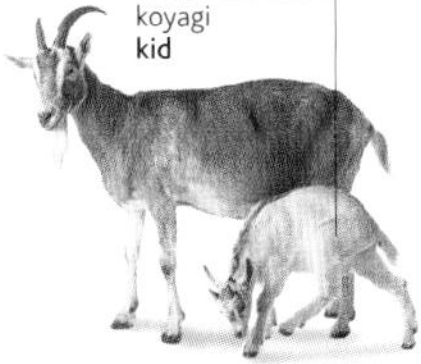

子山羊
koyagi
kid

山羊
yagi
goat

子馬
ko-uma
foal

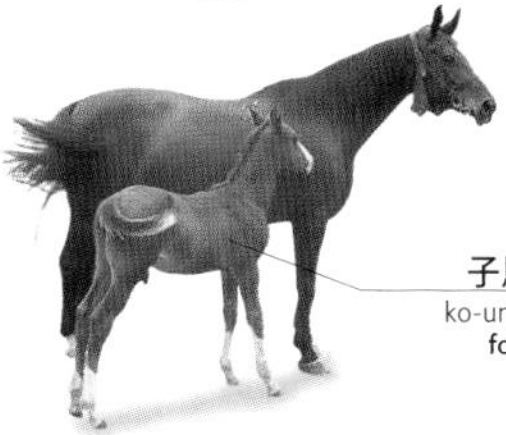

馬
uma
horse

驢馬
roba
donkey

雛
hiyoko
chick

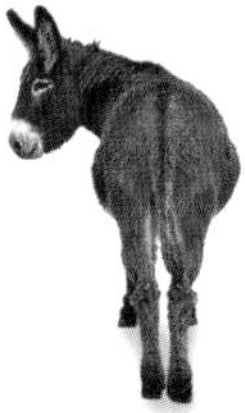

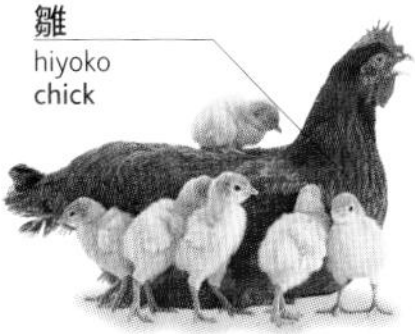

鶏
niwatori
chicken

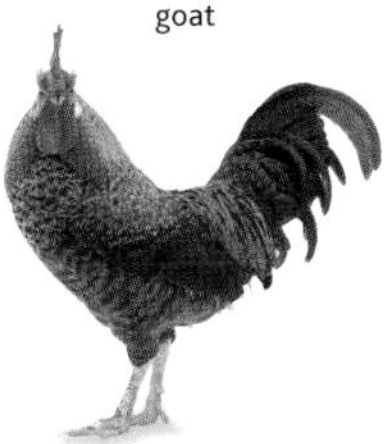

雄鶏
ondori
cockerel

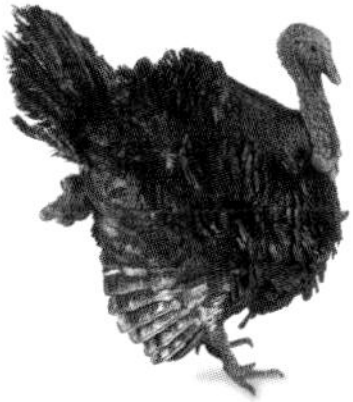

七面鳥
shichimenchō
turkey

子鴨
kogamo
duckling

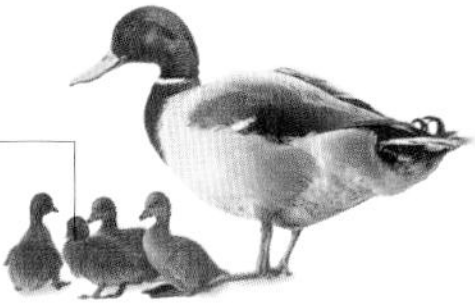

鴨
kamo
duck

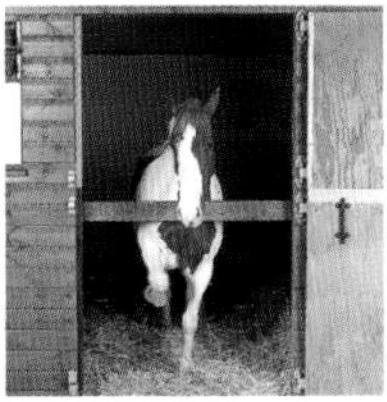

馬屋
umaya
stable

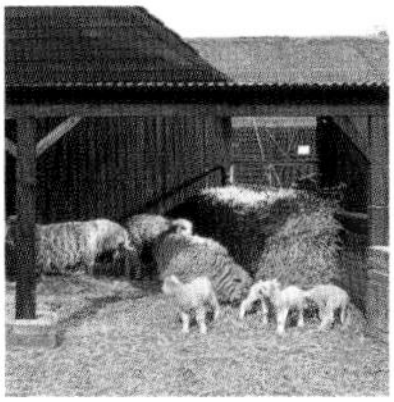

畜舎
chikusha
pen

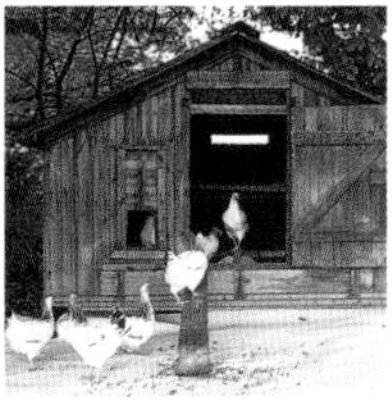

鳥小屋
torigoya
chicken coop

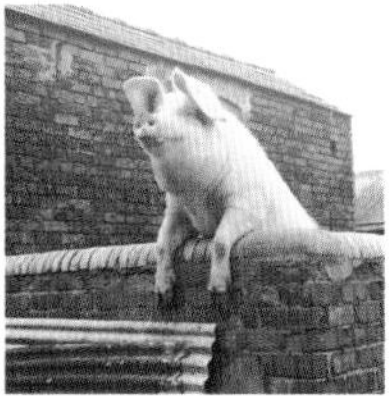

豚小屋
butagoya
pigsty

建設 kensetsu • construction

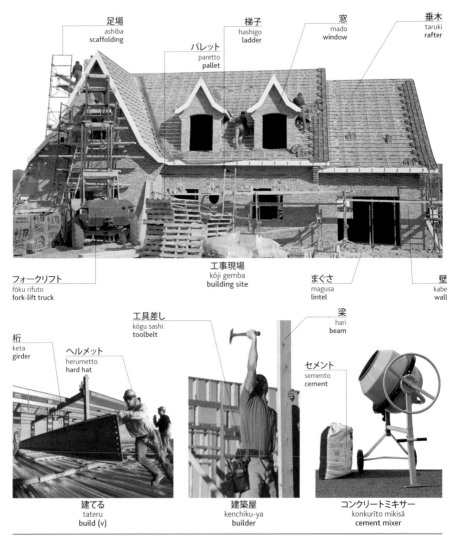

足場
ashiba
scaffolding

パレット
paretto
pallet

梯子
hashigo
ladder

窓
mado
window

垂木
taruki
rafter

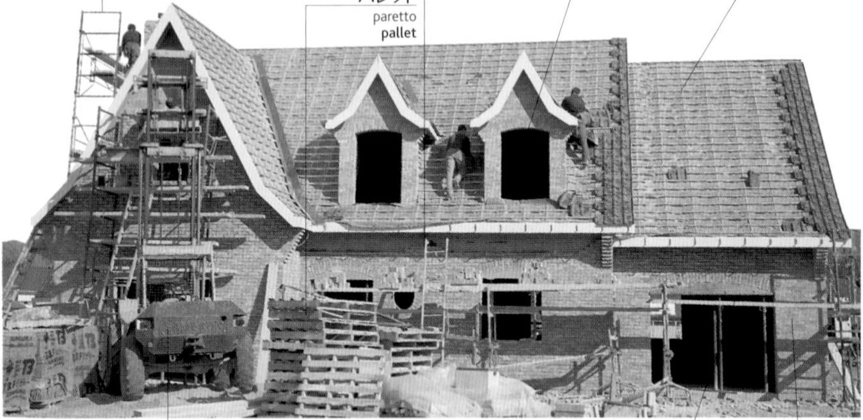

フォークリフト
fōku rifuto
fork-lift truck

工事現場
kōji gemba
building site

まぐさ
magusa
lintel

壁
kabe
wall

桁
keta
girder

ヘルメット
herumetto
hard hat

工具差し
kōgu sashi
toolbelt

梁
hari
beam

セメント
semento
cement

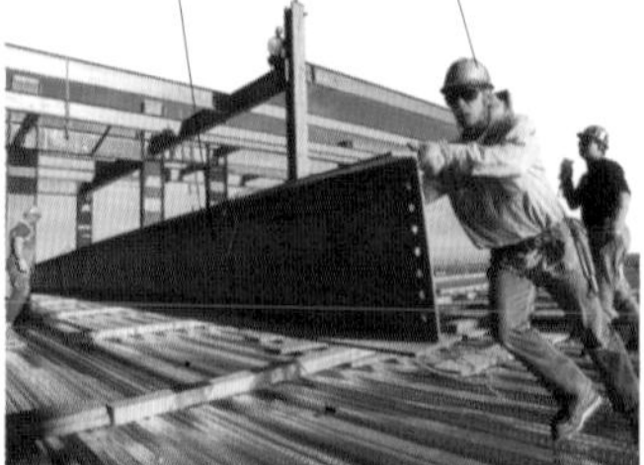

建てる
tateru
build (v)

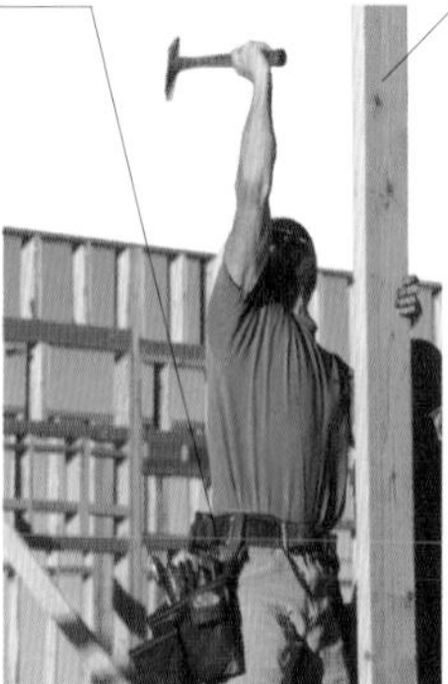

建築屋
kenchiku-ya
builder

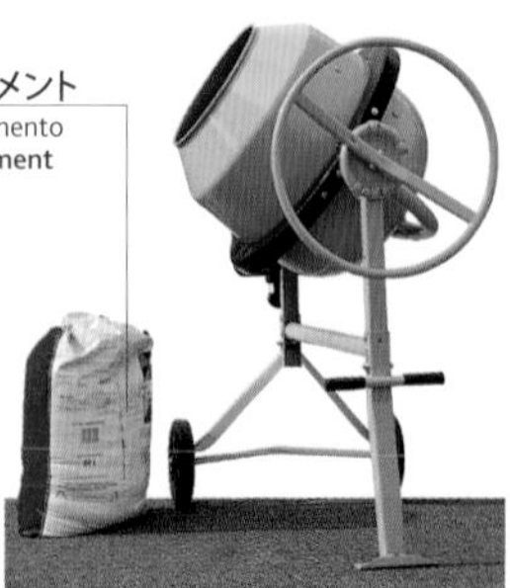

コンクリートミキサー
konkurīto mikisā
cement mixer

建築材料 kenchiku zairyō • **materials**

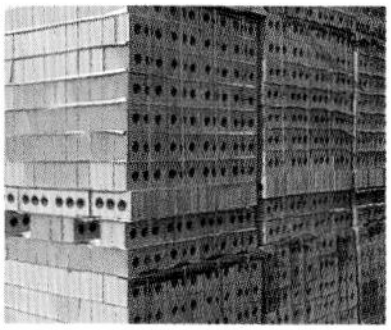

煉瓦
renga
brick

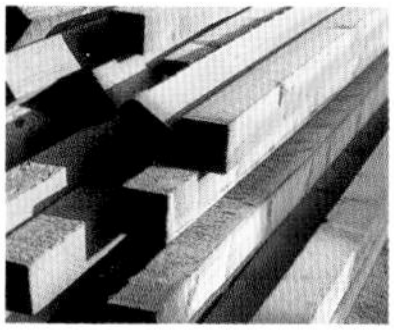

材木
zaimoku
timber

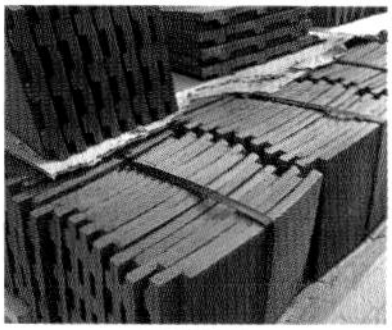

屋根瓦
yane-gawara
roof tile

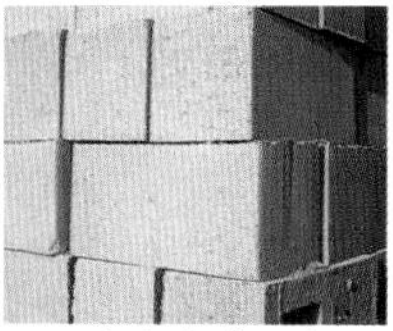

コンクリートブロック
konkurīto burokku
concrete block

道具 dōgu • **tools**

モルタル
morutaru
mortar

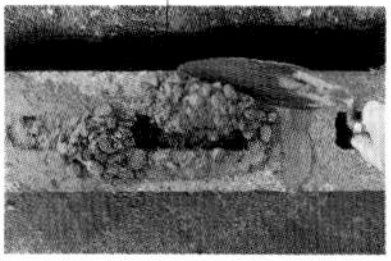

こて
kote
trowel

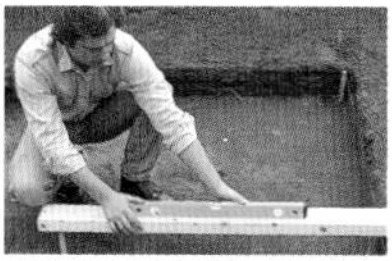

水平器
suiheiki
spirit level

柄
e
handle

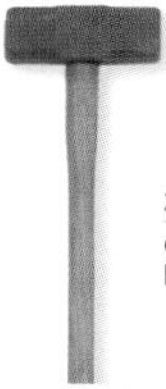

大ハンマー
ōhanmā
sledgehammer

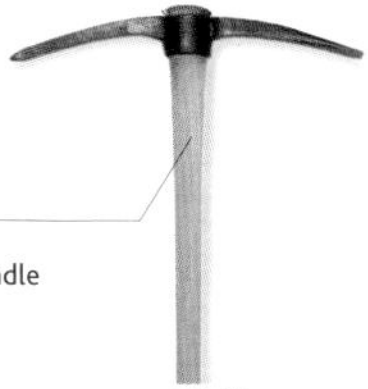

つるはし
tsuruhashi
pickaxe

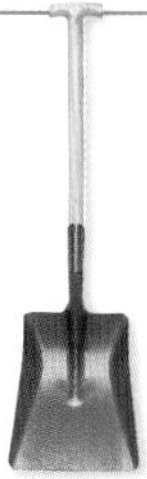

スコップ
sukoppu
shovel

機械 kikai • **machinery**

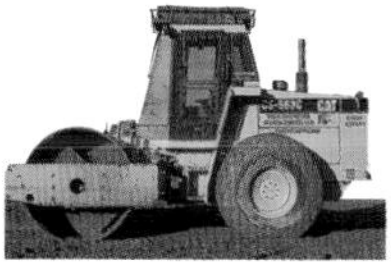

ローラー
rōrā
roller

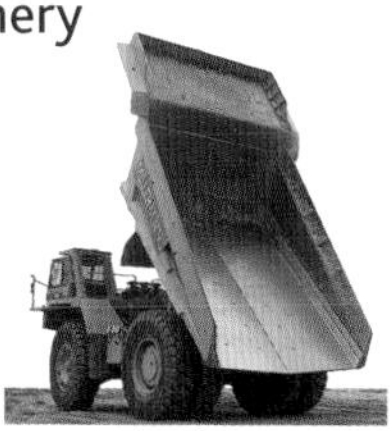

ダンプカー
dampukā
dumper truck

フック
fukku
hook

アウトリガー
autorigā
support

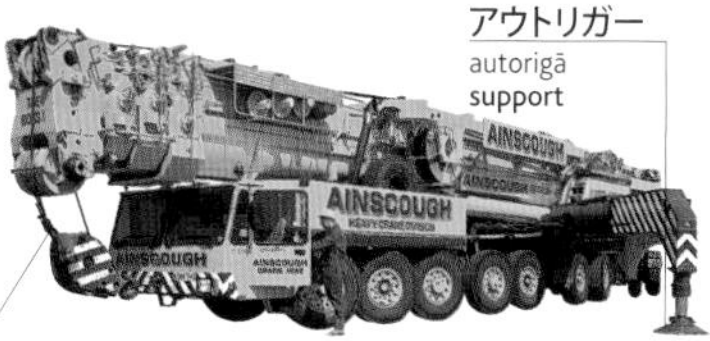

クレーン車 kurēn-sha I **crane**

道路工事 dōro kōji • **roadworks**

タールマック
tārumakku
tarmac

三角コーン
sankaku-kōn
cone

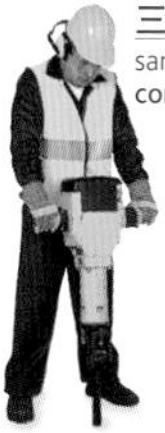

空気ドリル
kūki-doriru
pneumatic drill

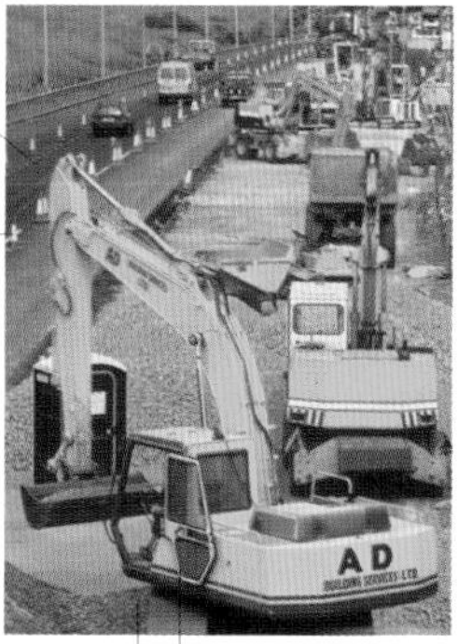

再舗装
saihosō
resurfacing

掘削機
kussakuki
mechanical digger

職業1 shokugyō • occupations 1

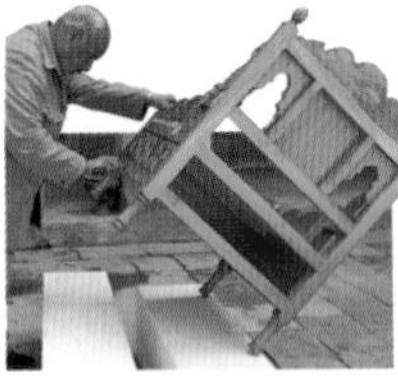

大工
daiku
carpenter

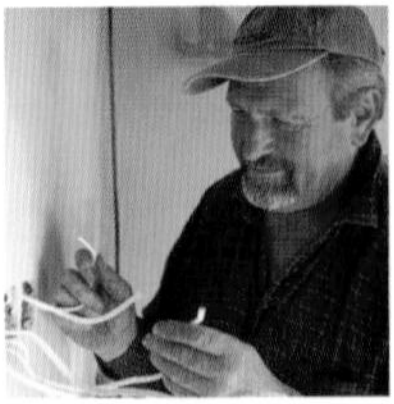

電気工
denkikō
electrician

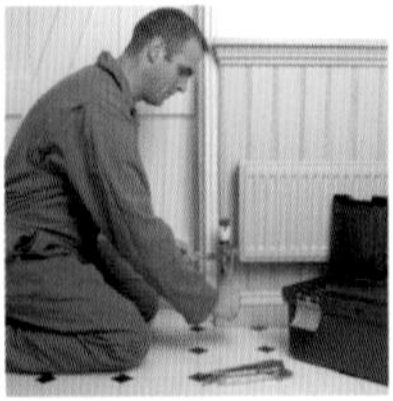

配管工
haikankō
plumber

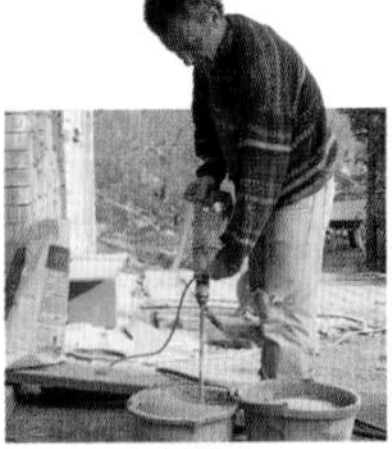

建築屋
kenchiku-ya
builder

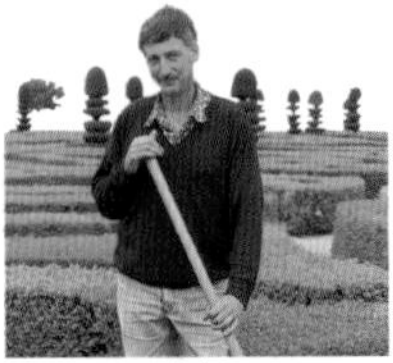

庭師
niwashi
gardener

掃除機
sōjiki
vacuum cleaner

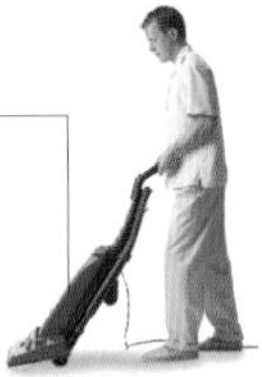

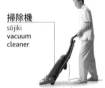

掃除夫
sōjifu
cleaner

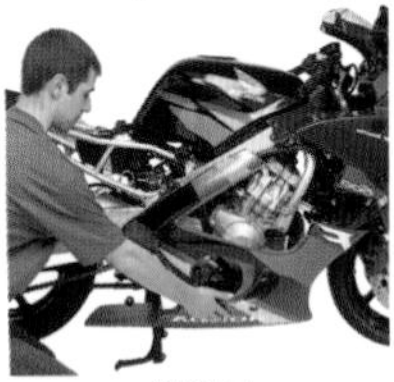

修理工
shūrikō
mechanic

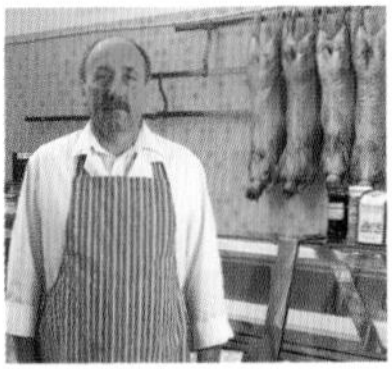

肉屋
nikuya
butcher

鋏
hasami
scissors

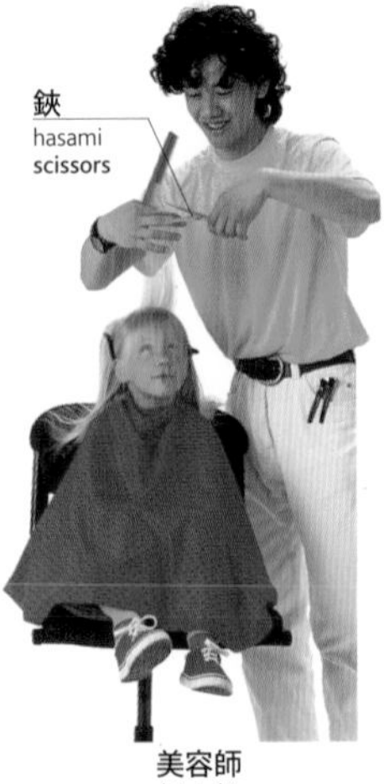

美容師
biyōshi
hairdresser

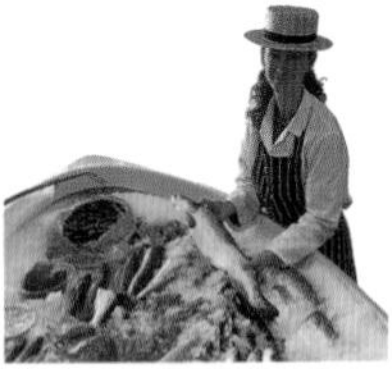

魚屋
sakanaya
fishmonger

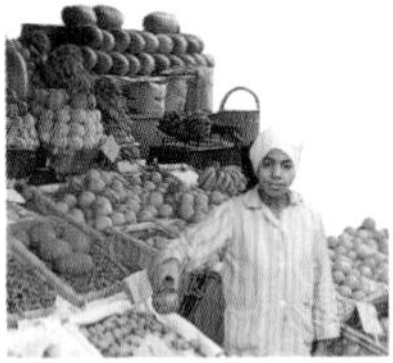

八百屋
yaoya
greengrocer

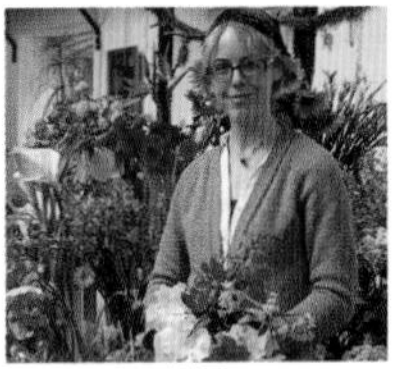

花屋
hanaya
florist

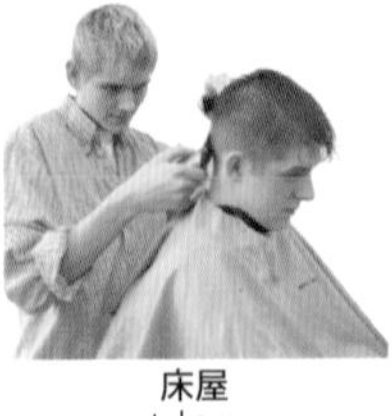

床屋
tokoya
barber

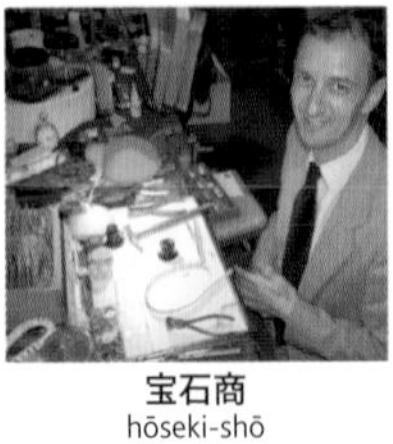

宝石商
hōseki-shō
jeweller

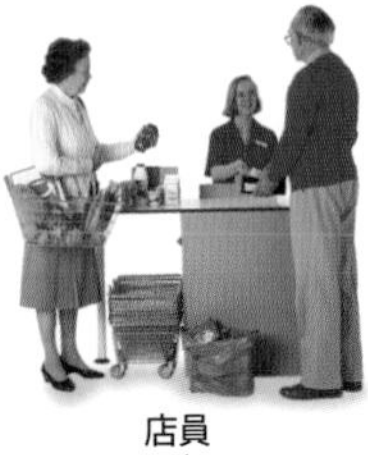

店員
ten'in
shop assistant

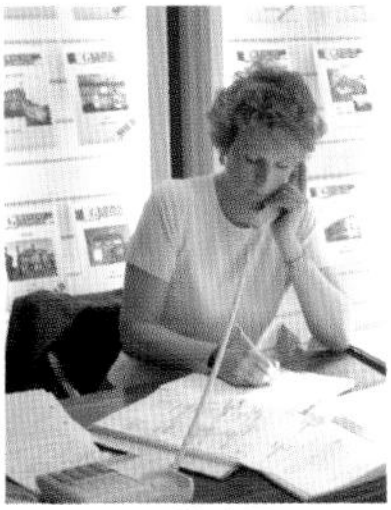

不動産屋
fudōsan-ya
estate agent

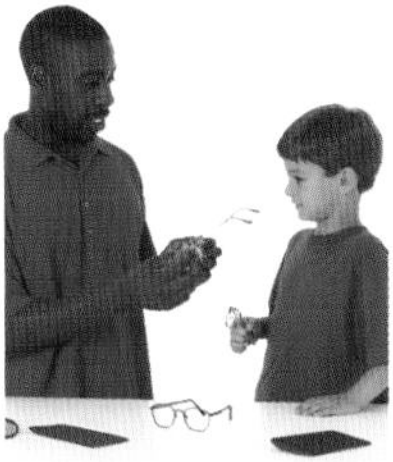

眼鏡屋
megane-ya
optician

マスク
masuku
mask

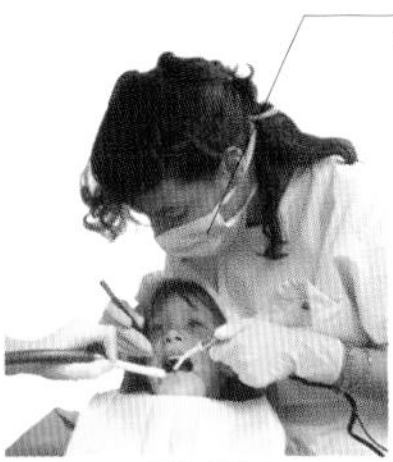

歯医者
haisha
dentist

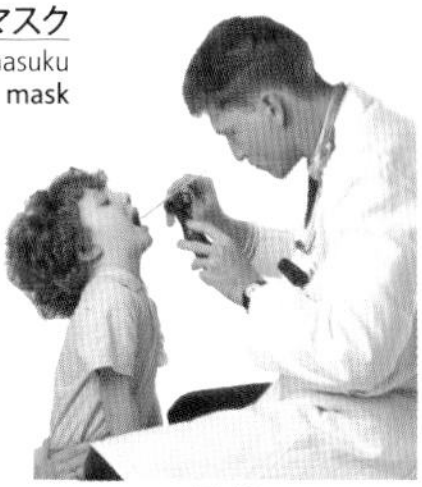

医者
isha
doctor

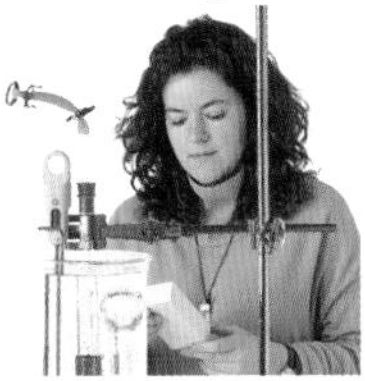

薬剤師
yakuzaishi
pharmacist

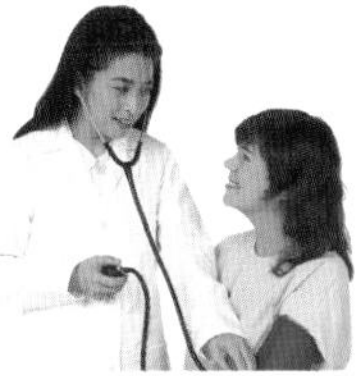

看護婦
kangofu
nurse

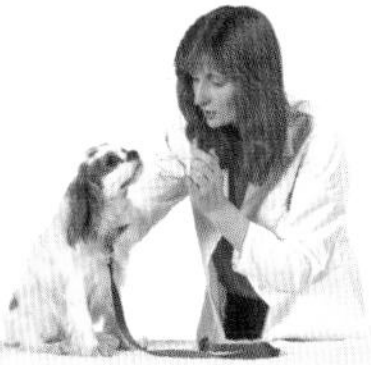

獣医
jūi
vet

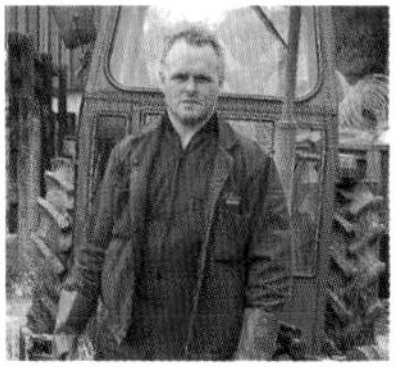

農夫
nōfu
farmer

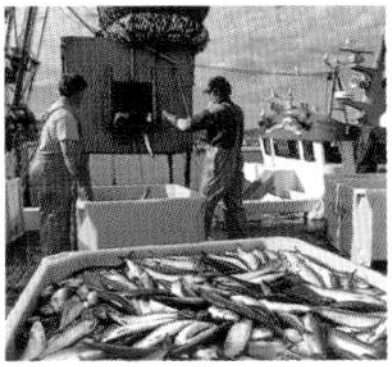

漁師
ryōshi
fisherman

マシンガン
mashin-gan
machine-gun

名札
nafuda
identity badge

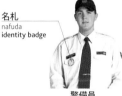

制服
seifuku
uniform

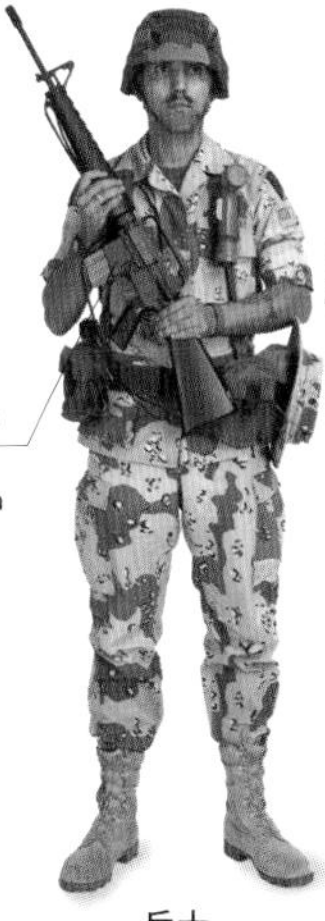

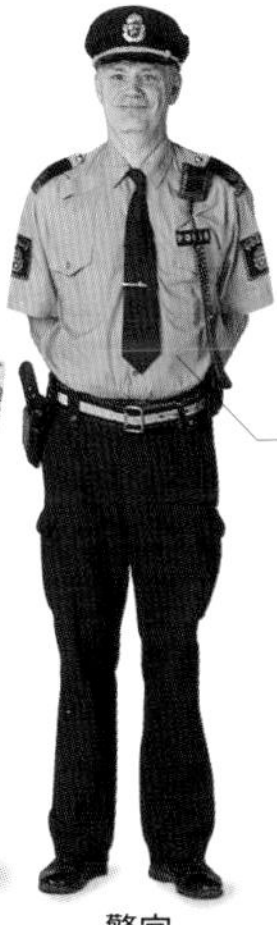

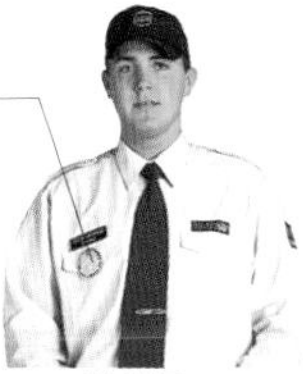

警備員
keibi'in
security guard

船員
sen'in
sailor

兵士
heishi
soldier

警官
keikan
policeman

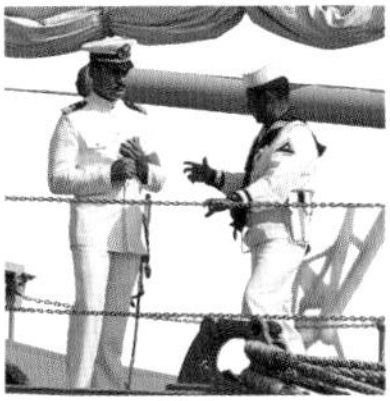

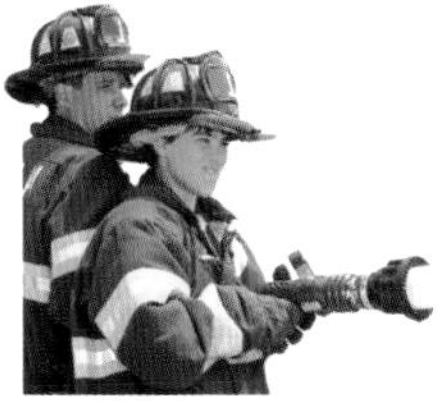

消防士
shōbōshi
fireman

職業2 shokugyō • occupations 2

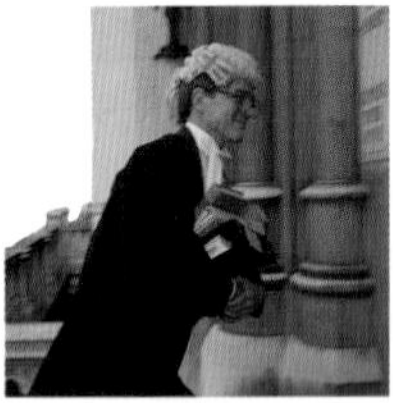

弁護士
bengoshi
lawyer

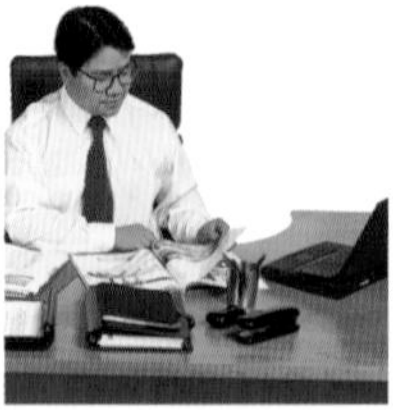

会計士
kaikeishi
accountant

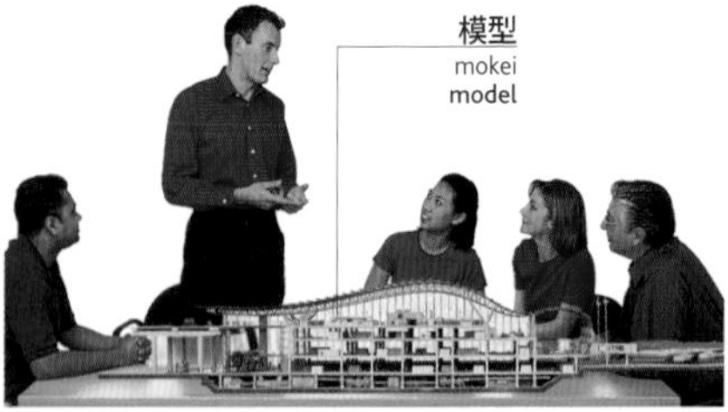

模型
mokei
model

建築家 kenchikuka I architect

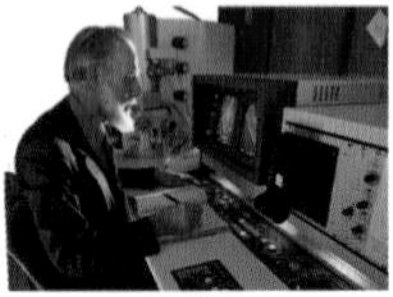

科学者
kagakusha
scientist

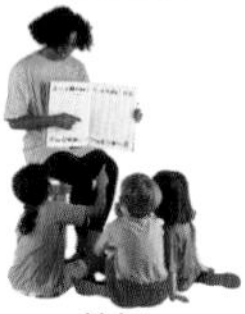

教師
kyōshi
teacher

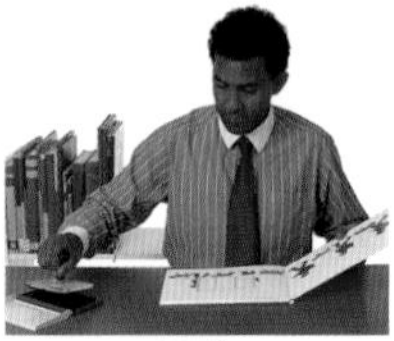

司書
shisho
librarian

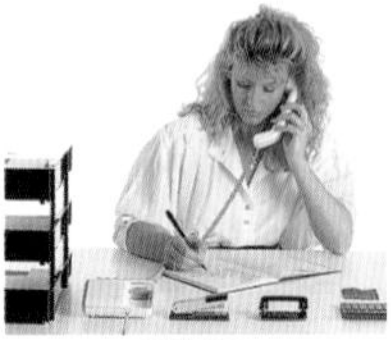

受付係
uketsuke gakari
receptionist

郵便鞄
yūbin kaban
mailbag

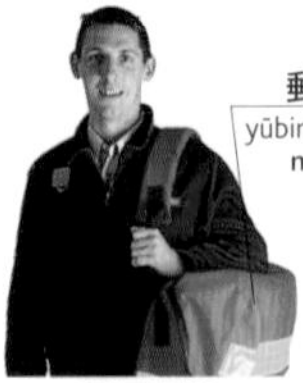

郵便配達
yūbinhaitatsu
postman

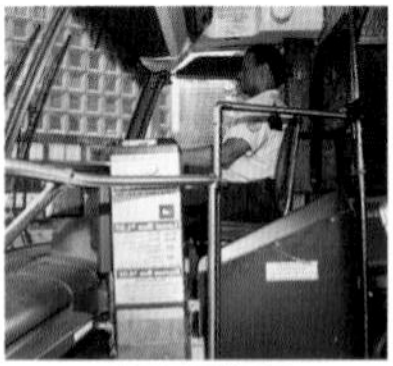

バスの運転手
basu no untenshu
bus driver

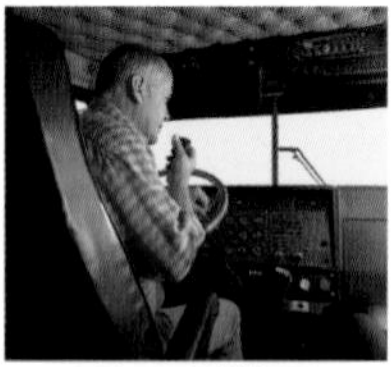

トラックの運転手
torakku no untenshu
lorry driver

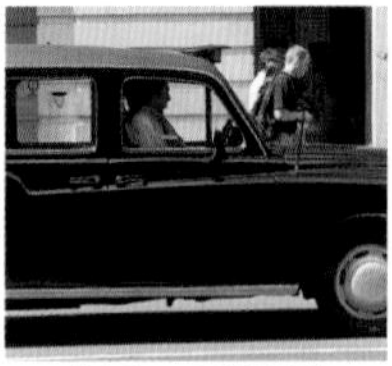

タクシーの運転手
takushī no untenshu
taxi driver

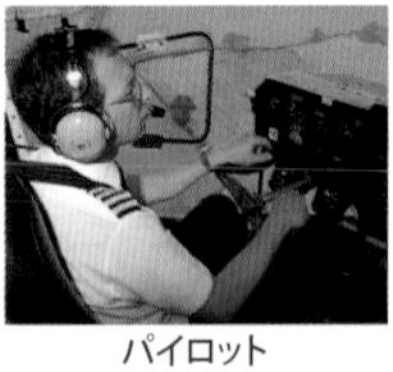

パイロット
pairotto
pilot

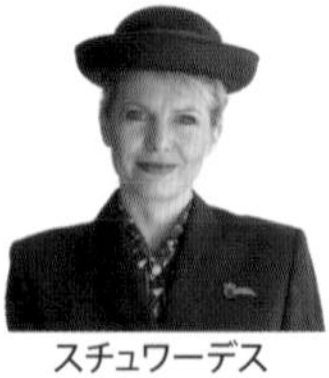

スチュワーデス
suchuwādesu
air stewardess

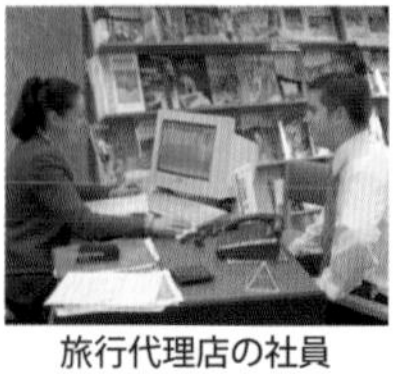

旅行代理店の社員
ryokō dairiten no shain
travel agent

シェフの帽子
shefu no bōshi
chef's hat

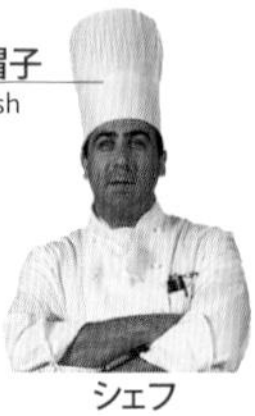

シェフ
shefu
chef

チュチュ
chuchu
tutu

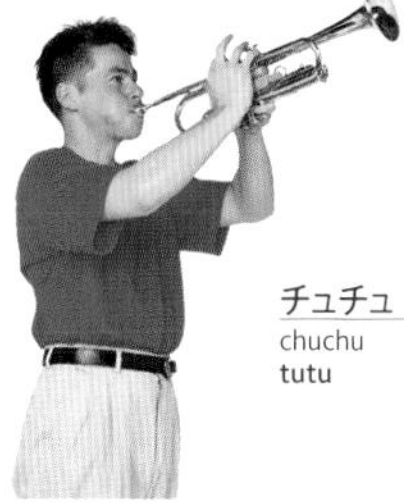

音楽家
ongakuka
musician

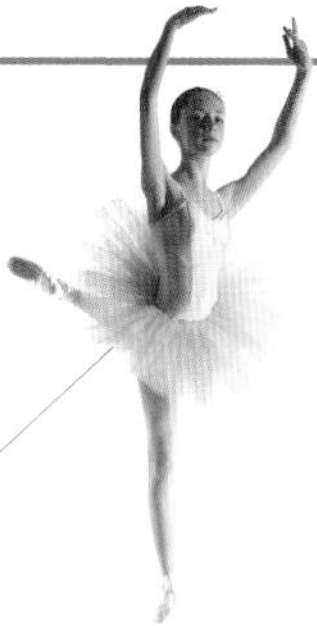

ダンサー
dansā
dancer

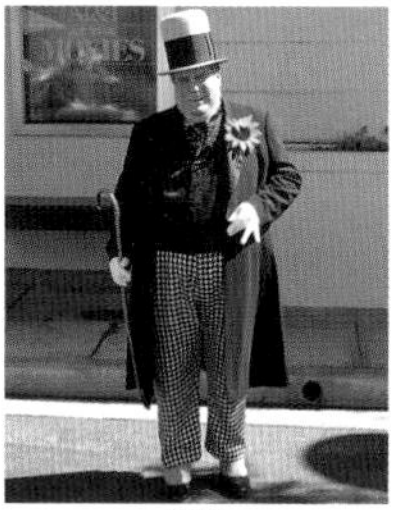

俳優
haiyū
actor

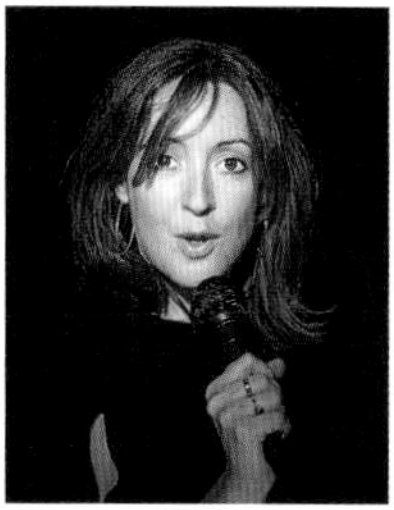

歌手
kashu
singer

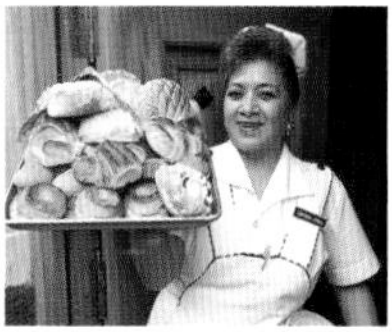

ウェイトレス
weitoresu
waitress

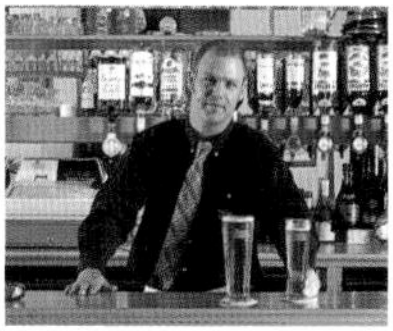

バーテン
bāten
barman

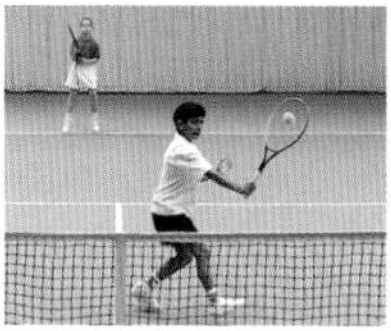

スポーツマン
supōtsuman
sportsman

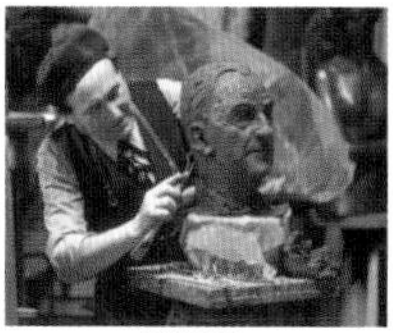

彫刻家
chōkokuka
sculptor

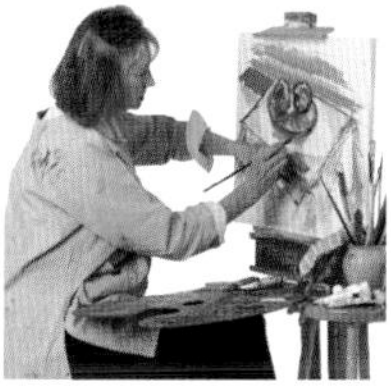

画家
gaka
painter

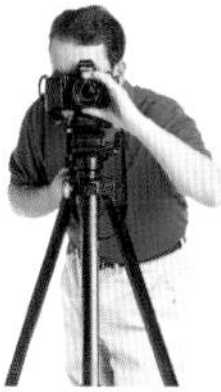

写真家
shashinka
photographer

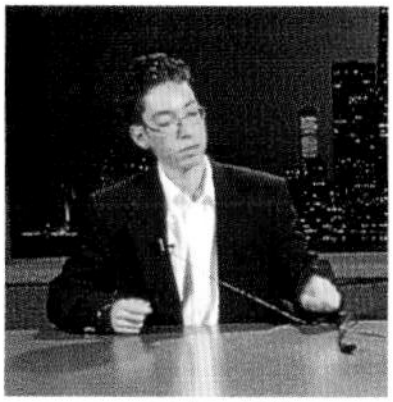

ニュースキャスター
nyūsukyasutā
newsreader

メモ
memo
notes

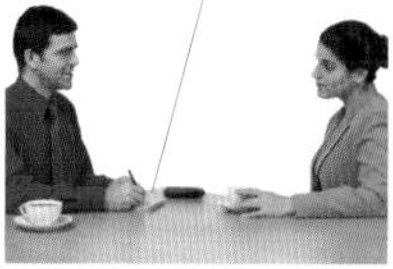

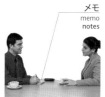

ジャーナリスト
jānarisuto
journalist

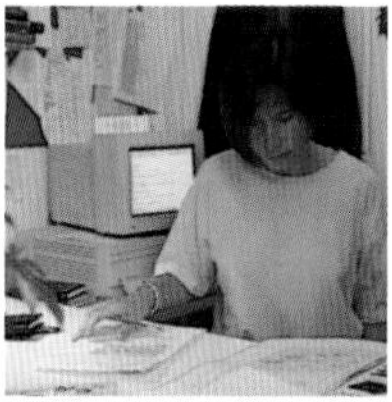

編集者
henshū-sha
editor

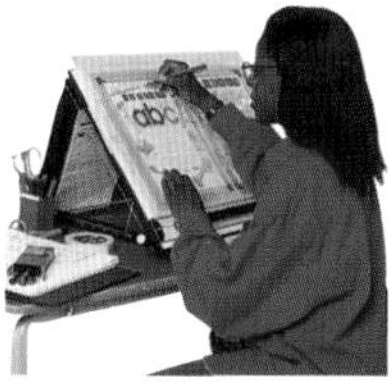

デザイナー
dezainā
designer

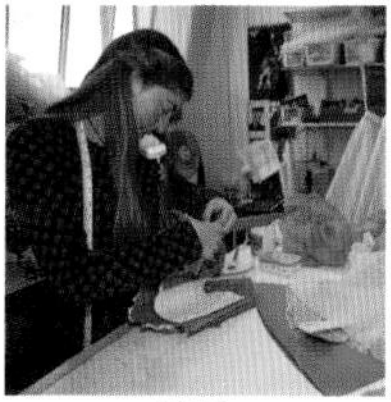

針子
hariko
seamstress

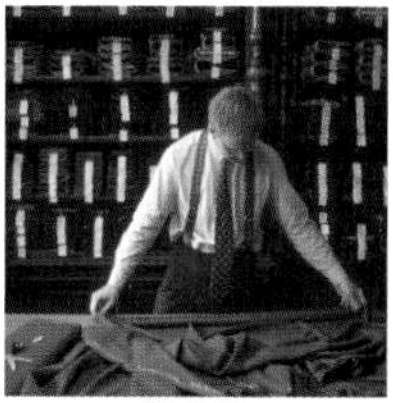

仕立屋
shitateya
tailor

交通 kōtsū
transport

道路 dōro • roads

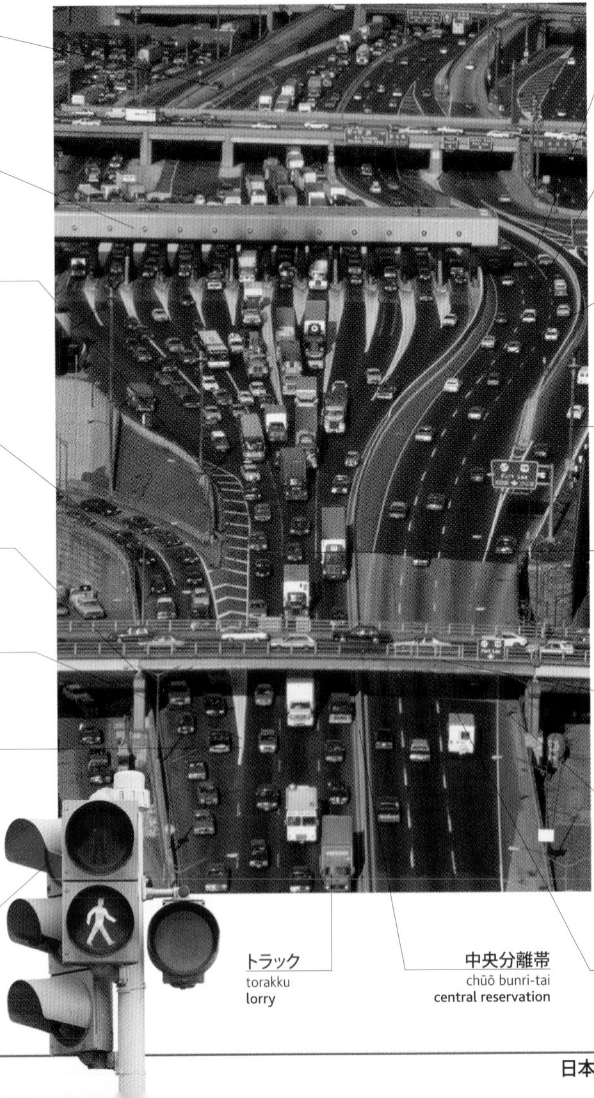

高速道路
kōsoku dōro
motorway

料金所
ryōkin-jo
toll booth

路面標識
romen hyōshiki
road markings

出入路
shutsunyū-ro
slip road

一方通行
ippōt-sūkō
one-way

分岐帯
bunki-tai
divider

ジャンクション
jankushon
junction

信号
shingō
traffic light

走行車線
sōkō shasen
inside lane

中央車線
chūō shasen
middle lane

追い越し車線
oikoshi shasen
outside lane

出口ランプ
deguchi rampu
exit ramp

交通
kōtsū
traffic

高架道路
kōka dōro
flyover

路肩
rokata
hard shoulder

トラック
torakku
lorry

中央分離帯
chūō bunri-tai
central reservation

ガード下通路
gādo shita tsūro
underpass

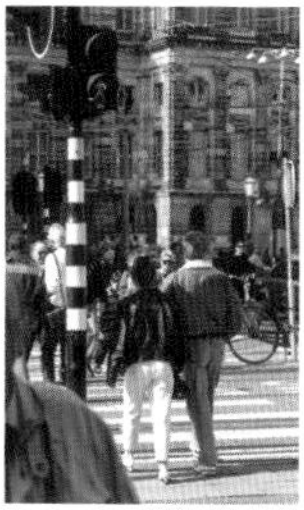

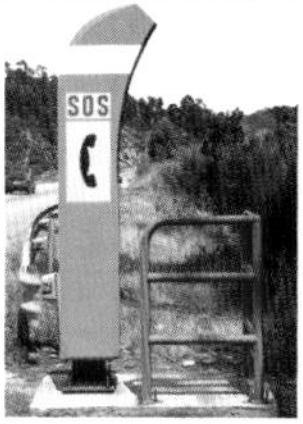

緊急電話
kinkyū denwa
emergency phone

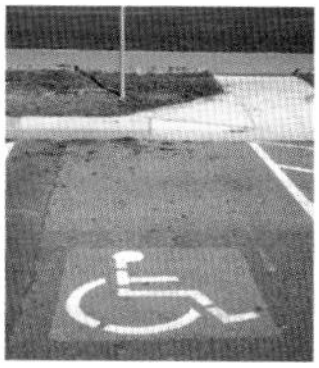

身体障害者用駐車スペース
shintaishōgaisha-yō
chūsha supēsu
disabled parking

横断歩道
ōdan hodō
pedestrian crossing

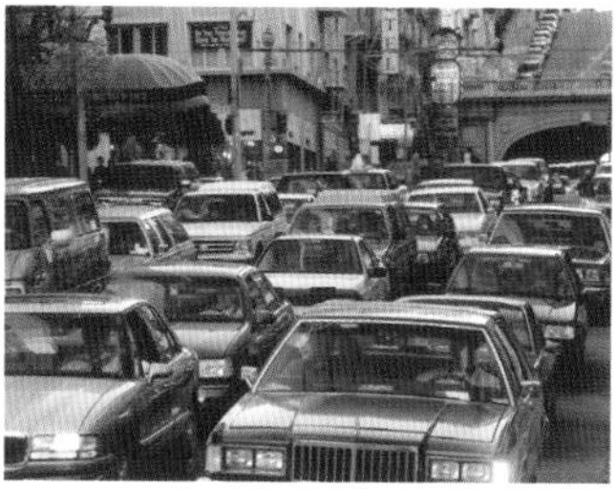

交通渋滞
kōtsū jūtai
traffic jam

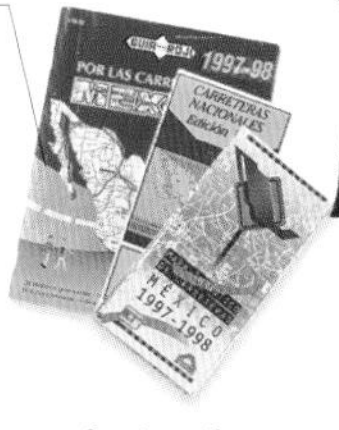

地図
chizu
map

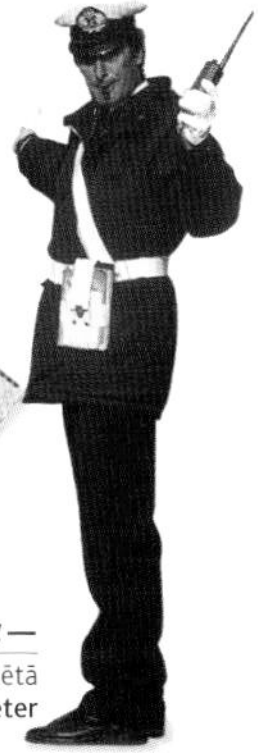

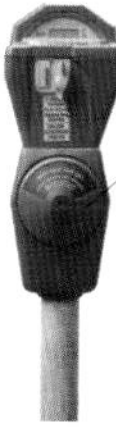

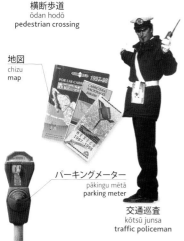

パーキングメーター
pākingu mētā
parking meter

交通巡査
kōtsū junsa
traffic policeman

関連用語 kanrenyōgo • vocabulary

環状交差点
kanjō kōsaten
roundabout

往復分離道路
ōfuku bunri dōro
dual
carriageway

追い越す
oikosu
overtake (v)

迂回路
ukairo
diversion

駐車する
chūsha suru
park (v)

レッカー移動
rekkā idō
tow away (v)

道路工事
dōro kōji
roadworks

運転する
unten suru
drive (v)

これは...へ行く道ですか。
kore wa ... e iku
michi desuka?
Is this the road to...?

ガードレール
gādo rēru
crash barrier

バックする
bakku suru
reverse (v)

どこに駐車できますか。
dokoni chūsha dekimasuka?
Where can I park?

道路標識 dōro hyōshiki • road signs

進入禁止
shinnyū kinshi
no entry

制限速度
seigen sokudo
speed limit

危険
kiken
hazard

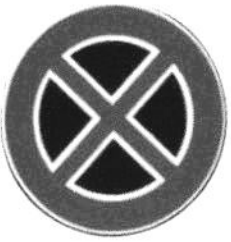

停車禁止
teisha kinshi
no stopping

右折禁止
jusetsu kinshi
no right turn

バス basu • bus

運転席
unten seki
driver's seat

手摺
tesuri
handrail

自動ドア
jidō doa
automatic door

前輪
zenrin
front wheel

トランクルーム
toranku rūmu
luggage hold

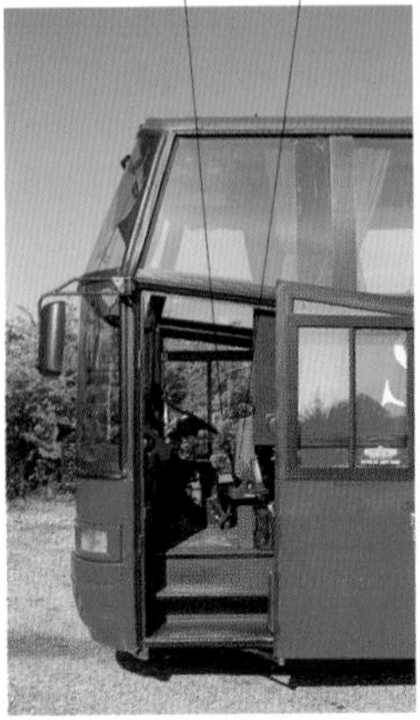

ドア doa **I door**

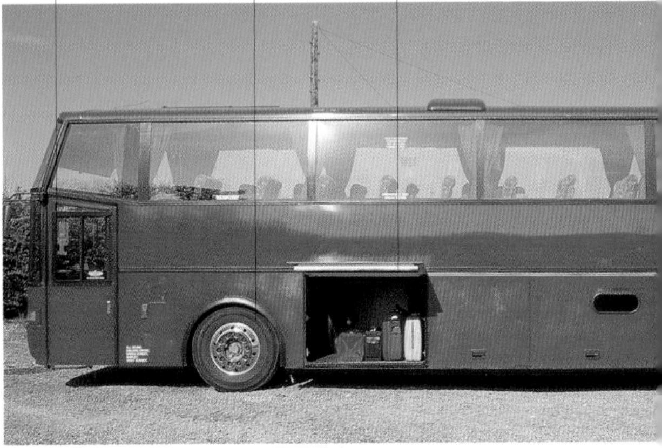

長距離バス chōkyori basu **I coach**

バスの種類 basu no shurui • types of buses

路線番号
rosen bangō
route number

運転手
untenshu
driver

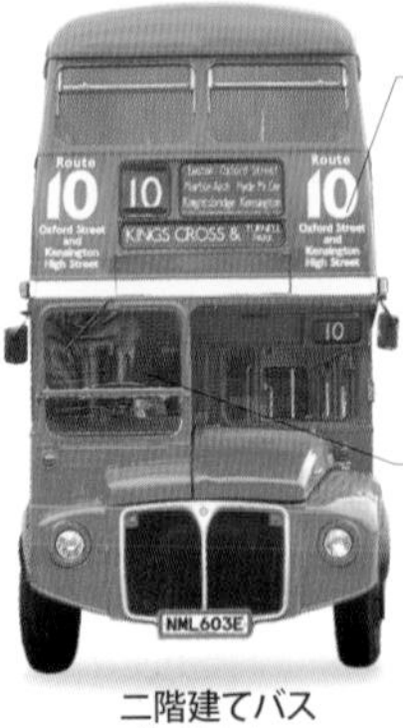

二階建てバス
nikaidate basu
double-decker bus

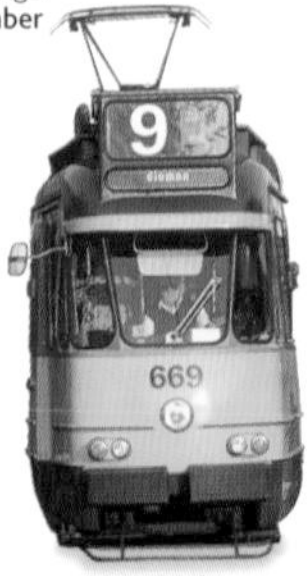

路面電車
romen densha
tram

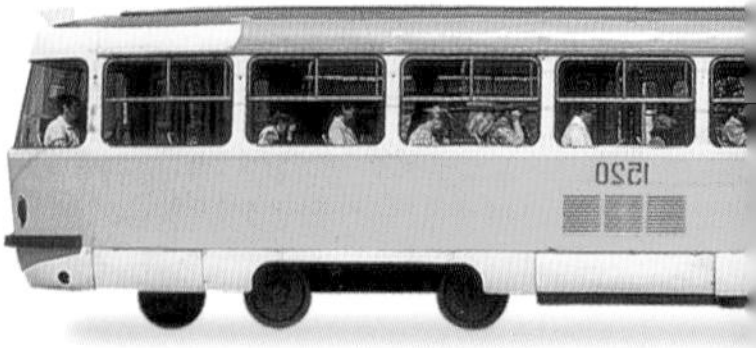

トロリーバス
tororī basu
trolley bus

スクールバス sukūru basu **I school bus**

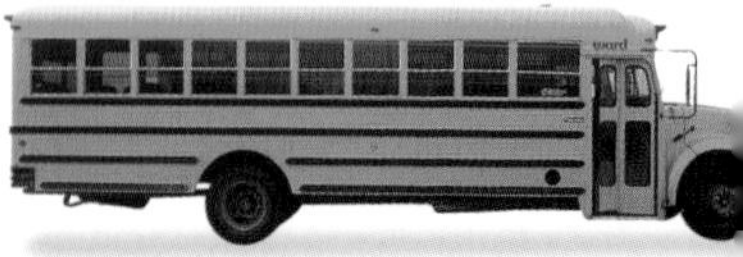

後輪
kōrin
rear wheel

窓
mado
window

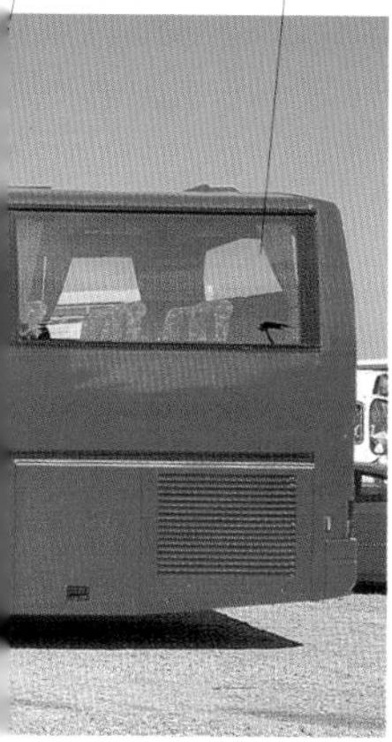

停車ボタン
teisha botan
stop button

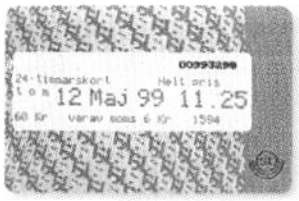

乗車券
jōshaken
bus ticket

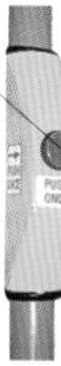

ベル
beru
bell

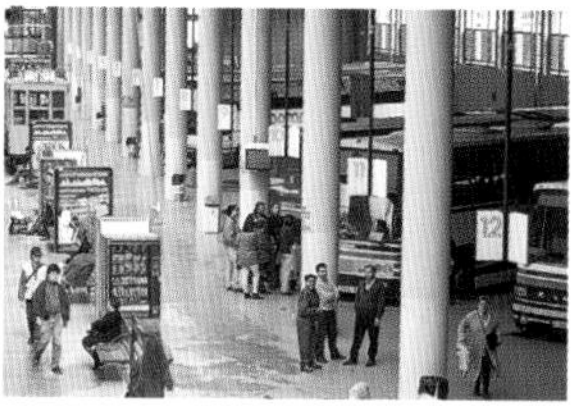

バスターミナル
basu tāminaru
bus station

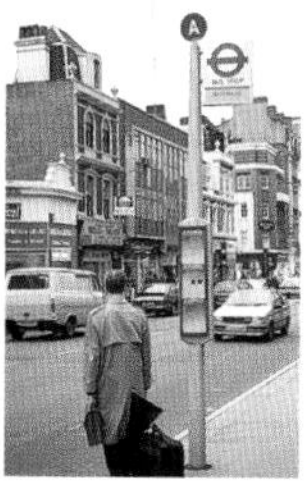

バス停
basu-tei
bus stop

関連用語 kanrenyōgo · vocabulary

料金 ryōkin fare	車椅子対応 kurumaisu taiō wheelchair access
時刻表 jikokuhyō timetable	バス待合所 basu machiai-jo bus shelter

...で停まりますか。
... de tomarimasuka?
Do you stop at...?

...へ行くのは、どのバスですか。
... e ikunowa dono basu desuka?
Which bus goes to...?

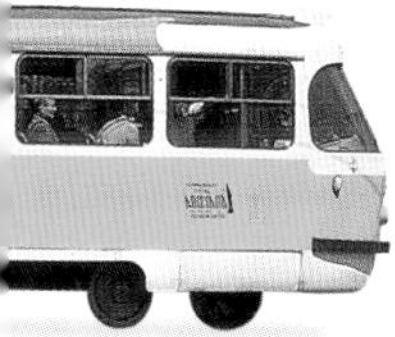

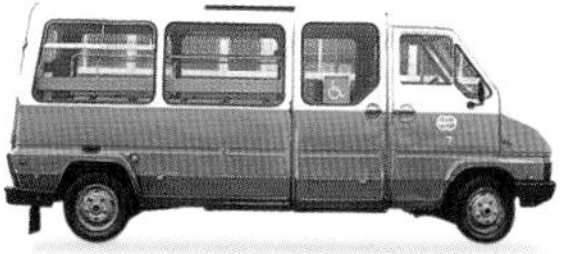

マイクロバス
maikuro basu
minibus

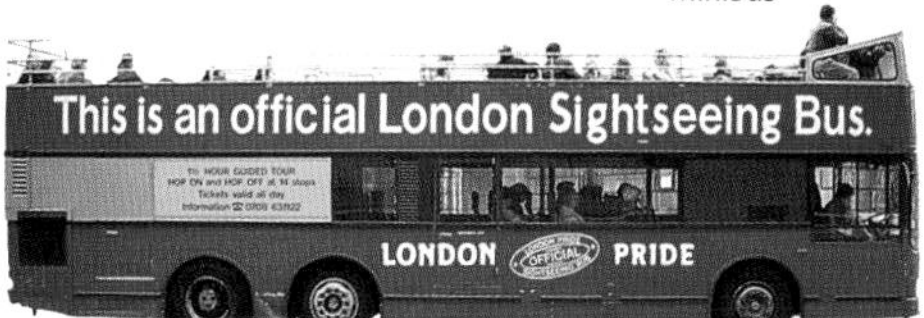

観光バス kankō basu | tourist bus

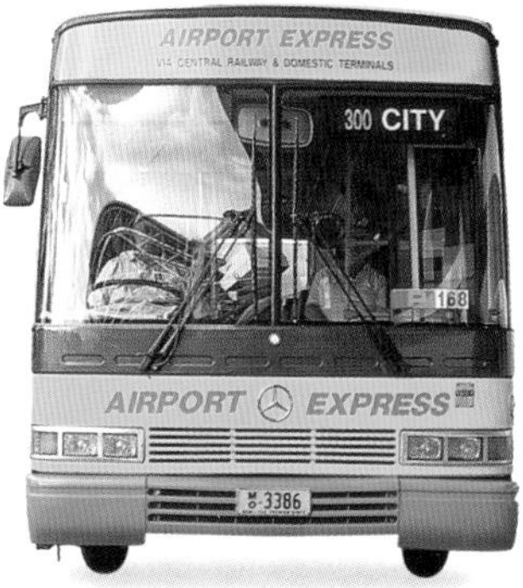

シャトルバス shatoru basu | shuttle bus

自動車1 jidōsha • car 1

外装 gaisō • exterior

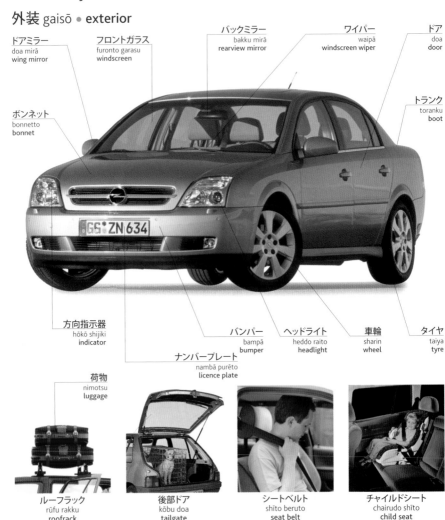

ドアミラー
doa mirā
wing mirror

フロントガラス
furonto garasu
windscreen

バックミラー
bakku mirā
rearview mirror

ワイパー
waipā
windscreen wiper

ドア
doa
door

ボンネット
bonnetto
bonnet

トランク
toranku
boot

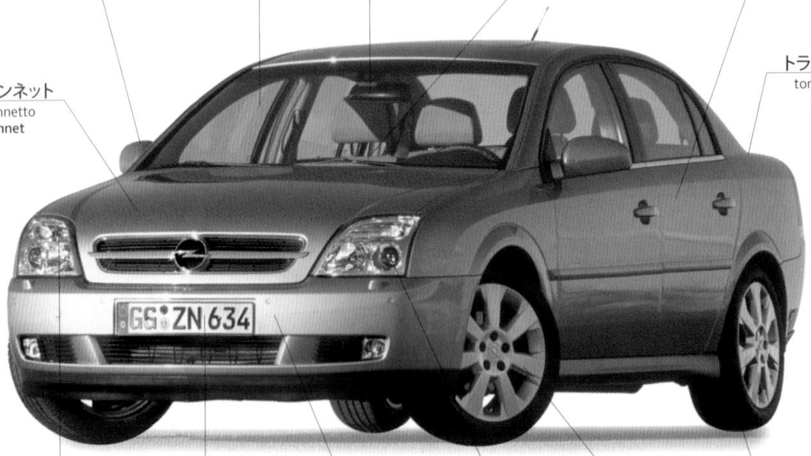

方向指示器
hōkō shijiki
indicator

バンパー
bampā
bumper

ヘッドライト
heddo raito
headlight

車輪
sharin
wheel

タイヤ
taiya
tyre

ナンバープレート
nambā purēto
licence plate

荷物
nimotsu
luggage

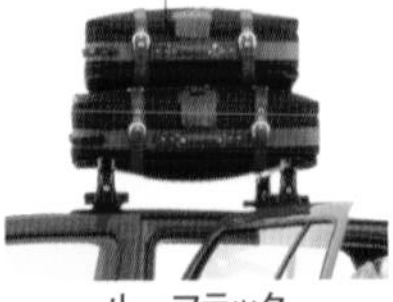

ルーフラック
rūfu rakku
roofrack

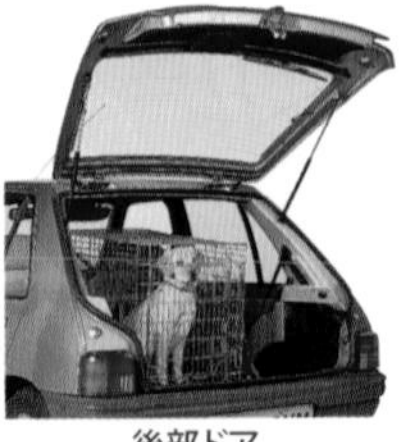

後部ドア
kōbu doa
tailgate

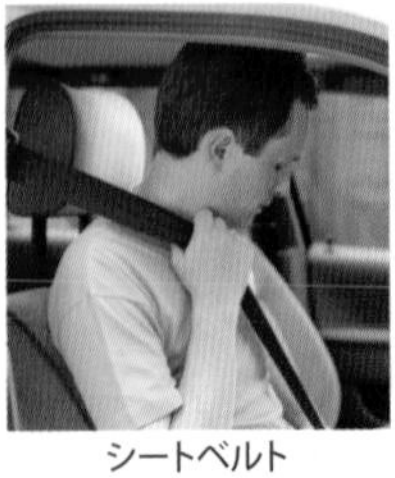

シートベルト
shīto beruto
seat belt

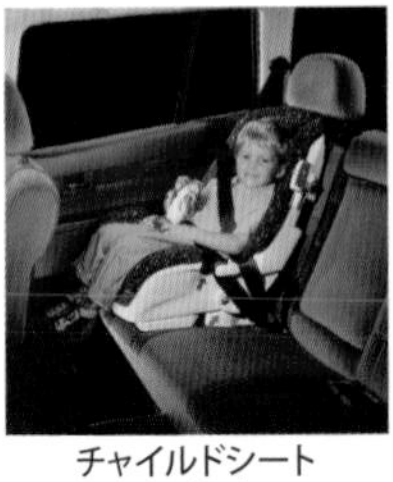

チャイルドシート
chairudo shīto
child seat

車の種類 kuruma no shurui・types

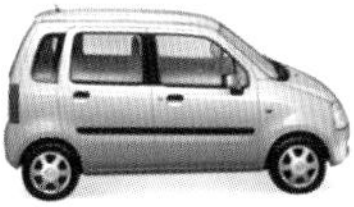

コンパクトカー
kompakuto kā
small car

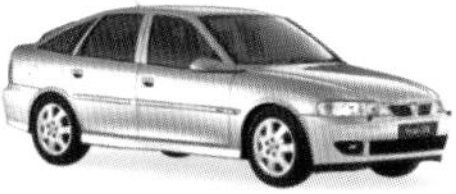

ハッチバック
hatchibakku
hatchback

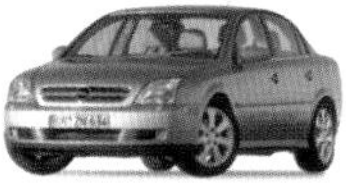

セダン
sedan
saloon

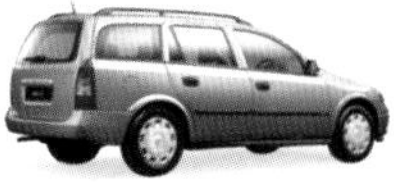

ステーションワゴン
sutēshonwagon
estate

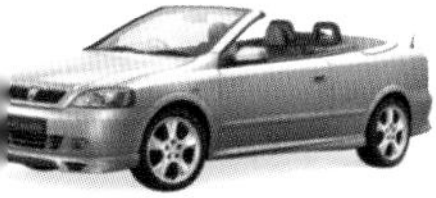

オープンカー
ōpun kā
convertible

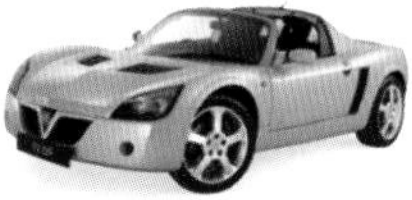

スポーツカー
supōtsu kā
sports car

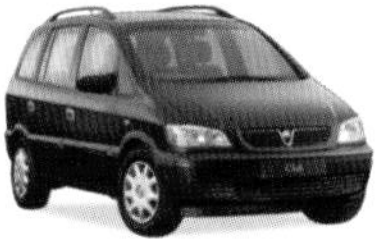

ワンボックスカー
wambokkusu kā
people carrier

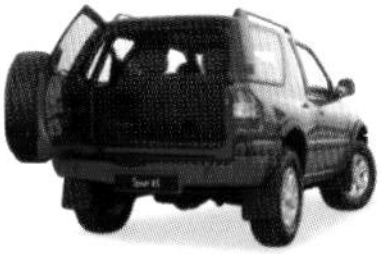

四輪駆動車
yonrin kudōsha
four-wheel drive

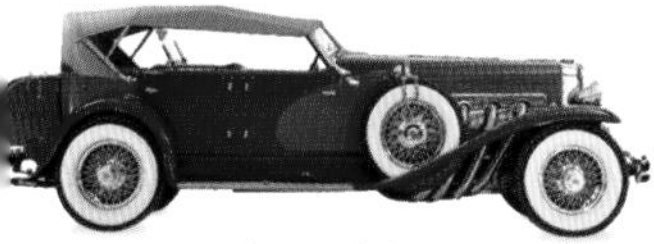

クラシックカー
kurashikku kā
vintage

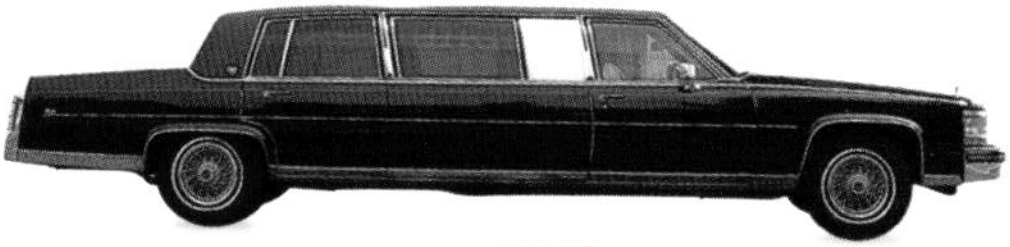

リムジン
rimujin
limousine

ガソリンスタンド gasorin sutando・petrol station

ガソリンポンプ
gasorin pompu
petrol pump

価格
kakaku
price

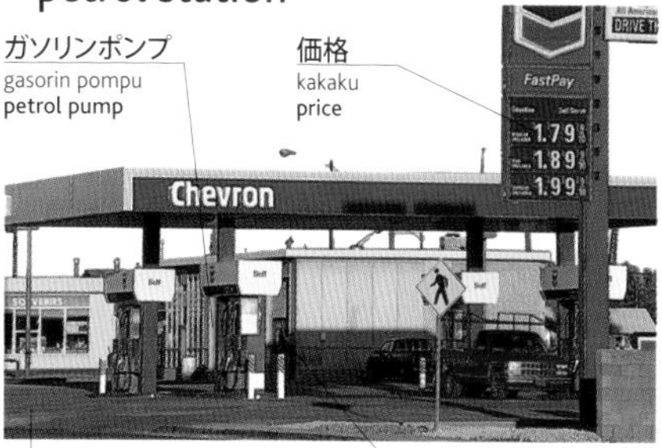

給油場
kyūyujō
forecourt

給気装置
kyūki sōchi
air supply

関連用語 kanrenyōgo・vocabulary

オイル oiru oil	**有鉛** yūen leaded	**洗車** sensha car wash
ガソリン gasorin petrol	**ディーゼル** dīzeru diesel	**不凍剤** futōzai antifreeze
無鉛 muen unleaded	**整備工場** seibi kōjō garage	**フロントガラス洗浄液** furonto-garasu senjōeki screenwash

満タンお願いします。
mantan onegaishimasu.
Fill the tank, please.

自動車 2 jidōsha ∙ car 2

内装 naisō ∙ interior

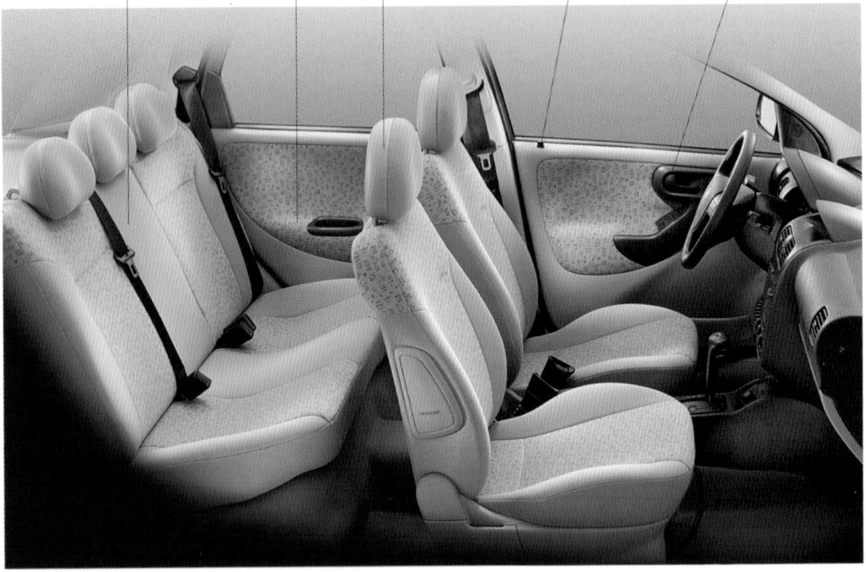

後部座席
kōbu zaseki
back seat

アームレスト
āmu resuto
armrest

ヘッドレスト
heddo resuto
headrest

ドアロック
doa rokku
door lock

ドアハンドル
doa handoru
handle

関連用語 kanrenyōgo ∙ vocabulary

ツードア tsū doa two-door	フォードア fō doa four-door	オートマ ōtoma automatic	ブレーキ burēki brake	アクセル akuseru accelerator
スリードア surī doa three-door	マニュアル manyuaru manual	イグニッション igunisshon ignition	クラッチ kuratchi clutch	エアコン eakon air conditioning

…への行き方を教えてください。
… eno ikikata o oshiete kudasai?
Can you tell me the way to…?

駐車場はどこですか。
chūshajō wa doko desuka?
Where is the car park?

ここに駐車できますか。
kokoni chūsha dekimasuka?
Can I park here?

日本語 nihongo ∙ english

操作系 sōsakei • controls

ハンドル
handoru
steering
wheel

クラクション
kurakushon
horn

ダッシュボード
dasshubōdo
dashboard

ハザードランプ
hazādo rampu
hazard lights

カーナビ
kānabi
satellite navigation

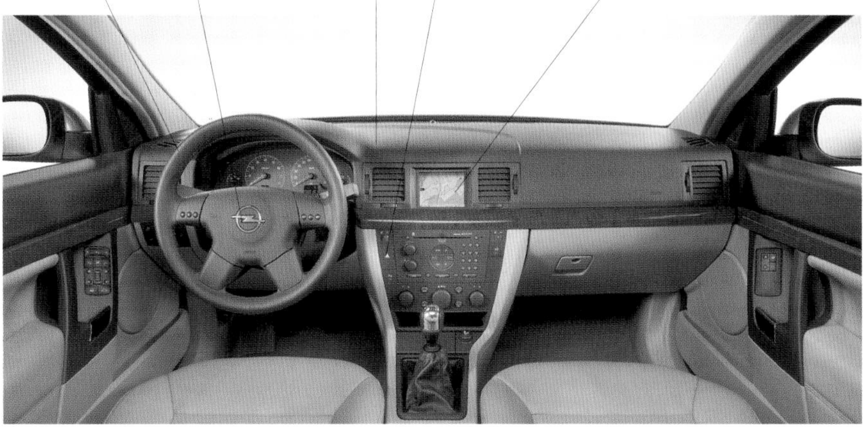

左ハンドル hidari handoru | left-hand drive

水温計
suionkei
temperature gauge

タコメーター
takomētā
rev counter

速度計
sokudokei
speedometer

燃料計
nenryōkei
fuel gauge

カーオーディオ
kā ōdio
car stereo

ライトスイッチ
raito suitchi
lights switch

オドメーター
odomētā
odometer

ヒーター調節
hītā chōsetsu
heater controls

エアバッグ
eabaggu
air bag

変速レバー
hensoku rebā
gearstick

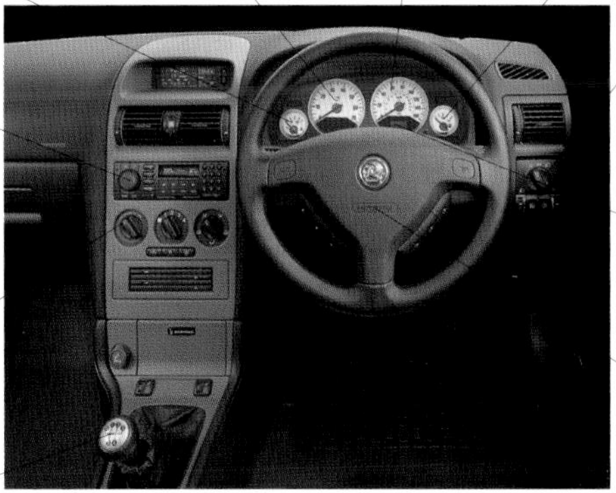

右ハンドル migi handoru | right-hand drive

自動車 3 jidōsha • car 3

機械構造 kikaikōzō • mechanics

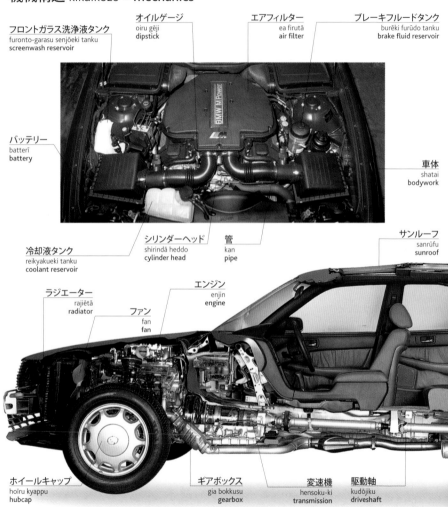

フロントガラス洗浄液タンク
furonto-garasu senjōeki tanku
screenwash reservoir

オイルゲージ
oiru gēji
dipstick

エアフィルター
ea firutā
air filter

ブレーキフルードタンク
burēki furūdo tanku
brake fluid reservoir

バッテリー
batterī
battery

車体
shatai
bodywork

冷却液タンク
reikyakueki tanku
coolant reservoir

シリンダーヘッド
shirindā heddo
cylinder head

管
kan
pipe

サンルーフ
sanrūfu
sunroof

ラジエーター
rajiētā
radiator

ファン
fan
fan

エンジン
enjin
engine

ホイールキャップ
hoīru kyappu
hubcap

ギアボックス
gia bokkusu
gearbox

変速機
hensoku-ki
transmission

駆動軸
kudōjiku
driveshaft

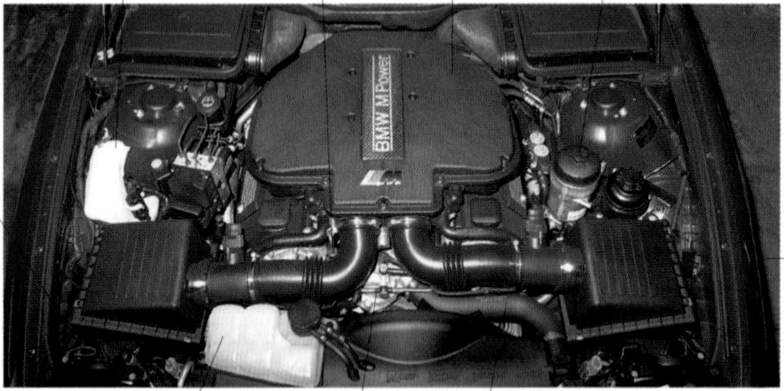

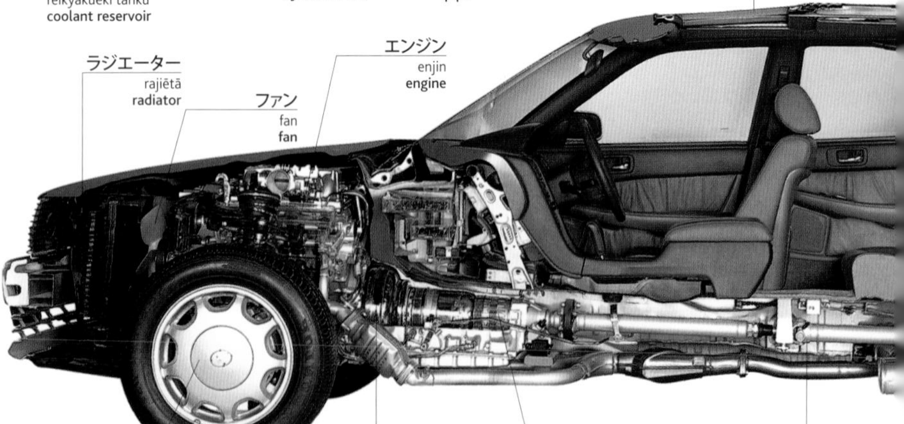

パンク panku • puncture

スペアタイヤ
supea taiya
spare tyre

レンチ
renchi
wrench

ホイールナット
hoīru natto
wheel nuts

ジャッキ
jakki
jack

タイヤを交換する
taiya o kōkan suru
change a wheel (v)

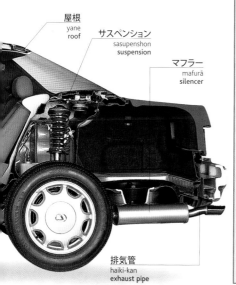

屋根
yane
roof

サスペンション
sasupenshon
suspension

マフラー
mafurā
silencer

排気管
haiki-kan
exhaust pipe

関連用語 kanrenyōgo • vocabulary

自動車事故
jidōsha jiko
car accident

故障
koshō
breakdown

保険
hoken
insurance

牽引車
ken'insha
tow truck

修理工
shūrikō
mechanic

タイヤ空気圧
taiya kūkiatsu
tyre pressure

ヒューズボックス
hyūzu bokkusu
fuse box

スパークプラグ
supāku puragu
spark plug

ファンベルト
fam beruto
fan belt

燃料タンク
nenryō tanku
petrol tank

タイミング
taimingu
timing

ターボチャージャー
tābochājā
turbocharger

配電器
haidenki
distributor

シャシー
shashī
chassis

ハンドブレーキ
handoburēki
handbrake

オルタネータ
orutanēta
alternator

カムベルト
kamu beruto
cam belt

車が故障しました。
kuruma ga koshō shimashita.
I've broken down.

車がスタートしません。
kuruma ga sutāto shimasen.
My car won't start.

修理はできますか。
shūri wa dekimasuka?
Do you do repairs?

エンジンがオーバーヒートしています。
enjin ga ōbāhīto shite imasu.
The engine is overheating.

オートバイ ōtobai ● **motorbike**

ヘルメット
herumetto
helmet

方向指示器
hōkō shijiki
indicator

速度計
sokudokei
speedometer

ブレーキ
burēki
brake

クラッチ
kuratchi
clutch

クラクション
kurakushon
horn

スロットル
surottoru
throttle

キャリア
kyaria
carrier

操作系
sōsakei
controls

リフレクター
rifurekutā
reflector

後部座席
kōbu zaseki
pillion

シート
shīto
seat

エンジン
enjin
engine

燃料タンク
nenryō tanku
fuel tank

テールランプ
tēru rampu
tail light

排気管
haiki kan
exhaust pipe

マフラー
mafurā
silencer

オイルタンク
oiru tanku
oil tank

ギアボックス
gia bokkusu
gearbox

エアフィルター
ea firutā
air filter

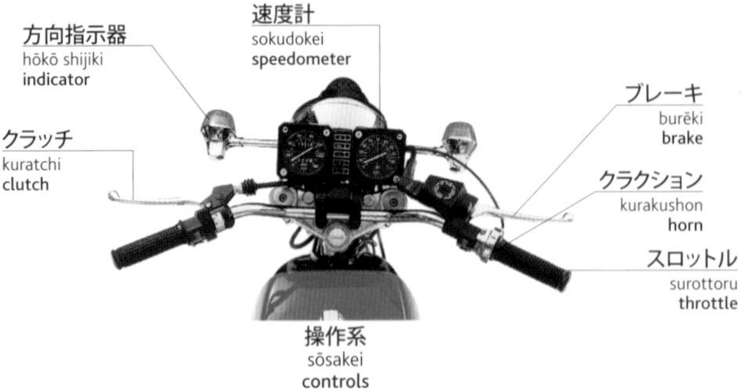

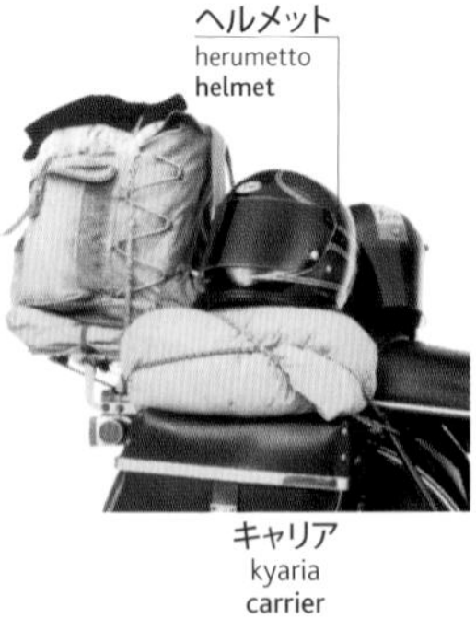

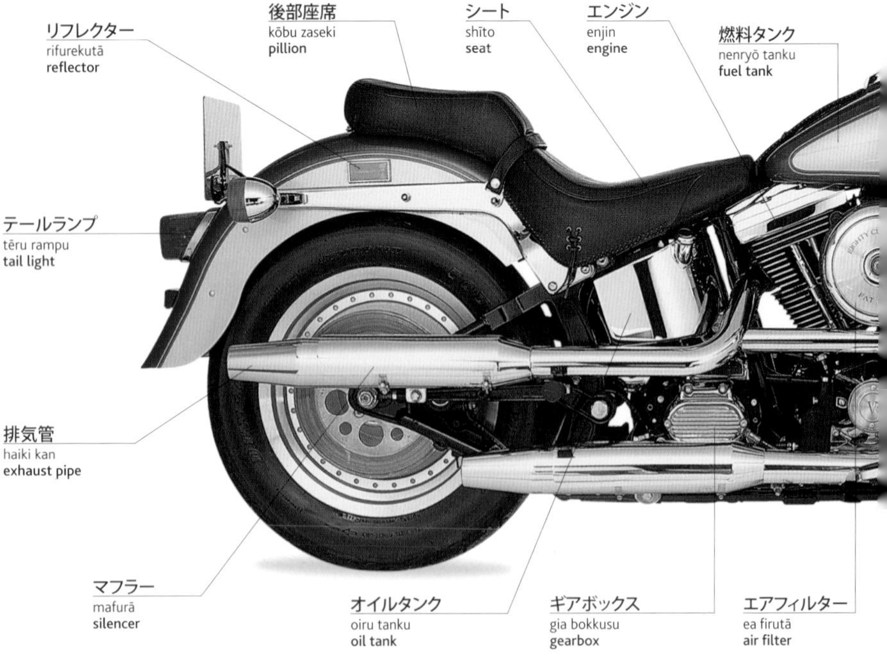

バイザー
baizā
visor

革ジャン
kawajan
leathers

反射材
hanshazai
reflector strap

膝当て
hiza'ate
knee pad

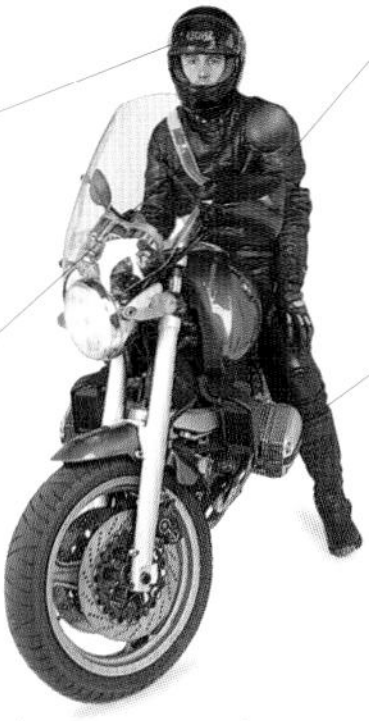

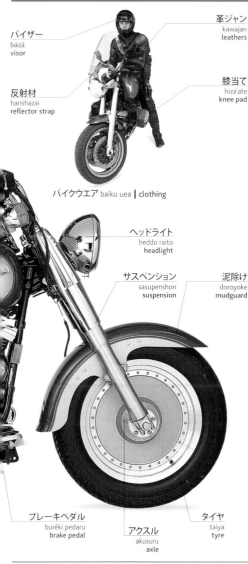

バイクウエア baiku uea | clothing

ヘッドライト
heddo raito
headlight

サスペンション
sasupenshon
suspension

泥除け
doroyoke
mudguard

ブレーキペダル
burēki pedaru
brake pedal

アクスル
akusuru
axle

タイヤ
taiya
tyre

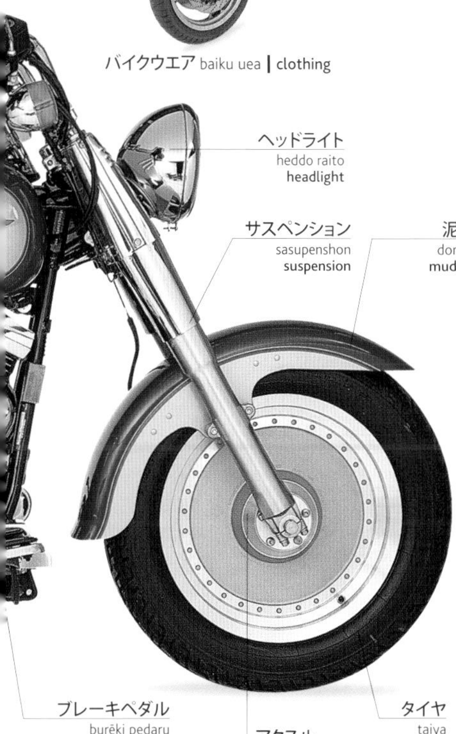

種類 shurui • types

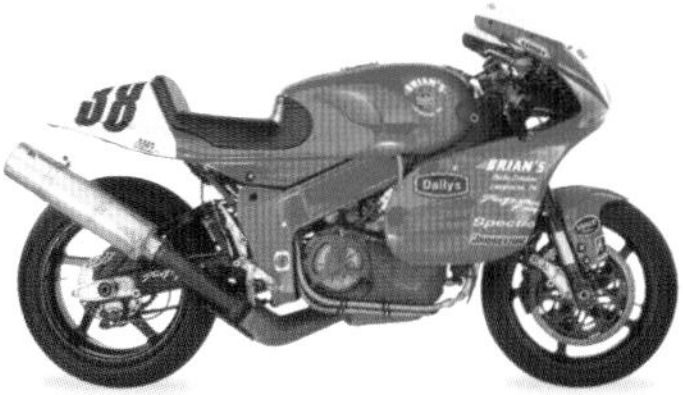

レーシングバイク rēshingu baiku | racing bike

ウインドシールド
uindo-shīrudo
windshield

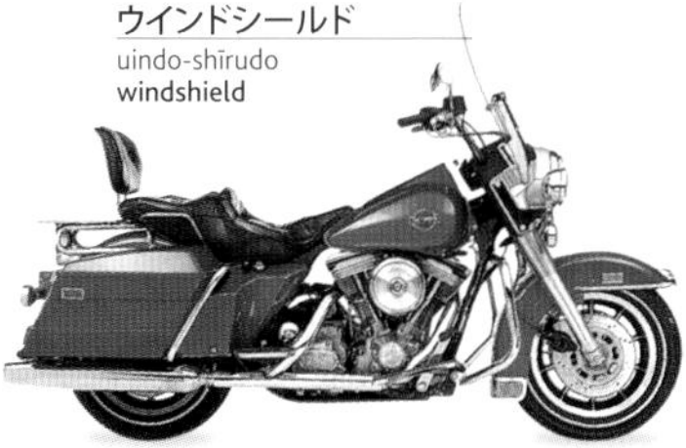

ツアラー tsuarā | tourer

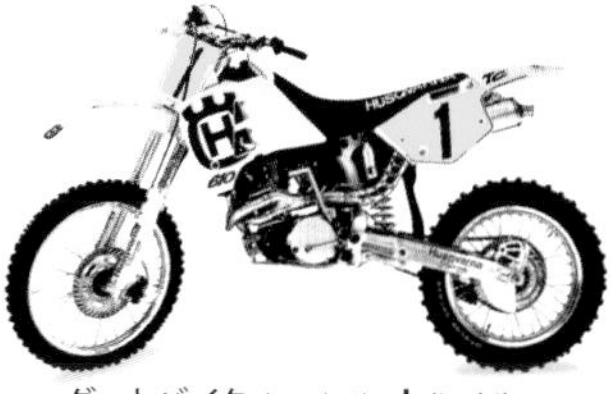

ダートバイク dāto baiku | dirt bike

スタンド
sutando
stand

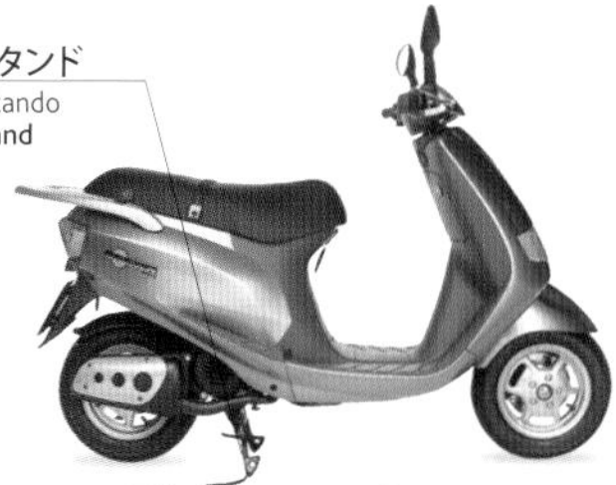

スクーター sukūtā | scooter

自転車 jitensha • bicycle

サドル
sadoru
saddle

シートピラー
shīto pirā
seat post

水筒
suitō
water bottle

フレーム
furēmu
frame

ブレーキ
burēki
brake

ハブ
habu
hub

変速機
hensoku-ki
gears

リム
rimu
rim

タイヤ
taiya
tyre

チェーン
chēn
chain

ペダル
pedaru
pedal

コグ
kogu
cog

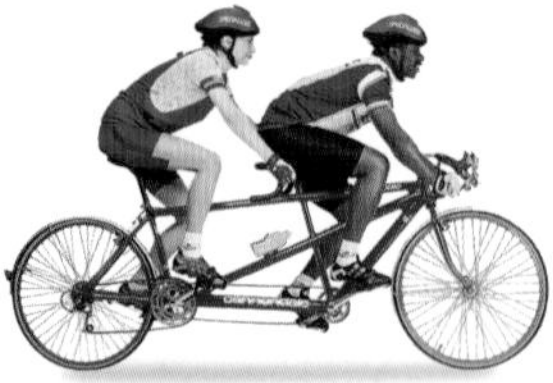

タンデム自転車 tandemu jitensha
tandem

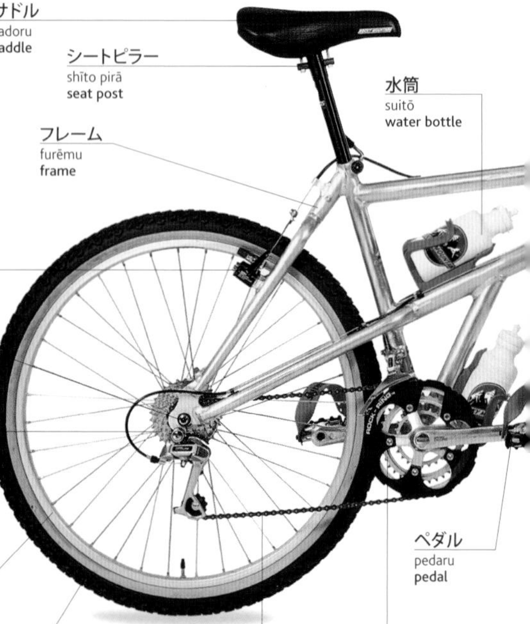

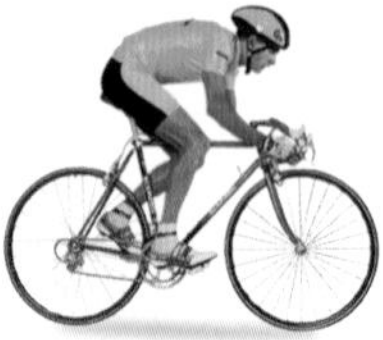

ロードレーサー
rōdo rēsā
racing bike

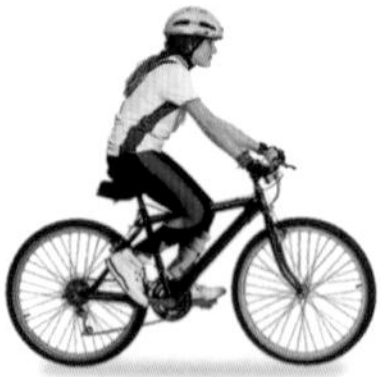

マウンテンバイク
maunten baiku
mountain bike

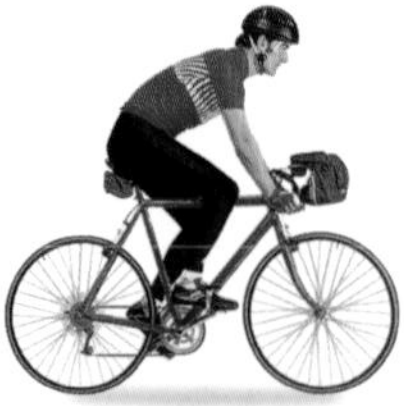

ツーリング自転車
tsūringu jitensha
touring bike

ヘルメット
herumetto
helmet

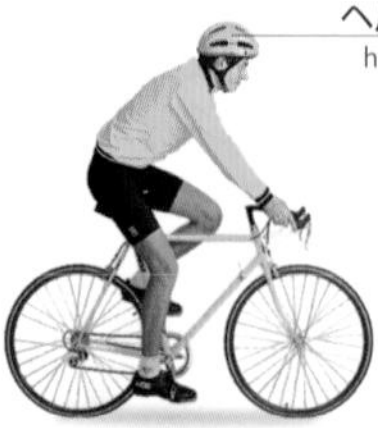

ロードバイク
rōdo baiku
road bike

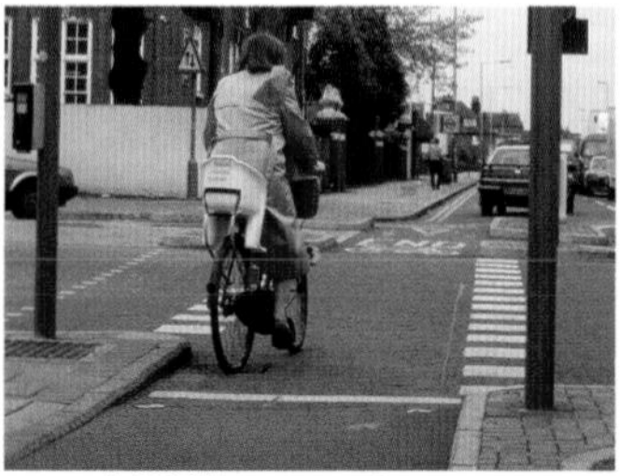

自転車道 jitensha-dō | cycle lane

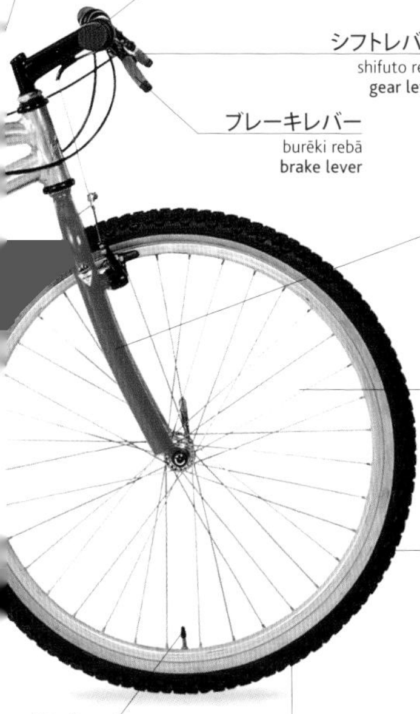

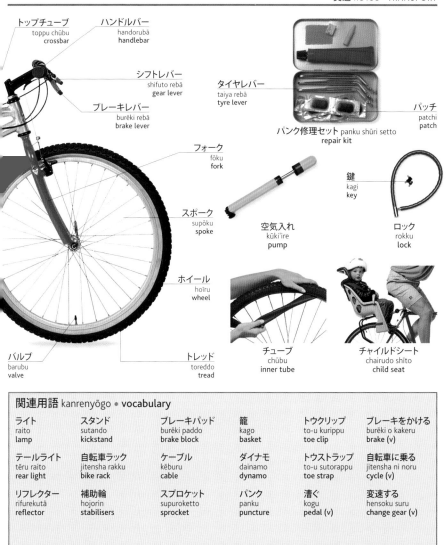

トップチューブ
toppu chūbu
crossbar

ハンドルバー
handorubā
handlebar

シフトレバー
shifuto rebā
gear lever

ブレーキレバー
burēki rebā
brake lever

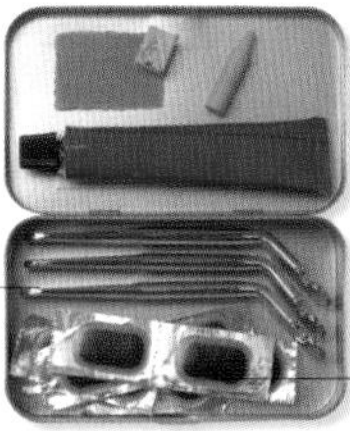

タイヤレバー
taiya rebā
tyre lever

パッチ
patchi
patch

パンク修理セット panku shūri setto
repair kit

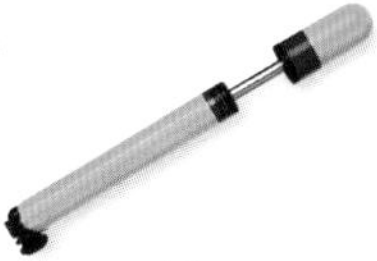

フォーク
fōku
fork

鍵
kagi
key

スポーク
supōku
spoke

空気入れ
kūki'ire
pump

ロック
rokku
lock

ホイール
hoīru
wheel

バルブ
barubu
valve

トレッド
toreddo
tread

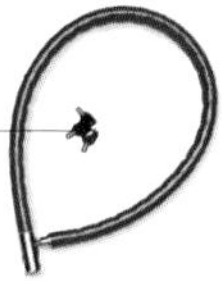

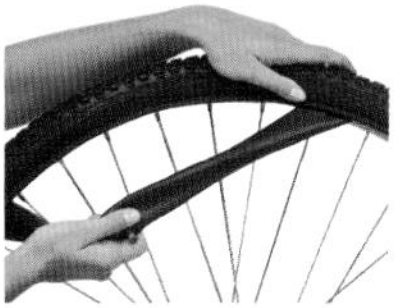

チューブ
chūbu
inner tube

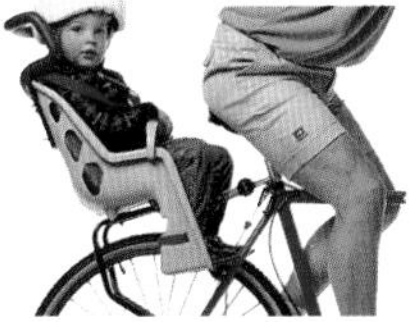

チャイルドシート
chairudo shīto
child seat

関連用語 kanrenyōgo • vocabulary

ライト
raito
lamp

スタンド
sutando
kickstand

ブレーキパッド
burēki paddo
brake block

籠
kago
basket

トウクリップ
to-u kurippu
toe clip

ブレーキをかける
burēki o kakeru
brake (v)

テールライト
tēru raito
rear light

自転車ラック
jitensha rakku
bike rack

ケーブル
kēburu
cable

ダイナモ
dainamo
dynamo

トウストラップ
to-u sutorappu
toe strap

自転車に乗る
jitensha ni noru
cycle (v)

リフレクター
rifurekutā
reflector

補助輪
hojorin
stabilisers

スプロケット
supuroketto
sprocket

パンク
panku
puncture

漕ぐ
kogu
pedal (v)

変速する
hensoku suru
change gear (v)

列車 ressha • train

客車
kyakusha
carriage

ホーム
hōmu
platform

カート
kāto
trolley

ホーム番号
hōmu bangō
platform number

通勤者
tsūkinsha
commuter

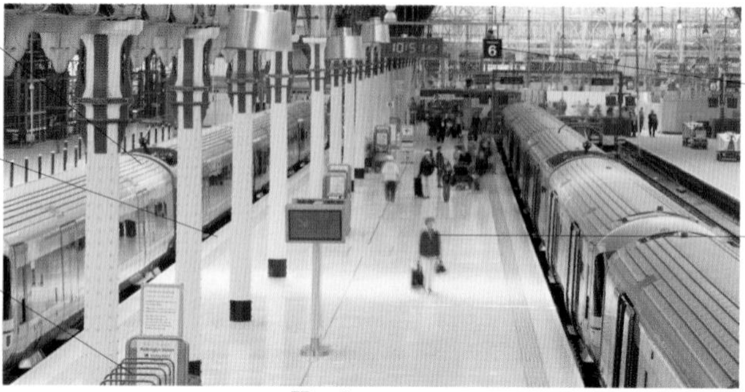

駅 eki | train station

列車の種類 ressha no shurui • types of train

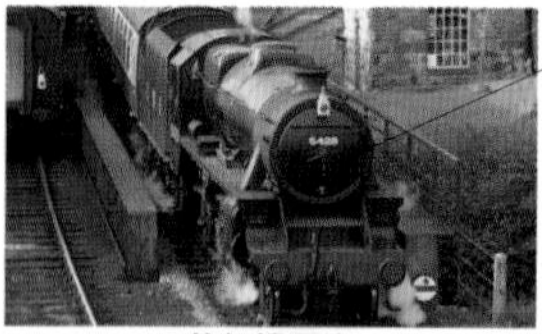

エンジン
enjin
engine

運転室
unten shitsu
driver's cab

レール
rēru
rail

蒸気機関車
jōki kikansha
steam train

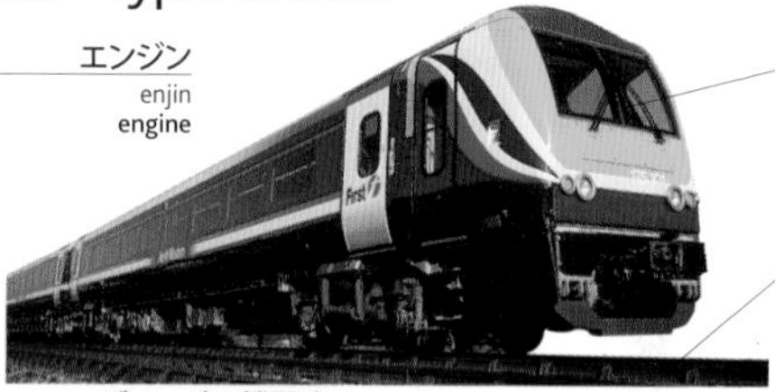

ディーゼル機関車 dīzeru kikansha | diesel train

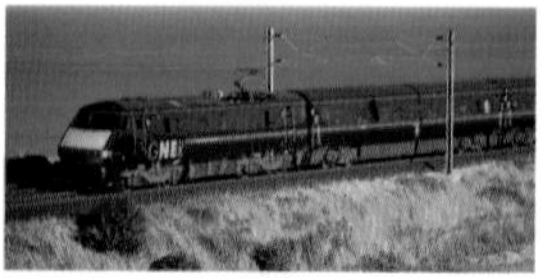

電車
densha
electric train

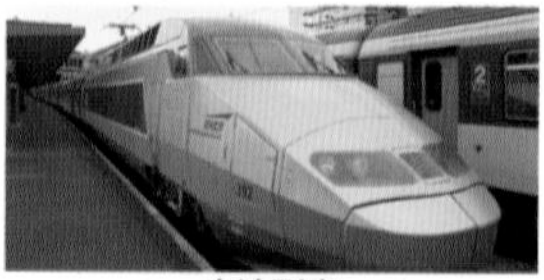

高速列車
kōsoku ressha
high-speed train

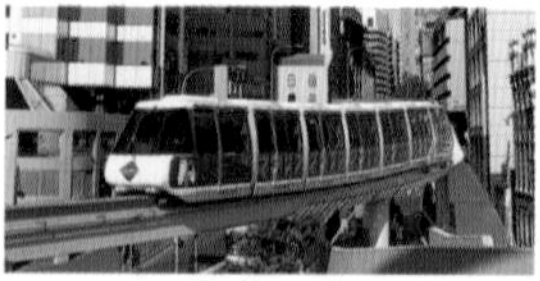

モノレール
monorēru
monorail

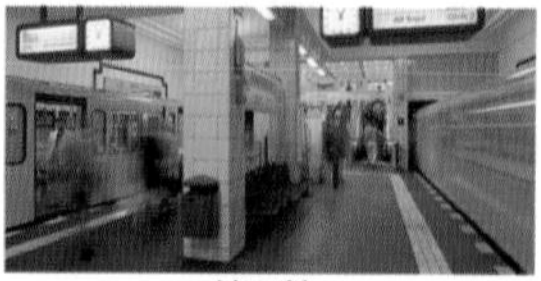

地下鉄
chikatetsu
underground train

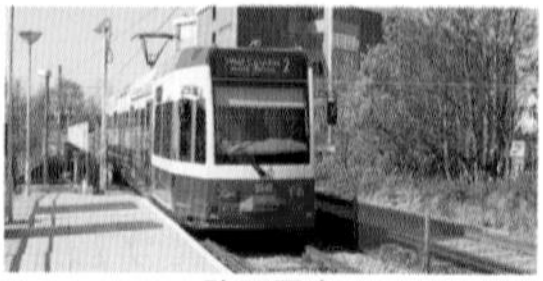

路面電車
romen densha
tram

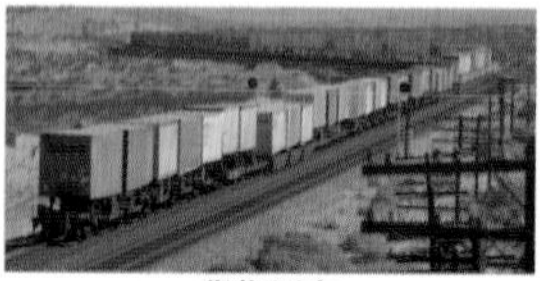

貨物列車
kamotsu ressha
freight train

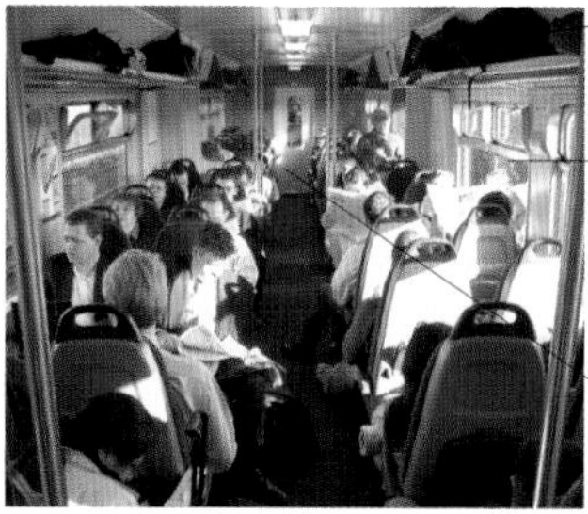

網棚
amidana
luggage rack

車窓
shasô
window

線路
senro
track

扉
tobira
door

座席
zaseki
seat

客室
kyakushitsu
compartment

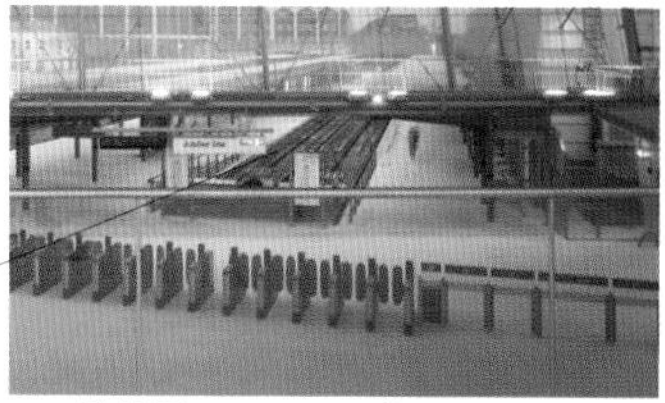

改札口 kaisatsu-guchi | ticket barrier

拡声装置
kakusei sôchi
public address system

時刻表
jikokuhyô
timetable

41213
KUPONG 7.00 kr
Typ 1109
Serie 964

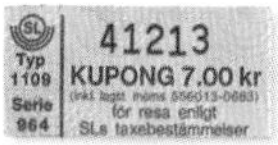

切符
kippu
ticket

食堂車 shokudô-sha | dining car

コンコース konkôsu | concourse

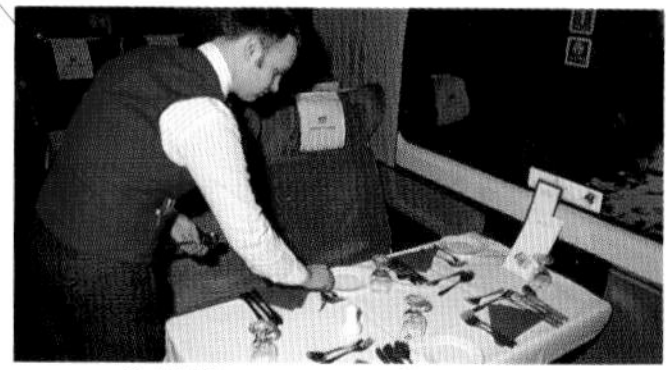

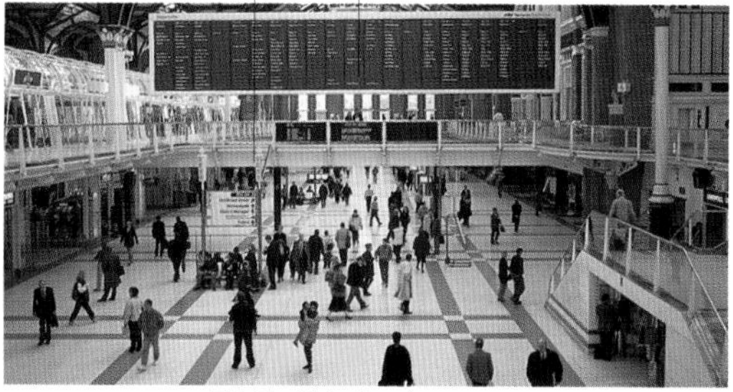

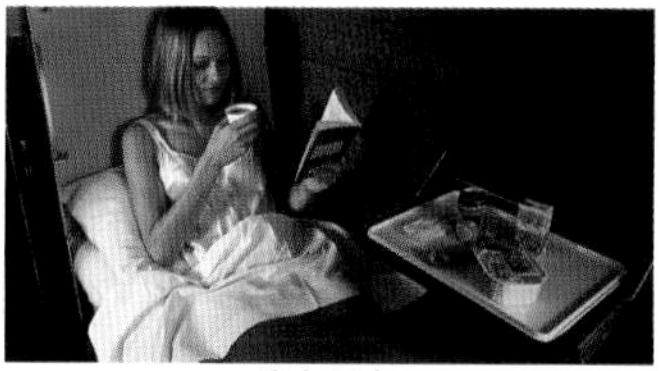

寝台個室
shindai koshitsu
sleeping compartment

関連用語 kanrenyôgo • vocabulary

鉄道網
tetsudô-mô
rail network

地下鉄路線図
chikatetsu rosenzu
underground map

切符売場
kippu uriba
ticket office

通電レール
tsûden rêru
live rail

インターシティ列車
intâshiti ressha
inter-city train

遅れ
okure
delay

検札員
kensatsuin
ticket inspector

信号
shingô
signal

新幹線
shinkansen
bullet train

料金
ryôkin
fare

乗り換える
norikaeru
change (v)

非常レバー
hijô rebâ
emergency lever

航空機 kōkūki • aircraft

定期旅客機 teiki-ryokakki • airliner

機首
kishu
nose

操縦室
sōjū shitsu
cockpit

エンジン
enjin
engine

機体
kitai
fuselage

翼
tsubasa
wing

尾翼
biyoku
tail

方向舵
hōkōda
rudder

ドア
doa
exit

前輪
zenrin
nosewheel

着陸装置
chakuriku sōchi
landing gear

補助翼
hojoyoku
aileron

垂直安定板
suichoku-anteiban
fin

水平尾翼
suihei-biyoku
tailplane

キャビン kyabin • cabin

非常口
hijō guchi
emergency exit

乗務員
jōmuin
flight attendant

荷物入れ
nimotsuire
overhead locker

窓
mado
window

換気口
kankikō
air vent

読書灯
dokusho-tō
reading light

座席
zaseki
seat

列
retsu
row

肘掛け
hijikake
armrest

通路
tsūro
aisle

テーブル
tēburu
tray-table

背もたれ
semotare
seat back

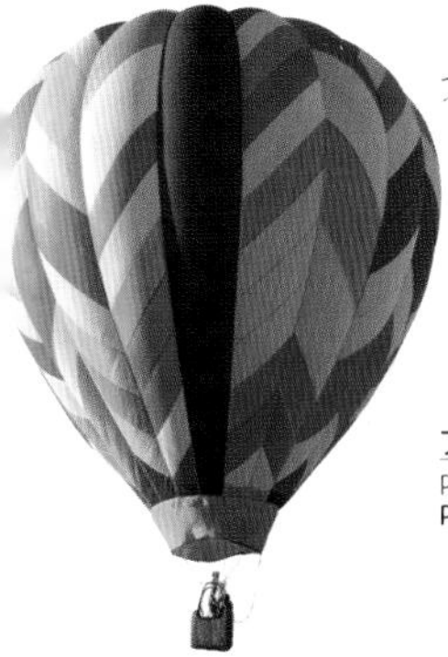

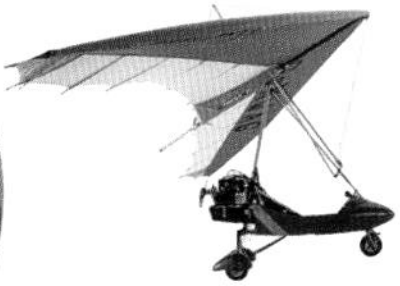

マイクロライト
maikuroraito
microlight

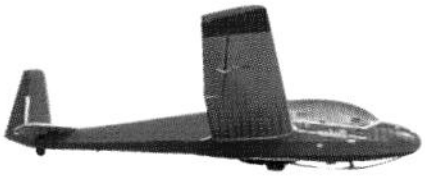

グライダー
guraidā
glider

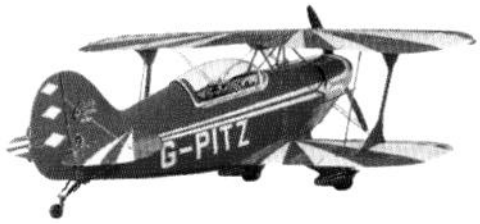

複葉機
fukuyōki
biplane

プロペラ
puropera
propeller

熱気球
netsukikyū
hot-air balloon

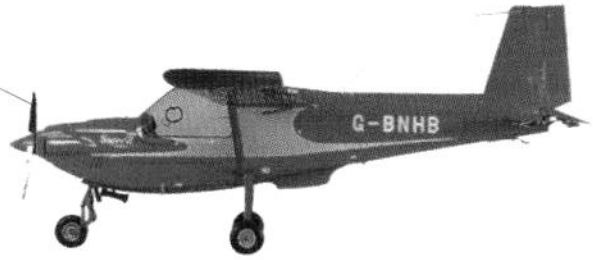

軽飛行機
keihikōki
light aircraft

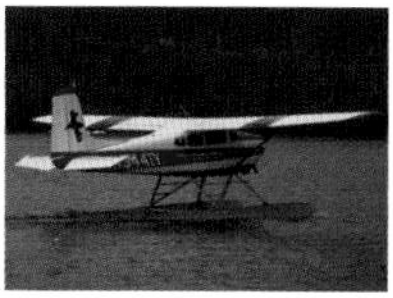

水上飛行機
suijō hikōki
sea plane

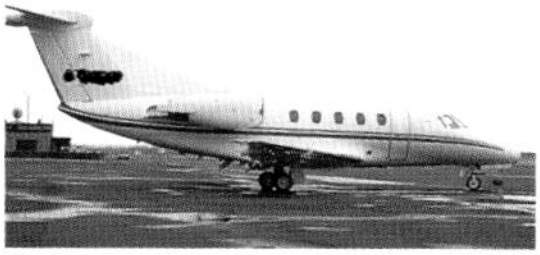

自家用ジェット機
jikayō jettoki
private jet

ローターブレード
rōtā burēdo
rotor blade

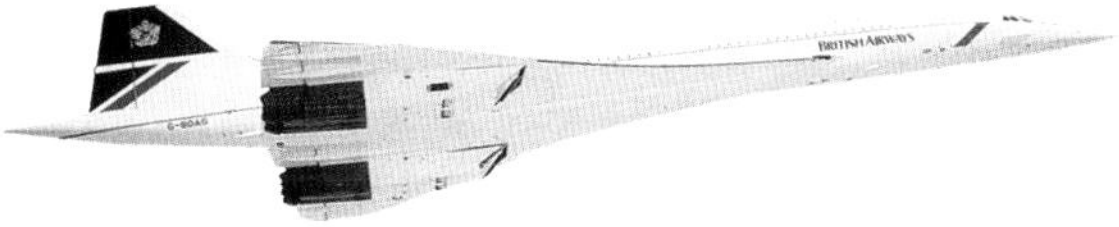

超音波ジェット機
chōompa jettoki
supersonic jet

ミサイル
misairu
missile

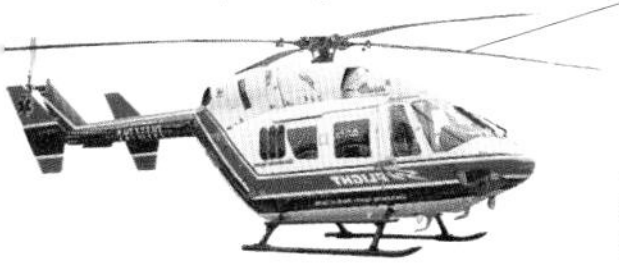

ヘリコプター
herikoputā
helicopter

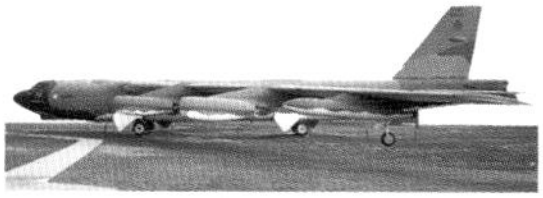

爆撃機
bakugekiki
bomber

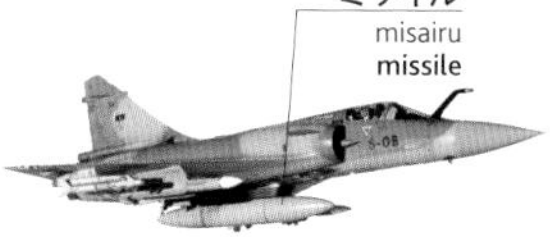

戦闘機
sentōki
fighter plane

関連用語 kanrenyōgo • vocabulary

パイロット pairotto **pilot**	離陸する ririku suru **take off (v)**	着陸する chakuriku suru **land (v)**	エコノミークラス ekonomī kurasu **economy class**	手荷物 tenimotsu **hand luggage**
副操縦士 fukusōjūshi **co-pilot**	飛ぶ tobu **fly (v)**	高度 kōdo **altitude**	ビジネスクラス bijinesu kurasu **business class**	シートベルト shīto beruto **seat belt**

空港 kūkō • airport

エプロン
epuron
apron

牽引車
ken'insha
baggage trailer

ターミナル
tāminaru
terminal

作業車
sagyō-sha
service vehicle

通路
tsūro
walkway

定期旅客機 teiki ryokakki | **airliner**

関連用語 kanrenyōgo • vocabulary

滑走路
kassōro
runway

便名
binmei
flight number

カルーセル
karūseru
carousel

休暇
kyūka
holiday

国際便
kokusai bin
international flight

出入国管理
shutsunyūkoku kanri
immigration

警備
keibi
security

チェックインする
chekkuin suru
check in (v)

国内便
kokunai bin
domestic flight

税関
zeikan
customs

レントゲン検査装置
rentogen kensa sōchi
X-ray machine

管制塔
kanseitō
control tower

乗り継ぎ
noritsugi
connection

超過荷物
chōka nimotsu
excess baggage

旅行パンフレット
ryokō panfuretto
holiday brochure

飛行機を予約する
hikōki o yoyaku suru
book a flight (v)

手荷物
tenimotsu
hand luggage

荷物
nimotsu
luggage

カート
kāto
trolley

チェクインデスク
chekuin desuku
check-in desk

旅券 ryoken | passport

ビザ
biza
visa

入国審査
nyūkoku shinsa
passport control

搭乗券
tōjōken
boarding pass

航空券
kōkūken
ticket

ゲート番号
gēto bangō
gate number

出発便
shuppatsu bin
departures

出発ロビー
shuppatsu robī
departure lounge

目的地
mokutekichi
destination

到着便
tōchaku bin
arrivals

案内板
annai-ban
information screen

免税店
menzeiten
duty-free shop

荷物引き渡し
nimotsu hikiwatashi
baggage reclaim

タクシー乗り場
takushī noriba
taxi rank

レンタカー
rentakā
car hire

船 fune • ship

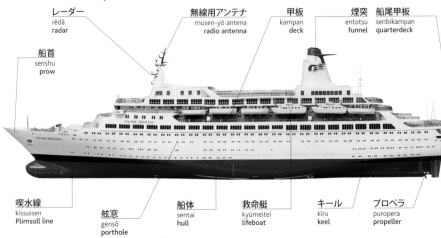

レーダー
rēdā
radar

無線用アンテナ
musen-yō antena
radio antenna

甲板
kampan
deck

煙突
entotsu
funnel

船尾甲板
senbikampan
quarterdeck

船首
senshu
prow

喫水線
kissuisen
Plimsoll line

舷窓
gensō
porthole

船体
sentai
hull

救命艇
kyūmeitei
lifeboat

キール
kīru
keel

プロペラ
puropera
propeller

海洋定期船 kaiyō teikisen | ocean liner

船橋
senkyō
bridge

機関室
kikan shitsu
engine room

船室
senshitsu
cabin

調理室
chōri shitsu
galley

関連用語 kanrenyōgo • vocabulary

ドック
dokku
dock

ウィンドラス
windorasu
windlass

港湾
kōwan
port

船長
senchō
captain

舷門
genmon
gangway

高速モーターボート
kōsoku mōtābōto
speedboat

錨
ikari
anchor

ボート
bōto
rowing boat

係船柱
keisenchū
bollard

カヌー
kanū
canoe

その他の船舶 sonota no sempaku • other ships

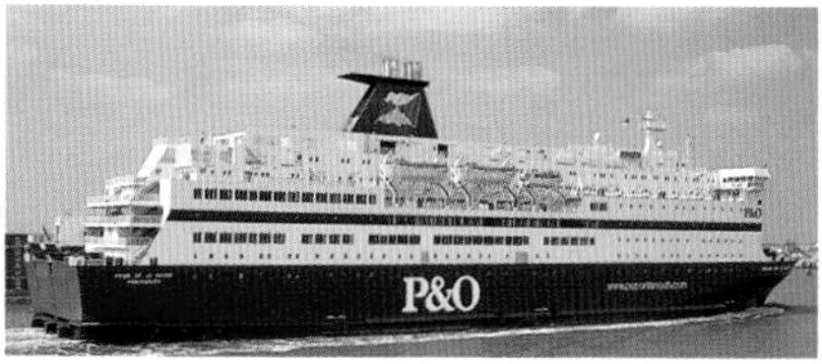

フェリー
ferī
ferry

船外機
sengaiki
outboard motor

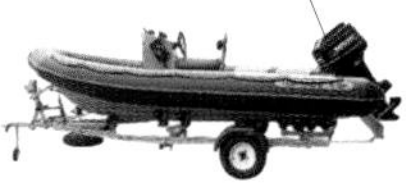

ゴムボート
gomubōto
inflatable dinghy

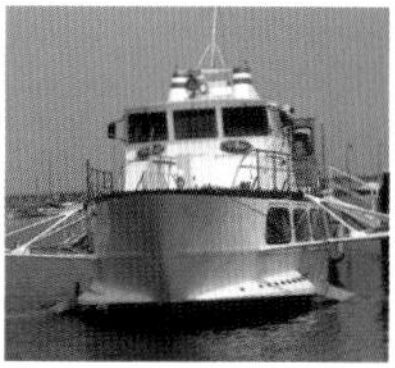

水中翼船
suichūyoku-sen
hydrofoil

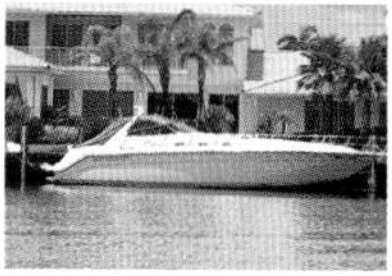

ヨット
yotto
yacht

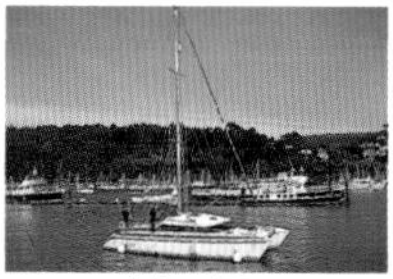

カタマラン
katamaran
catamaran

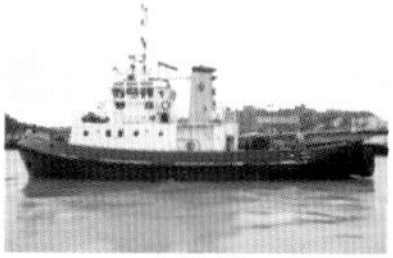

曳航船
eikō-sen
tug boat

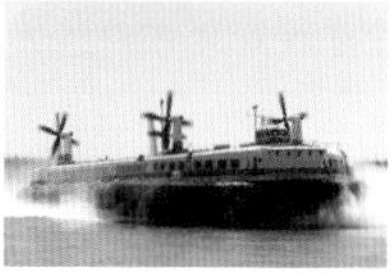

ホバークラフト
hobākurafuto
hovercraft

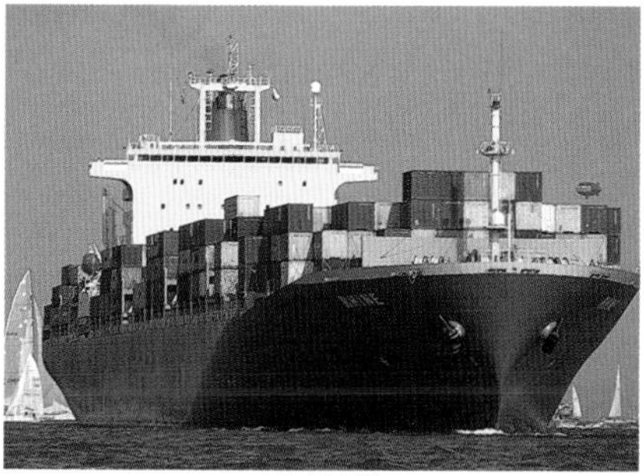

コンテナ船
kontena-sen
container ship

索具
sakugu
rigging

船倉
sensō
hold

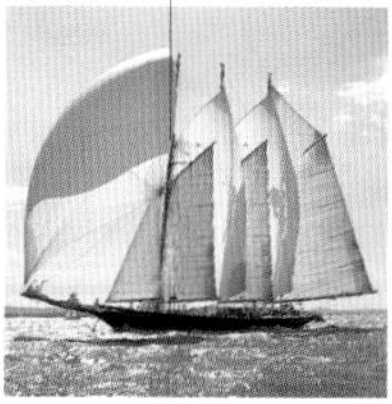

帆船
hansen
sailboat

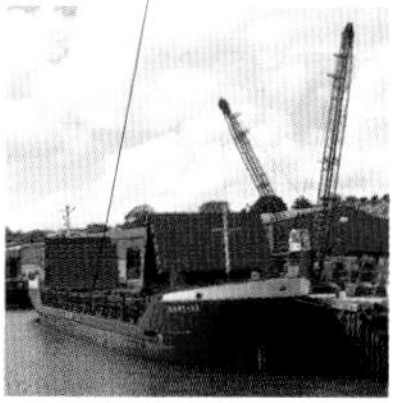

貨物船
kamotsu-sen
freighter

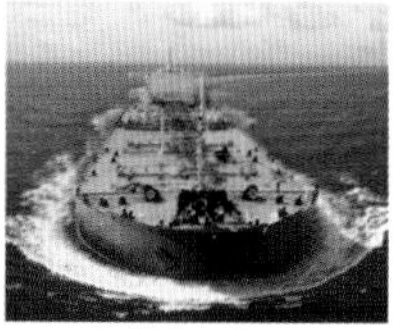

石油タンカー
sekiyu tankā
oil tanker

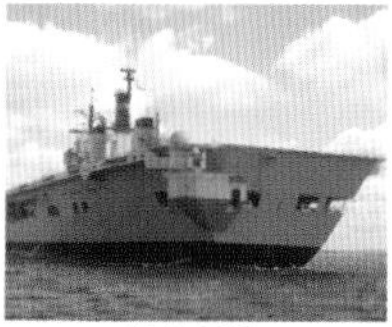

航空母艦
kōkū bokan
aircraft carrier

戦艦
senkan
battleship

展望塔
tembōtō
conning tower

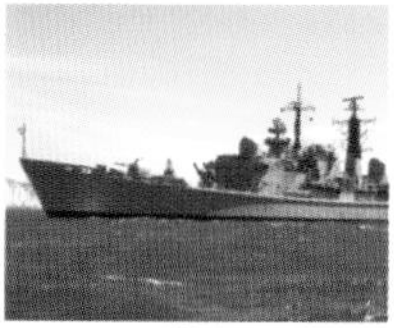

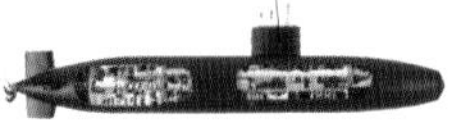

潜水艦
sensuikan
submarine

港湾 kōwan • port

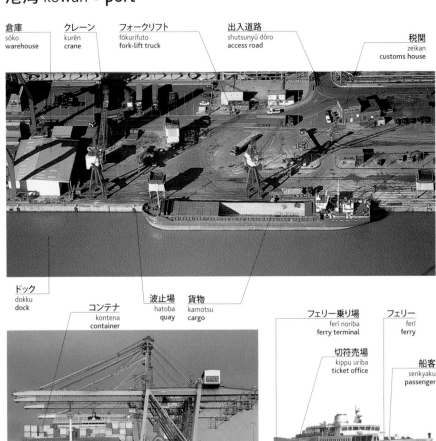

倉庫
sōko
warehouse

クレーン
kurēn
crane

フォークリフト
fōkurifuto
fork-lift truck

出入道路
shutsunyū dōro
access road

税関
zeikan
customs house

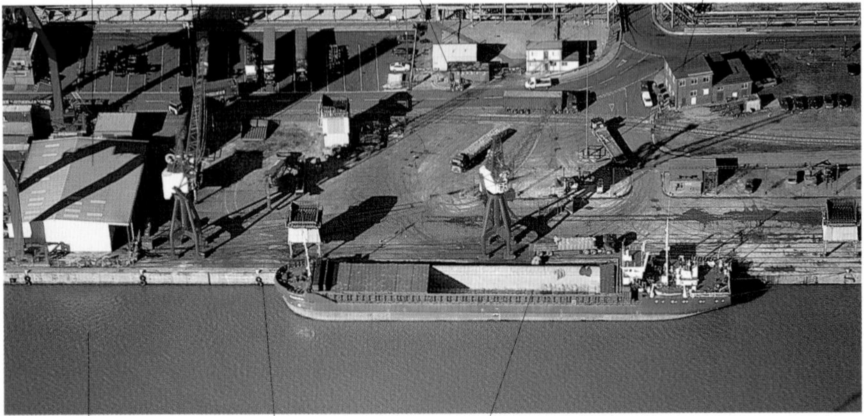

ドック
dokku
dock

コンテナ
kontena
container

波止場
hatoba
quay

貨物
kamotsu
cargo

フェリー乗り場
ferī noriba
ferry terminal

フェリー
ferī
ferry

切符売場
kippu uriba
ticket office

船客
senkyaku
passenger

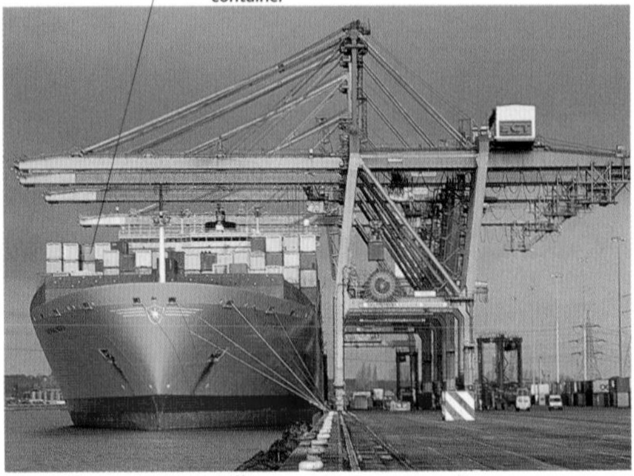

コンテナ港 kontena-kō | container port

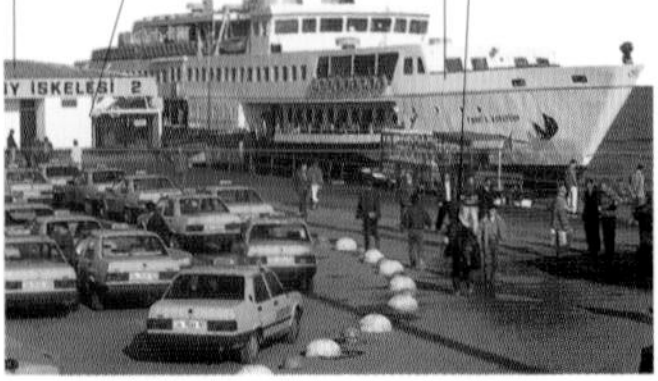

船客港 senkyaku-kō | passenger port

網
ami
net

漁船
gyosen
fishing boat

係留索具
keiryū sakugu
mooring

マリーナ marīna | marina

漁港 gyokō | fishing port

港 minato | harbour

桟橋 sambashi | pier

防波堤
bōhatei
jetty

造船所
zōsen jo
shipyard

ランプ
rampu
lamp

灯台
tōdai
lighthouse

ブイ
bui
buoy

関連用語 kanrenyōgo • vocabulary

沿岸警備隊
engan keibitai
coastguard

港長
kōchō
harbour master

錨を下ろす
ikari o orosu
drop anchor (v)

乾ドック
kandokku
dry dock

係留する
keiryū suru
moor (v)

波止場につける
hatoba ni tsukeru
dock (v)

乗船する
jōsen suru
board (v)

下船する
gesen suru
disembark (v)

出港する
shukkō suru
set sail (v)

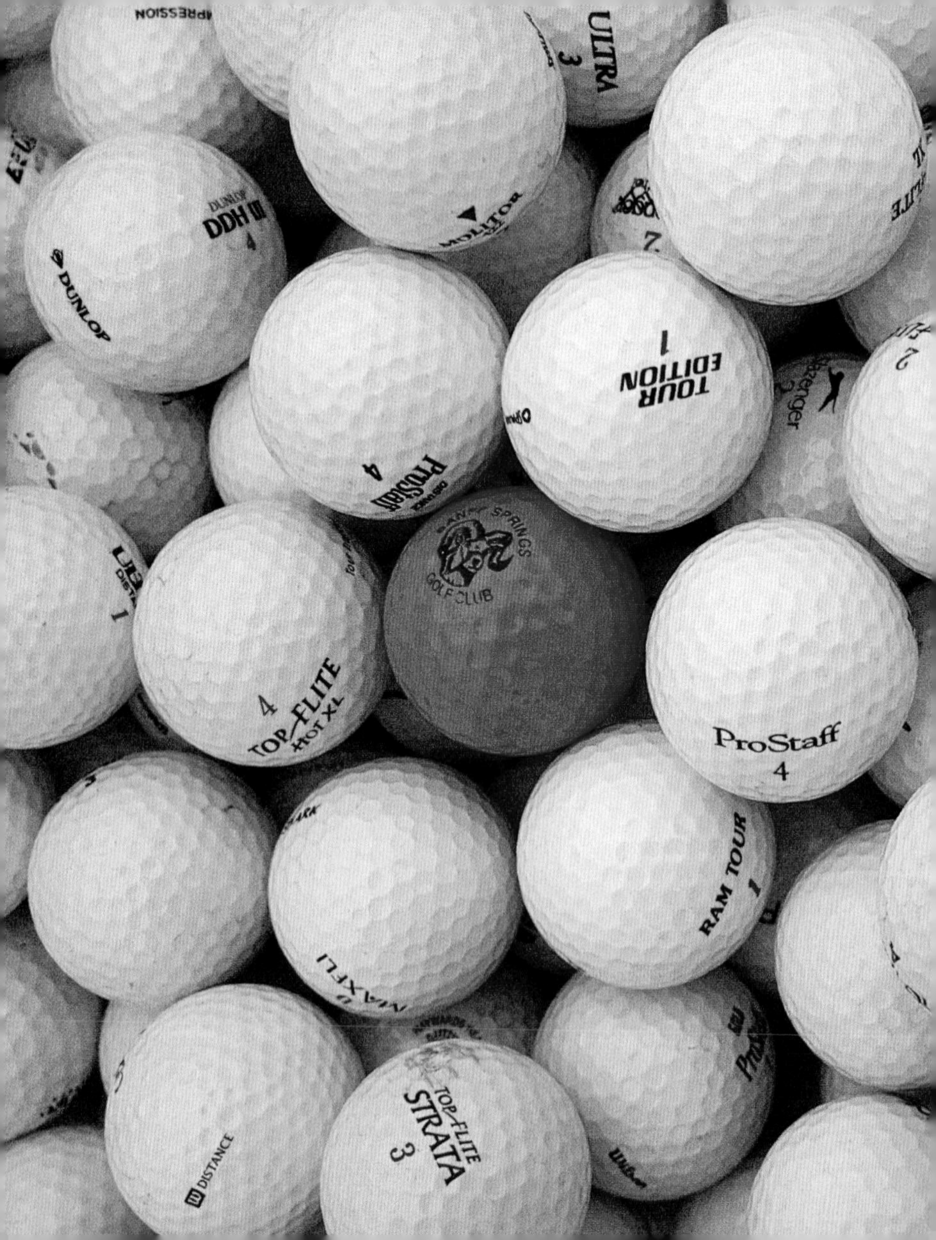

ULTRA
3
DUNLOP
DDH III
DUNLOP
MOLITOR
TOUR
EDITION
1
ProStaff
4
SPRINGS
GOLF CLUB
TOP-FLITE
HOT XL
4
ProStaff
4
RAM TOUR
1
MAXFLI
TOP-FLITE
STRATA
3
DISTANCE

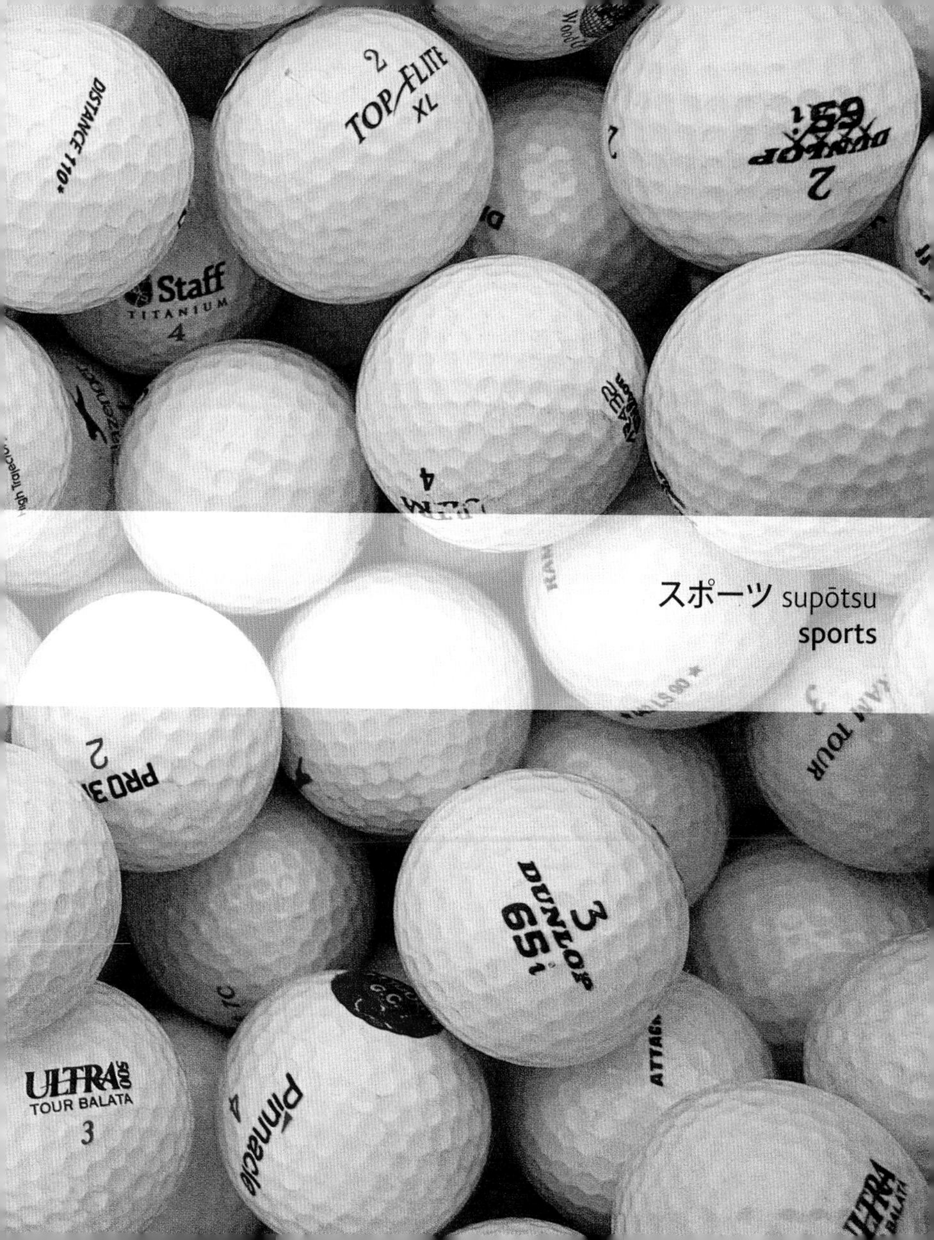

スポーツ supōtsu
sports

アメリカンフットボール amerikan futtobōru
• American football

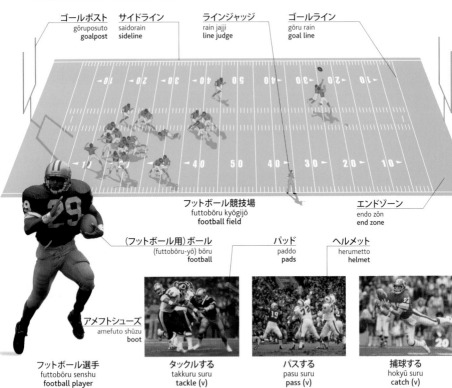

ゴールポスト
gōruposuto
goalpost

サイドライン
saidorain
sideline

ラインジャッジ
rain jajji
line judge

ゴールライン
gōru rain
goal line

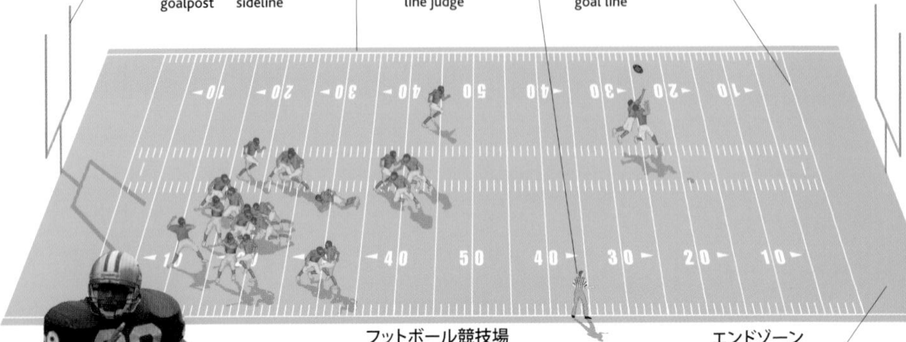

フットボール競技場
futtobōru kyōgijō
football field

エンドゾーン
endo zōn
end zone

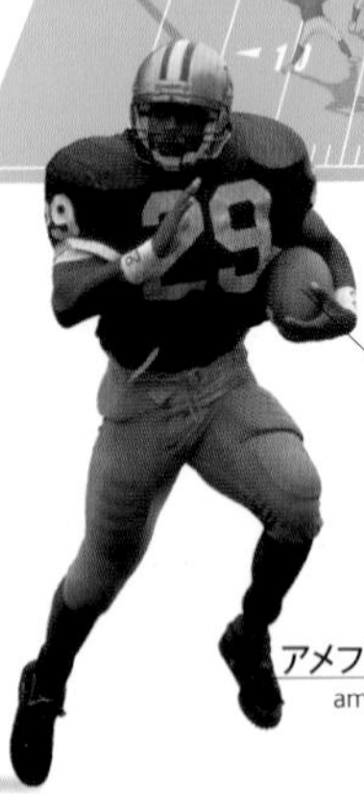

（フットボール用）ボール
(futtobōru-yō) bōru
football

パッド
paddo
pads

ヘルメット
herumetto
helmet

アメフトシューズ
amefuto shūzu
boot

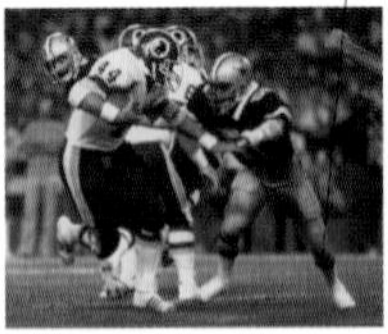

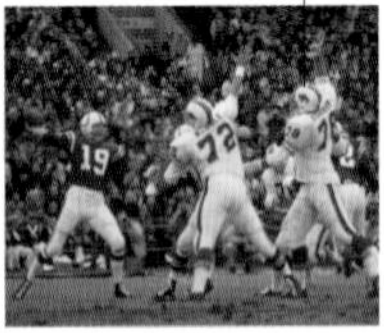

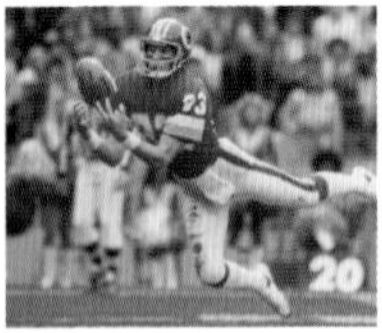

フットボール選手
futtobōru senshu
football player

タックルする
takkuru suru
tackle (v)

パスする
pasu suru
pass (v)

捕球する
hokyū suru
catch (v)

関連用語 kanrenyōgo • **vocabulary**

タイムアウト taimu auto **time out**	**チーム** chīmu **team**	**防御** bōgyo **defence**	**チアリーダー** chiarīdā **cheerleader**	**得点は何点ですか。** tokuten wa nanten desuka? **What is the score?**
ファンブル famburu **fumble**	**攻撃** kōgeki **attack**	**得点** tokuten **score**	**タッチダウン** tatchidaun **touchdown**	**どちらが勝っていますか。** dochira ga katte imasuka? **Who is winning?**

ラグビー ragubī • rugby

ー...ル
ōru
oal

インゴール
in-gōru
in-goal area

タッチライン
tatchi rain
touch line

フラッグポスト
furaggu posuto
flag

デッドボールライン
deddobōru rain
dead ball line

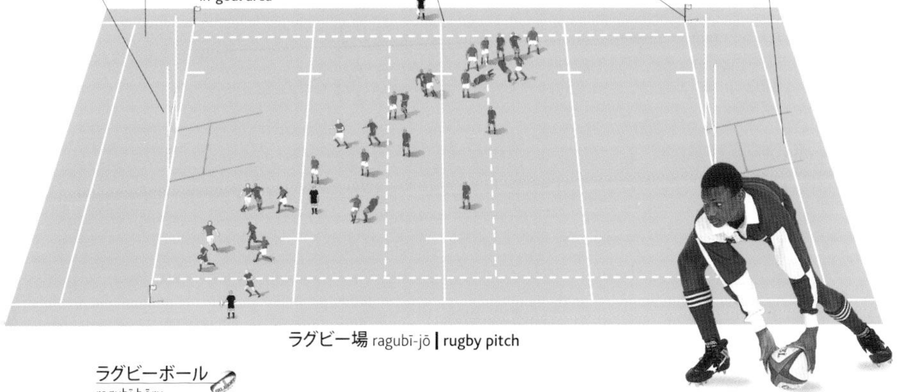

ラグビー場 ragubī-jō | rugby pitch

ラグビーボール
ragubī bōru
ball

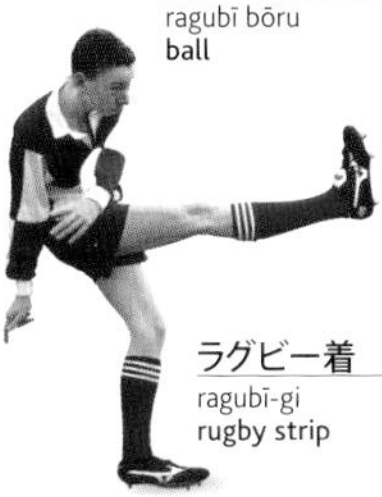

ラグビー着
ragubī-gi
rugby strip

投げる
nageru
throw (v)

蹴る
keru
kick (v)

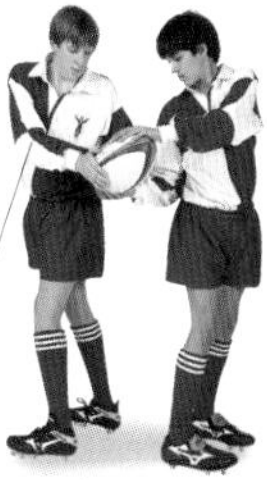

パスする
pasu suru
pass (v)

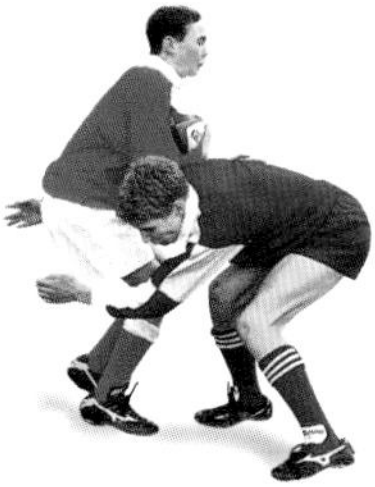

タックルする
takkuru suru
tackle (v)

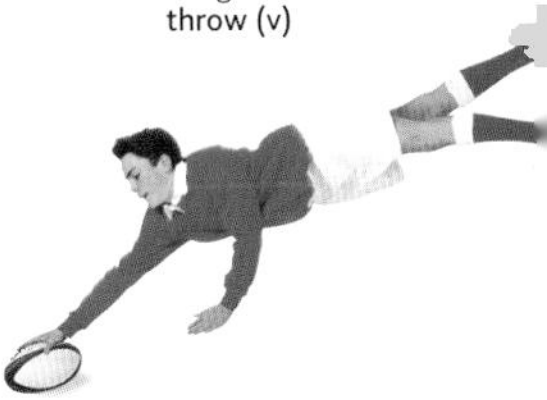

トライ
torai
try

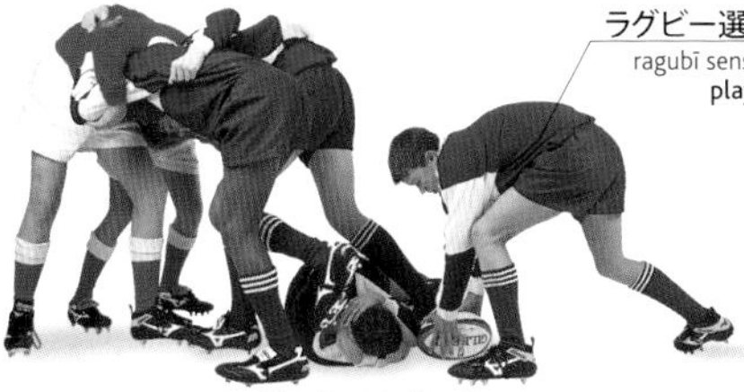

ラグビー選手
ragubī senshu
player

ラック rakku | ruck

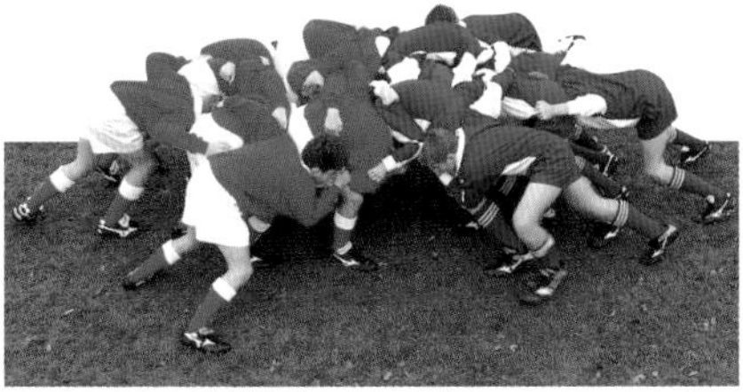

スクラム sukuramu | scrum

サッカー sakkā • soccer

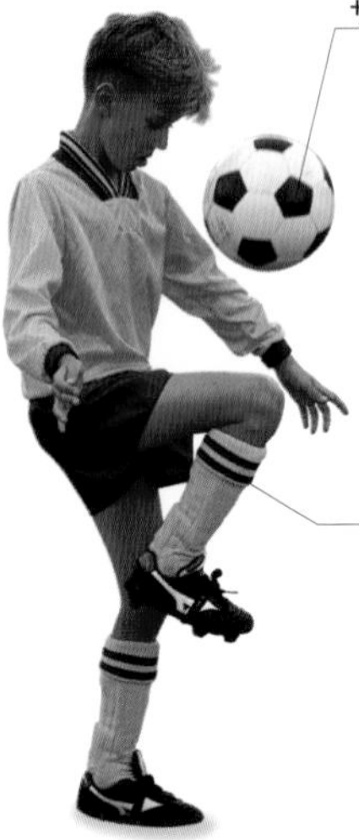

サッカーボール
sakkā bōru
football

ゴールキーパー
gōrukīpā
goalkeeper

サッカー着
sakkā-gi
football strip

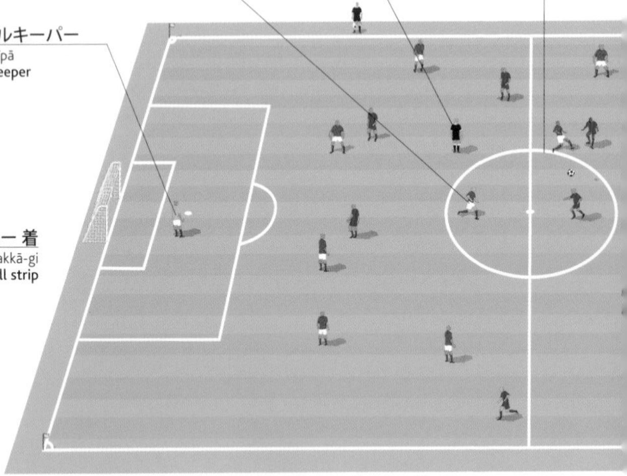

フォワード
fowādo
forward

審判
shimpan
referee

センターサークル
sentā sākuru
centre circle

サッカー選手
sakkā senshu
footballer

サッカー場
sakkā-jō
football pitch

ゴールポスト
gōruposuto
goalpost

ネット
netto
net

クロスバー
kurosubā
crossbar

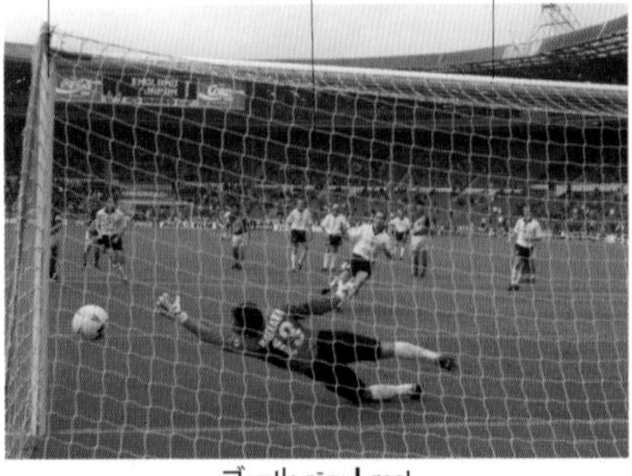

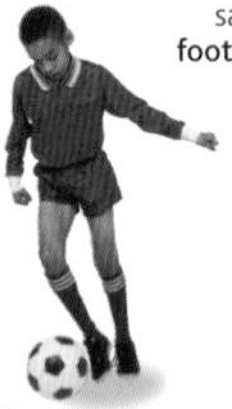

ドリブルする doriburu suru
dribble (v)

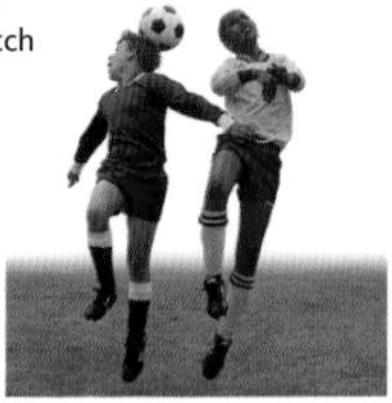

ヘディングする
hedingu suru
head (v)

壁
kabe
wall

ゴール gōru | goal

フリーキック furī kikku | free kick

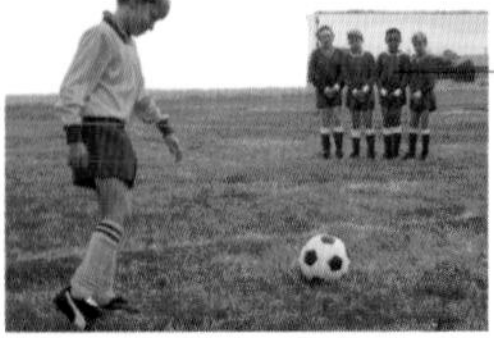

ペナルティエリア
penaruti eria
penalty area

ゴールライン
gōru rain
goal line

ゴールエリア
gōru eria
goal area

ゴール
gōru
goal

バック
bakku
defender

副審
fukushin
linesman

コーナーフラッグ
kōnā furaggu
corner flag

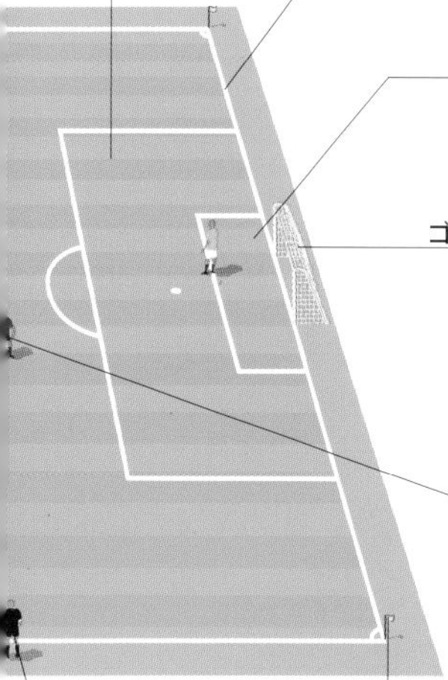

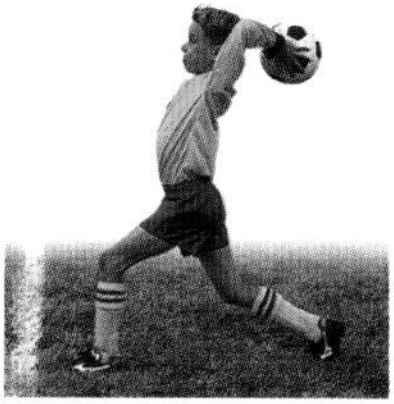

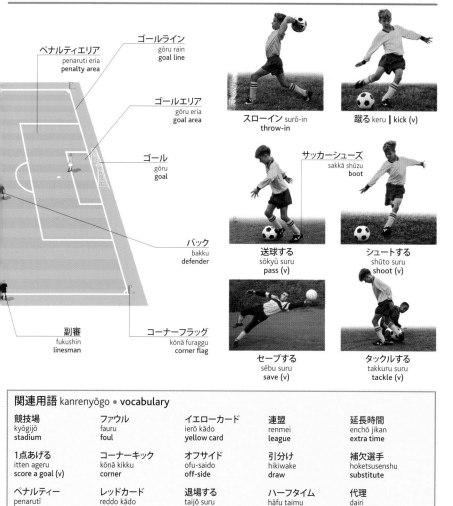

スローイン surō-in
throw-in

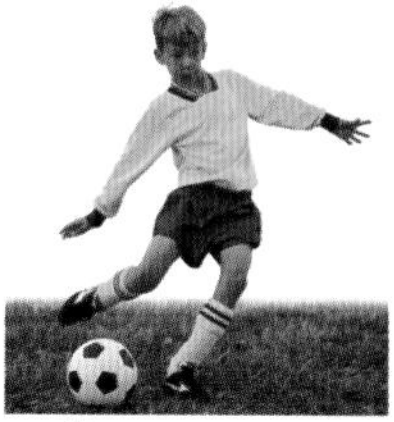

蹴る keru | **kick (v)**

サッカーシューズ
sakkā shūzu
boot

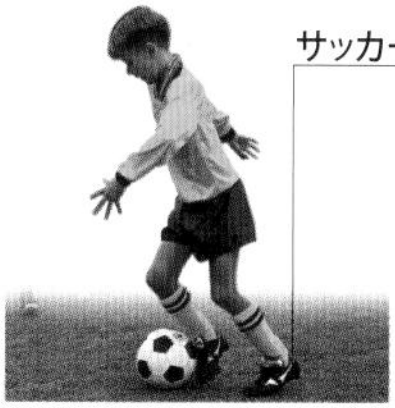

送球する
sōkyū suru
pass (v)

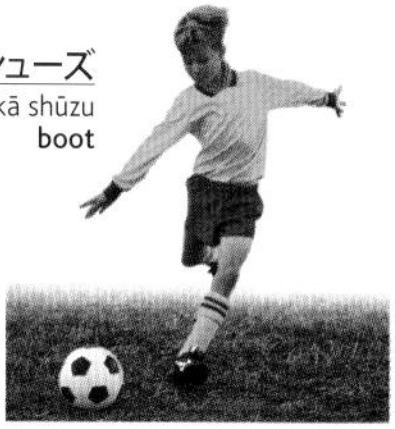

シュートする
shūto suru
shoot (v)

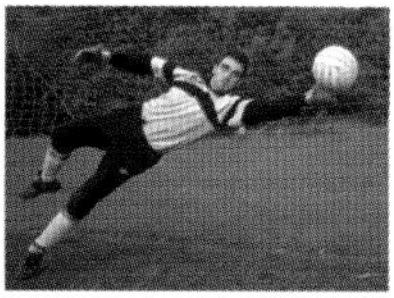

セーブする
sēbu suru
save (v)

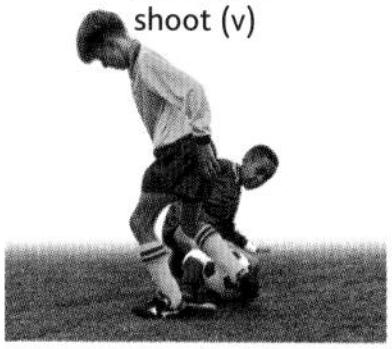

タックルする
takkuru suru
tackle (v)

関連用語 kanrenyōgo • vocabulary

競技場 kyōgijō **stadium**	**ファウル** fauru **foul**	**イエローカード** ierō kādo **yellow card**	**連盟** renmei **league**	**延長時間** enchō jikan **extra time**
1点あげる itten ageru **score a goal (v)**	**コーナーキック** kōnā kikku **corner**	**オフサイド** ofu-saido **off-side**	**引分け** hikiwake **draw**	**補欠選手** hoketsusenshu **substitute**
ペナルティー penarutī **penalty**	**レッドカード** reddo kādo **red card**	**退場する** taijō suru **send off (v)**	**ハーフタイム** hāfu taimu **half time**	**代理** dairi **substitution**

ホッケー hokkē • hockey

アイスホッケー aisu hokkē • ice hockey

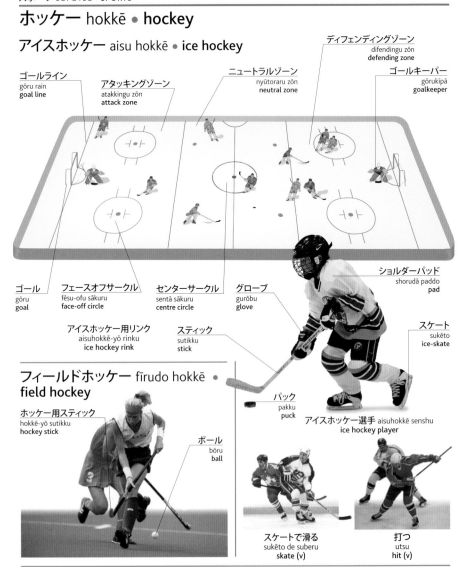

ディフェンディングゾーン
difendingu zōn
defending zone

ゴールライン
gōru rain
goal line

アタッキングゾーン
atakkingu zōn
attack zone

ニュートラルゾーン
nyūtoraru zōn
neutral zone

ゴールキーパー
gōrukīpā
goalkeeper

ゴール
gōru
goal

フェースオフサークル
fēsu-ofu sākuru
face-off circle

センターサークル
sentā sākuru
centre circle

グローブ
gurōbu
glove

ショルダーパッド
shorudā paddo
pad

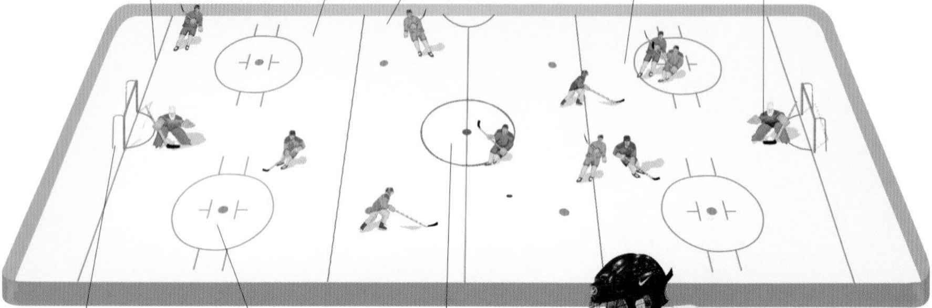

アイスホッケー用リンク
aisuhokkē-yō rinku
ice hockey rink

スティック
sutikku
stick

スケート
sukēto
ice-skate

フィールドホッケー fīrudo hokkē • field hockey

ホッケー用スティック
hokkē-yō sutikku
hockey stick

ボール
bōru
ball

パック
pakku
puck

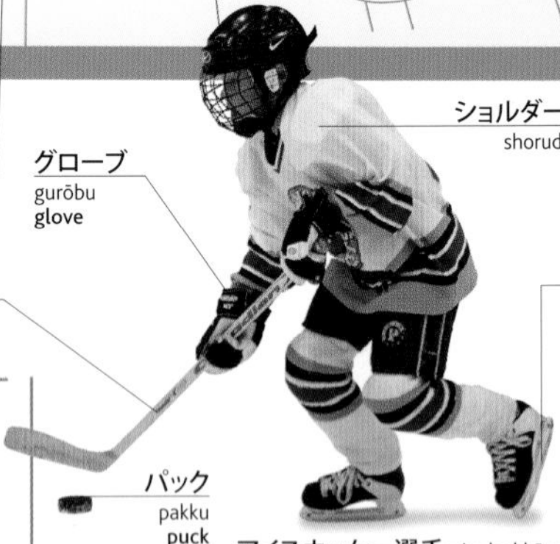

アイスホッケー選手 aisuhokkē senshu
ice hockey player

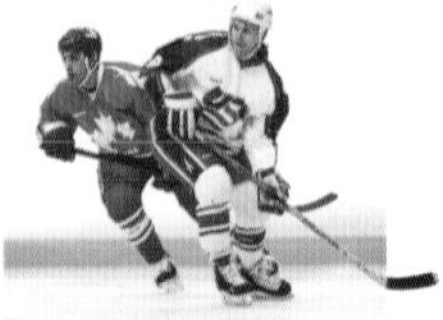

スケートで滑る
sukēto de suberu
skate (v)

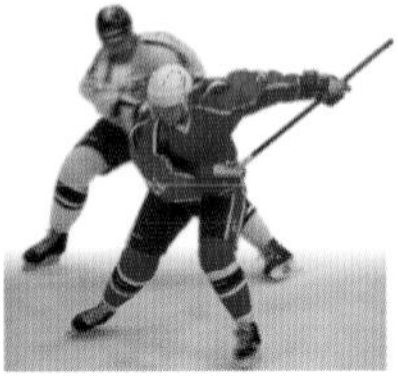

打つ
utsu
hit (v)

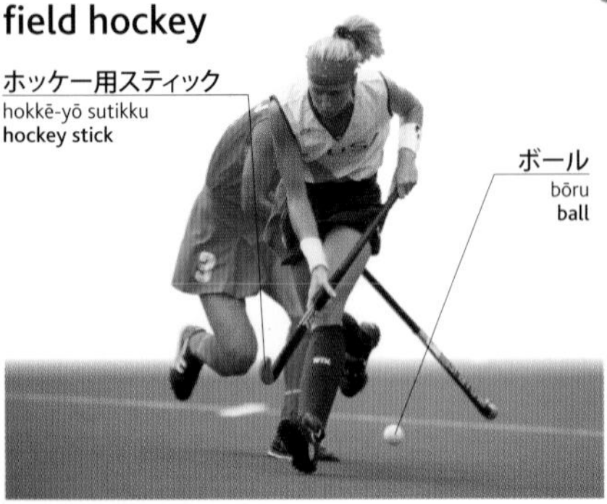

クリケット kuriketto ● cricket

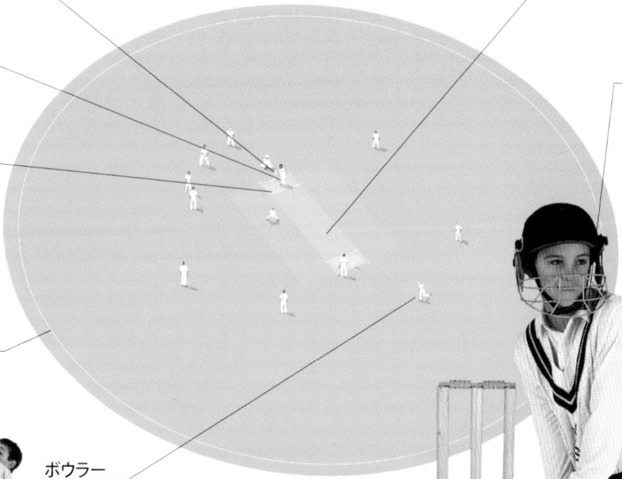

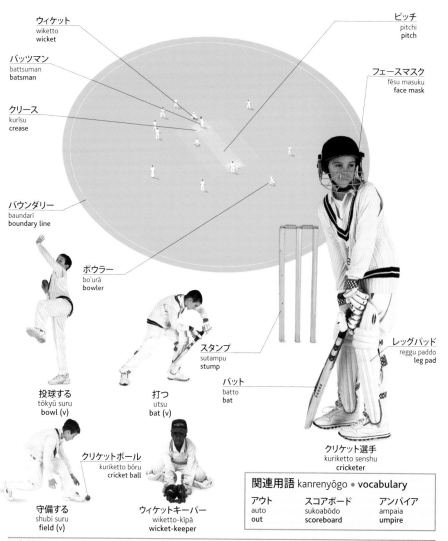

ウィケット
wiketto
wicket

ピッチ
pitchi
pitch

バッツマン
battsuman
batsman

フェースマスク
fēsu masuku
face mask

クリース
kurīsu
crease

バウンダリー
baundarī
boundary line

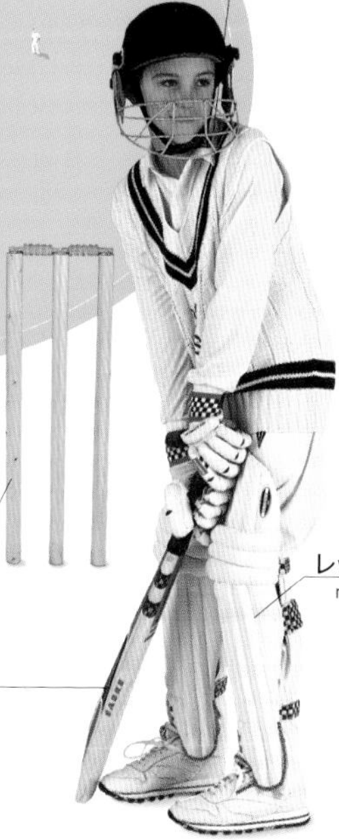

ボウラー
bo'urā
bowler

スタンプ
sutampu
stump

レッグパッド
reggu paddo
leg pad

バット
batto
bat

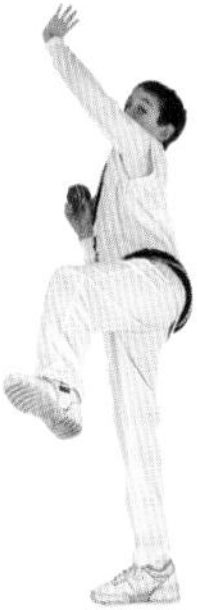

投球する
tōkyū suru
bowl (v)

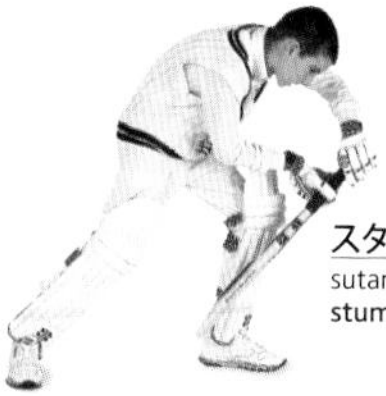

打つ
utsu
bat (v)

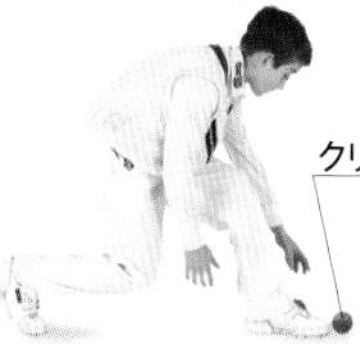

クリケットボール
kuriketto bōru
cricket ball

クリケット選手
kuriketto senshu
cricketer

守備する
shubi suru
field (v)

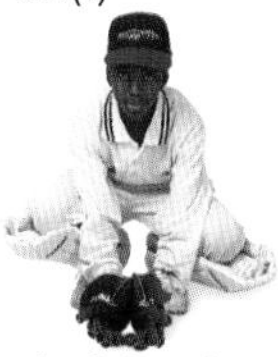

ウィケットキーパー
wiketto-kīpā
wicket-keeper

関連用語 kanrenyōgo ● vocabulary		
アウト	スコアボード	アンパイア
auto	sukoabōdo	ampaia
out	**scoreboard**	**umpire**

バスケットボール basukettobōru • **basketball**

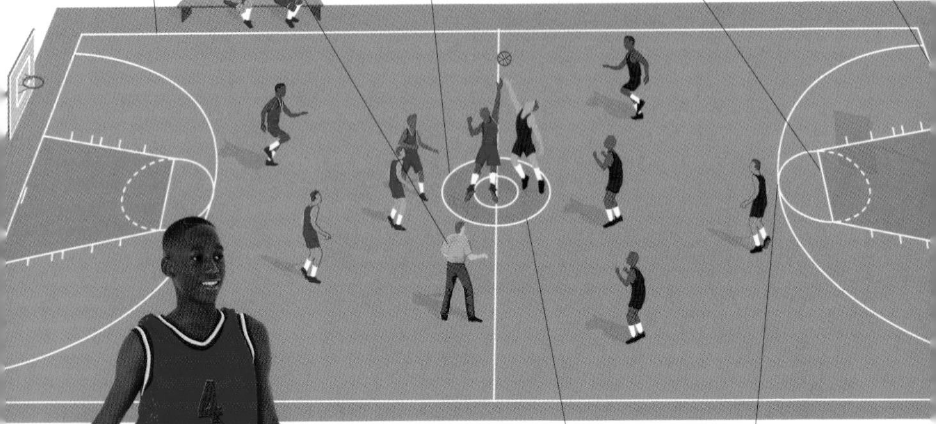

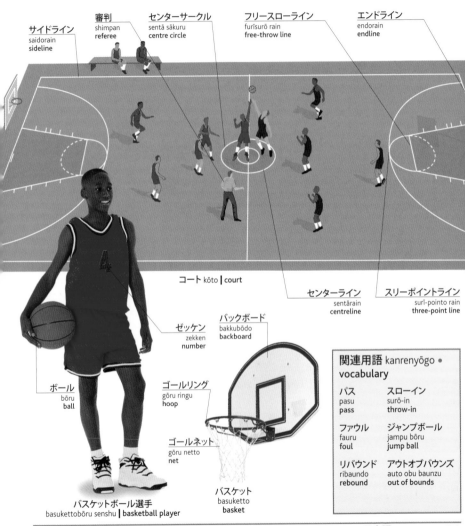

サイドライン
saidorain
sideline

審判
shimpan
referee

センターサークル
sentā sākuru
centre circle

フリースローライン
furīsurō rain
free-throw line

エンドライン
endorain
endline

コート kōto | court

センターライン
sentārain
centreline

スリーポイントライン
surī-pointo rain
three-point line

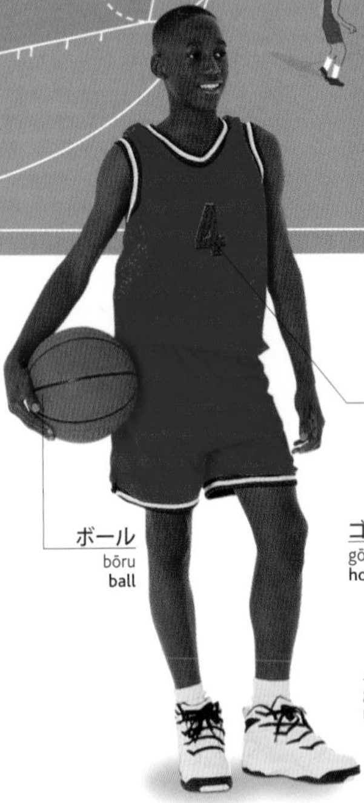

ゼッケン
zekken
number

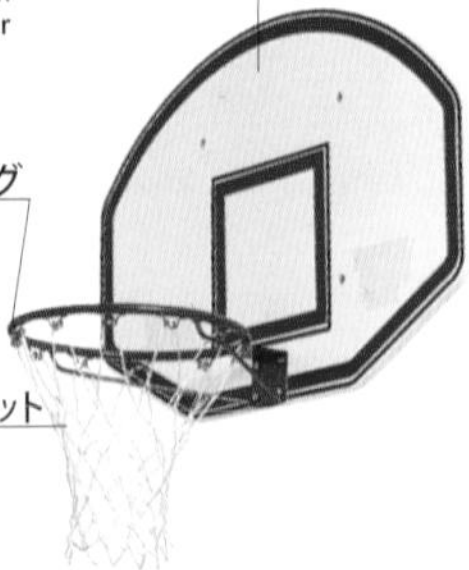

バックボード
bakkubōdo
backboard

ボール
bōru
ball

ゴールリング
gōru ringu
hoop

ゴールネット
gōru netto
net

バスケット
basuketto
basket

バスケットボール選手
basukettobōru senshu | basketball player

関連用語 kanrenyōgo • vocabulary

パス pasu **pass**	スローイン surō-in **throw-in**
ファウル fauru **foul**	ジャンプボール jampu bōru **jump ball**
リバウンド ribaundo **rebound**	アウトオブバウンズ auto obu baunzu **out of bounds**

動作 dōsa • actions

投げる
nageru
throw (v)

受ける
ukeru
catch (v)

シュートする
shūto suru
shoot (v)

ジャンプする
jampu suru
jump (v)

マークする
māku suru
mark (v)

ブロックする
burokku suru
block (v)

バウンドする
baundo suru
bounce (v)

ダンクシュートする
dankushūto suru
dunk (v)

バレーボール barēbōru • volleyball

ブロックする
burokku suru
block (v)

ネット
netto
net

レシーブする
reshību suru
dig (v)

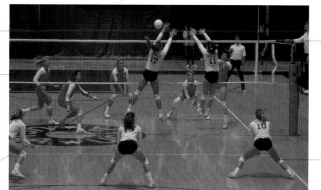

審判
shimpan
referee

サポーター
sapōtā
knee support

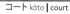

コート kōto | **court**

野球 yakyū • baseball

球場 kyūjō • field

左翼
sayoku
left field

内野
naiya
infield

センター
sentā
centre field

バット
batto
bat

ヘルメット
herumetto
helmet

三塁手
sanruishu
third baseman

ピッチャーマウンド
pitchā maundo
pitcher's mound

ホームベース
hōmu bēsu
home plate

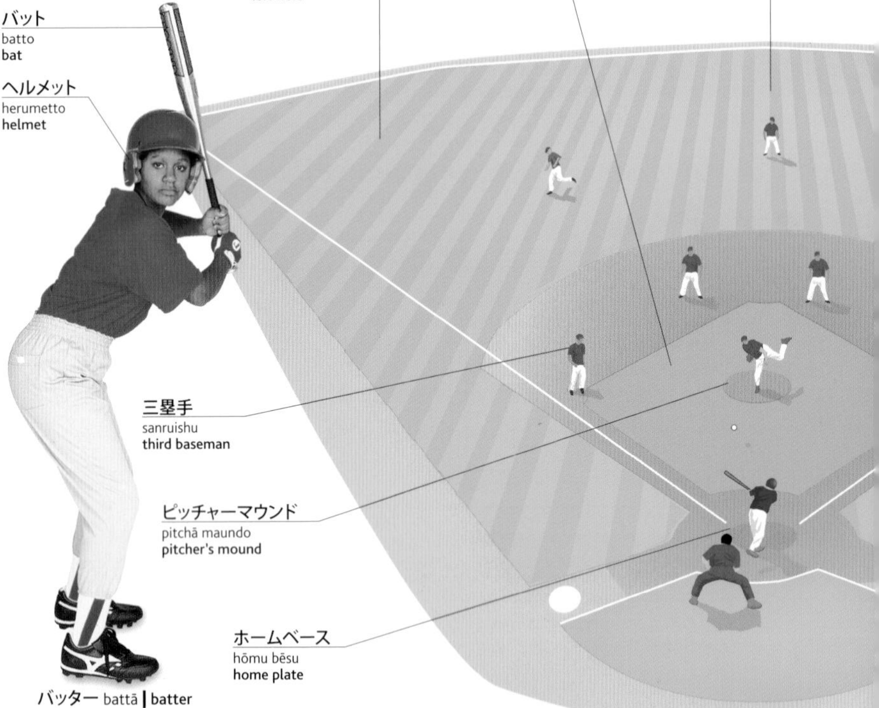

バッター battā **|** batter

関連用語 kanrenyōgo • vocabulary

イニング	セーフ	ファウルボール
iningu	sēfu	fauru bōru
inning	**safe**	**foul ball**
ラン	アウト	ストライク
ran	auto	sutoraiku
run	**out**	**strike**

ミット mitto
mitt

ボール
bōru
ball

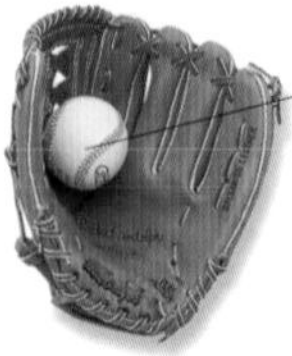

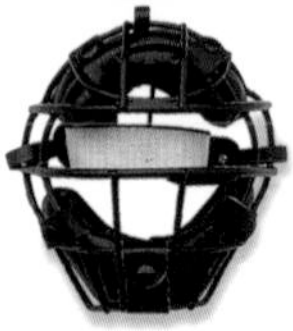

マスク masuku
mask

外野
gaiya
outfield

右翼
uyoku
right field

ファウルライン
fauru rain
foul line

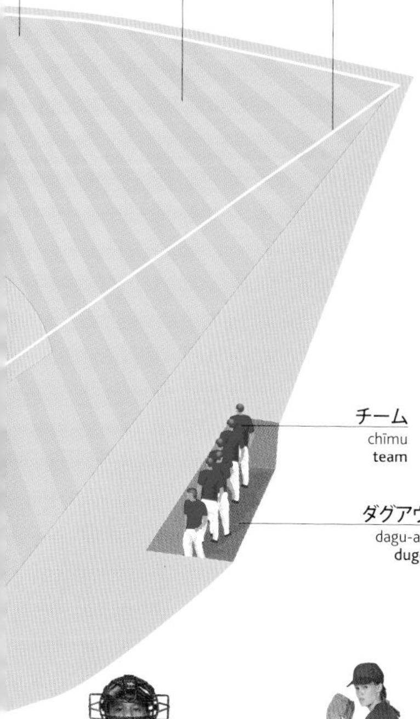

チーム
chīmu
team

ダグアウト
dagu-auto
dugout

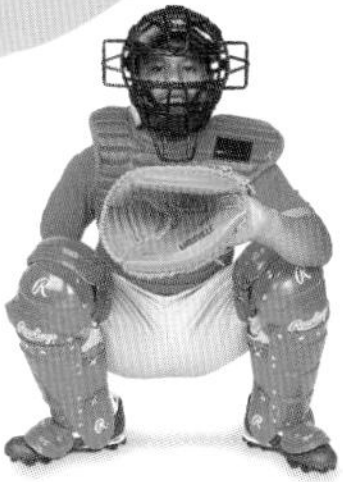

キャッチャー kyatchā
catcher

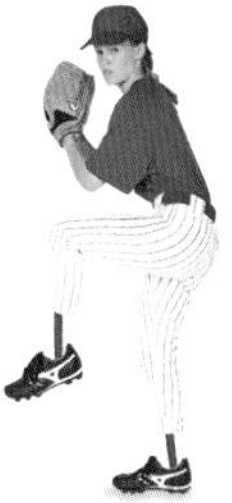

ピッチャー pitchā
pitcher

動作 dōsa • actions

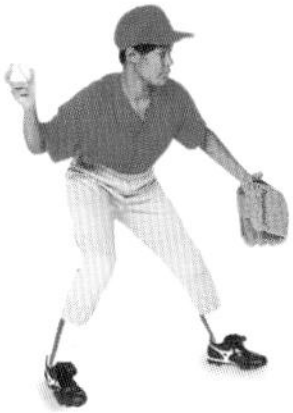

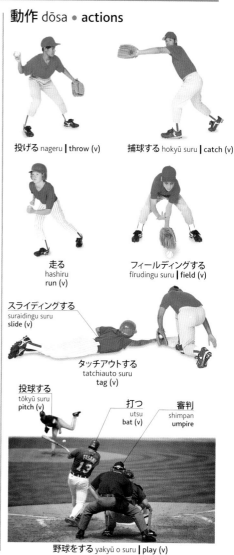

投げる nageru | throw (v)

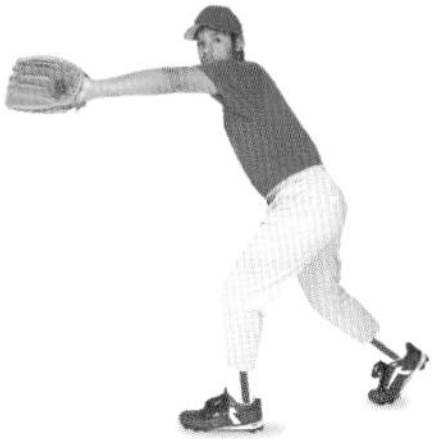

捕球する hokyū suru | catch (v)

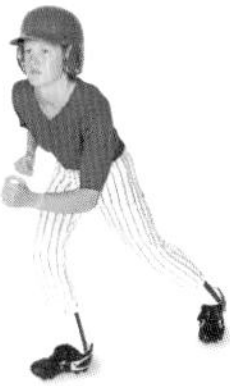

走る
hashiru
run (v)

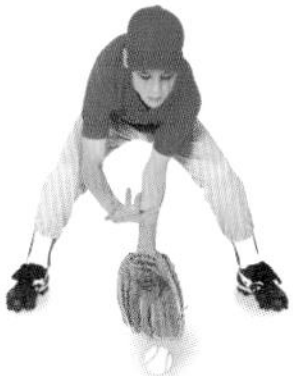

フィールディングする
fīrudingu suru | field (v)

スライディングする
suraidingu suru
slide (v)

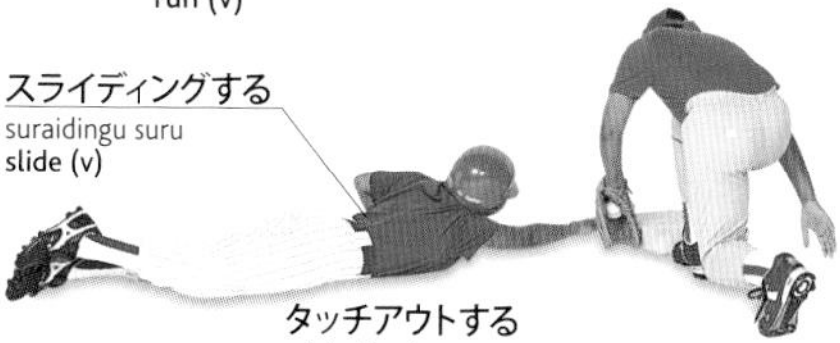

タッチアウトする
tatchiauto suru
tag (v)

投球する
tōkyū suru
pitch (v)

打つ
utsu
bat (v)

審判
shimpan
umpire

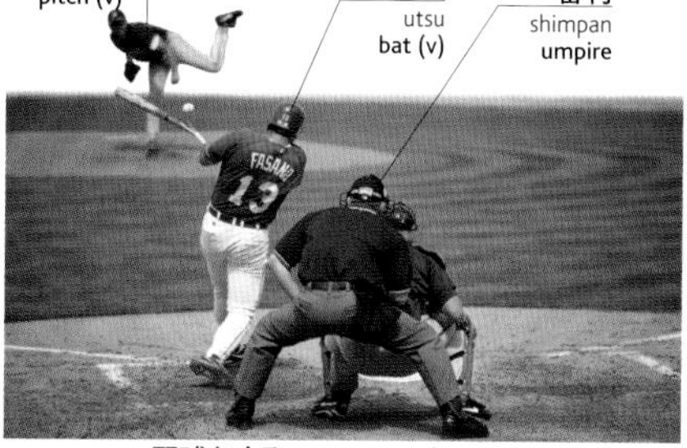

野球をする yakyū o suru | play (v)

テニス tenisu • tennis

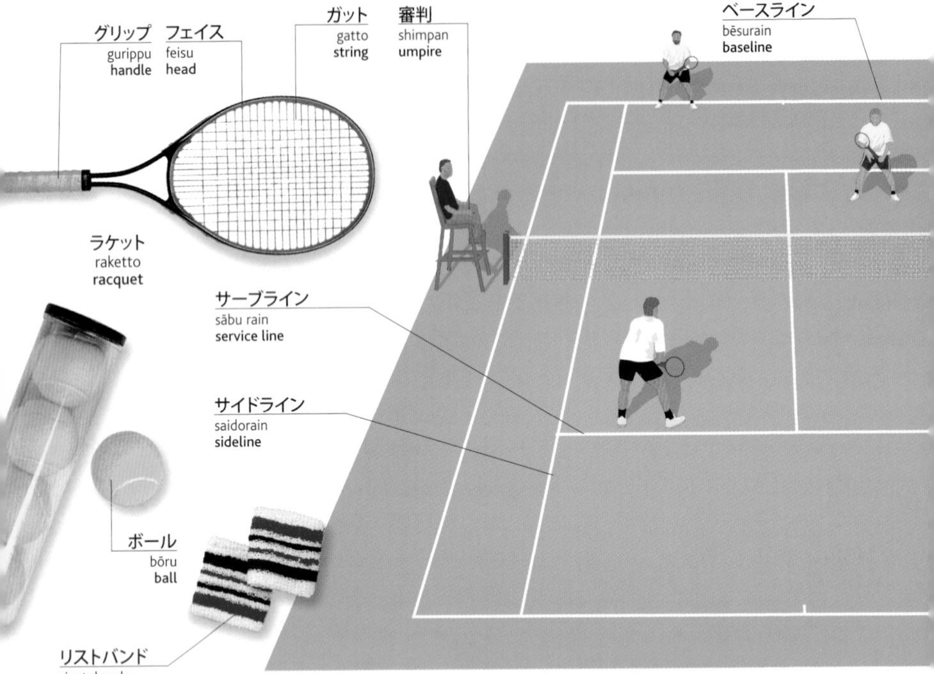

グリップ
gurippu
handle

フェイス
feisu
head

ガット
gatto
string

審判
shimpan
umpire

ベースライン
bêsurain
baseline

ラケット
raketto
racquet

サーブライン
sâbu rain
service line

サイドライン
saidorain
sideline

ボール
bôru
ball

リストバンド
risutobando
wristband

テニスコート tenisu kôto | tennis court

関連用語 kanrenyôgo • vocabulary

シングルス shingurusu singles	**セット** setto set	**ラブ** rabu love	**フォルト** foruto fault	**スライス** suraisu slice	**線審** senshin linesman
ダブルス daburusu doubles	**マッチ** matchi match	**デュース** dyûsu deuce	**エース** êsu ace	**ラリー** rarî rally	**選手権** senshuken championship
ゲーム gêmu game	**タイブレーク** taiburêku tiebreak	**アドバンテージ** adobantêji advantage	**ドロップショット** doroppu shotto dropshot	**レット** retto! let!	**スピン** supin spin

ネット
netto
net

スマッシュ
sumasshu
smash

ボールボーイ
bōrubōi
ballboy

サーブ する
sābu suru
serve (v)

テニス靴
tenisu-gutsu
tennis shoes

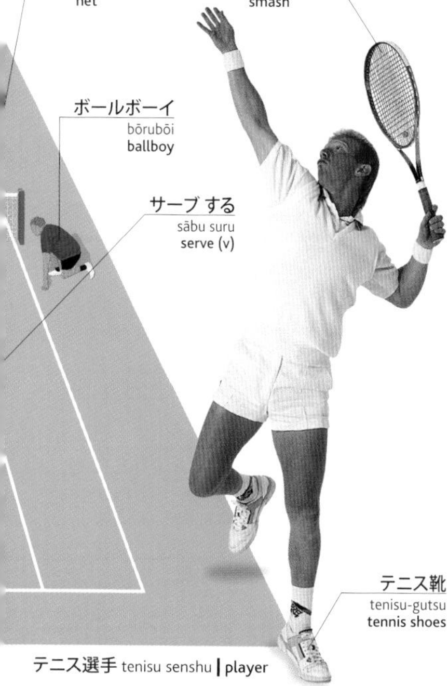

テニス選手 tenisu senshu | player

ストローク sutorōku • strokes

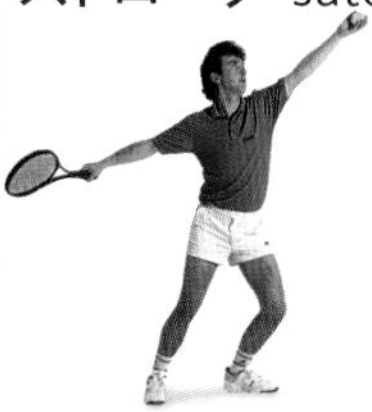

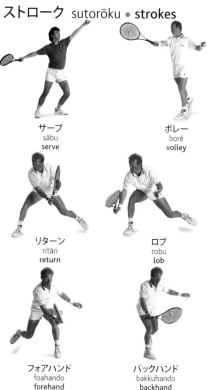

サーブ
sābu
serve

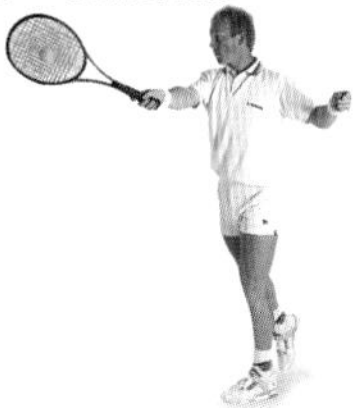

ボレー
borē
volley

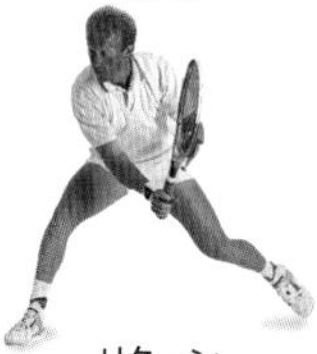

リターン
ritān
return

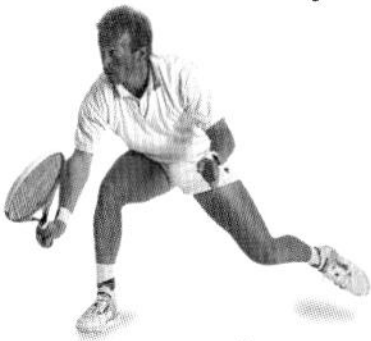

ロブ
robu
lob

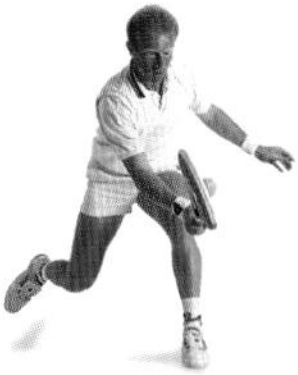

フォアハンド
foahando
forehand

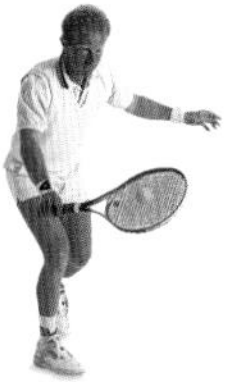

バックハンド
bakkuhando
backhand

ラケットスポーツ raketto supōtsu • racquet games

シャトル
shatoru
shuttlecock

ラケット
raketto
bat

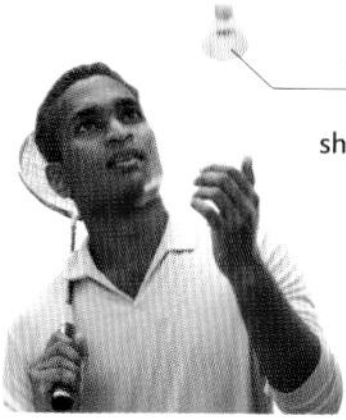

バドミントン
badominton
badminton

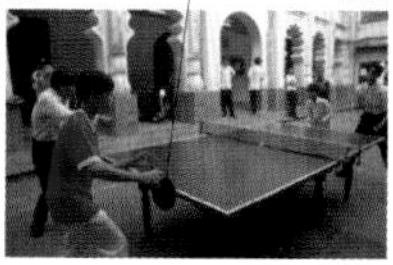

卓球
takkyū
table tennis

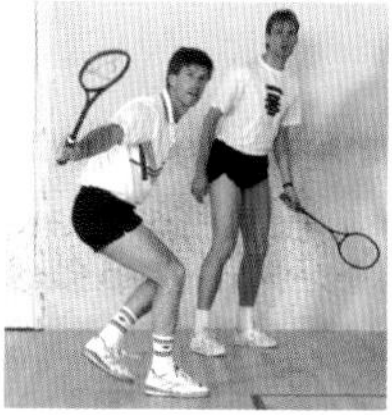

スカッシュ
sukasshu
squash

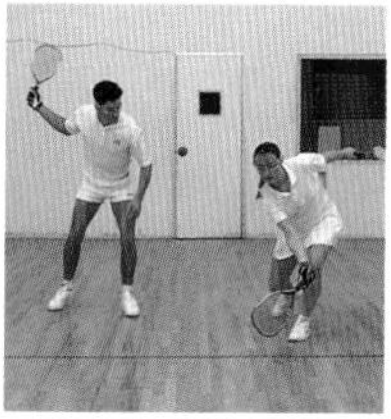

ラケットボール
rakettobōru
racquetball

ゴルフ gorufu • golf

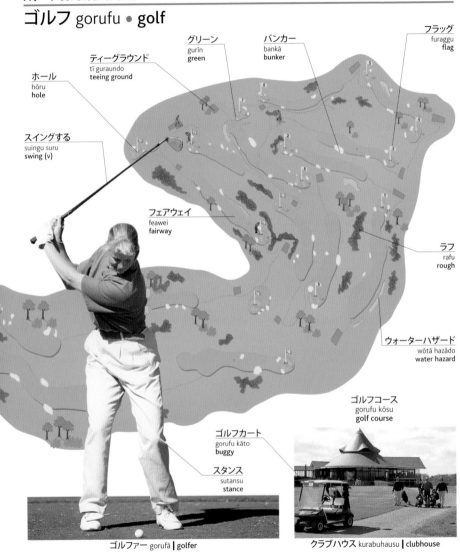

ホール
hōru
hole

ティーグラウンド
tī guraundo
teeing ground

グリーン
gurīn
green

バンカー
bankā
bunker

フラッグ
furaggu
flag

スイングする
suingu suru
swing (v)

フェアウェイ
feawei
fairway

ラフ
rafu
rough

ウォーターハザード
wōtā hazādo
water hazard

ゴルフコース
gorufu kōsu
golf course

ゴルフカート
gorufu kāto
buggy

スタンス
sutansu
stance

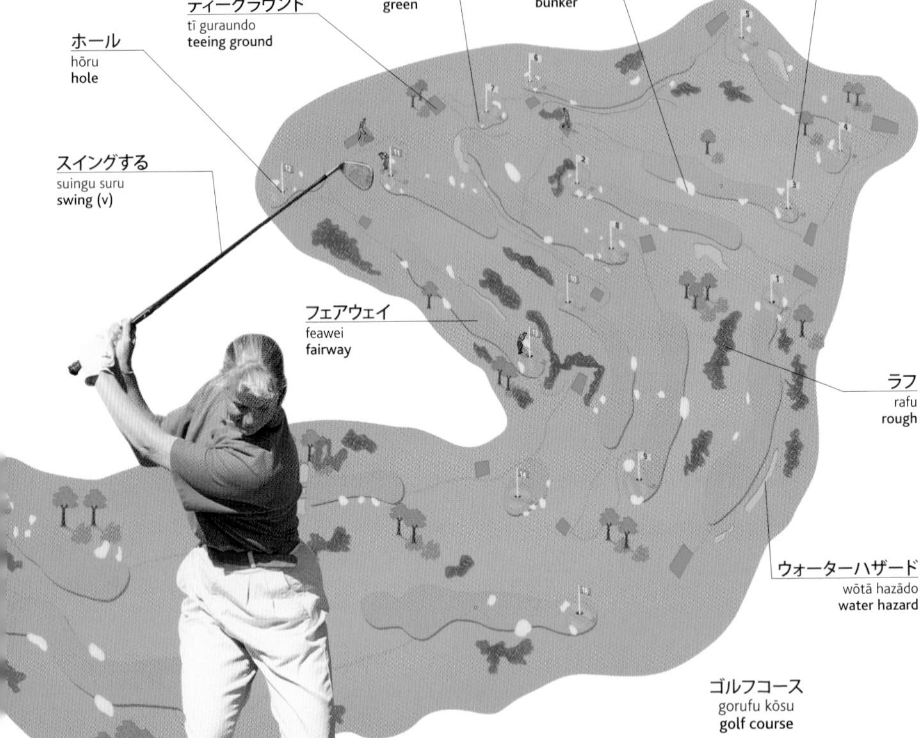

ゴルファー gorufā | golfer

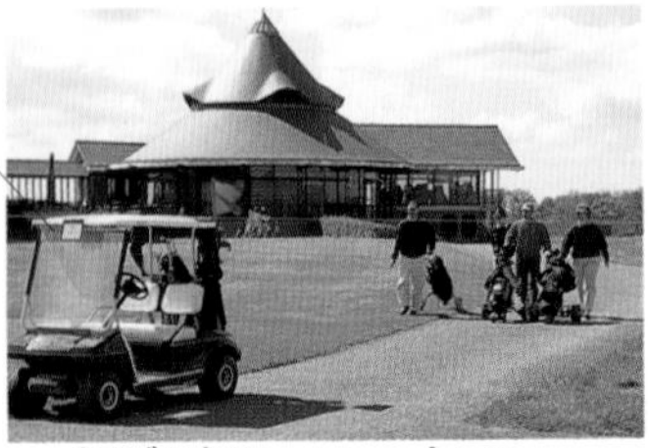

クラブハウス kurabuhausu | clubhouse

用具 yōgu • equipment

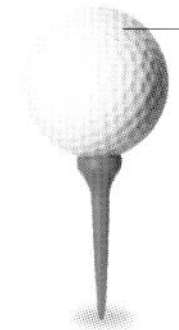

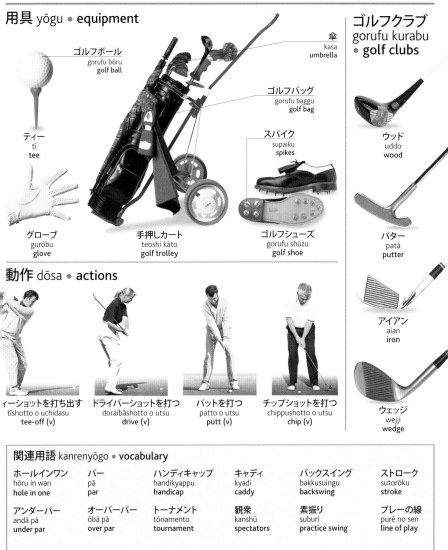

ゴルフボール
gorufu bōru
golf ball

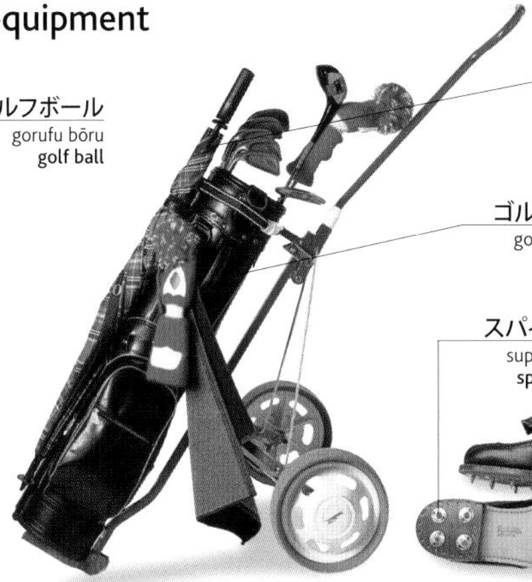

傘
kasa
umbrella

ゴルフバッグ
gorufu baggu
golf bag

ティー
tī
tee

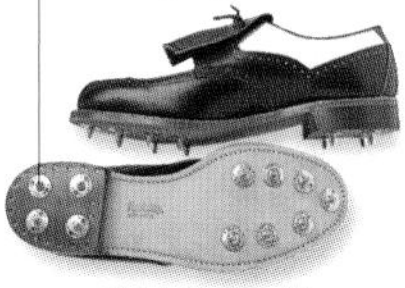

スパイク
supaiku
spikes

グローブ
gurōbu
glove

手押しカート
teoshi kāto
golf trolley

ゴルフシューズ
gorufu shūzu
golf shoe

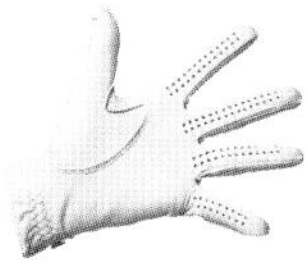

ゴルフクラブ
gorufu kurabu
• **golf clubs**

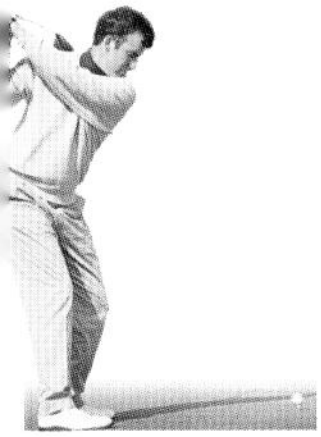

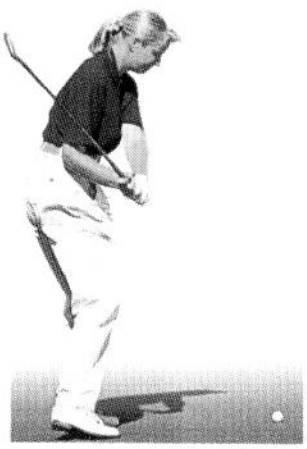

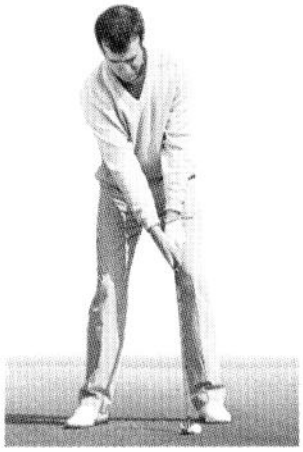

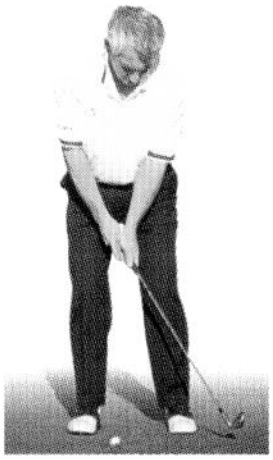

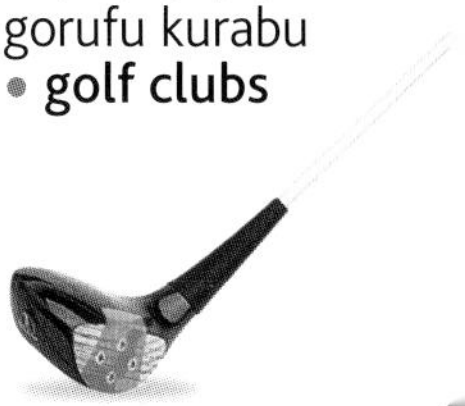

ウッド
uddo
wood

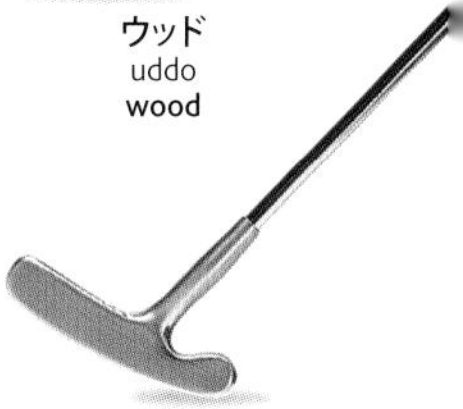

パター
patā
putter

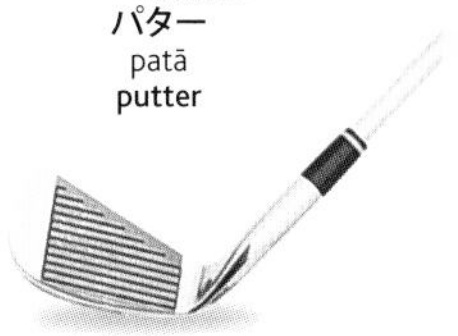

アイアン
aian
iron

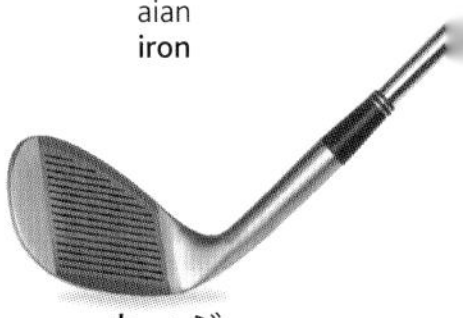

ウェッジ
wejji
wedge

動作 dōsa • actions

ィーショットを打ち出す
tīshotto o uchidasu
tee-off (v)

ドライバーショットを打つ
doraibāshotto o utsu
drive (v)

パットを打つ
patto o utsu
putt (v)

チップショットを打つ
chippushotto o utsu
chip (v)

関連用語 kanrenyōgo • vocabulary

ホールインワン hōru in wan **hole in one**	パー pā **par**	ハンディキャップ handikyappu **handicap**	キャディ kyadi **caddy**	バックスイング bakkusuingu **backswing**	ストローク sutorōku **stroke**
アンダーパー andā pā **under par**	オーバーパー ōbā pā **over par**	トーナメント tōnamento **tournament**	観衆 kanshū **spectators**	素振り suburi **practice swing**	プレーの線 purē no sen **line of play**

陸上競技 rikujō kyōgi • athletics

レーン
rēn
lane

トラック
torakku
track

ゴール
gōru
finishing line

スタートライン
sutāto rain
starting line

グランド
gurando
field

陸上競技者
rikujō kyōgi-sha
athlete

短距離走者
tankyori sōsha
sprinter

スターティングブロック
sutātingu burokku
starting blocks

円盤投げ
emban-nage
discus

砲丸投げ
hōgannage
shotput

槍投げ
yarinage
javelin

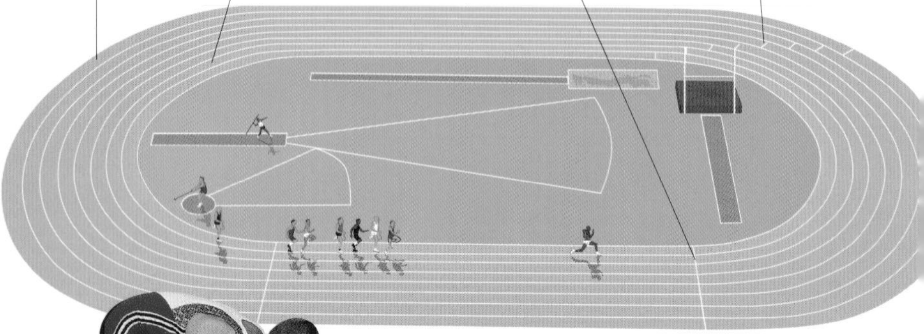

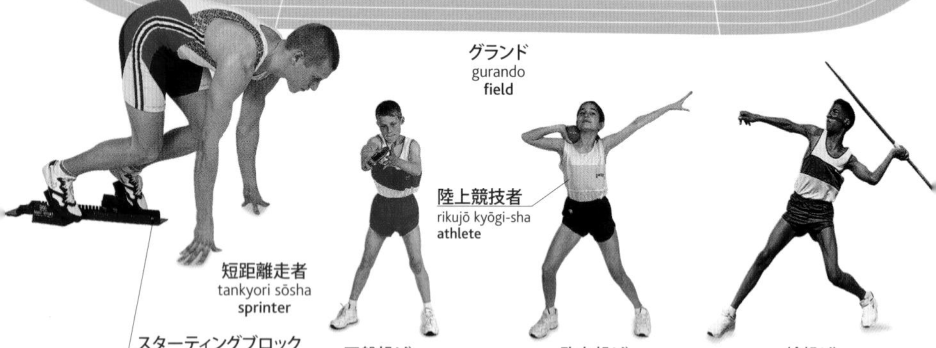

関連用語 kanrenyōgo • vocabulary

競争 kyōsō race	記録 kiroku record	写真判定 shashin hantei photo finish	棒高跳び bōtakatobi pole vault
時間 jikan time	記録を破る kiroku o yaburu break a record (v)	マラソン marason marathon	自己最高記録 jiko saikō kiroku personal best

ストップウォッチ
sutoppuwotchi
stopwatch

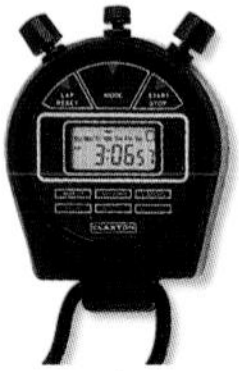

バトン
baton
baton

バー
bā
crossbar

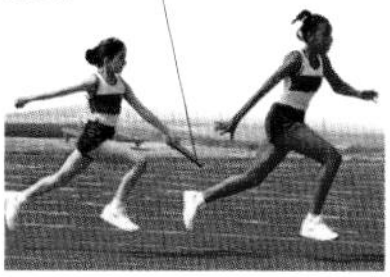

リレー競争
rirē kyōsō
relay race

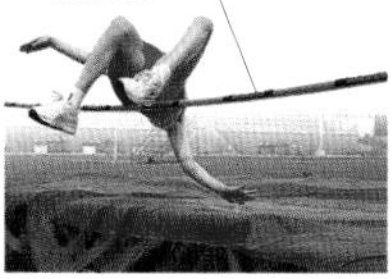

走り高跳び
hashiritakatobi
high jump

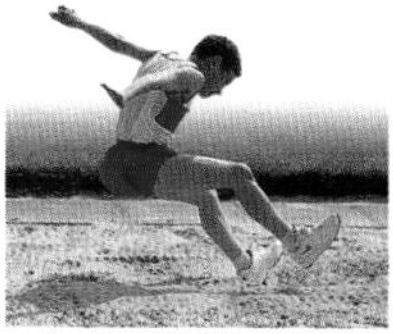

走り幅跳び
hashirihabatobi
long jump

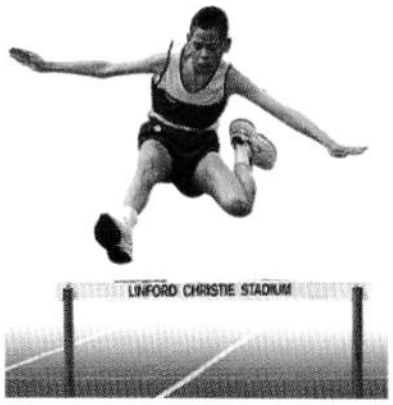

ハードル走
hādorusō
hurdles

体操競技 taisō kyōgi • **gymnastics**

跳躍板
chōyaku-ban
springboard

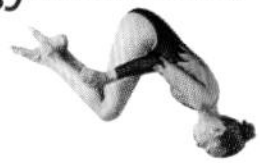

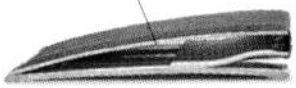

体操選手
taisō senshu
gymnast

跳馬
chōba
horse

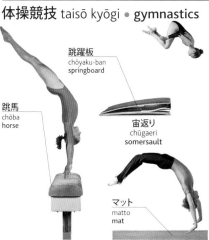

宙返り
chūgaeri
somersault

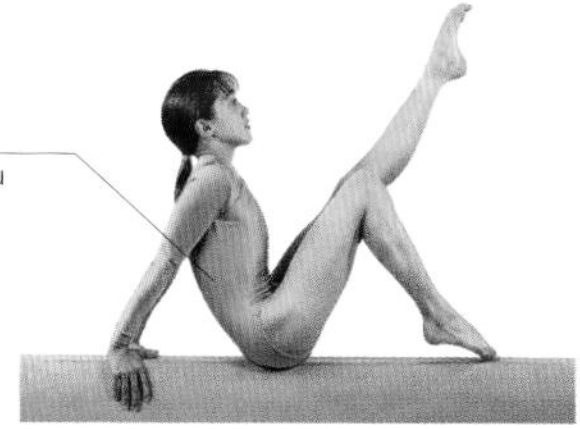

平均台 heikindai | **beam**

リボン
ribon
ribbon

マット
matto
mat

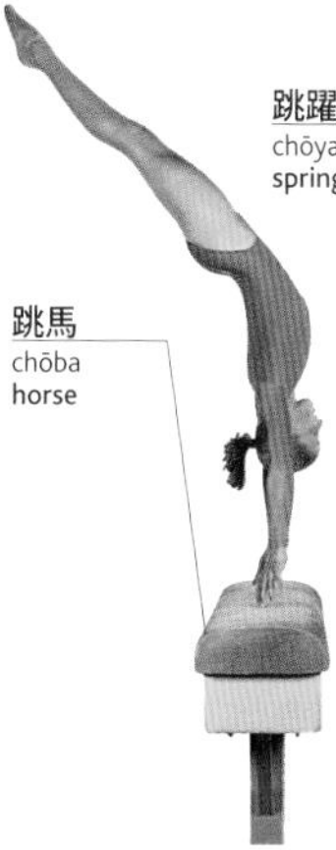

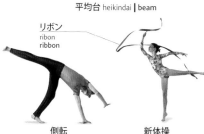

跳馬 (項目)
chōba (kōmoku)
vault

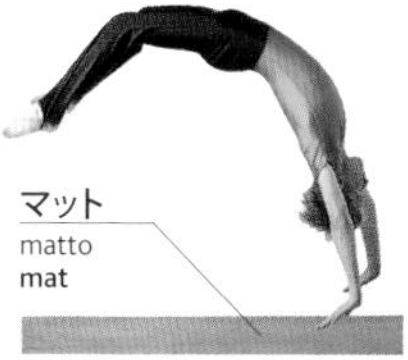

床運動
yuka undō
floor exercises

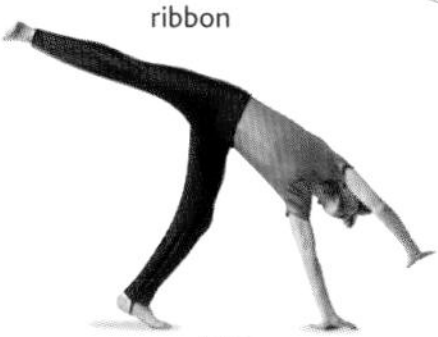

側転
sokuten
tumble

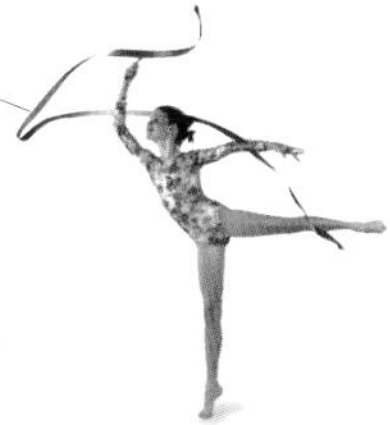

新体操
shintaishō
rhythmic gymnastics

関連用語 kanrenyōgo • **vocabulary**

鉄棒 tetsubō **horizontal bar**	**鞍馬** amba **pommel horse**	**吊り輪** tsuriwa **rings**	**メダル** medaru **medals**	**銀** gin **silver**
平行棒 heikōbō **parallel bars**	**段違い平行棒** danchigai heikōbō **asymmetric bars**	**表彰台** hyōshō dai **podium**	**金** kin **gold**	**銅** dō **bronze**

格闘技 kakutōgi • combat sports

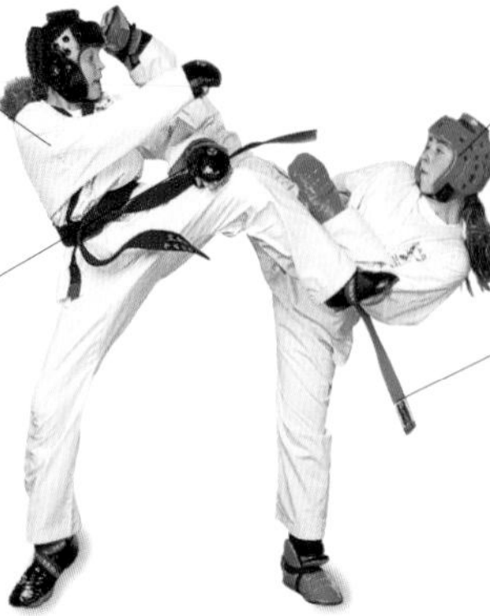

相手
aite
opponent

ヘッドガード
heddogādo
guard

帯
obi
belt

ミット
mitto
glove

テコンドー tekondō | tae-kwon-do

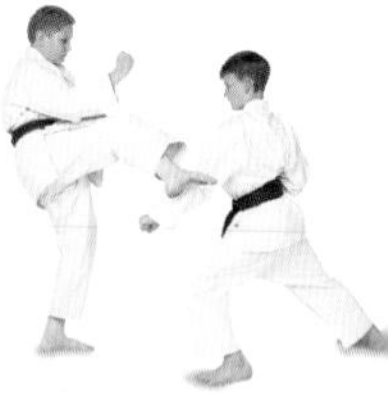

空手 karate | karate

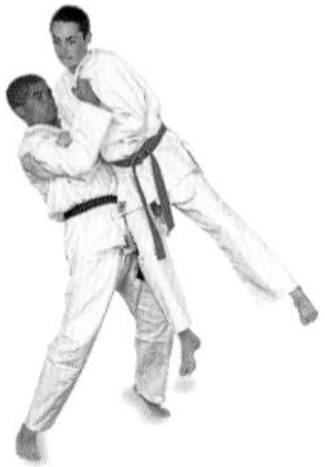

柔道 jūdō | judo

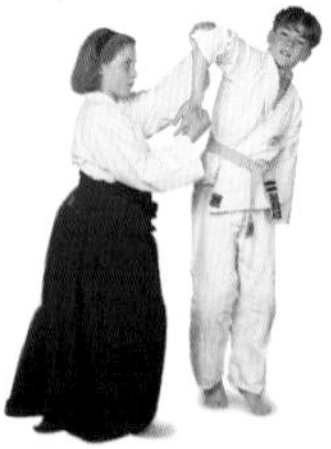

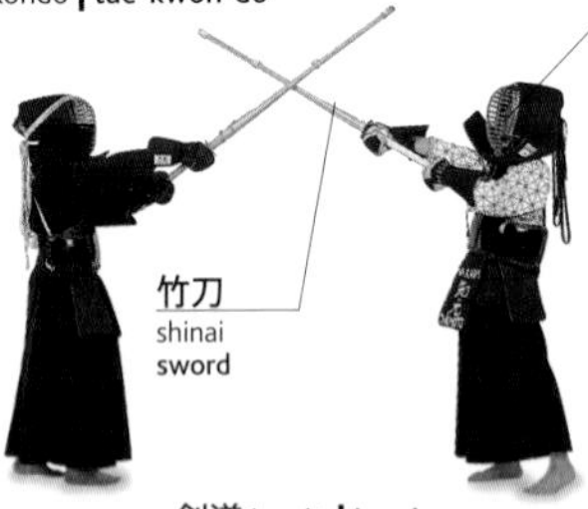

面
men
mask

竹刀
shinai
sword

合気道 aikidō | aikido

剣道 kendō | kendo

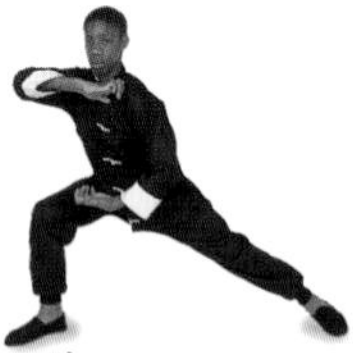

カンフー kanfū
kung fu

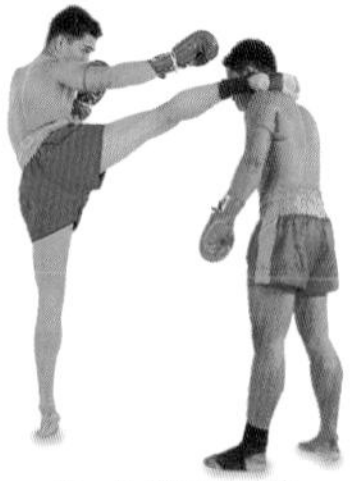

キックボクシング
kikkubokushingu | kickboxing

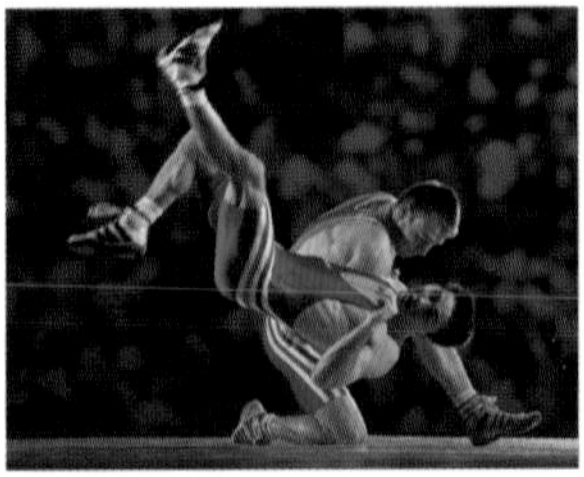

レスリング resuringu | wrestling

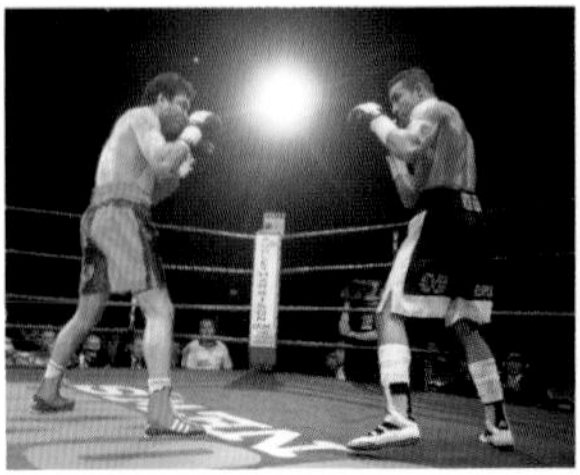

ボクシング bokushingu | boxing

技 waza • actions

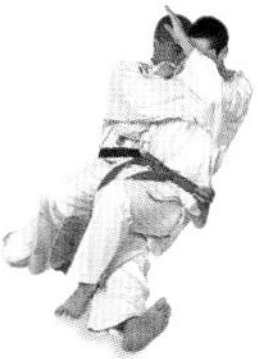

袈裟固 kesagatame | fall

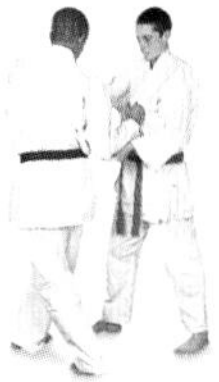

襟掴み erizukami | hold

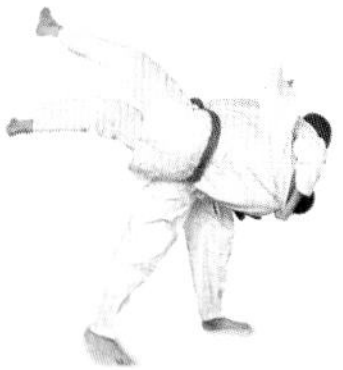

投げ nage | throw

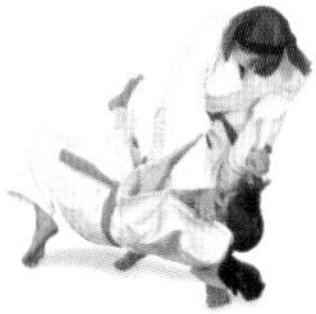

抑え osae | pin

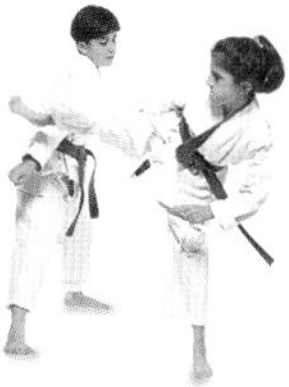

蹴り keri | kick

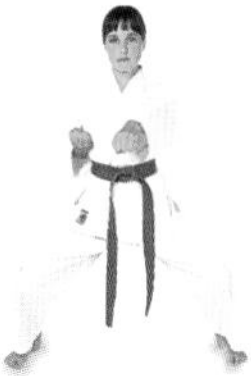

突き tsuki | punch

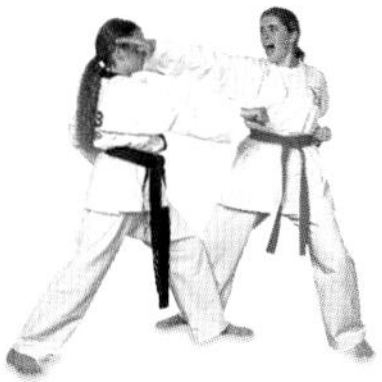

払い harai | strike

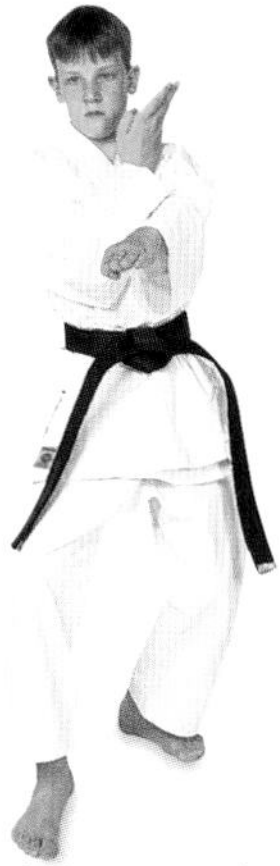

手刀打ち shutō uchi | chop

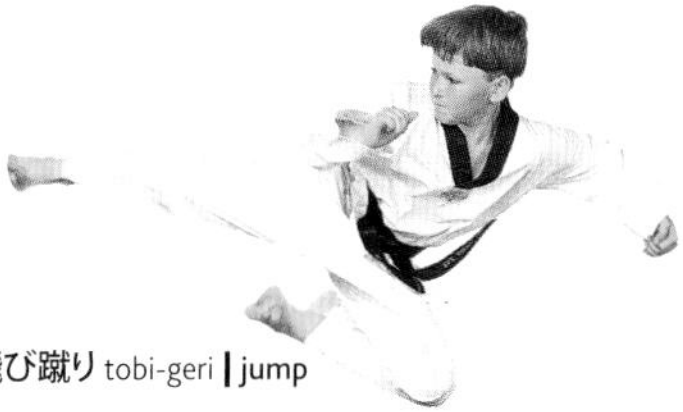

飛び蹴り tobi-geri | jump

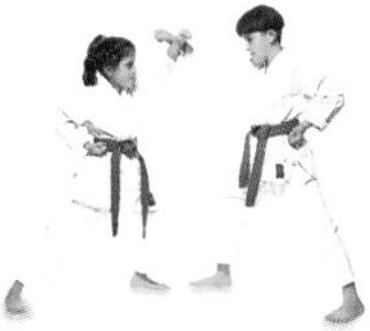

受け uke | block

関連用語 kanrenyōgo • vocabulary

リング
ringu
boxing ring

グローブ
gurōbu
boxing gloves

マウスピース
mausu pīsu
mouth guard

ラウンド
raundo
round

試合
shiai
bout

練習試合
renshū-jiai
sparring

拳
kobushi
fist

ノックアウト
nokku auto
knock out

パンチバッグ
panchi baggu
punch bag

黒帯
kuro obi
black belt

護身
goshin
self defence

武道
budō
martial arts

カポエイラ
kapoeira
capoeira

相撲
sumō
sumo wrestling

太極拳
taikyokuken
tai-chi

水泳 suiei ● swimming
水泳用品 suiei yōhin ● equipment

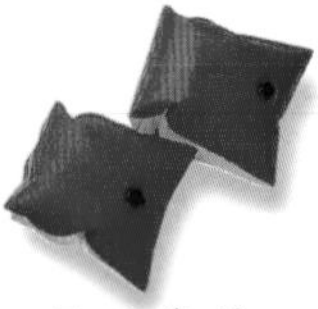

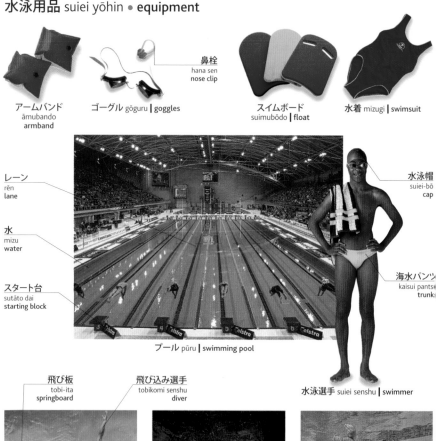

アームバンド
āmubando
armband

ゴーグル gōguru | **goggles**

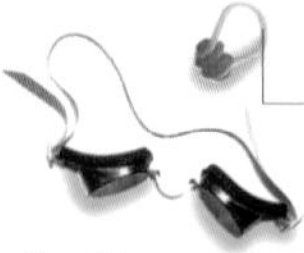

鼻栓
hana sen
nose clip

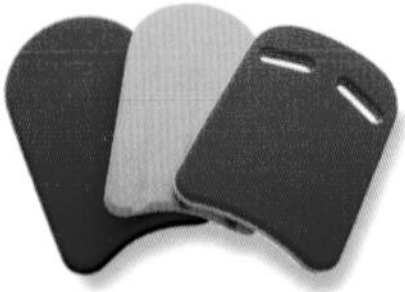

スイムボード
suimubōdo | **float**

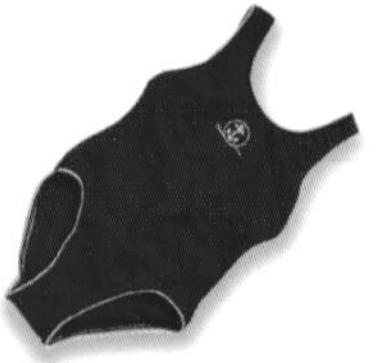

水着 mizugi | **swimsuit**

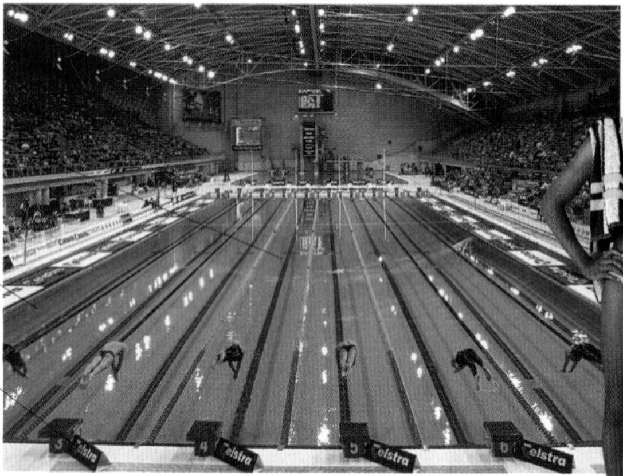

レーン
rēn
lane

水
mizu
water

スタート台
sutāto dai
starting block

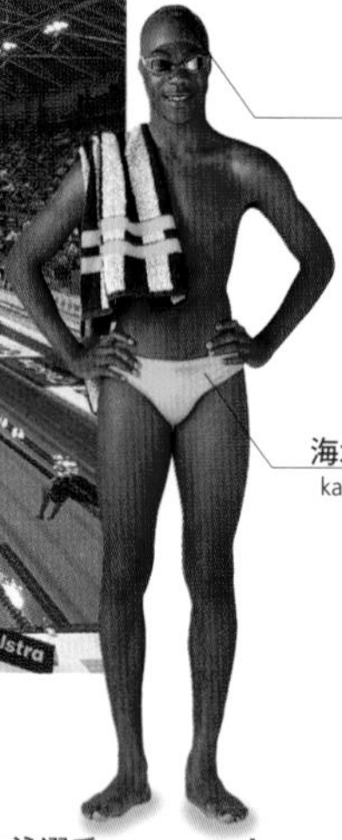

水泳帽
suiei-bō
cap

海水パンツ
kaisui pants
trunk

プール pūru | **swimming pool**

水泳選手 suiei senshu | **swimmer**

飛び板
tobi-ita
springboard

飛び込み選手
tobikomi senshu
diver

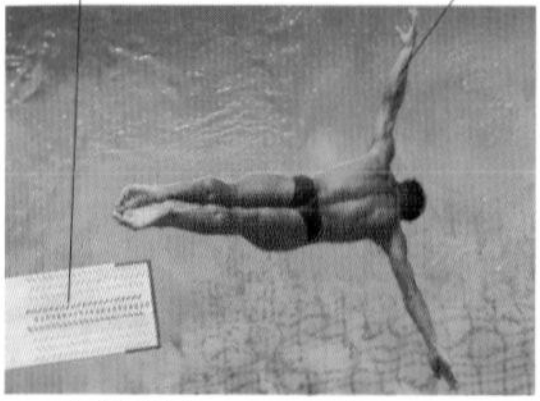

飛び込む tobikomu | **dive (v)**

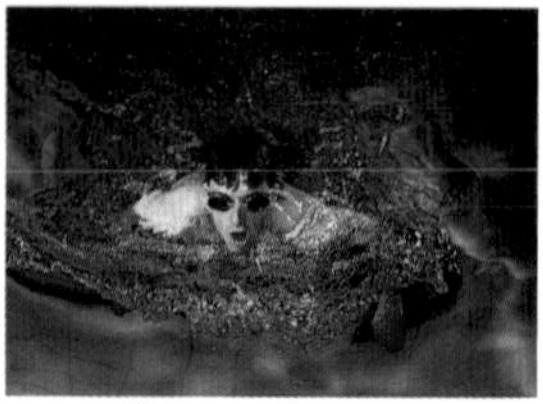

泳ぐ oyogu | **swim (v)**

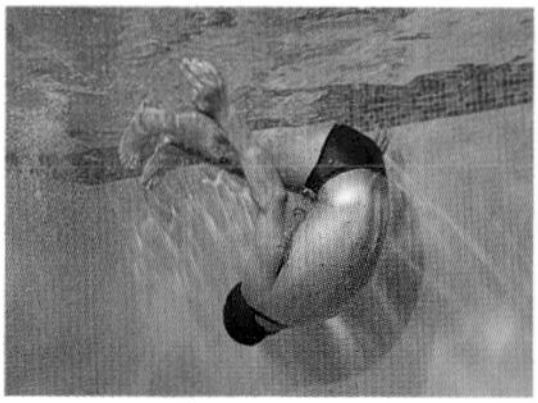

回転 kaiten | **turn**

泳法 eihō • styles

クロール kurōru | front crawl

平泳ぎ hiraoyogi | breaststroke

かき
kaki
stroke

蹴り
keri
kick

背泳ぎ seoyogi | backstroke

バタフライ batafurai | butterfly

スキューバダイビング sukyūba daibingu • scuba diving

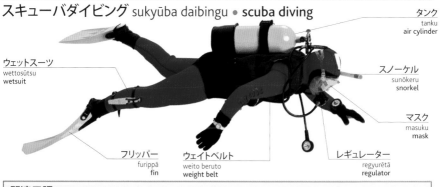

タンク
tanku
air cylinder

ウェットスーツ
wettosūtsu
wetsuit

スノーケル
sunōkeru
snorkel

マスク
masuku
mask

フリッパー
furippā
fin

ウェイトベルト
weito beruto
weight belt

レギュレーター
regyurētā
regulator

関連用語 kanrenyōgo • vocabulary

飛び込み tobikomi dive	立ち泳ぎする tachioyogi suru tread water (v)	ロッカー rokkā lockers	水球 suikyū water polo	浅瀬 asase shallow end	こむら返り komuragaeri cramp
高飛び込み takatobikomi high dive	飛び込みスタート tobikomi sutāto racing dive	救助員 kyūjo-in lifeguard	深み fukami deep end	シンクロナイズドスイミング shinkuronaizudo suimingu synchronized swimming	溺れる oboreru drown (v)

セーリング sēringu ● sailing

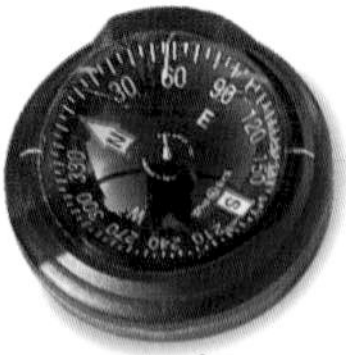

コンパス
kompasu
compass

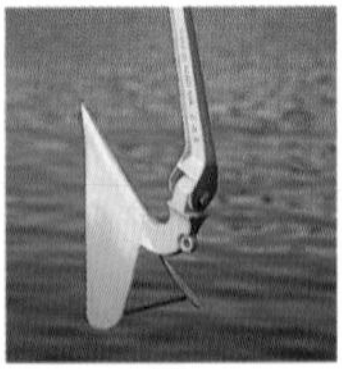

錨
ikari
anchor

マスト
masuto
mast

リギン
rigin
rigging

ヘッドセール
heddosēru
headsail

主帆
shuhan
mainsail

クリート
kurīto
cleat

サイドデッキ
saido dekki
sidedeck

船首
senshu
bow

ブーム
būmu
boom

船尾
sembi
stern

舵棒
kaji bō
tiller

船体
sentai
hull

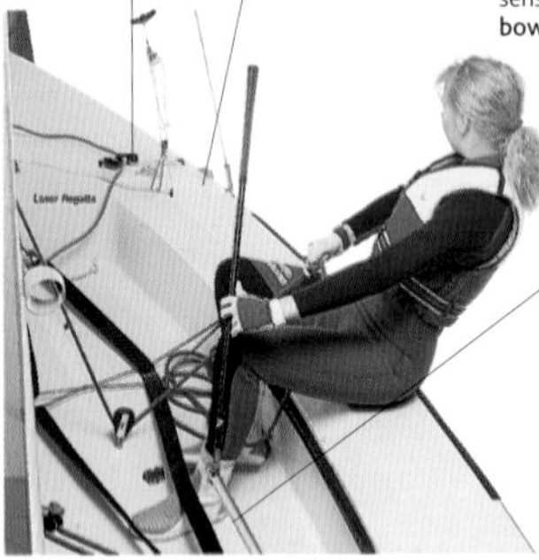

航行する kōkō suru | navigate (v)

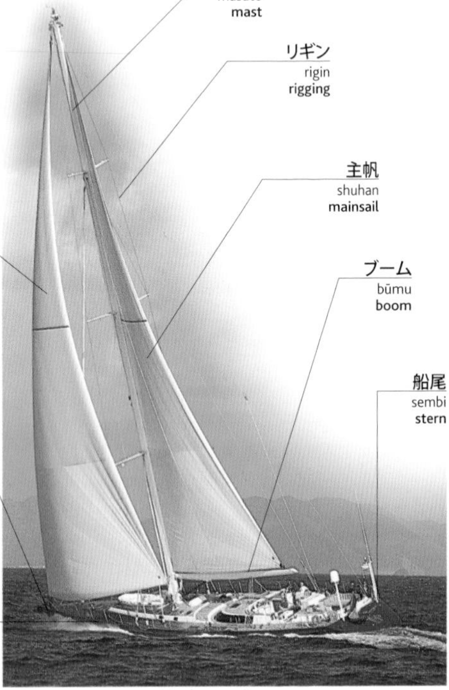

ヨット yotto | yacht

安全用具 anzen yōgu ● safety

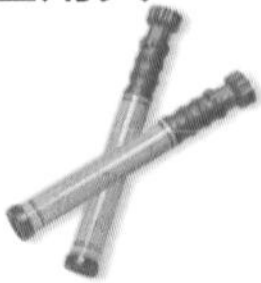

照明弾
shōmeidan
flare

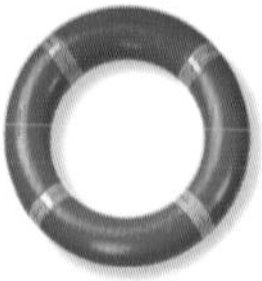

救命ブイ
kyūmei bui
lifebuoy

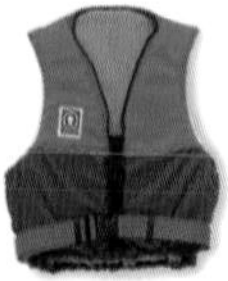

救命胴衣
kyūmei dōi
life jacket

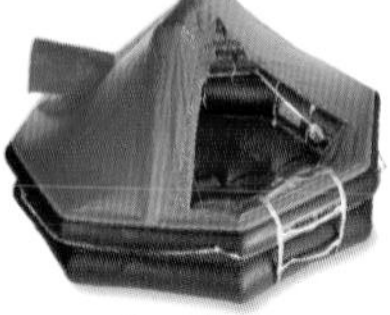

救命ボート
kyūmei bōto
life raft

水上スポーツ suijō supōtsu • **watersports**

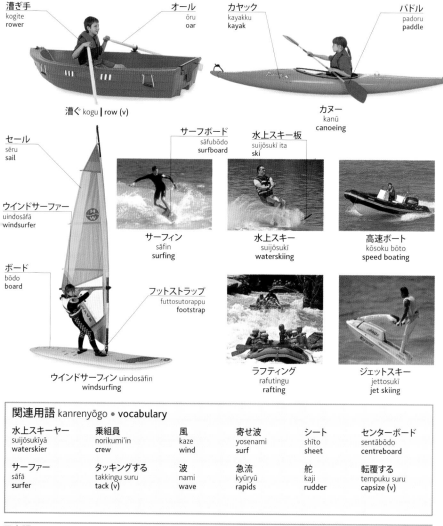

漕ぎ手
kogite
rower

オール
ōru
oar

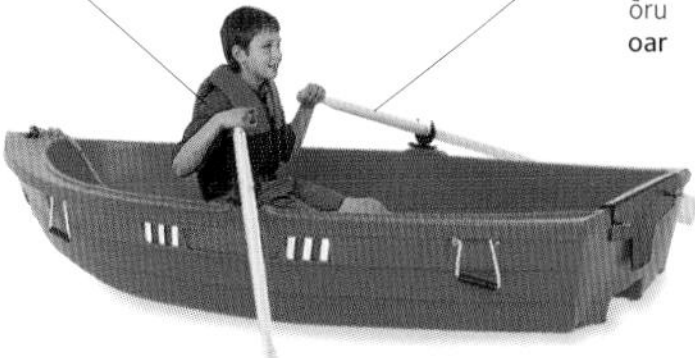

カヤック
kayakku
kayak

パドル
padoru
paddle

漕ぐ kogu | **row (v)**

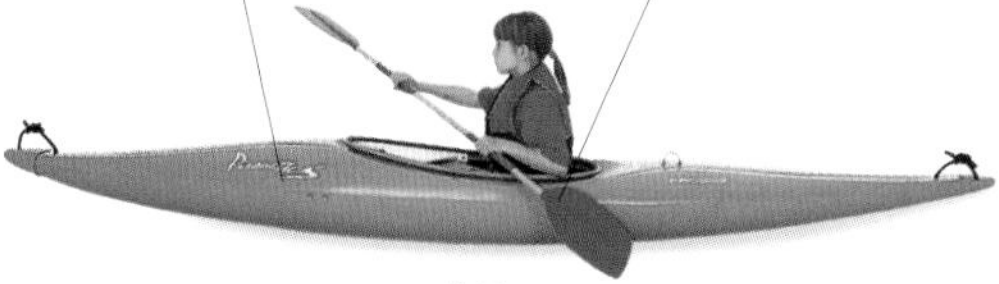

カヌー
kanū
canoeing

セール
sēru
sail

サーフボード
sāfubōdo
surfboard

水上スキー板
suijōsukī ita
ski

ウインドサーファー
uindosāfā
windsurfer

ボード
bōdo
board

フットストラップ
futtosutorappu
footstrap

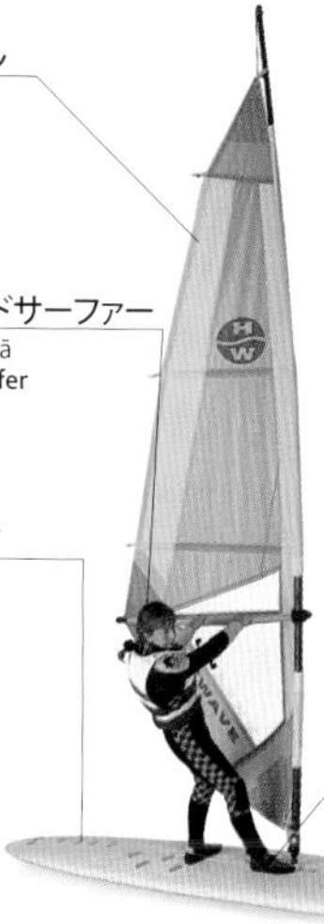

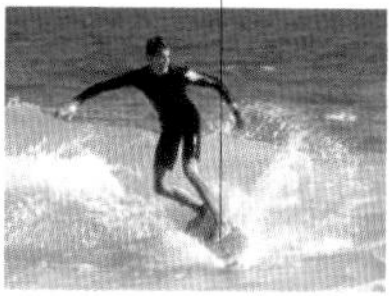

サーフィン
sāfin
surfing

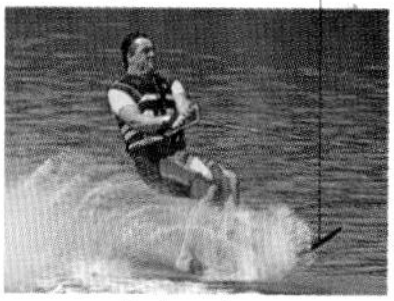

水上スキー
suijōsukī
waterskiing

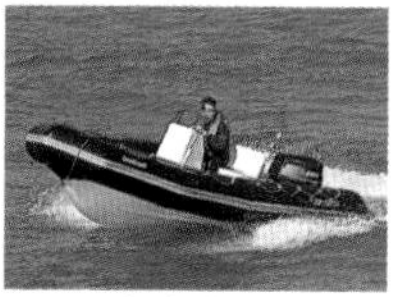

高速ボート
kōsoku bōto
speed boating

ウインドサーフィン uindosāfin
windsurfing

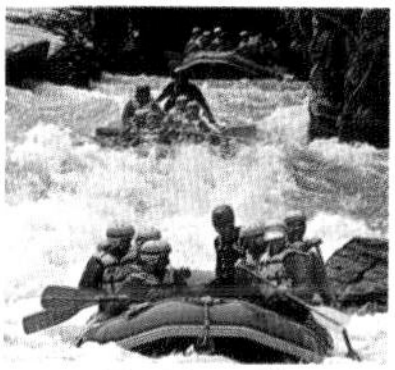

ラフティング
rafutingu
rafting

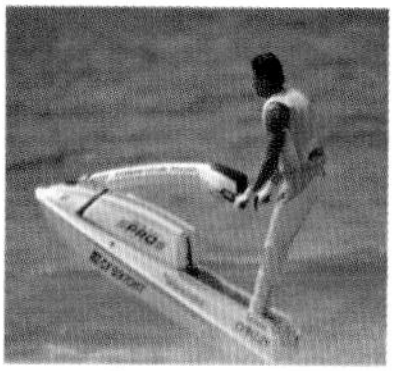

ジェットスキー
jettosukī
jet skiing

関連用語 kanrenyōgo • **vocabulary**

水上スキーヤー suijōsukīyā **waterskier**	乗組員 norikumi'in **crew**	風 kaze **wind**	寄せ波 yosenami **surf**	シート shīto **sheet**	センターボード sentābōdo **centreboard**
サーファー sāfā **surfer**	タッキングする takkingu suru **tack (v)**	波 nami **wave**	急流 kyūryū **rapids**	舵 kaji **rudder**	転覆する tempuku suru **capsize (v)**

乗馬 jōba • horse riding

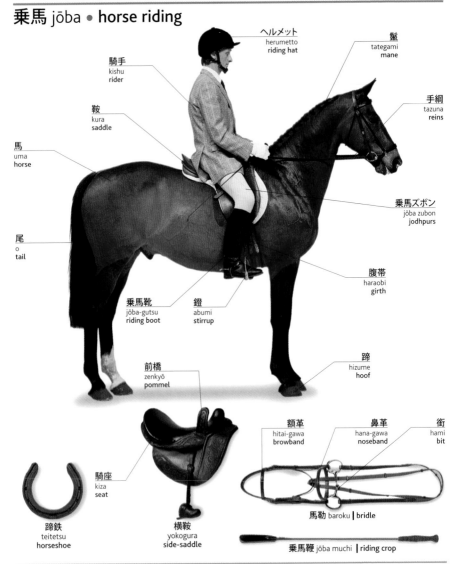

ヘルメット
herumetto
riding hat

鬣
tategami
mane

騎手
kishu
rider

手綱
tazuna
reins

鞍
kura
saddle

馬
uma
horse

乗馬ズボン
jōba zubon
jodhpurs

尾
o
tail

腹帯
haraobi
girth

乗馬靴
jōba-gutsu
riding boot

鐙
abumi
stirrup

蹄
hizume
hoof

前橋
zenkyō
pommel

額革
hitai-gawa
browband

鼻革
hana-gawa
noseband

銜
hami
bit

騎座
kiza
seat

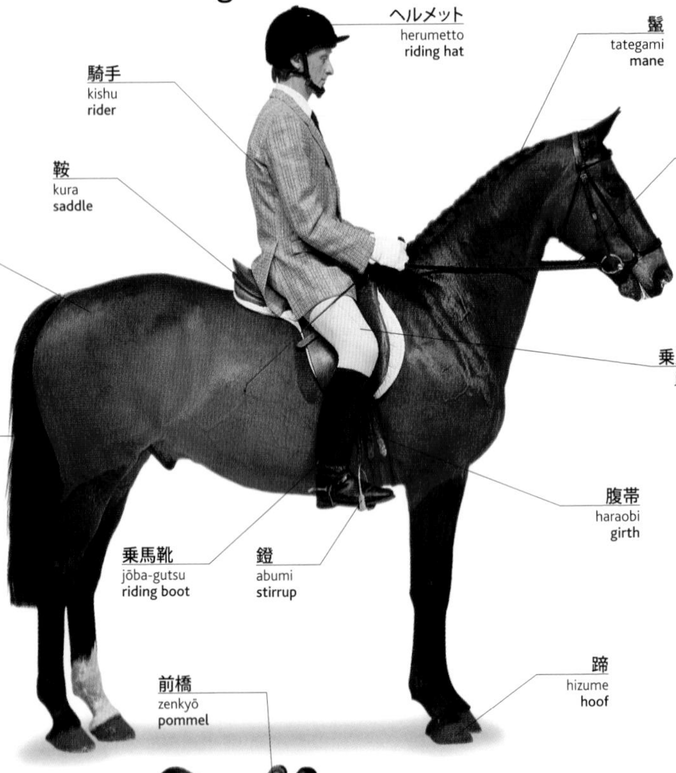

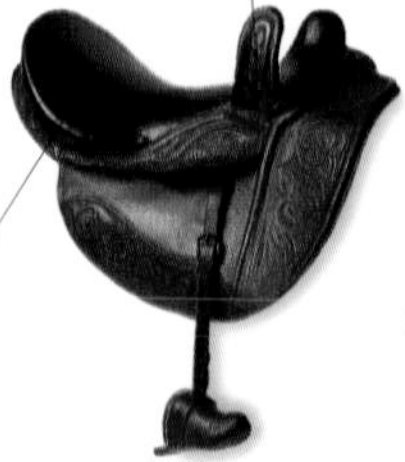

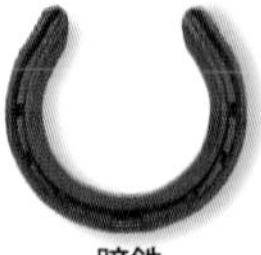

蹄鉄
teitetsu
horseshoe

横鞍
yokogura
side-saddle

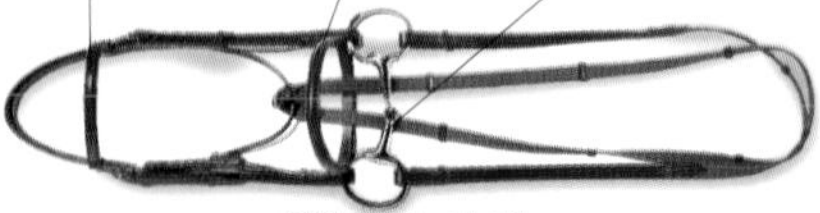

馬勒 baroku | bridle

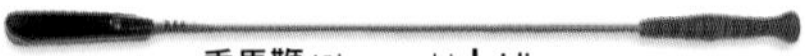

乗馬鞭 jōba muchi | riding crop

競技 kyōgi • events

競走馬
kyōsōba
racehorse

障害物
shōgaibutsu
fence

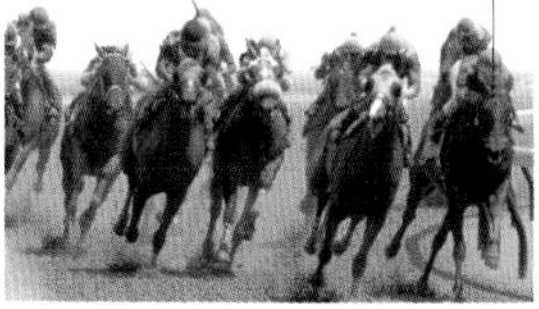
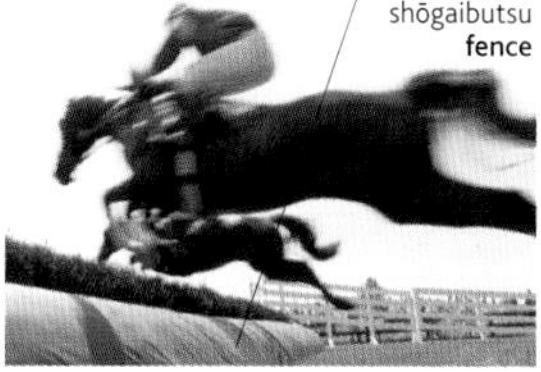
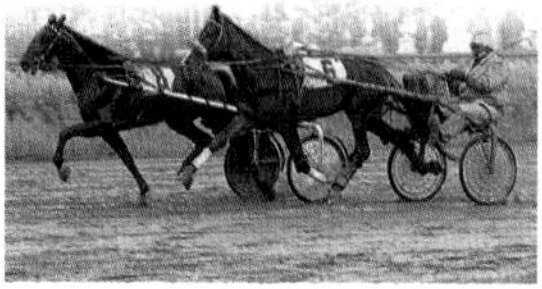

競馬
keiba
horse race

障害競走
shōgai kyōsō
steeplechase

繋駕競走
keiga kyōsō
harness race

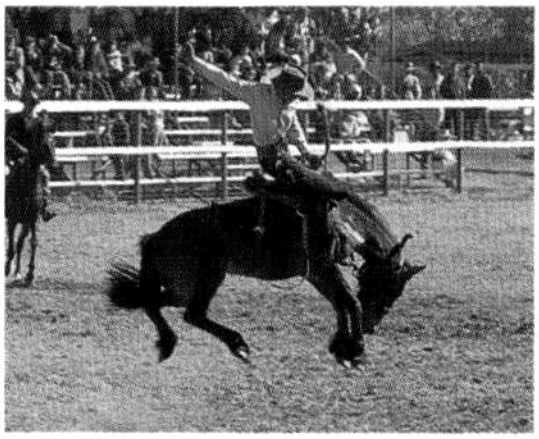
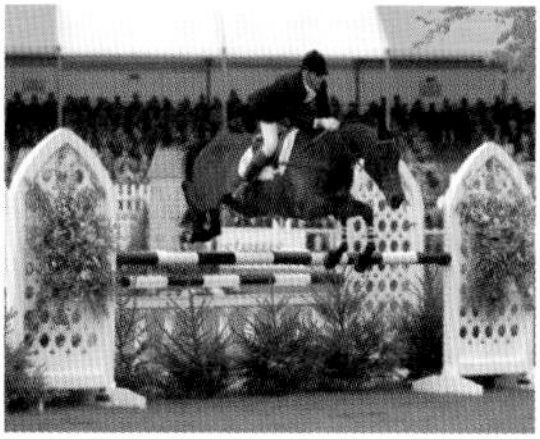
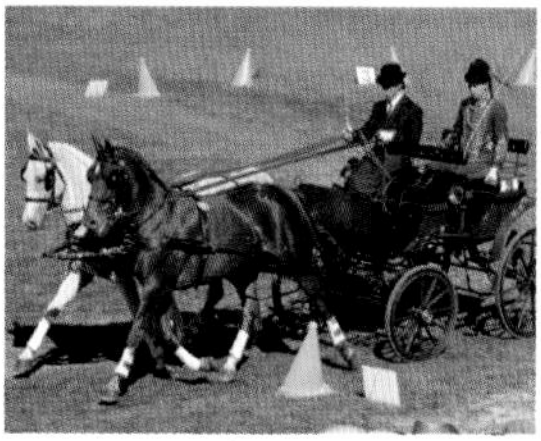

ロデオ
rodeo
rodeo

障害飛越
shōgai hietsu
showjumping

馬車レース
basha rēsu
carriage race

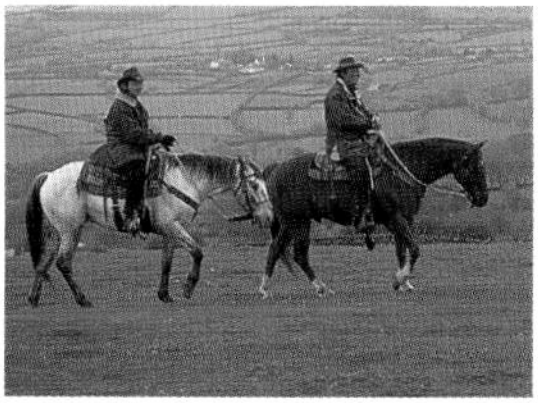
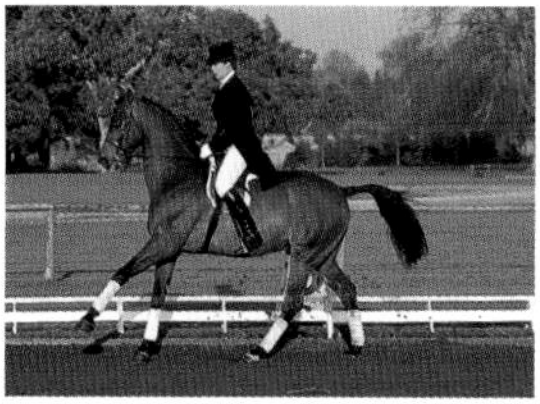
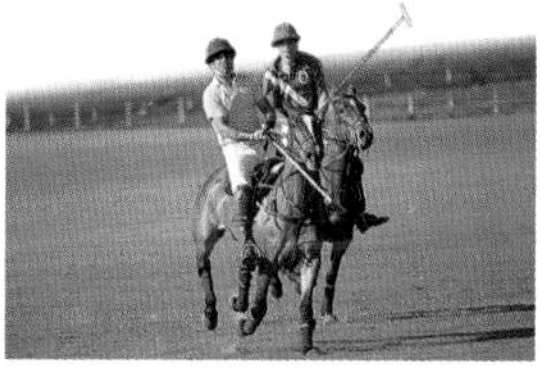

トレッキング torekkingu | trekking

馬場馬術 baba bajutsu | dressage

ポロ poro | polo

関連用語 kanrenyōgo • vocabulary

常歩 namiashi **walk**	駆歩 kakeashi **canter**	ジャンプ jampu **jump**	端綱 hazuna **halter**	パドック padokku **paddock**	平地競走 heichi kyōsō **flat race**
速歩 haya'ashi **trot**	襲歩 shūho **gallop**	馬手 umate **groom**	馬屋 umaya **stable**	アリーナ arīna **arena**	競馬場 keibajō **racecourse**

釣り tsuri • fishing

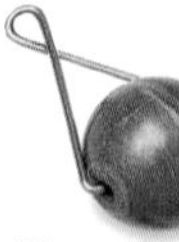

錘 omori | weight

返し
kaeshi
barb

穴
ana
eye

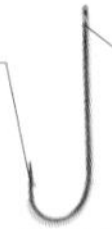

釣り針
tsuribari
fishhook

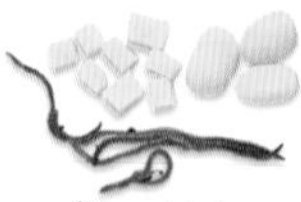

餌 esa | bait

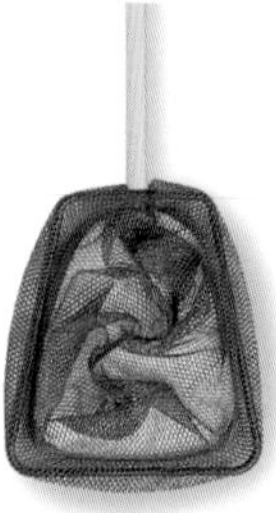

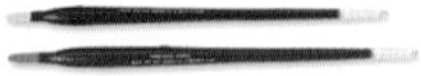

浮き
uki
float

フライ
furai
fly

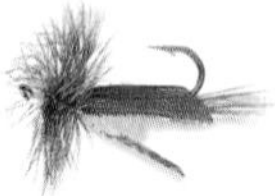

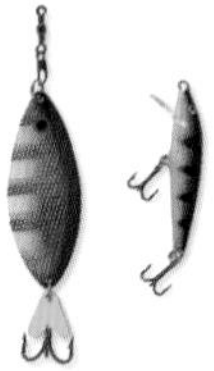

手綱
tamo
landing net

ルアー
ruā
lure

フラシ
furashi
keep net

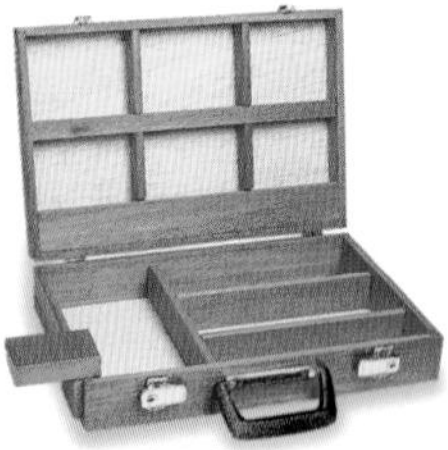

タックルボックス
takkuru bokkusu
tackle box

釣り糸
tsuri'ito
line

釣り竿
tsurizao
fishing rod

リール
rīru
reel

ウェーダー
wēdā
waders

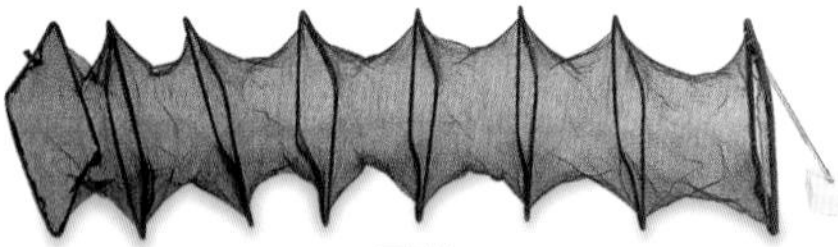

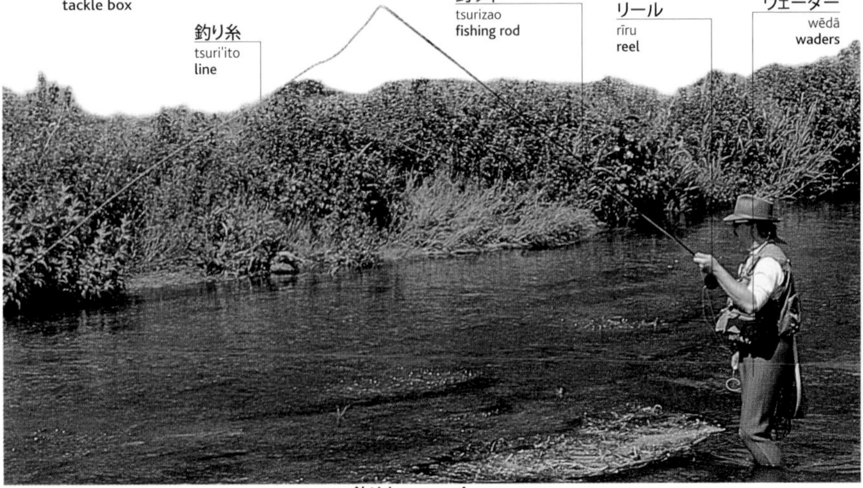

釣り人 tsuribito | angler

釣りの種類 tsuri no shurui • types of fishing

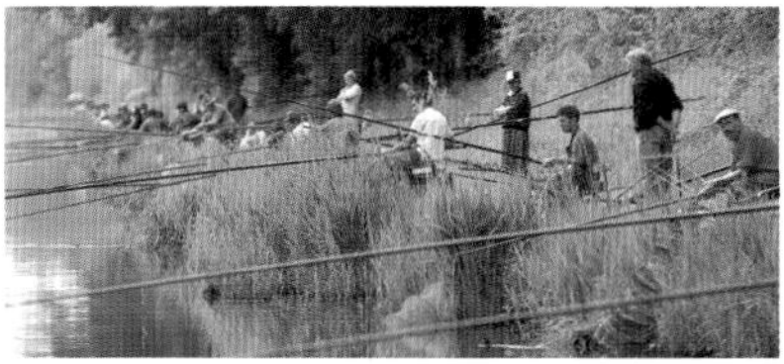

淡水釣り
tansui-zuri
freshwater fishing

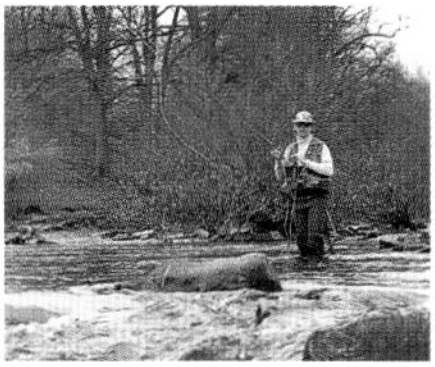

フライフィッシング
furai fisshingu
fly fishing

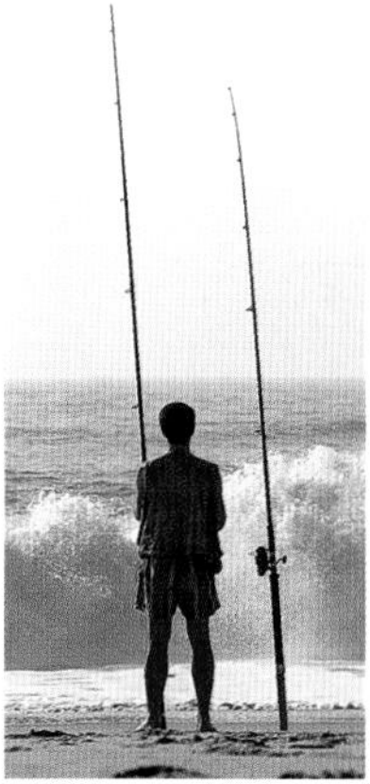

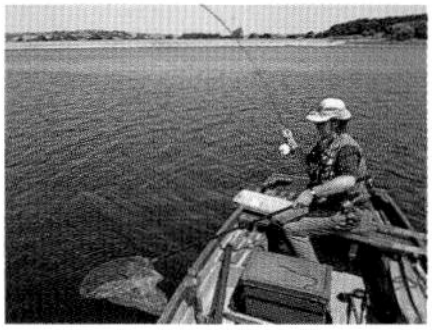

スポーツフィッシング
supōtsu fisshingu
sport fishing

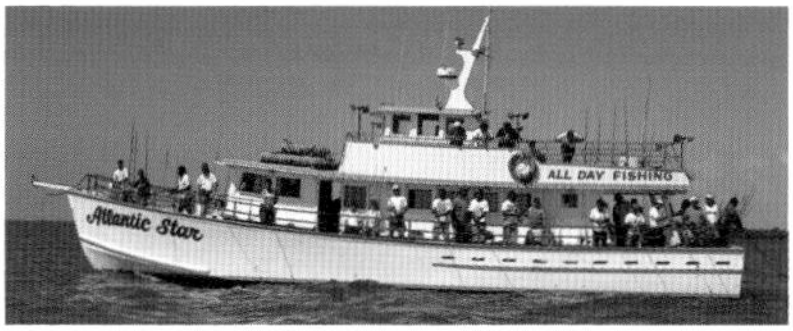

深海釣り
shinkai-zuri
deep sea fishing

磯釣り
isozuri
surfcasting

動作 dōsa • activities

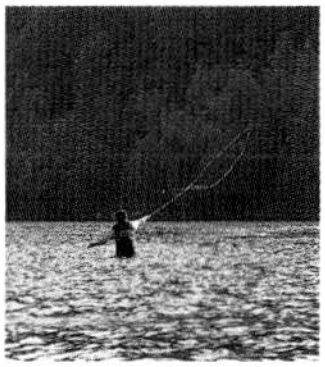

投げる
nageru
cast (v)

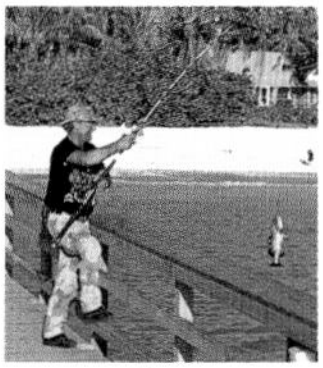

釣る
tsuru
catch (v)

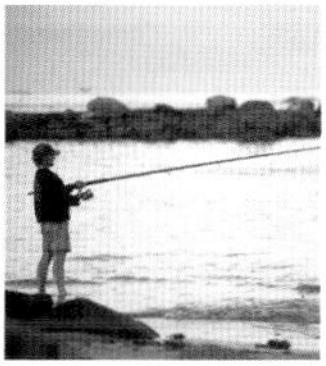

引き寄せる
hikiyoseru
reel in (v)

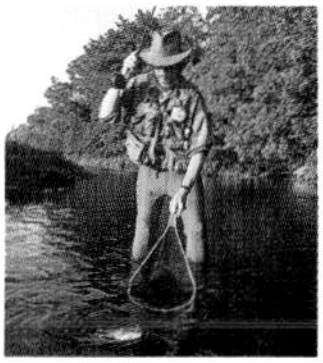

網打ちする
amiuchi suru
net (v)

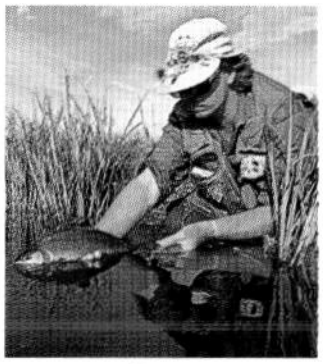

放す
hanasu
release (v)

関連用語 kanrenyōgo • vocabulary

誘き寄せる obikiyoseru bait (v)	タックル takkuru tackle	雨具 amagu waterproofs	釣り許可証 tsuri kyokashō fishing permit	魚籠 biku creel
針にかかる hari ni kakaru bite (v)	スプール supūru spool	竿 sao pole	海釣り umizuri marine fishing	ヤス漁 yasu ryō spearfishing

スキー sukī • skiing

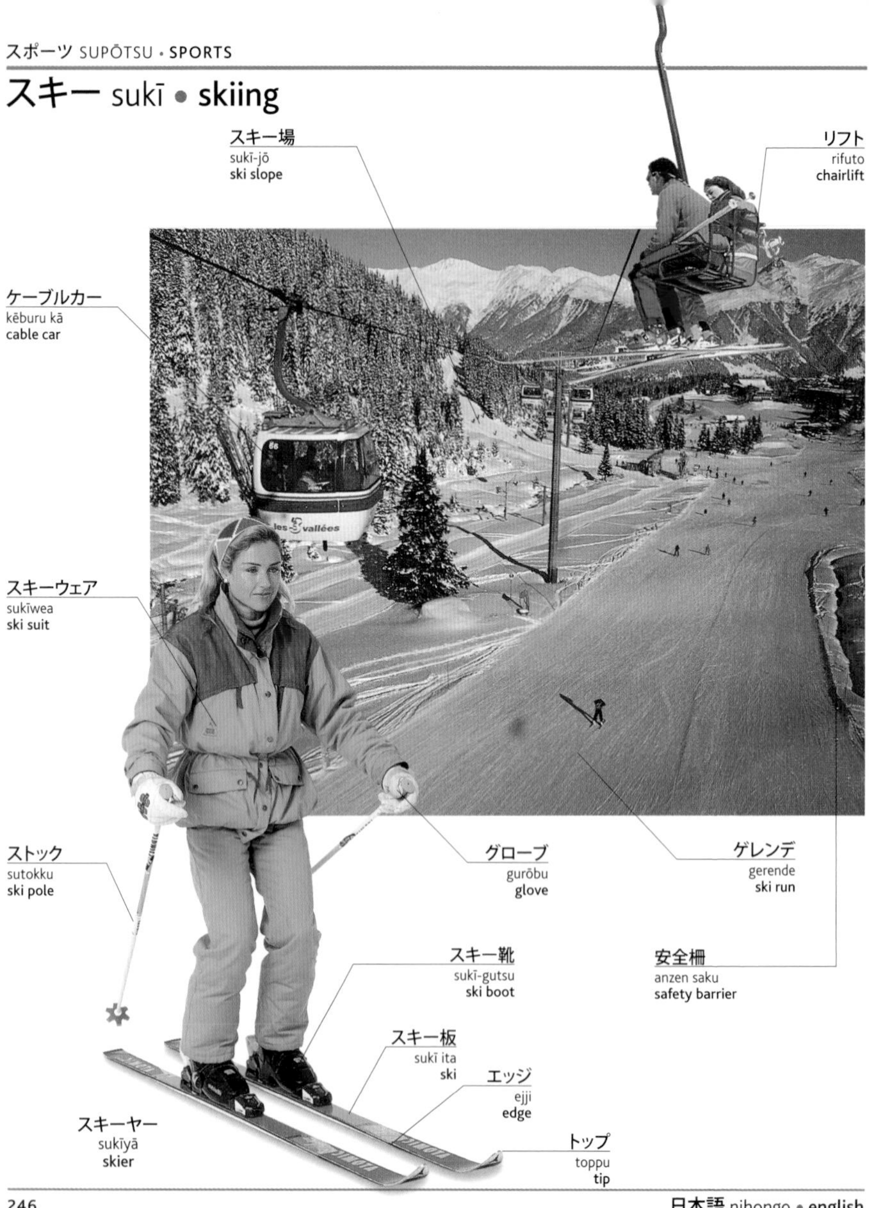

スキー場
sukī-jō
ski slope

リフト
rifuto
chairlift

ケーブルカー
kēburu kā
cable car

スキーウェア
sukīwea
ski suit

ストック
sutokku
ski pole

グローブ
gurōbu
glove

ゲレンデ
gerende
ski run

スキー靴
sukī-gutsu
ski boot

安全柵
anzen saku
safety barrier

スキー板
sukī ita
ski

エッジ
ejji
edge

スキーヤー
sukīyā
skier

トップ
toppu
tip

競技 kyōgi ● events

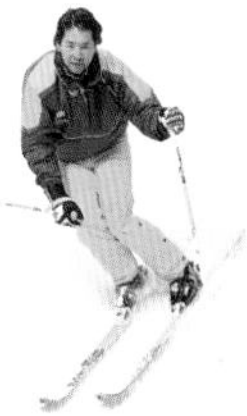

滑降
kakkō
downhill skiing

旗門
kimon
gate

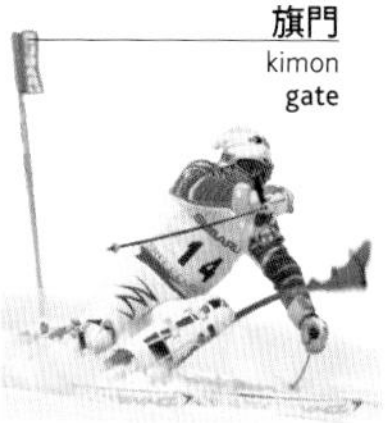

回転
kaiten
slalom

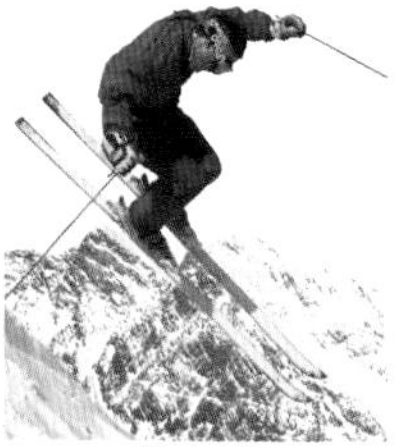

ジャンプ
jampu
ski jump

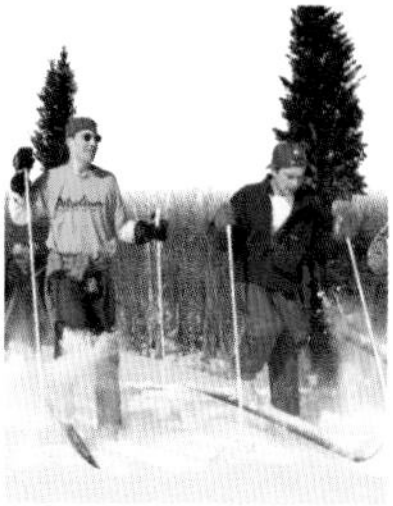

クロスカントリー
kurosu-kantorī
cross-country skiing

ウィンタースポーツ wintā supōtsu ● winter sports

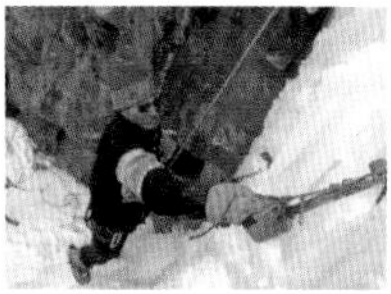

アイスクライミング
aisu kuraimingu
ice climbing

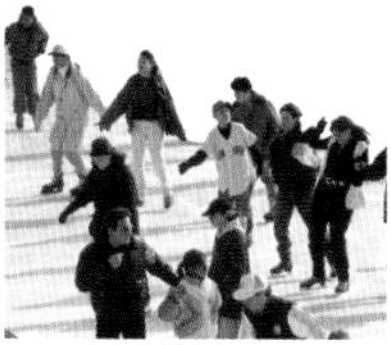

アイススケート
aisu sukēto
ice-skating

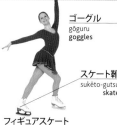

ゴーグル
gōguru
goggles

スケート靴
sukēto-gutsu
skate

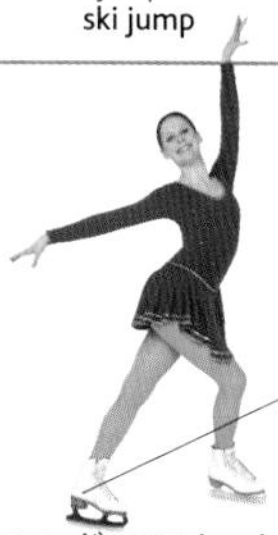

フィギュアスケート
figyuasukēto
figure skating

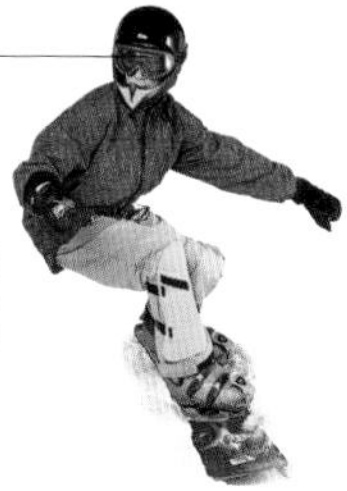

スノーボード
sunōbōdo
snowboarding

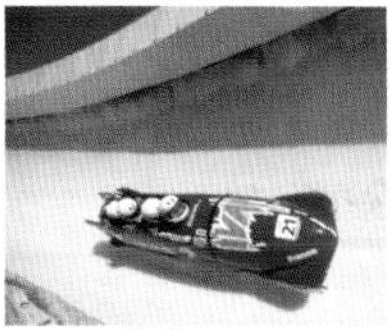

ボブスレー
bobusurē
bobsleigh

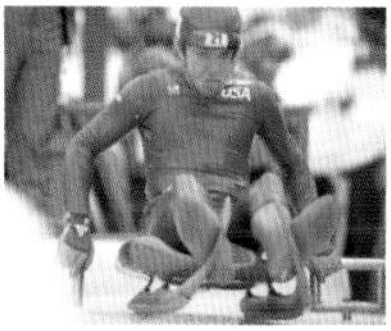

リュージュ
ryūju
luge

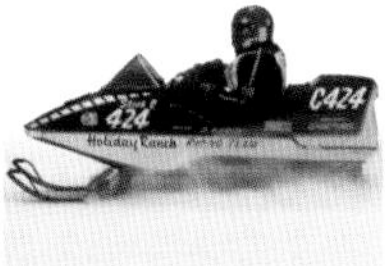

スノーモービル
sunōmōbiru
snowmobile

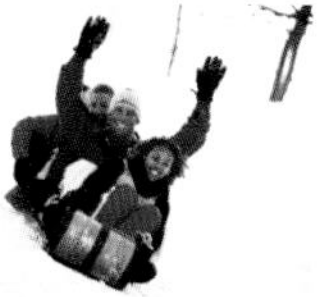

そり滑り
sori suberi
sledding

関連用語 kanrenyōgo ● vocabulary

アルペンスキー
arupen sukī
alpine skiing

大回転
daikaiten
giant slalom

ゲレンデ外
gerende-gai
off-piste

カーリング
kāringu
curling

犬ぞり滑り
inu-zori suberi
dog sledding

スピードスケート
supīdo sukēto
speed skating

バイアスロン
baiasuron
biathlon

雪崩
nadare
avalanche

他のスポーツ ta no supōtsu • other sports

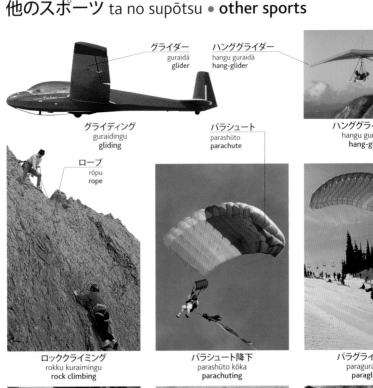

グライダー
guraidā
glider

ハンググライダー
hangu guraidā
hang-glider

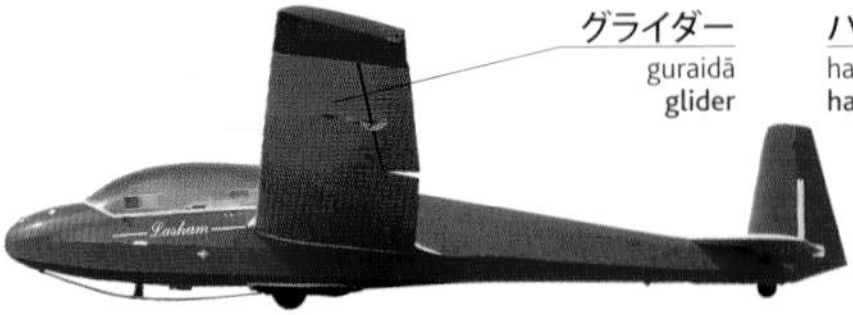

グライディング
guraidingu
gliding

パラシュート
parashūto
parachute

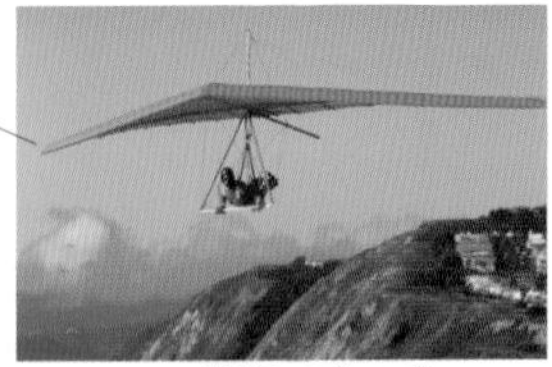

ハンググライディング
hangu guraidingu
hang-gliding

ロープ
rōpu
rope

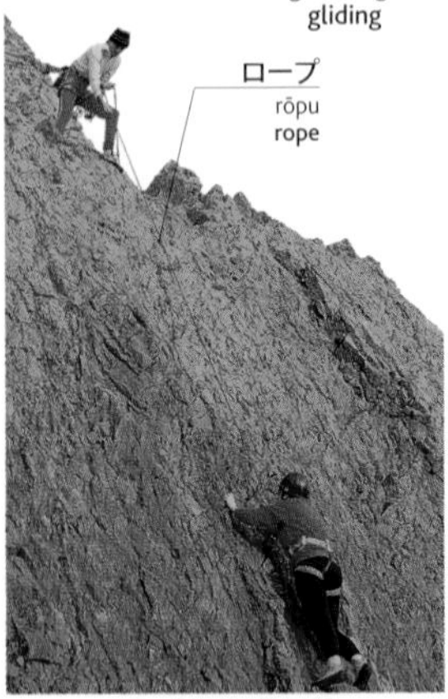

ロッククライミング
rokku kuraimingu
rock climbing

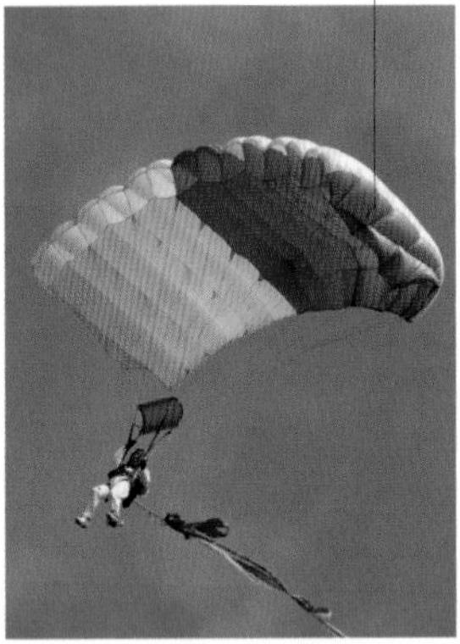

パラシュート降下
parashūto kōka
parachuting

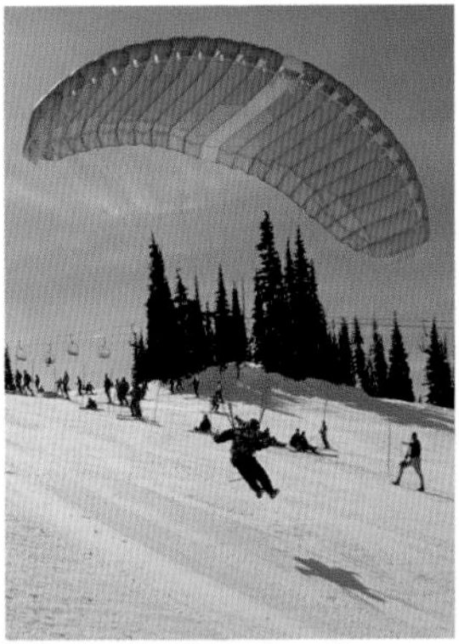

パラグライディング
paraguraidingu
paragliding

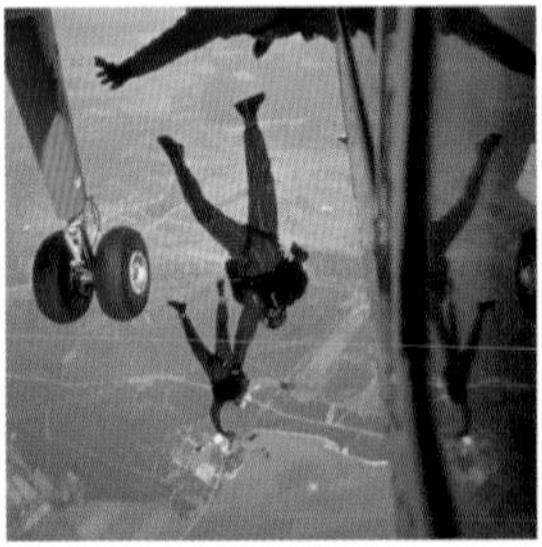

スカイダイビング
sukaidaibingu
skydiving

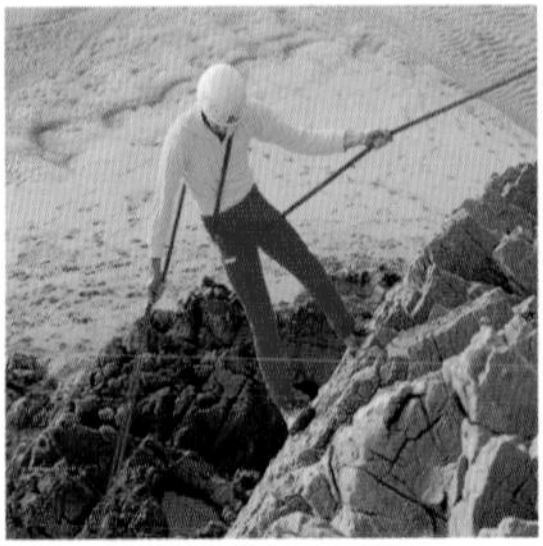

アブザイレン
abuzairen
abseiling

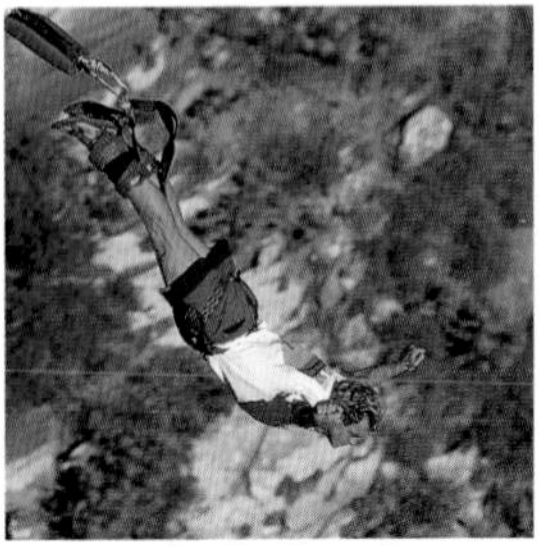

バンジージャンプ
banjī jampu
bungee jumping

レーサー
rēsā
racing driver

ラリー
rarī
rally driving

自動車レース
jidōsha rēsu
motor racing

モトクロス
motokurosu
motorcross

オートバイレース
ōtobai rēsu
motorbike racing

スケートボード
sukētobōdo
skateboard

ローラースケート靴
rōrāsukēto-gutsu
rollerskate

スティック
sutikku
stick

マスク
masuku
mask

フルーレ
furūre
foil

スケートボード乗り
sukētobōdo-nori
skateboarding

ローラースケート
rōrāsukēto
roller skating

ラクロス
rakurosu
lacrosse

フェンシング
fenshingu
fencing

ピン
pin
pin

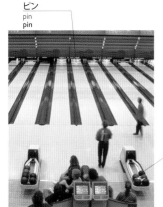

弓
yumi
bow

的
mato
target

矢
ya
arrow

矢筒
yazutsu
quiver

洋弓
yōkyū
archery

ターゲット射撃
tāgetto shageki
target shooting

ボール
bōru
bowling ball

ボウリング
bo'uringu
bowling

プール
pūru
pool

スヌーカー
sunūkā
snooker

フィットネス fittonesu ● **fitness**

エアロバイク
earobaiku
exercise bike

フィットネス器具
fittonesu kigu
gym machine

ベンチ
benchi
bench

フリーウェイト
furī weito
free weights

バー
bā
bar

スポーツジム
supōtsu jimu
gym

ローイングマシーン
rōingu mashīn
rowing machine

トレッドミル
toreddomiru
treadmill

クロストレーナー
kurosu torēnā
cross trainer

パーソナルトレーナー
pāsonaru torēnā
personal trainer

ステッパー
suteppā
step machine

プール
pūru
swimming pool

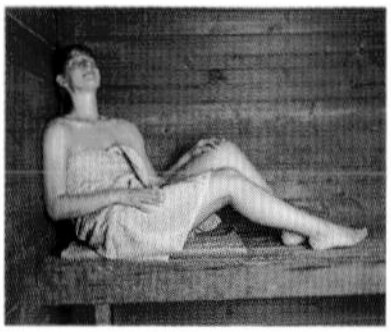

サウナ
sauna
sauna

運動 undō • exercises

ストレッチ
sutoretchi
stretch

ランジ
ranji
lunge

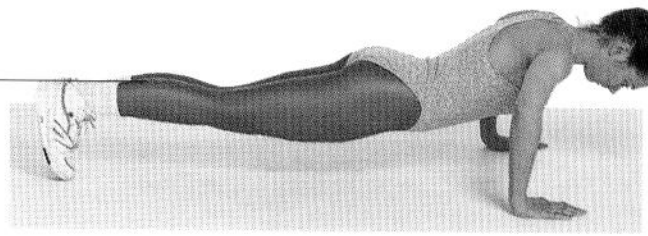

タイツ
taitsu
tights

腕立て伏せ
udetatefuse
press-up

ダンベル
danberu
dumbbell

スクワット
sukuwatto
squat

腹筋運動
fukkin undō
sit-up

アームカール
āmu kāru
bicep curl

レッグプレス
reggu puresu
leg press

チェストプレス
chesuto puresu
chest press

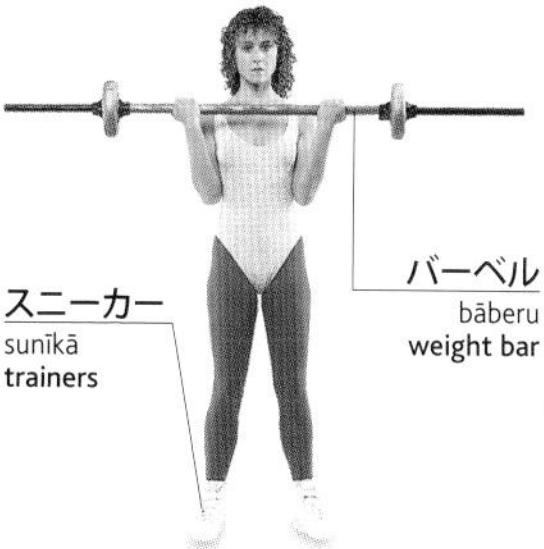

スニーカー
sunīkā
trainers

バーベル
bāberu
weight bar

ウェイトトレーニング
weito torēningu
weight training

ランニングシャツ
ranningu shatsu
vest

ジョギング
jogingu
jogging

エアロビクス
earobikusu
aerobics

関連用語 kanrenyōgo • vocabulary

トレーニングする torēningu suru **train (v)**	その場でジョギングする sono ba de jogingu suru **jog on the spot (v)**	伸ばす nobasu **extend (v)**	ピラティス piratisu **Pilates**	サーキットトレーニング sākitto torēningu **circuit training**
準備運動をする jumbi undō o suru **warm up (v)**	動かす ugokasu **flex (v)**	懸垂する kensui suru **pull up (v)**	ボクササイズ bokusasaizu **boxercise**	縄跳び nawatobi **skipping**

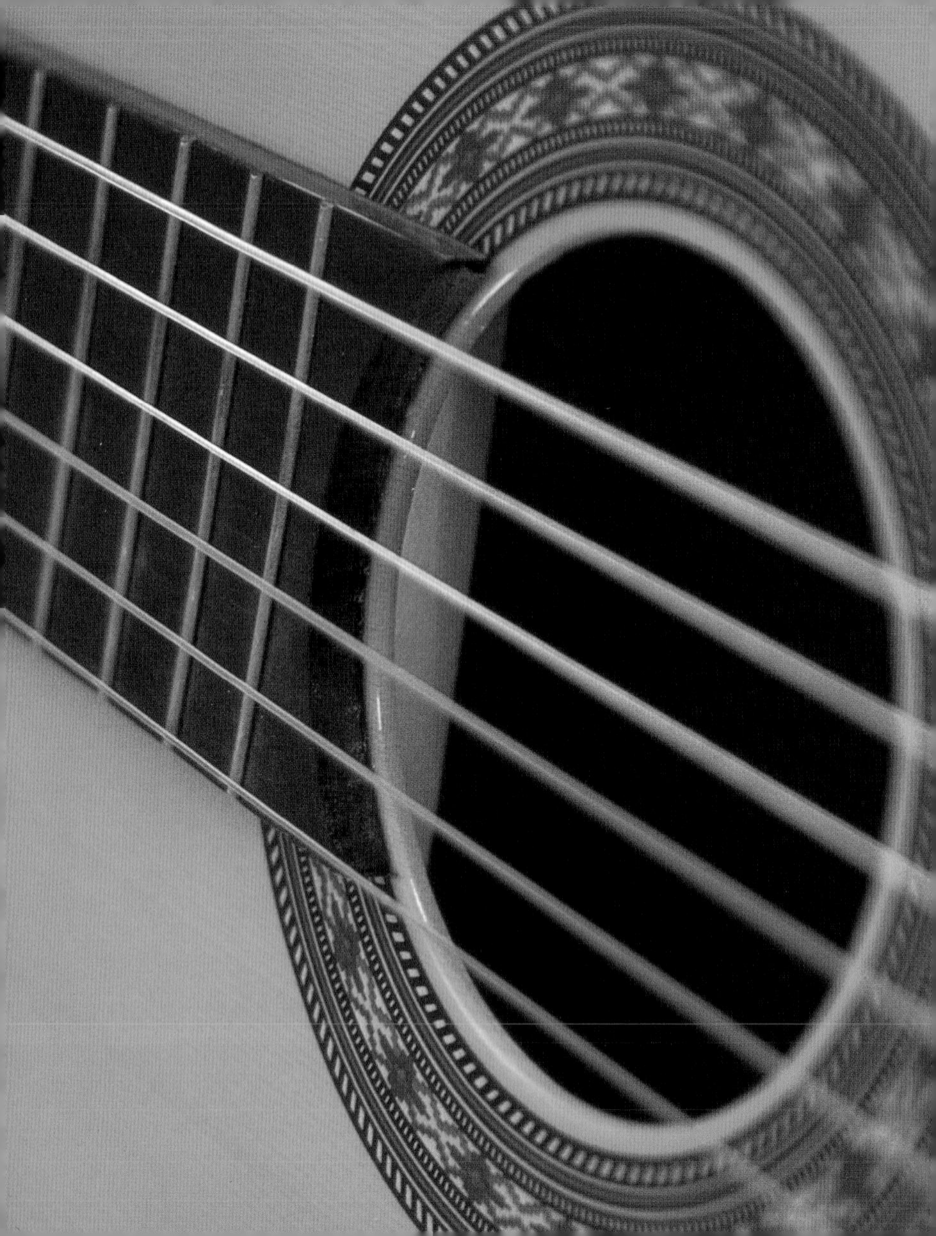

娯楽 goraku
leisure

劇場 gekijō • theatre

幕
maku
curtain

袖
sode
wings

セット
setto
set

観客
kankyaku
audience

オーケストラ
ōkesutora
orchestra

舞台 butai | **stage**

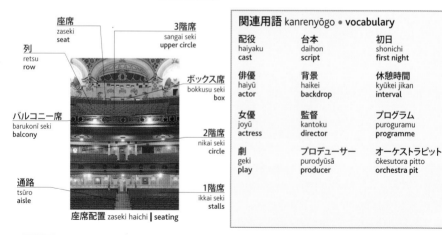

座席
zaseki
seat

列
retsu
row

3階席
sangai seki
upper circle

ボックス席
bokkusu seki
box

バルコニー席
barukonī seki
balcony

2階席
nikai seki
circle

通路
tsūro
aisle

1階席
ikkai seki
stalls

座席配置 zaseki haichi | **seating**

関連用語 kanrenyōgo • vocabulary

配役 haiyaku **cast**	台本 daihon **script**	初日 shonichi **first night**
俳優 haiyū **actor**	背景 haikei **backdrop**	休憩時間 kyūkei jikan **interval**
女優 joyū **actress**	監督 kantoku **director**	プログラム puroguramu **programme**
劇 geki **play**	プロデューサー purodyūsā **producer**	オーケストラピット ōkesutora pitto **orchestra pit**

音楽会 ongakukai | concert

ミュージカル myūjikaru | musical

衣装
ishō
costume

バレエ barē | ballet

関連用語 kanrenyōgo • vocabulary

案内係
annai-gakari
usher

クラシック音楽
kurashikku ongaku
classical music

楽譜
gakufu
musical score

サウンドトラック
saundotorakku
soundtrack

拍手する
hakushu suru
applaud (v)

アンコール
ankōru
encore

今晩のチケットを2枚ください。
konban no chiketto o ni-mai kudasai.
I'd like two tickets for tonight's performance.

何時に始まりますか。
nanji ni hajimarimasuka?
What time does it start?

オペラ opera | opera

映画 eiga • cinema

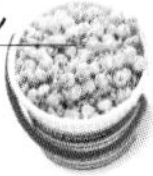

ポップコーン
poppukōn
popcorn

チケット売場
chiketto uriba
box office

ポスター
posutā
poster

ロビー
robī
lobby

映画館
eigakan
cinema hall

映写幕
eishamaku
screen

関連用語 kanrenyōgo • vocabulary

コメディ
komedi
comedy

スリラー
surirā
thriller

ホラー映画
horā eiga
horror film

西部劇
seibugeki
western

恋愛物語
ren'ai monogatari
romance

SF映画
esu-efu eiga
science fiction film

冒険
bōken
adventure

アニメ映画
anime eiga
animated film

オーケストラ ōkesutora • orchestra

弦楽器 gengakki • strings

ハープ
hāpu
harp

指揮者
shikisha
conductor

コントラバス
kontorabasu
double bass

バイオリン
baiorin
violin

指揮台
shiki dai
podium

ビオラ
biora
viola

チェロ
chero
cello

楽譜
gakufu
score

ト音記号
to'on kigō
treble clef

音符
ompu
note

五線譜
gosenfu
staff

ヘ音記号
heon kigō
bass clef

ピアノ piano | piano

記譜法 kifuhō | notation

関連用語 kanrenyōgo • vocabulary

序曲 jokyoku overture	ソナタ sonata sonata	休止符 kyūshifu rest	シャープ shāpu sharp	本位記号 hon'i kigō natural	音階 onkai scale
交響曲 kōkyōkyoku symphony	楽器 gakki instruments	ピッチ pitchi pitch	フラット furatto flat	小節 shōsetsu bar	指揮棒 shikibō baton

木管楽器 mokkan gakki • **woodwind**

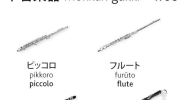

ピッコロ
pikkoro
piccolo

フルート
furūto
flute

オーボエ
ōboe
oboe

イングリッシュホルン
ingurisshu horun
cor anglais

クラリネット
kurarinetto
clarinet

バスクラリネット
basu kurarinetto
bass clarinet

ファゴット
fagotto
bassoon

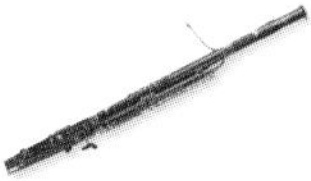

コントラファゴット
kontora fagotto
double bassoon

サクソフォン
sakusofon
saxophone

打楽器 dagakki • **percussion**

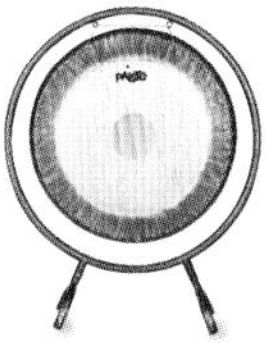

ボンゴ
bongo
bongos

スネアドラム
sunea doramu
snare drum

ケトルドラム
ketorudoramu
kettledrum

銅鑼
dora
gong

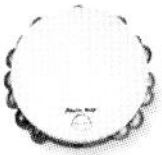

トライアングル
toraianguru
triangle

マラカス
marakasu
maracas

シンバル
shimbaru
cymbals

タンバリン
tambarin
tambourine

ビブラフォン
biburafon
vibraphone

金管楽器 kinkan gakki • **brass**

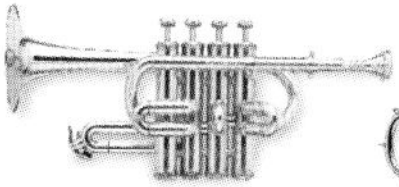

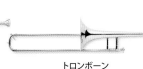

トランペット
torampetto
trumpet

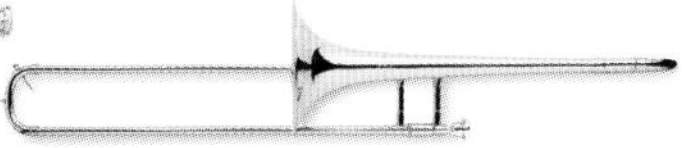

トロンボーン
toronbōn
trombone

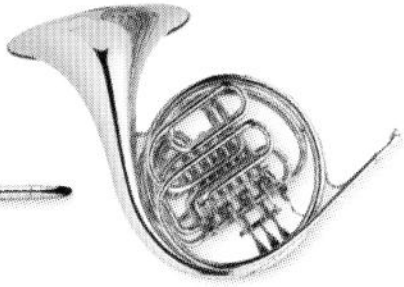

フレンチホルン
furenchi horun
French horn

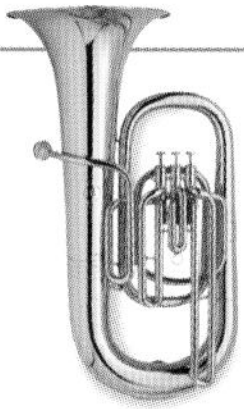

チューバ
chūba
tuba

コンサート konsāto • concert

マイク
maiku
microphone

リードシンガー
rīdo shingā
lead singer

ドラマー
doramā
drummer

ギタリスト
gitarisuto
guitarist

ファン
fan
fans

ベーシスト
bēshisuto
bass guitarist

スピーカー
supīkā
speaker

ロックコンサート rokku konsāto | rock concert

楽器 gakki • instruments

ピックアップ
pikkuappu
pickup

ネック
nekku
neck

フレット
furetto
fret

ペグ
pegu
tuning peg

弦
gen
string

ブリッジ
burijji
bridge

ドラム
doramu
drum

ベースギター
bēsu gitā
bass guitar

キーボード
kībōdo
keyboard

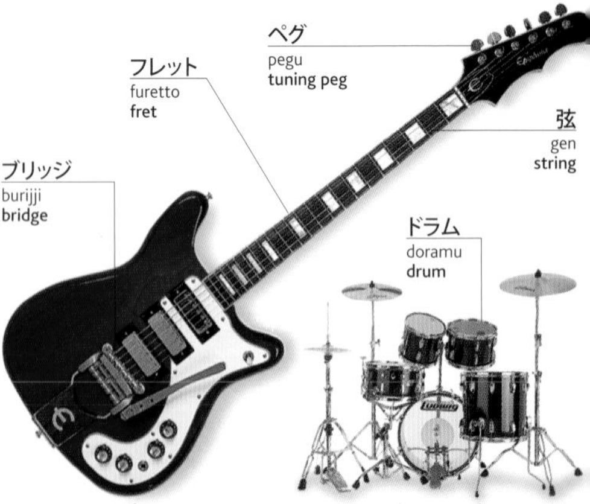

エレキギター
erekigitā
electric guitar

ドラムセット
doramu setto
drum kit

音楽ジャンル ongaku janru • **musical styles**

ジャズ jazu | **jazz**

ブルース burūsu | **blues**

パンク panku | **punk**

フォーク fōku | **folk music**

ポップス poppusu | **pop**

ダンス dansu | **dance**

ラップ rappu | **rap**

ヘビーメタル hebī metaru
heavy metal

クラシック kurasshikku
classical music

関連用語 kanrenyōgo • **vocabulary**

歌	歌詞	メロディー	ビート	レゲエ	カントリー	スポットライト
uta	kashi	merodī	bīto	rege'e	kantorī	supottoraito
song	**lyrics**	**melody**	**beat**	**reggae**	**country**	**spotlight**

観光 kankō ● sightseeing

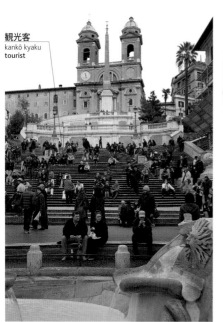

観光客
kankō kyaku
tourist

観光名所 kankō meisho | **tourist attraction**

観光ルート
kankō rūto
itinerary

オープントップ
ōpun toppu
open-top

観光バス kankō basu | **tour bus**

観光ガイド
kankō gaido
tour guide

小像
shōzō
statuette

ガイド付きツアー
gaido-tsuki tsuā
guided tour

土産物
miyagemono
souvenirs

関連用語 kanrenyōgo ● **vocabulary**

開館 kaikan **open**	観光案内書 kankō annaisho **guide book**	カムコーダー kamukōdā **camcorder**	左 hidari **left**	…は、どこですか。 … wa doko desuka? **Where is…?**
閉館 heikan **closed**	フィルム firumu **film**	カメラ kamera **camera**	右 migi **right**	道に迷ってしまいました。 michi ni mayotte shimaimashita. **I'm lost.**
入場料 nyūjō-ryō **entrance fee**	電池 denchi **batteries**	行き方 ikikata **directions**	まっすぐ massugu **straight on**	…への行き方を教えてください。 … e no ikikata o oshiete kudasai. **Can you tell me the way to…?**

名所 meisho • **attractions**

絵画
kaiga
painting

展示品
tenji-hin
exhibit

展覧会
tenrankai
exhibition

旧跡
kyūseki
famous ruin

美術館
bijutsukan
art gallery

記念碑
kinenhi
monument

博物館
hakubutsukan
museum

歴史的建造物
rekishi-teki kenzōbutsu
historic building

カジノ
kajino
casino

庭園
teien
gardens

国立公園
kokuritsu kōen
national park

案内 annai • **information**

時間
jikan
times

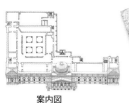

案内図
annai zu
floor plan

地図
chizu
map

時刻表
jikokuhyō
timetable

観光案内所
kankō annai-jo
tourist information

野外活動 yagai katsudō • outdoor activities

歩道
hodō
footpath

日時計
hidokei
sundial

カフェ
kafe
café

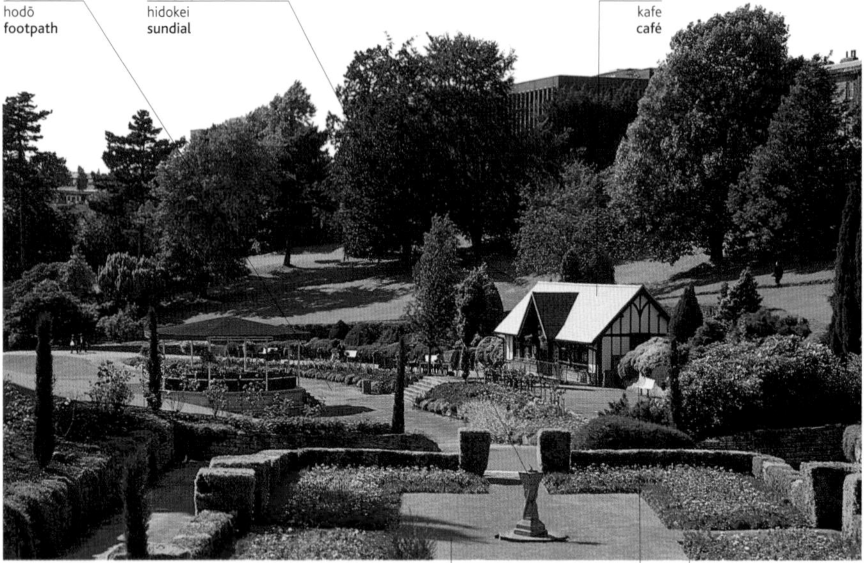

公園 kōen | park

芝生
shibafu
grass

ベンチ
benchi
bench

平面幾何学式庭園
heimen kikagaku-shiki teien
formal gardens

ジェットコースター
jetto kōsutā
roller coaster

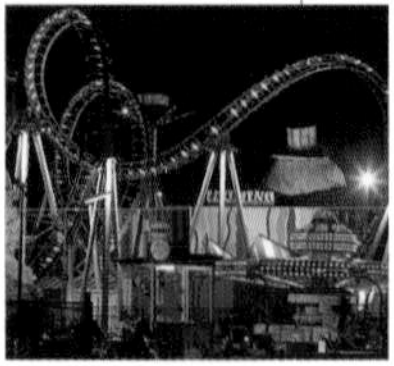

遊園地
yūenchi
fairground

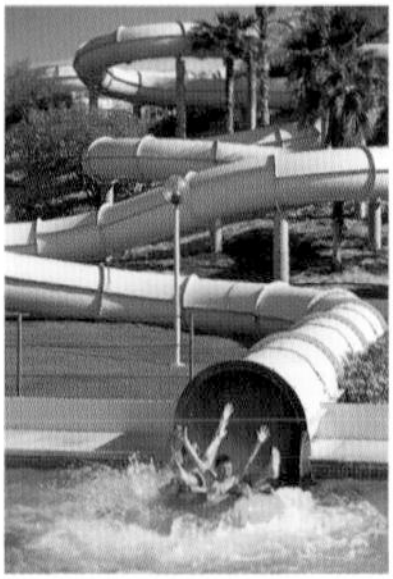

テーマパーク
tēma pāku
theme park

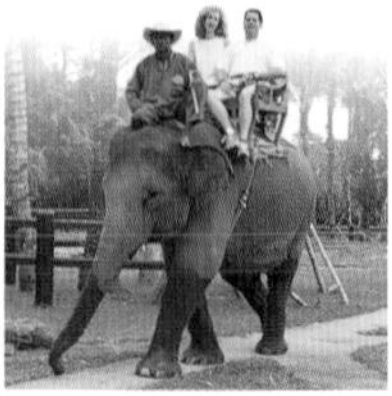

サファリパーク
safari pāku
safari park

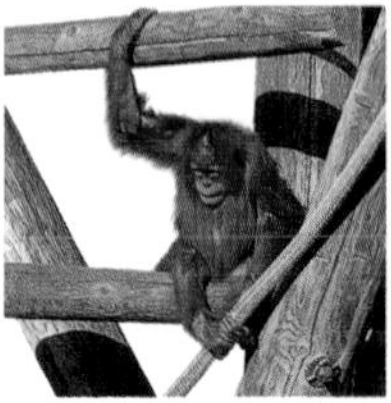

動物園
dōbutsuen
zoo

活動 katsudō · activities

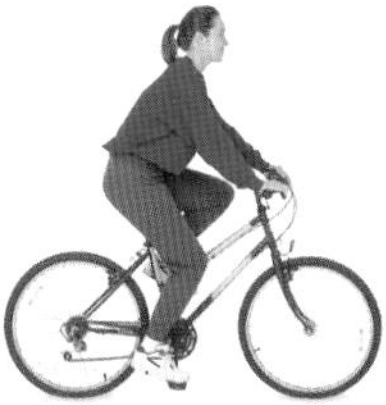

サイクリング
saikuringu
cycling

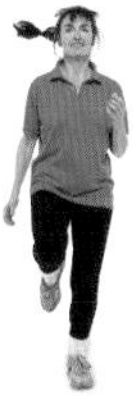

ジョギング
jogingu
jogging

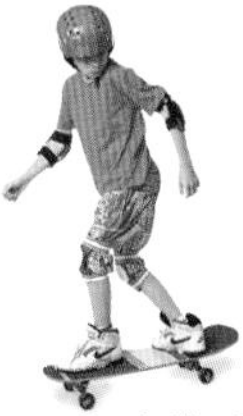

スケートボード
sukētobōdo
skateboarding

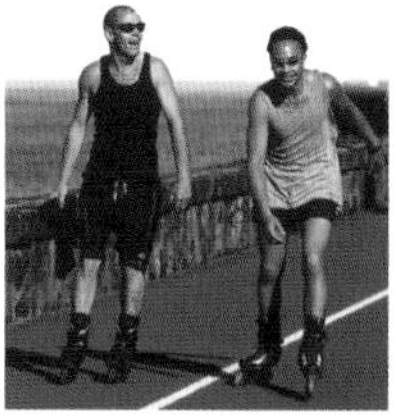

ローラーブレード
rōrāburēdo
rollerblading

乗馬道
jōba-dō
bridle path

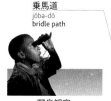

バスケット
basuketto
hamper

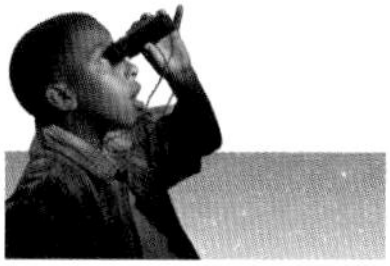

野鳥観察
yachō kansatsu
bird watching

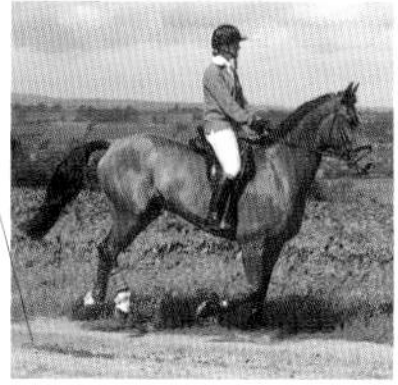

乗馬
jōba
horse riding

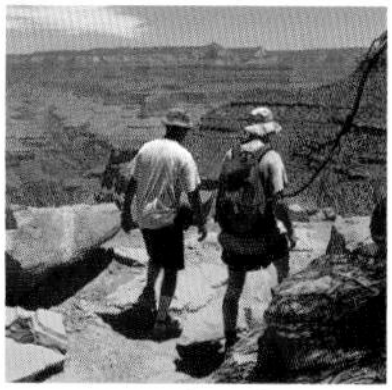

ハイキング
haikingu
hiking

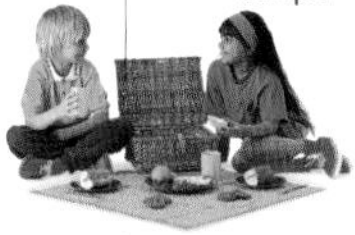

ピクニック
pikunikku
picnic

遊び場 asobiba · playground

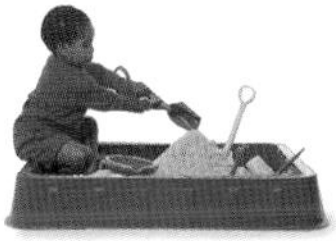

砂場
sunaba
sandpit

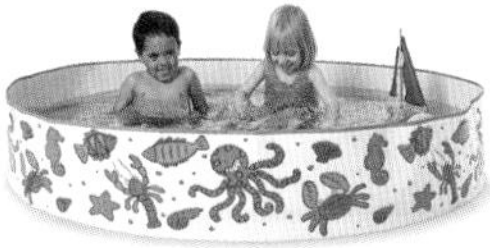

水浴びプール
mizuabi pūru
paddling pool

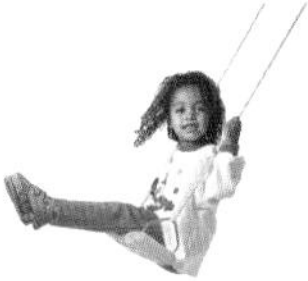

ブランコ
buranko
swings

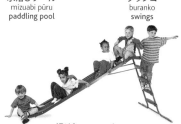

シーソー shīsō | **seesaw**

滑り台 suberidai | **slide**

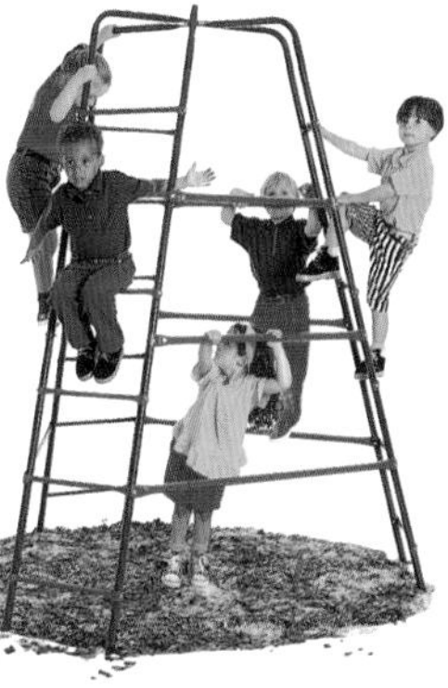

ジャングルジム janguru jimu
climbing frame

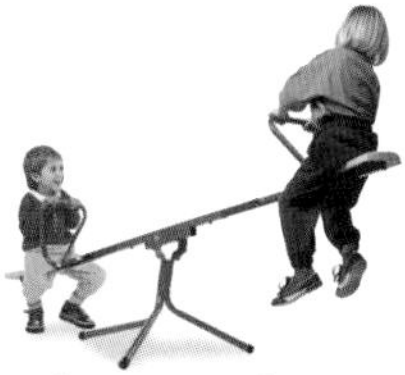

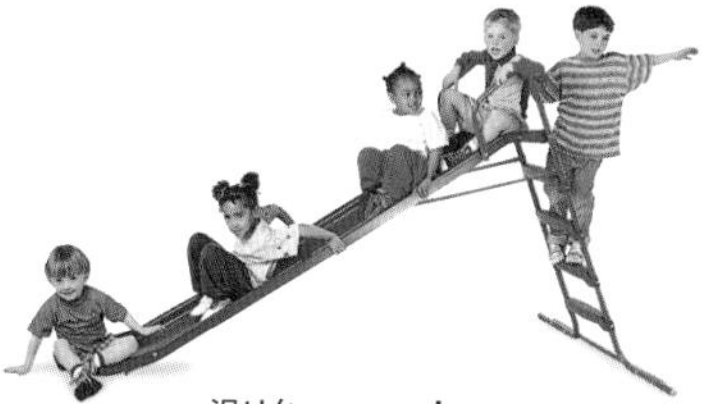

海辺 umibe • beach

ホテル
hoteru
hotel

ビーチパラソル
bīchi parasoru
beach umbrella

海の家
umi no ie
beach hut

砂
suna
sand

波
nami
wave

海
umi
sea

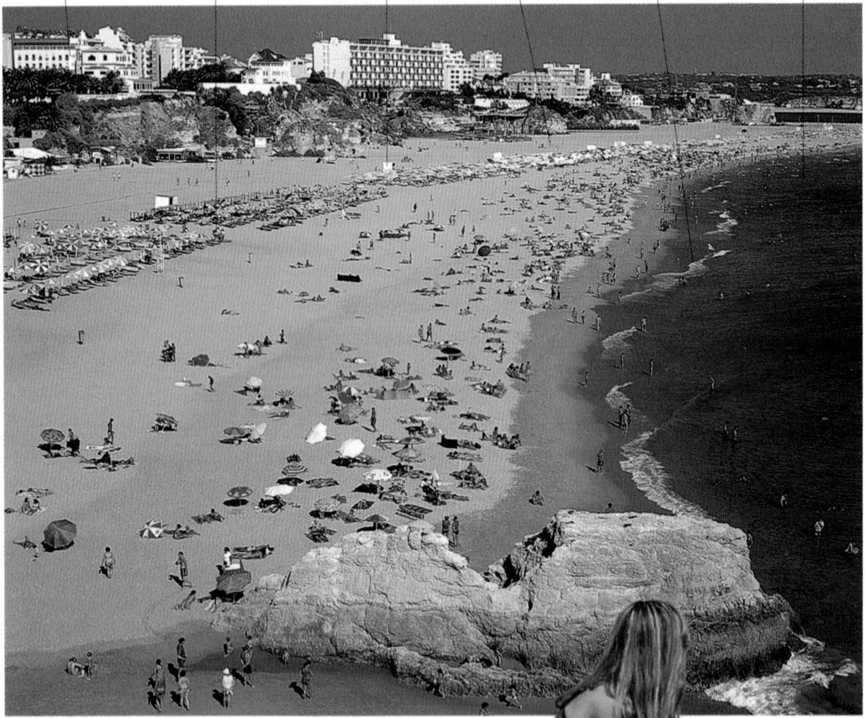

ビーチバッグ
bīchi baggu
beach bag

ビキニ
bikini
bikini

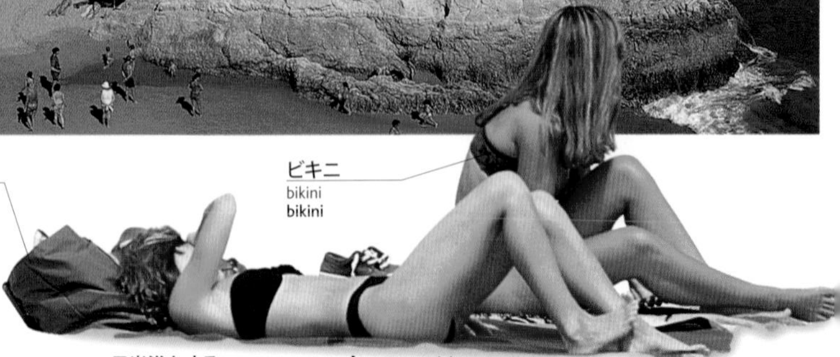

日光浴をする nikkōyoku o suru **|** sunbathe (v)

監視員
kanshi'in
lifeguard

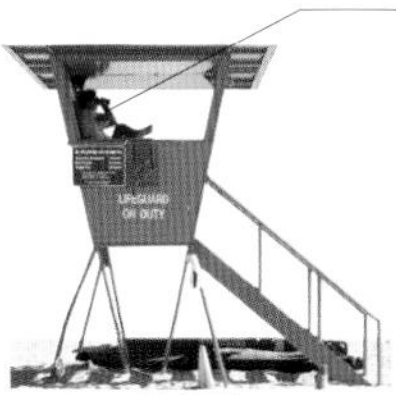

監視塔
kanshitō
lifeguard tower

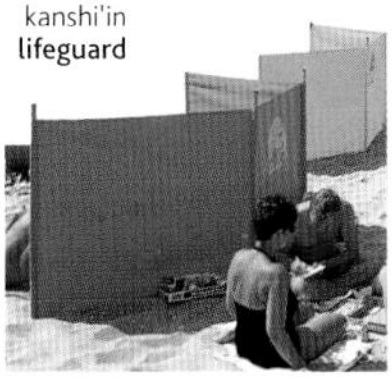

防風フェンス
bōfū fensu
windbreak

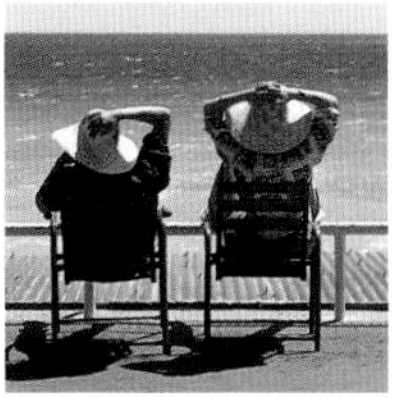

遊歩道
yūhodō
promenade

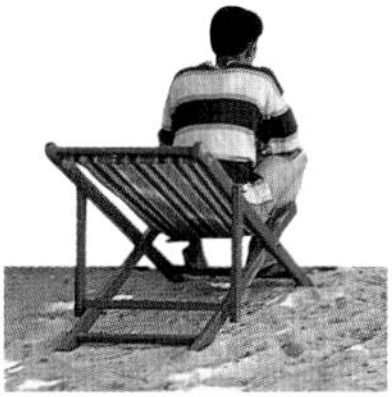

デッキチェア
dekki chea
deck chair

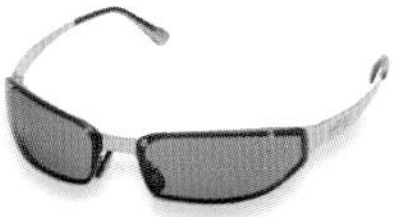

サングラス
sangurasu
sunglasses

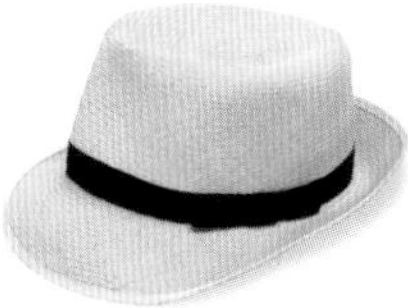

日除け帽
hiyoke-bō
sunhat

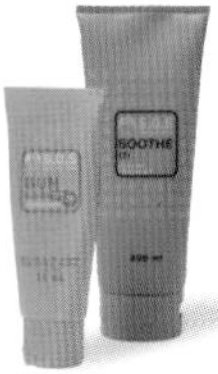

日焼けローション
hiyake rōshon
suntan lotion

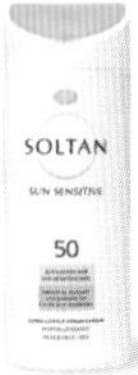

日焼け止め
hiyakedome
sunblock

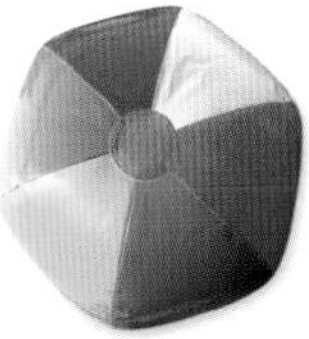

ビーチボール
bīchi bōru
beach ball

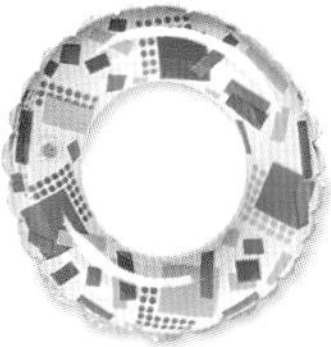

浮き輪
ukiwa
rubber ring

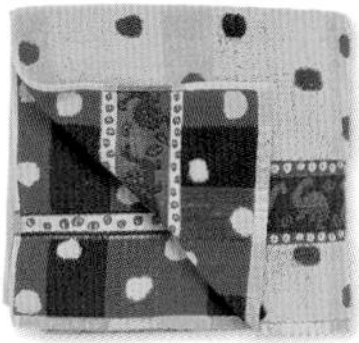

ビーチタオル
bīchi taoru
beach towel

水着
mizugi
swimsuit

シャベル
shaberu
spade

バケツ
baketsu
bucket

砂の城
suna no shiro
sandcastle

貝殻
kaigara
shell

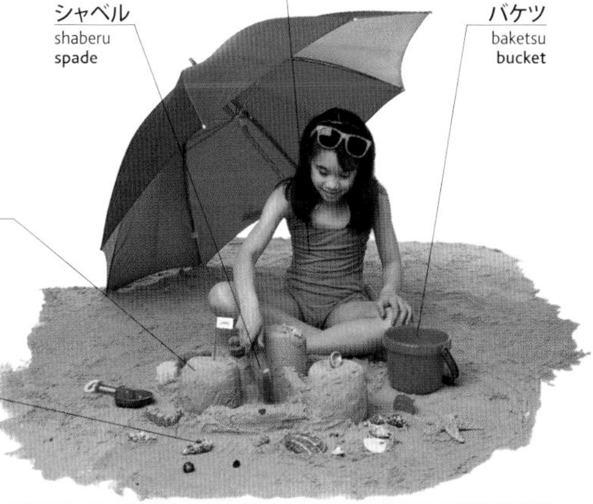

キャンプ kyampu • camping

トイレ
toire
toilets

ゴミ置場
gomi okiba
waste disposal

シャワー棟
shawā tō
shower block

電源装置
dengen sōchi
electric hook-up

フライシート
furaishīto
flysheet

ペグ
pegu
tent peg

ロープ
rōpu
guy rope

キャンピングトレーラー
kyampingu torērā
caravan

キャンプ場 kyampujō | campsite

関連用語 kanrenyōgo • vocabulary

キャンプする
kyampu suru
camp (v)

サイト
saito
pitch

ピクニックベンチ
pikunikku benchi
picnic bench

炭
sumi
charcoal

管理事務所
kanri jimusho
site manager's office

テントを張る
tento o haru
pitch a tent (v)

ハンモック
hammokku
hammock

着火剤
chakka-zai
firelighter

空きサイトあり
aki saito ari
pitches available

ポール
pōru
tent pole

キャンピングカー
kyampingu kā
camper van

火をつける
hi o tsukeru
light a fire (v)

空きなし
aki nashi
full

キャンプベッド
kyampu beddo
camp bed

トレーラー
torērā
trailer

キャンプファイヤー
kyampufaiyā
campfire

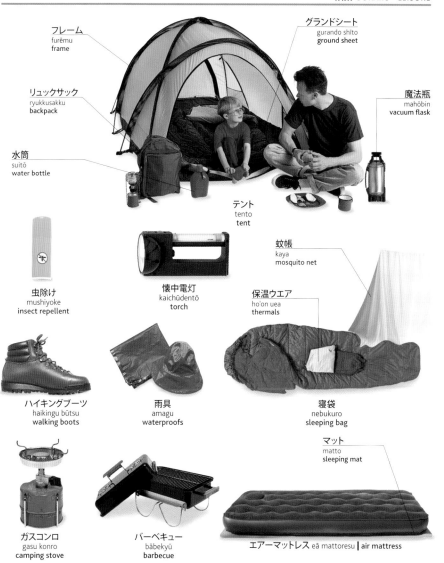

フレーム
furēmu
frame

グランドシート
gurando shīto
ground sheet

リュックサック
ryukkusakku
backpack

魔法瓶
mahōbin
vacuum flask

水筒
suitō
water bottle

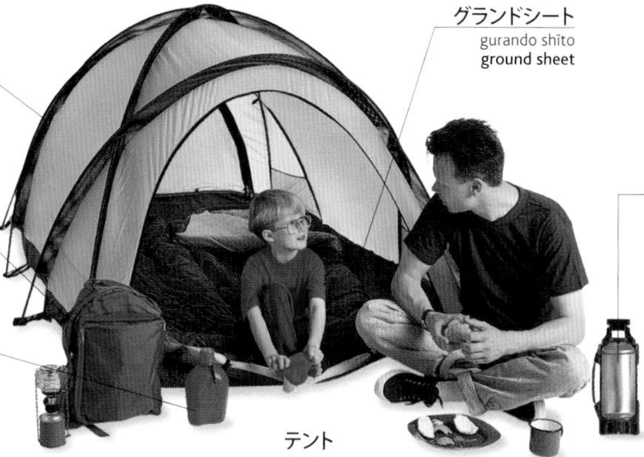

テント
tento
tent

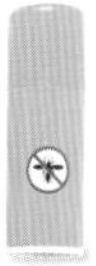

虫除け
mushiyoke
insect repellent

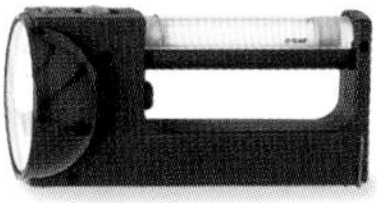

懐中電灯
kaichūdentō
torch

蚊帳
kaya
mosquito net

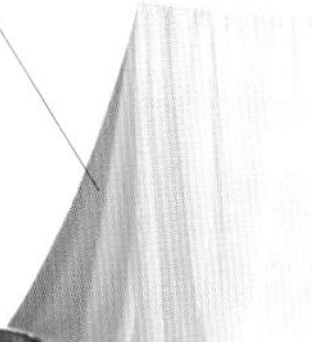

保温ウエア
ho'on uea
thermals

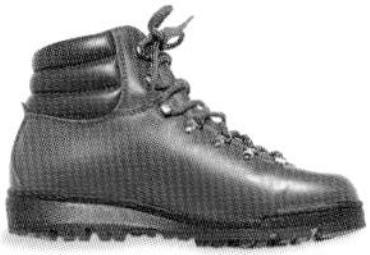

ハイキングブーツ
haikingu būtsu
walking boots

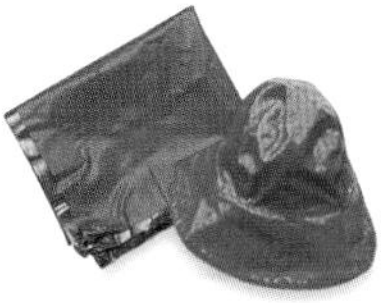

雨具
amagu
waterproofs

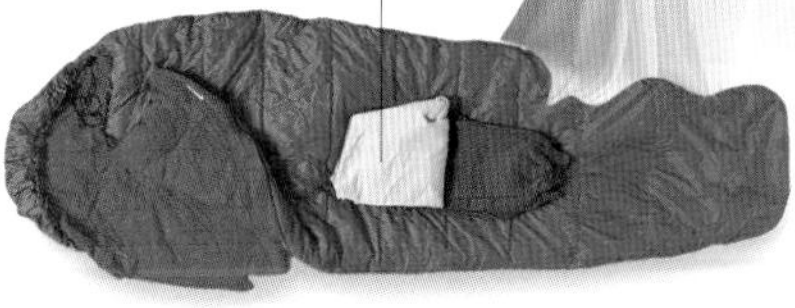

寝袋
nebukuro
sleeping bag

マット
matto
sleeping mat

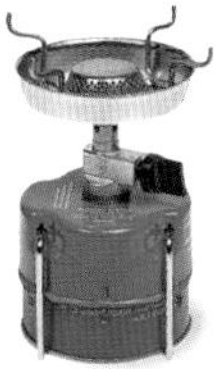

ガスコンロ
gasu konro
camping stove

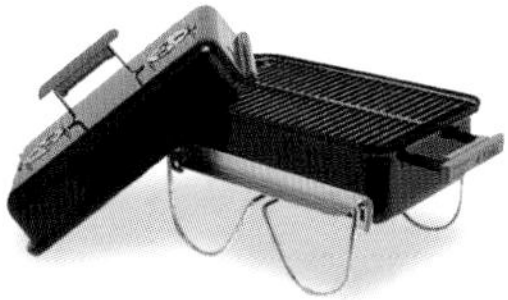

バーベキュー
bābekyū
barbecue

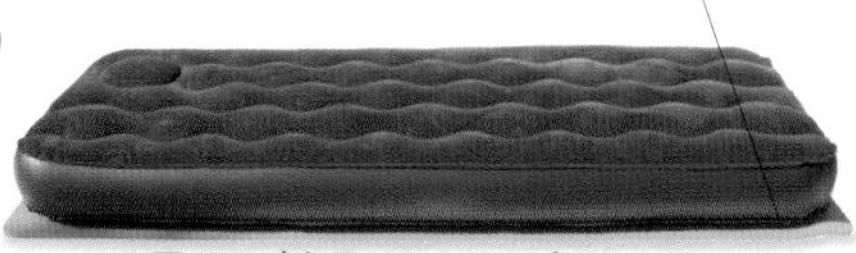

エアーマットレス eā mattoresu | air mattress

娯楽家電 goraku kaden • home entertainment

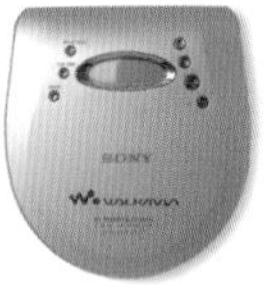

ポータブルCDプレーヤー
pōtaburu shī-dī purēyā
personal CD player

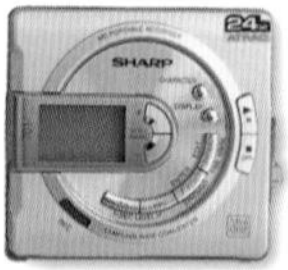

ミニディスクレコーダー
mini disuku rekōdā
mini disk recorder

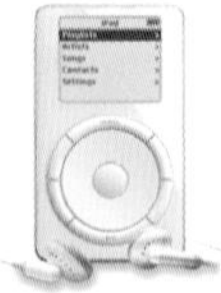

MP3プレーヤー
emu-pī-surī purēyā
MP3 player

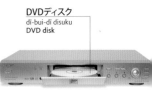

DVDディスク
dī-bui-dī disuku
DVD disk

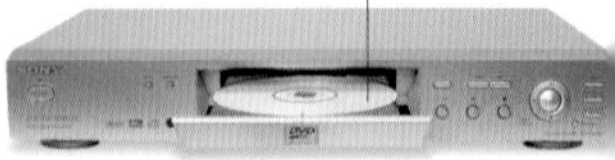

DVDプレーヤー
dī-bui-dī purēyā
DVD player

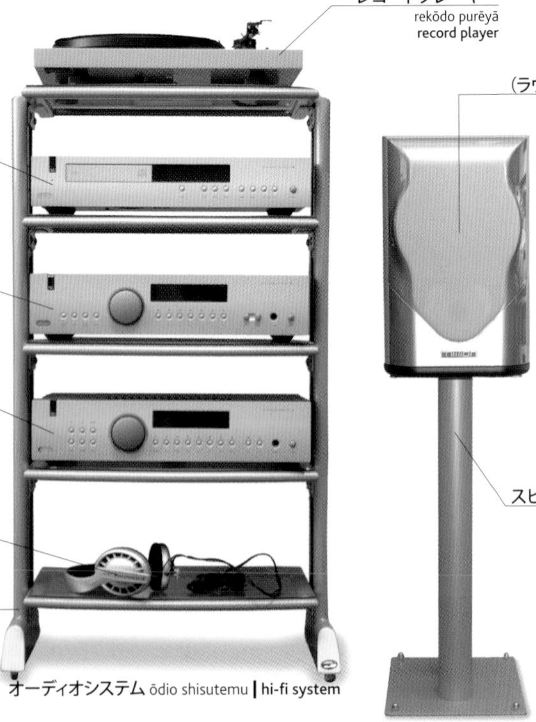

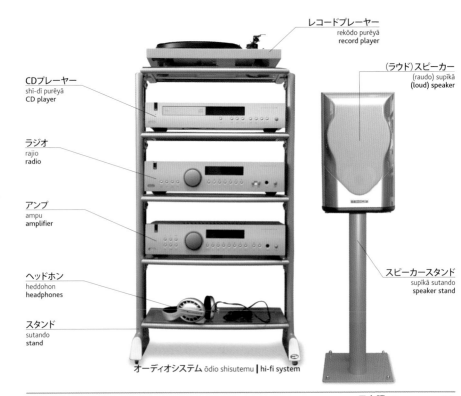

レコードプレーヤー
rekōdo purēyā
record player

CDプレーヤー
shī-dī purēyā
CD player

ラジオ
rajio
radio

アンプ
ampu
amplifier

ヘッドホン
heddohon
headphones

スタンド
sutando
stand

(ラウド)スピーカー
(raudo) supīkā
(loud) speaker

スピーカースタンド
supīkā sutando
speaker stand

オーディオシステム ōdio shisutemu | hi-fi system

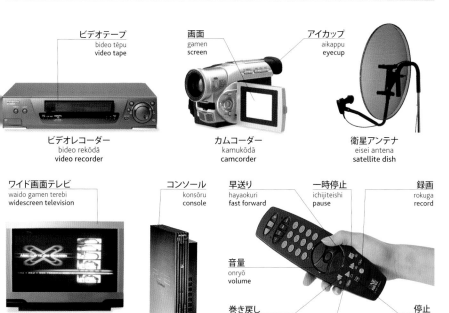

ビデオテープ
bideo têpu
video tape

画面
gamen
screen

アイカップ
aikappu
eyecup

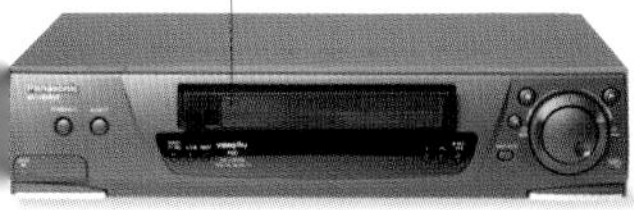

ビデオレコーダー
bideo rekôdâ
video recorder

カムコーダー
kamukôdâ
camcorder

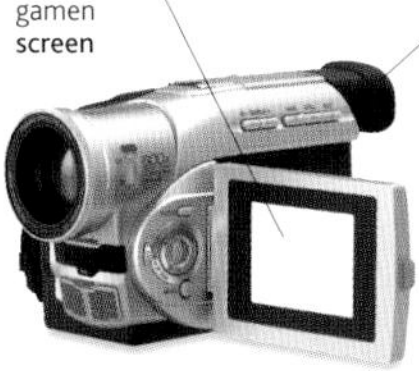

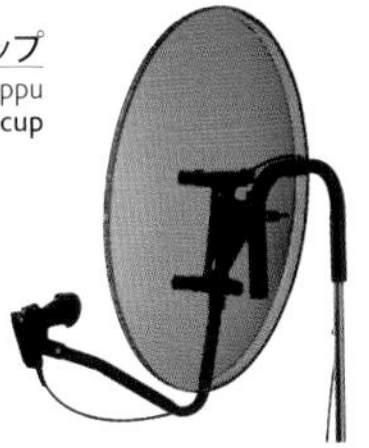

衛星アンテナ
eisei antena
satellite dish

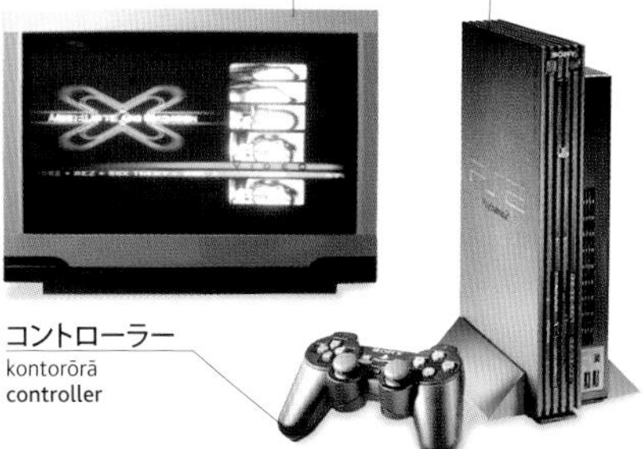

ワイド画面テレビ
waido gamen terebi
widescreen television

コンソール
konsôru
console

早送り
hayaokuri
fast forward

一時停止
ichijiteishi
pause

録画
rokuga
record

音量
onryô
volume

巻き戻し
makimodoshi
rewind

停止
teishi
stop

再生
saisei
play

コントローラー
kontorôrâ
controller

テレビゲーム terebi gêmu | **video game**

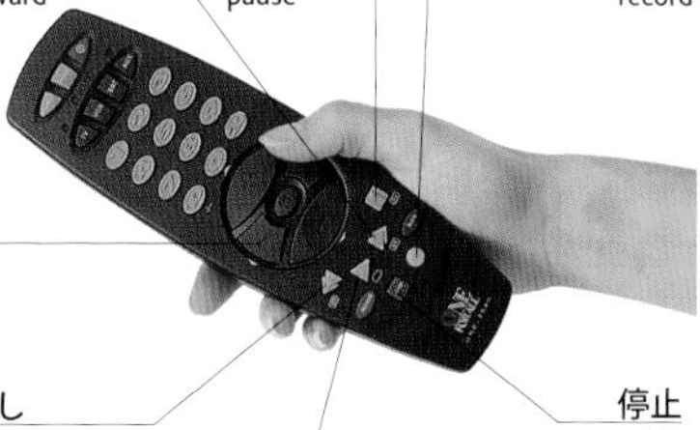

リモコン rimokon | **remote control**

関連用語 kanrenyôgo ● vocabulary

コンパクトディスク kompakuto disuku **compact disc**	長編映画 chôhen eiga **feature film**	番組 bangumi **programme**	有料チャンネル yûryô channeru **pay per view channel**	テレビを見る terebi o miru **watch television (v)**
カセットテープ kasetto têpu **cassette tape**	コマーシャル komâsharu **advertisement**	ステレオ sutereo **stereo**	チャンネルを替える channeru o kaeru **change channel (v)**	テレビを消す terebi o kesu **turn the television off (v)**
カセットプレーヤー kasetto purêyâ **cassette player**	ディジタル dijitaru **digital**	ケーブルテレビ kêburu terebi **cable television**	テレビを点ける terebi o tsukeru **turn the television on (v)**	ラジオをつける rajio o tsukeru **tune the radio (v)**

写真 shashin ● photography

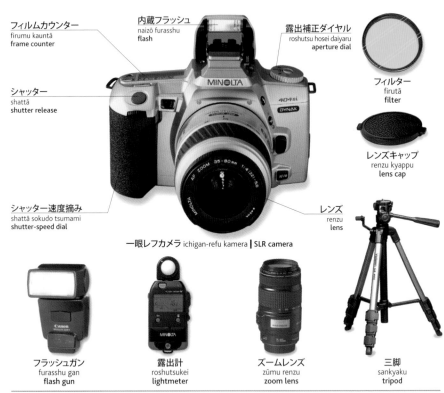

フィルムカウンター
firumu kauntā
frame counter

内蔵フラッシュ
naizō furasshu
flash

露出補正ダイヤル
roshutsu hosei daiyaru
aperture dial

シャッター
shattā
shutter release

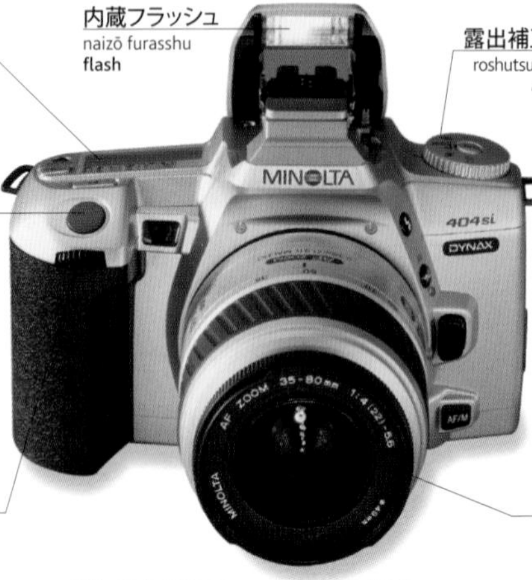

シャッター速度摘み
shattā sokudo tsumami
shutter-speed dial

レンズ
renzu
lens

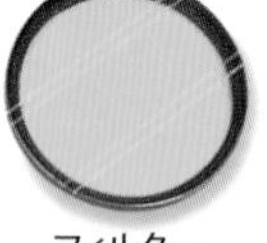

フィルター
firutā
filter

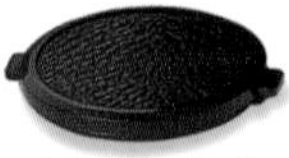

レンズキャップ
renzu kyappu
lens cap

一眼レフカメラ ichigan-refu kamera | SLR camera

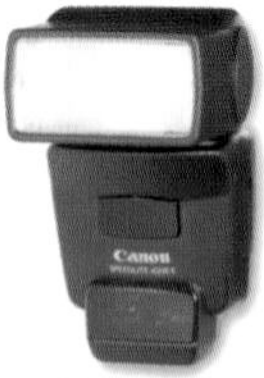

フラッシュガン
furasshu gan
flash gun

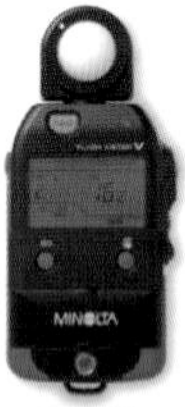

露出計
roshutsukei
lightmeter

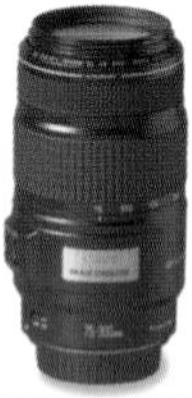

ズームレンズ
zūmu renzu
zoom lens

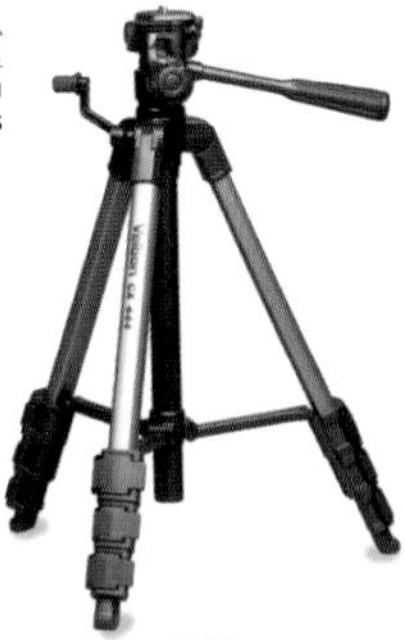

三脚
sankyaku
tripod

カメラの種類 kamera no shurui ● types of camera

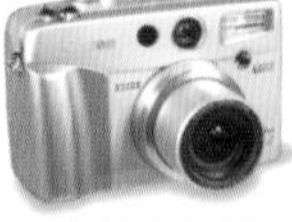

デジタルカメラ
dejitaru kamera
digital camera

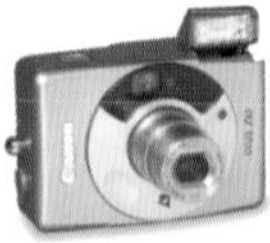

APSカメラ
ē-pī-esu kamera
APS camera

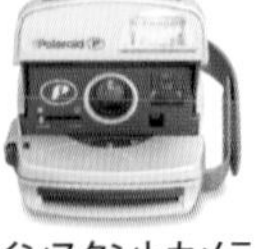

インスタントカメラ
insutanto kamera
instant camera

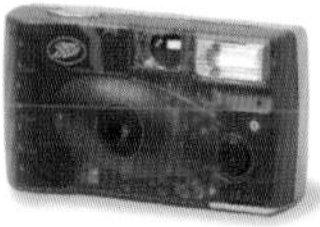

使い捨てカメラ
tsukaisute kamera
disposable camera

写真撮影 shashin satsuei ● **photograph**

フィルム
firumu
film

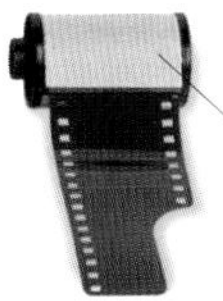

スプール
supūru
film spool

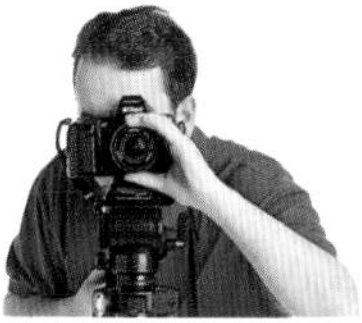

ピントを合わせる
pinto o awaseru
focus (v)

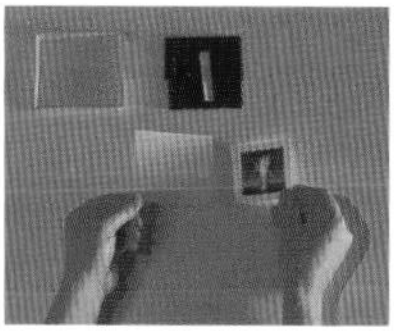

現像する
genzō suru
develop (v)

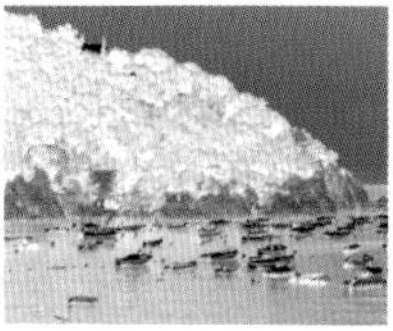

ネガ
nega
negative

ランドスケープ
randosukēpu
landscape

ポートレート
pōtorēto
portrait

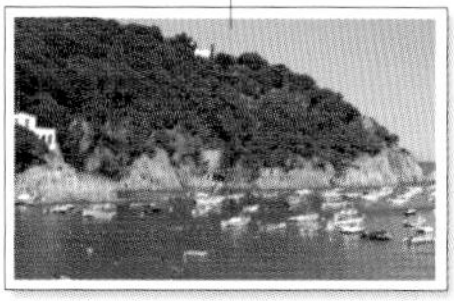

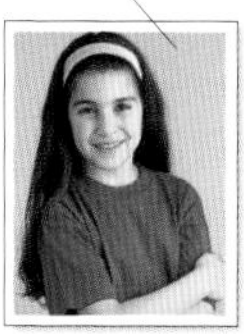

写真 shashin **|** photograph

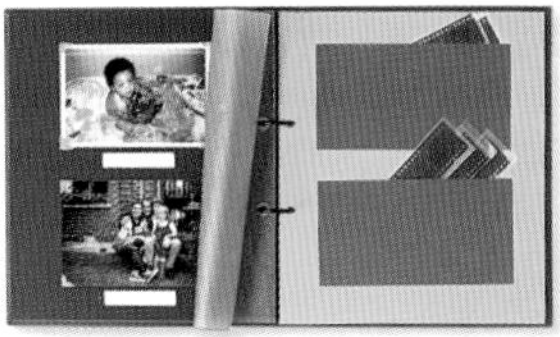

アルバム
arubamu
photo album

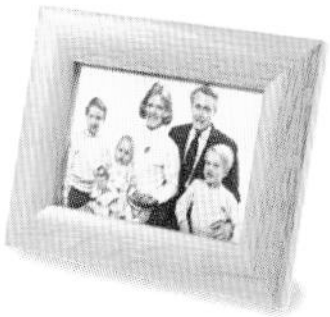

写真用額縁
shashin-yō gakubuchi
photo frame

問題 mondai ● **problems**

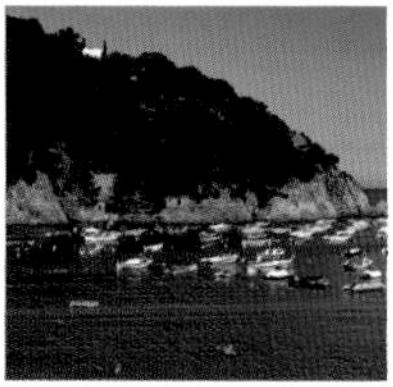

露出不足
roshutsu-busoku
underexposed

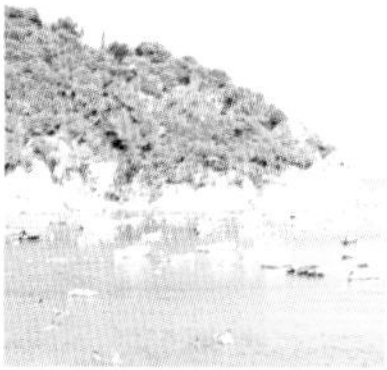

露出オーバー
roshutsu-ōbā
overexposed

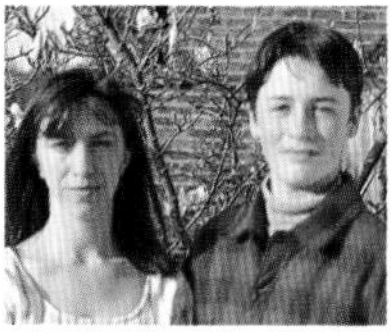

ピンぼけ
pimboke
out of focus

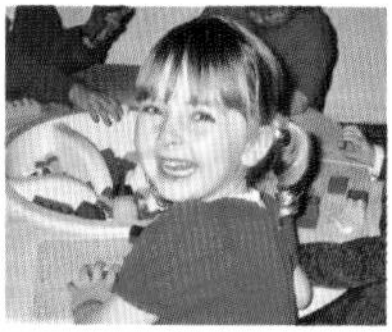

赤目
akame
red eye

関連用語 kanrenyōgo ● **vocabulary**

ファインダー faindā **viewfinder**	**印画** inga **print**
カメラケース kamera kēsu **camera case**	**無光沢** mukōtaku **matte**
露出 roshutsu **exposure**	**光沢** kōtaku **gloss**
暗室 anshitsu **darkroom**	**引き伸ばし** hikinobashi **enlargement**
メモリカード memori kādo **memory card**	**印画紙** ingashi **photo paper**

このフィルムを現像してください。
kono firumu o genzō shite kudasai.
I'd like this film processed.

ゲーム gēmu • games

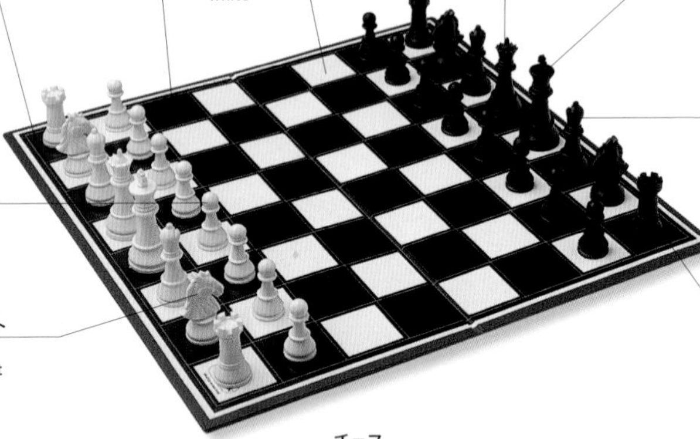

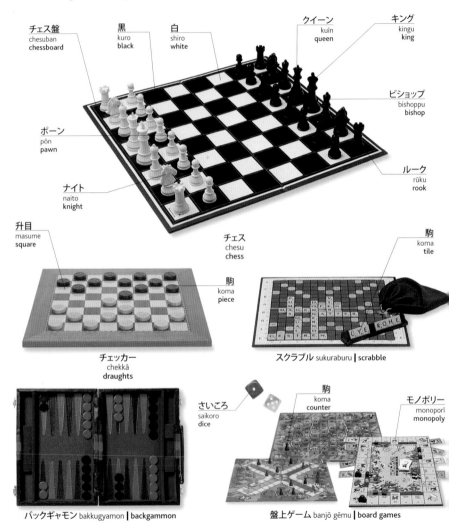

チェス盤
chesuban
chessboard

黒
kuro
black

白
shiro
white

クイーン
kuīn
queen

キング
kingu
king

ビショップ
bishoppu
bishop

ポーン
pōn
pawn

ナイト
naito
knight

ルーク
rūku
rook

升目
masume
square

チェス
chesu
chess

駒
koma
tile

駒
koma
piece

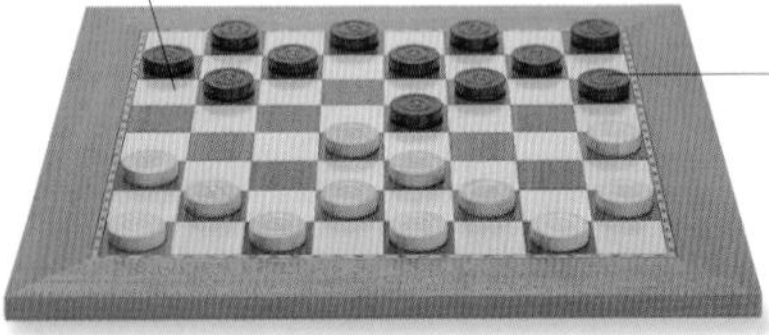

チェッカー
chekkā
draughts

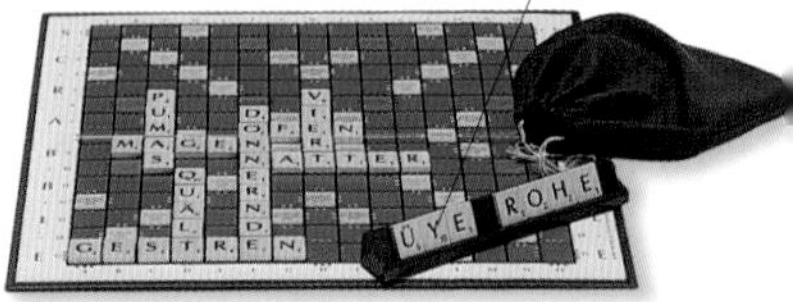

スクラブル sukuraburu | scrabble

さいころ
saikoro
dice

駒
koma
counter

モノポリー
monoporī
monopoly

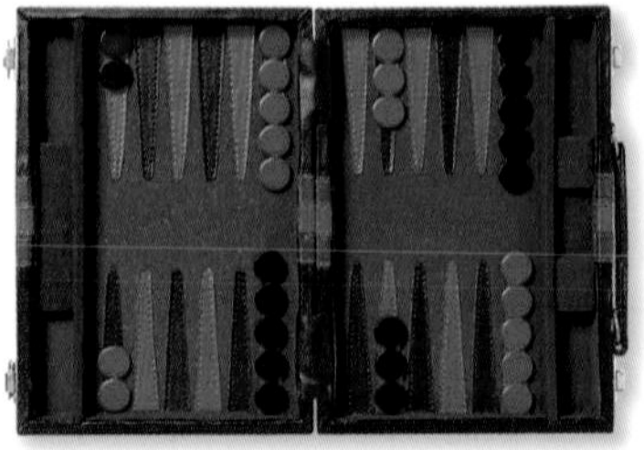

バックギャモン bakkugyamon | backgammon

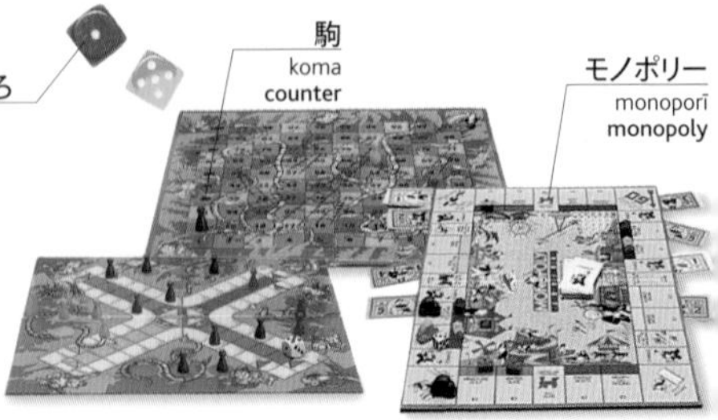

盤上ゲーム banjō gēmu | board games

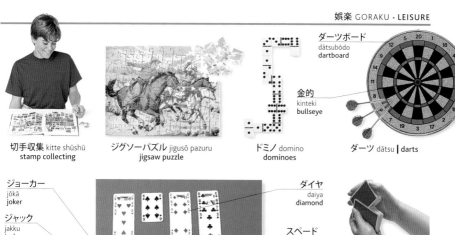

ダーツボード
dātsubōdo
dartboard

金的
kinteki
bullseye

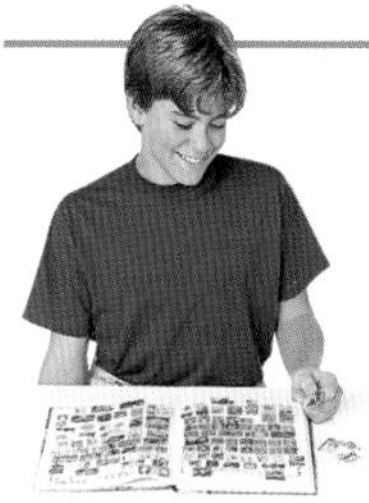

切手収集 kitte shūshū
stamp collecting

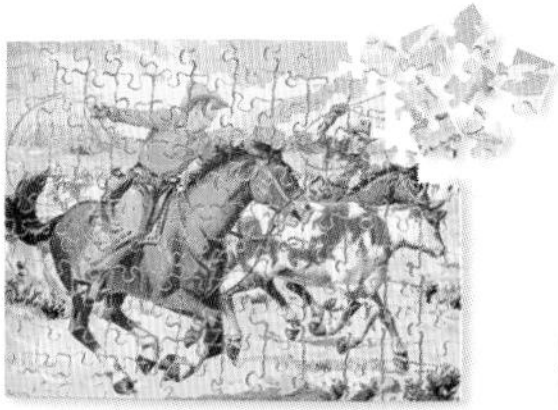

ジグソーパズル jigusō pazuru
jigsaw puzzle

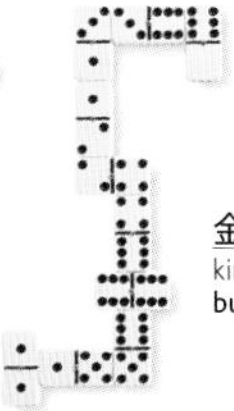

ドミノ domino
dominoes

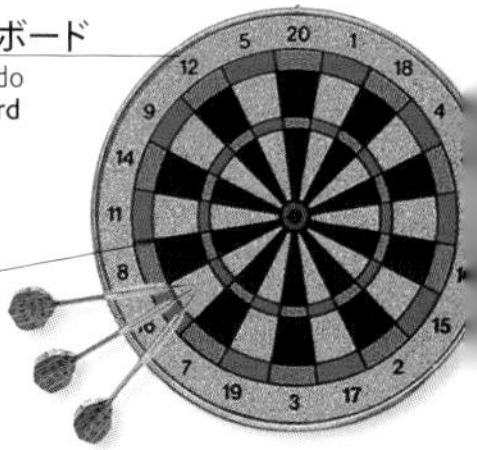

ダーツ dātsu | darts

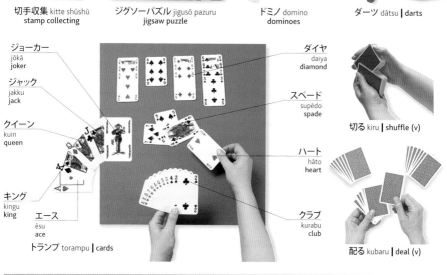

ジョーカー
jōkā
joker

ジャック
jakku
jack

クイーン
kuin
queen

キング
kingu
king

エース
ēsu
ace

ダイヤ
daiya
diamond

スペード
supēdo
spade

切る kiru | shuffle (v)

ハート
hāto
heart

クラブ
kurabu
club

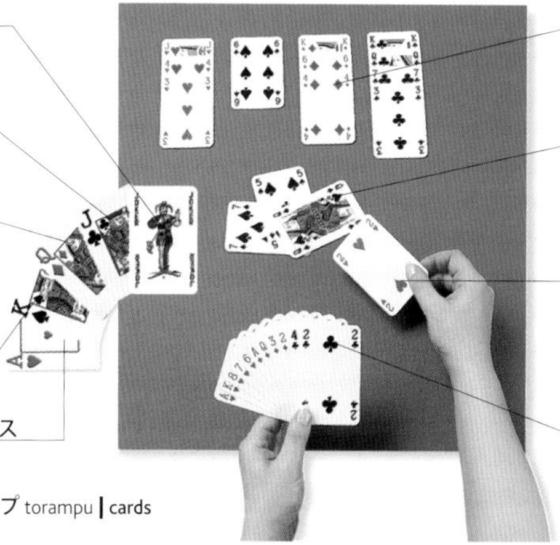

トランプ torampu | cards

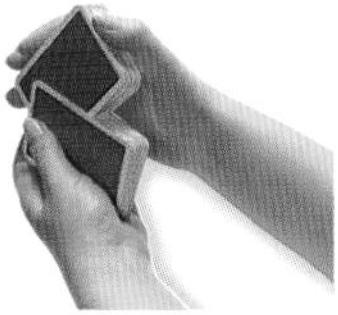

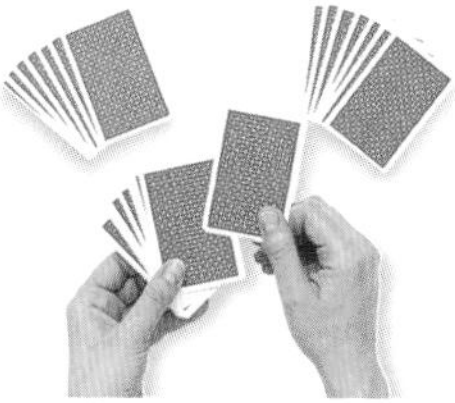

配る kubaru | deal (v)

関連用語 kanrenyōgo • vocabulary

手 te move	勝つ katsu win (v)	敗者 haisha loser	点 ten point	ブリッジ burijji bridge	さいころを転がしてください。 saikoro o korogashite kudasai. Roll the dice.
遊ぶ asobu play (v)	勝者 shōsha winner	ゲーム gēmu game	得点 tokuten score	トランプ一組 torampu hito-kumi pack of cards	誰の番ですか。 dare no ban desuka? Whose turn is it?
プレーヤー purēyā player	負ける makeru lose (v)	賭け kake bet	ポーカー pōkā poker	スート sūto suit	貴方の番です。 anata no ban desu. It's your move.

美術と工芸1 bijutsu to kōgei ● arts and crafts 1

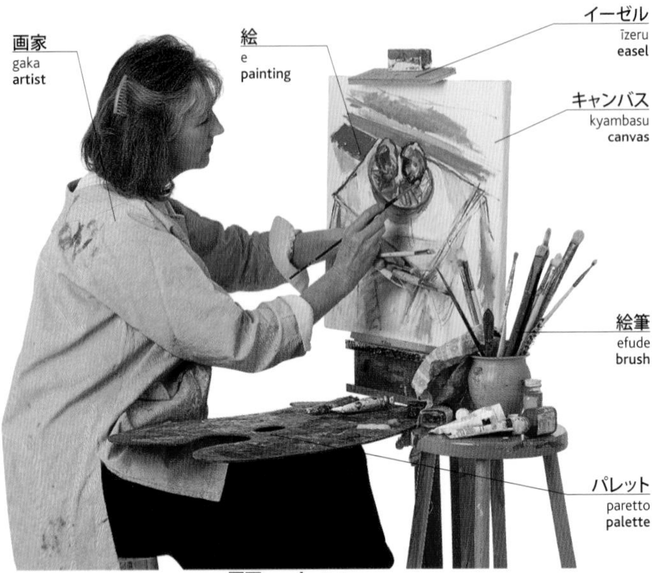

画家
gaka
artist

絵
e
painting

イーゼル
īzeru
easel

キャンバス
kyambasu
canvas

絵筆
efude
brush

パレット
paretto
palette

図画 zuga | painting

絵具 enogu ● paints

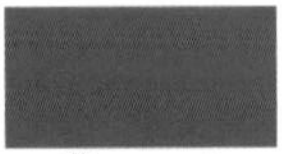

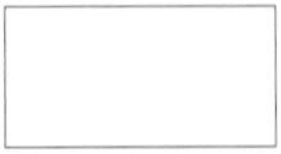

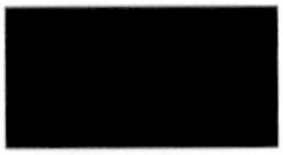

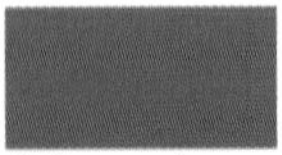

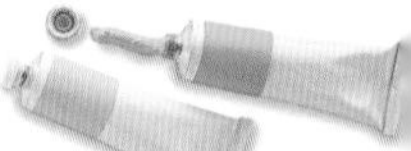

油絵具
abura enogu
oil paints

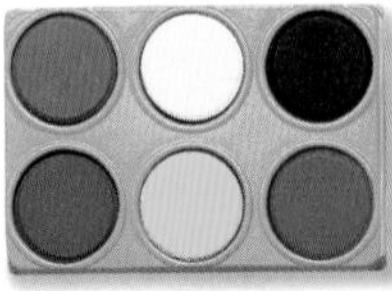

水彩絵具
suisai enogu
watercolour paint

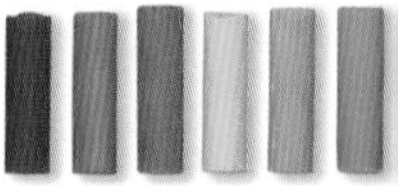

パステル
pasuteru
pastels

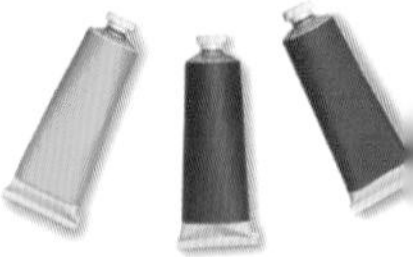

アクリル絵具
akuriru enogu
acrylic paint

ポスターカラー posutā karā
poster paint

色 iro ● colours

赤 aka | red

青 ao | blue

黄色 ki'iro
yellow

緑 midori | green

オレンジ色 orenji iro
orange

紫 murasaki
purple

白 shiro | white

黒 kuro | black

灰色 hai'iro | grey

ピンク pinku
pink

茶色 chairo | brown

藍色 ai'iro
indigo

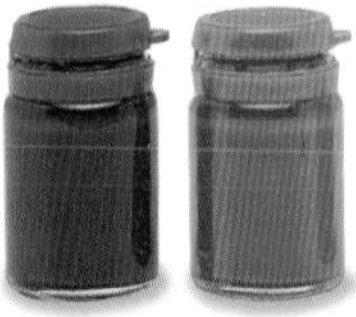

他の工芸 ta no kōgei • other crafts

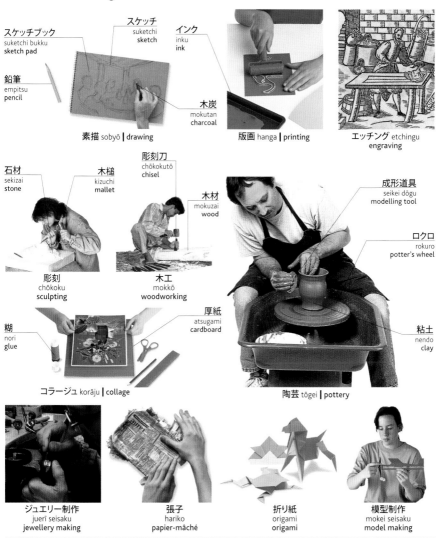

スケッチブック
suketchi bukku
sketch pad

鉛筆
empitsu
pencil

スケッチ
suketchi
sketch

インク
inku
ink

木炭
mokutan
charcoal

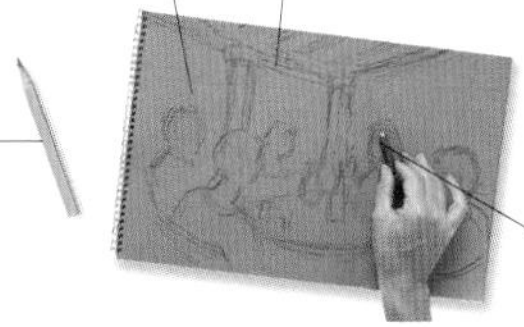

素描 sobyō | drawing

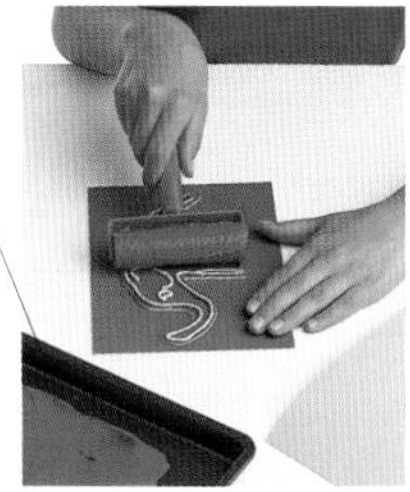

版画 hanga | printing

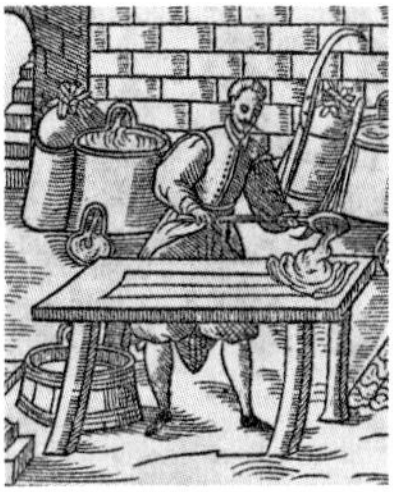

エッチング etchingu
engraving

石材
sekizai
stone

木槌
kizuchi
mallet

彫刻刀
chōkokutō
chisel

木材
mokuzai
wood

成形道具
seikei dōgu
modelling tool

ロクロ
rokuro
potter's wheel

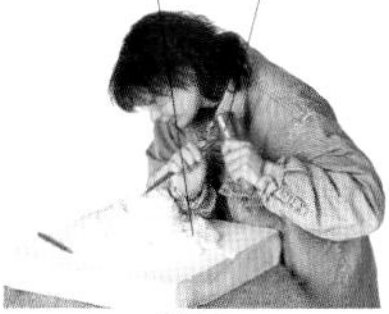

彫刻
chōkoku
sculpting

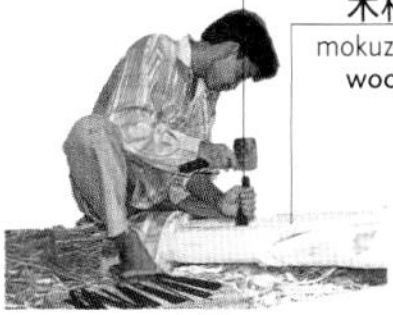

木工
mokkō
woodworking

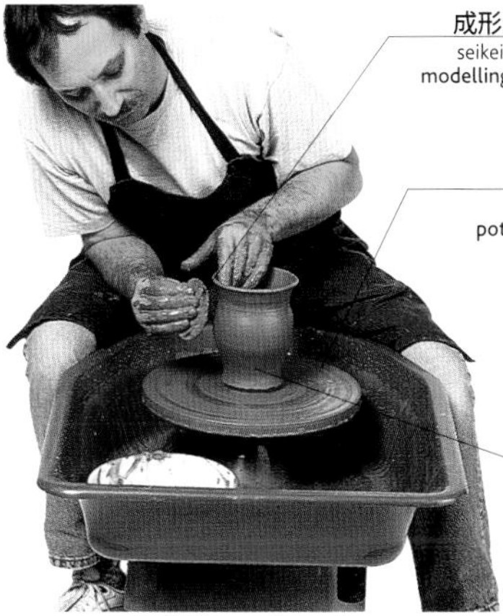

糊
nori
glue

厚紙
atsugami
cardboard

粘土
nendo
clay

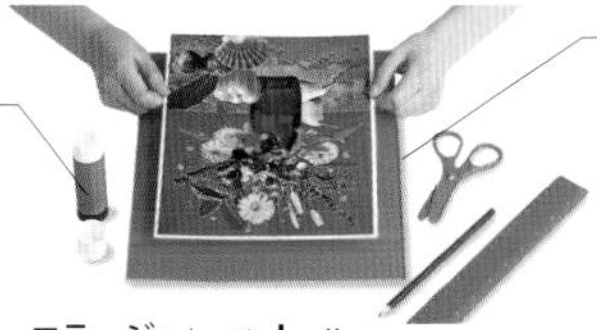

コラージュ korāju | collage

陶芸 tōgei | pottery

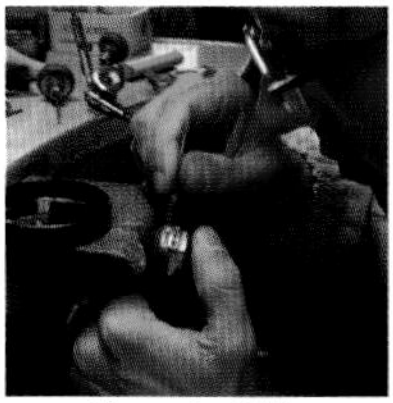

ジュエリー制作
juerī seisaku
jewellery making

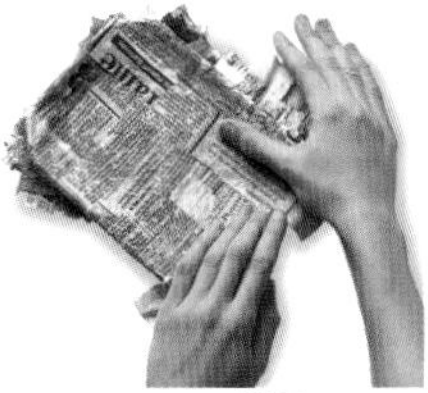

張子
hariko
papier-mâché

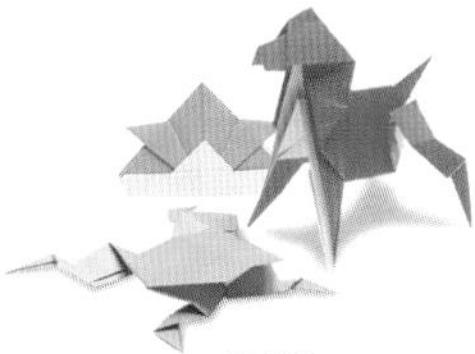

折り紙
origami
origami

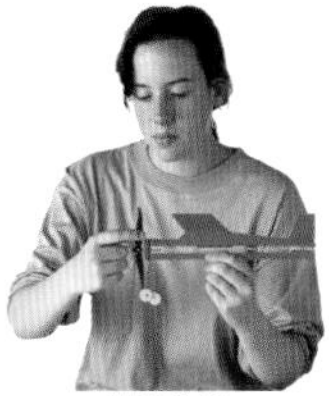

模型制作
mokei seisaku
model making

美術と工芸2 bijutsu to kōgei • arts and crafts 2

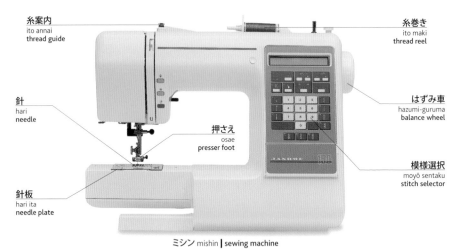

糸案内
ito annai
thread guide

糸巻き
ito maki
thread reel

針
hari
needle

はずみ車
hazumi-guruma
balance wheel

押さえ
osae
presser foot

模様選択
moyō sentaku
stitch selector

針板
hari ita
needle plate

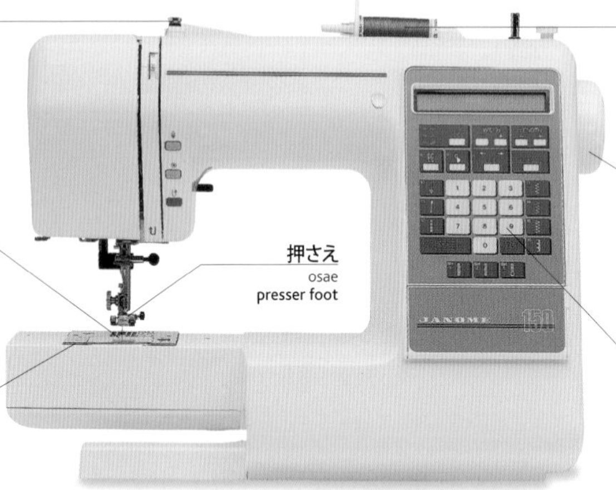

ミシン mishin | sewing machine

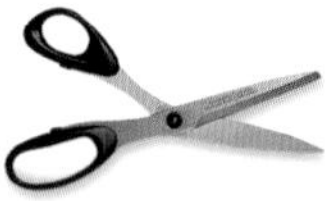

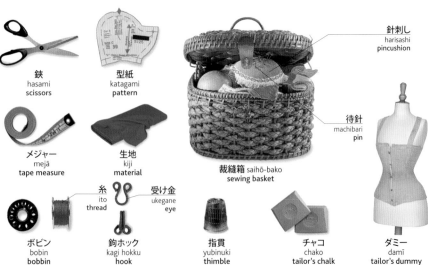

鋏
hasami
scissors

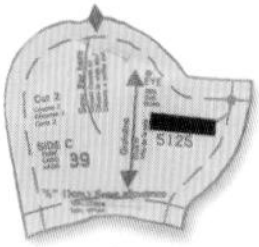

型紙
katagami
pattern

針刺し
harisashi
pincushion

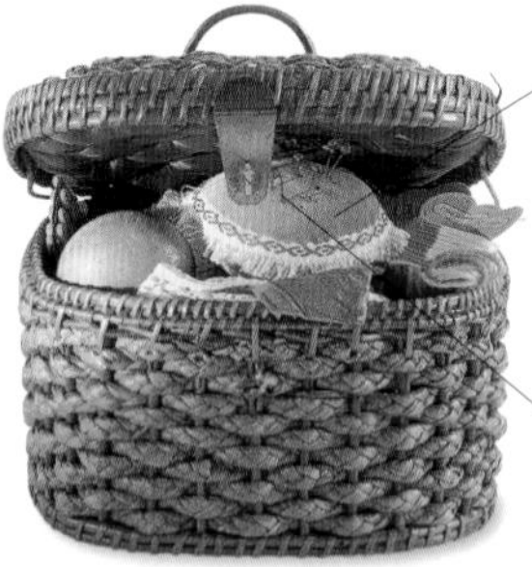

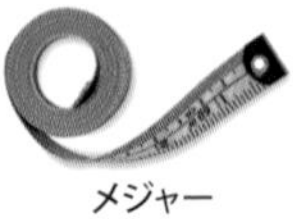

メジャー
mejā
tape measure

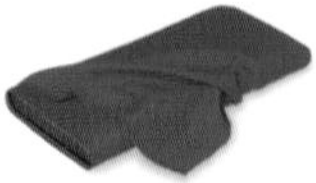

生地
kiji
material

待針
machibari
pin

糸
ito
thread

受け金
ukegane
eye

裁縫箱 saihō-bako
sewing basket

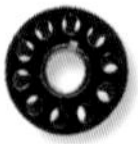

ボビン
bobin
bobbin

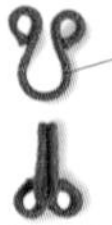

鉤ホック
kagi hokku
hook

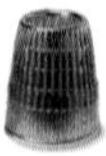

指貫
yubinuki
thimble

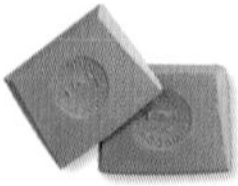

チャコ
chako
tailor's chalk

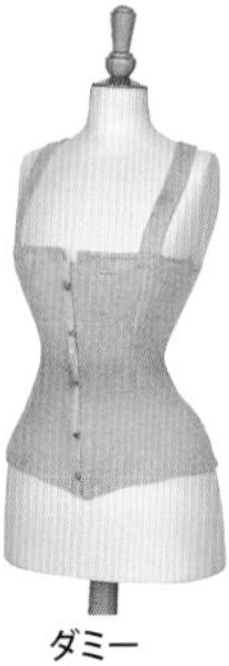

ダミー
damī
tailor's dummy

縫い目
nuime
stitch

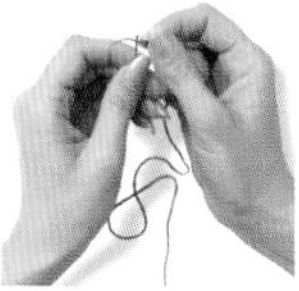

糸を通す
ito o tōsu
thread (v)

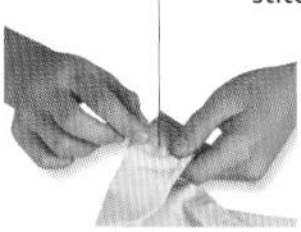

縫う
nu'u
sew (v)

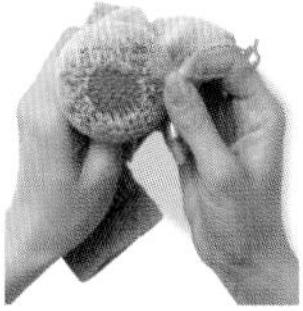

繕う
tsukurō
darn (v)

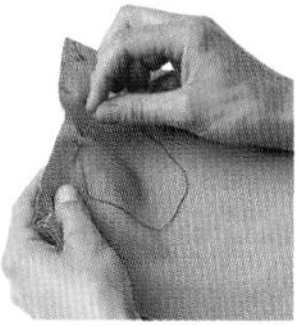

仮縫いする
karinui suru
tack (v)

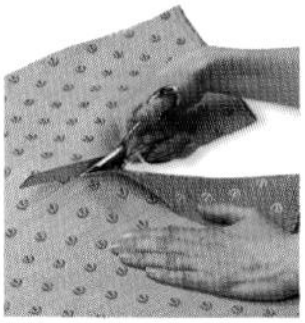

切る
kiru
cut (v)

かぎ針
kagibari
crochet hook

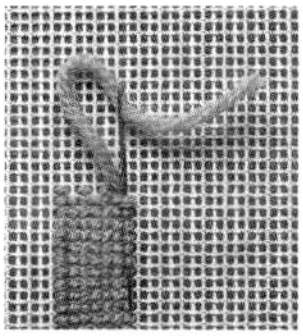

ニードルポイント
nīdorupointo
needlepoint

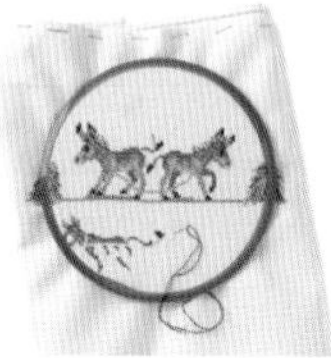

刺繍
shishū
embroidery

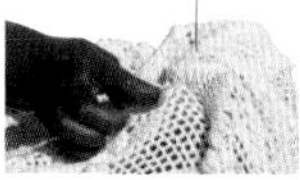

かぎ針編み
kagibariami
crochet

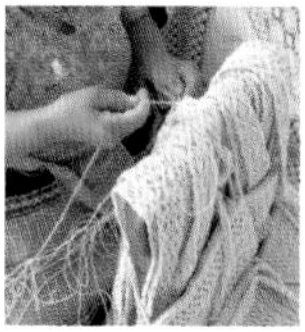

マクラメ
makurame
macramé

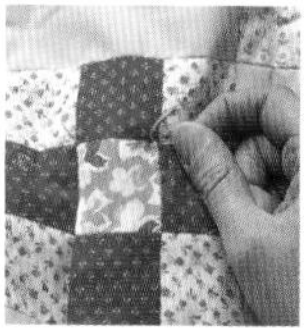

パッチワーク
patchiwāku
patchwork

レース用ボビン
rēsu-yō bobin
lace bobbin

機
hata
loom

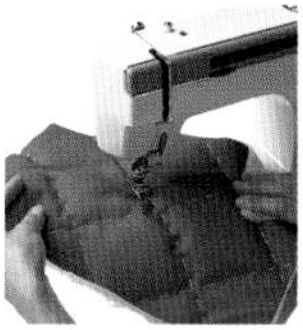

キルティング
kirutingu
quilting

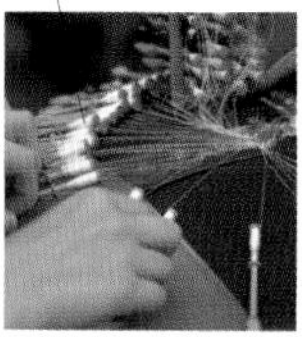

レース編み
rēsuami
lace-making

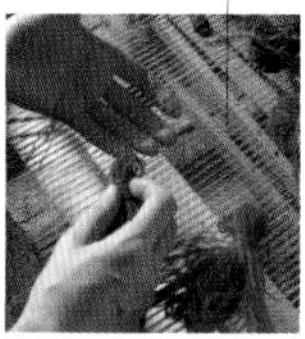

機織り
hataori
weaving

関連用語 kanrenyōgo • vocabulary

ほどく
hodoku
unpick (v)

ナイロン
nairon
nylon

布地
nunoji
fabric

絹
kinu
silk

綿
men
cotton

デザイナー
dezainā
designer

リネン
rinen
linen

ファッション
fasshon
fashion

ポリエステル
poriesuteru
polyester

ファスナー
fasunā
zip

編み針
amibari
knitting needle

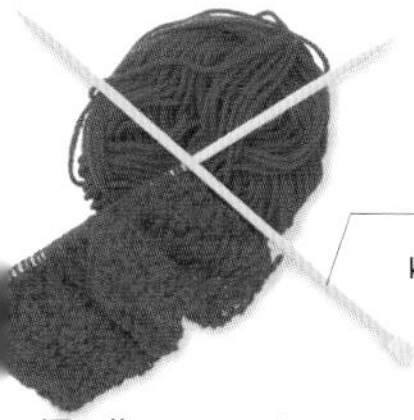

編み物 amimono | knitting

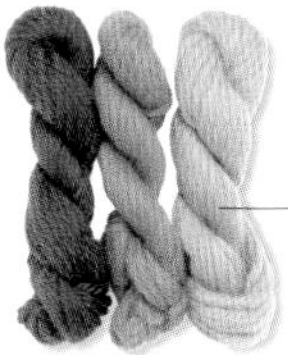

毛糸
keito
wool

かせ kase | skein

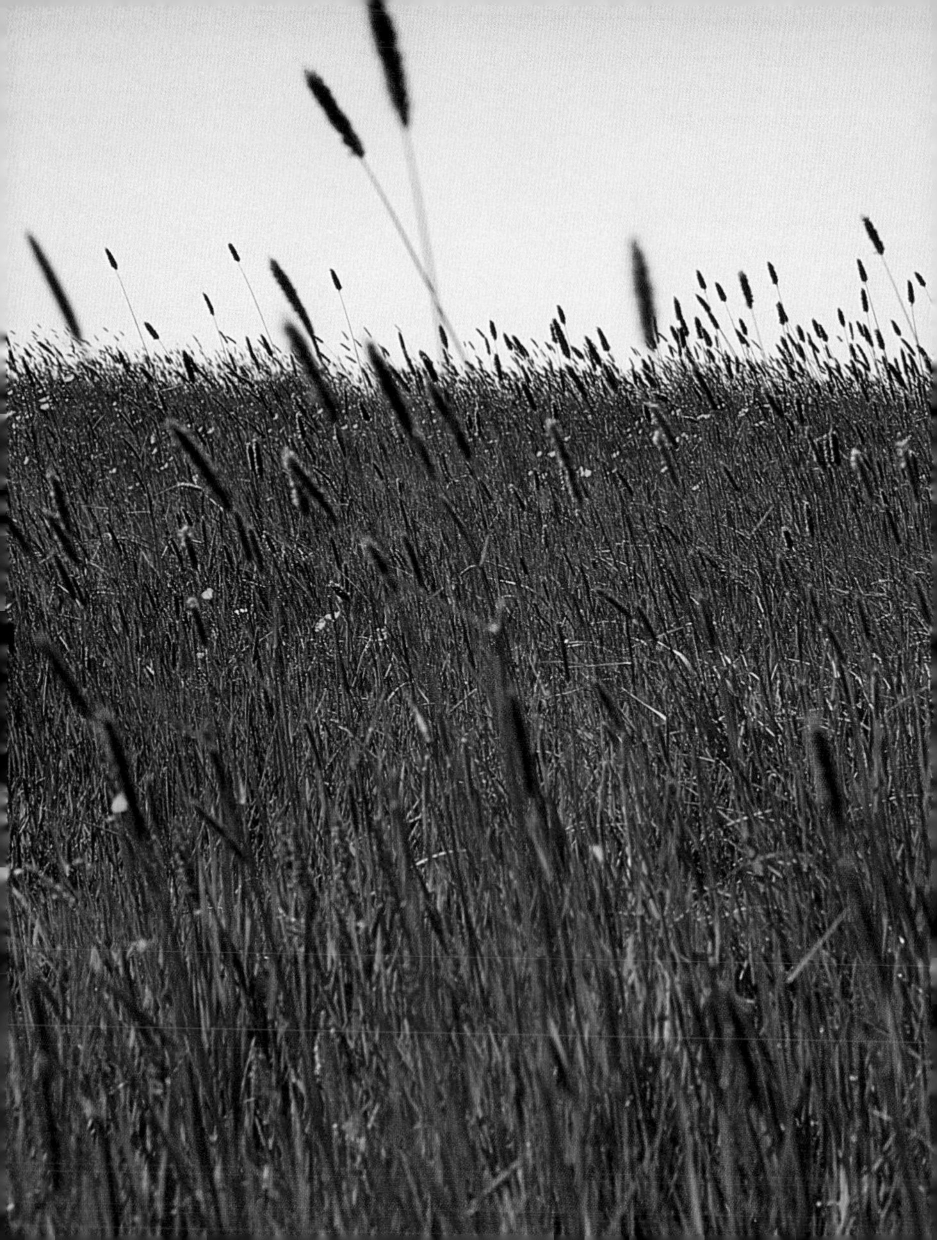

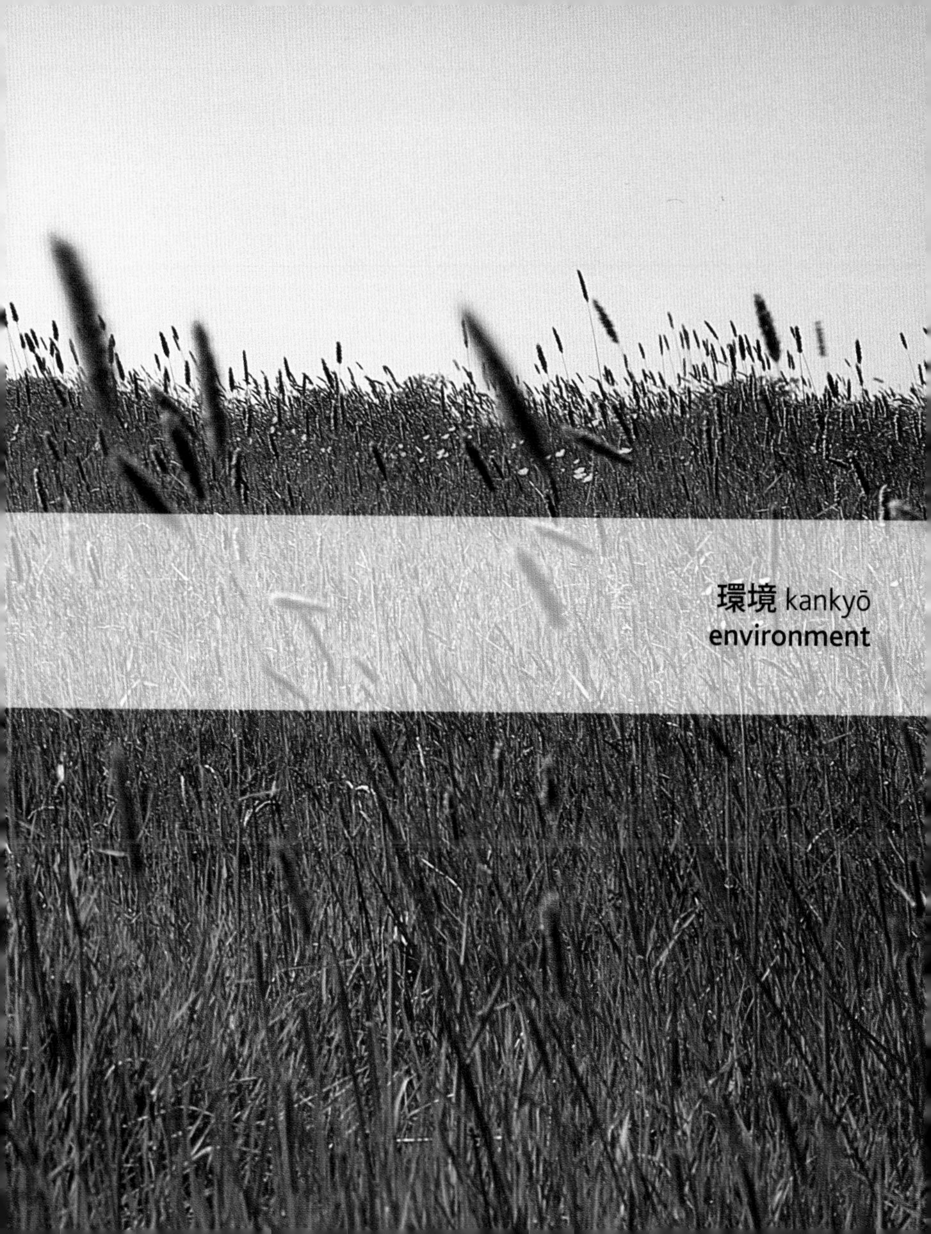

環境 kankyō
environment

宇宙空間 uchūkūkan • space

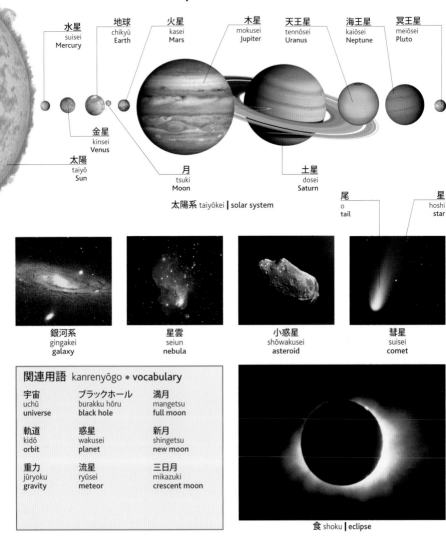

水星
suisei
Mercury

地球
chikyū
Earth

火星
kasei
Mars

木星
mokusei
Jupiter

天王星
tennōsei
Uranus

海王星
kaiōsei
Neptune

冥王星
meiōsei
Pluto

金星
kinsei
Venus

太陽
taiyō
Sun

月
tsuki
Moon

土星
dosei
Saturn

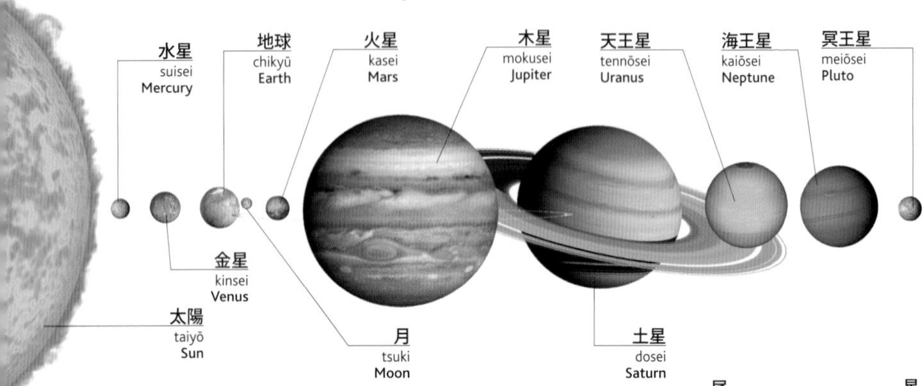

太陽系 taiyōkei | **solar system**

尾
o
tail

星
hoshi
star

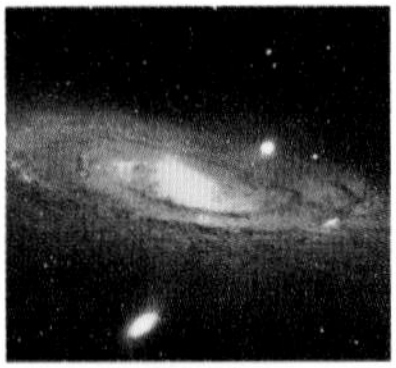

銀河系
gingakei
galaxy

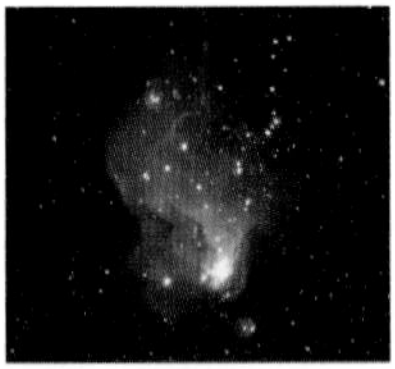

星雲
seiun
nebula

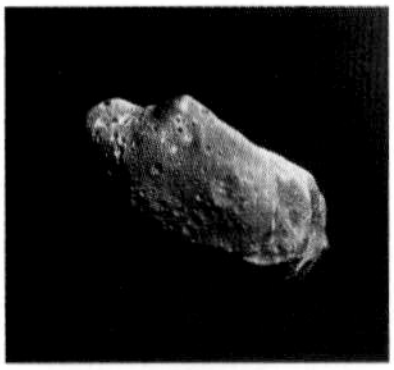

小惑星
shōwakusei
asteroid

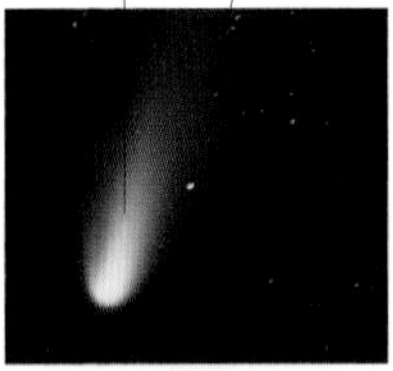

彗星
suisei
comet

関連用語 kanrenyōgo • vocabulary

宇宙 uchū universe	ブラックホール burakku hōru black hole	満月 mangetsu full moon
軌道 kidō orbit	惑星 wakusei planet	新月 shingetsu new moon
重力 jūryoku gravity	流星 ryūsei meteor	三日月 mikazuki crescent moon

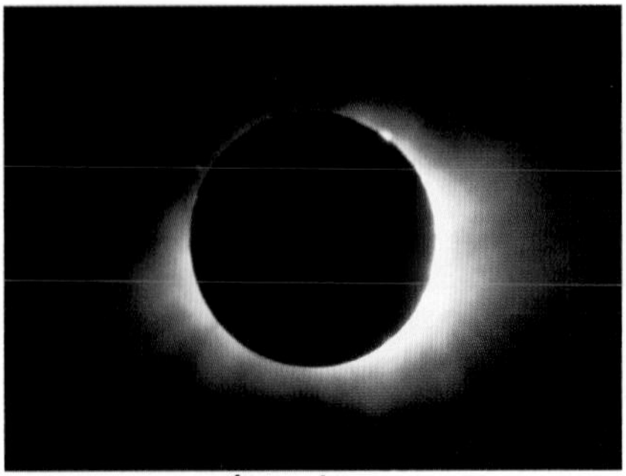

食 shoku | **eclipse**

宇宙探検 uchū tanken • **space exploration**

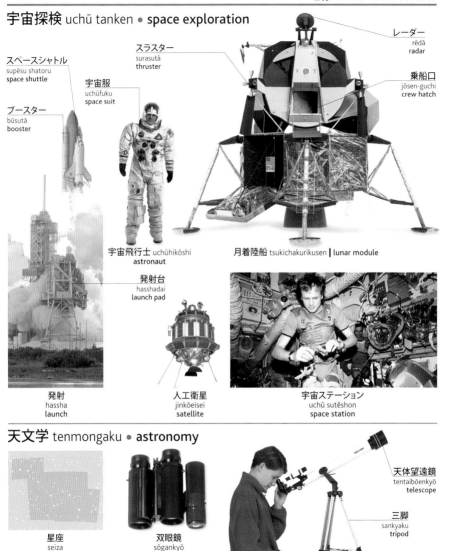

レーダー
rēdā
radar

スラスター
surasutā
thruster

スペースシャトル
supēsu shatoru
space shuttle

宇宙服
uchūfuku
space suit

ブースター
būsutā
booster

乗船口
jōsen-guchi
crew hatch

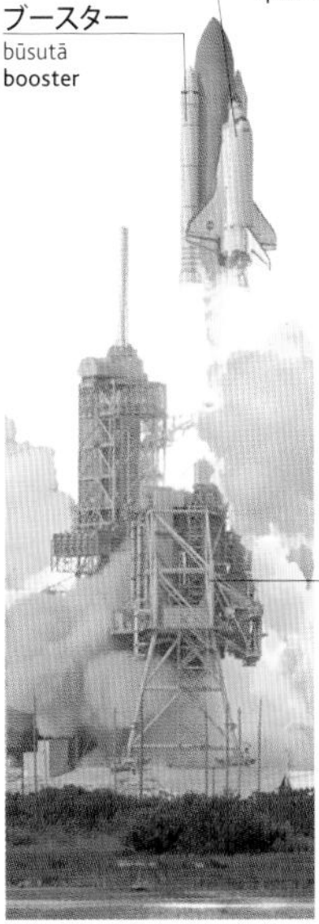

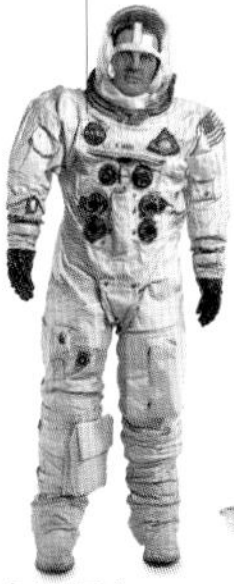

宇宙飛行士 uchūhikōshi
astronaut

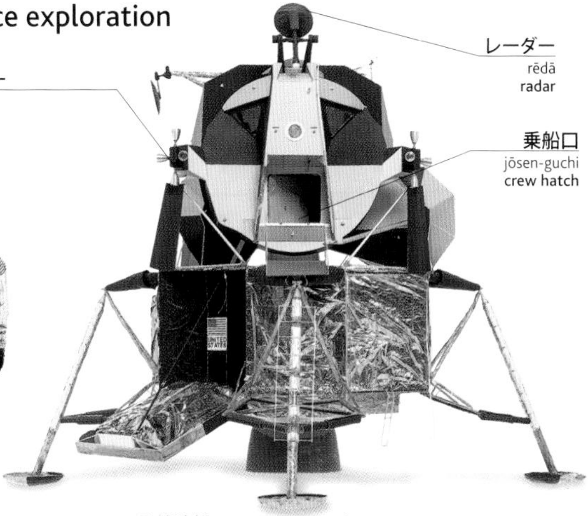

月着陸船 tsukichakurikusen **|** lunar module

発射台
hasshadai
launch pad

発射
hassha
launch

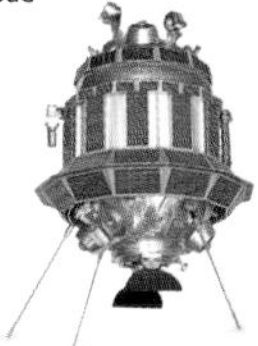

人工衛星
jinkōeisei
satellite

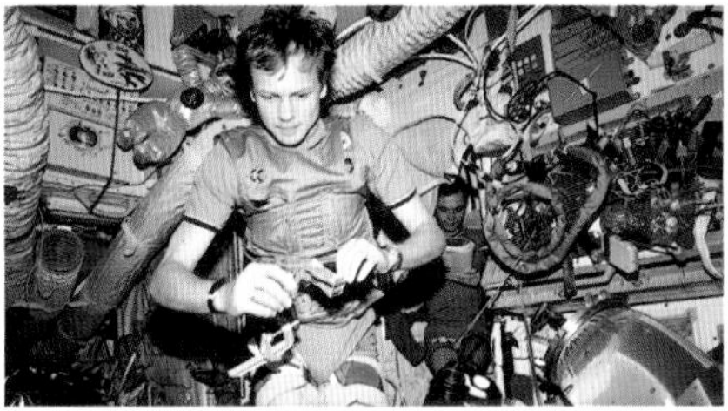

宇宙ステーション
uchū sutēshon
space station

天文学 tenmongaku • **astronomy**

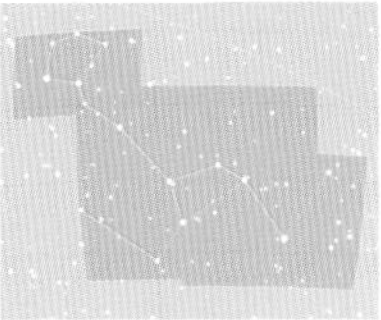

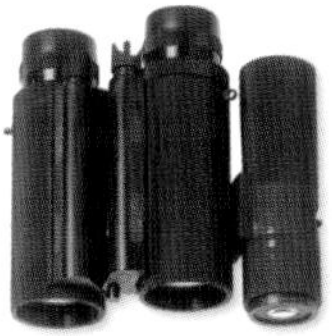

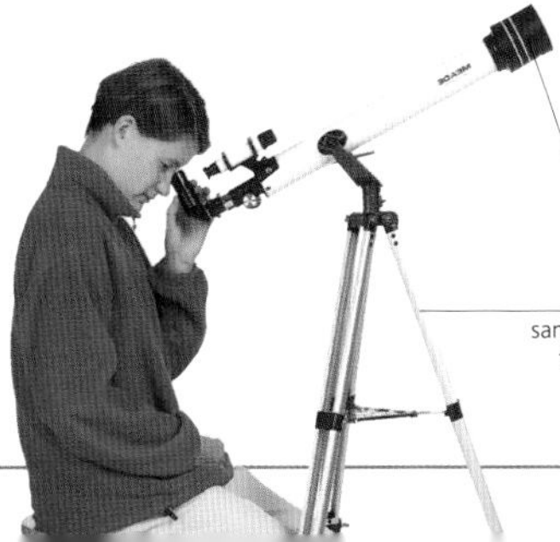

天体望遠鏡
tentaibōenkyō
telescope

三脚
sankyaku
tripod

星座
seiza
constellation

双眼鏡
sōgankyō
binoculars

地球 chikyū ● Earth

極地
kyokuchi
pole

陸地
rikuchi
land

大洋
taiyō
ocean

山脈
sanmyaku
mountain range

海
umi
sea

半島
hantō
peninsula

大陸
tairiku
continent

島
shima
island

大気圏
taikiken
atmosphere

地殻
chikaku
crust

マントル
mantoru
mantle

内核
naikaku
inner core

外核
gaikaku
outer core

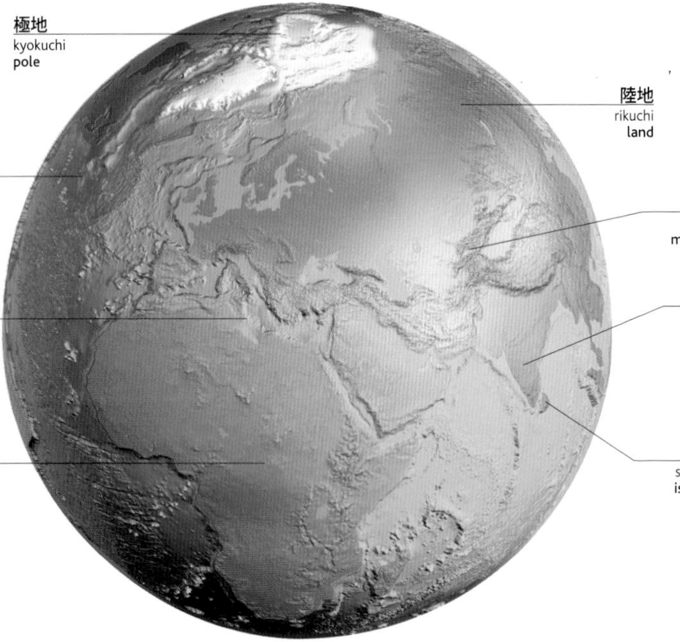

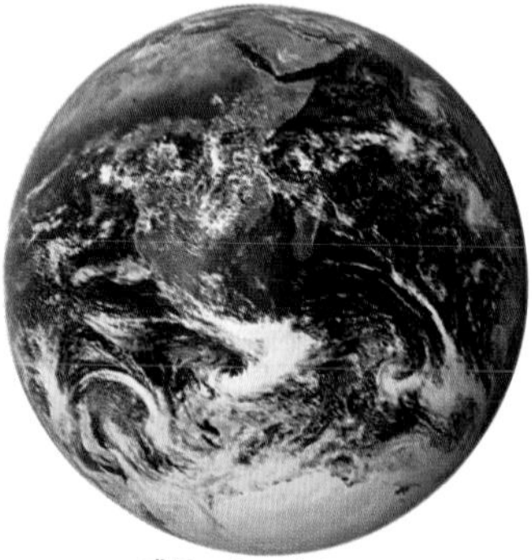

惑星 wakusei **|** planet

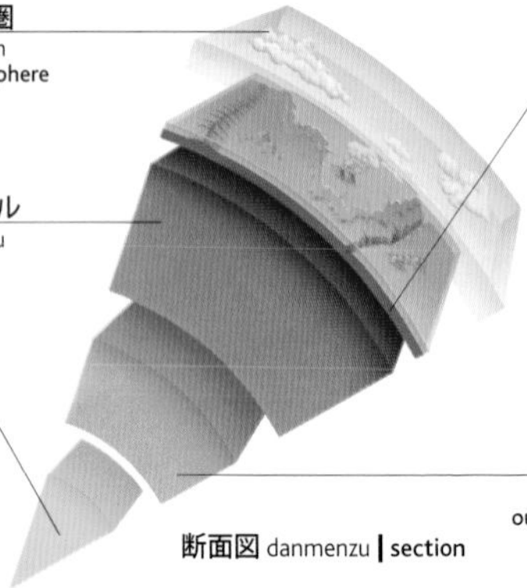

断面図 danmenzu **|** section

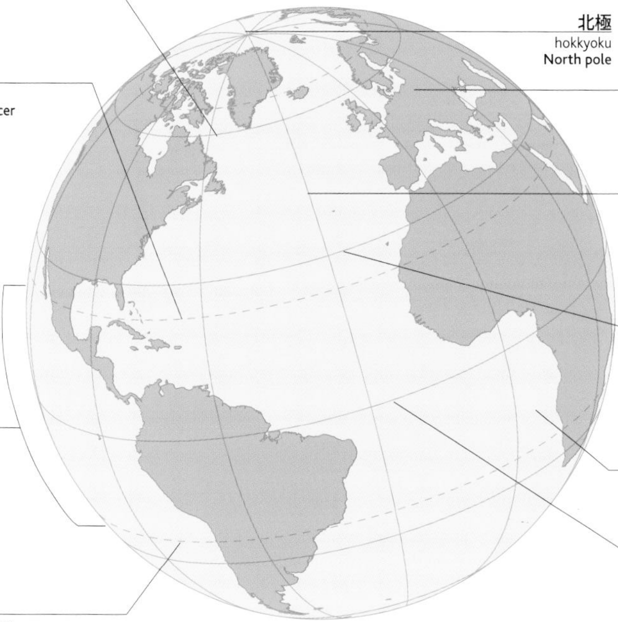

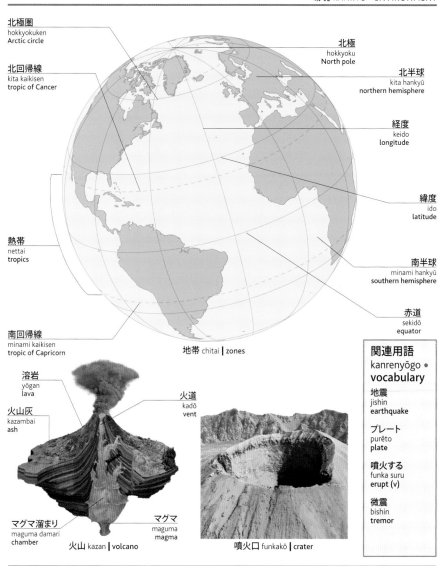

北極圏
hokkyokuken
Arctic circle

北回帰線
kita kaikisen
tropic of Cancer

熱帯
nettai
tropics

南回帰線
minami kaikisen
tropic of Capricorn

北極
hokkyoku
North pole

北半球
kita hankyū
northern hemisphere

経度
keido
longitude

緯度
ido
latitude

南半球
minami hankyū
southern hemisphere

赤道
sekidō
equator

地帯 chitai | zones

溶岩
yōgan
lava

火山灰
kazambai
ash

火道
kadō
vent

マグマ溜まり
maguma damari
chamber

マグマ
maguma
magma

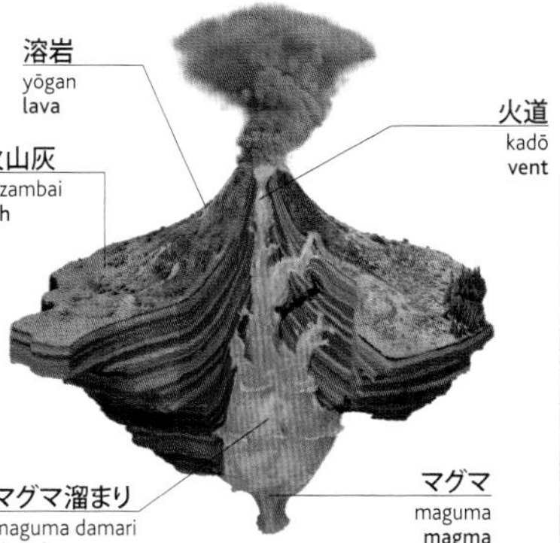

火山 kazan | volcano

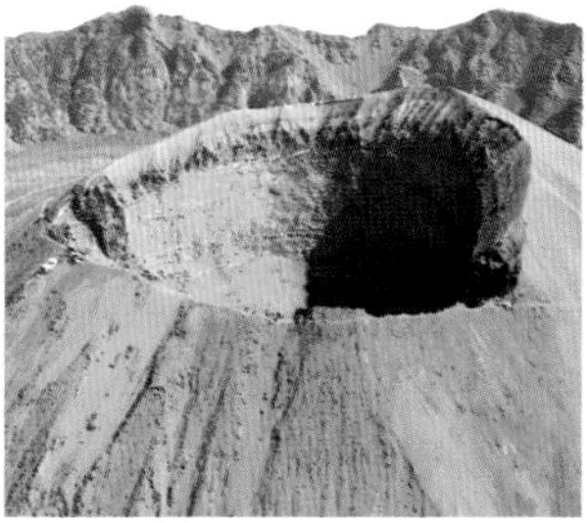

噴火口 funkakō | crater

関連用語
kanrenyōgo •
vocabulary

地震
jishin
earthquake

プレート
purēto
plate

噴火する
funka suru
erupt (v)

微震
bishin
tremor

地勢 chisei • landscape

山
yama
mountain

斜面
shamen
slope

川岸
kawagishi
bank

川
kawa
river

急流
kyūryū
rapids

岩
iwa
rocks

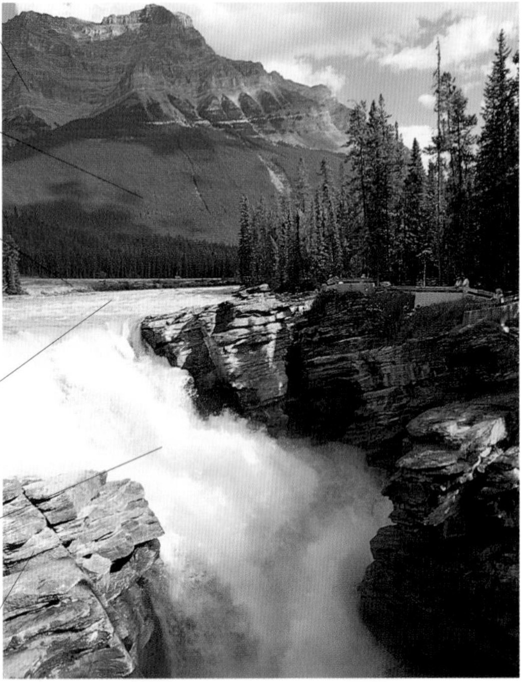

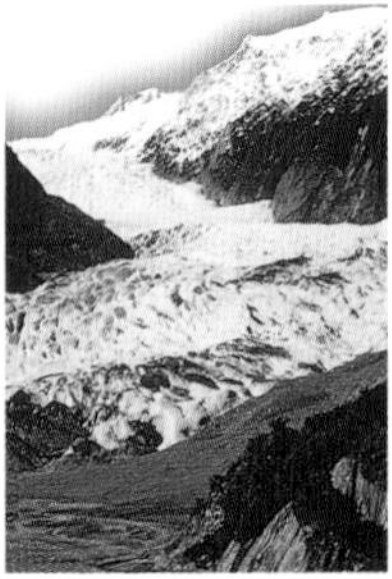

氷河
hyōga
glacier

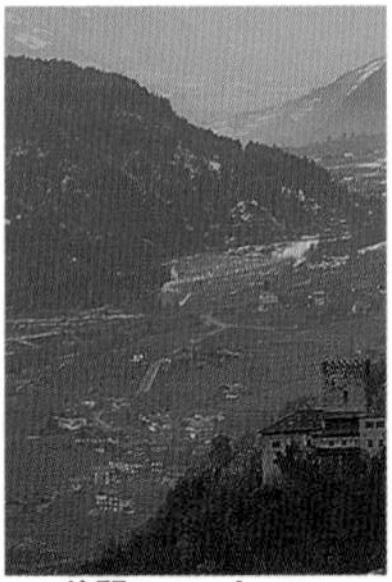

谷間 tanima | **valley**

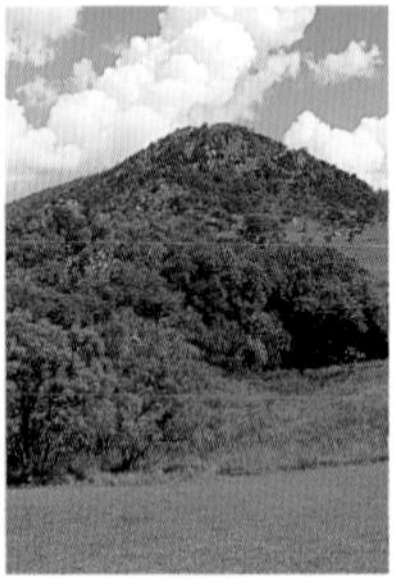

丘陵
kyūryō
hill

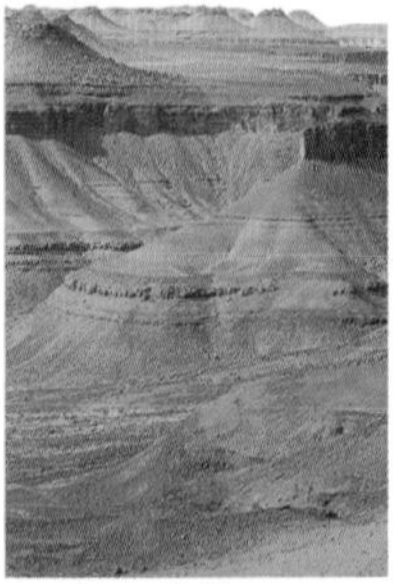

台地
daichi
plateau

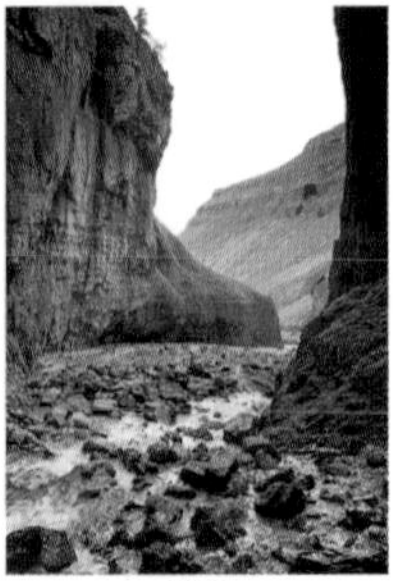

渓谷
keikoku
gorge

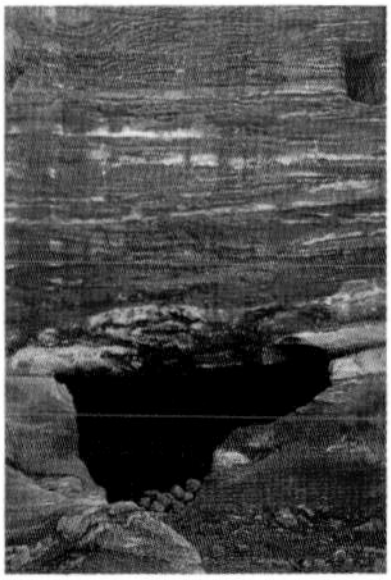

洞窟
dōkutsu
cave

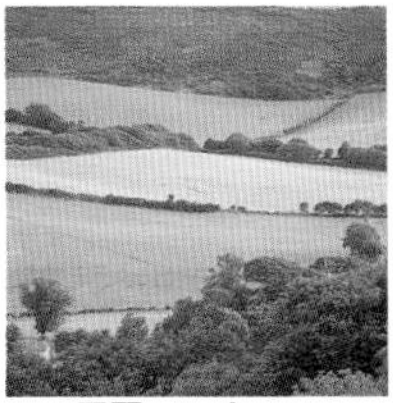

平野 heiya | plain

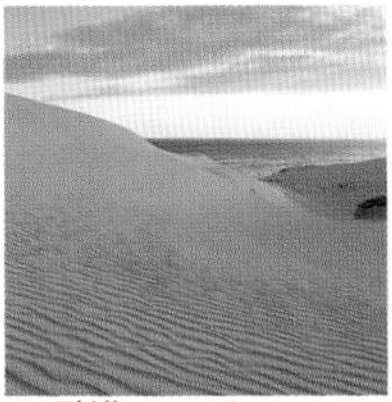

砂漠 sabaku | desert

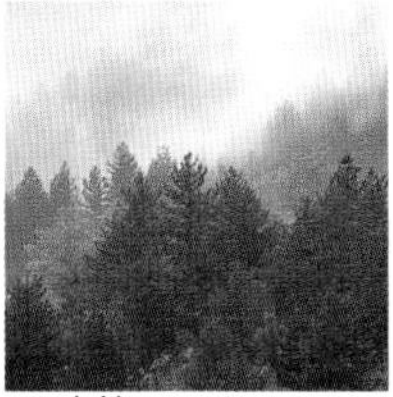

森林 shinrin | forest

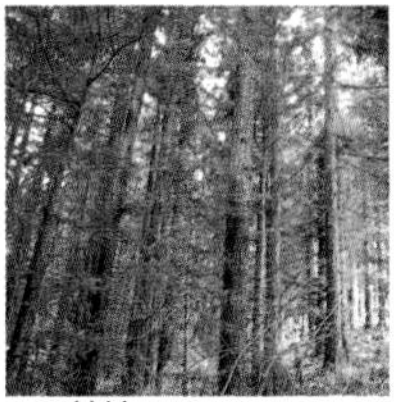

林地 rinchi | wood

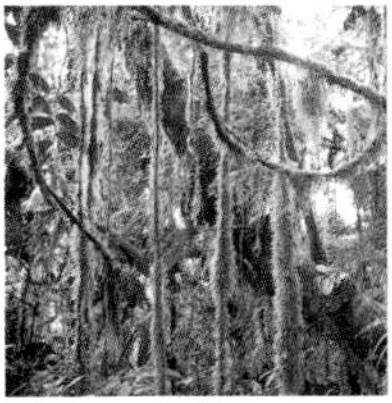

雨林
urin
rainforest

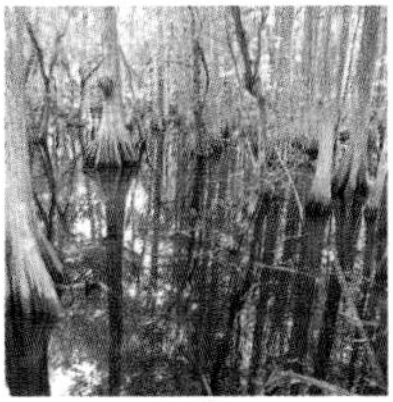

湿地
shitchi
swamp

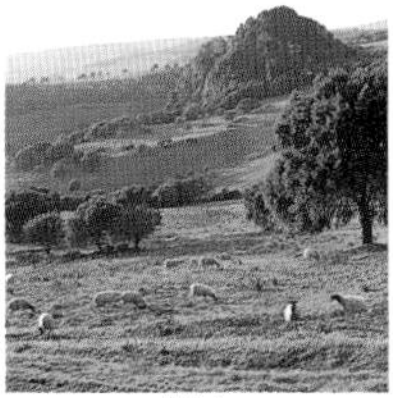

草地
kusachi
meadow

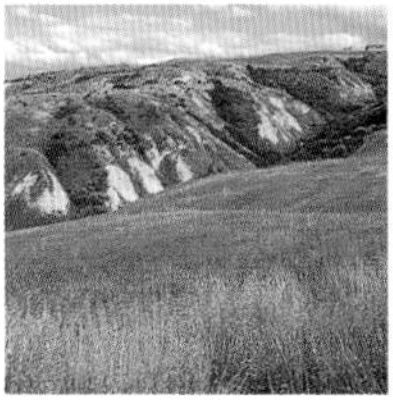

草原
sōgen
grassland

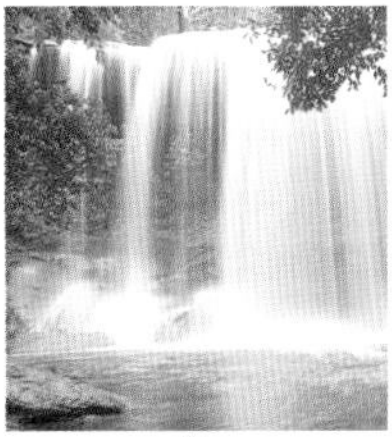

滝
taki
waterfall

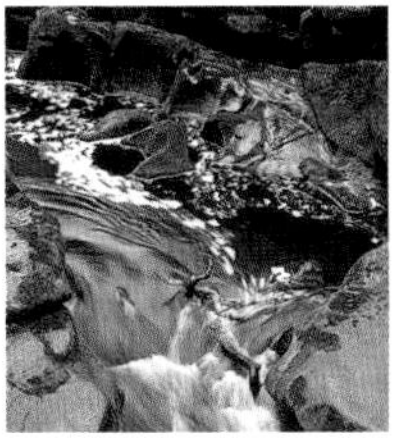

渓流
keiryū
stream

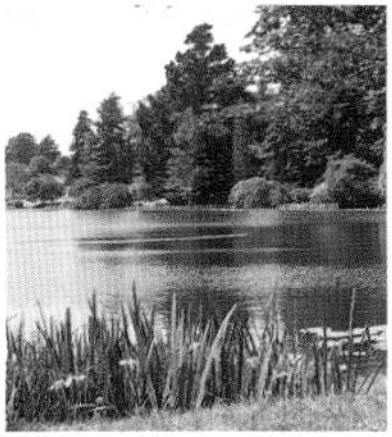

湖
mizu'umi
lake

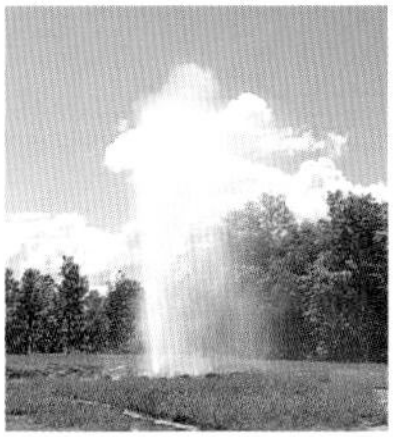

間欠泉
kanketsusen
geyser

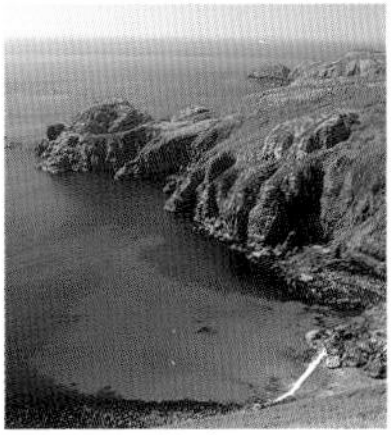

海岸
kaigan
coast

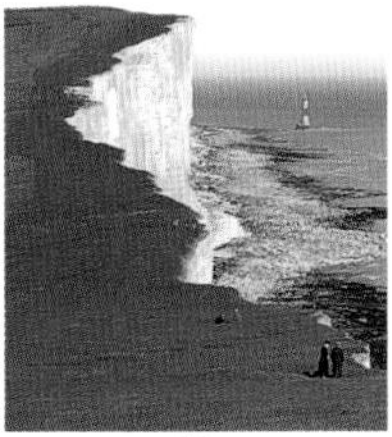

崖
gake
cliff

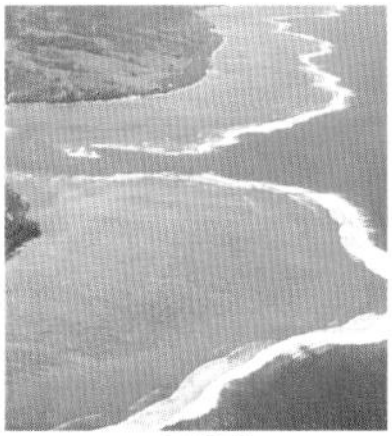

珊瑚礁
sangoshō
coral reef

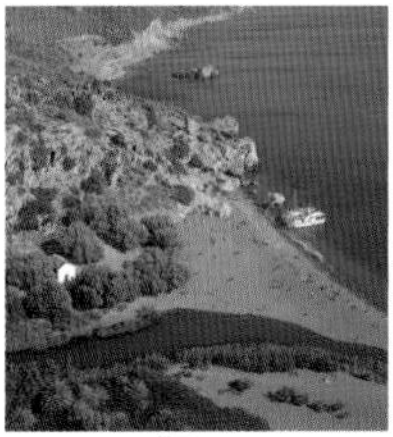

河口
kakō
estuary

気象 kishō ● weather

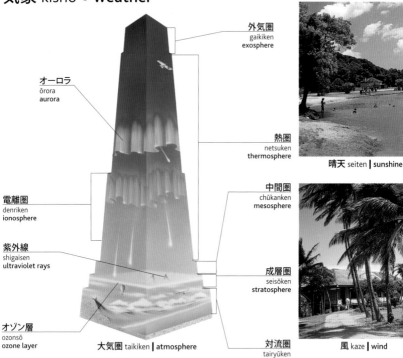

外気圏
gaikiken
exosphere

オーロラ
ōrora
aurora

熱圏
netsuken
thermosphere

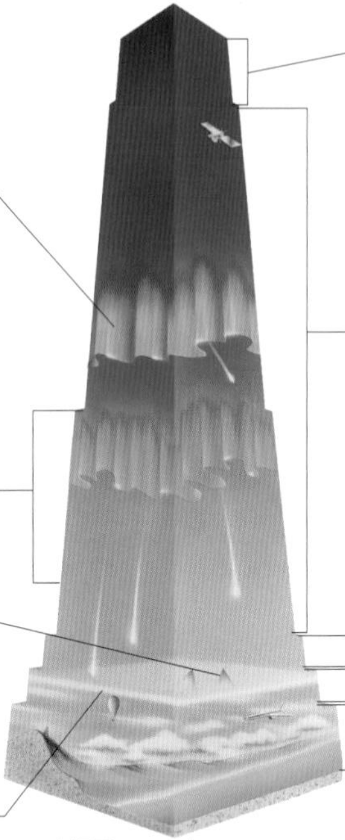

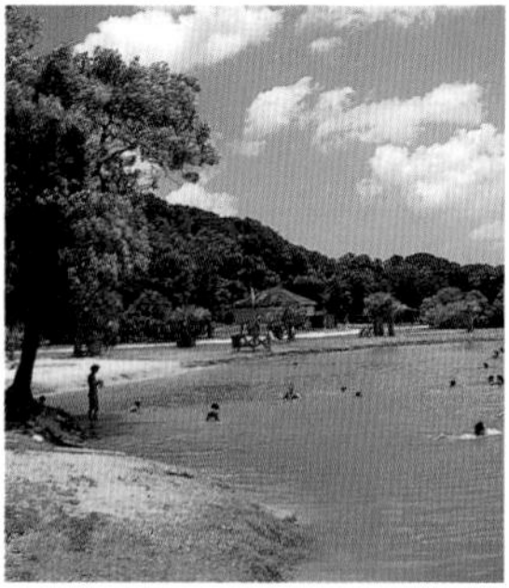

晴天 seiten | sunshine

中間圏
chūkanken
mesosphere

電離圏
denriken
ionosphere

紫外線
shigaisen
ultraviolet rays

成層圏
seisōken
stratosphere

オゾン層
ozonsō
ozone layer

大気圏 taikiken | atmosphere

対流圏
tairyūken
troposphere

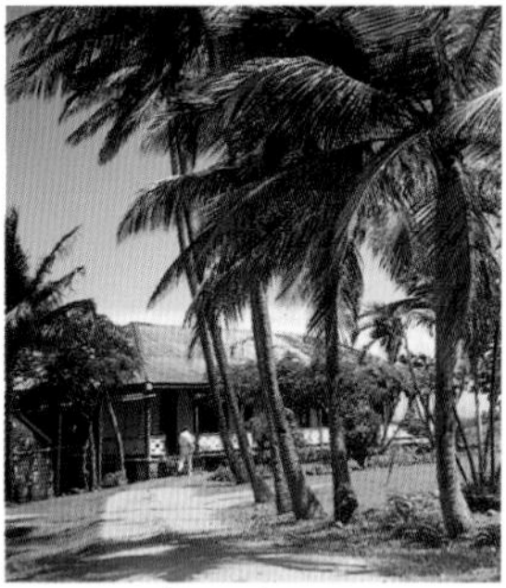

風 kaze | wind

関連用語 kanrenyōgo ● vocabulary

霙 mizore sleet	晴れ hare sunny	寒い samui cold	雨がちな ame-gachi na wet	強風 kyōfū gale	暑い/寒いです。 atsui/samui desu. I'm hot/cold.
雹 hyō hail	曇り kumori cloudy	暖かい atatakai warm	湿気の多い shikke no ōi humid	気温 kion temperature	雨が降っています。 ame ga futte imasu. It's raining.
雷 kaminari thunder	暑い atsui hot	乾燥した kansō shita dry	風の強い kaze no tsuyoi windy	台風 taifū typhoon	… 度です。 … do desu. It's … degrees.

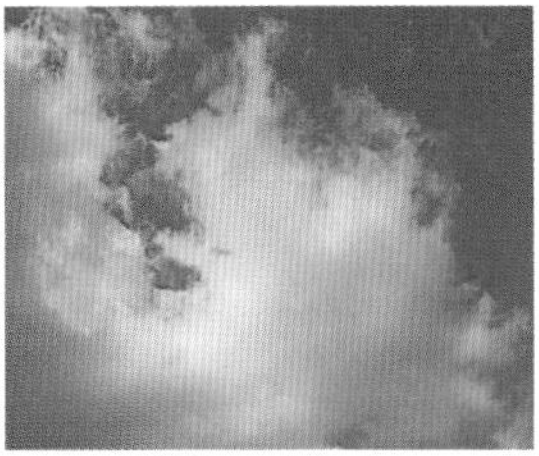

雲 kumo | cloud

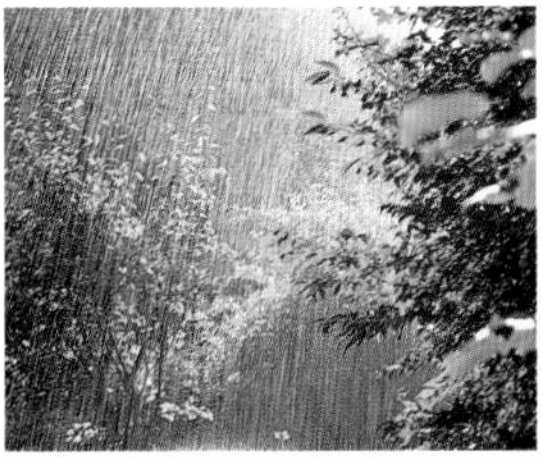

稲妻
inazuma
lightning

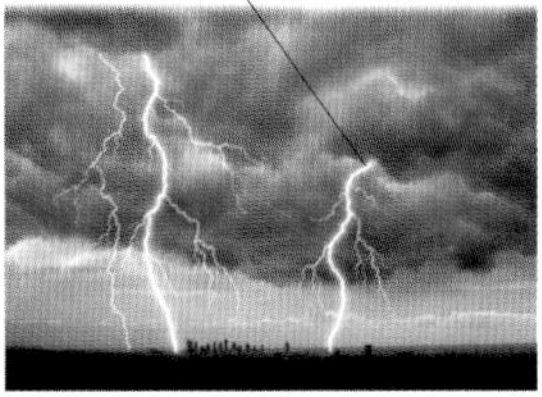

嵐 arashi | storm

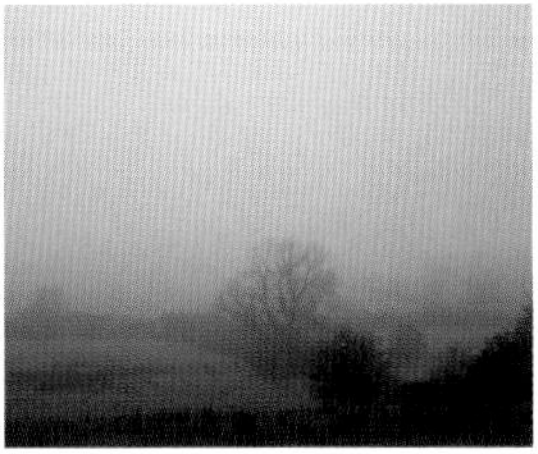

靄 moya | mist

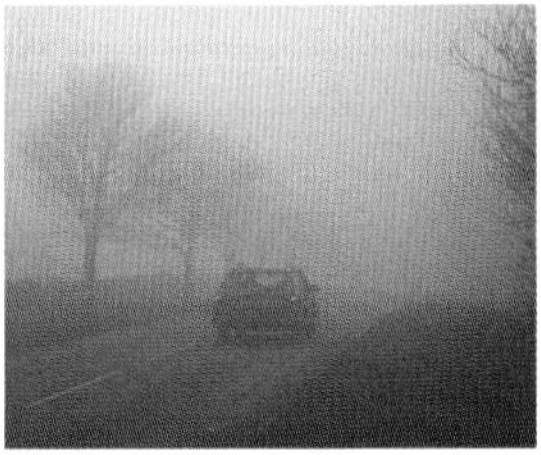

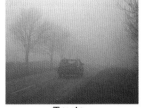

霧 kiri | fog

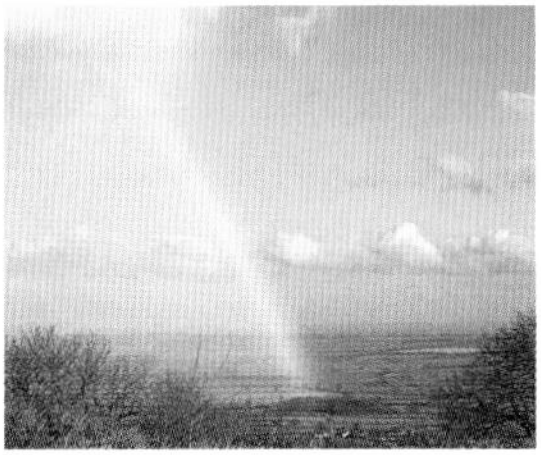

虹 niji | rainbow

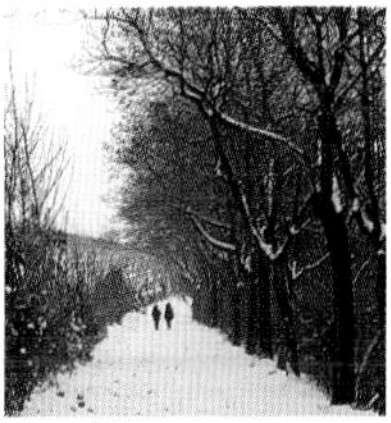

雪 yuki | snow

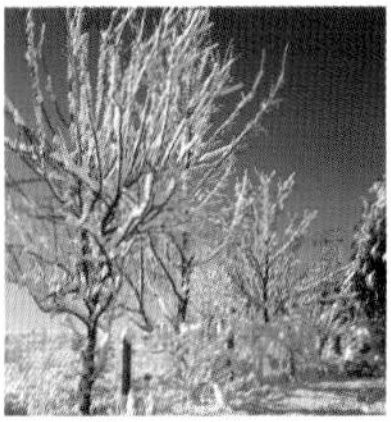

霜 shimo | frost

氷柱
tsurara
icicle

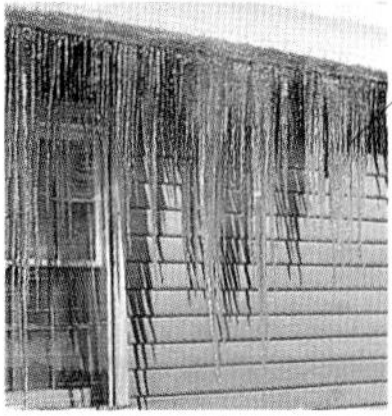

氷 kōri | ice

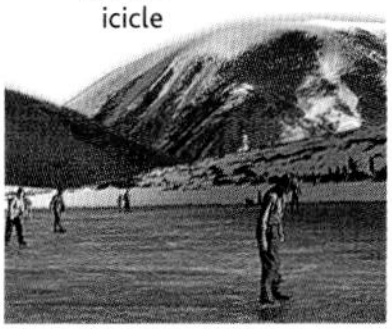

氷結 hyōketsu | freeze

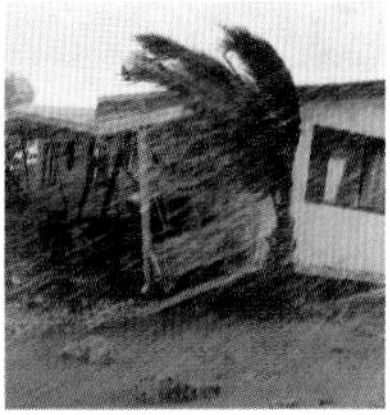

ハリケーン harikēn
hurricane

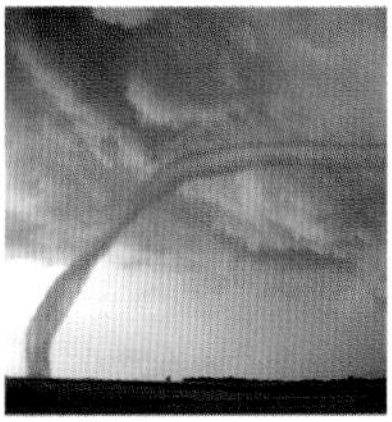

旋風 tsumujikaze
tornado

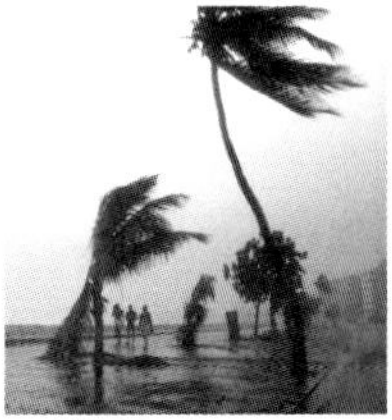

モンスーン monsūn
monsoon

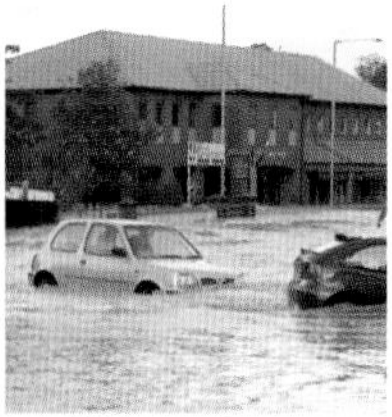

洪水 kōzui | flood

岩石 ganseki • rocks

火成岩 kaseigan • igneous

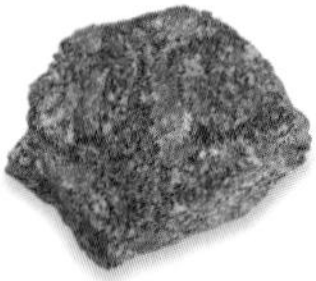

花崗岩
kakōgan
granite

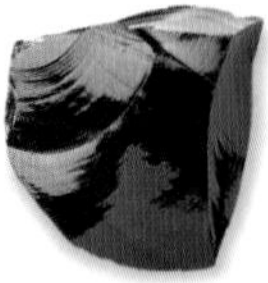

黒曜石
kokuyōseki
obsidian

玄武岩
gembugan
basalt

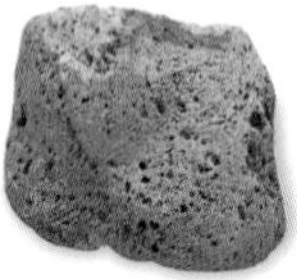

軽石
karuishi
pumice

堆積岩 taisekigan • sedimentary

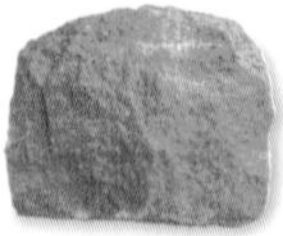

砂岩
sagan
sandstone

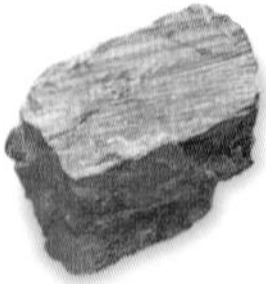

石灰岩
sekkaigan
limestone

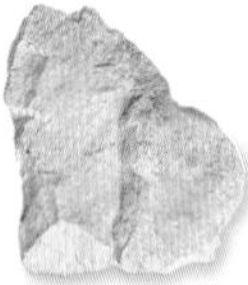

白亜
hakua
chalk

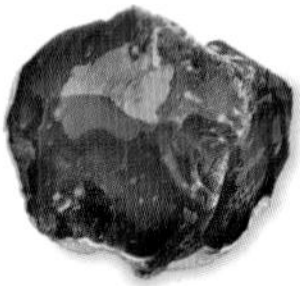

燧石
suiseki
flint

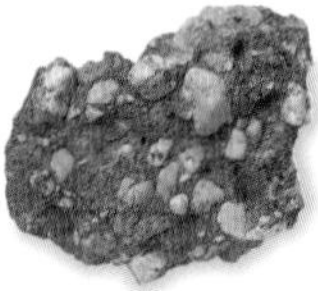

礫岩
rekigan
conglomerate

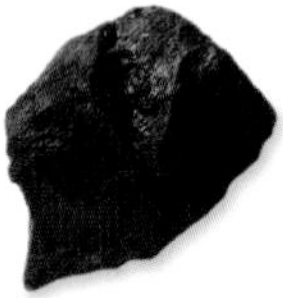

石炭
sekitan
coal

変成岩 henseigan • metamorphic

粘板岩
nembangan
slate

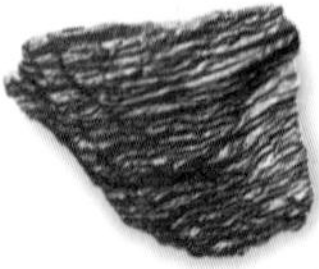

片岩
hengan
schist

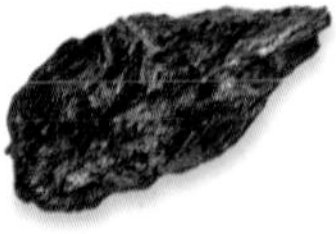

片麻岩
henmagan
gneiss

大理石
dairiseki
marble

宝石 hōseki • gems

ルビー
rubī
ruby

アクアマリン
akuamarin
aquamarine

アメジスト
amejisuto
amethyst

ダイヤモンド
daiyamondo
diamond

翡翠
hisui
jade

ジェット
jetto
jet

エメラルド
emerarudo
emerald

オパール
opāru
opal

サファイア
safaia
sapphire

トルマリン
torumarin
tourmaline

ムーンストーン
mūnsutōn
moonstone

ガーネット
gānetto
garnet

トパーズ
topāzu
topaz

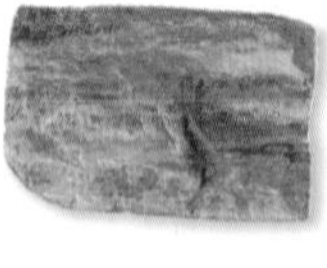

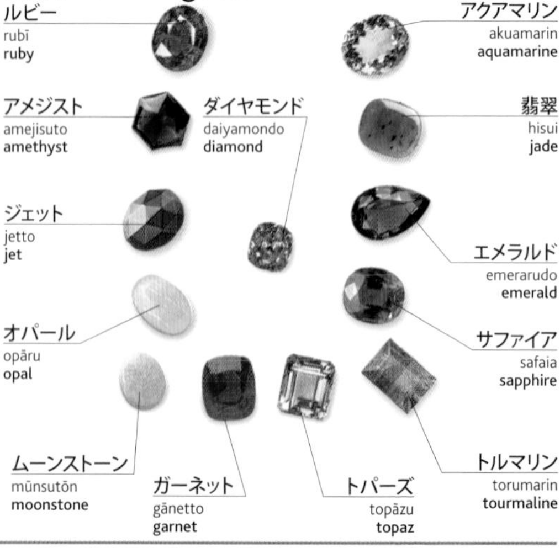

鉱石 kōseki • minerals

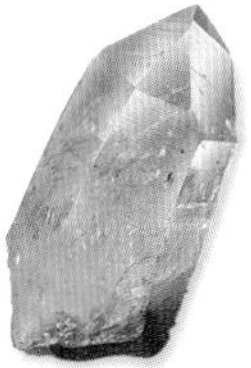

石英
sekiei
quartz

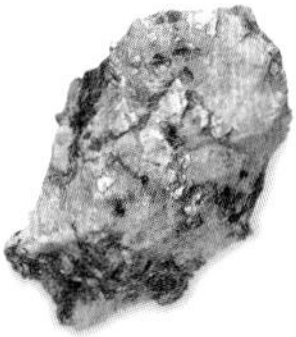

雲母
unmo
mica

硫黄
iō
sulphur

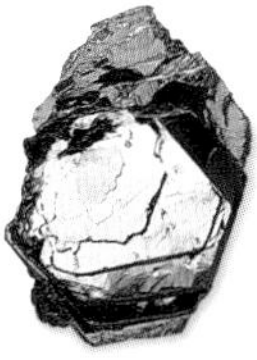

ヘマタイト
hemataito
hematite

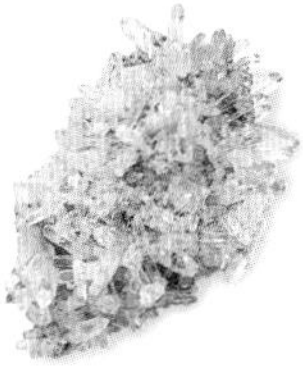

方解石
hōkaiseki
calcite

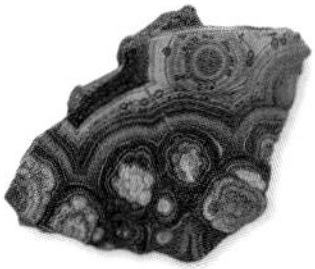

孔雀石
kujakuseki
malachite

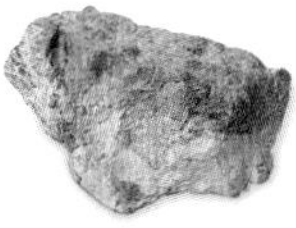

トルコ石
torukoishi
turquoise

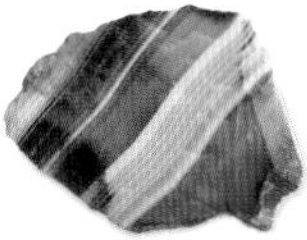

縞瑪瑙
shimamenō
onyx

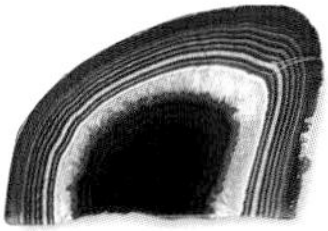

瑪瑙
menō
agate

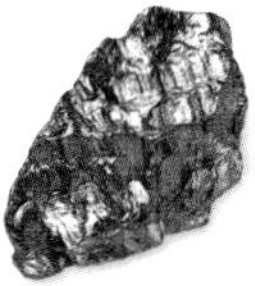

黒鉛
kokuen
graphite

金属 kinzoku • metals

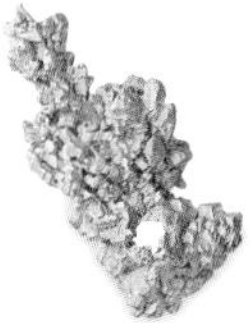

金
kin
gold

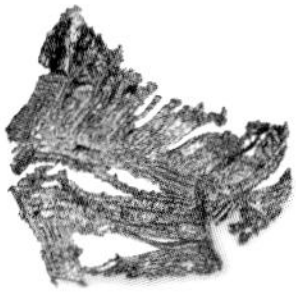

銀
gin
silver

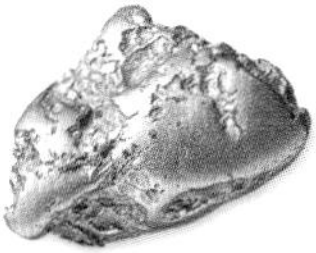

プラチナ
purachina
platinum

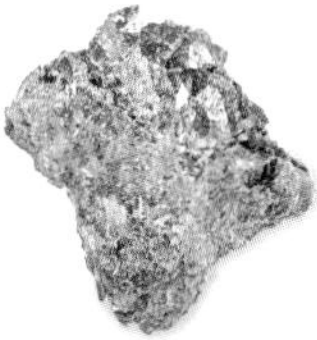

ニッケル
nikkeru
nickel

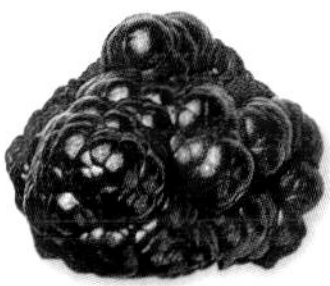

鉄
tetsu
iron

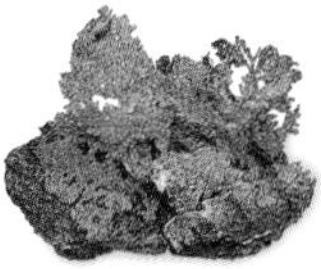

銅
dō
copper

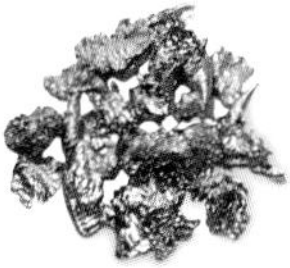

錫
suzu
tin

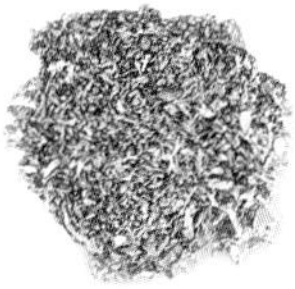

アルミニウム
aruminiumu
aluminium

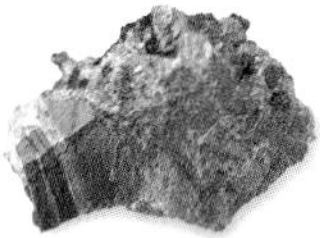

水銀
suigin
mercury

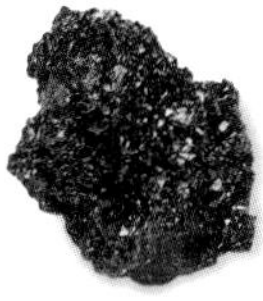

亜鉛
aen
zinc

動物1 dōbutsu • animals 1
哺乳類 honyūrui • mammals

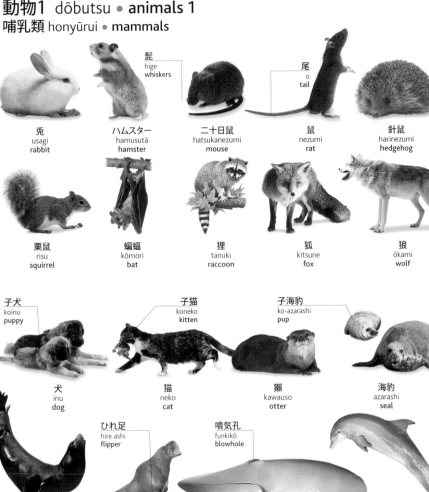

髭
hige
whiskers

尾
o
tail

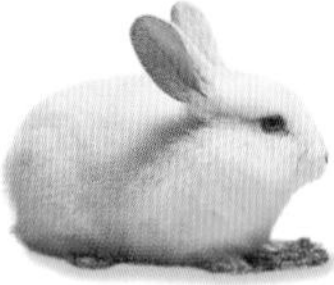

兎
usagi
rabbit

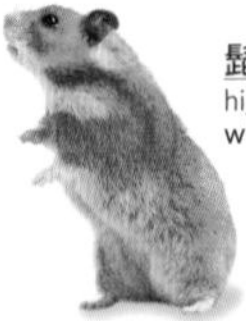

ハムスター
hamusutā
hamster

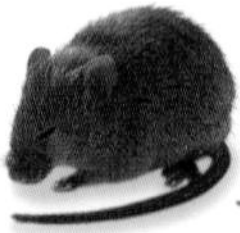

二十日鼠
hatsukanezumi
mouse

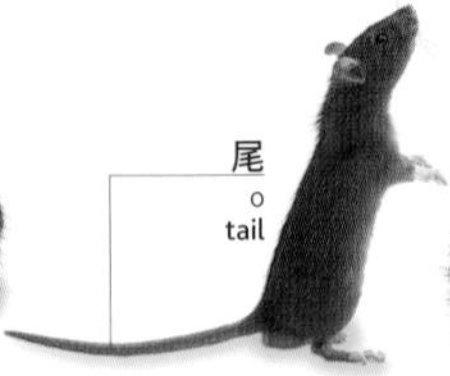

鼠
nezumi
rat

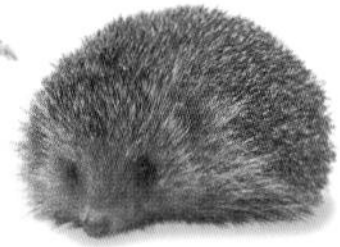

針鼠
harinezumi
hedgehog

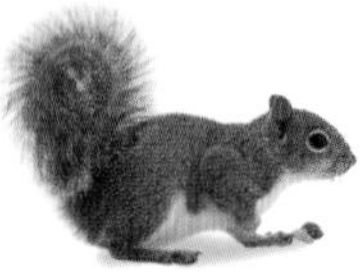

栗鼠
risu
squirrel

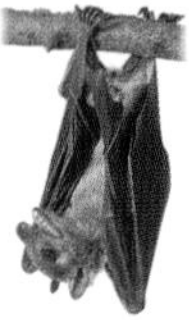

蝙蝠
kōmori
bat

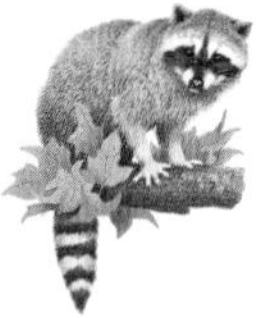

狸
tanuki
raccoon

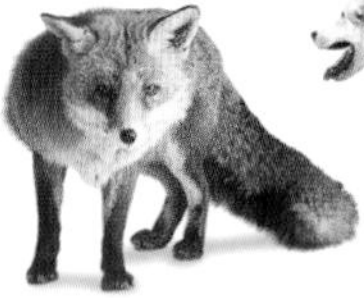

狐
kitsune
fox

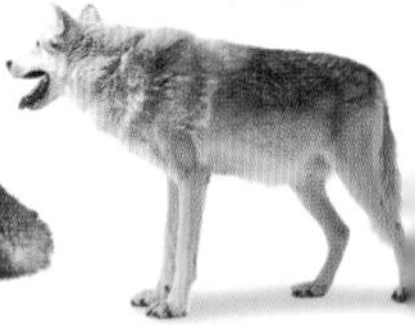

狼
ōkami
wolf

子犬
koinu
puppy

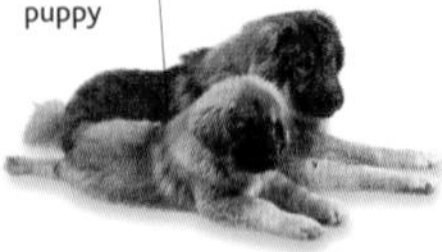

子猫
koneko
kitten

子海豹
ko-azarashi
pup

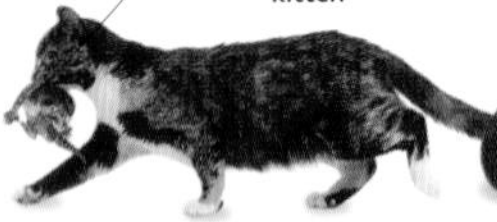

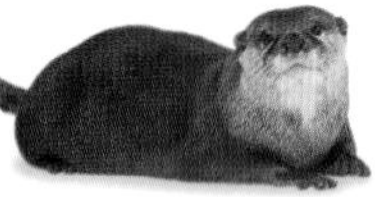

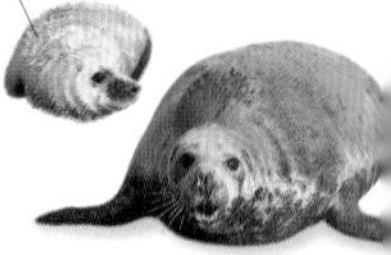

犬
inu
dog

猫
neko
cat

獺
kawauso
otter

海豹
azarashi
seal

ひれ足
hire ashi
flipper

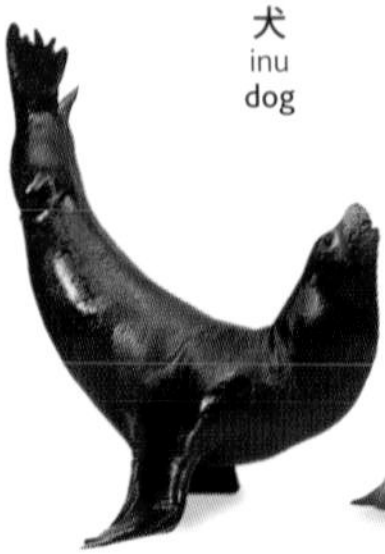

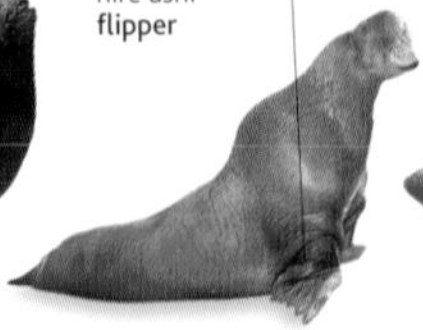

噴気孔
funkikō
blowhole

海驢
ashika
sea lion

海象
seiuchi
walrus

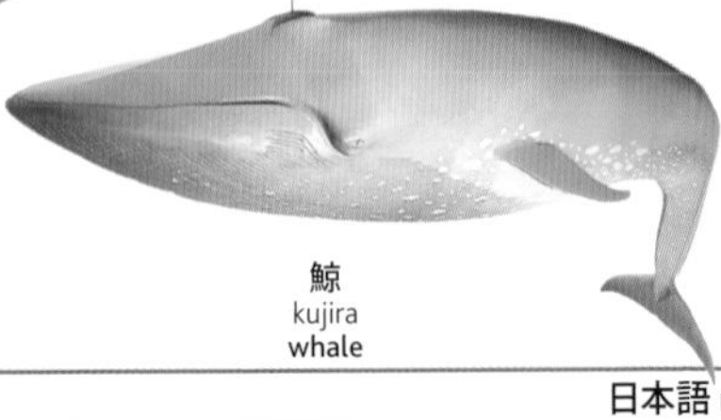

鯨
kujira
whale

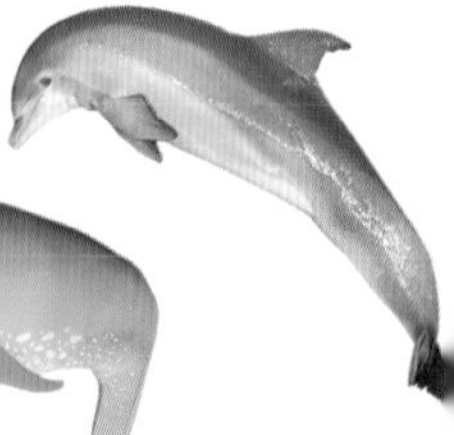

海豚
iruka
dolphin

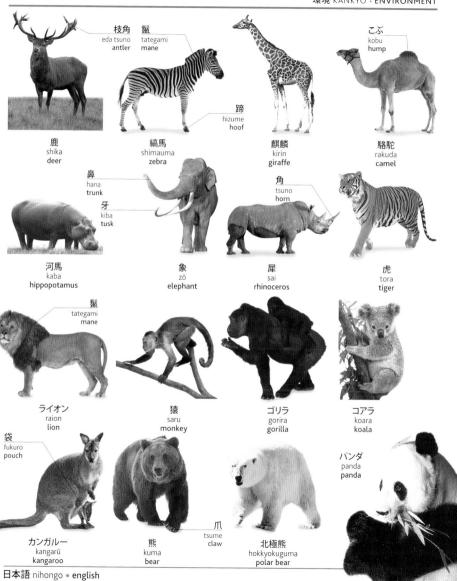

枝角
eda tsuno
antler

鬣
tategami
mane

こぶ
kobu
hump

蹄
hizume
hoof

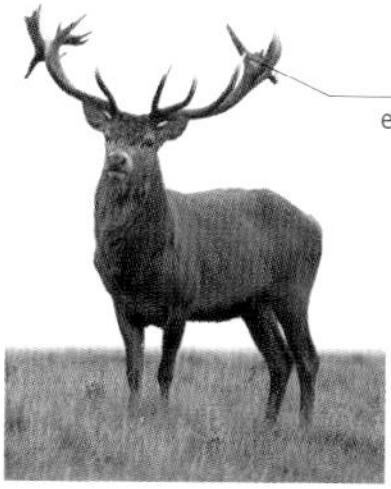

鹿
shika
deer

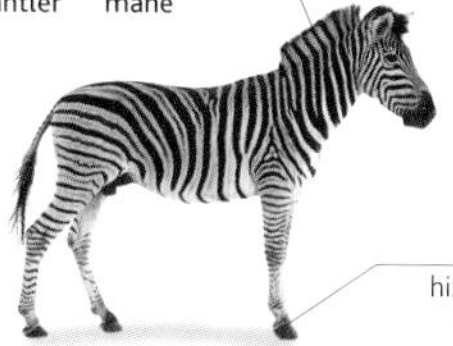

縞馬
shimauma
zebra

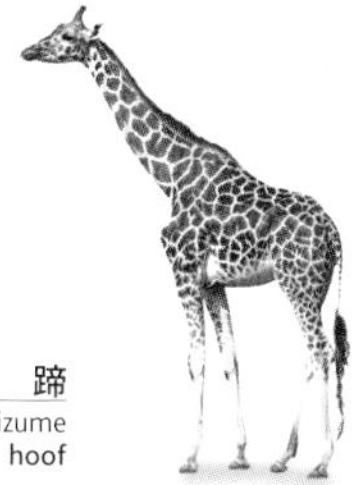

麒麟
kirin
giraffe

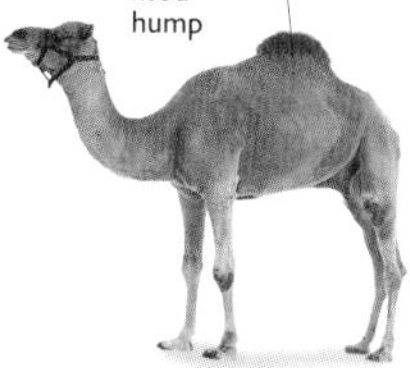

駱駝
rakuda
camel

鼻
hana
trunk

牙
kiba
tusk

角
tsuno
horn

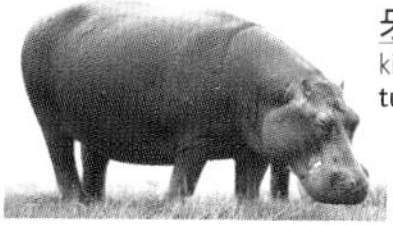

河馬
kaba
hippopotamus

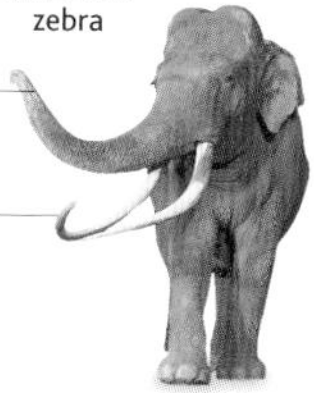

象
zō
elephant

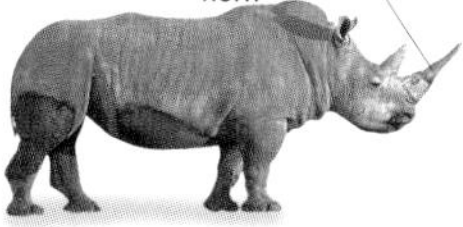

犀
sai
rhinoceros

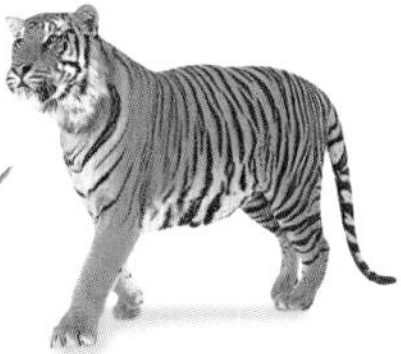

虎
tora
tiger

鬣
tategami
mane

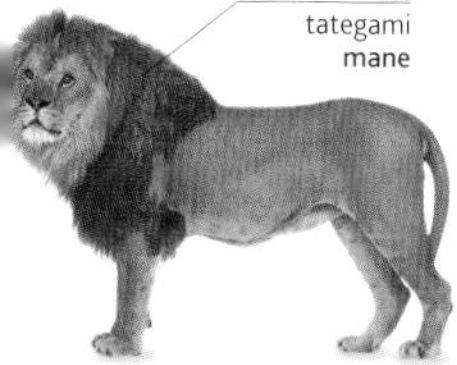

ライオン
raion
lion

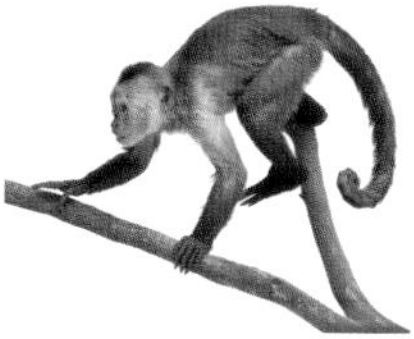

猿
saru
monkey

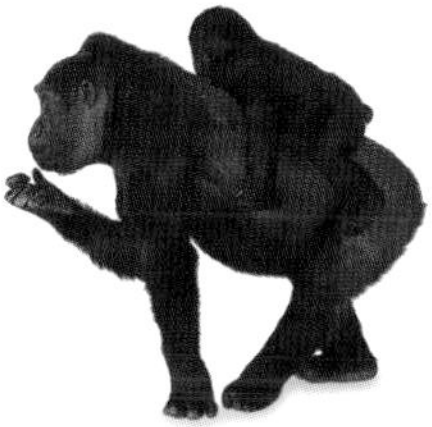

ゴリラ
gorira
gorilla

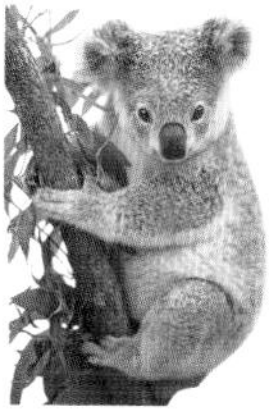

コアラ
koara
koala

袋
fukuro
pouch

パンダ
panda
panda

爪
tsume
claw

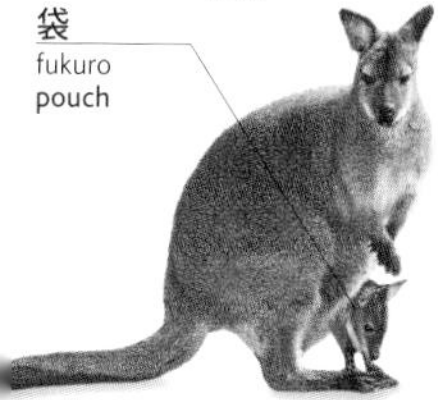

カンガルー
kangarū
kangaroo

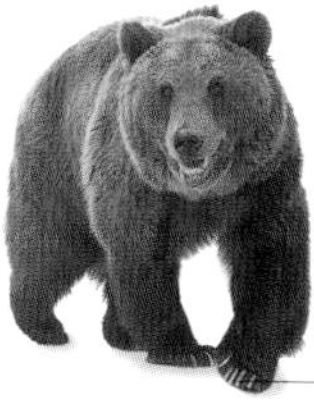

熊
kuma
bear

北極熊
hokkyokuguma
polar bear

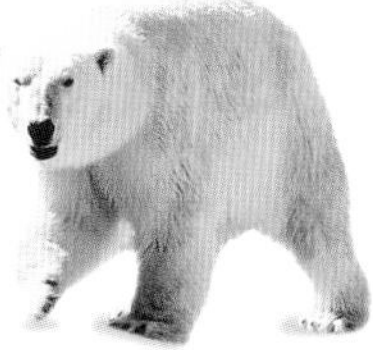

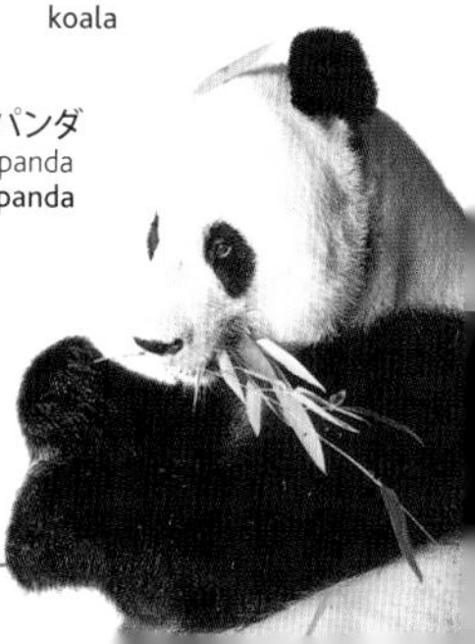

動物2 dōbutsu ● animals 2
鳥類 chōrui ● birds

尾
o
tail

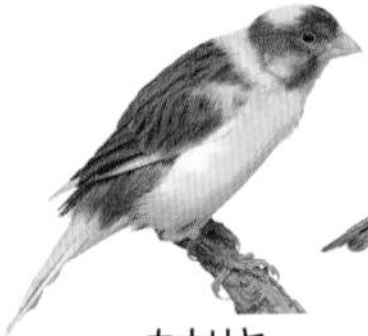

カナリヤ
kanariya
canary

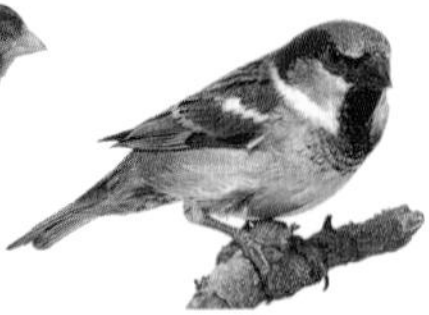

雀
suzume
sparrow

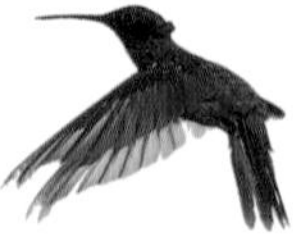

蜂鳥
hachidori
hummingbird

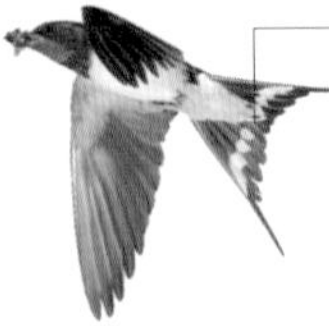

燕
tsubame
swallow

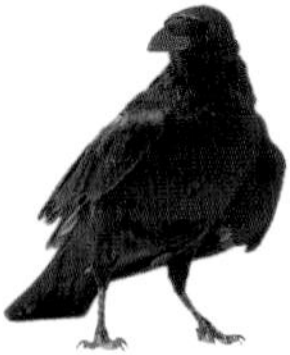

烏
karasu
crow

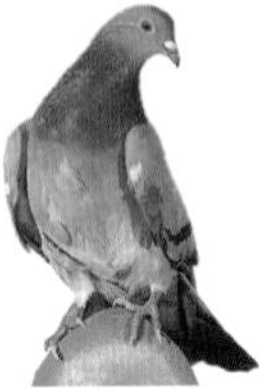

鳩
hato
pigeon

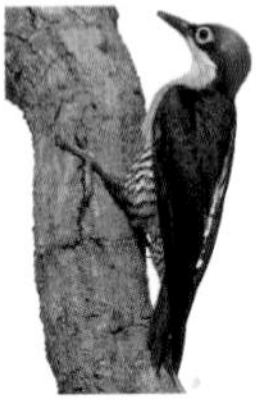

啄木鳥
kitsutsuki
woodpecker

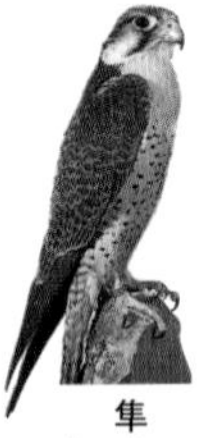

隼
hayabusa
falcon

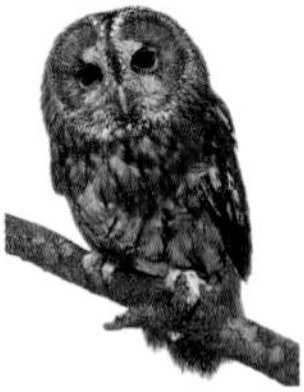

梟
fukurō
owl

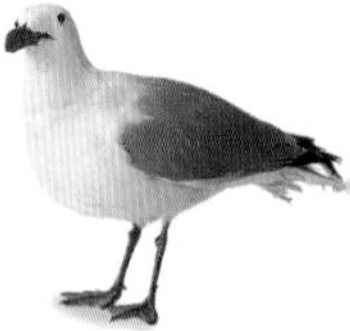

鴎
kamome
gull

鷲
washi
eagle

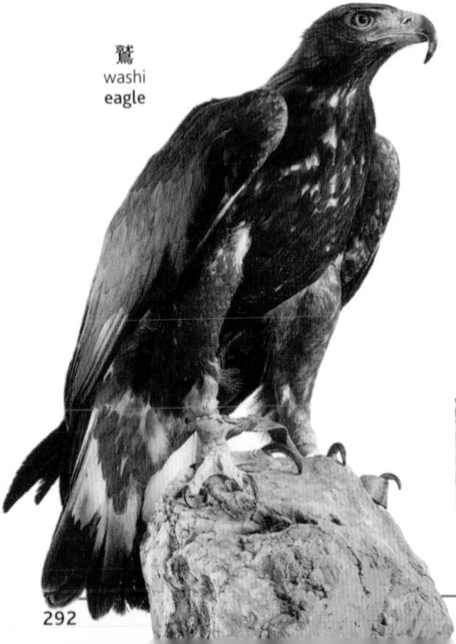

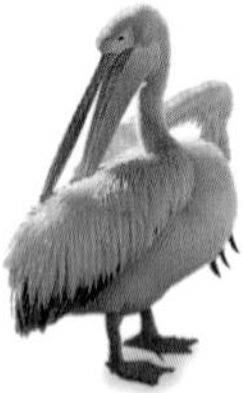

ペリカン
perikan
pelican

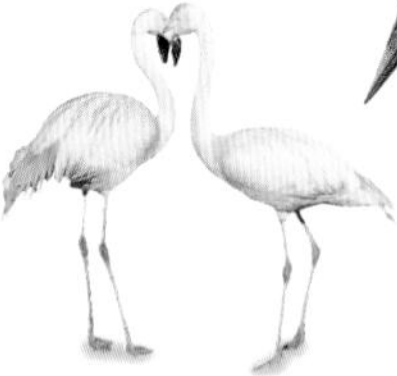

フラミンゴ
furamingo
flamingo

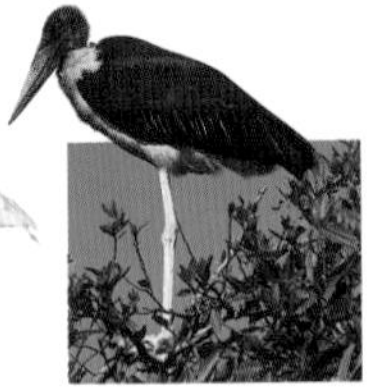

鸛
kōnotori
stork

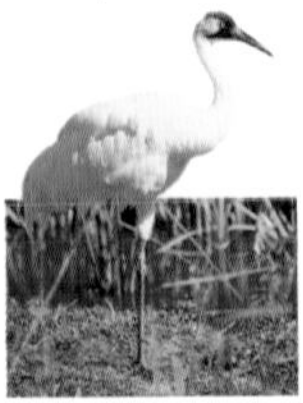

鶴
tsuru
crane

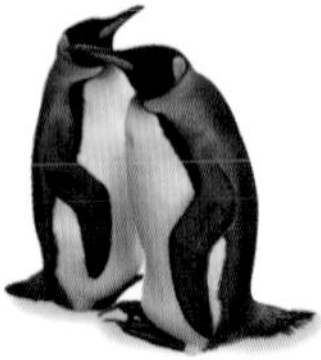

ペンギン
pengin
penguin

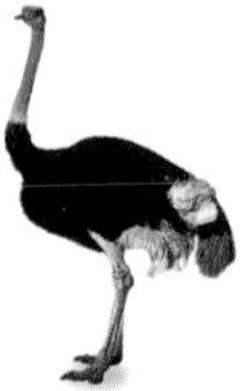

駝鳥
dachō
ostrich

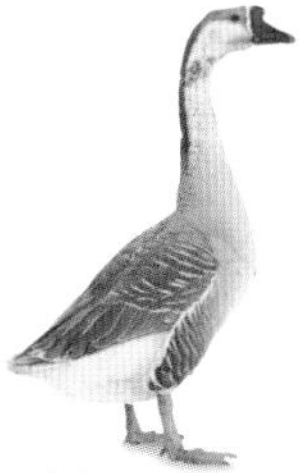

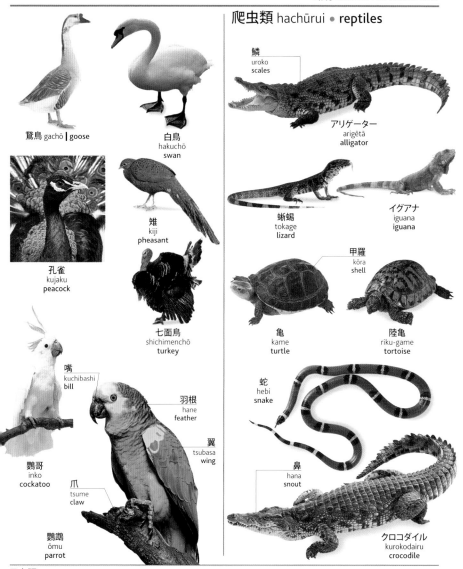

鷲鳥 gachō | goose

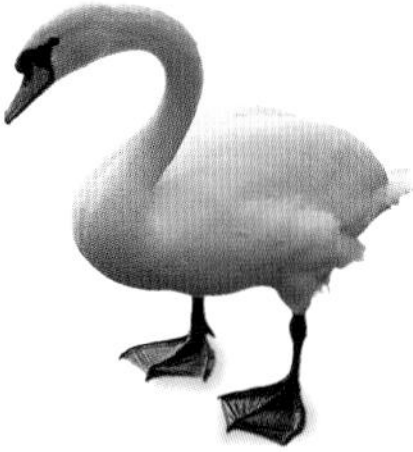

白鳥
hakuchō
swan

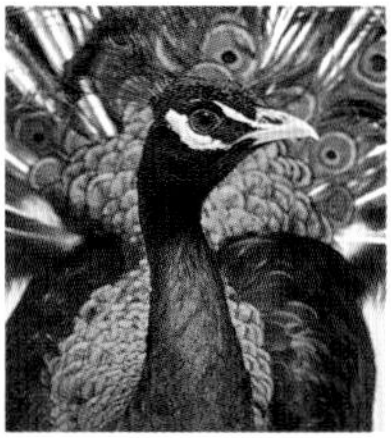

孔雀
kujaku
peacock

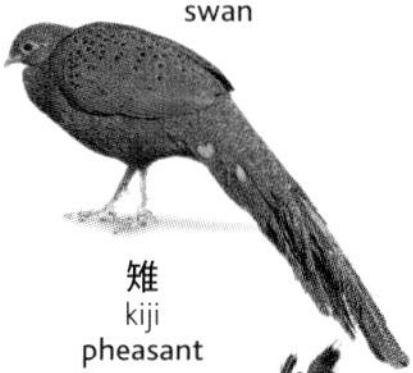

雉
kiji
pheasant

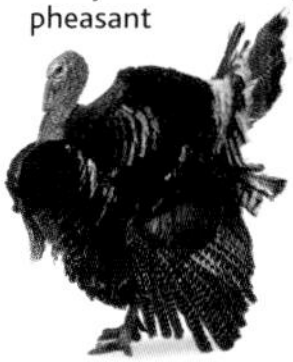

七面鳥
shichimenchō
turkey

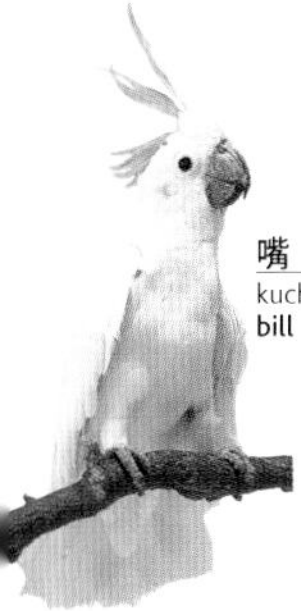

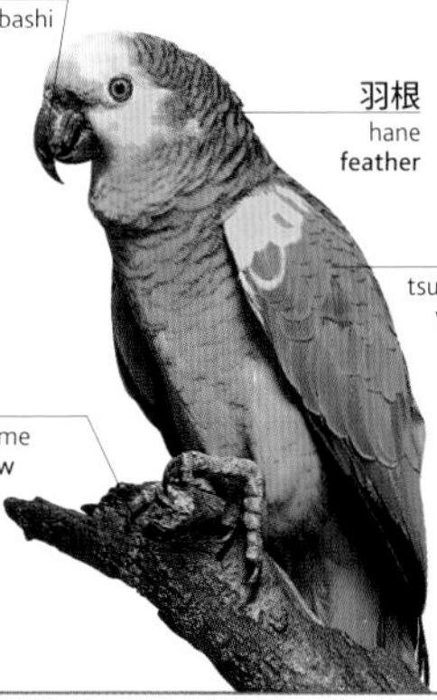

嘴
kuchibashi
bill

羽根
hane
feather

翼
tsubasa
wing

爪
tsume
claw

鸚哥
inko
cockatoo

鸚鵡
ōmu
parrot

爬虫類 hachūrui • reptiles

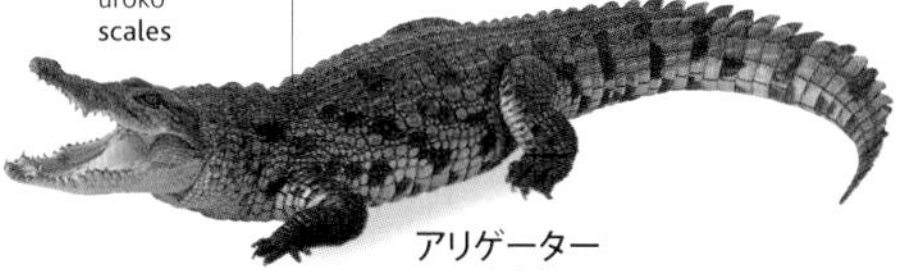

鱗
uroko
scales

アリゲーター
arigētā
alligator

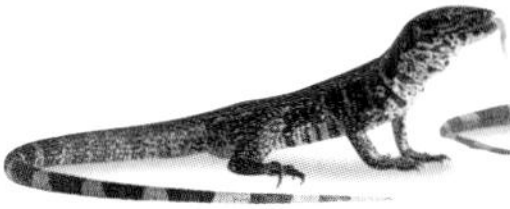

蜥蜴
tokage
lizard

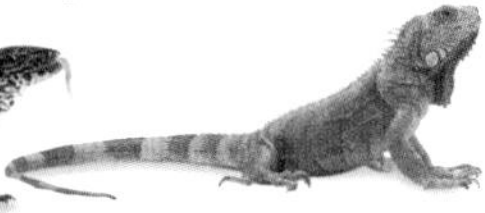

イグアナ
iguana
iguana

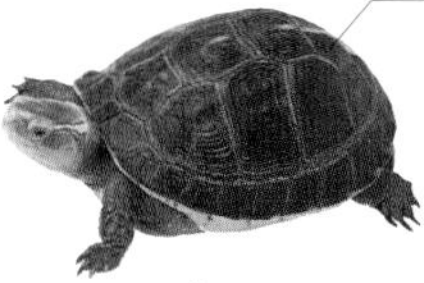

甲羅
kōra
shell

亀
kame
turtle

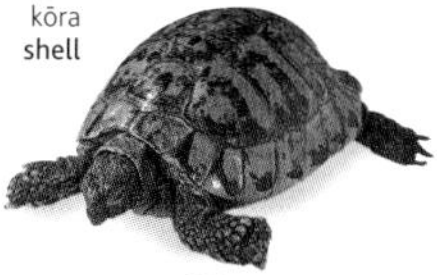

陸亀
riku-game
tortoise

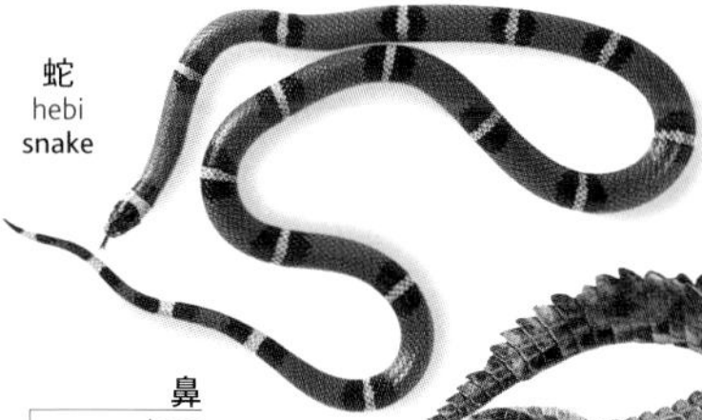

蛇
hebi
snake

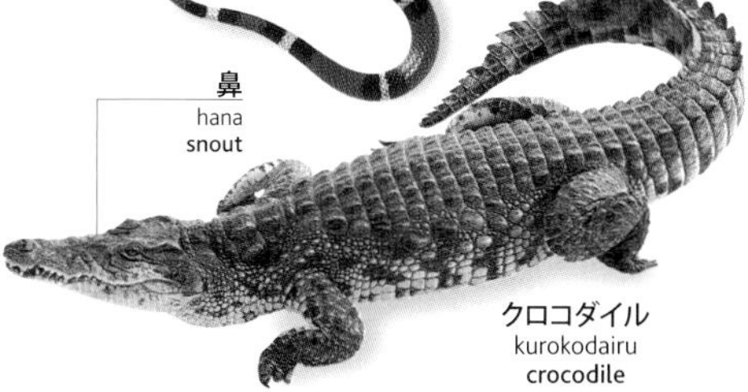

鼻
hana
snout

クロコダイル
kurokodairu
crocodile

動物3 dōbutsu • animals 3

両生類 ryōseirui • amphibians

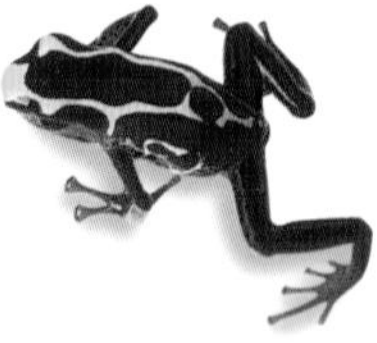

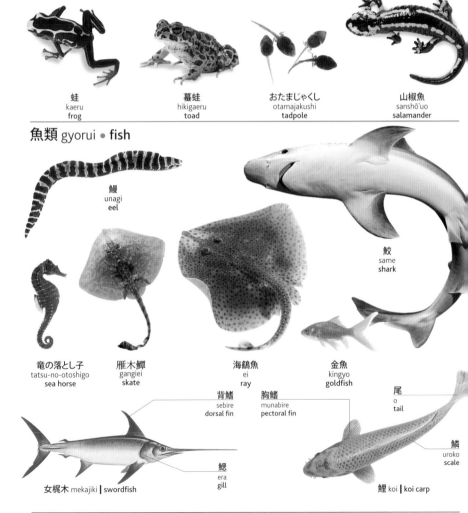

蛙
kaeru
frog

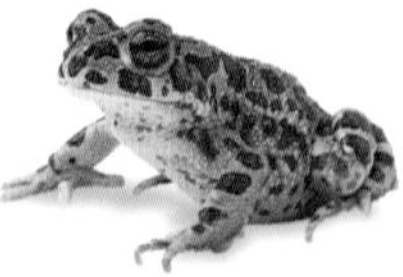

蟇蛙
hikigaeru
toad

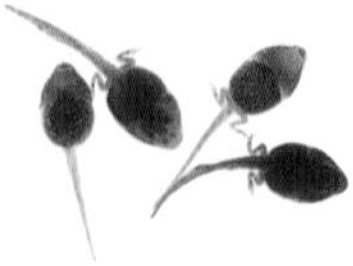

おたまじゃくし
otamajakushi
tadpole

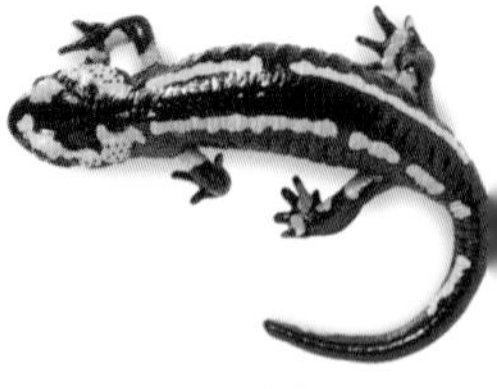

山椒魚
sanshō'uo
salamander

魚類 gyorui • fish

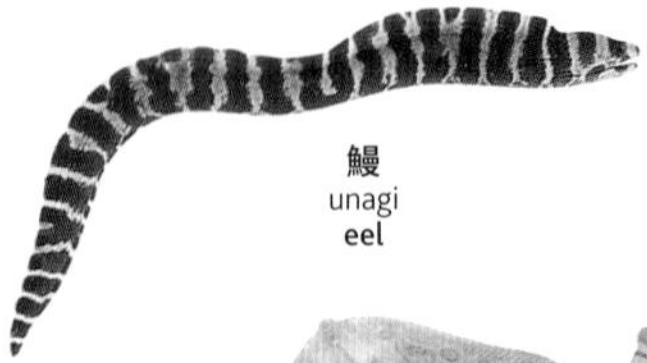

鰻
unagi
eel

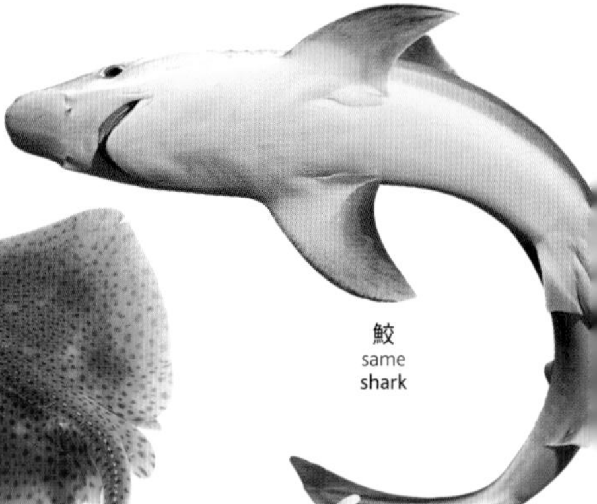

鮫
same
shark

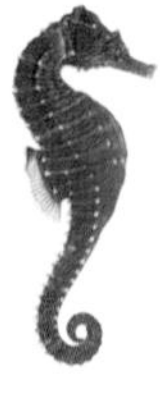

竜の落とし子
tatsu-no-otoshigo
sea horse

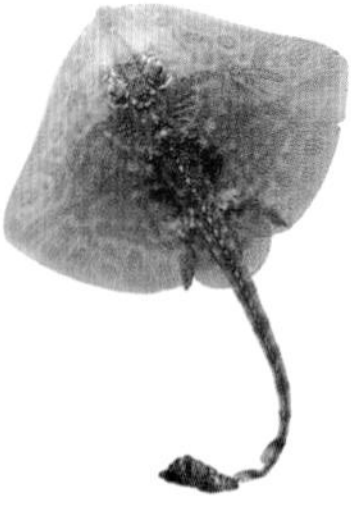

雁木鱏
gangiei
skate

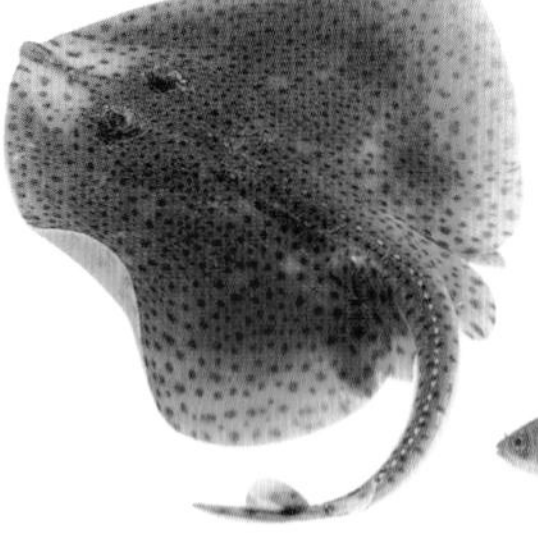

海鷂魚
ei
ray

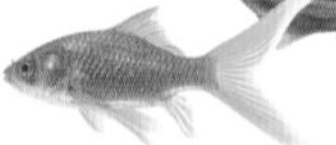

金魚
kingyo
goldfish

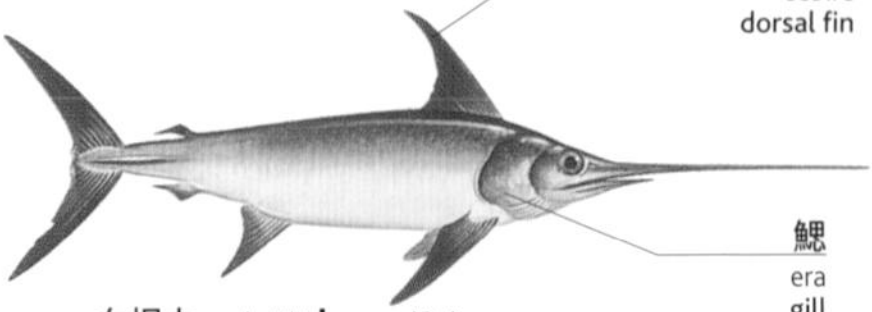

背鰭
sebire
dorsal fin

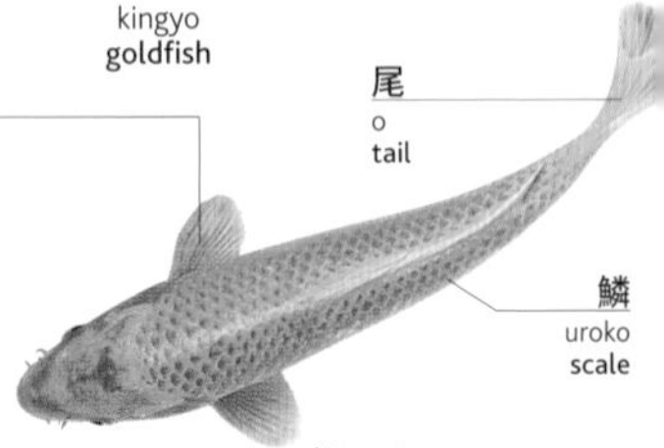

胸鰭
munabire
pectoral fin

尾
o
tail

鰓
era
gill

鱗
uroko
scale

女梶木 mekajiki | **swordfish**

鯉 koi | **koi carp**

無脊椎動物 musekitsui dōbutsu • invertebrates

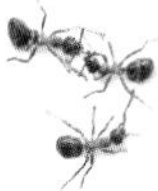

蟻
ari
ant

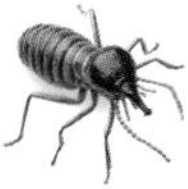

白蟻
shiroari
termite

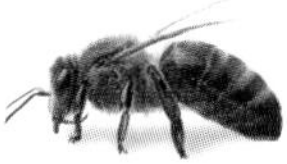

蜜蜂
mitsubachi
bee

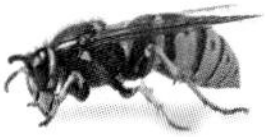

蜂
hachi
wasp

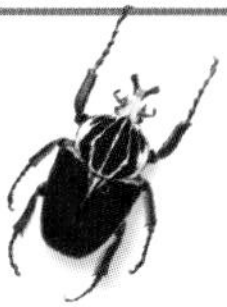

甲虫
kabutomushi
beetle

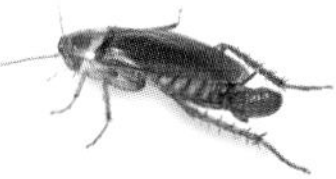

ゴキブリ
gokiburi
cockroach

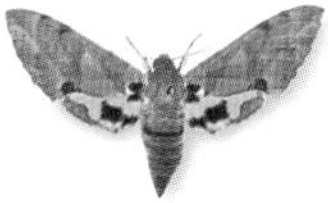

蛾
ga
moth

触角
shokkaku
antenna

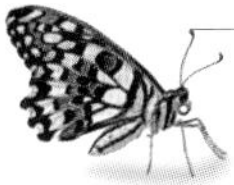

蝶
chō
butterfly

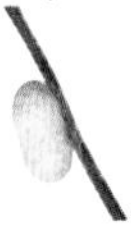

繭
mayu
cocoon

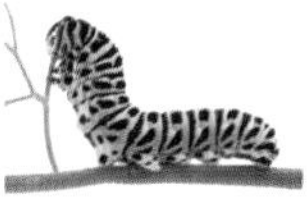

芋虫
imomushi
caterpillar

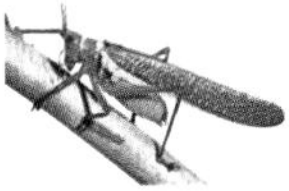

蟋蟀 kōrogi | cricket

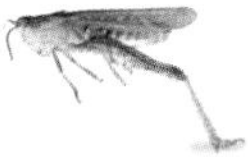

蝗
inago
grasshopper

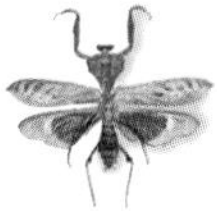

蟷螂
kamakiri
praying mantis

毒針
dokubari
sting

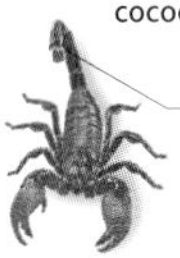

蠍
sasori
scorpion

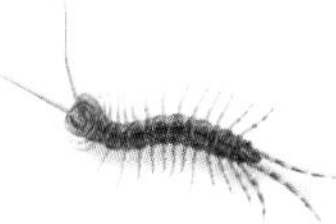

百足
mukade
centipede

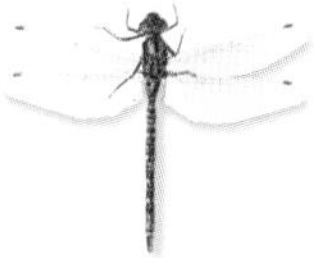

蜻蛉
tombo
dragonfly

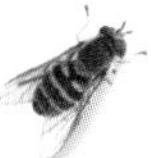

蠅
hae
fly

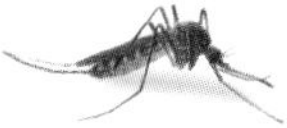

蚊
ka
mosquito

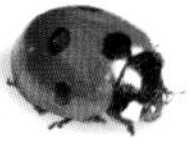

天道虫
tentōmushi
ladybird

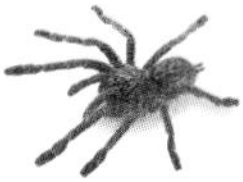

蜘蛛
kumo
spider

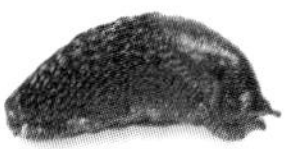

蛞蝓
namekuji
slug

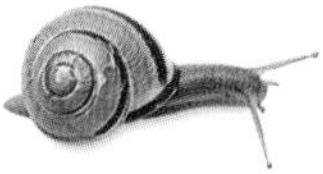

蝸牛
katatsumuri
snail

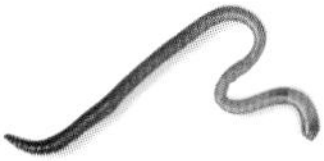

蚯蚓 mimizu | worm

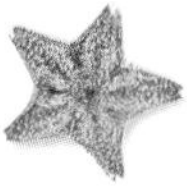

海星
hitode
starfish

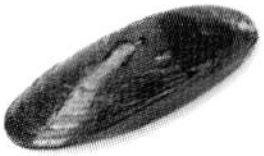

紫貽貝
murasaki igai
mussel

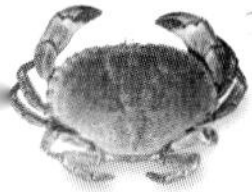

蟹 kani | crab

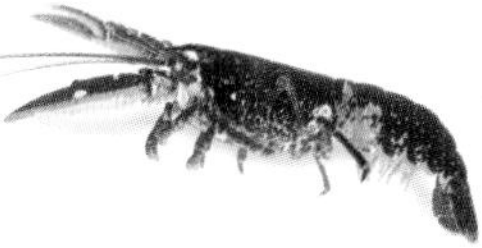

ロブスター robusutā
lobster

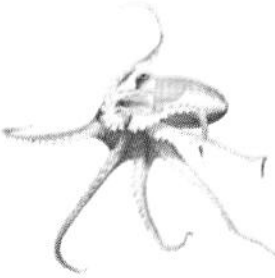

蛸 tako | octopus

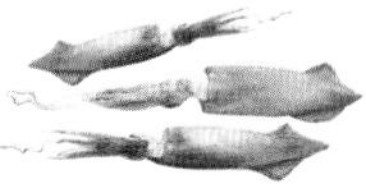

烏賊 ika | squid

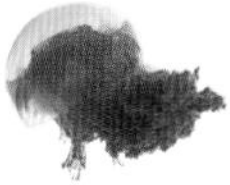

水母 kurage | jellyfish

植物 shokubutsu • plants

木 ki • tree

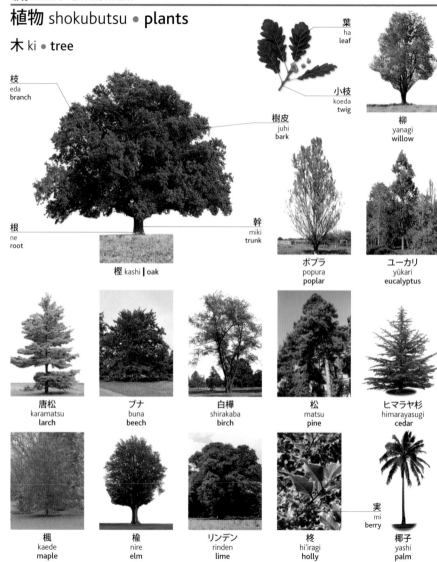

枝
eda
branch

葉
ha
leaf

小枝
koeda
twig

樹皮
juhi
bark

根
ne
root

幹
miki
trunk

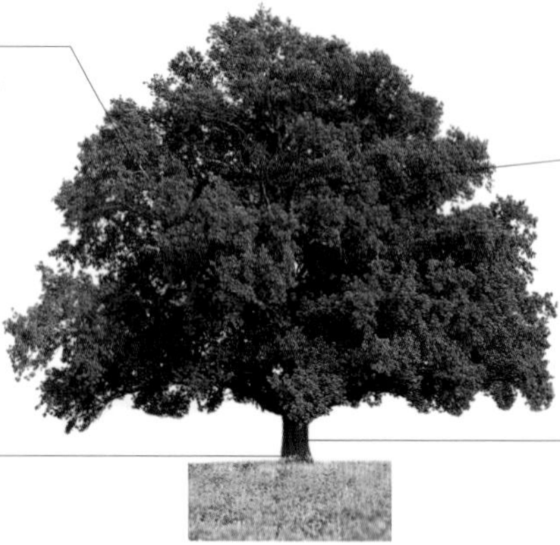

樫 kashi | oak

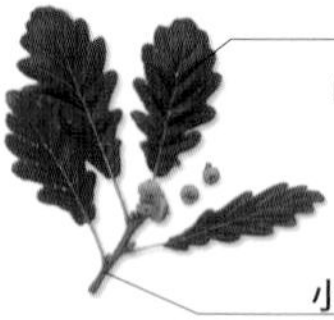

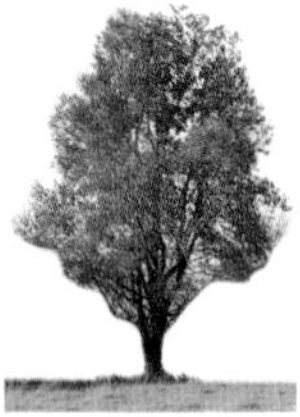

柳
yanagi
willow

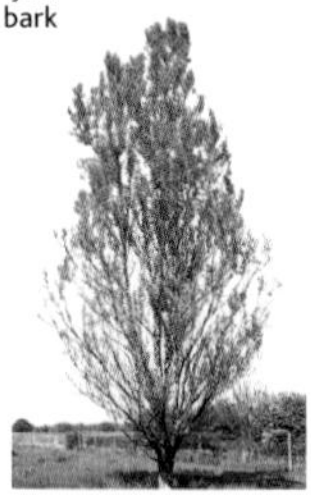

ポプラ
popura
poplar

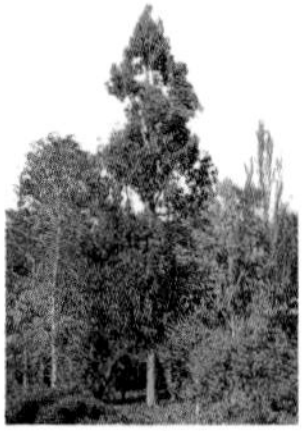

ユーカリ
yūkari
eucalyptus

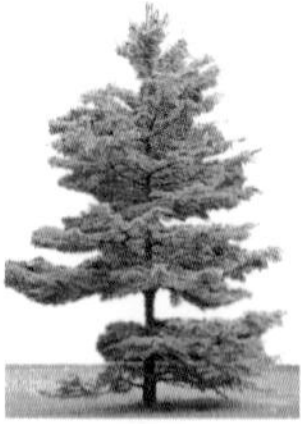

唐松
karamatsu
larch

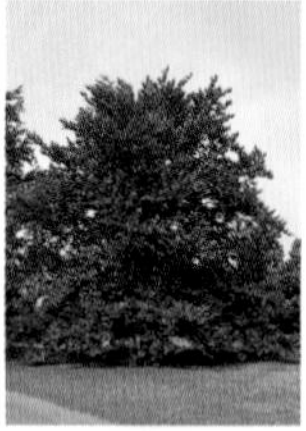

ブナ
buna
beech

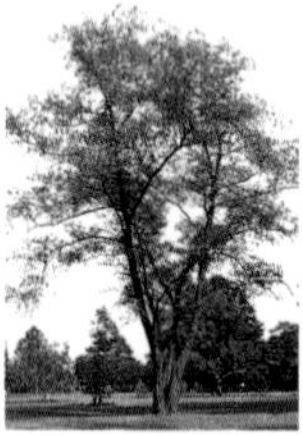

白樺
shirakaba
birch

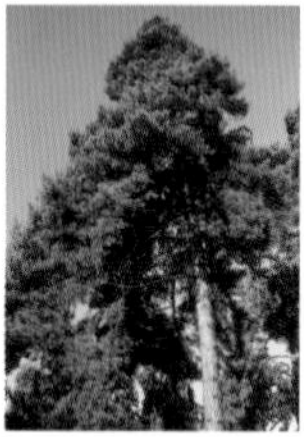

松
matsu
pine

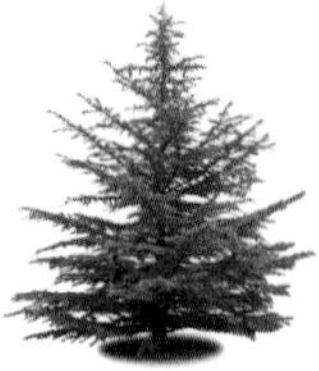

ヒマラヤ杉
himarayasugi
cedar

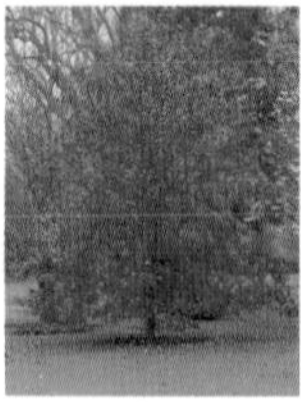

楓
kaede
maple

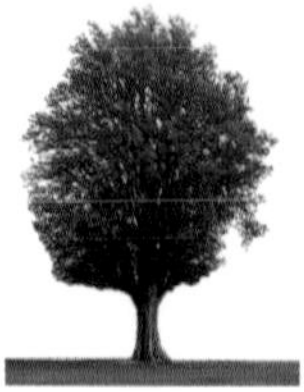

楡
nire
elm

リンデン
rinden
lime

柊
hi'iragi
holly

実
mi
berry

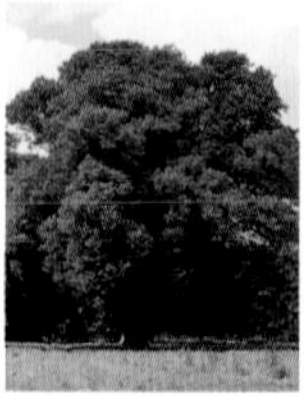

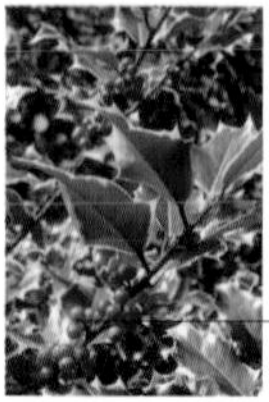

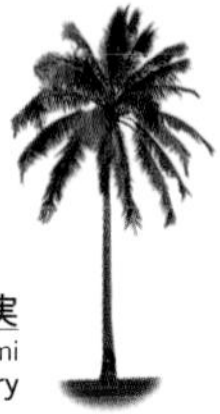

椰子
yashi
palm

顕花植物 kenkashokubutsu・flowering plant

花
hana
flower

雄蕊
oshibe
stamen

花弁
hanabira
petal

萼
gaku
calyx

分枝
bunshi
stalk

茎
kuki
stem

蕾
tsubomi
bud

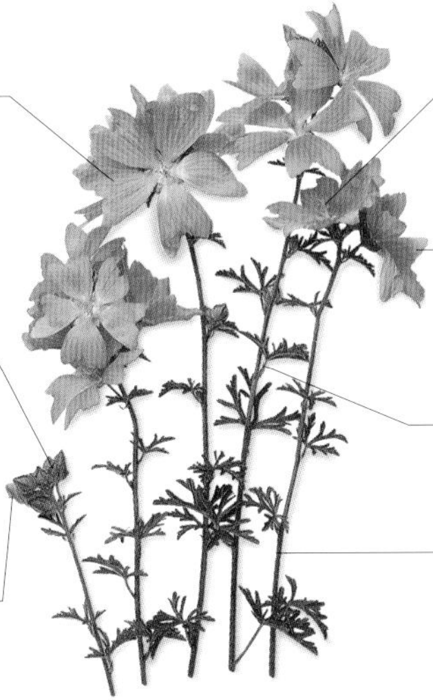

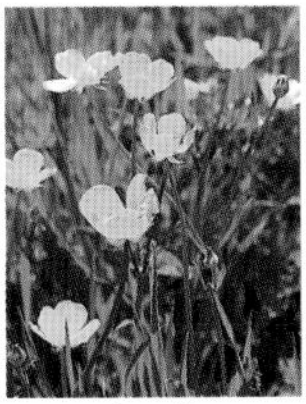

金鳳花
kimpōge
buttercup

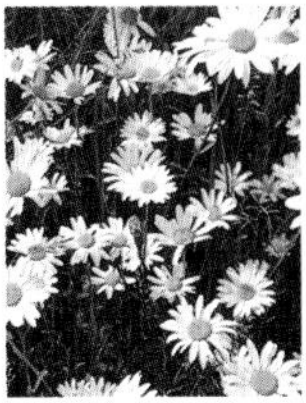

雛菊
hinagiku
daisy

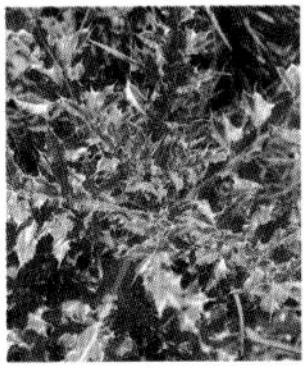

薊
azami
thistle

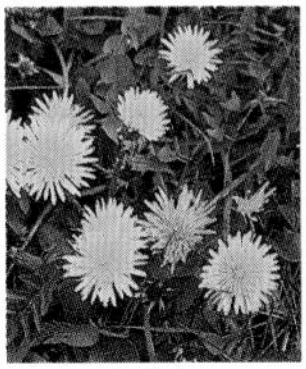

蒲公英
tampopo
dandelion

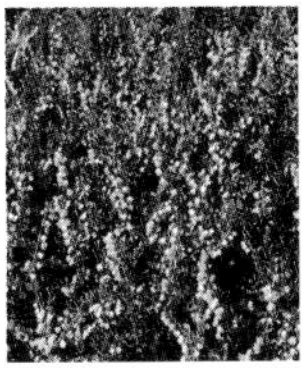

ヒース
hīsu
heather

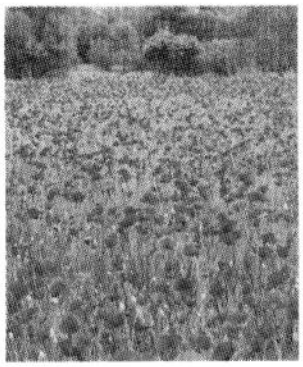

芥子
keshi
poppy

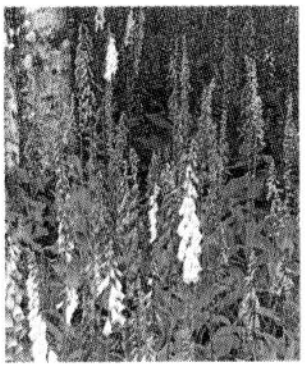

狐の手袋
kitsune-no-tebukuro
foxglove

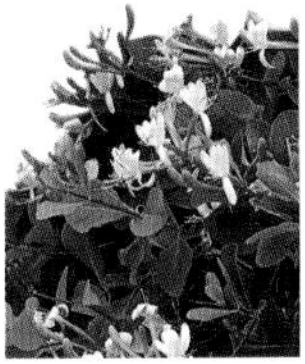

忍冬
suikazura
honeysuckle

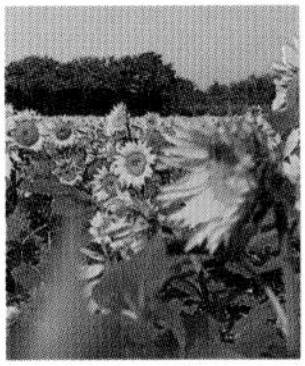

向日葵
himawari
sunflower

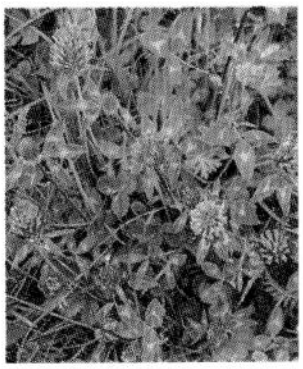

クローバー
kurōbā
clover

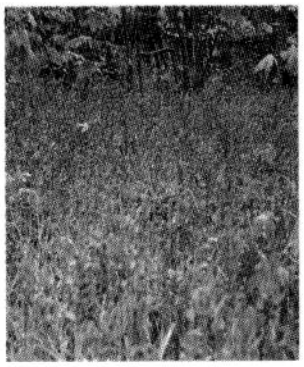

釣鐘水仙
tsurigane suisen
bluebells

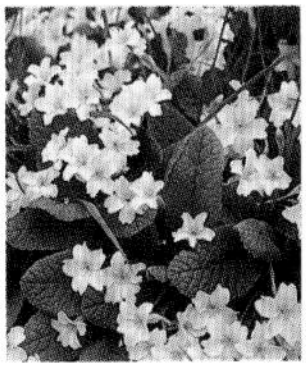

桜草
sakurasō
primrose

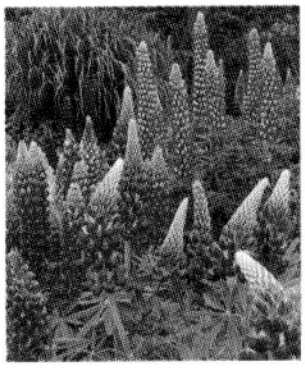

ルーピン
rūpin
lupins

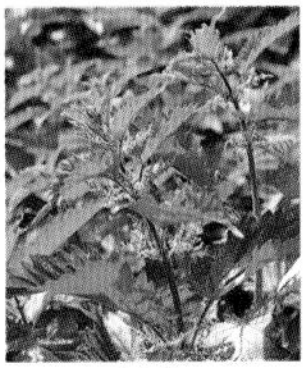

刺草
irakusa
nettle

市街 shigai • town

通り
tōri
street

縁石
fuchi'ishi
kerb

街角
machikado
street corner

商店
shōten
shop

交差点
kōsaten
intersection

一方通行
ippōtsūkō
one-way system

歩道
hodō
pavement

オフィスビル
ofisu biru
office block

マンション
manshon
apartment block

路地
roji
alley

駐車場
chūshajō
car park

道路標識
dōro hyōshiki
street sign

ボラード
borādo
bollard

街灯
gaitō
street light

建物 tatemono • buildings

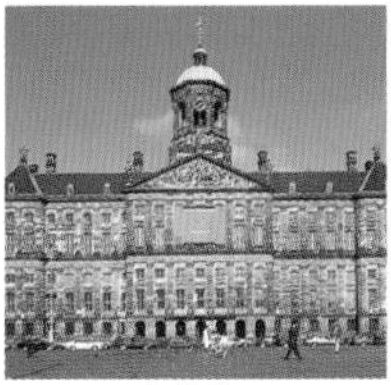

市庁舎
shichōsha
town hall

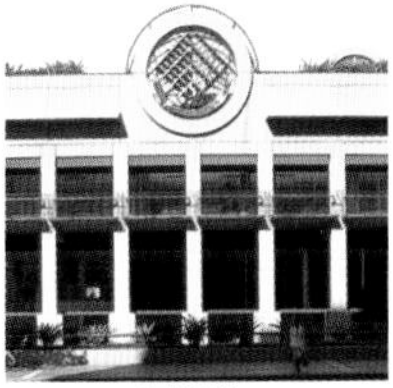

図書館
toshokan
library

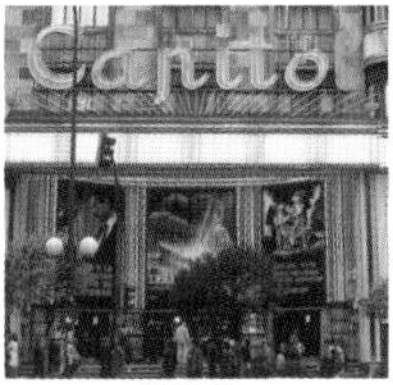

映画館
eigakan
cinema

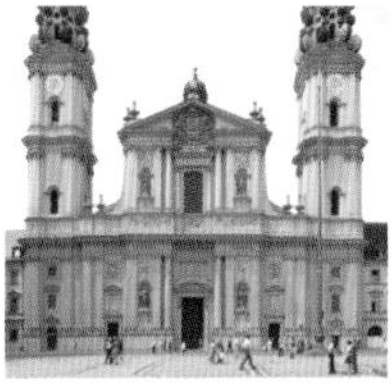

劇場
gekijō
theatre

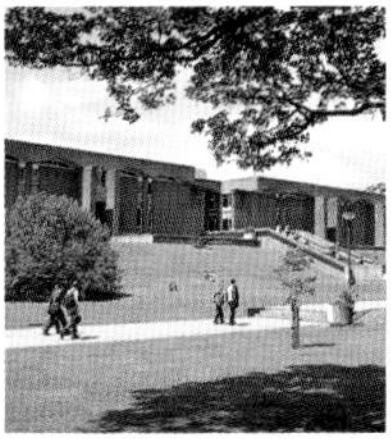

大学
daigaku
university

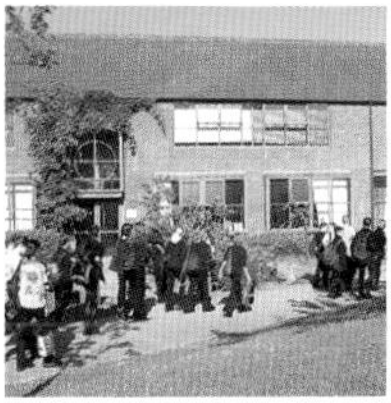

学校
gakkō
school

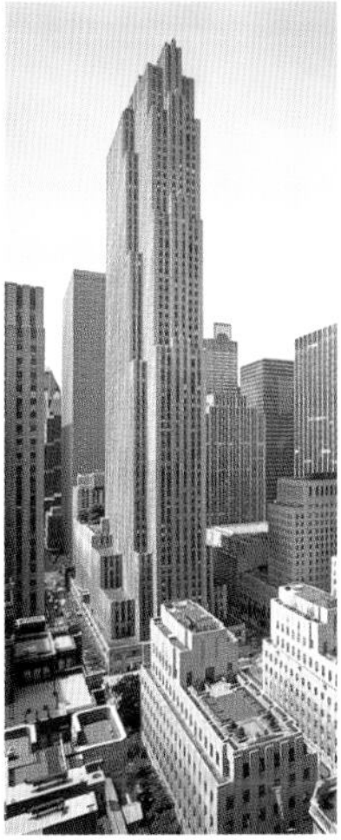

摩天楼
matenrō
skyscraper

区域 kuiki • areas

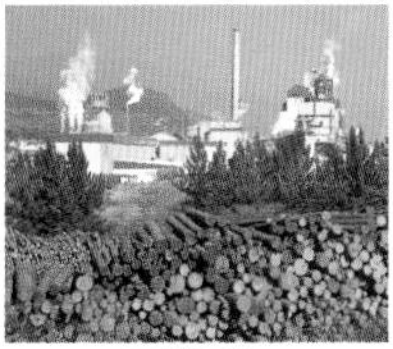

工業団地
kōgyōdanchi
industrial estate

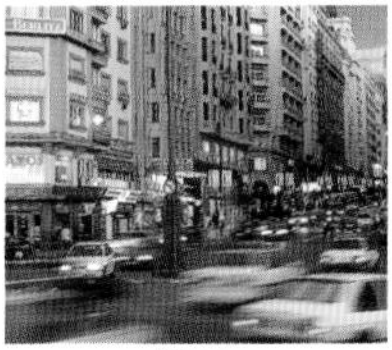

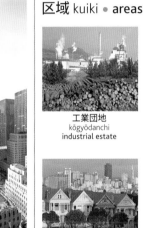

都市
toshi
city

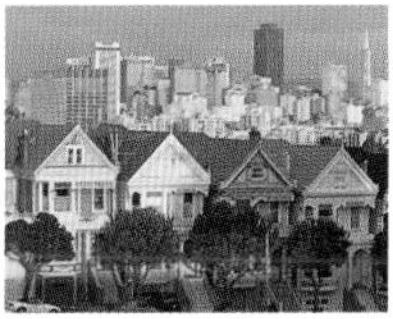

郊外
kōgai
suburb

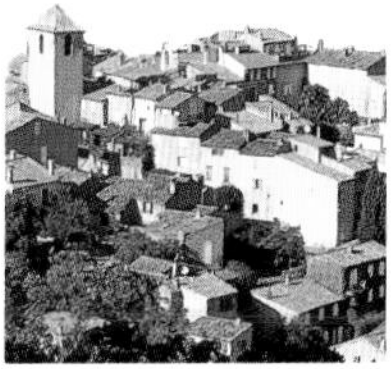

村
mura
village

関連用語 kanrenyōgo • vocabulary

歩行者天国 hokōsha-tengoku pedestrian zone	**脇道** wakimichi side street	**マンホール** manhōru manhole	**排水溝** haisuikō gutter	**教会** kyōkai church
大通り ōdōri avenue	**広場** hiroba square	**バス停** basutei bus stop	**工場** kōjō factory	**下水道** gesuidō drain

---

建築 kenchiku • architecture

建物と構造 tatemono to kōzō • buildings and structures

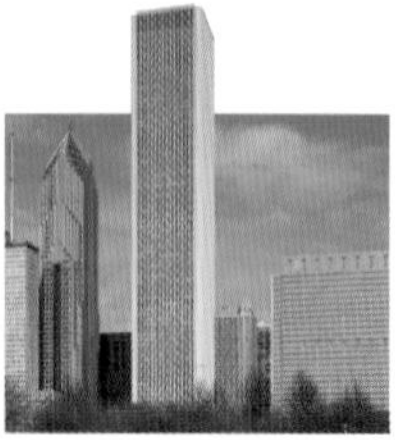

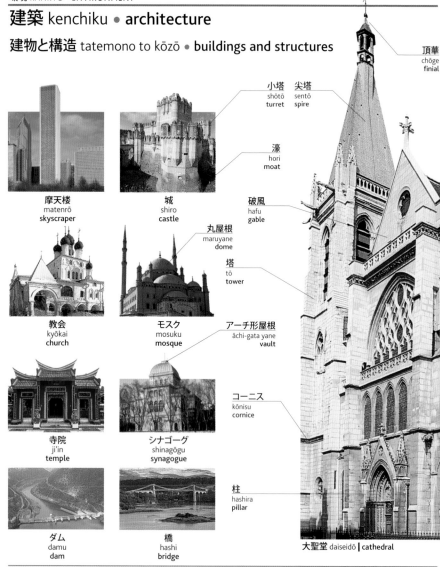

摩天楼
matenrō
skyscraper

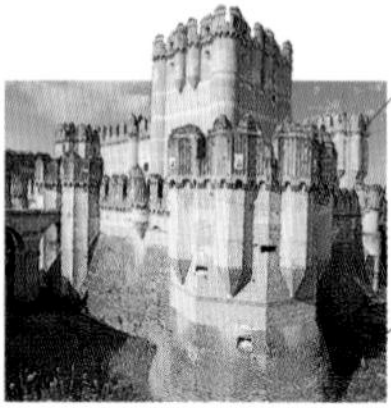

城
shiro
castle

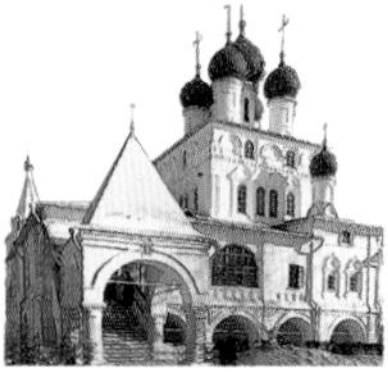

教会
kyōkai
church

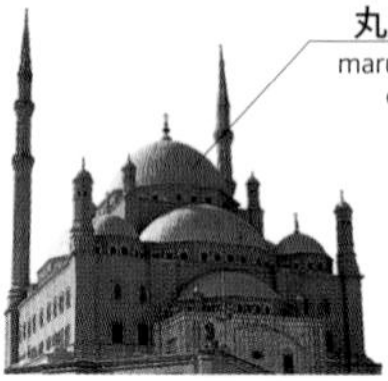

モスク
mosuku
mosque

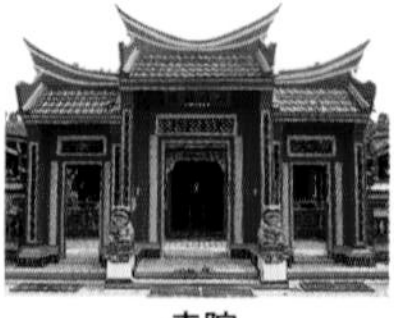

寺院
ji'in
temple

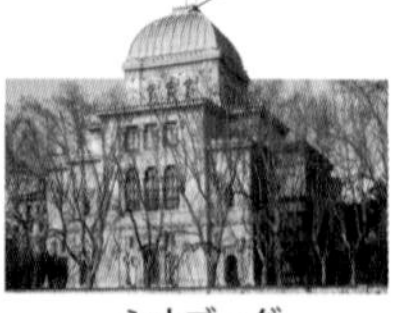

シナゴーグ
shinagōgu
synagogue

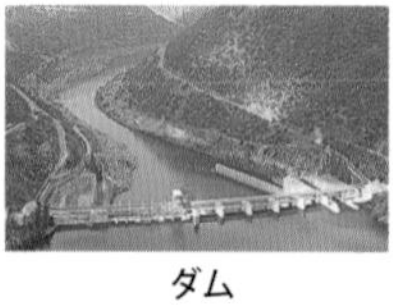

ダム
damu
dam

橋
hashi
bridge

頂華
chōge
finial

小塔
shōtō
turret

尖塔
sentō
spire

濠
hori
moat

破風
hafu
gable

丸屋根
maruyane
dome

塔
tō
tower

アーチ形屋根
āchi-gata yane
vault

コーニス
kōnisu
cornice

柱
hashira
pillar

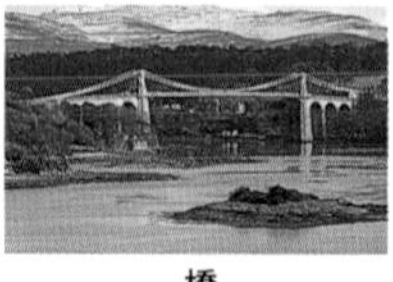

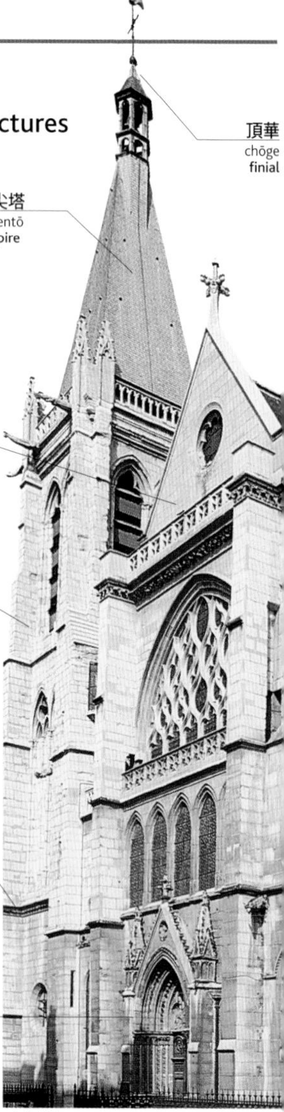

大聖堂 daiseidō | cathedral

建築様式 kenchiku yōshiki • styles

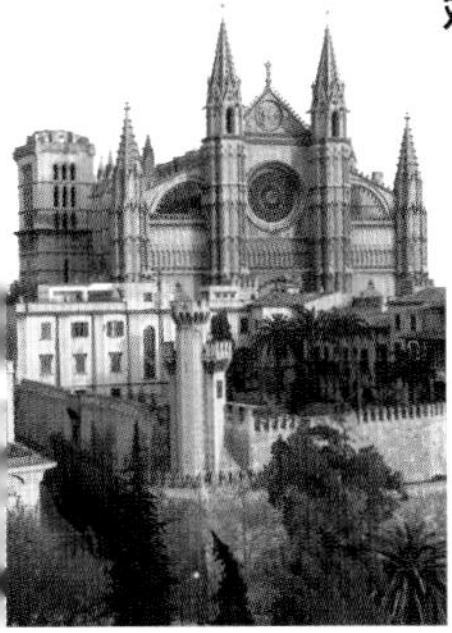

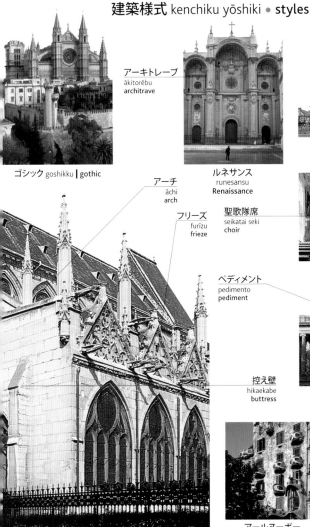

ゴシック goshikku | **gothic**

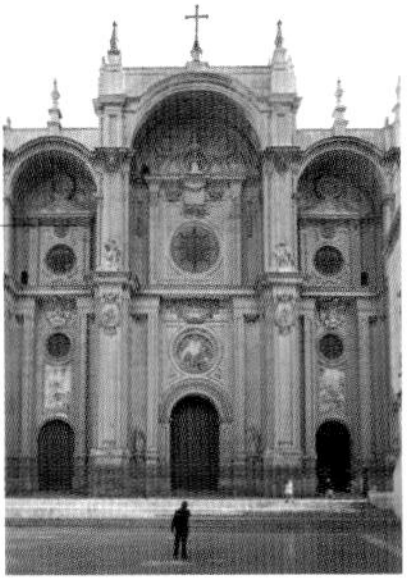

アーキトレーブ
ākitorēbu
architrave

ルネサンス
runesansu
Renaissance

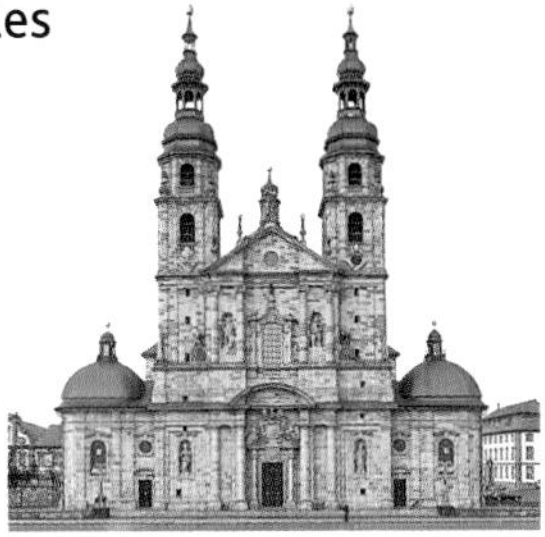

バロック
barokku
baroque

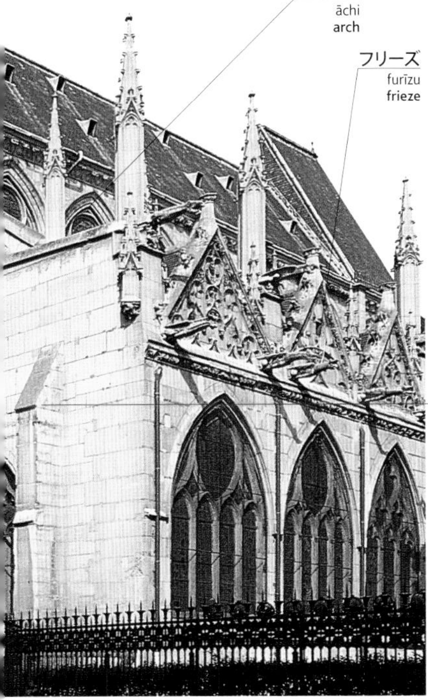

アーチ
āchi
arch

フリーズ
furīzu
frieze

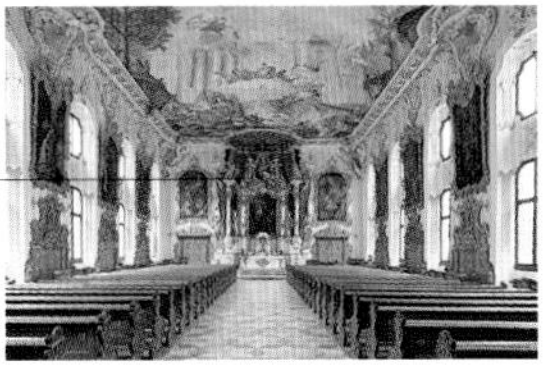

聖歌隊席
seikatai seki
choir

ロココ
rokoko
rococo

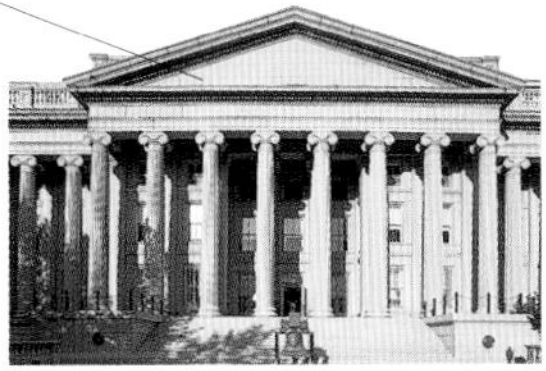

ペディメント
pedimento
pediment

控え壁
hikaekabe
buttress

新古典主義
shinkotenshugi
neoclassical

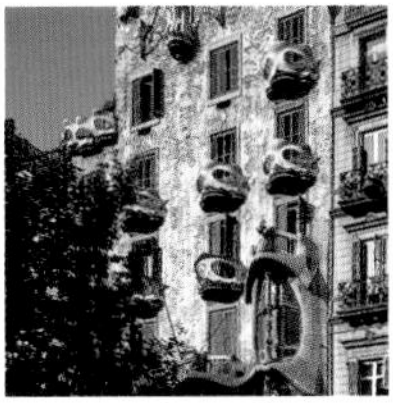

アールヌーボー
āru nūbō
art nouveau

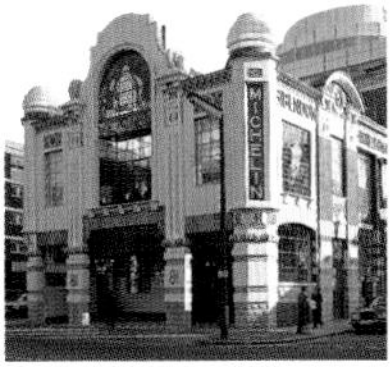

アールデコ
āru deko
art deco

参考資料 sankō shiryō
reference

時間 jikan • time

長針
chōshin
minute hand

短針
tanshin
hour hand

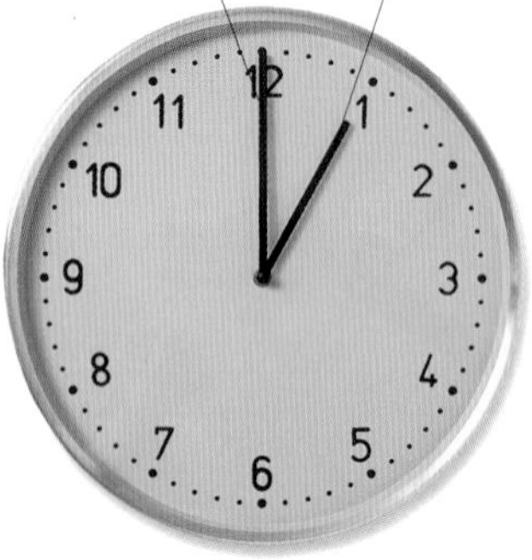

時計
tokei
clock

関連用語 kanrenyōgo • vocabulary

秒 byō second	現在 genzai now	15分 jūgo-fun a quarter of an hour
分 fun minute	後 nochi later	20分 nijuppun twenty minutes
時 ji hour	30分 sanjuppun half an hour	40分 yonjuppun forty minutes

今、何時ですか。
ima nanji desuka?
What time is it?

3時です。
san-ji desu.
It's three o'clock.

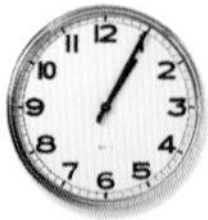

1時5分
ichi-ji go-fun
five past one

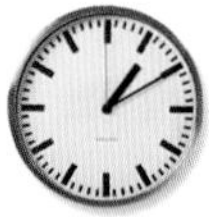

1時10分
ichi-ji juppun
ten past one

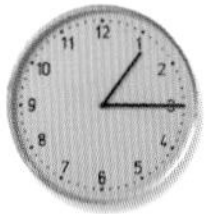

1時15分
ichi-ji jūgo-fun
quarter past one

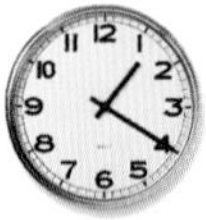

1時20分
ichi-ji nijuppun
twenty past one

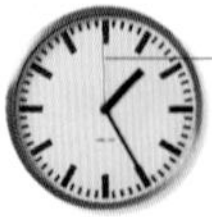

秒針
byōshin
second hand

1時25分
ichi-ji nijūgo-fun
twenty five past one

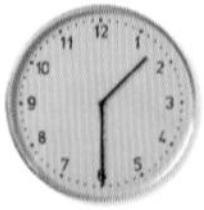

1時半
ichi-ji han
half past one

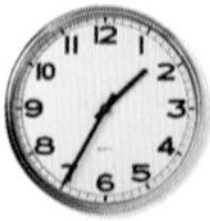

1時35分
ichi-ji sanjūgo-fun
twenty five to two

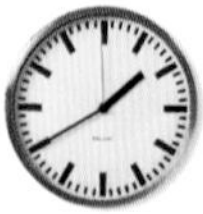

1時40分前
ichi-ji yonjuppun
twenty to two

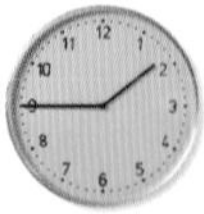

2時15分前
ni-ji jūgo-fun mae
quarter to two

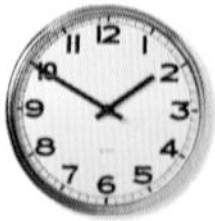

2時10分前
ni-ji juppun mae
ten to two

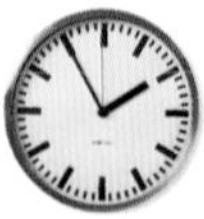

2時5分前
ni-ji go-fun mae
five to two

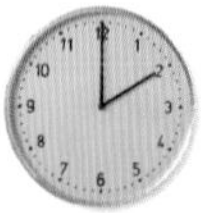

2時
ni-ji
two o'clock

日中と夜 nitchū to yoru • **night and day**

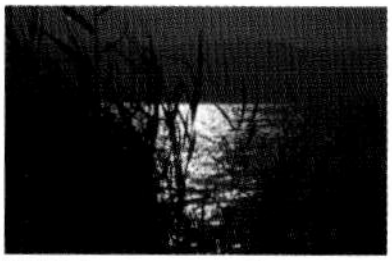

真夜中 mayonaka | midnight

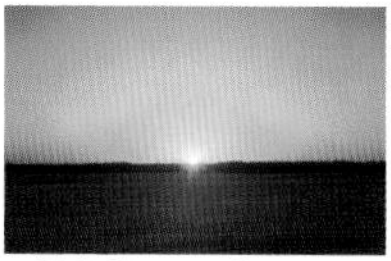

日の出 hinode | sunrise

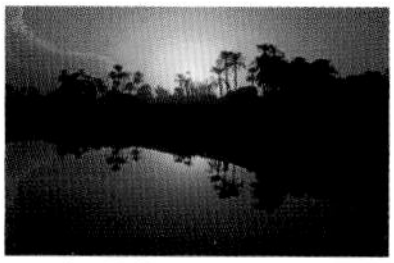

夜明け yoake | dawn

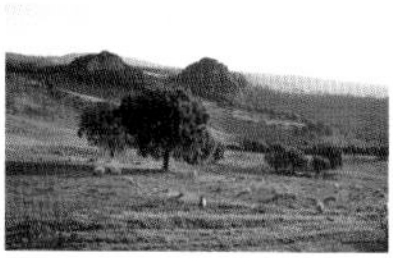

朝 asa | morning

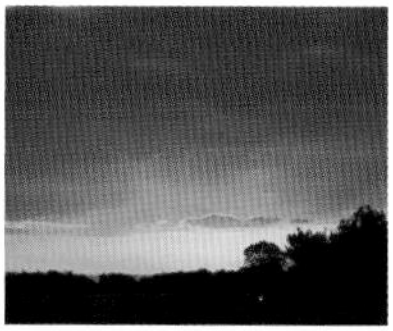

日没
nichibotsu
sunset

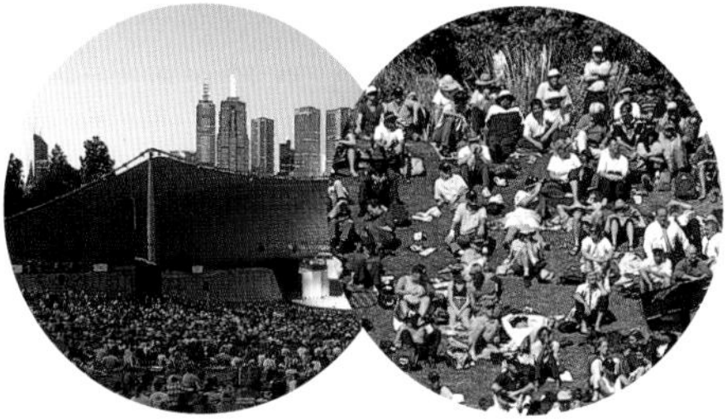

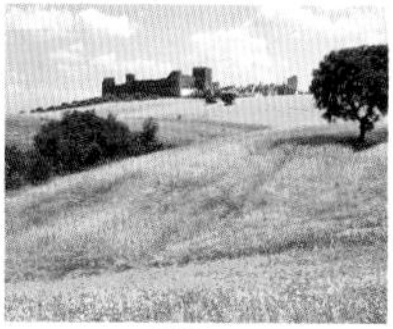

正午
shōgo
midday

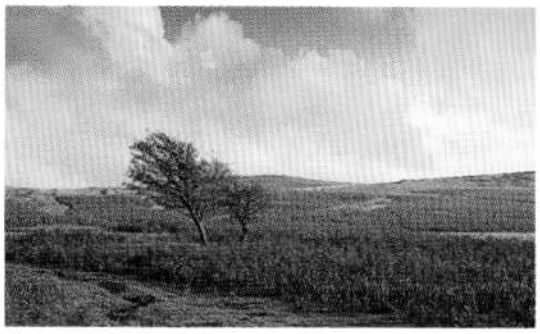

夕暮れ yūgure | dusk

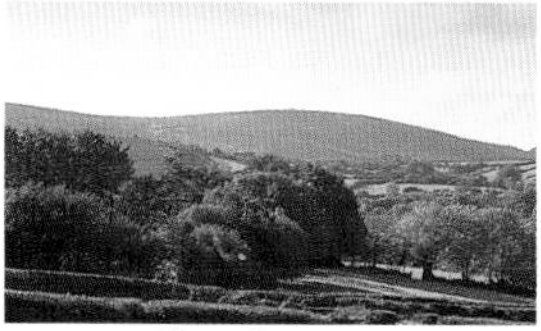

晩 ban | evening

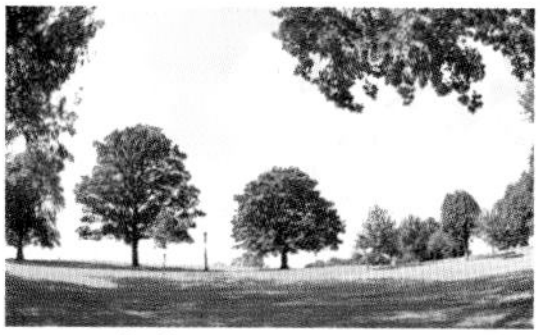

午後 gogo | afternoon

関連用語 kanrenyōgo • **vocabulary**

早い
hayai
early

早いですね。
hayai desune.
You're early.

時間通りに来てください。
jikan-dōri ni kite kudasai.
Please be on time.

何時に終わりますか。
nanji ni owarimasuka?
What time does it finish?

時間通り
jikan-dōri
on time

遅刻です。
chikoku desu.
You're late.

また後で。
mata ato de.
I'll see you later.

遅くなってきました。
osokunatte kimashita.
It's getting late.

遅い
osoi
late

もうすぐ到着します。
mōsugu tōchaku shimasu.
I'll be there soon.

何時に始まりますか。
nanji ni hajimarimasuka?
What time does it start?

時間は、どのくらいかかりますか。
jikan wa donokurai kakarimasuka?
How long will it last?

カレンダー karendā ● calendar

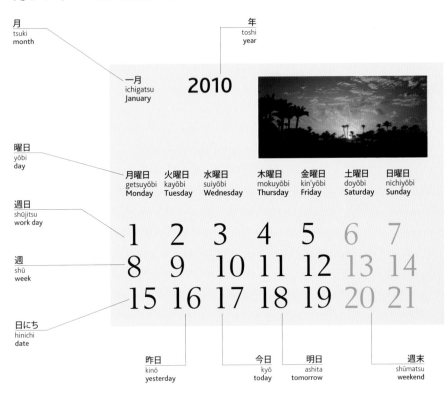

月
tsuki
month

年
toshi
year

一月
ichigatsu
January

2010

曜日
yōbi
day

週日
shūjitsu
work day

週
shū
week

日にち
hinichi
date

月曜日	火曜日	水曜日	木曜日	金曜日	土曜日	日曜日
getsuyōbi	kayōbi	suiyōbi	mokuyōbi	kin'yōbi	doyōbi	nichiyōbi
Monday	**Tuesday**	**Wednesday**	**Thursday**	**Friday**	**Saturday**	**Sunday**
1	2	3	4	5	6	7
8	9	10	11	12	13	14
15	16	17	18	19	20	21

昨日
kinō
yesterday

今日
kyō
today

明日
ashita
tomorrow

週末
shūmatsu
weekend

関連用語 kanrenyōgo ● vocabulary

一月	三月	五月	七月	九月	十一月
ichigatsu	sangatsu	gogatsu	shichigatsu	kugatsu	jūichigatsu
January	March	May	July	September	November
二月	四月	六月	八月	十月	十二月
nigatsu	shigatsu	rokugatsu	hachigatsu	jūgatsu	jūnigatsu
February	April	June	August	October	December

年 toshi • years

1900 一九〇〇年 sen kyūhyaku nen • nineteen hundred

1901 一九〇一年 sen kyūhyaku ichi nen • nineteen hundred and one

1910 一九一〇年 sen kyūhyaku jū nen • nineteen ten

2000 二〇〇〇年 nisen nen • two thousand

2001 二〇〇一年 nisen ichi nen • two thousand and one

季節 kisetsu • seasons

春
haru
spring

夏
natsu
summer

秋
aki
autumn

冬
fuyu
winter

関連用語 kanrenyōgo • vocabulary

世紀
seiki
century

十年間
jūnenkan
decade

千年間
sennenkan
millennium

二週間
nishūkan
fortnight

今週
konshū
this week

先週
senshū
last week

来週
raishū
next week

一昨日
ototoi
the day before yesterday

明後日
asatte
the day after tomorrow

毎週
maishū
weekly

毎月
maitsuki
monthly

毎年
maitoshi
annual

今日は何日ですか。
kyō wa nannichi desuka?
What's the date today?

2002年2月17日です。
nisen ni nen nigatsu jūshichi nichi desu.
It's February seventeenth, two thousand and two.

数字 sūji • numbers

0	零 rei • **zero**	
1	一 ichi • **one**	
2	二 ni • **two**	
3	三 san • **three**	
4	四 shi/yon • **four**	
5	五 go • **five**	
6	六 roku • **six**	
7	七 shichi/nana • **seven**	
8	八 hachi • **eight**	
9	九 ku/kyū • **nine**	
10	十 jū • **ten**	
11	十一 jūichi • **eleven**	
12	十二 jūni • **twelve**	
13	十三 jūsan • **thirteen**	
14	十四 jūshi/jūyon • **fourteen**	
15	十五 jūgo • **fifteen**	
16	十六 jūroku • **sixteen**	
17	十七 jūshichi/jūnana • **seventeen**	
18	十八 jūhachi • **eighteen**	
19	十九 jūku/jūkyū • **nineteen**	
20	二十 nijū • **twenty**	
21	二十一 nijūichi • **twenty-one**	
22	二十二 nijūni • **twenty-two**	
30	三十 sanjū • **thirty**	
40	四十 shijū/yonjū • **forty**	
50	五十 gojū • **fifty**	
60	六十 rokujū • **sixty**	
70	七十 shichijū/nanajū • **seventy**	
80	八十 hachijū • **eighty**	
90	九十 kyūjū • **ninety**	
100	百 hyaku • **one hundred**	
110	百十 hyakujū • **one hundred and ten**	
200	二百 nihyaku • **two hundred**	
300	三百 sambyaku • **three hundred**	
400	四百 yonhyaku • **four hundred**	
500	五百 gohyaku • **five hundred**	
600	六百 roppyaku • **six hundred**	
700	七百 nanahyaku • **seven hundred**	
800	八百 happyaku • **eight hundred**	
900	九百 kyūhyaku • **nine hundred**	

1,000 千 sen • one thousand

10,000 一万 ichiman • ten thousand

20,000 二万 niman • twenty thousand

50,000 五万 goman • fifty thousand

55,500 五万五千五百 goman gosen gohyaku • fifty-five thousand five hundred

100,000 十万 jūman • one hundred thousand

1,000,000 百万 hyakuman • one million

1,000,000,000 十億 jūoku • one billion

一番目 ichi banme • first

二番目 ni banme • second

三番目 san banme • third

四番目 yon banme • fourth

五番目 go banme • fifth

六番目 roku banme • sixth

七番目 nana banme • seventh

八番目 hachi banme • eighth

九番目 kyū banme • ninth

十番目 jū banme • tenth

十一番目 jūichi banme • eleventh

十二番目 jūni banme • twelfth

十三番目 jūsan banme • thirteenth

十四番目 jūyon banme • fourteenth

十五番目 jūgo banme • fifteenth

十六番目 jūroku banme • sixteenth

十七番目 jūnana banme • seventeenth

十八番目 jūhachi banme • eighteenth

十九番目 jūkyū banme • nineteenth

二十番目 nijū banme • twentieth

二十一番目 nijūichi banme • twenty-first

二十二番目 nijūni banme • twenty-second

二十三番目 nijūsan banme • twenty-third

三十番目 sanjū banme • thirtieth

四十番目 yonjū banme • fortieth

五十番目 gojū banme • fiftieth

六十番目 rokujū banme • sixtieth

七十番目 nanajū banme • seventieth

八十番目 hachijū banme • eightieth

九十番目 kyūjū banme • ninetieth

百番目 hyaku banme • one hundredth

計量 keiryō • weights and measures

面積 menseki • area

平方フィート
heihō fīto
square foot

平方メートル
heihō mētoru
square metre

距離 kyori • distance

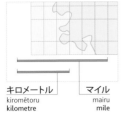

キロメートル
kiromētoru
kilometre

マイル
mairu
mile

ポンド
pondo
pound

オンス
onsu
ounce

キログラム
kiroguramu
kilogram

グラム
guramu
gram

秤 hakari | scales

関連用語 kanrenyōgo • vocabulary

ヤード yādo **yard**	**トン** ton **tonne**	**測る** hakaru **measure (v)**
メートル mētoru **metre**	**ミリグラム** miriguramu **milligram**	**量る** hakaru **weigh (v)**

長さ nagasa • length

フィート
fīto
foot

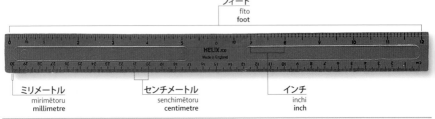

ミリメートル
mirimētoru
millimetre

センチメートル
senchimētoru
centimetre

インチ
inchi
inch

日本語 nihongo • english

容量 yōryō • capacity

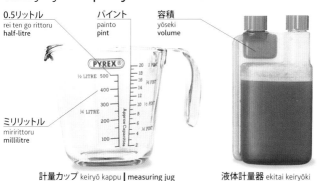

0.5リットル
rei ten go rittoru
half-litre

パイント
painto
pint

容積
yōseki
volume

ミリリットル
miririttoru
millilitre

計量カップ keiryō kappu | measuring jug

液体計量器 ekitai keiryōki
liquid measure

容器 yōki • container

紙パック
kami pakku
carton

包み
tsutsumi
packet

瓶
bin
bottle

袋
fukuro
bag

カップ形容器
kappu-gata yōki | tub

広口瓶 hirokuchi bin | jar

缶
kan
can

缶詰容器 kanzume yōki | tin

霧吹き kirifuki | liquid dispenser

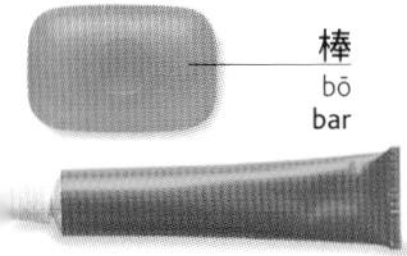

棒
bō
bar

チューブ
chūbu
tube

ロール
rōru
roll

パック
pakku
pack

スプレー缶
supurē kan
spray can

世界地図 sekai chizu • **world map**

北海
hokkai
North Sea

北極海
hokkyokukai
Arctic Ocean

ロッキー山脈
rokkī sanmyaku
Rocky Mountains

カリブ海
karibukai
Caribbean Sea

アマゾニア
amazonia
Amazonia

太平洋
taiheiyō
Pacific Ocean

北
kita
north

西
nishi
west

東
higashi
east

コンパス
kompasu
compass

アンデス山脈
andesu sanmyaku
Andes

大西洋
taiseiyō
Atlantic Ocean

南
minami
south

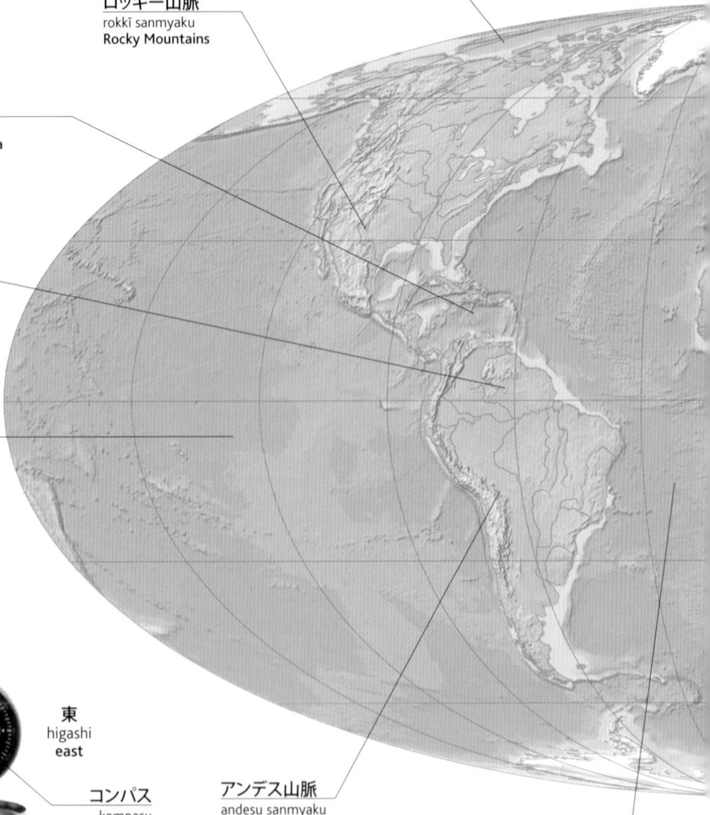

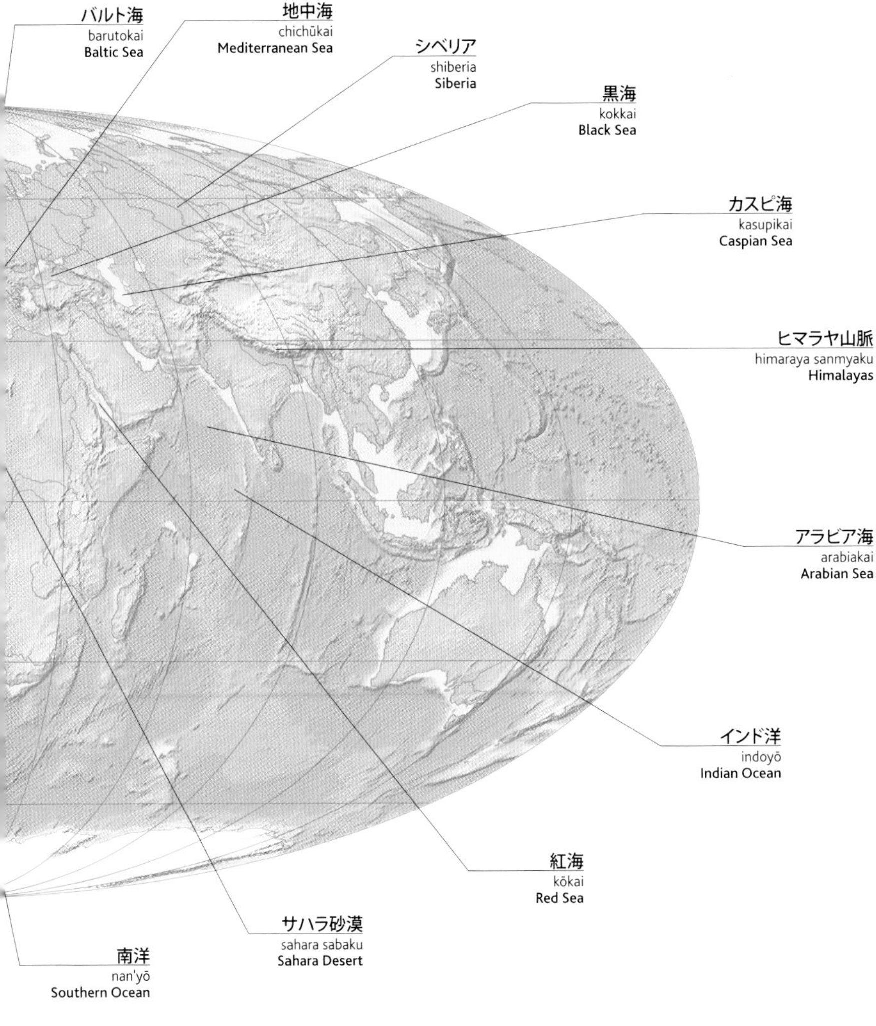

バルト海
barutokai
Baltic Sea

地中海
chichūkai
Mediterranean Sea

シベリア
shiberia
Siberia

黒海
kokkai
Black Sea

カスピ海
kasupikai
Caspian Sea

ヒマラヤ山脈
himaraya sanmyaku
Himalayas

アラビア海
arabiakai
Arabian Sea

インド洋
indoyō
Indian Ocean

紅海
kōkai
Red Sea

サハラ砂漠
sahara sabaku
Sahara Desert

南洋
nan'yō
Southern Ocean

北米と中米 hokubei to chūbei • **North and Central America**

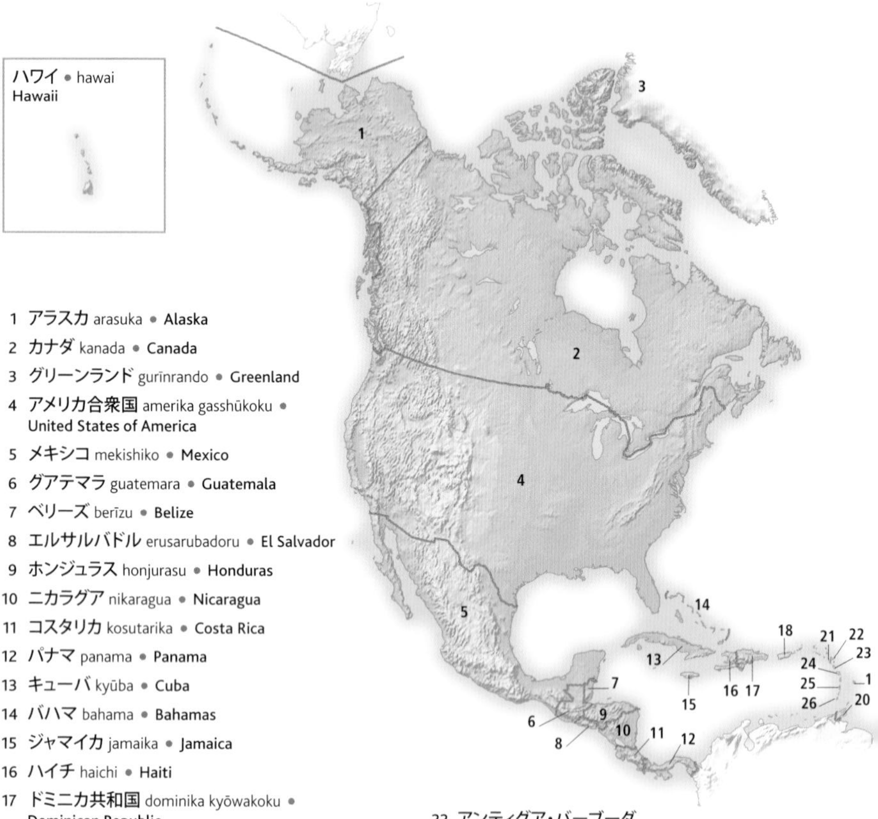

ハワイ • hawai
Hawaii

1　アラスカ arasuka • **Alaska**

2　カナダ kanada • **Canada**

3　グリーンランド gurīnrando • **Greenland**

4　アメリカ合衆国 amerika gasshūkoku •
United States of America

5　メキシコ mekishiko • **Mexico**

6　グアテマラ guatemara • **Guatemala**

7　ベリーズ berīzu • **Belize**

8　エルサルバドル erusarubadoru • **El Salvador**

9　ホンジュラス honjurasu • **Honduras**

10　ニカラグア nikaragua • **Nicaragua**

11　コスタリカ kosutarika • **Costa Rica**

12　パナマ panama • **Panama**

13　キューバ kyūba • **Cuba**

14　バハマ bahama • **Bahamas**

15　ジャマイカ jamaika • **Jamaica**

16　ハイチ haichi • **Haiti**

17　ドミニカ共和国 dominika kyōwakoku •
Dominican Republic

18　プエルトリコ puerutoriko • **Puerto Rico**

19　バルバドス barubadosu • **Barbados**

20　トリニダード・トバゴ torinidādo tobago •
Trinidad and Tobago

21　セントクリストファー・ネーヴィス sentokurisutofā nēvisu •
St Kitts and Nevis

22　アンティグア・バーブーダ
antigua bābūda • **Antigua and Barbuda**

23　ドミニカ dominika • **Dominica**

24　セントルシア sentorushia • **St Lucia**

24　セントビンセント及びグレナディーン諸島 sentobinsento
oyobi gurenadīn shotō • **St Vincent and The Grenadines**

26　グレナダ gurenada • **Grenada**

南米 nambei • South America

1 ベネズエラ benezuera • **Venezuela**

2 コロンビア korombia • **Colombia**

3 エクアドル ekuadoru • **Ecuador**

4 ペルー perū • **Peru**

5 ガラパゴス諸島 garapagosu shotō •
Galapagos Islands

6 ギアナ giana • **Guyana**

7 スリナム surinamu • **Suriname**

8 仏領ギアナ futsuryō giana •
French Guiana

9 ブラジル burajiru • **Brazil**

10 ボリビア boribia • **Bolivia**

11 チリ chiri • **Chile**

12 アルゼンチン aruzenchin • **Argentina**

13 パラグアイ paraguai • **Paraguay**

14 ウルグアイ uruguai • **Uruguay**

15 フォークランド諸島 fōkurando shotō •
Falkland Islands

関連用語 kanrenyōgo • vocabulary

国 kuni **country**	地方 chihō **province**	地帯 chitai **zone**
国家 kokka **nation**	領土 ryōdo **territory**	地区 chiku **district**
大陸 tairiku **continent**	植民地 shokuminchi **colony**	地域 chi'iki **region**
州 shū **state**	公国 kōkoku **principality**	首都 shuto **capital**

ヨーロッパ yōroppa • Europe

1 アイルランド airurando • Ireland

2 英国 eikoku • United Kingdom

3 ポルトガル porutogaru • Portugal

4 スペイン supein • Spain

5 バレアレス諸島 barearesu shotō • Balearic Islands

6 アンドラ andora • Andorra

7 フランス furansu • France

8 ベルギー berugī • Belgium

9 オランダ oranda • Netherlands

10 ルクセンブルク rukusemburuku • Luxembourg

11 ドイツ doitsu • Germany

12 デンマーク denmāku • Denmark

13 ノルウェー noruwē • Norway

14 スウェーデン suwēden • Sweden

15 フィンランド finrando • Finland

16 エストニア esutonia • Estonia

17 ラトビア ratobia • Latvia

18 リトアニア ritoania • Lithuania

19 カリーニングラード karīningurādo • Kaliningrad

20 ポーランド pōrando • Poland

21 チェコ共和国 cheko kyōwakoku • Czech Republic

22 オーストリア ōsutoria • Austria

23 リヒテンシュタイン rihitenshutain • Liechtenstein

24 スイス suisu • Switzerland

25 イタリア itaria • Italy

26 モナコ monako • Monaco

27 コルシカ korushika • Corsica

28 サルディニア sarudinia • Sardinia

29 サンマリノ sanmarino • San Marino

30 バチカン市国 bachikan shikoku • Vatican City

31 シチリア shichiria • Sicily

32 マルタ maruta • Malta

33 スロベニア surobenia • Slovenia

34 クロアチア kuroachia • Croatia

35 ハンガリー hangarī • Hungary

36 スロバキア surobakia • Slovakia

37 ウクライナ ukuraina • Ukraine

38 ベラルーシ berarūshi • Belarus

39 モルドバ morudoba • Moldova

40 ルーマニア rūmania • Romania

41 セルビア serubia • Serbia

42 ボスニア・ヘルツェゴビナ bosunia herutsegobina • Bosnia and Herzegovina

43 アルバニア arubania • Albania

44 マケドニア makedonia • Macedonia

45 ブルガリア burugaria • Bulgaria

46 ギリシャ girisha • Greece

47 コソボ kosobo • Kosovo

48 モンテネグロ monteneguro • Montenegro

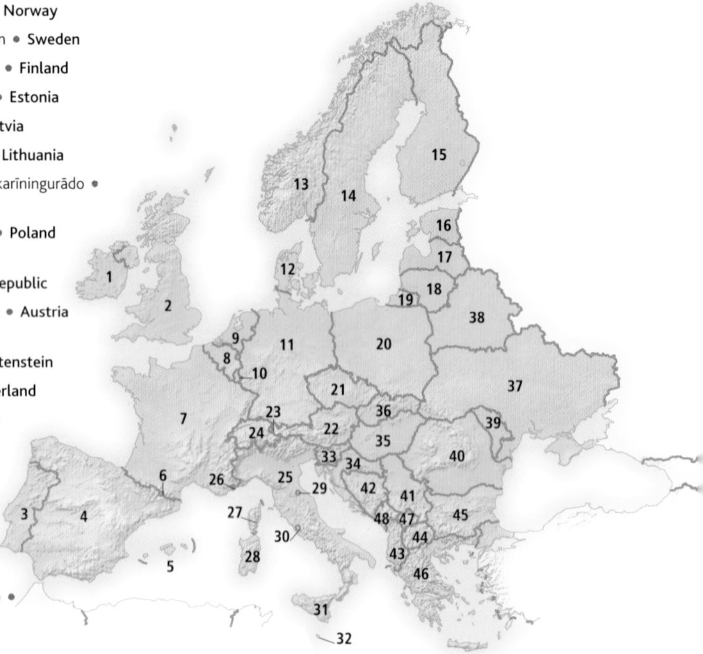

アフリカ afurika • **Africa**

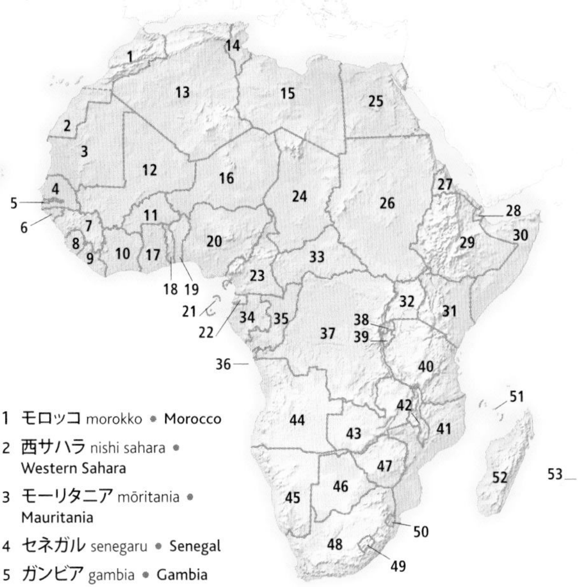

1 モロッコ morokko • Morocco

2 西サハラ nishi sahara • Western Sahara

3 モーリタニア mōritania • Mauritania

4 セネガル senegaru • Senegal

5 ガンビア gambia • Gambia

6 ギニアビサウ giniabisau • Guinea-Bissau

7 ギニア ginia • Guinea

8 シエラレオネ shierareone • Sierra Leone

9 リベリア riberia • Liberia

10 コートジボワール kōtojibowāru • Ivory Coast

11 ブルキナファソ burukinafaso • Burkina Faso

12 マリ mari • Mali

13 アルジェリア arujeria • Algeria

14 チュニジア chunijia • Tunisia

15 リビア ribia • Libya

16 ニジェール nijēru • Niger

17 ガーナ gāna • Ghana

18 トーゴ tōgo • Togo

19 ベニン benin • Benin

20 ナイジェリア naijeria • Nigeria

21 サントメ・プリンシペ santome purinshipe • Sao Tome and Principe

22 赤道ギニア sekidō ginia • Equatorial Guinea

23 カメルーン kamerūn • Cameroon

24 チャド chado • Chad

25 エジプト ejiputo • Egypt

26 スーダン sūdan • Sudan

27 エリトリア eritoria • Eritrea

28 ジブチ jipuchi • Djibouti

29 エチオピア echiopia • Ethiopia

30 ソマリア somaria • Somalia

31 ケニア kenia • Kenya

32 ウガンダ uganda • Uganda

33 中央アフリカ共和国 chūō afurika kyōwakoku • Central African Republic

34 ガボン gabon • Gabon

35 コンゴ kongo • Congo

36 カビンダ kabinda • Cabinda

37 コンゴ民主共和国 kongo minshu kyōwakoku • Democratic Republic of the Congo

38 ルワンダ ruwanda • Rwanda

39 ブルンジ burunji • Burundi

40 モザンビーク mizambīku • Mozambique

41 タンザニア tanzania • Tanzania

42 マラウィ marawi • Malawi

43 ザンビア zambia • Zambia

44 アンゴラ angora • Angola

45 ナミビア namibia • Namibia

46 ボツワナ botsuwana • Botswana

47 ジンバブエ jimbabue • Zimbabwe

48 南アフリカ minami afurika • South Africa

49 レソト resoto • Lesotho

50 スワジランド suwajirando • Swaziland

51 コモロ komoro • Comoros

52 マダガスカル madagasukaru • Madagascar

53 モーリシャス mōrishasu • Mauritius

アジア ajia • Asia

1 トルコ toruko • Turkey

2 キプロス kipurosu • Cyprus

3 ロシア連邦 roshia rempō • Russian Federation

4 グルジア gurujia • Georgia

5 アルメニア arumenia • Armenia

6 アゼルバイジャン azerubaijan • Azerbaijan

7 イラン iran • Iran

8 イラク iraku • Iraq

9 シリア shiria • Syria

10 レバノン rebanon • Lebanon

11 イスラエル isuraeru • Israel

12 ヨルダン yorudan • Jordan

13 サウジアラビア saujiarabia • Saudi Arabia

14 クウェート kuwēto • Kuwait

15 バーレーン bārēn • Bahrain

16 カタール katāru • Qatar

17 アラブ首長国連邦 arabu shuchō-koku rempō • United Arab Emirates

18 オマーン omān • Oman

19 イエメン iemen • Yemen

20 カザフスタン kazafusutan • Kazakhstan

21 ウズベキスタン uzubekisutan • Uzbekistan

22 トルクメニスタン torukumenisutan • Turkmenistan

23 アフガニスタン afuganisutan • Afghanistan

24 タジキスタン tajikisutan • Tajikistan

25 キルギスタン kirigisutan • Kyrgyzstan

26 パキスタン pakisutan • Pakistan

27 インド indo • India

28 モルディブ morudibu • Maldives

29 スリランカ suriranka • Sri Lanka

30 中国 chūgoku • China

31 モンゴル mongoru • Mongolia

32 北朝鮮 kita chōsen • North Korea

33 韓国 kankoku • South Korea

34 日本 nihon • Japan

35 ネパール nepāru • Nepal

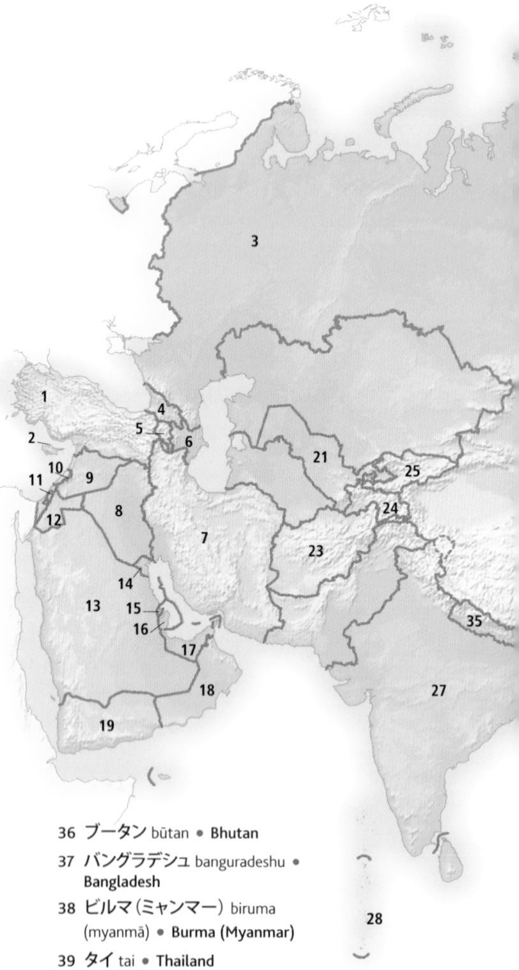

36 ブータン būtan • Bhutan

37 バングラデシュ banguradeshu • Bangladesh

38 ビルマ（ミャンマー）biruma (myanmā) • Burma (Myanmar)

39 タイ tai • Thailand

40 ラオス raosu • Laos

41 ベトナム betonamu • Viet Nam

42 カンボジア kambojia • Cambodia

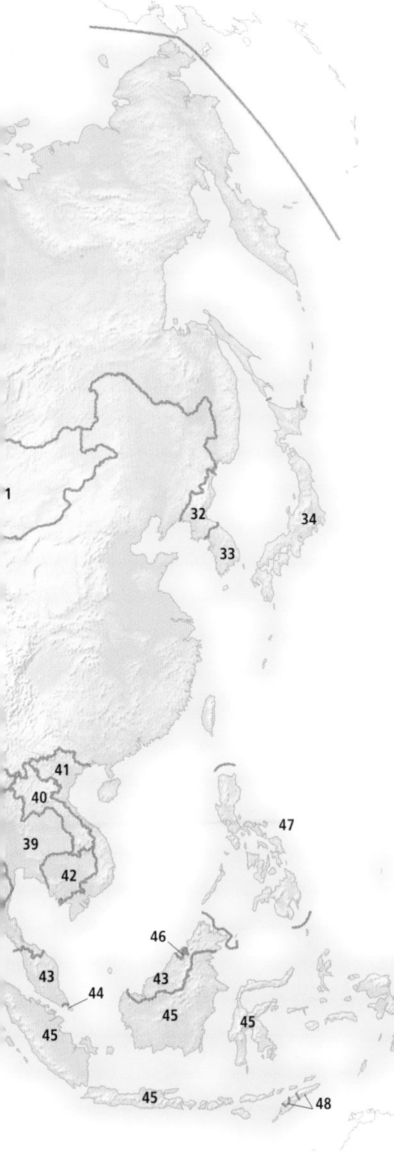

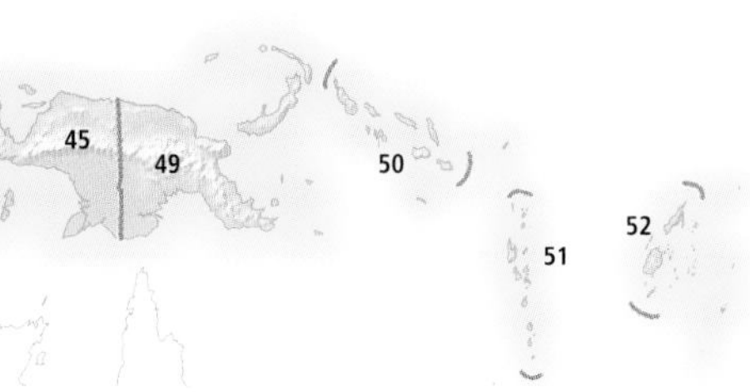

オーストラレーシア
ōsutorarēshia · **Australasia**

1 オーストラリア ōsutoraria · **Australia**

2 タスマニア tasumania · **Tasmania**

3 ニュージーランド nyūjīrando · **New Zealand**

43 マレーシア marēshia · **Malaysia**

44 シンガポール shingapōru · **Singapore**

45 インドネシア indoneshia · **Indonesia**

46 ブルネイ burunei · **Brunei**

47 フィリピン firipin · **Philippines**

48 東ティモール higashi timōru · **East Timor**

49 パプアニューギニア papuanyūginia · **Papua New Guinea**

50 ソロモン諸島 soromon shotō · **Solomon Islands**

51 バヌアツ banuatsu · **Vanuatu**

52 フィジー fijī · **Fiji**

不変化詞と反義語 fuhenkashi to hangigo •
particles and antonyms

... へ
... e
to ...

...から
... kara
from ...

...から離れて
... kara hanarete
away from...

...に向かって
... ni mukatte
towards ...

...の上方
... no jōhō
over ...

...の下方
... no kahō
under ...

...に沿って
... ni sotte
along ...

...を横切って
... o yokogitte
across ...

...の前
... no mae
in front of ...

...の後ろ
... no ushiro
behind ...

...と一緒に
... to issho ni
with ...

...なしで
... nashi de
without ...

...の上へ
... no ue e
onto ...

...の中へ
... no naka e
into ...

...以前
... izen
before ...

...以後
... igo
after ...

中
naka
in

外
soto
out

...までに
... made ni
by ...

...まで
... made
until ...

真上
maue
above

真下
mashita
below

早い
hayai
early

遅い
osoi
late

内側
uchigawa
inside

外側
sotogawa
outside

今
ima
now

後ほど
nochihodo
later

上へ
ue e
up

下へ
shita e
down

いつも
itsumo
always

決して...ない
kesshite ... nai
never

...で
... de
at ...

...の向こう
... no mukō
beyond ...

頻繁に
himpan ni
often

稀に
mare ni
rarely

...を通って
... o tōtte
through ...

...を回って
... o mawatte
around ...

昨日
kinō
yesterday

明日
ashita
tomorrow

...の上
... no ue
on top of ...

...の側
... no soba
beside ...

最初
saisho
first

最後
saigo
last

...の間
... no aida
between ...

...の向かい側
... no mukaigawa
opposite ...

あらゆる
arayuru
every

いくつかの
ikutsuka no
some

近い
chikai
near

遠い
tōi
far

およそ
oyoso
about

丁度
chōdo
exactly

ここ
koko
here

あそこ
asoko
there

少し
sukoshi
a little

沢山
takusan
a lot

大きい ōkī **large**	小さい chīsai **small**	熱い atsui **hot**	冷たい tsumetai **cold**
幅の広い haba no hiroi **wide**	幅の狭い haba no semai **narrow**	開いた hiraita **open**	閉まった shimatta **closed**
背の高い se no takai **tall**	背の低い se no hikui **short**	満ちた michita **full**	空の kara no **empty**
高い takai **high**	低い hikui **low**	新しい atarashī **new**	古い furui **old**
厚い atsui **thick**	薄い usui **thin**	明るい akarui **bright**	暗い kurai **dark**
軽い karui **light**	重い omoi **heavy**	簡単な kantan na **easy**	難しい muzukashī **difficult**
硬い katai **hard**	柔らかい yawarakai **soft**	空き aki **free**	使用中 shiyō-chū **occupied**
湿った shimetta **wet**	乾いた kawaita **dry**	強い tsuyoi **strong**	弱い yowai **weak**
良い yoi **good**	悪い warui **bad**	太い futoi **fat**	細い hosoi **thin**
速い hayai **fast**	ゆっくりした yukkurishita **slow**	若い wakai **young**	老いた oita **old**
正しい tadashī **correct**	誤った ayamatta **wrong**	より良い yori yoi **better**	もっと悪い motto warui **worse**
きれいな kirei na **clean**	汚い kitanai **dirty**	黒 kuro **black**	白 shiro **white**
美しい utsukushī **beautiful**	醜い minikui **ugly**	面白い omoshiroi **interesting**	つまらない tsumaranai **boring**
高価な kōka na **expensive**	安い yasui **cheap**	病気の byōki no **sick**	健康な kenkō na **well**
静かな shizuka na **quiet**	うるさい urusai **noisy**	始め hajime **beginning**	終わり owari **end**

便利な表現 benri na hyōgen • useful phrases

基本的表現
kihonteki hyōgen
• essential phrases

はい
hai
Yes

いいえ
īe
No

多分
tabun
Maybe

どうぞ
dōzo
Please

ありがとう
arigatō
Thank you

どういたしまして
dō itashimashite
You're welcome

すみません
sumimasen
Excuse me

ごめんなさい
gomen nasai
I'm sorry

...しないでください
... shinaide kudasai
Don't ...

オーケー
ōkē
OK

それで結構です
sorede kekkō desu
That's fine

そうです
sōdesu
That's correct

違います
chigaimasu
That's wrong

挨拶 aisatsu •
greetings

もしもし
moshimoshi
Hello (on telephone)

さようなら
sayōnara
Goodbye

おはようございます
ohayō gozaimasu
Good morning

こんにちは
konnichiwa
Good afternoon

こんばんは
kombanwa
Good evening

おやすみなさい
oyasuminasai
Good night

お元気ですか
o-genki desuka
How are you?

私は...です
watashi wa ... desu
My name is ...

お名前は何ですか
o-namae wa nan desuka?
What is your name?

彼/彼女のお名前は
kare/kanojo no o-namae wa?
What is his/her name?

...をご紹介します
... o go-shōkai shimasu
May I introduce...

こちらは...です
kochira wa ... desu
This is...

初めまして
hajimemashite
Pleased to meet you

また後で
mata ato de
See you later

標識 hyōshiki • signs

観光案内所
kankō annai-jo
Tourist information

入口
iriguchi
Entrance

出口
deguchi
Exit

非常口
hijōguchi
Emergency exit

押す
osu
Push

危険
kiken
Danger

禁煙
kin'en
No smoking

故障中
koshōchū
Out of order

開館時間
kaikan jikan
Opening times

入場無料
nyūjō muryō
Free admission

全日営業
zennichi eigyō
Open all day

割引料金
waribiki ryōkin
Reduced price

特売
tokubai
Sale

ノックしてください
nokku shite kudasai
Knock before entering

芝生立ち入り禁止
shibafu tachi'iri kinshi
Keep off the grass

援助 enjo • help

助けてください
tasukete kudasai
Please help me

分かりません
wakarimasen
I don't understand

知りません
shirimasen
I don't know

英語/日本語を話せますか
eigo/nihongo o hanasemasuka?
Do you speak English/Japanese?

英語を話せます
eigo hanasemasu
I speak English

スペイン語を話せます
supeingo o hanasemasu
I speak Spanish

もっとゆっくり言ってください
motto yukkuri itte kudasai
Please speak more slowly

書いてください
kaite kudasai
Please write it down for me

...をなくしました
... o nakushimashita
I have lost...

道案内 michi annai • directions

道に迷いました
michi ni mayoimashita
I am lost

...はどこですか
... wa doko desuka?
Where is the...?

最寄りの...はどこですか
moyori no ... wa doko desuka?
Where is the nearest...?

お手洗いはどこですか
o-tearai wa doko desuka?
Where are the toilets?

右です
migi desu
To the right

左です
hidari desu
To the left

まっすぐです
massugu desu
Straight ahead

...は、どのくらい離れていますか
... wa donokurai hanarete imasuka
How far is...?

...への行き方を教えてください
... e no ikikata o oshiete kudasai
How do I get to...?

道路標識 dōro hyōshiki • road signs

注意
chūi
Caution

進入禁止
shinnyū kinshi
No entry

スピード落せ
supīdo otose
Slow down

迂回路
ukairo
Diversion

右側通行
migigawa tsūkō
Keep to the right

高速道路
kōsokudōro
Motorway

駐車禁止
chūsha kinshi
No parking

通行禁止
tsūkō kinshi
No through road

道路工事中
dōro kōji-chū
Roadworks

一方通行
ippōtsūkō
One-way street

譲れ
yuzure
Give way

止まれ
tomare
Stop

屈折あり
kussetsu ari
Dangerous bend

宿泊 shukuhaku • accommodation

予約してあります
yoyaku shite arimasu
I have a reservation

朝食は何時ですか
chōshoku wa nanji desuka
What time is breakfast?

食堂はどこですか
shokudō wa doko desuka?
Where is the dining room?

私の部屋は...号室です
watashi no heya wa ...-gōshitsu desu
My room number is...

...時に戻ります
... ji ni modorimasu
I'll be back at...o'clock

飲食 inshoku • eating and drinking

乾杯!
kampai
Cheers!

美味しい/不味いです
oishī/mazui desu
It's delicious/awful

お酒は飲めません
o-sake wa nomemasen
I don't drink

煙草は吸いません
tabako wa suimasen
I don't smoke

肉は食べません
niku wa tabemasen
I don't eat meat

もう結構です
mō kekkō desu
No more for me, thank you

もう少し、いただけますか
mō sukoshi itadakemasuka
May I have some more?

会計をお願いします
kaikei o onegaishimasu
Please give us the bill

領収書をください
ryōshūsho o kudasai
Please give us a receipt

禁煙席
kin'en seki
No-smoking area

健康 kenkō • health

体調が優れません
taichō ga suguremasen
I don't feel well

気分が悪いです
kibun ga warui desu
I feel sick

最寄りの医者の電話番号は何ですか
moyori no isha no denwabangō wa nan desuka?
What is the telephone number of the nearest doctor?

ここが痛いです
koko ga itai desu
It hurts here

熱があります
netsu ga arimasu
I have a temperature

妊娠...ヶ月です
ninshin ...-kagetsu desu
I'm...months pregnant

...の処方箋をください
... no shohōsen o kudasai
I need a prescription for...

普段は...を飲みます
fudan wa ... o nomimasu
I normally take ...

...にアレルギーがあります
... ni arerugī ga arimasu
I'm allergic to ...

大丈夫ですか
daijōbu desuka?
Will he/she be all right?

日本語索引 nihongo sakuin • Japanese index

A

abaraniku 119
abokado 128
abumi 242
abura 142
abura enogu 274
abura hada 41
abura shitsu 39
abura-zuke 143
aburami 119
abuzairen 248
āchi 85, 301
āchi-gata yane 300
adobantēji 230
aen 289
aen mekki 79
afuganisutan 318
afurika 317
afutāsankea 108
afutāshēbu 73
ageru 67
ageta 159
ago 14
agurifurūtsu 126
ahiru no tamago 137
ai yū dī 21
aʾiiro 274
aian 233
aiburow- burashi 40
aiburow-penshiru 40
aikappu 269
aikidō 236
aikon 177
airainā 40
airon 76
airon o kakeru 76
airondai 76
airurando 316
aisatsu 322
aishadō 40
aishingu 141
aisu baketsu 150
aisu hokkē 224
aisu kōhī 148
aisu kuraimingu 247
aisu sukēto 247
aisu tī 149
aisuhokkē senshu 224
aisuhokkē-yō rinku 224
aisukurīmu 137, 149
aisukurīmu sukūpu 68
aite 236
ajia 318
aka 274
aka (wain) 145
aka chikori 123
aka rentiru 131
aka tōgarashi 124
akachairo 39
akachan 30
akachan-yō taijūkei 53
akage 39

akame 271
akami niku 118
akarui 321
akashia 110
aki 31, 307, 321
akiresuken 16
akiru 25
ākitorēbu 301
akuamarin 288
akubi suru 25
akuriru enogu 274
akuseru 200
akusesarī 36
akusuru 205
ama 184
amadoi 58
amagu 245, 267
amai 124, 127, 155
amakawa 15
amazonia 312
amba 235
ame 287
ame-gachi na 286
amefuto shūzu 220
amejisuto 288
amerika gasshūkoku 314
amerikan futtobōru 220
ameya 113
ami 217
amiagegutsu 37
amibari 277
amidana 209
amimono 277
amiuchi suru 245
āmondo 129, 151
āmondo oiru 134
ampaia 225
ampea 60
ampu 268
āmu kāru 251
āmu resuto 200
āmubando 238
āmuchea 63
ana 244
ana o akeru 79
anaʾake panchi 173
anaʾaki supūn 68
andā pā 233
andesu sanmyaku 312
andora 316
angora 317
anime 178
anime eiga 255
ankō 120
ankōru 255
annai 261
annai zu 261
annai-ban 213
annai-gakari 255
anorakku 31, 33
anshitsu 271
anshō bangō 96

antigua bābūda 314
anzempin 47
anzen gōguru 167
anzen saku 246
anzen yōgu 240
anzen yōhin 75
anzu 126
ao 274
aoi 129
apurikēshon 176
arabiakai 313
arabiki mugi 130
arabu shūchō-koku rempō 318
arakaruto 152
araseitō 110
arashi 287
arasuka 314
arau 38, 77
arayuru 320
arenjimento 111
arerugī 44
ari 295
arigatō 322
arigētā 293
arīna 243
aromaterapī 55
āru deko 301
āru nūbō 301
arubamu 271
arubania 316
arufarufa 184
arujeria 317
arukōru inryō 145
arumenia 318
aruminiumu 289
arupen sukī 247
aruzenchin 315
asa 305
asari 121
asase 239
asatsuki 133
asatte 307
ashi 12, 13, 15, 64, 119
ashi no kō 15
ashi no kō no uchigawa 15
ashi no koyubi 15
ashi no oyayubi 15
ashi no tsume 15
ashiba 186
ashika 290
ashikubi 13, 15
ashisutanto 24
ashita 306, 320
ashiura 15
ashiyubi 15
asobi 75
asobiba 263
asobu 273
asoko 320
atakkingu zōn 224
atama 12, 19, 80
atarashii 130, 321

atatakai 286
atatakai nomimono 144
atatamenaosu 154
ātichōku 124
atopīsei hifuen 44
atoriumu 104
atsu-giri 121
atsugami 275
atsui 286, 321
atsuryoku barubu 61
auto 225, 228
auto obu baunzu 226
autorigā 187
awa 148
awadateki 68
awadateru 67
awaseru 179
ayamatta 321
ayame 110
ayuruvēda 55
aza 46
azami 297
azarashi 290
aze 183
azerubaijan 318
azuki 131

B

bā 150, 235, 250
bā sutsūru 150
baba bajutsu 243
bābekyū 267
bāberu 251
baburu basu 73
bachikan shikoku 316
badominton 231
bāga mīru 154
bagetto 138
baggu 37
bahama 314
baiasuron 247
baiku uea 205
baiorin 256
baishin'in 180
baishin'in seki 180
baito 176
baizā 205
bajiriko 133
bajji 94
baketsu 77, 82, 265
bakku 223
bakku mirā 198
bakku suru 195
bakkubōdo 226
bakkugyamon 272
bakkuhando 231
bakkuru 36
bakkusuingu 233
bākōdo 106
bākōdo yomitori sōchi 106
bakuga inryō 144
bakugekiki 211

bampā 198
ban 305
banana 128
bandoēdo 47
banebakari 166
bangō annai 99
bangumi 269
bangumi seisaku 178
banguradeshu 318
banira 132
banji jampu 248
banjō gēmu 272
bankā 232
bansōkō 47
banuatsu 319
banzu 155
bappu 139
bara 89, 110
barē 255
barearesu shotō 316
barēbōru 227
barokku 301
baroku 242
barubadosu 314
barubu 207
barukonī seki 254
barumitsubā 26
barusamiko su 135
barutokai 313
basha rēsu 243
basshi 50
basu 196
basu kurarinetto 257
basu machiai-jo 197
basu matto 72
basu no untenshu 190
basu tāminaru 197
basu taoru 73
basu-tei 197
basuketto 95, 226, 263
basukettobōru 226
basukettobōru senshu 226
basuku 35
basurōbu 73
basutei 299
batā 137, 156
batafurai 239
batāmiruku 137
batānetto sukuwasshu 125
bāten 150, 191
baton 235
battā 228
batterī 202
batto 225, 228
battsuman 225
baundarī 225
baundo suru 227
bayonetto-shiki 60
bebī basu 74
bebī gēto 75
bebī kea 74
bebī monitā 75

bebī rūmu 104
bebī suringu 75
bebī yōhin 107
bebī-yō magu kappu 75
bebībeddo 74
bebīgurō 30
bebīkā 75
bebīsākuru 75
beddo 70, 71
beddo bampā 74
beddo sukāto 71
beddokabā 70
beddomēkingu suru 71
beddosaido rampu 70
beddosaido tēburu 70
bēguru 139
beji bāgā 155
bēkingu torei 69
bēkon 118, 157
benchi 250, 262
beneshan buraindo 63
benezuera 315
bengoshi 180, 190
benin 317
benki 61, 72
bentō 154
benza 61, 72
beranda 59
berarūshi 316
berīzu 314
bero 37
beru 197
bēru 35
berugī 316
beruto 32, 36
beruto kombea 106
bēshisuto 258
bēsu 99
bēsu gitā 258
bēsurain 230
besuto 33, 35
betonamu 318
biburafon 257
bīchi baggu 264
bīchi bōru 265
bīchi parasoru 264
bīchi taoru 265
bide 72
bideo denwa 99
bideo rekōdā 269
bideo tēpu 269
bihin 38
bijimesu'ūman 175
bijinesu 175
bijinesu kurasu 211
bijinesu pātonā 24
bijinesu ranchi 175
bijinesuman 175
bijutsu 162
bijutsu daigaku 169
bijutsu to kōgei 274
bijutsukan 261
bijutsushi 169
bīkā 167
bikini 264
bikotsu 17
biku 245

bin 134, 135, 311
bīniru tai 89
binkan hada 41
binmei 212
binzume furūtsu 135
binzume shokuhin 134
biora 256
bīru 145, 151
biruma (myanmā) 318
bishin 283
bishō 25
bishoppu 272
bisuketto 141
bitā 145
bīto 259
bītorūto 125
biyō 40
biyōin 115
biyoku 210
biyōshi 188
biza 213
bō 311
bō-tsuki kyandī 113
bōrā 221
bobin 276
bobu 39
bobusurē 247
bodi rōshon 73
bōdo 241
bōfū fensu 265
bōfuzai 83
bōgyo 220
bōhan beru 58
bōhatei 217
bōifurendo 24
boirā 61
bōken 255
bokkusu seki 254
bōkō 20, 94
bokusasaizu 251
bokusāshōtsu 33
bokushingu 236
bokusō-chi 182
bokuyō nōjō 183
bongo 257
bonnetto 198
bōrādo 298
borē 231
boribia 315
bōringu 249
bōru 65, 75, 112, 220, 224,
    226, 228, 230, 249
bōrubōi 231
bōsai ono 95
bōshi 36
boshikyū 15
bosunia herutsegobina 316
bōtakatobi 234
botan 32, 111
botanhōru 32
botchangari 39
bōto 214
botoru 61
botsuwana 317
budō 127, 237
budō abura 134

budō no ki 183
budōen 183
bui 217
buinekku 33
būke 35, 111
būkegaruni 132
bumben 52
bumbetsu yunitto 61
bumbo 165
bumbōgu 105
būmu 240
būmumaiku 179
buna 296
bundoki 165
bungaku 162, 169
bunki-tai 194
bunrui-dana 100
bunryō 151
bunshi 165, 297
bunsū 165
bunzen bānā 166
burajā 35
burajiru 315
burajirunattsu 129
burakku hōru 280
burakku kōhī 148
burakku pudingu 157
burakkuberī 127
burakkukaranto 127
burandē 145
buranko 263
burashi 40, 77
burashi o kakeru 38
burausu 34
burauza 177
bureddo naifu 68
burēdo 66
burēki 200, 204, 206
burēki furūdo tanku 202
burēki o kakeru 207
burēki paddo 207
burēki pedaru 205
burēki rebā 207
buresuretto 36
burezā 33
burī chīzu 142
burīfu 33
burīfukēsu 37
burijji 258, 273
buriosshu 157
burō suru 38
burōchi 36
burōka 97
burokkori 123
burokku suru 227
burondo 39
burū chīzu 136
burūberī 127
burugaria 316
burukinafaso 317
burunei 319
burunetto 39
burunji 317
burūsu 259
būsutā 281
buta 185
butagoya 185

butai 254
būtan 318
butaniku 118
būti 30
butikku 115
butsuri 162
butsurigaku 169
buyō gakuin 169
byō 304
byōin 48
byōki 44
byōki no 321
byōri-ka 49
byōshin 304
byōshitsu 48
byuffe 152

C
cha 184
chado 317
chairo 274
chairudo shīto 198, 207
chakka-zai 266
chakku 78
chako 276
chakuriku sōchi 210
chakuriku suru 211
chan 23
channeru 178
channeru o kaeru 269
chatsune 135
chawan 64
chedā chīzu 142
chekkā 272
chekkuauto 106
chekkuin suru 212
cheko kyōwakoku 316
chekuin desuku 213
chēn 36, 206
chero 256
chesu 272
chesuban 272
chesuto puresu 251
chī'iki 315
chiarīdā 220
chibusa 12
chichi 22
chichi o shiboru 183
chichūkai 313
chihō 315
chijin 24
chikai 320
chikaku 282
chikashitsu 58
chikatetsu 208
chikatetsu rosenzu 209
chiketto uriba 255
chikin bāgā 155
chikin nagetto 155
chikori 122
chiku 315
chikubi 12, 75
chikusha 185
chikyū 280, 282
chīmu 220, 229
chimei 85
chingensai 123

chinjutsu-sho 180
chinsei-zai 109
chippu 152
chippubōdo 79
chippushotto o utsu 233
chiri 162
chiritori 77
chīsai 321
chisei 284
chissoku suru 47
chitai 283, 315
chitsu 20
chizu 195, 261
chīzu 136, 156
chō 295
chōba 235
chōdo 320
chōge 300
chōha 179
chōhen eiga 269
chōhōkei 164
chōji 125
chōka hikidashi 96
chōka nimotsu 212
chokin 96
chokkei 164
chokobā 113
chōkoku 275
chōkokuka 191
chōkokutō 275
chokorēto 113
chokorēto chippusu 141
chokorēto kēki 140
chokorēto mirukusēki 149
chokorēto o kabuseta 140
chokorēto supureddo 135
chōku 162
chokuchō 21
chokuryū denryū 60
chokusen 165
chōkyori basu 196
chōnekutai 36
chōompa (kensa) 52
chōompa jettoki 211
choppu 119
chōri 67
chōri niku 143
chōri shitsu 214
chōri yōgu 68
chōri-zumi niku 118
chōridai 66
choriso 143
chōrui 292
chōryū 130
chōsa 94
chōsei taku 179
chōshin 304
chōshinki 45
chōshoku 64, 156
chōshoku byuffe 156
chōshoku no tēburu 156
chōshoku torei 101
chōshoku-tsuki 101
chosui tanku 61
chōten 164
chōyaku-ban 235
chōzai shitsu 108

日本語索引

chūba 257
chūbei 314
chūbu 207, 311
chuchu 191
chūdoku 46
chūgaeri 235
chūgoku 318
chūha 179
chūi 323
chūka nabe 69
chūkanken 286
chūko hambaiten 115
chūmon suru 153
chunijia 317
chūō afurika kyōwakoku 317
chūō bunri-tai 194
chūō enzan shori sōchi 176
chūō shasen 194
chūrippu 111
chūsha 48
chūsha kinshi 323
chūsha suru 195
chūsha-bari 109
chūshajō 298
chūshaki 109, 167
chūshin 164
chūshoku 64
chūshukotsu 17
chūsokkotsu 17

D

daburu 151
daburu beddo 71
daburu kurīmu 137
daburu rūmu 100
daburusu 230
dachō 292
daenkei 164
daffurukōto 31
dagakki 257
dagu-auto 229
daichi 284
daichō 18
daidenkin 16
daidokoro 66
daidokoro yōhin 105
daigaku 168, 299
daigakuin 169
daigakusei 169
daihon 254
daikaiten 247
daikei 164
daiku 188
daimei 168
dainamo 207
dainingu rūmu 64
daiō 127
dairi 223
dairiseki 288
daiseidō 300
daitai ryōhō 54
daitaikotsu 17
daiuikyō 133
daiya 273
daiyamondo 288
daizu 131
damī 276

dampukā 187
damu 300
danberu 251
danchigai heikōbō 235
dankushūto suru 227
danmenzu 282
danro 63
dansā 191
dansei 12, 13, 21, 23
dansei fuku 32
danshi seito 162
dansu 259
dasshubōdo 201
dassui suru 76
dassuiki 76
dasutā 77
dāto baiku 205
dātsu 273
dātsubōdo 273
daunrōdo suru 177
de 320
debitto kādo 96
deddobōru rain 221
deguchi 322
deguchi rampu 194
dejitaru kamera 270
dekki 85
dekki chea 265
dempō 98
den'atsu 60
denchi 167, 260
denchi pakku 78
dengen 60
dengen kēburu 176
dengen sōchi 266
denki doriru 78
denki kamisori 73
denki kigu 66
denki seihin 105, 107
denki setsubi 60
denki yakan 66
denkikō 188
denkimōfu 71
denkyū 60
denmāku 316
denriken 286
denryoku 60
denryokuryō-kei 60
densen 60
densha 208
denshimēru 177
denshirenji 66
denshitechō 175
dentaku 165
dentaru furosu 50, 72
dentaru furosu de sōji suru 50
denwa 99, 172
denwa ni deru 99
denwa suru 99
deodoranto 73, 108
depāto 105
derikatessen 107, 142
desukutoppu 177
desukutoppu ōganaizā 172
dezainā 191, 277
dezāto 153

dezāto wagon 152
dī-bui-dī disuku 268
dī-bui-dī purēyā 268
difendingu zōn 224
dijitaru 269
dijon masutādo 135
diru 133
disuku 176
disuku jokkī 179
diwāri 27
dīzeru 199
dīzeru kikansha 208
dō 235, 289
doa 196, 198, 210
doa handoru 200
doa mirā 198
doa rokku 200
doachēn 59
doanokkā 59
dōbā karei 120
dōbutsu 290, 292, 294
dōbutsuen 262
dōbutsugaku 169
dōgu 187
dōgubako 80
doitsu 316
dojō 85
dokku 214, 216
dōkō 51
dokubari 295
dokusho risuto 168
dokusho-tō 210
dōkutsu 284
dokyumentarī 178
dokyumento fairu 173
dōmā 58
dominika 314
dominika kyōwakoku 314
domino 273
dōmyaku 19
donabe 69
donaru 25
donguri kabocha 125
dora 257
dorai furawā 111
dorai furūtsu 129, 156
doraibā 80
doraibā bitto 80
doraibāshotto o utsu 233
doramā 258
doramu 258
doramu setto 258
doresshingu o kaketa 159
doriburu suru 222
doriru 50
doriru bitto 78, 80
dōro 194
dōro hyōshiki 195, 298, 323
dōro kōji 187, 195
dōro kōji-chū 323
doroppu shotto 230
doroyoke 205
dōru hausu 75
dōryō 24
dosei 280
dōtsuki noko 81
doyōbi 306

dōzo 322
dyūsu 230

E

e 36, 62, 187, 274, 320
ē tī emu 97
ē-pī-esu kamera 270
ea firutā 202, 204
eā mattoresu 267
eabaggu 201
eakon 200
earobaiku 250
earobikusu 251
echiopia 317
eda 296
eda tsuno 291
edage 39
edamu chīzu 142
edawake suru 91
efude 274
egaku 162
eggu kappu 65, 137
ehagaki 112
ei 294
eiga 255
eiga no setto 179
eigakan 255, 299
eigyō bu 175
eihō 239
eikō-sen 215
eikoku 316
eisei antena 269
eishamaku 255
ejiputo 317
ejji 246
eki 208
ekika 127
ekitai keiryōki 311
ekitai senzai 77
ekitai-gusuri 109
ekonomi kurasu 211
ekuadoru 315
ekubo 15
ekuiti 97
ekurea 140
emarushon 83
emban-nage 234
embosu kabegami 83
emerarudo 288
empitsu 163, 275
empitsu-kezuri 163
emu di efu 79
emu-pī-surī purēyā 268
enamerushitsu 50
enchō jikan 223
enchō kōdō 78
enchō suru 168
enchū 164
endaibu 123
endo zōn 220
endōmame 122
endorain 226
engan-keibitai 217
engei 90
engei sentā 115
engei yōhin 88
engei-yō tebukuro 89

enjin 202, 204, 208, 210
enjo 322
enkei 164
enkin ryōyō 51
enko 164
enogu 274
enshi 51
enshū 164
ensui 164
entotsu 58, 214
epuron 30, 50, 69, 212
era 294
erebētā 59, 100, 104
erekigitā 258
eri 32
eritoria 317
erizukami 237
erusarubadoru 314
esa 244
esa o ataeru 183
esharotto 125
ēsu 230, 273
esu-efu eiga 255
esukarētā 104
esupuresso 148
esute 41
esutonia 316
etchingu 275
etsuran shitsu 168
etsuran suru 177

F

fagotto 257
faindā 271
fairingu kyabinetto 172
fairu 172, 177
faiyā sukurīn 63
fakkusu 172
fam beruto 203
famburu 220
fan 202, 258
fandēshon 40
fanhītā 60
fasshon 277
fasunā 277
fāsuto fūdo 154
fauru 223, 226
fauru bōru 228
fauru rain 229
feawei 232
feijoa 128
feisu 230
fenshingu 249
fenugurīku 132
ferī 215, 216
ferī noriba 216
fēsharu 41
fēsu kurīmu 73
fēsu masuku 225
fēsu pakku 41
fēsu-ofu sākuru 224
figyuasukēto 247
fiji 319
finrando 316
firamento 60
firipin 319
firo pesutorī 140

firudingu suru 229
firudo hokkē 224
firumu kauntā 270
firumu 260, 271
firutā 270
firutā kōhī 148
fito 310
fittonesu 250
fittonesu kigu 250
fō doa 200
foahando 231
fōku 65, 88, 153, 207
fōku 259
fōku rifuto 186
fōkurando shotō 315
fōkurifuto 216
fōmaru-na teien 84
fonto 177
foruda 177
foruto 230
fowādo 222
fuan 25
fuchi'ishi 298
fudansō 123
fudebako 163
fūdo 31, 75
fūdopurosessā 66
fudōsan-ya 115, 189
fuhenkashi 320
fujin fuku 105
fujin-ka 49
fujinka-i 52
fukami 239
fuke 39
fukikesu 141
fukkatsusai 27
fukkin 16
fukkin undō 251
fukku 187
fuku 77
fukuboku 47
fukurahagi 13
fukurashiko-iri komugiko 139
fukureru 151
fukuro 291, 311
fukurō 292
fukusayō 109
fukusha suru 172
fukushin 223
fukutsū 44
fukuyōki 211
fukyoku 167
fuminshō 71
fun 304
fune 214
funinshō 20
funka suru 283
funkakō 283
funkikō 290
funmatsu senzai 77
funnyū 137
funōshō 20
funsui 85
furaggu 232

furaggu posuto 221
furai 244
furai fisshingu 245
furaido chikin 155
furaido poteto 154
furaigaeshi 68
furaipan 69
furaishito 266
furajore mame 131
furamingo 292
furan 142
furansu 316
furashi 244
furasshu gan 270
furasuko 166
furatto 256
furatto uddo bitto 80
furattobureddo 139
furēku 132
furēmu 51, 206, 267
furenchi horun 257
furenchi purītsu 39
furenchi tōsuto 157
furetto 258
furī kikku 222
furī weito 250
furījia 110
furippā 239
furippu chāto 174
furīsu 74
furīsurō rain 226
furīzu 301
furo ni hairu 72
furonto 100
furonto garasu 198
furonto garasu senjōeki 199
furonto-gakari 100
furorentin 141
furōzun yōguruto 137
furui 89, 321
furui ni kakeru 91, 138
furūre 249
furūto 257
furūtsu gamu 113
furūtsu kēki 140
furūtsu pan 139
furūtsu sarada 157
furūtsu taruto 140
furūtsu yōguruto 157
fusa 122, 126
fūsui 55
fusuma 130
futa 61, 66, 69
futago 23
fūtō 98, 173
futoi 321
futomomo 12
futon 71
futōzai 199
futsū 39, 99
futsuryō giana 315
futsūyokin kōza 96
futtobōdo 71
futtobōru kyōgijō 220
futtobōru senshu 220
futtosutorappu 241
fuyu 31, 307

G
ga 295
gābera 110
gabon 317
gabyō 173
gaba 49
gachō 119, 293
gachō no tamago 137
gādo rēru 195
gādo shita tsūro 194
gaido-tsuki tsuā 260
gaika 97
gaikaku 282
gaikan 28
gaikiken 286
gaikokugo 162
gairaikanja 48
gaishoku 146
gaishutsu 75
gaisō 198
gaitō 298
gaiya 229
gaka 191, 274
gake 285
gakki 256, 258
gakkō 162, 299
gakkō no seifuku 162
gakkotsu 17
gaku 297
gakubu 169
gakubuchi 62
gakufu 255, 256
gakugyō 162
gakui 169
gakui-rombun 169
gakumen kingaku 97
gakunen 163
gakusei ryō 168
gakusei shokudō 168
gakushū 160
gambia 317
gamen 97, 176, 269
gamu 113
gan-ka 49
gāna 317
gānetto 288
gangiei 120, 294
gangiei no hire 120
ganka 49
ganseki 288
garagara 74
gārando 111
garapagosu shotō 315
garasu bin 166
garasubō 167
garasusei 69
gārikku puresu 68
garon 311
gārufurendo 24
gasorin 199
gasorin pompu 199
gasorin sutando 199
gasu konro 267
gasubānā 61
gasuketto 61
gasurenji 67
gātā 35

gatto 230
gaun 38
gazai-ya 115
gāze 47
gedan 141
geka 49
geka-i 48
geki 254
gekijō 254, 299
gekkei 20
gembugan 288
gēmu 230, 272, 273
gēmu bangumi 178
gen 258
gengakki 256
genkan 59
genkan matto 59
genkan-tō 58
genmai 130
genmon 214
gensō 214
genzai 304
genzō suru 271
gerende 246
gerende-gai 247
geri 44, 109
gesen suru 217
gesuidō 299
gēto bangō 213
getsuyōbi 306
gezai 109
gia bokkusu 202, 204
giana 315
gibo 23
gibusu 46
gichō o tsutomeru 174
gidai 174
gifu 23
gifuto shoppu 114
gijiroku 174
gikyōdai 23
gin 235, 289
gingakei 280
ginia 317
giniabisau 317
ginkō 96
ginkō furikomi 96
ginkō tesūryō 96
giri no shimai 23
girisha 316
gishigishi 123
gitarisuto 258
go 308
go banme 309
gōban 79
gogatsu 306
gogo 305
gōguru 238, 247
gohan 158
gohan-jawan 64
gohyaku 308
gojū 308
gojū banme 309
gokakkei 164
gokiburi 295
goma 131
goma'abura 134

goman 309
goman gosen gohyaku 309
gomi okiba 266
gomibako 61, 67, 172, 177
gomishori 61
gomishori-ki 61
gomubōto 215
gomuin 173
gomunagagutsu 89
gomuzōri 37
goraku 252
goraku kaden 268
gorira 291
gōru 221, 222, 223, 224, 234
gōru eria 223
gōru netto 226
gōru rain 220, 223, 224
gōru ringu 226
gorufā 232
gorufu 232
gorufu baggu 233
gorufu bōru 233
gorufu kāto 232
gorufu kōsu 232
gorufu kurabu 233
gorufu shūzu 233
gōrukīpā 222, 224
gōruposuto 220, 222
gōsei sen'i 31
gosenfu 256
goshigoshi arau 77
goshikku 301
goshin 237
gu 140, 155
guaba 128
guatemara 314
gun'yō 110
guraidā 211, 248
guraidingu 248
gurajiorusu 110
guramu 310
guranari bureddo 139
gurando 234
gurando kabā 87
gurando shīto 267
gurasu 150, 152
guratan-zara 69
gurauto 83
gurē 39
gurenada 314
gurēpu jūsu 144
gurēpufurūtsu 126
gurēzu o nuru 139
gurīn 232
gurin pīsu 131
gurīn sarada 158
gurīnrando 314
gurippu 230
gurirupan 69
gurōbu 224, 233, 237, 246
gurū gan 78
gurujia 318
gurūpu ryōhō 55
gūzuberī 127
gyokō 217
gyōmu 183
gyōretsu 27

日本語索引

gyorui 294
gyosen 217
gyūniku 118
gyūnyū 136, 156
gyūnyū kāton 136

H

ha 50, 89, 122, 296
ha no teire 72
haba 165
haba no hiroi 321
haba no semai 321
habu 206
hābu 86, 133, 134
hābu cha 149
hābu no bōda kadan 85
hābu to kōshinryō 132
hābu-en 84
haburashi 72
hachi 295, 308
hachi banme 309
hachidori 292
hachigatsu 306
hachijū 308
hachijū banme 309
hachō 179
hachūrui 293
hada no iro 41
hadagi 30, 33
hādo chīzu 136
hādo doraibu 176
hādobōdo 79
hādorusō 235
hādowea 176
hae 295
hafu 300
hāfu taimu 223
hagasu 82
hageatama 39
haguki 50
haha 22
hai 18, 52, 322
hai'iro 274
haichea 75
haichi 314
haidenki 203
haigūsha 23
haihīru 37
haikan setsubi 61
haikankō 188
haikei 254
haiki-kan 203, 204
haikingu 263
haikingu būtsu 37, 267
hairaito 39
hairan 20, 52
haisha 50, 189
haisui 91
haisuikan 61
haisuikō 72, 299
haisuikoku 61
haita 50
haitatsu 98
haitō 97
haiyaku 254
haiyū 179, 191, 254
haizara 150

hajime 321
hakari 69, 98, 118, 310
hakaru 310
hakase gō 169
hake 69, 83
hakike 44
hakka 133
hakka ame 113
hakkakkei 164
hakkō saseru 139
hako-gata fairu 173
hakozume chokorēto 113
haku 44, 77, 90
hakua 288
hakubutsukan 261
hakuchō 293
hakumai 130
hakunaishō 51
hakurikiko 139
hakusai 122
hakushu suru 255
hamaki 112
hambāgā 154, 155
hambāgā-ya 154
hami 242
hamigaki suru 50
hamigaki yōhin 108
hamigakiko 72
hammokku 266
hamu 119, 143, 156
hamusutā 290
hamusutoringukin 16
hana 14, 110, 291, 293, 297
hana no ana 14
hana sen 238
hana-gawa 242
hanabira 297
hanaji 44
hanareya 182
hanashiau 163
hanashigai no 118
hanasu 245
hanataba 111
hanawa 111
hanaya 110, 188
handa 79, 81
handagote 81
handazuke suru 79
hando doriru 78, 81
hando fōku 89
hando taoru 73
handobaggu 37
handoburēki 203
handoru 201
handorubā 207
hane 60, 293
hanebuton 71
hanemūn 26
hanga 275
hangā 70
hangari 316
hangigo 320
hangingu basuketto 84
hangu guraidā 248
hangu guraidingu 248
hanikamu 25, 134

hankachi 36
hankei 164
hanken 96
hanketsu 181
hansen 215
hanshakyō 50, 167
hanshazai 205
hantō 282
hanzai 94
hanzai-reki 181
hanzai-sha 181
hanzubon 30
happō 144
happyaku 308
hāpu 256
hara 12
harai 237
haraobi 242
hare 286
hari 186, 276
hari ita 276
hari ni kakaru 245
hari ryōhō 55
harigane 79
harikēn 287
hariko 191, 275
harinezumi 290
harisashi 276
harowīn 27
haru 307
hasami 38, 47, 82, 188, 276
hashi 64, 300
hashigo 95, 186
hashika 44
hashira 300
hashirihabatobi 235
hashiritakatobi 235
hashiru 229
hassha 281
hasshadai 281
hasui suru 52
hata 277
hatake 182
hataori 277
hatchibakku 199
hato 292
hatoba 216
hatoba ni tsukeru 217
hatsudenki 60
hatsukanezumi 290
hatsunetsutai 61
hawai 314
haya'ashi 242
hayabusa 292
hayai 305, 320, 321
hayaokuri 269
hazādo rampu 209
hazukashī 25
hazumi-guruma 276
hazuna 243
hea karā 39
heabando 38
heaburashi 38
headoraiyā 38
heakarā 40
heapin 38

heasupurē 38
heatai 39
hebi 293
hebī metaru 259
hechima 73
heddo raito 198, 205
heddo resuto 200
heddobōdo 70
heddogādo 236
heddohon 268
heddosēru 240
hedingu suru 222
heichi kyōsō 243
heihō fīto 310
heihō mētoru 310
heikan 260
heikindai 235
heikōbō 235
heikōsen 165
heikōshihenkei 164
heimen kikagaku-shiki teien 262
heimenzukei 164
heishi 189
heiya 285
hekimen shōmei 62
hemataito 289
hen'atsuki 60
hengan 288
henkyaku-bi 168
henmagan 288
henseigan 288
henshū-sha 191
hensoku ki 202, 206
hensoku rebā 201
hensoku suru 207
henzutsū 44
heon kigō 256
hera 68, 167
herikoputā 211
herumetto 95, 186, 204, 206, 220, 228, 242
heso 12
hesono'o 52
heya 58
heya bangō 100
heya no kagi 100
hēzerunattsu 129
hēzerunattsu oiru 134
hi o tsukeru 266
hi'iragi 296
hidari 260
hidari desu 323
hidari handoru 201
hidokei 262
hifu 14
hifu-ka 49
hifukukin 16
higashi 312
higashi timōru 319
hige 290
higesori 73
higesori kurīmu 73
higisha 180
hiji 13
hijikake 210
hijō kaidan 95

hijō rebā 209
hijō-guchi 210, 322
hikaekabe 301
hikidashi 66, 70, 172
hikigaeru 294
hikiniku 119
hikinobashi 271
hikiwake 223
hikiyoseru 245
hikōki o yoyaku suru 212
hikoku-gawa 181
hikokunin 181
hikotsu 17
hiku 165
hikui 321
himaraya sanmyaku 313
himarayasugi 296
himawari 184, 297
himawari abura 134
himawari no tane 131
himeji 120
himpan ni 320
hinagiku 110, 297
hinichi 306
hinin 21
hinode 305
hinyōki kei 19
hinyōki-ka 49
hiraita 321
hiraoyogi 239
hiraya 58
hire ashi 290
hire niku 119
hiroba 299
hirokuchi bin 311
hiryō 91
hiryō o yaru 91
hishi no mi 124
hishigata 164
hīsu 297
hisui 288
hītā 60
hītā chōsetsu 201
hitai 14
hitai-gawa 242
hito 10
hitode 295
hitokire 140
hitoribun 64
hitosashiyubi 15
hitsuji 185
hitsuji no mure 183
hiyake 41, 46
hiyake rōshon 265
hiyakedome 108, 265
hiyoko 185
hiyoko mame 131
hiza 12
hiza-take 34
hiza'ate 205
hizō 18
hizume 242, 291
hō 14
ho'on uea 267
ho'onzai 61
hobākurafuto 215

hōbeni 40
hochikisu 173
hōchō 68
hōchō togi-ki 68
hodō 262, 298
hōdō 178
hodoku 277
hofuku shokubutsu 87
hōgaku 169
hōgannage 234
hōgō 52
hogo megane 81
hōhi 21
hoikuki 53
hoippu kurīmu 137
hoīru 207
hoīru kyappu 202
hoīru natto 203
hojorin 207
hojoyoku 210
hōkaiseki 289
hoken 203
hoketsusenshu 223
hōki 77
hokkai 312
hokkē 224
hokkē-yō sutikku 224
hokkyoku 283
hokkyokuguma 291
hokkyokukai 312
hokkyokuken 283
hōkō shijiki 198, 204
hōkōda 210
hōkokusho 174
hokori o harau 77
hokoru 25
hokōsha-tengoku 299
hokubei 314
hokuro 14
hokyū suru 220, 229
homeopashī 55
homojinaizu 137
hōmu 208
hōmu bangō 208
hōmu bēsu 228
hōmu bu 175
hon 168
hon'i kigō 256
hon'ya 115
hondana 63
hone 17, 119, 121
hone o totta 121
honjurasu 314
honsha 175
honsō-gaku 55
honyūbin 75
honyūrui 290
horā eiga 255
hōrensō 123
hori 300
hōritsu 180
hōritsu jimusho 180
hōritsu sōdan 180
horu 90
hōru 232
hōru in wan 233
horumon 20

hōrutā nekku 35
hōseki 36, 288
hōseki-bako 36
hōseki-shō 188
hōseki-ten 114
hoshakukin 181
hōshasen-ka 49
hoshi 280
hoshibudō 129
hoshikusa 184
hōsō 179
hōsō suru 178
hōsō-shi 111
hosoi 321
hosshin 44
hōsu 89, 95
hōsu rīru 89
hōtai 47
hotategai 121
hōtei 180
hōtei kakari-kan 180
hotto doggu 155
hotto kokoa 144, 156
howaitingu 120
howaito 39
howaito chokorēto 113
howaitokaranto 127
hozon shori 118, 143, 159
hozon suru 177
hyakkajiten 163
hyaku 308
hyaku banme 309
hyakubunritsu 165
hyakujū 308
hyakuman 309
hyō 286
hyōdo 85
hyōga 284
hyōhakuzai 77
hyōketsu 287
hyōshiki 322
hyōshō dai 235
hyūzu 60
hyūzu bokkusu 203

I

i 18
ibiki o kaku 71
ibuningudoresu 34
ichi 308
ichi banme 309
ichi-ji han 304
ichi-ji jūgo-fun 304
ichiba 115
ichigan-refu kamera 270
ichigatsu 306
ichigo 127
ichigo no mirukusēki 149
ichijiku 129
ichijiteishi 269
ichiman 309
ichinensō 86
ichirin daisha 88
ido 283
ie 322
iemen 318

ierō kādo 223
igaku 169
igo 320
iguana 293
igunisshon 200
igusa 86
ika 121, 295
ikari 214, 240
ikari o orosu 217
ike 85
ikegaki 182
ikikata 260
ikkai 104
ikkai seki 254
ikkodate 58
ikōru 165
ikutsuka no 320
ima 62, 320
imin suru 26
imomushi 295
in-gōru 221
inago 295
inazuma 287
inchi 310
indekkusu 173
indo 318
indoneshia 319
indoyō 313
infuruenza 44
inga 271
ingashi 271
ingenmame 122, 313
ingurisshu burekkufāsuto 157
ingurisshu horun 257
ingurisshu masutādo 135
iningu 228
inko 293
inku 275
innō 21
insatsu suru 172
insei shokubutsu 87
inshin 20
insurin 109
insutanto kamera 270
insutanto shokuhin 107
insutōru suru 177
intabyūā 179
intāhon 59
intānetto 177
intāshiti ressha 209
intō 19
inu 290
inu-zori suberi 247
iō 289
ippōtsūkō 194, 298, 323
iraku 318
irakusa 297
iran 318
ireba 50
ireru 76
irezumi 41
iriguchi 59, 322
iro 274
iro-empitsu 163
iroai 41
iroguro 41
irojiro 41

iruka 290
iryō bumon 49
iryō sentā 168
ise ebi 121
isha 45, 189
ishikifumei 47
ishō 255
isozuri 245
isu 64
isuraeru 318
itachoko 113
itameru 67
itameta 159
itami-dome 47, 109
itaria 316
ito 276
ito annai 276
ito maki 276
ito o tōsu 277
itoko 22
itonoko 81
itsū 44
itsumo 320
itta 129
itten ageru 223
iwa 284
iwashi 120
iyakuhin 109
iyaringu 36
izen 320
īzeru 174, 274

J

jagaimo 124
jaguchi 61, 66
jaketto 34
jakki 203
jakku 273
jamaika 314
jampu 243, 247
jampu bōru 226
jampu suru 227
jamu 156
jānarisuto 191
janguru jimu 263
jankushon 194
jari 88
jazu 259
jeru 38, 109
jetto 288
jetto kōsutā 262
jettosukī 241
ji 304
ji'in 300
jibi'inkō-ka 49
jidō doa 196
jidō hikiotoshi 96
jidōsha 198, 200
jidōsha jiko 203
jidōsha rēsu 249
jigusō 78
jigusō pazuru 273
jikan 234, 261, 304
jikan-dōri 305
jikayō jettoki 211
jikken 166
jikken shitsu 166

jiko 46
jiko saikō kiroku 234
jikokuhyō 197, 209, 261
jimbabue 317
jimu 101
jimu kiki 172
jimu yōhin 173
jimusho 172, 174
jin 145
jinji bu 175
jinkōeisei 281
jinsei 26
jintai 17
jintai keitō 19
jintonikku 151
jintsū 52
jintsū sokushin suru 53
jinzō 18, 199
jioputā 51
jīpan 31
jipuchi 317
jishaku 167
jishin 25, 283
jisho 163
jitensha 206
jitensha ni noru 207
jitensha rakku 207
jitensha-dō 206
jizai supana 80
jō 59
jōba 242, 263
jōba muchi 242
jōba zubon 242
jōba-dō 263
jōba-gutsu 242
jōgi 163, 165
jogingu 251, 263
jōkā 273
jōki kikansha 208
jokō eki 41
jokyoku 256
jōmuin 210
jōmyaku 19
jōro 89
jōryokuju 86
jōsampu 53
josei 12, 20, 23
josei fuku 34
jōsen suru 217
jōsen-guchi 281
jōshaken 197
joshi seito 162
jōso 181
josō suru 91
josōzai 91, 183
jōwankotsu 17
joyū 254
jōzai 109
jū 308
jū banme 309
jūden-shiki doriru 78
jūdō 236
juerī seisaku 275
jūgatsu 306
jūgo 308
jūgo banme 309
jūgo-fun 304

jugyō 163
jūgyōin 24, 175
jūgyōin meibo 175
jūhachi 308
jūhachi banme 309
juhi 296
jūi 189
jūichi 308
jūichi banme 309
jūichigatsu 306
jūku/jūkyū 308
jūkyū banme 309
jūman 309
jumbi undō o suru 251
jūnan shiagezai 76
jūnana banme 309
jūnenkan 307
jūni 308
jūni banme 309
jūnigatsu 306
jūnishichō 18
junkan kei 19
junyū 53
junyū burajā 53
junyū suru 53
jūoku 309
jūroku 308
jūroku banme 309
jūryoku 280
jūsan 308
jūsan banme 309
jusei 20
jūshi/jūyon 308
jūshichi/jūnana 308
jushin suru 177
jushin-bako 177
jūsho 98
jūsu 149
jutai 52
jūtaku 58
jūtaku rōn 96
jūtaku-nai setsubi 60
jūtan 63
jūtenzai 83
juwaki 99
jūyon banme 309

K
ka 295
kā ōdio 201
ka'atsutai 45
kaba 291
kaban uriba 104
kabe 58, 186, 222
kabegami 82, 177
kabegami o harikaeru 82
kabegami o haru 82
kabegami-bake 82
kabegami-yō nori 82
kabin 63, 111
kabinda 317
kābingu fōku 68
kabocha 125
kabocha no tane 131
kabu 97, 124
kabuka 97
kabushiki 97

kabutomushi 295
kachiku 182, 185
kachinko 179
kadan 85, 90
kādigan 32
kadō 283
kādo 27
kādo sōnyū-guchi 97
kādo-shiki kōshū-denwa 99
kaede 296
kaeru 294
kaeshi 244
kagaku 162, 166
kagakusha 190
kagami 63, 71
kagi 59, 207
kagi hokku 276
kagibari 277
kagibariami 277
kago 106, 207
kagu 105
kaguya 115
kai'in sekkai 52
kaibaoke 183
kaichūdentō 267
kaidan 59
kaidan no tesuri 59
kaiga 261
kaigan 285
kaigara 265
kaigi 174
kaigi shitsu 174
kaigi wa nanji desuka 174
kaijo bumben 53
kaikan 260
kaikan jikan 322
kaikei 152
kaikeishi 97, 190
kaimono 102
kaimono-bukuro 106
kaiōsei 280
kairopurakutikku 54
kaisambutsu 121
kaisatsu-guchi 209
kaisha 175
kaisui pantsu 238
kaiten 238, 247
kaiten isu 172
kaitō suru 67
kaiyō teikisen 214
kaji 95, 241
kaji bō 240
kajino 261
kajū 127
kajuaruwea 33, 34
kajuen 183
kakaku 199
kakaku hyō 154
kakashi 184
kakato 13, 15, 37
kake 273
kakeashi 243
kakeru 165

kaki 121, 128, 239
kakimawasu 67
kakine 85, 90, 182
kakitome yūbin 98
kakkō 247
kakō 285
kakō kokumotsu 130
kakōgan 288
kaku 162
kaku-gōri 151
kakudai suru 172
kakudo 164
kakumaku 51
kakusei sōchi 209
kakushitsu jokyo suru 41
kakusui 164
kakuteru 151
kakutōgi 236
kamakiri 295
kamanbēru chīzu 142
kamban 104
kambō 181
kambōjia 318
kambu 174
kame 293
kamera 178, 260, 270
kamera dai 178
kamera kēsu 271
kamera-ya 115
kameraman 178
kamerūn 317
kami 14, 38
kami omutsu 30
kami pakku 311
kami yasuri 81
kamigata 39
kamikizu 46
kaminari 286
kamisori no ha 73
kamiyui 38
kamo 119, 185
kamome 292
kamomīru cha 149
kamotsu 216
kamotsu ressha 208
kamotsu-sen 215
kampai 323
kampan 214
kampari 145
kamu beruto 203
kamukōda 260, 269
kan 145, 202, 311
kan inryō 154
kan'yō shokubutsu 87
kānabi 201
kanada 314
kanamonoya 114
kanariya 292
kanashī 25
kanazuchi 80
kanden 46
kandokku 217
kānēshon 110
kanfū 236
kangarū 291
kangofu 45, 48, 52, 189
karai 124

kānibaru 27
kaniku 124, 127, 129
kanja 45
kanjō 25
kanjō kōsaten 195
kanjuku 129
kanketsusen 285
kankikō 210
kankin suru 97
kankiri 68
kankisen 66
kankitsu rui 126
kankō 260
kankō annai-jo 261, 322
kankō annaisho 260
kankō basu 197, 260
kankō gaido 260
kankō kyaku 260
kankō meisho 260
kankō rūto 260
kankoku 318
kankyaku 254
kankyō 278
kanmi supureddo 134
kanna 81
kanna o kakeru 79
kannakuzu 78
kannuki 59
kanri jimusho 266
kansan ritsu 97
kanseitō 212
kansen 44
kansetsu 17
kanshasai 27
kanshi 53, 167
kanshi'in 265
kanshitō 265
kanshu 181
kanshū 233
kansō 129, 130
kansō hada 41
kansō shita 286
kansō shitsu 39
kansōki 76
kantan na 321
kantoku 254
kantori 259
kanū 214, 241
kanzō 18
kanzō ame 113
kanzume 107
kanzume yōki 311
kao 14
kaori no aru 130
kāpetto 71
kapoeira 237
kappu-gata yōki 311
kappuru 24
kapuchīno 148
kapuseru 109
kara 129, 130, 137
kārā 38
kara hanarete 320
kara no 321
kara o muita 129
karada 12
karai 124

karakuchi 145
karamatsu 296
karanto 129
karashi no tane 131
karasu 292
karasumugi 130
karate 236
karē 158
karēko 132
karendā 306
kari'ireru 183
karibukai 312
karidashi 168
karifurawā 124
karikomi-basami 89
karikomu 90
kāringu 247
kariningurādo 316
karinui suru 277
kariru 168
karishakuhō 181
kāru 39
kāru airon 38
karudamon 132
karui 321
karuishi 73, 288
karūseru 212
karushiumu 109
karute 48
kasa 36, 233
kasai keihōki 95
kase 277
kasei 280
kaseigan 288
kasetto purēyā 269
kasetto tēpu 269
kashi 113, 259, 296
kashi rui 107
kashidashi kauntā 168
kashiya 113
kashu 191
kashūnattsu 129, 151
kassōro 212
kasu 58
kasumisō 110
kasupikai 313
kasutādo 140
kasutādo kurīmu 140
kasutamā sābisu 104
kata 13
katagami 276
katai 129, 129, 321
katamaran 215
katamari niku 119
katāru 318
katate nabe 69
katatsumuri 295
katei 56, 62
katei saien 85
katei yōhin 107
kāten 63
katēteru 53
kāto 100, 106, 208, 213
katsu 273
katsudō 263
katsura 39
kattā 80

kattā naifu 81
kattēji chīzu 136
katto suru 38
kaunserā 55
kauntā 96, 98, 100, 142, 150
kawa 119, 126, 127, 128, 136, 142, 284
kawa o muita 121
kawa o muku 67
kawagishi 284
kawagutsu 32, 37
kawaita 321
kawajan 205
kawakasu 76
kawamuki-ki 68
kawauso 290
kaya 267
kayakku 241
kayōbi 306
kazafusutan 318
kazambai 283
kazan 283
kazari 141
kazan 283
kaze 44, 241, 286
kazoeru 165
kazoku 22
keana 15
kebabu 155, 258
kēburu 79, 207
kēburu kā 246
kēburu terebi 269
kechappu 135
kega 46
keiba 243
keibajō 243
keibatsu 181
keibi 212
keibi'in 189
keibō 94
keibu 52, 94
keido 283
keiga kyōsō 243
keihikōki 211
keiji 94
keijiban 173
keikan 94, 189
keikoku 284
keikōtō 94
keikotsu 17
keimusho 181
keiran 137
keiri bu 175
keiryō 310
keiryō jagu 69
keiryō kappu 311
keiryō supūn 109
keiryōki 150
keiryū 285
keiryū sakugu 217
keiryū suru 217
keisatsu 94
keisatsusho 94
keisei-geka 49
keisenchū 214
keishō 23

keitai denwa 99
keitai mēru 99
keito 277
keitsui 17
keizaigaku 169
kēki 140
kēki to dezāto 140
kēki yaki-gata 69
kēki-zukuri 69
kēkiya 114
kekka 49
kekkon hirōen 26
kekkon suru 26
kekkonshiki 26, 35
kembikyō 167
kemuri 95
kemuri hōchiki 95
ken 17
ken'insha 203, 212
kenchiku 300
kenchiku yōshiki 301
kenchiku zairyō 187
kenchiku-ya 186, 188
kenchikuka 190
kendō 236
kenia 317
kenjū 94
kenkasei teiboku 87
kenkashokubutsu 297
kenkō 42, 44, 323
kenkō na 321
kenkō shokuhin-ten 115
kenkōkotsu 17
kenkyū 169
kenma suru 82
kensa 49
kensaku suru 177
kensatsuin 209
kensetsu 186
kenshi 50
kensui suru 251
kenuki 40
kēpā 143
keri 237, 239
keru 221, 223
kēru 123
kesagatame 237
keshi 297
keshi no mi 138
keshi'in 98
keshigomu 163
keshōdai 71
keshōhin 41, 105, 107
keshōsui 41
kessai-bako 172
kesshite nai 320
kessoku himo 89
kēsu 51
keta 186
ketchappu 154
ketorudoramu 257
ketsuatsu 44
ketsuatsukei 45
ketsueki kensa 48
kezuru 79
ki 86, 296
kī 176

ki'iro 274
kiba 291
kibi 130
kībōdo 172, 176, 258
kidō 280
kifuhō 256
kiji 119, 276, 289
kikagaku 165
kikai 187
kikaikōzō 202
kikan 18
kikan shitsu 214
kiken 195, 322
kikkubokushingu 236
kiku 110
kikuimo 125
kimi 157
kimon 247
kimono 35
kimpōge 297
kin 235, 289
kin'en 322
kin'en seki 152, 323
kin'yōbi 306
kin'yū 128
kin'yū adobaizā 97
kinembi 26
kinenhi 261
kingaku 96
kingu 272, 273
kingyo 294
kinkan 126
kinkan gakki 257
kinkyū chiryō-shitsu 48
kinkyū denwa 195
kinkyūjitai 46
kinniku 16
kinō 306, 320
kinoa 130
kinri 96
kinsei 280
kinsen 97
kinshi 51
kintei surippu 77
kinteki 273
kintoki mame 131
kinu 277
kinzoku 79, 289
kinzoku-yō bitto 80
kion 286
kipaddo 97, 99
kippu 209
kippu uriba 209, 216
kipurosu 318
kirei na 321
kiri 287
kirieda 91
kirifuki 89, 311
kirigisutan 318
kirikizu 46
kirimi 119, 121
kirin 291
kiroguramu 310
kiroku 234
kiroku o yaburu 234
kirōmētoru 310

kiru 67, 79, 273, 277
kiru 214
kirutingu 277
kiruto 71
kisetsu 307
kisetsu mono 129
kishō 286
kishu 210, 242
kiso-gawa 180
kissuisen 214
kita 312
kita chōsen 318
kita hankyū 283
kita kaikisen 283
kitai 210
kitanai 321
kitchin 152
kitsuen 112
kitsuen seki 152
kitsune 290
kitsune-no-tebukuro 297
kitsutsuki 292
kitte 98, 112
kitte shūshū 273
kiwi 128
kiza 242
kizami-tabako 112
kizetsu suru 25
kizu 46
kizuchi 275
ko-azarashi 290
ko-uma 185
ko-ushi 185
kō'unki 182
koara 291
kōbo 138
kobu 291
kōbu doa 198
kōbu zaseki 200
kōbu zaseki 204
kobushi 15, 237
kobuta 185
kōcha 144, 149, 156
kochira ga ue 98
kōchō 217
kōchō sensei 163
kodachitomato 128
kodara 120
kōdo 211
kōdō 169
kodomo 23, 31
kodomo fuku 30
kodomo no ie 75
kodomo yōhin uriba 104
kodomobeya 74
kōdoresu denwa 99
koeda 296
kōen 262
kōenshō-zai 109
kōfun suru 25
kōgai 19, 299
kōgaku 169
kogamo 185
kōgeki 220
kogite 241
kogitte 96
kogitte-chō 172

kogu 206, 207, 241
kōgu sashi 186
kōgu-dana 78
kōgyōdanchi 299
kōhaikin 16
kōhan-bi 180
kōhi 144, 148, 153, 156, 184
kōhi mēkā 148, 150
kōhi mirukusēki 149
kōhi supūn 153
kōhi tēburu 62
kōhi-fun 144
kōhi-mame 144
kōhikappu 65
kohitsuji 185
koi 294
koin randori 115
koinu 290
kōji gemba 186
kōjō 299
kōjōsen 18
kōka 97
kōka na 321
kōka-shiki kōshū-denwa 99
kōkai 313
kokan 12
kōkanshu 99
kōkka 315
kokkai 313
kokkaku 17
koko 320
kōkō suru 240
kokoa paudā 148
kōkoku 315
kokonattsu 129
kokotto 69
kōkū bokan 215
kokuban 162
kōkūbin 98
kokuen 289
kōkūken 213
kōkūki 210
kokunai bin 212
kokuritsu kōen 261
kokurui 130
kokuryū 130
kokusai bin 212
kokuso 94
kokuyōseki 288
kōkyaku sābisu bu 175
kōkyōkyoku 256
kokyū 47
kokyūki kei 19
koma 272
kōmaku-gai masui 52
komamono 105
kōmāsharu 269
kombain 182
kombanwa 322
kome 130, 184
komedi 255
komekami 14
komezu 135
kōmi abura 134
komi shefu 152

komichi 58, 85
kōmori 290
komoro 317
kompakuto 40
kompakuto disuku 269
kompakuto kā 199
kompakuto mirā 40
kompasu 165, 240, 312
kompyūta 176
komugi 130, 184
komugiko 138
komuragaeri 239
komyunikēshon 98
kōn yu 135
kon'yakusha 24
kon'yakusha 24
kona chīzu 136
kōnā furaggu 223
kōnā kikku 223
kona-gusuri 109
kondishonā 38
kondōmu 21
koneko 290
koneru 138
kongo 317
kongo minshu kyōwakoku 317
kōnisu 300
konkōsu 209
konkurīto burokku 187
konkurīto mikisā 186
konnichiwa 322
kōnotori 292
konran suru 25
konro 67
konsāto 258
konsento 60
konshīrā 40
konshū 307
konsome 158
konsōru 269
kontakutorenzu 51
kontena 216
kontena-sen 215
kontenakō 216
kontora fagotto 257
kontorabasu 256
kontorōrā 269
koppu rui 65
kōra 144, 293
korāju 275
korekuto kōru 99
kōri 120, 287
kōri nashi 151
kōri to remon 151
kōri-basami 150
kōri-iri 151
koriandā 133
kōrin 197
kōrogi 295
koromia 315
kōrudopuresu yu 135
koruku sen 134
koruku sennuki 150
kōrurabi 123
korusetto 35
korushika 316
kōryū denryū 60

kōsai 51
kōsaku nōjō 183
kōsaten 298
kōseki 289
koshi 12, 169
kōshi niku 118
kōshinryō 132
koshitsu 48
koshō 64, 152, 203
koshō no mi 132
koshōchū 322
kosobo 316
kōsoku bōto 241
kōsoku dōro 194, 323
kōsoku mōtābōto 214
kōsoku ressha 208
kossetsu 46
kōsu ryōri 153
kōsui 41
kōsui uriba 105
kosuritoru 77
kosuru 77
kōsutā 150
kosutarika 314
kotae 163
kotaeru 163
kōtaku 271
kote 187
kotēji gāden 84
kōto 32, 226, ,227
kōtō 19
kōtōgai 19
kōtojibowāru 317
kōtsū 192, 194
kōtsū junsa 195
kōtsū jūtai 195
kotsuban 17,
kotsufun 88
kotton bōru 41
kottōya 114
kowagaru 25
kōwan 214, 216
kowaremono 98
koyagi 185
koyōnushi 24
koyubi 15
kōza bangō 96
kōzai 79
kōzan shokubutsu 87
kozara 65
kōzui 287
kozutsumi 99
ku/kyū 308
kubaru 273
kubi 12
kubisuji 13
kuchi 14
kuchibashi 293
kuchibeni 40
kuchibiru 14
kudamono 107, 126, 128
kudamono jūsu 156
kudamono kago 126
kudōjiku 202
kūfuku 64
kugatsu 306

kugi 80
kui 90
kuiki 299
kuīn 272, 273
kujaku 293
kujakuseki 289
kujira 290
kuki 111, 122, 297
kūki ni sarasu 91
kūki-doriru 187
kūki'ire 207
kukki 113
kūkō 212
kuma 291
kumade 88
kumin 132
kumo 287, 295
kumori 286
kuni 315
kunsei 118, 121, 143, 159
kunsei nishin 157
kuōto 311
kura 242
kurabu 273
kurabu-sando 155
kurabuhausu 232
kurafuto naifu 82
kurage 295
kurai 321
kuraianto 180
kurakushon 201, 204
kurampu 78, 166
kuranberī 127
kurarinetto 257
kurashikku kā 199
kurashikku ongaku 255
kurasshikku 259
kurasupu 36
kuratchi 200, 204
kurejitto kādo 96
kurementin 126
kurēn 216
kurēn-sha 187
kurenzā 41
kurēpu 155
kureson 123
kuri 129
kuriketto 225
kuriketto bōru 225
kuriketto senshu 225
kurīmu 109, 140, 157
kurīmu chīzu 136
kurīmu hachimitsu 134
kurīmu pai 141
kūringu rakku 69
kurīningu-ya 115
kurippubōdo 173
kurīsu 225
kurisumasu 27
kurisupu bureddo 139, 156
kurīto 240
kuritorisu 20
kuro 272, 274, 321
kuro komugiko 138
kuro obi 237
kuro orību 143
kuro pan 139, 149

kuroachia 316
kurōbā 297
kurobīru 145
kurōbu 133
kurokami 39
kurokodairu 293
kurome mame 131
kurōru 239
kurosu torēnā 250
kurosu-kantorī 247
kurosubā 222
kurowassan 156
kurubushi-take 34
kurumaebi 121
kurumaisu 48
kurumaisu taiō 197
kurumi 129
kurumi abura 134
kusa 87
kusachi 285
kusatta 127
kushami 44
kushi 38, 68
kushi de suku 38
kussakuki 187
kusukusu 130
kusuriyubi 15
kutsu 34, 37
kutsu uriba 104
kutsuhimo 37
kutsuhimo ana 37
kutsushita 33
kutsuya 114
kutsuzoko 37
kuwa 88
kuwēto 318
kyabetsu 123
kyabin 210
kyadi 233
kyaku 38, 64, 96, 104, 106, 152
kyakusha 208
kyakushitsu 100, 209
kyakushitsu-zuki basurūmu 100
kyambasu 274
kyamisōru 35
kyampasu 168
kyampingu kā 266
kyampingu torērā 266
kyampu 266
kyampu beddo 266
kyampu suru 266
kyampufaiyā 266
kyampujō 266
kyappu 21
kyarameru 113
kyarawei shido 131
kyaria 204
kyarīkotto 75
kyaserōru nabe 69
kyatatsu 82
kyatchā 229
kyō 306
kyōdai 22
kyōfū 286
kyōgi 243, 247

kyōgijō 223
kyōkai 299, 300
kyōkaku 17
kyōkasho 163
kyōkin 16
kyōkotsu 17
kyokuchi 282
kyokusen 165
kyori 310
kyōriki 139
kyōshi 190
kyōshitsu 162
kyōsō 234
kyōsōba 243
kyōtsui 17
kyū 164
kyū banme 309
kyūba 314
kyūba ribure 151
kyūhyaku 308
kyūin kappu 81
kyūji suru 64
kyūji-yō supūn 68
kyūjō 228
kyūjo-in 239
kyūjū 308
kyūjū banme 309
kyūka 212
kyūkei jikan 254
kyūki sōchi 199
kyūkon shokubutsu 86
kyūkyū iryō tai'in 94
kyūkyū sosei 47
kyūkyūbako 47
kyūkyūsha 94
kyūmei bōto 240
kyūmei bui 240
kyūmei dōi 240
kyūmeitei 214
kyūnyūki 44, 109
kyūri 125
kyūryō 175, 284
kyūryū 241, 284
kyūseki 261
kyūshi 50
kyūshi torei 172
kyūshika 256
kyūsui-kō 61
kyūsuikan 61
kyūyujō 199

M
mabuta 51
machiai-shitsu 45
machibari 276
machikado 298
madagasukaru 317
made 320
made ni 320
mado 58, 186, 197, 210
madoguchi 96, 98
madorā 150
mafin 140
mafin-gata 69
mafurā 31, 203, 204
māgarin 137
mago 23

日本
語
索
引

mago musuko 22
mago musume 22
magu kappu 65
maguma 283
maguneshiumu 109
maguro 120
magusa 186
mahōbin 267
maiku 179, 258
maikuro basu 197
maikuroraito 211
mainasu 60, 165
mairu 310
maishū 307
maitā bokkusu 81
maitoshi 307
maitsuki 307
majipan 141
majoramu 133
makademianattsu 129
makedonia 316
makeru 273
makijaku 80
makimodoshi 269
maku 67, 254
māku suru 227
makurakabā 71
makurame 277
mama chichi 23
mama haha 23
mama musuko 23
mama musume 23
mamerui 130, 131
mampuku 64
manabu 163
manaita 68
manchego chīzu 142
manējā 24, 174
manga-bon 112
mangetsu 280
mangō 128
manhōru 299
manikyua 41
manriki 78
manshon 59, 298
manshon-tō 59
mantoru 282
mantorupīsu 63
manyuaru 200
marakasu 257
marason 234
marawi 317
mare ni 320
marēshia 318
mari 317
marīna 217
marine 143, 159
maruchi bitamin 109
marugoto 129, 132
marui kogata pan 140
marukubi 33
marumero 128
marunoko 78
maruta 316

maruyane 300
mashin-gan 189
mashita 320
mashumaro 113
massāji 54
masshurūmu 125
massugu 260
masu 120
masui-shi 48
masukara 40
masukingu tēpu 83
masuku 189, 228, 239, 249
masume 272
masutādo 155
masuto 240
matchi 112, 230
mategai 121
matenrō 299, 300
matīni 151
mato 249
matsu 296
matsu no mi 129
matsuge 14, 51
matsuri 27
matto 54, 235, 267
mattoresu 70, 74
maue 320
maunten baiku 206
mausu 176
mausu pīsu 237
mausu wosshu 72
mayonaka 305
mayonēzu 135
mayu 295
mayuge 14, 51
mazeru 67, 138
me 14, 51
medama kurippu 173
medamayaki 157
medaru 235
megane 51
megane-ten 51
megane-ya 189
mei 23
meiōsei 280
meirei 180
meisho 261
meisō 54
mejā 276
mejā kappu 150
mekajiki 120, 294
mekishiko 314
mekyabetsu 123
mēkyappu 40
memo 175, 191
memori 176
memori kādo 271
men 158, 164, 236, 277
menka 184
menkai jikan 48
menō 289
menseki 165, 310
menyū 148, 153, 154
menyūbā 177
menzeiten 213
mēpuru shiroppu 137
merange 140

merodī 259
meron 127
mēru adoresu 177
mēru akaunto 177
messēji 100
messhu kāten 63
mesu 167
mēsu 132
mētoru 310
meushi 185
mezamashi o kakeru 71
mezamashi-dokei 70
mezameru 71
mi 122, 296
michi annai 323
michita 321
midori 274
midori orību 143
migaku 77
migi 260
migi desu 323
migi handoru 201
mijikai 32
mijukuji 52
mikazuki 280
mikessai-bako 172
miki 296
mikisā 66
mikishingu bōru 66, 69
mikkusu sarada 158
mimi 14, 139
mimizu 295
minami 312
minami afurika 317
minami hankyū 283
minami kaikisen 283
minato 217
mineraru wōtā 144
mini disuku rekōda 268
minibā 101
minikui 321
minto tī 149
mippū bin 135
miriguramu 310
mirimētoru 310
mirittorru 311
miruku 136
miruku chokorēto 113
miruku kōhī 148
miruku tī 149
mirukusēki 137, 149
misairu 211
mishin 276
mītobōru 158
miton 30
mītopai 158
mitsuami 39
mitsubachi 295
mitto 228
mitto 236
miyagemono 260
mizambīku 317
mizore 286
mizu 144, 238
mizu jetto 95
mizu o hiku 183
mizu o yaru 90

mizu'umi 285
mizuabi pūru 263
mizubukure 46
mizugi 238, 265
mizuhane bōshi-ban 66
mizukiri zaru 68
mizukiridai 67
mizukusa 86
mizumizushī 127
mizusashi 65, 151
mizuyari 89
mobīru 74
mochikaeri 154
mōchō 18
modemu 176
moderu 169
mōfu 71, 74
mokei 190
mokei seisaku 275
mokkan gakki 257
mokkō 275
mokkō-yō doriru bitto 80
mokkō-yō setchakuzai 78
mōkon 39
mokusei 280
mokusei supūn 68
mokutan 275
mokutekichi 213
mokuyōbi 306
mokuzai 79, 275
mokuzai chakushokuzai 79
mōmaku 51
momo 126, 128
momoniku 119
mon 85, 182
monako 316
mondai 271
mongōika 121
mongoru 318
monitā 53, 172, 176
monohoshi-yō rōpu 76
monoporī 272
monorēru 208
monsūn 287
montāju shashin 181
monteneguro 316
moppu 77
mōrishasu 317
mōritania 317
morokko 317
mōrudingu 63
mōrudoba 316
morutaru 187
moruto su 135
moshimoshi 322
mōshitate 94
mosuku 300
mōtā 88
motokurosu 249
motsarera chīzu 142
motto warui 321
moya 287
moyashi 122
moyō sentaku 276
mu-shibō 137
muchiuchishō 46

muen 137, 199
mujitsu 181
mukade 295
mukiebi 120
muko 22
mukōtaku 271
munabire 294
mune 12
muneniku 119
mūnsutōn 288
mura 299
murasaki 274
murasaki igai 295
mure 183
mūrugai 121
musekitsui dōbutsu 295
musen-yō antena 214
mushi-sasare 46
mushiba 50
mushita 159
mushiyoke 108, 267
musu 67
mūsu 141
musuko 22
musume 22
muzai 181
muzukashī 321
myakuhaku 47
myūjikaru 255

N
nadare 247
nae 91
nafuda 189
nagagutsu 31
nagai 32
nagasa 165, 310
nagashi 66
nagashidai 61, 72
nage 237
nageru 221, 227, 229, 245
naibumpi kei 19
naibumpi-ka 49
naifu 65
naijeria 317
naikaku 282
nairon 277
naisō 200
naisō kōji 82
naisō kōji shokunin 82
naito 272
naitogaun 31, 32, 35
naiya 228
naizō 18, 118
naizō furasshu 270
naka 320
nakaniwa 58, 84
nakayubi 15
naku 25
nama 124, 129
nama chīzu 136
nama kuriīmu 137
namaniku 142
nambā purēto 198
nambei 315
namekuji 295
nami 241, 264

namiashi 243
namibia 317
namida 51
namigata 139
nan 139
nan'yō 313
nana 308
nana banme 309
nanahyaku 308
nanajū 308
nanajū banme 309
nankō 47, 109
nankotsu 17
nanzai 79
napukin 65, 152
napukin ringu 65
nashi de 320
nasu 125
natane 184
natane abura 135
natauri 124
natsu 31, 307
natsume 129
natsumeggu 132
natto 80
nattsu 129, 151
nawatobi 251
naya 85
naya 182
ne 50, 124, 296
nebukuro 267
nedan 152
nega 271
negurije 31, 35
neji 80
nekku 258
nekkurain 34
nekkuresu 36
neko 290
nekutai 32
nekutaipin 36
nekutarin 126
nemaki 31
nembangan 288
nendo 85, 275
nenryō tanku 204
nenryōkei 201
nenryōtanku 203
nenza 46
neōi suru 91
nepāru 318
neru 71
netsu 44
netsuken 286
netsukikyū 211
nettai 283
nettai kajitsu 129
netto 222, 227, 231
nettowāku 176
nezumi 290
ni 308
ni banme 309
ni mukatte 320
ni sotte 320
ni-ji 304
nichibotsu 305
nichiyōbi 306

nídoru penchi 80
nídorupointo 277
nigai 124
nigatsu 306
nihon 318
nihyaku 308
nijēru 317
niji 287
nijimasu 120
nijū 308
nijū banme 309
nijūichi 308
nijūichi banme 309
nijūni 308
nijūni banme 309
nijuppun 304
nijūsan banme 309
nikai 104
nikai seki 254
nikaidate basu 196
nikaragua 314
nikkeru 289
nikkōyoku o suru 264
nikomu 67
nikonda 159
niku 107, 118
niku fukku 118
nikukiribōchō 68
nikutataki 68
nikuya 114, 118, 188
niman 309
nimotsu 100, 198, 213
nimotsu hikiwatashi 213
nimotsuire 210
nin 129
ninensō 86
ningen kankei 24
ningyō 75
ninjin 124
ninniku 125, 132
ninshin 52
ninshin dekiru 20
ninshin shiteiru 52
ninshin suru 20
ninshin tesuto 52
niranegi 125
nire 296
nisen nen 307
nishi 312
nishi sahara 317
nishoku-tsuki 101
nishūkan 307
nisu 79, 83
nitchū 305
nitōkin 16
niwa 84
niwa no akusento 84
niwa no shokubutsu 86
niwa no yōshiki 84
niwashi 188
niwatori 185
no aida 320
no jōhō 320
no kahō 320
no mae 320
no mukaigawa 320
no mukō 320

no naka e 320
no soba 320
no ue 320
no ue e 320
no ushiro 320
nobasu 251
nochi 304
nōchi 182
nochihodo 320
nodo 19
nodo ame 109
nodobotoke 19
nōfu 182, 189
nōjō 182
nōka 182
nōka no niwa 182
noki 58
nokku auto 237
nokogiri-ba 78
nomi 81
nomimono 107, 144, 156
nori 275
nori-zuke dai 82
noribake 82
norikaeru 209
norikumi'in 241
noritsugi 212
noruwē 316
noshibō 69
nōshintō 46
nōsorōbu 34
nōsuki 195
nōto 163, 172, 173
nōto o toru 163
nōtopasokon 175, 176
nozuru 89
nu'u 277
nugā 113
nuigurumi 75
nuime 34, 277
nunoji 277
nyō kan 21
nyōdō 20
nyōdō 20
nyūbachi 167
nyūbō 167
nyūeki 41
nyūgaku jimukyoku 168
nyūgaku suru 26
nyūin 48
nyūji 23
nyūjirando 319
nyūjō muryō 322
nyūjō-ryō 260
nyūkin suru 96
nyūkin-sho 96
nyūkoku shinsa 213
nyūseihin 107, 136
nyūsū 178
nyūsukyasutā 179, 191
nyūtō 137
nyūtoraru zōn 224

O

o 121, 242, 280, 290, 292, 294
o mawatte 320
o tōtte 320
o yokogitte 320

o-susume ryōri 152
o-tearai 104
o-tsumami 151
o-ushi 185
oba 22
ōbā pā 233
ōbāfurō kan 61
ōbāheddo purojekutā 163
ōbāōru 30
obi 236
obikiyoseru 245
ōboe 257
oboreru 239
ōbun 66
ōbunmitto 69
ōdan hodō 195
odango 39
ōdio shisutemu 268
odomētā 201
ōdōri 299
odoriba 59
odoroku 25
ōdotoware 41
ofisu 24
ofisu biru 298
ofu saido 223
ōfuku bunri dōro 195
ōhanmā 187
ohayō gozaimasu 322
ohyō no kirimi 120
oi 23
oikoshi shasen 194
oikosu 195
oiru 199
oiru gēji 202
oiru tanku 204
oita 321
oiwai 27, 140
oiwai-yō kēki 141
oji 22
ōkakumaku 19
ōkami 290
okan 44
ōkē 322
ōkesutora 254, 256
ōkesutora pitto 254
ōki 321
okiru 71
okoru 25
okosama menyū 153
okujō teien 84
okura 122
okure 209
okuyuki 165
ōkyū teate 47
ōmān 318
omaru 74
omocha 75, 105
omocha kago 75
omoi 321
omori 166, 244
omoshiroi 321
ompu 256
ōmu 293
ōmugi 130, 184
omuretsu 158
omutsu 30, 75

omutsu kabā 30
omutsu kabure kurīmu 74
omutsu kae baggu 75
omutsu kae shito 74
ondokei 167
ondori 185
ongaku 162
ongaku gakkō 169
ongaku janru 259
ongakuka 191
ongakukai 255
onigiri 154
ōningu 148
onkai 256
onna no ko 23
onrain 177
onryō 179, 269
onsei messēji 99
onshitsu 85
onsu 310
onsui tanku 61
onsui tappu 72
opāru 288
opera 255
ōpun kā 199
ōpun toppu 260
ōpun-sando 155
oranda 316
oregano 133
orenji 126
orenji iro 274
orenji jūsu 149
orenjiēdo 144
orību 151
oribuyu 134
origami 275
orimage genkin 98
ōrora 286
oroshigane 68
oroshita 121
ōru 241
ōrusupaisu 132
orutanēta 203
osae 237, 276
osage 39
oshibe 297
oshikomi gōtō 94
oshiri fuki 74
oshiroi 40
osoi 305, 320
osu 322
ōsutorarēshia 319
ōsutoraria 319
ōsutoria 316
otafukukaze 44
otama 68
otamajakushi 294
ōtobai 204
ōtobai rēsu 249
otoko no ko 23
ōtoma 200
otona 23
ototoi 307
otsuri 99
otto 22
owari 321
ōya 58

yasuminasai 322
yayubi 15
yyogu 238
yoso 320
azara 65
zonsō 286

ぅ
ぁ 233
waddo 53, 220
vadokku 243
vadoru 241
vafu 40
vāgora 84
vai 143
vai kiji 140
vai yaki-zara 69
vainappuru 128
vainappuru jūsu 149
vainto 311
vaipu 112
vaipu kattā 81
vairotto 190, 211
vajama 33
vākingu mētā 195
vakisutan 318
vakku 224, 311
vāma 39
van 138, 157
van kiji 138
van rui 107
van shokunin 139
van-zukuri 138
van'ya 114, 138
vanama 314
vanchi baggu 237
vanda 291
vankēki 157
vanko 139
vanku 203, 207, 259
vanku shūri setto 207
vansuto 34, 35
vanti 35
vanti rainā 108
vapaia 128
vapuanyūginia 319
vapurika 132
varaguai 315
varaguraidingu 248
varashūto 248
varashūto kōka 248
varasoru 148
varetto 186, 274
varittoshita 127
varumetto yashi no shin 122
varumezan chīzu 142
vaseri 133
vasokon 172
vāsonaru torēnā 250
vasshonfurūtsu 128
vasu 226
vasu suru 220, 221
vasuta 158
vasuteru 274
vatā 233
vatchi 207

patchiwāku 277
pate 142, 156
patokā 94
patto o utsu 221
paudā 132
pedaru 61, 206
pedikyua 41
pedimento 301
pegu 258, 266
pemparu 24
pen 163
penarutī 223
penaruti eria 223
penchi 80
pendanto 36
pengin 292
penisu 21
penki 83
pensaki 163
pēpā napukin 154
peparoni 142
perikan 292
perū 315
pessarī 21
pesutori 140, 149
petto fūdo 107
petto shoppu 115
piano 256
pikannattsu 129
pikkoro 257
pikkuappu 258
pikkunmikkusu 113
pikunikku 263
pikunikku benchi 266
pikurusu 159
pīman 124
pimboke 271
pin 60, 249
pīnattsu 129, 151
pīnattsubatā 135
pinku 274
pinsetto 47, 167
pinto o awaseru 271
pipetto 167
piratisu 251
piru 21
pisutachio 129
pita pan 139
pitchā 229
pitchā maundo 228
pitchi 225, 256
piza 154, 155
piza-ya 154
pōchi 58
pōkā 273
poketto 32
pōn 272
pondo 310
ponītēru 39
poppukōn 255
poppusu 259
popura 296
popuri 111
pōrando 316
poriesuteru 277
porijji 157
poro 243

pōru 266
porutogaru 316
posutā 255
posutā karā 274
pōtā 100
pōtaburu shī-dī purēyā 268
poteto chippusu 113, 151
poteto masshā 68
pōto 176
pōtoforio 97
pōtorēto 271
pōtowain 145
puchi tomato 124
pudingu raisu 130
puerutoriko 314
purachina 289
puragu 60
puraimā 83
puramu 126
purasu 60, 165
purasu doraibā 80
purattofōmu shūzu 37
purē no sen 233
purēto 283
purēyā 268, 273
purezentā 174
purezentēshon 174
purezento 27
purin 141
purinta 172, 176
purodyūsā 254
puroguramu 176, 254
purojekutā 174
puropera 211, 214
purosessa 176
puroshutto 143
pūru 101, 238, 249, 250

R
raberu 89, 172
rabu 230
radisshu 124
rafu 232
rafutingu 241
ragubī 221
ragubī bōru 221
ragubī senshu 221
ragubī-gī 221
ragubī-jō 221
raibu 178
raimame 122, 131
raimu 126
raimugi pan 138
rain jajji 220
raion 291
raishū 307
raisu pudingu 140
raitā 112
raito 207
raito suitchi 201
rajiētā 60, 202
rajio 179, 268
rajio kyoku 179
rajio o tsukeru 269
raketto 230, 231
raketto supōtsu 231
raketobōru 231

rakkasei yu 135
rakku 221
rakuda 291
rakunōjō 183
rakurosu 249
rakuyōju 86
ramadān 27
ramikin 69
rampaku 137
rampu 62, 217
rampusutēki 119
ramu 176
ramu niku 118
ramushu 145
ran 111, 228
ran'ō 137
ranchon matto 64
randosukēpu 271
ranhō 20
ranjerī 35, 105
ranji 251
rankan 20
ranningu shatsu 251
ranshi 20, 51
ransō 20
raosu 318
raperu 32
rappu 259
rappu-sando 155
rarī 230, 249
ratobia 316
raudo supīkā 268
raundo 237
razuberī 127
razuberī jamu 134
rebā 61, 118, 150
rebā'āchi-shiki fairu 173
rebanon 318
rēdā 214, 281
reddo kādo 223
reddokaranto 127
rege'e 259
reggu paddo 225
reggu puresu 251
reginsu 31
regyurētā 239
rei 308
rei ten go rittoru 311
reijō 180
reiki ryōhō 55
reikyakueki tanku 202
reinkōto 31, 32
reishi 128
reisui tappu 72
reitō 121, 124
reitō shokuhin 107
reitō suru 67
reitōko 67
reitōreizōko 67
reizōko 67
reji 106, 150
reji-gakari 106
rēki 88
rekigan 288
rekishi 162
rekishi-teki kenzōbutsu 261
rekkā idō 195

rekōdo-ten 115
remon 126
remon garei 120
remon kādo 134
remon tī 149
remonēdo 144
remongurasu 133
rēn 234, 238
ren'ai monogatari 255
ren'ai suru 26
renchi 81, 203
renga 187
renmei 223
rennyū 136
renshū-jiai 237
rentakā 213
rentogen 48
rentogen byuā 45
rentogen kensa sōchi 212
rentogen shashin 50
renzoku dorama 178
renzu 51, 270
renzu kēsu 51
renzu kyappu 270
renzumame 131
repōtā 179
rēru 208
rēsā 249
reshību suru 227
rēshingu baiku 205
resoto 317
ressha 208
restoran 101
rēsu 35
rēsu-yō bobin 277
rēsuami 277
resuringu 236
resutoran 152
retāheddo 173
retasu 123
retsu 210, 254
retto 230
ribaundo 226
riberia 317
ribia 317
ribon 27, 39, 111, 141, 235
rīdo shingā 258
rifu tī 144
rifurekusorojī 54
rifurekutā 204, 207
rifuretto 96
rifuto 246
rigakuryōhō-ka 49
rigin 240
rihitenshutain 316
rikon 26
riku-game 293
rikuchi 282
rikujō kyōgi 234
rikujō kyōgi-sha 234
rikyūru 145
rīmā 80
rimokon 269
rimpa kei 19
rimu 206
rimujin 199
rinchi 285

日本語索引

rinden 296
rinen 277
ringo 126
ringo jūsu 149
ringo no shin nuki-ki 68
ringo su 135
ringoshu 145
ringu 237
ringu tai 89
rinjin 24
rinku 36
rippōtai 164
rippu burashi 40
rippu gurosu 40
rippu rainā 40
rirakusēshon 55
rirē kyōsō 235
ririku suru 211
rīru 244
risaikuru bokkusu 61
risu 290
risutobando 230
ritān 231
ritoania 316
rittaizukei 164
rittoru 311
roba 185
rōbai suru 25
robī 100, 255
robu 231
rōbu 169
robusutā 121, 295
rodeo 243
rōdo baiku 206
rōdo rēsā 206
rōganberī 127
rogo 31
roguon suru 177
rōingu mashīn 250
roji 298
rojō kafe 148
rokata 194
rokettosarada 123
rokkā 239
rokkaku-bō renchi 80
rokkakukei 164
rokkankin 16
rokkī sanmyaku 312
rokkotsu 17
rokku 207
rokku konsāto 258
rokku kuraimingu 248
rokoko 301
roku 308
roku banme 309
rokuga 178, 269
rokugatsu 306
rokujū 308
rokujū banme 309
rokuon sutajio 179
rokuro 275
romen densha 196, 208
romen hyōshiki 194
rompāsu 30
rōn 96
roppyaku 308
rōpu 248, 266

rōrā 83, 187
rōrā ukezara 83
rōrāburēdo 263
rōrāsukēto 249
rōrāsukēto-gutsu 249
rōrie 133
rōru 311
rōru sukurīn 63
rōrupan 139, 143
rosen bangō 196
roshi 167
roshia rempō 318
roshutsu 271
roshutsu hosei daiyaru 270
roshutsu-busoku 271
roshutsu-ōbā 271
roshutsukei 270
rōsoku 133
rōsuto 158
rōsuto suru 67
rōtā burēdo 211
roten 154
rōto 166
roze (wain) 145
rōzumarī 133
ruā 244
rubī 288
rūfu rakku 198
rūku 272
rukusemburuku 316
rūmania 316
rūmu sābisu 101
runesansu 301
rūpin 297
rusuban denwa 99
rūtā 78
rutabaga 125
rutsubo 166
ruwanda 317
ryōchō 119
ryōdo 315
ryōgaejo 97
ryōhōshi 55
ryoken 213
ryōkin 197, 209
ryōkin-jo 194
ryokō dairiten 114, 190
ryokō kogitte 97
ryokō panfuretto 212
ryokōkaban 37
ryokucha 149
ryokutō 131
ryōseirui 294
ryōshi 189
ryōshin 23
ryōshūsho 152
ryūchijō 94
ryūju 247
ryukkusakku 31, 37, 267
ryūsei 280
ryūzan 52

S

saba 120
sābā 176
sabaku 285
sābisu purobaida 177

sābisu-ryō 152
saboten 87
sābu 231
sābu rain 230
sābu suru 231
sadoru 206
sāfā 241
safaia 288
safari pāku 262
sāfin 241
sāfubōdo 241
safuran 132
sagan 288
sagefuri 82
sagyō-sha 212
sagyōba 78
sagyōdai 78
sahara sabaku 313
sai 291
saibai suru 91
saibankan 180
saibansho shokuin 180
saido dekki 240
saido ōdā 153
saidorain 220, 226, 230
saien 182
saifu 37
saigo 320
saihō-bako 276
saihosō 187
saijōdan 141
saikoro 272
saikuringu 263
saimin ryōhō 55
sairen 94
sairo 183
saisei 269
saisho 320
saito 266
sakago 52
sakana 107, 120
sakana no kunsei 143
sakanaya 114, 120, 188
sakaya 115
sake 120, 152
sākitto torēningu 251
sakkā 222
sakkā bōru 222
sakkā senshu 222
sakkā shūzu 223
sakkā-gi 31, 222
sakkā-jō 222
sakkin 47
sakotsu 17
saku 74, 85
sakubun 163
sakugu 215
sakumotsu 183, 184
sakunyū-ki 53
sakurambo 126
sakurasō 297
sakusofon 257
sambashi 217
sambedo 41
sambyaku 308
same 294
sāmosutatto 61

samui 286
san 23, 308
san banme 309
sandā 78
sandaru 31, 37
sandoitchi 155
sandoitchi uriba 143
sandopēpā 83
sangai 104
sangai seki 254
sangatsu 306
sangoshō 285
sangurasu 51, 265
sanhanki 52
sanjū 308
sanjū banme 309
sanjuppun 304
sanka 49
sanka byōtō 48
sanka-i 52
sankakkei 164
sankaku-kōn 187
sankakufu 46
sankakujōgi 165
sankakukin 16
sankō shiryō 302
sankyaku 166, 270, 281
sanmarino 316
sanmyaku 282
sanrūfu 202
sanruishu 228
sanshō'uo 294
sanshoku-tsuki 101
sansū 165
sansukurīn 108
santōkin 16
santome purinshipe 317
sao 245
sapōtā 227
sapurimento 55
sara 65
sara'arai-ki 66
sarada 149
sarada doresshingu 158
sarada yu 135
sarami 142
sāroinsutēki 119
saru 291
sarudinia 316
sarutana rēzun 129
sasaebō 89, 91
sashidashinin jūsho 98
sashimi 121
sasori 295
sasu 90
sasupenshon 203, 205
satchūzai 89, 183
satōkibi 184
satōzuke kudamono 129
satsuire 37
satsuma mikan 126
satsumaimo 125
saujiarabia 318
sauna 250
saundo enjinia 179
saundotorakku 255
sawā kurīmu 137

sawādo buredo 139
saya 122
sayoku 228
sayōnara 322
se no hikui 321
se no takai 321
sebire 294
sebone 17
sēbu suru 223
sedai 23
sedan 199
sēfu 228
sei kansenshō 20
seibi kōjō 199
seibugeki 255
seibutsu 162
seichō dankai 23
seifuku 94, 189
seigen sokudo 195
seihatsu suru 39
seihyōshitsu 67
seijigaku 169
seikatai seki 301
seikei dōgu 275
seikei-geka 49
seiki 12, 307
seikō 20
seikotsu ryōhō 54
seikyoku 167
seinō 21
seiri yōhin 108
seiri-yō napukin 108
seiseki 163
seishi 20
seishi suru 91
seishin-ka 49
seishoku 20
seishokuki 20
seishokuki kei 19
seisō 21
seisōken 286
seitai 19
seiten 286
seito 162
seiuchi 290
seiun 280
seiyōwasabi 125
seiyu 55
seiza 281
sēji 133
sekai chizu 312
seki 44
sekidō 283
sekidō ginia 317
sekidome 108
sekiei 289
sekika 126
sekitan 288
sekitei 84
sekiyu tankā 215
sekizai 275
sekizai-yō doriru bitto 80
sekkai-shitsu dojō 85
sekkaigan 288
sekken 73
sekken-zara 73
sekyuriti bitto 80

sembankakō suru 79
sembi 240
semento 186
semidetatchi 58
semihādo chīzu 136
semisofuto chīzu 136
semorina 130
semotare 64, 210
sempatsu 39
sempūki 60
sen 19, 72, 165, 309
sen kyūhyaku ichi nen 307
sen kyūhyaku jū nen 307
sen kyūhyaku nen 307
sen'i 127
sen'in 189
senaka 13
senaka arai burashi 73
senaka no kubomi 13
senbikampan 214
senchimētoru 310
senchō 214
senegaru 317
sengaiki 215
senjō eki 51
senkan 215
senkyaku 216
senkyaku-kō 216
senkyō 214
senmon'i 49
senmongakkō 169
sennenkan 307
sennuki 68, 150
senrei 26
senro 209
sensei 54, 162
sensha 199
senshin 230
senshitsu 214
senshu 214, 240, 307
senshuken 230
sensō 215
sensuikan 215
sentā 228
sentā sākuru 222, 224, 226
sentābōdo 241
sentai 214, 240
sentakki 76
sentaku 76
sentaku kansōki 76
sentaku-basami 76
sentakukago 76
sentakumono 76
sentakumono ire 76
sentan 36, 122
sentārain 226
sentei noko 89
sentei-basami 89
sentō 300
sentobinsento oyobi gurenadin
  shotō 314
sentōki 211
sentokurisutofā névisu 314
sentorushia 314
senza 77

seoyogi 239
seramikku konro 66
sēringu 240
serori 122
seroriakku 124
serotēpu 173
sēru 241
serubia 316
serufu tanningu kurīmu 41
sesshi 50
sētā 33
setchi pin 60
setsugan renzu 167
setsuzoku suru 177
setto 178, 230, 254
setto suru 38
shaberu 265
shābetto 141
shachō 175
shadamben 61
shahen 164
shakkotsu 17
shako 58
shakuyanin 58
shamen 284
shampan 145
shampū 38
shampū dai 38
shāpu 256
shārē 166
sharin 198
sharin-tsuki tanka 48
shasei kan 21
shashī 203
shashin 270, 271
shashin hantei 234
shashin satsuei 271
shashin-yō gakubuchi 271
shashinka 191
shasō 209
shatai 202
shatoru 231
shatoru basu 197
shattā 270
shattā sokudo tsumami 270
shawā 72
shawā doa 72
shawā jeru 73
shawā kāten 72
shawā o abiru 72
shawā tō 266
shawāheddo 72
shefu 152, 190
shefu no bōshi 190
shēkā 150
sherī 145
shī-dī purēyā 268
shi 308
shiai 237
shiatsu 54
shiatsu ryōhō 55
shiba de ōu 90
shibafu 85, 90, 262
shibakari suru 90
shibakariki 88, 90
shiberia 313
shibori bukuro 69

shichaku shitsu 104
shichi 308
shichigatsu 306
shichijū 308
shichimenchō 119, 185, 293
shichiria 316
shichōsha 299
shichū 158
shida 86
shierareone 317
shifuto rebā 207
shigai 298
shigaisen 286
shigatsu 306
shigoto 170
shiharai 96
shiharau 153
shihei 97
shijōkaihatsu bu 175
shijū 308
shika 291
shika kenshin 50
shika niku 118
shika rentogen 50
shika yunitto 50
shikai-sha 178
shikakkei 164
shikame-zura 25
shikan 50
shiken 163
shikenkan 166
shikenkan-tate 166
shiki dai 256
shiki'ishi 85
shikibetsu bandō 53
shikibō 256
shikiri kādo 173
shikisha 256
shikke no ōi 286
shikkui 83
shikkui o nuru 82
shikō 57
shikyū 20, 52
shikyū keibu kakuchō 52
shikyūkei 20
shima 282
shima hōzuki 128
shimai 22
shimamenō 289
shimatta 321
shimauma 291
shimbaru 257
shimbun 112, 178
shimbun hambaiten 112
shimetta 321
shimo 287
shimon 94
shimpai suru 25
shimpan 222, 226, 227, 229, 230
shin 122, 127, 173
shin kyabetsu 123
shin'yōju 86
shinai 236
shinamon 133
shinchō-kei 45
shindai koshitsu 209

shindo 91
shingapōru 318
shingetsu 280
shingō 194, 209
shingu 74
shingu taoru rui 105
shinguru 151
shinguru beddo 71
shinguru kurīmu 137
shinguru rūmu 100
shingurusu 230
shinjaga 124
shinju no kubikazari 36
shinkai-zuri 245
shinkansen 209
shinkei 19, 50
shinkei kei 19
shinkei-ka 49
shinkotenshugi 301
shinkū kappu 53
shinkuronaizudo suimingu 239
shinnyū kinshi 195, 323
shinri ryōhō 55
shinrin 285
shinrui 23
shinryō-shitsu 45
shinryōjo 48
shinsatsu 45
shinseiji 53
shinsen 121, 127
shinshi fuku 105
shinshitsu 70
shintaishō 235
shintaishōgaisha-yō chūsha
  supēsu 195
shinu 26
shinzō 18, 119
shinzōbyō-ka 49
shinzōhossa 44
shio 64, 129, 152
shio-furi 121
shio-iri 137
shioaji 155
shiomizu-zuke 143
shiozuke 143
shirā 83
shirakaba 296
shiretsu kyōsei burijji 50
shiri 13
shiria 318
shiriaru 156
shirindā heddo 202
shirīzu bangumi 178
shiro 145, 272, 274, 300, 321
shiro komugiko 138
shiro pan 139
shiroari 295
shiromi niku 118
shiroppu 109
shiroppu-zuke 159
shirudo 80
shiryō dai 167
shiryoku 51
shiryoku kensa 51
shisha 175
shishinkei 51

shisho 168, 190
shishū 277
shisō 263
shisshin suru 44
shisutemu 176
shisutemu techō 173
shita 19
shita e 320
shitagi 32
shitagoshirae shita tori 119
shītake 124
shitanuri 83
shitateya 115, 191
shitchi 285
shitenchō 96
shito 204, 241
shito beruto 198, 211
shito pirā 206
shitsu 71, 74
shitsugaikotsu 17
shitsumon 163
shitsumon suru 163
shiwa 15
shiwa tori 41
shiyō kigen 109
shiyō-chū 321
shizen ryōhō 55
shizuka na 321
shoberu 88
shōbōsha 95
shōbōshi 95, 189
shōbōsho 95
shōbōtai 95
shōchō 18
shōdoku eki 47, 51
shōdoku waipu 47
shōga 125, 133
shōgai hietsu 243
shōgai kyōsō 243
shōgaibutsu 243
shōgakuhin 169
shōgatsu 27
shōgeki o ukeru 25
shōgo 305
shohōsen 45
shoka 168
shōkai 49
shōkaki 95
shōkaki kei 19
shōkasen 95
shōken torihiki-jo 97
shokkaku 295
shokki 64
shokki rui 65
shokkidana 62
shokku 47
shōko 181
shoku 280
shokubutsu 296
shokudō 19
shokudō-sha 209
shokugyō 188, 190
shokuhin uriba 105
shokuji 64, 75, 158
shokuminchi 315
shokumu 92
shokupan no katamari 139

日本語索引

shokuryohin 106
shokuryohin-ten 114
shokuyō abura 134
shokuzenshu 153
shōkyūshi 50
shomei 96, 98
shōmei 178
shōmei kigu 105
shōmeidan 240
shōmen genkan 58
shōni byōtō 48
shōni-ka 49
shonichi 254
shōnin 180
shoppingu sentā 104
shorudā paddo 35, 224
shorudābaggu 37
shosai 63
shōsetsu 256
shōsha 273
shōten 298
shōten chōsetsu nobu 167
shōtō 300
shōtorihiki 175
shōwakusei 280
shōyu 135
shōzō 260
shū 306, 315
shū-gawa 140
shubi suru 225
shukketsu 46
shukkin irai-sho 96
shukkō suru 217
shukudai 163
shukuhaku kyaku 100
shukuhaku-sha meibo 100
shukushō suru 172
shūmatsu 306
shuppatsu bin 213
shuppatsu robī 213
shūrikō 188, 203
shusai 153
shūshi gō 169
shūshoku suru 26
shūsō baggu 88
shussan 53
shussan mae 52
shussan suru 26
shussei shōmeisho 26
shussei-ji taijū 53
shusseki suru 174
shussui-kō 61
shutchō 175
shuto 315
shūto suru 223, 227
shutō uchi 237
shutsunyū dōro 216
shutsunyū-ro 194

shutsunyūkoku kanri 212
sobakasu 15
sobo 22
sōbōkin 16
sobyō 275
sōda pan 139
sōdasui 144
sode 34, 254
sodeguchi 32
sofa 62
sofa beddo 63
sofu 22
sofubo 23
sofuto 176
sofuto chīzu 136
sofuto dorinku 144, 154
sōgankyō 281
sōgen 285
sōji 77
sōji dōgu 77
sōji sābisu 101
sōjifu 188
sōjiki 77, 188
sōju shitsu 210
soketto 80
soketto renchi 80
sokki-sha 181
sōko 216
sōkō shasen 194
sokudokei 201, 204
sokutei 165
sokuten 235
sōkyū suru 223
somaria 317
sonata 256
sonota no mise 114
soramame 122, 313
sori suberi 247
soromon shotō 319
sōsakei 201, 204
sōsēji 118, 155, 157
sōshiki 26
sōshin suru 177
sōshingu 36
sōshō anken 180
sosogu 67
sōsu 135, 143, 155
soto 320
sotogawa 320
sotsugyō suru 26
sotsugyō-rombun 169
sotsugyō-shiki 169
sotsugyō-shōsho 169
sotsugyōsei 169
su 135, 142
suberidai 263
suburi 233
suchiru'ūru 81
suchuwādesu 190
sūdan 317
suettopantsu 33
sufure 109
sūgaku 162, 164
sūgaku yōhin 165
sugikoshimatsuri 27
suichi ryōhō 55
suichoku-anteiban 210

suichokusen 165
suichūyoku-sen 215
suidōsui 144
suiei 238
suiei senshu 238
suiei yōhin 238
suiei-bō 238
suigin 289
suihei-biyoku 210
suiheiki 187
suijō hikōki 211
suijō supōtsu 241
suijōsuki 241
suijōsuki ita 241
suijōsukiya 241
suika 127
suikazura 297
suikeiki 80
suikomi hōsu 77
suikyū 239
suimin 74
suimin'yaku 109
suimubōdo 238
suingu suru 232
suionkei 201
suisai enogu 274
suisei 280
suiseki 288
suisen 111
suishitsu 61
suishō ryōhō 55
suishōtai 51
suisu 316
suitchi 60
suitō 44, 206, 267
suīto chokorēto 113
suitō-gakari 96
suiyōbi 306
suiyōsei 109
suizō 18
suji 126
sūji 308
sukāfu 36
sukī 246
sukī ita 246
suki-gutsu 246
suki-jō 246
sukimu miruku 136
sukinkea 108
sukīwea 246
sukīya 246
sukoabōdo 225
sukoppu 89, 187
sukoshi 307
sukotchi 151
sukūpu 149
sukuraburu 272

sukuramburu eggu 157
sukuramu 221
sukurēpā 82
sukurōrubā 177
sukūru basu 196
sukuryū doraibā 151
sukūtā 205
sukuwatto 251
sukyan 48, 52
sukyanā 176
sukyūba daibingu 239
sumasshu 231
sumi 266
sumimasen 322
sumō 237
sumomo 129
sumpō 165
suna 264
suna no shiro 265
sunaba 263
sunakku bā 148
sunappu 30
sunatsuchi 85
sune 12
sunea doramu 257
sunīkā 31, 37, 251
sunōbōdo 247
sunōkeru 239
sunōmōbiru 247
sunōsūtsu 30
sunūkā 249
supaiku 233
supāku puragu 203
sūpāmāketto 106
supana 80
supea ribu 155
supea taiya 203
supēdo 273
supein 316
supēsu shatoru 281
supīdo kukku 130
supīdo otose 323
supīdo sukēto 247
supika 176, 258
supīkā sutando 268
supin 230
supoito 109, 167
supōku 207
suponji 73, 74, 83
suponji fingā 141
suponji kēki 140
supōtsu 218
supōtsu firudo 168
supōtsu fisshingu 245
supōtsu jaketto 33
supōtsu jimu 250
supōtsu kā 199
supōtsu yōhin 105
supōtsu-yō burajā 35
supōtsuman 191
supottoraito 259
suppai 127
sūpu 153, 158
supūn 65
supurē 109
supurē kan 311
supureddo 135

supuringu 71
supuringu onion 125
supurinkurā 89
supuritto pi 131
supuroketto 207
sūpuru 245, 271
sūpusupūn 65
sūpuzara 65
suraidingu suru 229
suraido 167
suraisā 139
suraisu 139, 230
suraisu shokupan 138
surakkusu 34
surasutā 281
surī doa 200
surī-pointo rain 226
suribachi 68
surikizu 46
surikogi 68
surinamu 315
suriorosu 67
surippa 31
surippon 37
surippu 35
surīpusūtsu 30
surirā 255
suriranka 318
surō-in 223, 226
surobakia 316
surobenia 316
surottoru 204
sushi 121
sūshiki 165
suso 32
susugu 76
sutaffudo orību 143
sutāfurūtsu 128
sutampu 225
sutampu dai 173
sutando 88, 166, 205, 207, 268
sutansu 232
sutātingu burokku 234
sutāto dai 238
sutāto rain 234
sutemu 112
sutenresu 79
sutenshiru 83
suteppā 250
sutereo 269
sutēshonwagon 199
sutikku 133, 224, 249
sutiru 144
sūto 273
sutokkingu 35
sutokku 246
sutoppā 166
sutoppuwotchi 234
sutoraiku 228
sutorappu 35, 37
sutorappuresu 34
sutorēnā 68
sutoresu 55
sutoretchi 251
sutorēto 39
sutorēto ni suru 39
sutorō 144, 154

sutorōku 231, 233
sūtsu 32
suwajirando 317
suwēden 316
suzu 289
suzuki 120
suzume 292

T

ta no kōgei 275
ta no supōtsu 248
tabako 112, 184
tabako hitohako 112
tabemono 116, 149
taberu 64
tābochājā 203
tabun 322
tachioyogi suru 239
tadashī 321
tagayasu 183
tāgetto shageki 249
tai 120, 318
tai'iku 162
tai'in 48
taiban 52
taiburēku 230
taibutsu renzu 167
taifū 286
taiheiyō 312
taihi 88
taihi-zumi 85
taiho 94
taiji 52
taijū suru 223
taijū-kei 45
taikakusen 164
taikiken 282, 286
taikyokuken 237
taimā 166
taimingu 203
taimu 133
taimu auto 220
tainetsusei 69
taionkei 45
tairiku 282, 315
tairu o haru 82
tairyūken 286
taiseiyō 312
taiseki 165
taisekigan 288
taishoku suru 26
taisō kyōgi 235
taisō senshu 235
taitsu 251
taiwan 319
taiya 198, 205, 206
taiya kūkiatsu 203
taiya o kōkan suru 203
taiya rebā 207
taiyō 280, 282
taiyōkei 280
ajikisutan 318
akai 321
akarakuji 112
akasa 165
akatobikomi 239
ake 86

takenoko 122
taki 285
takkingu suru 241
takkuru 245
takkuru bokkusu 244
takkuru suru 220, 221, 223
takkyū 231
tako 121, 295
takomētā 201
takuhai 99, 154
takusan 320
takushī no untenshu 190
takushī noriba 213
tamago 137
tamanegi 124
tambarin 257
tamburā 65
tameiki o tsuku 25
tāminaru 212
tamo 244
tampa 179
tampan 33
tampon 108
tampopo 123, 297
tan 118
tana 66, 67, 106
tandemu jitensha 206
tane 88, 122, 127, 128, 130, 131
tane o maku 183
tane o ueru 90
tane-iri pan 139
tanemaki torei 89
tanenashi 127
tanensō 86
tangutsu 37
taniku shokubutsu 87
tanima 284
tanjerin 126
tanjō 52
tanjō pātī 27
tanjōbi 27
tanjōbi kēki 141
tanjōbi kēki no rōsoku 141
tanka 94
tanku 239
tankyori sōsha 234
tanryū 130
tanshin 50, 304
tansu 70
tansui-zuri 245
tanuki 290
tanzania 317
taoru 73
taorukake 72
tappu 150
tara 120
taragon 133
taroimo 124
tarukamu paudā 73
taruki 186
tārumakku 187
taruto-gata 69
tasu 165
tasumania 319
tatchi rain 221
tatchiauto suru 229
tatchidaun 220

tategami 242, 291
tatemono 299
tatemono to kōzō 300
tateru 186
tatsu-no-otoshigo 294
tauhausu 58
taunhausu 58
tawara 184
tazuna 242
te 13, 15, 273
teate 47
tebaniku 119
tebiki noko 81
tebukuro 36
tēburu 64, 148, 210
tēburu settingu 65, 152
tēburukurosu 64
techō 175
tedibea 75
tefuron kakō 69
tegami 98
tei-shigeki sei 41
teian sho 174
teiden 60
teien 261
teiki kankōbutsu 168
teiki-ryokakki 210, 212
teimen 164
teiō sekkai 52
teionsakkin 137
teionsakkin shiteinai 137
teire suru 91
teisha botan 197
teisha kinshi 195
teishi 269
teishibō niku 178
teishibō-nyū 136
teitetsu 242
tejō 9
tekīra 145
tekondō 236
tekubi 13, 15
tekunikku 79
tēma pāku 262
tembin 166
tembōtō 215
tempu shorui 177
tempuku suru 241
ten 273
ten'in 104, 188
tenimotsu 211, 213
tenisu 230
tenisu kōto 230
tenisu senshu 231
tenisu-gutsu 231
tenji-hin 261
tenjō 62
tenkan 44
tenmongaku 281
tennai inshoku 154
tennen sen'i 31
tennōsei 280
tenohira 15
tenrankai 261
tentaibōenkyō 281
tenteki 53
tento 267
tento o haru 266

tentōmushi 295
teoshi suru 241
tēpu kattā 173
tērādo 35
terasu 58
terasu gāden 84
terasu kafe 148
terebi gēmu 269
terebi o kesu 269
terebi o miru 269
terebi o tsukeru 269
terebi sutajio 178
terepin-yu 83
teroppu 179
tēru raito 207
tēru rampu 204
tesuri 59, 196
tesūryō 97
tetsu 289
tetsubō 235
tetsubun 109
tetsudō-mō 209
tetsugaku 169
tī 233
tī baggu 144
tī guraundo 232
tīkappu 65
tīn'ējā 23
tīpotto 65
tīshatsu 30, 33
tishotto o uchidasu 233
tisshu 108
tisshu no hako 70
tīsupūn 65
tō 300
to issho ni 320
tō kurippu 207
tō sutorappu 207
to'on kigō 256
tobi-geri 237
tobi-ita 238
tobikomi 239
tobikomi senshu 238
tobikomi sutāto 239
tobikomu 238
tobira 209
tobu 211
tōbu gaishō 46
tōchaku bin 213
tōdai 217
todana 66
todana rokku 75
tofī 113
tōgarashi 132, 143
toge 46
tōgei 275
togi-bō 118
tōgo 317
togurubotan 31
tōhi 39
tōi 320
toiawase 168
toire 61, 266
toire burashi 72
toiretto pēpā 72
toishi 81
tōjiki 105

tōjōken 213
tokage 293
tokei 62, 304
tokei-tsuki rajio 70
toko ni tsuku 71
tōkotsu 17
tokoya 39, 188
tokubai 322
tokubaihin 106
tokuten 220, 273
tōkyū suru 225, 229
tomare 323
tomato 125, 157
tomato jūsu 144, 149
tombo 295
tomegane 37
tōmei hachimitsu 134
tomodachi ni naru 26
tōmorokoshi 122, 130, 184
tōmorokoshi pan 139
ton 310
tōnamento 233
tongu 167
tonikku wōtā 144
tōnyōbyō 44
topāzu 288
topiari 87
toppingu 155
toppu 246
toppu chūbu 207
tora 291
toraffuru 113
toragu 88
torai 221
toraianguru 257
toraifuru 141
torakku 194, 234
torakku no untenshu 190
torakkusūtsu 31, 32
torakutā 182
torampetto 257
torampu 273
torampu hito-kumi 273
toranku 198
toranku rūmu 196
toreddo 207
toreddomiru 250
torei 152, 154
torekkingu 243
torēn 35
torēnā 33
torēningu suru 251
torērā 266
torerisu 84
tori 119
tōri 298
torigoya 185
torihikisaki 175
torimā 88
torinidādo tobago 314
toriniku 119
toronbōn 257
tororī basu 196
toruko 318
torukoishi 289
torukumenisutan 318
torumarin 288

toryō baketsu 83
toryō-yō shinnā 83
toryufu 125
toshi 299, 306, 307
tōshi 97
tosho kādo 168
tosho mokuroku 168
toshokan 168, 299
tosō suru 83
tōsuto 157
tōsuto-sando 149
totte 37, 88, 106
tōyaku 109
tōzayokin kōza 96
tsū doa 200
tsuarā 205
tsubame 292
tsubasa 210, 293
tsubomi 111, 297
tsubu masutādo 135
tsubushita 132, 159
tsuchifumazu 15
tsūden rēru 209
tsūgaku kaban 162
tsugiki suru 91
tsuihi suru 90
tsuin rūmu 100
tsukaisute 109
tsukaisute kamera 270
tsukaisute kamisori 73
tsukeru 130
tsuki 237, 280, 306
tsukichakurikusen 281
tsūkinsha 208
tsūkō kinshi 323
tsukue 162, 172
tsukurō 277
tsuma 22
tsumaranai 321
tsume 15, 291, 293
tsumekiri 41
tsumekiri-basami 41
tsumemono 50, 159
tsumetai 321
tsumitoru 91
tsumu 91
tsumujikaze 287
tsunagi 83
tsunagu 91
tsuno 291
tsurara 287
tsuri 244
tsuri kyokashō 245
tsuri no shurui 245
tsuri'ito 244
tsuribari 244
tsuribito 244
tsurigane suisen 297
tsūringu jitensha 206
tsurisage-shiki forudā 173
tsuriwa 235
tsurizao 244
tsūro 106, 168, 210, 212, 254
tsuru 245, 292
tsurubā 177

tsuruhashi 187
tsurusei shokubutsu 87
tsutsugiri 121
tsutsumi 311
tsūwa-chū 99
tsuyadashi 83
tsuyadashizai 77
tsuyakeshi 83
tsuyoi 321
tsuzuru 162

U
ubaguruma 75
uchigawa 320
uchiwasaboten 128
uchū 280
uchū sutēshon 281
uchū tanken 281
uchūfuku 281
uchūhikōshi 281
uchūkūkan 280
uddo 233
ude 13, 95
udedokei 36
udetatefuse 251
ue e 320
ue-kaeru 91
ueki 87, 110
uekibachi 89
ueru 183
uesuto 12
uesutobando 35
ugai dai 50
uganda 317
ugokasu 251
uikyō 122, 133
uikyō no tane 133
uindo-shīrudo 205
uindoburēkā 33
uindosāfā 241
uindosāfin 241
uirusu 44
uisukī 145
ukairo 195, 323
uke 237
ukegane 276
ukeru 227
uketsuke-gakari 190
uki 244
ukidama 61
ukiwa 265
ukon 132
ukuraina 316
uma 185, 242
umareru 26
umate 243
umaya 185, 243
umeru 82
umi 264, 282
umi no ie 264
umibe 264
umizuri 245
unagi 294
undō 251
unmo 289
unten seki 196
unten shitsu 208

unten suru 195
untendai 95
untenshu 196
uraji 32
urauchi-gami 83
ureshī 25
uriba annai 104
urin 285
uroko 121, 293, 294
uroko o totta 121
uruguai 315
urusai 321
usagi 290
usagi niku 118
usetsu kinshi 195
usugiri 119
usui 321
uta 259
utsu 79, 224, 225, 229
utsukushī 321
uwagi 32
uwanuri 83
uwazara 310
uyoku 229
uzubekisutan 318
uzura 119
uzura mame 131
uzura tamago 137

W
waffuru 157
wagomu 173
wagon 172
waido gamen terebi 269
wain 145, 151
wain risuto 152
wain su 135
waingurasu 65
waipā 198
waishatsu 32
waiyā kappu 35
waiyā kattā 81
waiyā sutorippā 81
wakai 321
waki no shita 13
wakimichi 299
wakkusu 41
wakusei 280, 282
wambokkusu kā 199
wampīsu 31, 34
waniguchi kurippu 167
wanshotto 151
warau 25
waribiki ryōkin 322
waru 165
warui 321
wasabi 124
washi 292
wasshā 80
wata o totta 121
waza 237
webusaito 177
wēdā 244
wedingu kēki 141
wedingudoresu 35
weitā 148, 152
weito beruto 239

weito torēningu 251
weitoresu 191
wejji 233
wetto tisshu 108
wettosūtsu 239
wiketto 225
wiketto-kīpā 225
windō 177
windorasu 214
wintā supōtsu 247
wokka 145
wōtā gāden 84
wōtā hazādo 232

Y
ya 249
yachin 58
yachō kansatsu 263
yādo 310
yagai katsudō 262
yagi 185
yagi chīzu 142
yagi-nyū 136
yaita 159
yakedo 46
yakisoba 158
yakkyoku 108
yaku 67, 138
yakumi 135
yakusō 55
yakusō-zai 108
yakuzaishi 108, 189
yakyū 228
yakyū o suru 229
yakyūbō 36
yama 284
yamaimo 125
yanagi 296
yane 58, 203
yane-gawara 58, 187
yaneura-beya 58
yaoya 114, 188
yarinage 234
yasai 107, 122, 124
yasai-shitsu 67
yasei mai 130
yashi 296
yashi no ki 86
yasu ryō 245
yasui 321
yasuri 81
yawarakai 129, 321
yazutsu 249
yoake 305
yōbi 306
yobidashi botan 48
yobidashijō 180
yobirin 59
yobō-sesshu 45
yodarekake 30
yōfukudansu 70
yoga 54
yōgan 283
yōgisha 94, 181
yogoremono 76
yōgu 233
yōguruto 137

yōgyojō 183
yōhō 109
yoi 321
yoidome 109
yōji 30
yōjō shīto 83
yōkeijō 183
yōki 311
yōki-iri inryōsui 144
yokogura 242
yokushitsu 72
yokushitsu-yō kyabinetto 72
yokusō 72
yōkyū 249
yome 22
yomu 162
yon 308
yon banme 309
yōnashi 126
yonhyaku 308
yonjū 308
yonjū banme 309
yonjuppun 304
yonrin kudōsha 199
yontōkin 16
yōnyū 137
yori yoi 321
yoroido 58
yōroppa 316
yoru 305
yorudan 318
yōryō 109, 311
yōseki 311
yosenami 241
yōshi gaido 172
yōsui 52
yōsui senshi 52
yotei 175
yōtonjō 183
yōtsui 17
yotto 215, 240
yowai 321
yoyaku 45
yoyaku suru 168
yōzai 83
yubi no kansetsu 15
yūbim-bangō 98
yūbim-bukuro 98
yūbin haitaisunin 98
yūbin kaban 190
yūbin kawase 98
yūbin posuto 99
yūbin-uke 58, 99
yūbinhaitatsu 190
yūbinkyoku 98
yūbinkyoku-in 98
yubinuki 276
yubiwa 36
yuderu 67
yudeta 159
yudetamago 137, 157
yūen 199
yūenchi 262
yūgure 305
yūhodō 265
yuigonjō o kaku 26
yūjin 24

yuka 58, 62, 71
yuka undō 235
yūkari 296
yuki 287
yūki 91, 122
yūki gomi 61
yūki-sei 118
yukkurishita 321
yumi 249
yuminoko 81
yuri 110
yūryō channeru 269
yusei kan 21
yūshoku 64
yūsō-ryō 98
yusugu 38
yutampo 70
yutiriti rūmu 76
yūzai 181
yuzure 323

Z
zabuton 64, 152
zaijō 180
zaijōnimpi 180
zaimoku 187
zairyō 79
zakuro 128
zambia 317
zamen 64
zarugai 121
zaseki 209, 210, 254
zaseki haichi 254
zasshi 107, 112, 168
zassō 86
zassō kari-basami 88
zataku 152
zayaku 109
zei 96
zeikan 212, 216
zekken 226
zemu kurippu 173
zenkyō 242
zennyū 136
zenrin 196, 210
zenritsusen 21
zenryū 130
zenryū pan 139
zenryū-fun 138
zensai 153
zensoku 44
zentōdō 19
zentōkin 16
zenwan 12
zerībīnzu 113
zetsuen tēpu 81
zō 291
zōchiku bubun 58
zōen suru 91
zōsen-jo 217
zubon 32
zuga 274
zugaikotsu 17
zukkīni 125
zūmu renzu 270
zunō 19
zutsū 44

英語索引 eigo sakuin • English index

A

à la carte 152
abdomen 12
abdominals 16
above 320
abseiling 248
acacia 110
accelerator 200
access road 216
accessories 36, 38
accident 46
account number 96
accountant 97, 190
accounts department 175
accused 180
ace 230, 273
Achilles tendon 16
acorn squash 125
acquaintance 24
acquitted 181
across 320
acrylic paints 274
actions 237, 229, 227, 233, 183
activities 263, 245, 162, 77
actor 254, 191
actors 179
actress 254
acupressure 55
acupuncture 55
Adam's apple 19
add v 165
address 98
adhesive tape 47
adjustable spanner 80
admissions 168
admitted 48
aduki beans 131
adult 23
advantage 230
adventure 255
advertisement 269
aerate v 91
aerobics 251
Afghanistan 318
Africa 317
after 320
afternoon 305
aftershave 73
aftersun 108
agate 289
agenda 174
aikido 236
aileron 210
air bag 201
air conditioning 200
air cylinder 239
air filter 202, 204
air letter 98
air mattress 267
air stewardess 190
air supply 199
air vent 210

aircraft 210
aircraft carrier 215
airliner 210, 212
airport 212
aisle 106, 168, 210, 254
alarm clock 70
Alaska 314
Albania 316
alcoholic drinks 145
alfalfa 184
Algeria 317
allergy 44
alley 298
alligator 293
allspice 132
almond 129
almond oil 134
almonds 151
along 320
alpine 87
alpine skiing 247
alternating current 60
alternative therapy 54
alternator 203
altitude 211
aluminium 289
Amazonia 312
ambulance 94
American football 220
amethyst 288
amniocentesis 52
amniotic fluid 52
amount 96
amp 60
amphibians 294
amplifier 268
anaesthetist 48
anchor 214, 240
Andes 312
Andorra 316
angle 164
angler 244
Angola 317
angry 25
animals 292, 294
animated film 255
ankle 13, 15
ankle-length 34
anniversary 26
annual 86, 307
anorak 31, 33
answer 163
answer v 99, 163
answering machine 99
ant 295
antenatal 52
antenna 295
antifreeze 199, 203
Antigua and Barbuda 314
anti-inflammatory 109
antique shop 114
antiseptic 47
antiseptic wipe 47

anti-wrinkle 41
antler 291
apartment block 298
apéritif 153
aperture dial 270
apex 165
appeal 181
appearance 30
appendix 18
applaud v 255
apple 126
apple corer 68
apple juice 149
appliances 66
application 176
appointment 45, 175
apricot 126
April 306
apron 30, 50, 69, 212
APS camera 270
aquamarine 288
Arabian Sea 313
arable farm 183
arc 164
arch 15, 85, 301
archery 249
architect 190
architecture 300
architrave 301
Arctic circle 283
Arctic Ocean 312
area 165, 310
areas 299
arena 243
Argentina 315
arithmetic 165
arm 13
armband 238
armchair 63
armrest 200, 210
aromatherapy 55
around 320
arrangements 111
arrest 94
arrivals 213
arrow 249
art 162
art college 169
art gallery 261
art nouveau 301
art shop 115
artery 19
artichoke 124
artist 274
arts and crafts 274, 276
ash 283
ashtray 150
Asia 318
assault 94
assistant 24

assisted delivery 53
asteroid 280
asthma 44
astigmatism 51
astronaut 281
astronomy 281
asymmetric bars 235
at 320
athlete 234
athletics 234
Atlantic Ocean 312
atmosphere 282, 286
atrium 104
attachment 177
attack 220
attack zone 224
attend v 174
attic 58
attractions 261
aubergine 125
auburn 39
audience 254
August 306
aunt 22
aurora 286
Australasia 319
Australia 319
Austria 316
autocue 179
automatic 200
automatic door 196
autumn 31, 307
avalanche 247
avenue 299
avocado 128
awning 148
axe 95
axle 205
ayurveda 55
Azerbaijan 318

B

baby 23, 30
baby bath 74
baby care 74
baby changing facilities 104
baby monitor 75
baby products 107
baby sling 75
babygro 30
back 13
back brush 73
back seat 200
backboard 226
backdrop 254
backgammon 272
backhand 231
backpack 31, 37, 267
backstroke 239
backswing 233
bacon 118, 157
bad 321
badge 94

badminton 231
bag 311
bagel 139
baggage reclaim 213
baggage trailer 212
bags 37
baguette 138
Bahamas 314
bail 181
bait 244
bait v 245
bake v 67, 138
baked 159
baker 139
baker's 114
bakery 107, 138
baking 69
baking tray 69
balance wheel 276
balcony 59, 254
bald 39
bale 184
Balearic Islands 316
ball 15, 75, 221, 224, 226, 228, 230
ballboy 231
ballet 255
balsamic vinegar 135
Baltic Sea 313
bamboo 86,122
banana 128
bandage 47
Bangladesh 318
banister 59
bank 96, 284
bank charge 96
bank manager 96
bank transfer 96
bap 139
bar 150, 152, 250, 256, 311
bar code 106
bar counter 150
bar mitzvah 26
bar snacks 151
bar stool 150
barb 244
Barbados 314
barbecue 267
barber 39, 188
bark 296
barley 130, 184
barman 191
barn 182
baroque 301
bars 74
bartender 150
basalt 288
base 164, 229
base station 99
baseball 228
baseline 230
baseman 228

basement 58
basil 133
basin 50
basket 106, 207, 226
basket of fruit 126
basketball 226
basketball player 226
basque 35
bass clarinet 257
bass clef 256
bass guitar 258
bass guitarist 258
bassoon 257
bat 225, 228, 231, 290
bat v 225, 229
bath mat 72
bath towel 73
bathrobe 73
bathroom 72
bathtub 72
baton 235, 256
batsman 225
batter 228
batteries 260
battery 167, 202
battery pack 78
battleship 215
bay leaf 133
bayonet fitting 60
be born v 26
beach 264
beach bag 264
beach ball 265
beach hut 264
beach towel 265
beach umbrella 264
beaker 167
beam 186, 235
bean sprout 122
beans 131, 144
bear 291
beat 259
beauty 40, 105
beauty treatments 41
beaver 290
bed 70, 71
bed and breakfast 101
bedding 74
bedroom 70
bedside lamp 70
bedside table 70
bedspread 70
bee 295
beech 296
beef 118
beer 145,151
beer tap 150
beetle 295
beetroot 125
before 320
beginning 321
behind 320
Belarus 316
Belgium 316
Belize 314
bell 197
below 320
belt 32, 36, 236
bench 250, 262

Benin 317
berry 296
beside 320
bet 273
between 320
beyond 320
Bhutan 318
biathlon 247
bib 30
bicep curl 251
biceps 16
bicycle 206
bidet 72
biennial 86
bifocal 51
big toe 15
bike rack 207
bikini 264
bill 152, 293
binoculars 281
biology 162
biplane 211
birch 296
bird watching 263
birds 292
birth 52
birth weight 53
birth certificate 26
birthday 27
birthday cake 141
birthday candles 141
birthday party 27
biscuit 113
biscuits 141
bishop 272
bit 242
bit brace 78
bite 46
bite v 245
bitter 124, 145
black 39, 272, 274
black belt 237
black coffee 148
black hole 280
black olive 143
black pudding 157
Black Sea 313
black tea 149
blackberry 127
blackboard 162
blackcurrant 127
black-eyed beans 131
bladder 20
blade 60, 66, 78, 89
blanket 71, 74
blazer 33
bleach 77
blender 66
blister 46
block 237
block v 227
block of flats 59
blonde 39
blood pressure 44
blood pressure gauge 45
blood test 48
blouse 34
blow dry v 38

blow out v 141
blowhole 290
blue 274
blue cheese 136
bluebells 297
blueberry 127
blues 259
blusher 40
board 241
board v 217
board games 272
boarding pass 213
bob 39
bobbin 276
body 12
body lotion 73
body systems 19
bodywork 202
boil v 67
boiled egg 137, 157
boiled sweets 113
boiler 61
Bolivia 315
bollard 214, 298
bolt 59
bomber 211
bone 17, 119, 121
bone meal 88
boned 121
bongos 257
bonnet 198
book 168
book a flight v 212
book shop 115
bookshelf 63, 168
boom 95, 240
booster 281
boot 198, 220, 223
booties 30
bored 25
borrow v 168
Bosnia and Herzegovina 316
Botswana 317
bottle 61, 75, 135, 311
bottle opener 68, 150
bottled foods 134
bottled water 144
bottom tier 141
bounce v 227
boundary line 225
bouquet 35, 111
bouquet garni 132
bout 237
boutique 115
bow 240, 249
bow tie 36
bowl 61, 65, 112
bowl v 225
bowler 225
bowling 249
bowling ball 249
box 254
box file 173
box of chocolates 113
box of tissues 70
box office 255
boxer shorts 33

boxercise 251
boxing 236
boxing gloves 237
boxing ring 237
boy 23
boyfriend 24
bra 35
brace 50
bracelet 36
brain 19
brake 200, 204, 206
brake v 207
brake block 207
brake fluid reservoir 202
brake lever 207
brake pedal 205
bran 130
branch 175, 296
brandy 145
brass 256
Brazil 315
brazil nut 129
bread 157
bread knife 68
bread roll 143
breadcrumbs 139
breads 138
break a record v 234
break waters v 52
breakdown 203
breakfast 64, 156
breakfast buffet 156
breakfast cereals 107
breakfast table 156
breakfast tray 101
breast 12, 119
breast bone 17
breast pump 53
breastfeed v 53
breaststroke 239
breathing 47
breech 52
brick 187
bridge 15, 214, 258, 273, 300
bridle 242
bridle path 263
brie 142
briefcase 37
briefs 33, 35
brioche 157
broad bean 122
broad beans 131
broadcast 179
broadcast v 178
broccoli 123
brochure 175
brogue 37
bronze 235
brooch 36
broom 77
broth 158
brother 22
brother-in-law 23
browband 242
brown 274
brown bread 139, 149
brown flour 138
brown lentils 131

brown rice 130
browse v 177
browser 177
bruise 46
Brunei 319
brunette 39
brush 38, 40, 77, 83, 274
brush v 38, 50
brussel sprout 122
bubble bath 73
bucket 77, 82, 265
buckle 36
bud 111, 297
buffet 152
buggy 232
build v 186
builder 186, 188
building site 186
buildings 299
built-in wardrobe 71
bulb 86
Bulgaria 316
bull 185
bulldog clip 173
bullet train 209
bull-nose pliers 80
bullseye 273
bumper 74, 198
bun 39, 140, 155
bunch 111
bungalow 58
bungee jumping 248
bunker 232
bunsen burner 166
buoy 217
bureau de change 97
burger 154
burger bar 154
burger meal 154
burglar alarm 58
burglary 94
Burkina Faso 317
Burma (Myanmar) 318
burn 46
burner 67
Burundi 317
bus 196
bus driver 190
bus shelter 197
bus station 197
bus stop 197, 299
bus ticket 197
buses 196
business 175
business class 211
business deal 175
business lunch 175
business partner 24
business suit 32
business trip 175
businessman 175
businesswoman 175
butcher 118, 188
butcher's 114
butter 137, 156
butter beans 131
buttercup 297
butterfly 239, 295

english

buttermilk 137
butternut squash 125
buttock 13, 16
button 32
buttonhole 32
buttress 301
by 320
by airmail 98
bytes 176

C
cab 95
cabbage 123
cabin 210, 214
Cabinda 317
cabinet 66
cable 79, 207
cable car 246
cable television 269
cactus 87
caddy 233
caesarean section 52
café 148, 262
cafetière 65
cake shop 114
cake tin 69
cakes 140
calcite 289
calcium 109
calculator 165
calendar 306
calf 13, 16, 185
call button 48
calyx 297
cam belt 203
Cambodia 318
camcorder 260, 269
camel 291
camembert 142
camera 178, 260, 270
camera case 271
camera crane 178
camera shop 115
cameraman 178
Cameroon 317
camisole 35
camomile tea 149
camp v 266
camp bed 266
campari 145
camper van 266
campfire 266
camping 266
camping stove 267
campsite 266
campus 168
can 145, 311
can opener 68
Canada 314
canary 292
candied fruit 129
candle 63
cane 91
canes 89
canine 50
canned drink 154
canoe 214
canoeing 241

canter 243
canvas 274
cap 21, 36, 238
capacity 311
cape gooseberry 128
capers 143
capital 315
capoeira 237
cappuccino 148
capsize v 241
capsule 109
captain 214
car 198, 200
car accident 203
car hire 213
car park 298
car stereo 201
car wash 198
caramel 113
caravan 266
caraway 131
card 27
card phone 99
card slot 97
cardamom 132
cardboard 275
cardigan 32
cardiology 49
cardiovascular 19
cards 273
cargo 216
Caribbean Sea 312
carnation 110
carnival 27
carousel 212
carpenter 188
carpentry bits 80
carpet 71
carriage 208
carriage race 243
carrier 204
carrot 124
carrycot 75
cartilage 17
carton 311
cartoon 178
carve v 79
carving fork 68
case 51
cash v 97
cash machine 97
cashewnut 129
cashewnuts 151
cashier 96, 106
casino 261
Caspian Sea 313
casserole dish 69
cassette player 269
cassette tape 269
cast 254
cast v 245
castle 300
casual 34
casual wear 33
cat 290
catalogue 168
catamaran 215
cataract 51

catch v 220, 227, 229, 245
catcher 229
caterpillar 295
cathedral 300
catheter 53
cauliflower 124
cave 284
CD player 268
cedar 296
ceiling 62
celebration 140
celebration cakes 141
celebrations 27
celeriac 124
celery 122
cell 181
cello 256
cement 186
cement mixer 186
centimetre 310
centipede 295
Central African Republic 317
central processing unit 176
central reservation 194
centre 164
centre circle 222, 224, 226
centre field 228
centreboard 241
century 307
ceramic hob 66
cereal 130, 156
cervical vertebrae 17
cervix 20, 52
Chad 317
chain 36, 206
chair 64
chair v 174
chairlift 246
chalk 85, 162, 288
chamber 283
champagne 145
championship 230
change v 209
change a wheel v 203
change channel v 269
change gear v 207
changing bag 75
changing mat 74
changing room 104
channel 178
charcoal 266, 275
charge 94, 180
chart 48
chassis 203
check-in v 212
check-in desk 213
checkout 106
check-up 50
cheddar 142
cheek 14
cheerleader 220
cheese 136, 156
chef 152, 190
chef's hat 190
chemist 108
chemistry 162
cheque 96

chequebook 96
cherry 126
cherry tomato 124
chess 272
chessboard 272
chest 12
chest of drawers 70
chest press 251
chestnut 129
chewing gum 113
chick 185
chickpeas 131
chicken 119, 185
chicken burger 155
chicken coop 185
chicken nuggets 155
chicken pox 44
chicory 122
child 23, 31
child lock 75
child seat 198, 207
childbirth 53
children 23
children's clothing 30
children's department 104
children's ward 48
child's meal 153
Chile 315
chill 44
chilli 124, 132
chilli pepper 143
chimney 58
chin 14
China 318
china 105
Chinese leaves 122
chip v 233
chipboard 79
chiropractic 54
chisel 81, 275
chives 133
chocolate 113
chocolate bar 113
chocolate cake 140
chocolate chip 141
chocolate-coated 140
chocolate milkshake 149
chocolate spread 135
choir 301
choke v 47
chop 119, 237
chopping board 68
chopsticks 64
chorizo 143
choux pastry 140
christening 26
Christmas 27
chrysanthemum 110
chuck 78
church 298, 300
chutney 134
cider 145
cider vinegar 135
cigar 112
cigarettes 112
cinema 255, 299
cinema hall 255
cinnamon 133

circle 165, 254
circular saw 78
circuit training 251
circumference 164
cistern 61
citrus fruit 126
city 299
clam 121
clamp 78, 166
clamp stand 166
clapper board 179
clarinet 257
clasp 36
classical music 255, 259
classroom 162
claw 291
clay 85, 275
clean v 77
clean clothes 76
cleaned 121
cleaner 188
cleaning equipment 77
cleaning fluid 51
cleanser 41
clear honey 134
cleat 240
cleaver 68
clementine 126
client 38, 175, 180
cliff 285
climber 87
climbing frame 263
clinic 48
clipboard 173
clitoris 20
clock 62
clock radio 70
closed 260, 321
clothes line 76
clothes peg 76
clothing 205
cloud 287
cloudy 286
clove 125
clover 297
cloves 133
club 273
club sandwich 155
clubhouse 232
clutch 200, 204
coach 196
coal 288
coast 285
coaster 150
coastguard 217
coat 32
coat hanger 70
cockatoo 293
cockerel 185
cockle 121
cockpit 210
cockroach 295
cocktail 151
cocktail shaker 150
cocoa powder 148
coconut 129
cocoon 295
cod 120

coffee 144, 148, 153, 156, 184
coffee cup 65
coffee machine 148, 150
coffee milkshake 149
coffee spoon 153
coffee table 62
cog 206
coin 97
coin phone 99
coin return 99
cola 144
colander 68
cold 44, 286, 321
cold tap 72
cold-pressed oil 135
collage 275
collar 32
collar bone 17
colleague 24
collection 98
college 168
Colombia 315
colony 315
colouring pencil 163
colours 39, 274
comb 38
comb v 38
combat sports 236
combine harvester 182
comedy 255
comet 280
comic 112
commis chef 152
commission 97
communications 98
commuter 208
compact 40
compact disc 269
company 175
compartment 209
compass 165, 312, 240
complaint 94
complexion 41
compliments slip 173
compost 88
compost heap 85
computer 172, 176
concealer 40
conceive v 20
conception 52
concert 255, 258
concertina file 173
concourse 209
concrete block 187
concussion 46
condensed milk 136
conditioner 38
condom 21
conductor 256
cone 164, 187
confectioner 113
confectionery 107, 113
confident 25
confused 25
conglomerate 288
Congo 317

conifer 86
connect v 177
connection 212
conning tower 215
console 269
constellation 281
construction 186
consultant 49
consultation 45
contact lenses 51
container 216, 311
container port 216
container ship 215
continent 282, 315
contraception 21, 52
contraction 52
control tower 212
controller 269
controls 201, 204
convector heater 60
convenience food 107
convertible 199
conveyer belt 106
cooked meat 118, 143
cooking 67
coolant reservoir 202
cooling rack 69
co-pilot 211
copper 289
copy v 172
cor anglais 257
coral reef 285
cordless phone 99
core 127
coriander 133
cork 134
corkscrew 150
corn 130, 184
corn bread 139
corn oil 135
cornea 51
corner 223
corner flag 223
cornice 300
corset 35
Corsica 316
Costa Rica 314
costume 255
cot 74
cottage cheese 136
cottage garden 84
cotton 184, 277
cotton balls 41
cough 44
cough medicine 108
counsellor 55
count v 165
counter 96, 98, 100, 142, 272
country 259, 315
couple 24
courgette 125
courier 99
courses 153
court 226
court case 180
court date 180
court officer 180

court official 180
courtroom 180
courtyard 58, 84
couscous 130
cousin 22
cow 185
cow's milk 136
crab 121, 295
cracked wheat 130
cradle 95
craft knife 82
crafts 275
cramp 239
cramps 44
cranberry 127
crane 187, 216, 292
crash barrier 195
crater 283
crayfish 121
cream 109, 137, 140, 157
cream cheese 136
cream pie 141
crease 225
credit card 96
creel 245
creeper 87
crème caramel 141
crème patisserie 140
crêpe 155
crescent moon 280
crew 241
crew hatch 281
cricket 225, 295
cricket ball 225
cricketer 225
crime 94
criminal 181
criminal record 181
crisp 127
crispbread 139, 156
crisper 67
crisps 113, 151
Croatia 316
crochet 277
crochet hook 277
crockery 64
crockery 65
crocodile 293
crocodile clip 167
croissant 156
crop 39, 183
crops 184
cross trainer 250
crossbar 207, 222, 235
cross-country skiing 247
crow 292
crown 50
crown 306
crucible 166
crushed 132
crust 139, 282
cry v 25
crystal healing 55
Cuba 314
cube 164
cucumber 125
cuff 32, 45
cufflink 36
cultivate v 91

cultivator 182
cumin 132
curb 298
cured 118, 159, 143
curler 38
curling 247
curling tongs 38
curly 39
currant 129
current account 96
curry 158
curry powder 132
curtain 63, 254
curved 165
cushion 62
custard 140
customer 96, 104, 106, 152
customer service department 175
customer services 104
customs 212
customs house 216
cut 46
cut v 38, 79, 277
cuticle 15
cutlery 64
cuts 119
cutting 91
cuttlefish 121
cycle v 207
cycle lane 206
cycling 263
cylinder 164
cylinder head 202
cymbals 257
Cyprus 318
Czech Republic 316

D

daffodil 111
dairy 107
dairy farm 183
dairy produce 136
daisy 110, 297
dam 300
dance 259
dance academy 169
dancer 191
dandelion 123, 297
dandruff 39
dark 41, 321
darkroom 271
darn v 277
dartboard 273
darts 273
dashboard 201
date 129, 306
daughter 22
daughter-in-law 22
dawn 305
day 305, 306
dead ball line 221
deadhead v 91
deal v 273
debit card 96
decade 307
decay 50
December 306

deciduous 86
decimal 165
deck 214
deck chair 265
decking 85
decorating 82
decoration 141
decorator 82
deep end 239
deep-fried 159
deep sea fishing 245
deer 291
defence 181, 220
defendant 181
defender 223
defending zone 224
defrost v 67
degree 169
delay 209
deli 107
delicatessen 142
delivery 52, 98
deltoid 16
Democratic Republic of the Congo 317
Denmark 316
denomination 97
denominator 165
dental care 108
dental floss 50, 72
dental hygiene 72
dental x-ray 50
dentist 50, 189
dentist's chair 50
dentures 50
deodorant 73
deodorants 108
department 169
department store 105
departments 49
departure lounge 213
departures 213
depth 165
dermatology 49
descaled 121
desert 285
desiccated 129
designer 191, 277
desk 162, 172
desktop 177
desktop organizer 172
dessert 153
desserts 140
destination 213
detached 58
detective 94
detergent 77
deuce 230
develop v 271
diabetes 44
diagonal 164
dial v 99
diameter 164
diamond 273, 288
diaphragm 19, 21
diarrhoea 44, 109
diary 175

english

dice 272
dictionary 163
die v 26
diesel 199
diesel train 208
difficult 321
dig v 90, 227
digestive 19
digital 269
digital camera 270
dilation 52
dill 133
dimensions 165
dimple 15
dining car 209
dining room 64
dinner 64, 158
dinner plate 65
diopter 51
diploma 169
dipstick 202
direct current 60
direct debit 96
directions 260
director 254
directory enquiries 99
dirt bike 205
dirty washing 76
disabled parking 195
discharged 48
disconnected 99
discus 234
discuss v 163
disembark v 217
dishwasher 66
disinfectant solution 51
disk 176
dispensary 108
disposable 109
disposable camera 270
disposable nappy 30
disposable razor 73
dissertation 169
distance 310
distributor 203
district 315
dive 239
dive v 238
diver 238
diversion 195
divide v 165
divided by 165
dividends 97
divider 173, 194
divorce 26
Diwali 27
DJ 179
Djibouti 317
do not bend v 98
dock 214, 216
dock v 217
doctor 45, 189
doctorate 169
documentary 178
dog 290
dog sledding 247
doll 75
doll's house 75

dolphin 290
dome 300
domestic flight 212
Dominica 314
Dominican Republic 314
dominoes 273
donkey 185
door 196, 198, 209
door chain 59
door knob 59
door knocker 59
door lock 200
doorbell 59
doormat 59
dormer 58
dorsal fin 294
dosage 109
double 151
double bass 256
double bassoon 257
double bed 71
double cream 137
double room 100
double-decker bus
    196
doubles 230
dough 138
Dover sole 120
down 320
downhill skiing 247
download v 177
dragonfly 295
drain 61, 72, 299
drain cock 61
drainage 91
draining board 67
draughts 272
draw 223
draw v 162
drawer 66, 70, 172
drawer unit 172
drawing 275
drawing pin 173
dress 31, 34
dressage 243
dressed 159
dressed chicken 119
dressing 47, 158
dressing gown 31, 32
dressing table 71
dribble v 223
dried flowers 111
dried fruit 156
drill 50
drill v 79
drill bit 78
drill bits 80
drinking cup 75
drinking fountain 262
drinks 107, 144, 156
drip 53
drive v 195, 233
driver 196
driver's cab 208
driver's seat 196
driveshaft 202
drop anchor v 217
dropper 109, 167

drops 109
dropshot 230
drown v 239
drum 258
drum kit 258
drummer 258
dry 39, 41, 130, 145, 286,
    321
dry v 76
dry cleaners 115
dry dock 217
dual carriageway 195
duck 119, 185
duck egg 137
duckling 185
duffel coat 31
dugout 229
dumbbell 251
dumper truck 187
dungarees 30
dunk v 227
duodenum 18
dusk 305
dust 77
dust v 77
dustpan 77
duster 77
dustsheet 83
duty-free shop 213
duvet 71
DVD disk 269
DVD player 268
dyed 39
dynamo 207

E

eagle 292
ear 14
early 305, 320
earring 36
Earth 280, 282
earthenware dish 69
earthing 60
earthquake 283
easel 174, 274
east 312
East Timor 319
Easter 27
easy 321
easy cook 130
eat v 64
eat-in 154
eating 75
eau de toilette 41
eaves 58
éclair 140
eclipse 280
economics 169
economy class 211
Ecuador 315
eczema 44
Edam 142
edge 246
editor 191
eel 294
egg 20
egg cup 65, 137
egg white 137
eggs 137

Egypt 317
eight 308
eight hundred 308
eighteen 308
eighteenth 309
eighth 309
eightieth 309
eighty 308
ejaculatory duct 21
El Salvador 314
elbow 13
electric blanket 71
electric drill 78
electric guitar 258
electric razor 73
electric shock 46
electric train 208
electrical goods 105, 107
electrician 188
electricity 60
electricity meter 60
elephant 291
eleven 308
eleventh 309
elm 296
email 98, 177
email account 177
email address 177
embarrassed 25
embossed paper 83
embroidery 277
embryo 52
emerald 288
emergency 46
emergency lever 209
emergency exit 210
emergency phone 195
emergency room 48
emergency services 94
emigrate v 26
emotions 25
employee 24
employer 24
empty 321
emulsion 83
enamel 50
encore 255
encyclopedia 163
end 321
end zone 220
endive 123
endline 226
endocrine 19
endocrinology 49
engaged/busy 99
engaged couple 24
engine 202, 204, 208, 210
engine room 214
engineering 169
English breakfast 157
english mustard 135
engraving 275
enlarge v 172
enlargement 271
enquiries 168
ENT 49
entrance 59
entrance fee 260

envelope 98, 173
environment 280
epidural 52
epiglottis 19
epilepsy 44
episiotomy 52
equals 165
equation 165
equator 283
equipment 233, 238
equipment 165
Equitorial Guinea 317
equity 97
Eritrea 317
erupt v 283
escalator 104
espresso 148
essay 163
essential oils 55
estate 199
estate agent 189
estate agent's 115
Estonia 316
estuary 285
Ethiopia 317
eucalyptus 296
Europe 316
evening 305
evening dress 34
events 243, 247
evergreen 86
evidence 181
examination 163
excess baggage 212
exchange rate 97
excited 25
excuse me 322
executive 174
exercise bike 250
exercises 251
exfoliate v 41
exhaust pipe 203, 204
exhibit v 261
exhibition 261
exit 210
exit ramp 194
exosphere 286
expectant 52
experiment 166
expiry date 109
exposure 271
extend v 251
extension 58
extension lead 78
exterior 198
extra time 223
extraction 50
extractor 66
eye 14, 51, 244, 276
eye shadow 40
eye test 51
eyebrow 14, 51
eyebrow brush 40
eyebrow pencil 40
eyecup 269
eyelash 14, 51
eyelet 37
eyelid 51

eyeliner 40
eyepiece 167

F

fabric 277
fabric conditioner 76
face 14
face cream 73
face mask 225
face pack 41
face powder 40
face-off circle 224
facial 41
factory 299
faint v 25, 44
fair 41
fairground 262
fairway 232
falcon 292
Falkland Islands 315
fall 237
fall in love v 26
Fallopian tube 20
family 22
famous ruin 261
fan 60, 202
fan belt 203
fans 258
far 320
fare 197, 209
farm 182, 183, 184
farmer 182, 189
farmhouse 182
farmland 182
farmyard 182
fashion 277
fast 321
fast food 154
fast forward 269
fastening 37
fat 119, 321
fat free 137
father 22
father-in-law 23
fault 230
fax 98, 172
fax machine 172
feather 293
feature film 269
February 306
feed v 183
feijoa 128
female 12, 20
feminine hygiene 108
femur 17
fence 85, 182, 243
fencing 249
feng shui 55
fennel 122, 133
fennel seeds 133
fenugreek 132
fern 86
ferry 215, 216
ferry terminal 216
fertilization 20
fertilize v 91
fertilizer 91
festivals 27

fever 44
fiancé 24
fiancée 24
fibre 127
fibula 17
field 182, 222, 228, 234
field v 225, 229
field hockey 224
fifteen 308
fifteenth 309
fifth 309
fiftieth 309
fifty 308
fifty five thousand, five
  hundred 309
fifty thousand 309
fig 129
fighter plane 211
figure skating 247
Fiji 319
filament 60
file 81, 172, 177
filing cabinet 172
fill v 82
filler 83
fillet 119, 121
filleted 121
filling 50, 140, 155
film 260, 271
film set 179
film spool 271
filo pastry 140
filter 270
filter coffee 148
filter paper 167
fin 210, 239
finance 97
financial advisor 97
fingerprint 94
finial 300
finishing line 234
Finland 316
fire 95
fire alarm 95
fire brigade 95
fire engine 95
fire escape 95
fire extinguisher 95
fire fighters 95
fire station 95
firelighter 266
fireman 189
fireplace 63
firm 124
first 309
first aid 47
first aid box 47
first floor 104
first night 254
fish 107, 120, 294
fish farm 183
fish slice 68
fisherman 189
fishhook 244
fishing 244, 245
fishing boat 217
fishing permit 245

fishing port 217
fishing rod 244
fishmonger 188
fishmonger's 114, 120
fist 15, 237
fitness 250
five 308
five hundred 308
flag 221, 232
flageolet beans 131
flakes 132
flamingo 292
flan 142
flan dish 69
flare 240
flash 270
flash gun 270
flask 166
flat 59, 256
flatbread 139
flat race 243
flat wood bit 80
flavoured oil 134
flax 184
fleece 74
flesh 124, 127, 129
flex v 251
flight attendant 210
flight number 213
flint 288
flipchart 174
flip-flop 37
flipper 290
float 238, 244
float ball 61
flock 183
flood 287
floor 58, 62, 71
floor exercises 235
floor plan 261
florentine 141
floret 122
florist 110, 188
floss v 50
flours 138
flower 297
flowerbed 85, 90
flowering plant 297
flowering shrub 87
flowers 110
flu 44
flute 139, 257
fly 244, 295
fly v 211
fly fishing 245
flyover 194
flysheet 266
foal 185
focus v 271
focusing knob 167
foetus 52
fog 287
foil 249
folder 177
foliage 110
folk music 259
follicle 20
font 177

food 118, 130, 149
food hall 105
food processor 66
foot 12, 15, 310
football 220, 222
football field 220
football player 220
football strip 31, 222
footballer 222
footboard 71
footpath 262
footstrap 241
for 320
forceps 53, 167
forearm 12
forecourt 199
forehand 231
forehead 14
foreign currency 97
foreskin 21
forest 285
fork 65, 88, 153, 207
fork-lift truck 186, 216
formal garden 84
formal gardens 262
fortieth 309
fortnight 307
forty 308
forty minutes 304
forward 222
foul 222, 226
foul ball 228
foul line 229
foundation 40
fountain 85
four 308
four hundred 308
four-door 200
fourteen 308
fourteenth 309
fourth 309
four-wheel drive 199
fox 290
foxglove 297
fraction 165
fracture 46
fragile 98
fragranced 130
frame 51, 62, 206, 267
frame counter 270
France 316
freckle 15
free 321
free kick 222
free range 118
free weights 250
freesia 110
free-throw line 226
freeze 287
freeze v 67
freezer 67
freight train 208
freighter 215
French bean 122
french fries 154
French Guiana 315
French horn 257
french mustard 135

french pleat 39
French toast 157
frequency 179
fresh 121, 127, 130
fresh cheese 136
freshwater fishing 245
fret 258
fretsaw 81
Friday 306
fridge-freezer 67
fried 159
fried chicken 155
fried egg 157
fried noodles 158
friend 24
frieze 301
frog 294
from 320
front crawl 239
front door 58
front wheel 196
frontal 16
frost 287
froth 148
frown 25
frozen 121, 124
frozen food 107
frozen yoghurt 137
fruit 107, 126, 128
fruit bread 139
fruit cake 140
fruit farm 183
fruit gum 113
fruit juice 127, 156
fruit salad 157
fruit tart 140
fruit yoghurt 157
fry v 67
frying pan 69
fuel gauge 201
fuel tank 204
full 64, 266, 321
full board 101
full moon 280
fumble 220
funeral 26
funnel 166, 214
furniture shop 115
furrow 183
fuse 60
fuse box 60, 203
fuselage 210
futon 71

G

gable 300
Gabon 317
Galapagos Islands 315
galaxy 280
gale 286
galley 214
gallon 311
gallop 243
galvanised 79
Gambia 317
game 119, 230, 273
game show 178

english

games 272
gangway 214
garage 58, 199
garden 84
garden centre 115
garden features 84
garden pea 122
garden plants 86
garden styles 84
garden tools 88
gardener 188
gardening 90
gardening gloves 89
gardens 261
garland 111
garlic 125, 132
garlic press 68
garnet 288
garter 35
gas burner 61
gasket 61
gate 85, 182, 247
gate number 213
gauze 47, 167
gear lever 207
gearbox 202, 204
gears 206
gearstick 201
gel 38, 109
gems 288
generation 23
generator 60
genitals 12
geography 162
geometry 165
Georgia 318
gerbera 110
Germany 316
get a job v 26
get married v 26
get up v 71
geyser 285
Ghana 317
giant slalom 247
gifts shop 114
gill 294
gin 145
gin and tonic 151
ginger 39, 125, 133
giraffe 291
girder 186
girl 23
girlfriend 24
girth 242
glacier 284
gladiolus 110
gland 19
glass 69, 152
glass bottle 166
glass rod 167
glasses 51, 150
glassware 64
glaze v 139
glider 211, 248
gliding 248
gloss 83, 271
glove 224, 233, 236, 246
gloves 36

glue 275
glue gun 78
gneiss 288
go to bed v 71
go to sleep v 71
goal 221, 223, 224
goal area 223
goal line 220, 223, 224
goalkeeper 222, 224
goalpost 220, 222
goat 185
goat's cheese 142
goat's milk 136
goggles 238, 247
going out 75
gold 235, 289
goldfish 294
golf 232
golf bag 233
golf ball 233
golf clubs 233
golf course 232
golf shoe 233
golf trolley 233
golfer 232
gong 257
good 321
good afternoon 322
good evening 322
good morning 322
good night 322
goodbye 322
goose 119, 293
goose egg 137
gooseberry 127
gorge 284
gorilla 291
gothic 301
grade 163
graduate 169
graduate v 26
graduation ceremony 169
graft v 91
grains 130
gram 310
granary bread 139
grandchildren 23
granddaughter 22
grandfather 22
grandmother 22
grandparents 23
grandson 22
granite 288
grape juice 144
grapefruit 126
grapeseed oil 134
graphite 289
grass 86, 262
grass bag 88
grasshopper 295
grassland 285
grate v 67
grated cheese 136
grater 68
gratin dish 69
gravel 88
gravity 280

graze 46
greasy 39
Greece 316
green 129, 232, 274
green olive 143
green peas 131
green salad 158
green tea 149
greengrocer 188
greengrocer's 114
greenhouse 85
Greenland 314
grey 39, 274
grill v 67
grill pan 69
grilled 159
groceries 106
grocer's 114
groin 12
groom 243
ground 132
ground coffee 144
ground cover 87
ground floor 104
ground sheet 267
groundnut oil 135
group therapy 55
grout 83
guard 236
Guatemala 314
guava 128
guest 64, 100
guidebook 260
guided tour 260
guilty 181
Guinea 317
Guinea-Bissau 317
guitarist 258
gull 292
gum 50
gun 94
gutter 58, 299
guy rope 266
Guyana 315
gym 101, 250
gym machine 250
gymnast 235
gymnastics 235
gynaecologist 52
gynaecology 49
gypsophila 110

H

haberdashery 105
hacksaw 81
haddock 120
haemorrhage 46
hail 286
hair 14, 38
hair dye 40
hairband 38
hairdresser 38, 188
hairdresser's 115
hairdryer 38
hairpin 38
hairspray 38
hairtie 39

Haiti 314
half an hour 304
half board 101
half time 223
half-litre 311
hall of residence 168
halibut fillets 120
Halloween 27
hallway 59
halter 243
halter neck 35
ham 119, 143, 156
hammer 80
hammer v 79
hammock 266
hamper 263
hamster 290
hamstring 16
hand 13, 15
hand drill 81
hand fork 89
hand luggage 211, 213
hand rail 59
hand saw 89
hand towel 73
handbag 37
handbrake 203
handcuffs 94
handicap 233
handkerchief 36
handle 36, 88, 106, 187, 200, 230
handlebar 207
handles 37
handrail 196
handsaw 80
handset 99
hang v 82
hang-glider 248
hang-gliding 248
hanging basket 84
hanging file 173
happy 25
harbour 217
harbour master 217
hard 129, 321
hard cheese 136
hard drive 176
hard hat 186
hard shoulder 194
hardboard 79
hardware 176
hardware shop 114
hardwood 79
haricot beans 131
harness race 243
harp 256
harvest v 91, 183
hat 36
hatchback 199
have a baby v 26
Hawaii 314
hay 184
hayfever 44
hazard 195
hazard lights 201
hazelnut 129
hazelnut oil 134

head 12, 19, 81, 230
head v 222
head injury 46
head office 175
head teacher 163
headache 44
headboard 70
headlight 198, 205
headphones 268
headrest 200
headsail 240
health 44
health centre 168
health food shop 115
heart 18, 119, 122, 273
heart attack 44
heater 60
heater controls 201
heather 297
heating element 61
heavy 321
heavy metal 259
hedge 85, 90, 182
hedgehog 290
heel 13, 15, 37
height 165
height bar 45
helicopter 211
hello 322
helmet 95, 204, 206, 220, 224, 228
hem 34
hematite 289
hen's egg 137
herb 55, 86
herb garden 84
herbaceous border 85
herbal remedies 108
herbal tea 149
herbalism 55
herbicide 183
herbs 133, 134
herbs and spices 132
herd 183
hexagon 164
hi-fi system 268
high 321
high chair 75
high dive 239
high heel shoe 37
high jump 235
high speed train 208
highlights 39
hiking 263
hill 284
Himalayas 313
hip 12
hippopotamus 291
historic building 261
history 162
history of art 169
hit v 224
hob 67
hockey 224
hockey stick 224
hoe 88
hold 215, 237
holdall 37

english

hole 232
hole in one 233
hole punch 173
holiday 212
holiday brochure 212
holly 296
home 58
home delivery 154
home entertainment 268
home furnishings 105
home plate 228
homeopathy 55
homework 163
homogenised 137
Honduras 314
honeycomb 135
honeymoon 26
honeysuckle 297
hood 31, 75
hoof 242, 291
hook 187, 276
hoop 226, 277
horizontal bar 235
hormone 20
horn 201, 204, 291
horror film 255
horse 185, 235, 242
horse race 243
horse riding 242, 263
horseradish 125
horseshoe 242
hose 95
hose reel 89
hosepipe 89
hospital 48
hot 124, 286, 321
hot chocolate 144, 156
hot dog 155
hot drinks 144
hot tap 72
hot-air balloon 211
hotel 100, 264
hot-water bottle 70
hour 304
hour hand 304
house 58
household products 107
hovercraft 215
hub 206
hubcap 202
hull 214, 240
humerus 17
humid 286
hummingbird 292
hump 291
hundred 308
hundred and ten 308
hundred thousand 308
hundredth 309
Hungary 316
hungry 64
hurdles 235
hurricane 287
husband 22
husk 130
hydrant 95
hydrofoil 215
hydrotherapy 55

hypnotherapy 55
hypoallergenic 41
hypotenuse 164

I
ice 120, 287
ice and lemon 151
ice bucket 150
ice climbing 247
ice cream 149
ice cube 151
ice hockey 224
ice hockey player 224
ice hockey rink 224
ice maker 67
ice-cream 137
iced coffee 148
iced tea 149
ice-skate 224
ice-skating 247
icicle 287
icing 141
icon 177
identity badge 189
identity tag 53
igneous 288
ignition 200
iguana 293
illness 44
immigration 212
impotent 20
in 320
in brine 143
in front of 320
in oil 143
in sauce 159
in syrup 159
inbox 177
inch 310
incisor 50
incubator 53
index finger 15
India 318
Indian Ocean 312
indicator 198, 204
indigo 274
Indonesia 319
induce labour v 53
industrial estate 299
infection 44
infertile 20
infield 228
inflatable dinghy 215
information 261
information screen 213
in-goal area 221
inhaler 44, 109
injection 48
injury 46
ink 275
ink pad 173
inlet 61
inner core 282
inner tube 207
inning 228
innocent 181
inoculation 45
insect repellent 108, 267

inside 320
inside lane 194
insomnia 71
inspector 94
install v 177
instant camera 270
instep 15
instructions 109
instruments 256, 258
insulating tape 81
insulation 61
insulin 109
insurance 203
intensive care unit 48
inter-city train 209
intercom 59
intercostal 16
intercourse 20
interest rate 96
interior 200
internal systems 60
international flight 212
internet 177
intersection 298
interval 254
interviewer 179
into 320
in-tray 172
invertebrates 295
investigation 94
investment 97
ionosphere 286
Iran 318
Iraq 318
Ireland 316
iris 51, 110
iron 76, 109, 233, 289
iron v 76
ironing board 76
island 282
Israel 318
Italy 316
itinerary 260
IUD 21
Ivory Coast 317

J
jack 203, 273
jacket 32, 34
jade 288
jam 134, 156
Jamaica 314
January 306
Japan 318
Japanese tea cup 64
Japanese floor cushion 64, 152
Japanese horseradish 124
Japanese low table 152
jar 134, 311
javelin 234
jaw 14, 17
jazz 259
jeans 31
jelly bean 113
jellyfish 295
Jerusalem artichoke 125
jet 288

jet skiing 241
jetty 217
jeweller 188
jeweller's 114
jewellery 36
jewellery box 36
jewellery making 275
jigsaw 78
jigsaw puzzle 273
jodhpurs 242
jog on the spot 251
jogging 251, 263
joint 17, 119
joker 273
Jordan 318
journal 168
journalist 190
judge 180
judo 236
jug 65
juices and milkshakes 149
juicy 127
July 306
jump 237, 243
jump v 227
jump ball 226
junction 194
June 306
Jupiter 280
jury 180
jury box 180

K
kale 123
Kaliningrad 316
kangaroo 291
karate 236
kayak 241
Kazakhstan 318
kebab 155, 158
keel 214
keep net 244
kendo 236
Kenya 317
kernel 122, 129, 130
ketchup 135
kettle 66
kettledrum 257
key 59, 80, 176, 207
keyboard 172, 176, 258
keypad 97, 99
kick 237, 239
kick v 221, 223
kickboxing 236
kickstand 207
kid 185
kidney 18, 119
kilogram 310
kilometre 310
kimono 35
king 272, 273
king prawn 121
kippers 157
kitchen 66, 152
kitchen knife 68
kitchenware 68, 105
kitten 290
kiwifruit 128

knead v 138
knee 12
knee pad 205
knee support 227
kneecap 17
knee-length 34
knickers 35
knife 65, 80
knife sharpener 68, 118
knight 272
knitting 277
knitting needle 277
knock out 237
knuckle 15
koala 291
kohlrabi 123
koi carp 294
kumquat 126
kung fu 236
Kuwait 318
Kyrgyzstan 318

L
label 172
labels 89
labia 20
laboratory 166
lace 35, 37
lace bobbin 277
lace making 277
lace-up 37
lacrosse 249
lactose 137
ladder 95, 186
ladle 68
ladybird 295
lake 285
lamb 118, 185
lamp 62, 207, 217
land 282
land v 211
landing 59
landing gear 210
landing net 244
landlord 58
landscape 271, 284
landscape v 91
lane 234, 238
languages 162
Laos 318
lapel 32
laptop 175
larch 296
large 321
large intestine 18
larynx 19
last week 307
lat 16
late 305
later 304
latitude 283
Latvia 316
laugh v 25
launch 281
launch pad 281
launderette 115
laundry 76

english

laundry basket 76
laundry service 101
lava 283
law 169, 180
lawn 85, 90
lawn rake 88
lawnmower 88, 90
lawyer 180, 190
lawyer's office 180
laxative 109
lead singer 258
leaded 199
leaf 122, 296
leaflets 96
league 223
lean meat 118
learn v 163
leather shoe 37
leather shoes 32
leathers 205
Lebanon 318
lecture theatre 169
lecturer 169
leek 125
left 260
left field 228
left-hand drive 201
leg 12, 119
leg pad 225
leg press 251
legal advice 180
legal department 175
leggings 31
leisure 258, 254, 264
lemon 126
lemon curd 134
lemon grass 133
lemon sole 120
lemonade 144
length 165, 310
lens 270
lens (eye) 51
lens (glasses) 51
lens cap 270
lens case 51
Lesotho 317
lesson 163
let! 231
letter 98
letterbox 58, 99
letterhead 173
lettuce 123
lever 61, 150
lever arch file 173
Liberia 317
librarian 168, 190
library 168, 299
library card 168
Libya 317
licence plate 198
liquorice 113
lid 61, 66
Liechtenstein 316
life events 26
life jacket 240
life raft 240
lifeboat 214
lifebuoy 240

lifeguard 239, 265
lifeguard tower 265
lift 59, 100, 104
ligament 17
light 178, 321
light a fire v 266
light aircraft 211
light bulb 60
lighter 112
lighthouse 217
lighting 105
lightmeter 270
lightning 287
lights 94
lights switch 201
lily 110
lime 126, 296
limestone 288
limousine 199
line 244
line judge 220
line of play 233
linen 105, 277
linen basket 76
lines 165
linesman 223, 230
lingerie 35, 105
lining 32
lining paper 83
link 36
lintel 186
lion 291
lip 14
lip brush 40
lip gloss 40
lip liner 40
lipstick 40
liqueur 145
liquid 77
liquid dispenser 311
liquid measure 311
literature 162, 169
Lithuania 316
litre 311
little finger 15
little toe 15
live 60, 178
live rail 209
liver 18, 118
livestock 183, 185
living room 62
lizard 293
load v 76
loaf 139
loan 96, 168
loans desk 168
lob 230
lobby 100, 255
lobster 121, 295
lock 59, 207
lockers 239
log on v 177
loganberry 127
logo 31
loin 121
lollipop 113
long 32
long jump 235

long sight 51
long wave 179
long-grain 130
long-handled shears 88
longitude 283
loofah 73
loom 277
loose leaf tea 144
lorry 194
lorry driver 190
lose v 273
loser 273
lottery tickets 112
love 230
low 321
luge 247
luggage 100, 198, 213
luggage department 104
luggage hold 196
luggage rack 209
lumbar vertebrae 17
lunar module 281
lunch 64
lunch box 154
lung 18
lunge 251
lupins 297
lure 244
Luxembourg 316
lychee 128
lymphatic 19
lyrics 259

M

macadamia 129
mace 132
Macedonia 316
machine gun 189
machinery 187
mackerel 120
macramé 277
Madagascar 317
magazine 112
magazines 107
magma 283
magnesium 109
magnet 167
maid service 101
mailbag 98, 190
main course 153
mains supply 60
mainsail 240
make a will v 26
make friends v 26
make the bed v 71
make-up 40
making bread 138
malachite 288
Malawi 317
Malaysia 318
Maldives 318
male 12, 21
Mali 317
mallet 78, 275
malt vinegar 135
Malta 316
malted drink 144
mammals 290

man 23
manager 24, 174
managing director 175
manchego 142
mane 242, 291
mango 128
manhole 299
manicure 41
mantelpiece 63
mantle 282
manual 200
map 195, 261
maple 296
maple syrup 134
maracas 257
marathon 234
marble 288
March 306
margarine 137
marina 217
marinated 143, 159
marine fishing 245
marjoram 133
mark v 227
market 115
marketing department 175
marmalade 134, 156
marrow 124
Mars 280
marshmallow 113
martial arts 237
martini 151
marzipan 141
mascara 40
mashed 159
masher 68
mask 189, 228, 236, 239, 249
masking tape 83
masonry bit 80
massage 54
mast 240
masters 169
mat 54, 83, 235, 271
match 230
matches 112
material 276
materials 79, 187
maternity 49
maternity ward 48
maths 162, 164
mattress 70, 74
Mauritania 317
Mauritius 317
May 306
maybe 322
mayonnaise 135
MDF 79
meadow 285
meal 64
measles 44
measure 150, 151
measure v 165
measurements 165
measuring jug 69, 311
measuring spoon 109
meat 119
meat and poultry 106

meat tenderizer 68
meatballs 158
meathook 118
mechanic 188, 203
mechanical digger 187
mechanics 202
medals 235
media 178
medical examination 45
medication 109
medicine 109, 169
medicine cabinet 72
meditation 54
Mediterranean Sea 313
medium wave 179
meeting 174
meeting room 174
melody 259
melon 127
memory 176
men's clothing 32
men's wear 105
menstruation 20
menu 148, 153, 154
menubar 177
mercury 289
Mercury 280
meringue 140
mesosphere 286
messages 100
metacarpal 17
metal 79
metal bit 80
metals 289
metamorphic 288
metatarsal 17
meteor 280
metre 310
Mexico 314
mica 289
microlight 211
microphone 179, 258
microscope 167
microwave oven 66
midday 305
middle finger 15
middle lane 194
midnight 305
midwife 53
migraine 44
mile 310
milk 136, 156
milk v 183
milk carton 136
milk chocolate 113
milkshake 137
millennium 307
millet 130
milligram 310
millilitre 311
millimetre 310
mince 119
mineral 144
minerals 289
mini bar 101
mini disk recorder 268
minibus 197
mint 113, 133

mint tea 149
minus 165
minute 304
minute hand 304
minutes 174
mirror 40, 63, 71, 167
miscarriage 52
Miss 23
missile 211
mist 287
mitre block 81
mitt 228
mittens 30
mix v 67, 138
mixed salad 158
mixing bowl 66, 69
mixing desk 179
moat 300
mobile 74
mobile phone 99
model 169, 190
model making 275
modelling tool 275
modem 176
moisturizer 41
molar 50
Moldova 316
mole 14
Monaco 316
Monday 306
money 97
Mongolia 318
monitor 172, 176
monitor 53
monkey 291
monkfish 120
monopoly 272
monorail 208
monsoon 287
month 306
monthly 307
monument 261
Moon 280
moonstone 288
moor v 217
mooring 217
mop 77
morning 305
Morocco 317
mortar 68, 167, 187
mortgage 96
moses basket 74
mosque 300
mosquito 295
mosquito net 267
moth 295
mother 22
mother-in-law 23
motor 88
motor racing 249
motorbike 204
motorbike racing 249
motorcross 249
motorway 194
moulding 63
mountain 284
mountain bike 206
mountain range 282

mouse 176, 290
mousse 141
mouth 14
mouth guard 237
mouthwash 72
move 273
mow v 90
Mozambique 317
mozzarella 142
MP3 player 268
Mr 23
Mrs 23
mudguard 205
muffin 140
muffin tray 69
mug 65
mulch v 91
multiply v 165
multivitamin tablets 109
mumps 44
mung beans 131
muscles 16
museum 261
mushroom 125
music 162
music school 169
musical 255
musical score 255
musical styles 259
musician 191
mussel 121, 295
mustard 155
mustard seed 131
Myanmar 318

N

naan bread 139
nail 15, 80
nail clippers 41
nail file 41
nail scissors 41
nail varnish 41
nail varnish remover 41
Namibia 317
nape 13
napkin 65, 152
napkin ring 65
nappy 75
nappy rash cream 74
narrow 321
nation 315
national park 261
natural 256
natural fibre 31
naturopathy 55
nausea 44
navel 12
navigate v 240
near 320
nebula 280
neck 12, 258
neck brace 46
necklace 36
neckline 34
nectarine 126
needle 109, 276
needle plate 276
needle-nose pliers 80

needlepoint 277
negative 271
negative electrode 167
negligée 35
neighbour 24
neoclassical 301
Nepal 318
nephew 23
Neptune 280
nerve 19, 50
nervous 19, 25
net 217, 222, 226, 227, 231
net v 245
net curtain 63
Netherlands 316
nettle 297
network 176
neurology 49
neutral 60
neutral zone 224
new 321
new moon 280
new potato 124
New Year 27
New Zealand 319
newborn baby 53
news 178
newsagent 112
newspaper 112
newsreader 179, 191
next week 306
nib 163
Nicaragua 314
nickel 289
niece 23
Niger 317
Nigeria 317
night 305
nightdress 35
nightie 31
nightwear 31
nine 308
nine hundred 308
nineteen 308
nineteen hundred 307
nineteen hundred and one 307
nineteen ten 307
nineteenth 309
ninetieth 309
ninety 308
ninth 309
nipple 12
no 322
no entry 195
no right turn 195
no stopping 195
non-smoking section 152
non-stick 69
noodles 158
normal 39
north 312
North and Central America 314
North Korea 318
North pole 283
North Sea 312
northern hemisphere 283
Norway 316

nose 14, 210
nose clip 238
noseband 242
nosebleed 44
nosewheel 210
nostril 14
notation 256
note 97, 256
note pad 173
notebook 163, 172
notes 175, 191
notice board 173
nougat 113
November 306
now 304
nozzle 89
number 226
numbers 308
numerator 165
nurse 45, 48, 52, 189
nursing 53
nursing bra 53
nut 80
nutmeg 132
nuts 151
nuts and dried fruit 129
nylon 277

O

oak 296
oar 241
oats 130
objective lens 167
oboe 257
obsidian 288
obstetrician 52
occupations 188, 190
occupied 321
ocean 282
ocean liner 215
octagon 164
October 306
octopus 121, 295
odometer 201
oesophagus 19
off licence 115
offal 118
offers 106
office 24, 172, 174
office block 298
office equipment 172
office supplies 173
off-piste 247
off-side 223
oil 142, 199
oil paints 274
oil tank 204
oil tanker 215
oils 134
oily 41
ointment 47, 109
okra 122
old 321
olive oil 134
olives 151
Oman 318
omelette 158

on time 305
on top of 320
oncology 49
one 308
one billion 309
one million 309
one thousand 309
one-way 194
one-way system 298
onion 124
online 177
onto 320
onyx 289
opal 288
open 260, 321
open sandwich 155
open-top 260
opera 255
operating theatre 48
operation 48
operator 99
ophthalmology 49
opponent 236
opposite 320
optic 150
optic nerve 51
optician 51, 189
orange 126, 274
orange juice 148
orangeade 144
orbit 280
orchestra 254, 256
orchestra pit 254
orchid 111
order v 153
oregano 133
organic 91, 118, 122
organic waste 61
origami 275
ornamental 87
orthopedics 49
osteopathy 54
ostrich 292
otter 290
ounce 310
out 225, 228, 320
out of bounds 226
out of focus 271
outboard motor 215
outbuilding 182
outdoor activities 262
outer core 282
outfield 229
outlet 61
outpatient 48
outside 320
outside lane 194
out-tray 172
oval 164
ovary 20
oven 66
oven glove 69
ovenproof 69
over 320
over par 233
overalls 82
overdraft 96
overexposed 271

english

overflow pipe 61
overhead locker 210
overhead projector 163
overtake v 195
overture 256
ovulation 20, 52
owl 292
oyster 121
ozone layer 286

P
Pacific Ocean 312
pack 311
pack of cards 273
packet 311
packet of cigarettes 112
pad 224
paddle 241
paddling pool 263
paddock 242
pads 53, 220
paediatrics 49
painkiller 109
painkillers 47
paint 83
paint v 83
paint tin 83
paint tray 83
painter 191
painting 62, 261, 274
paints 274
pak-choi 123
Pakistan 318
palate 19
palette 274
pallet 186
palm 15, 86, 296
palm hearts 122
palmtop 175
pan 310
pan-fried 159
Panama 314
pancakes 157
pancreas 18
panda 291
panty liner 108
papaya 128
paper clip 173
paper guide 172
paper napkin 154
paper tray 172
papier-mâché 275
paprika 132
Papua New Guinea 319
par 233
parachute 248
parachuting 248
paragliding 248
Paraguay 315
parallel 165
parallel bars 235
parallelogram 164
paramedic 94
parcel 99
parents 23
park 262
park v 195
parking meter 195

parmesan 142
parole 181
parrot 293
parsley 133
parsnip 125
partner 23
pass 226
pass v 220, 223
passenger 216
passenger port 216
passion fruit 128
Passover 27
passport 213
passport control 213
pasta 158
pastels 274
pasteurized 137
pasting brush 82
pasting table 82
pastry 140, 149
pastry brush 69
pasture 182
patch 207
patchwork 277
pâté 142, 156
path 58, 85
pathology 49
patient 45
patio garden 85
pattern 276
pause 269
pavement 298
pavement café 148
paving 85
pawn 272
pay v 153
pay in v 96
pay per view channel 269
paying-in slips 96
payment 96
payroll 175
peach 126, 128
peacock 293
peanut 129
peanut butter 135
peanuts 151
pear 127
peas 131
pecan 129
pectoral 16
pectoral fin 294
pedal 61, 206
pedal v 207
pedestrian crossing 195
pedestrian zone 299
pedicure 41
pediment 301
peel v 67
peeled prawns 120
peeler 68
pelican 292
pelvis 17
pen 163, 185
penalty 222
penalty area 223
pencil 163, 275
pencil case 163
pencil sharpener 163

pendant 36
penfriend 24
penguin 292
peninsula 282
penis 21
pentagon 164
peony 111
people 12, 16
people carrier 199
pepper 64, 124, 152
peppercorn 132
pepperoni 142
percentage 165
percussion 257
perennial 86
perfume 41
perfumery 105
pergola 84
periodical 168
perm 39
perpendicular 165
persimmon 128
personal best 234
personal CD player 269
personal organizer 173, 175
personal trainer 250
personnel department 175
Peru 315
pesticide 89, 183
pestle 68, 167
pet food 107
pet shop 115
petal 297
petri dish 166
petrol 199
petrol pump 199
petrol station 199
petrol tank 203
pharmacist 108, 189
pharynx 19
pheasant 119, 293
phillips screwdriver 81
philosophy 169
Philippines 319
photo album 271
photo finish 234
photo frame 271
photofit 181
photographer 191
photograph 271
photograph v 271
photography 270
physical education 162
physics 162, 169
physiotherapy 49
piano 256
piccolo 257
pick v 91
pick and mix 113
pickaxe 187
pickled 159
pickup 258
picnic 263
picnic bench 266
pie 158
pie tin 69
piece 272
pier 217

pies 143
pig 185
pig farm 183
pigeon 292
pigeonhole 100
piglet 185
pigsty 185
pigtails 39
Pilates 251
pill 21, 109
pillar 300
pillion 204
pillow 70
pillowcase 71
pilot 190, 211
pin 60, 237, 249, 276
pin number 96
pincushion 276
pine 296
pine nut 129
pineapple 128
pineapple juice 149
pink 274
pint 311
pinto beans 131
pip 128
pipe 112, 202
pipe cutter 81
pipette 167
piping bag 69
pistachio 129
pitch 225, 256, 266
pitch v 229
pitch a tent v 266
pitcher 151, 229
pitcher's mound 228
pitches available 266
pith 126
pitta bread 139
pizza 154
pizza parlour 154
place mat 64
place setting 65
placenta 52
plain 285
plain chocolate 113
plain flour 139
plait 39
plane 81
plane v 79
planet 280, 282
plant v 183
plant pot 89
plants 86, 296
plaque 50
plaster 47, 83
plaster v 82
plastic bag 122
plastic pants 30
plastic surgery 49
plate 65, 283
plateau 284
platform 208
platform number 208
platform shoe 37
platinum 289
play 254, 269
play v 229, 273

player 221, 231, 273
playground 263
playhouse 75
playing 75
playpen 75
plea 180
please 322
Plimsoll line 214
plough v 183
plug 60, 72
plum 126
plumb line 82
plumber 188
plumbing 61
plunger 81
plus 165
Pluto 280
plywood 79
pneumatic drill 187
poach v 67
poached 159
pocket 32
pod 122
podium 235, 256
point 273
poisoning 46
poker 273
Poland 316
polar bear 291
pole 245, 282
pole vault 234
police 94
police car 94
police cell 94
police officer 94
police station 94
policeman 189
polish 77
polish v 77
politics 169
polo 243
polyester 277
pomegranate 128
pommel 242
pommel horse 235
pond 85
ponytail 39
pool 249
pop 259
popcorn 255
poplar 296
popper 30
poppy 297
poppy seeds 138
porch 58
porch light 58
pore 15
pork 118
porridge 156
port 145, 176, 214, 216
porter 100
portfolio 97
porthole 214
portion 64
portrait 271
Portugal 316
positive electrode 167
post office 98

postage 98
postal code 98
postal order 98
postal worker 98
postbox 99
postcard 112
poster 255
poster paint 274
postgraduate 169
postman 98, 190
postmark 98
pot plant 110
pot up v 91
potato 124
pot-pourri 111
potted plant 87
potter's wheel 275
pottery 275
potty 74
pouch 291
poultry 119
poultry farm 183
pound 310
pour v 67
powder 77, 109
powder puff 40
powdered milk 137
power 60
power cable 176
power cut 60
practice swing 233
pram 75
praying mantis 295
pregnancy 52
pregnancy test 52
pregnant 52
premature 52
premolar 50
prerecorded 178
prescription 45
present 27
presentation 174
presenter 178
preservative 83
preserved fruit 134
press 178
presser foot 276
press-up 251
pressure valve 61
price 152, 199
price list 154
prickly pear 128
primer 83
primrose 297
principality 315
print 271
print v 172
printer 172, 176
printing 275
prison 181
prison guard 181
private bathroom 100
private jet 211
private room 48
probe 50
problems 271
processed grains 130
procession 27

processor 176
producer 254
program 176
programme 254, 269
programming 178
projector 174
promenade 265
propagate v 91
propeller 211, 214
proposal 174
prosciutto 143
prosecution 180
prostate 21
protractor 165
proud 25
prove v 139
province 315
prow 215
prune 129
prune v 91
psychiatry 49
psychotherapy 55
public address system 209
puck 224
pudding rice 130
Puerto Rico 314
puff pastry 140
pull up v 251
pulp 127
pulse 47
pulses 130
pumice 288
pumice stone 73
pump 207
pumpkin 125
pumpkin seed 131
punch 237
punch bag 237
puncture 203, 207
pup 290
pupil 51, 162
puppy 290
purple 274
purse 37
pushchair 75
putt v 233
putter 233
pyjamas 33
pyramid 164

Q
Qatar 318
quadriceps 16
quail 119
quail egg 137
quart 311
quarter of an hour 304
quarterdeck 214
quartz 289
quay 216
queen 272, 273
question 163
question v 163
quilt 71
quilting 277
quince 128
quinoa 130
quiver 249

R
rabbit 118, 290
raccoon 290
race 234
racecourse 243
racehorse 243
racing bike 205, 206
racing dive 239
racing driver 249
rack 166
racquet 230
racquet games 231
racquetball 231
radar 214, 281
radiator 60, 202
radicchio 123
radio 179, 268
radio antenna 214
radio station 179
radiology 49
radish 124
radius 17, 164
rafter 186
rafting 241
rail 208
rail network 209
rain 287
rainbow 287
rainbow trout 120
raincoat 31, 32
rainforest 285
raisin 129
rake 88
rake v 90
rally 230
rally driving 249
RAM 176
Ramadan 26
ramekin 69
rap 259
rapeseed 184
rapeseed oil 135
rapids 240, 284
rash 44
rasher 119
raspberry 127
raspberry jam 134
rat 290
rattle 74
raw 124, 129
ray 294
razor blade 73
razor-shell 121
read v 162
reading light 210
reading list 168
reading room 168
reamer 80
rear light 207
rear wheel 197
rearview mirror 198
receipt 152
receive v 177
receiver 99
reception 100
receptionist 100, 190
rechargeable drill 78
record 234, 269

record player 268
record shop 115
recording studio 179
rectangle 164
rectum 21
recycling bin 61
red 145, 274
red card 223
red eye 271
red kidney beans 131
red lentils 131
red meat 118
red mullet 120
Red Sea 313
reduce v 172
reel 244
reel in v 245
refectory 168
referee 222, 226
referral 49
reflector 50, 204, 207
reflector strap 205
reflexology 54
refrigerator 67
reggae 259
region 315
register 100
registered post 98
regulator 239
reheat v 154
reiki 55
reins 242
relationships 24
relatives 23
relaxation 55
relay race 235
release v 245
remote control 269
Renaissance 301
renew v 168
rent 58
rent v 58
repair kit 207
report 174
reporter 179
reproduction 20
reproductive 19
reproductive organs 20
reptiles 293
research 169
reserve v 168
respiratory 19
rest 256
restaurant 101, 152
result 49
resurfacing 187
resuscitation 47
retina 51
retire v 26
return 231
return address 98
return date 168
rev counter 201
reverse v 195
reverse charge call 99
rewind 269
rhinoceros 291
rhombus 164

rhubarb 127
rhythmic gymnastics 235
rib 17, 119
rib cage 17
ribbon 27
ribbon 39, 111, 141, 235
ribs 155
rice 130, 158, 184
rice ball 154
rice bowl 64
rice pudding 140
rice vinegar 135
rice wine 152
rider 242
riding boot 242
riding crop 242
riding hat 242
rigging 215, 240
right 260
right field 229
right-hand drive 201
rim 206
rind 119, 127, 136, 142
ring 36
ring finger 15
ring ties 89
rings 235
rinse v 38, 76
ripe 129
rise v 139
river 284
road bike 206
road markings 194
road signs 195
roads 194
roadworks 187, 195
roast 158
roast v 67
roasted 129
robe 38, 169
rock climbing 248
rock concert 258
rock garden 84
rocket 123
rocks 284, 288
Rocky Mountains 312
rococo 301
rodeo 243
roll 139, 311
roll v 67
roller 83, 187
roller blind 63
roller coaster 262
roller skating 249
rollerblading 263
rollerskate 249
rolling pin 69
romance 255
Romania 316
romper suit 30
roof 58, 203
roof garden 84
roof tile 187
roofrack 198
rook 272
room 58
room key 100
room number 100

english

room service 101
rooms 100
root 50, 124, 296
roots 39
rope 248
rose 89, 110, 145
rosé 145
rosemary 133
rotor blade 211
rotten 127
rough 232
round 237
round neck 33
roundabout 195
route number 196
router 78
row 210, 254
row v 241
rower 241
rowing boat 214
rowing machine 250
rubber 163
rubber band 173
rubber boots 89
rubber ring 265
rubber stamp 173
rubbish bin 61, 67
ruby 288
ruck 221
rudder 210, 241
rug 63
rugby 221
rugby pitch 221
rugby strip 221
ruler 163, 165
rum 145
rum and coke 151
rump steak 119
run 228
run v 228
runner bean 122
runway 212
rush 86
Russian Federation 318
Rwanda 317
rye bread 138

S
sad 25
saddle 206, 242
safari park 262
safe 228
safety 75, 240
safety barrier 246
safety goggles 81, 167
safety pin 47
saffron 132
sage 133
Sahara Desert 313
sail 241
sailboat 215
sailing 240
sailor 189
salad 149
salamander 294
salami 142
salary 175
sales assistant 104

sales department 175
salmon 120
saloon 199
salt 64, 152
salted 121, 129, 137, 143
San Marino 316
sand 85, 264
sand v 82
sandal 37
sandals 31
sandcastle 265
sander 78
sandpaper 81, 83
sandpit 263
sandstone 288
sandwich 155
sandwich counter 143
sanitary towel 108
São Tomé and Principe 317
sapphire 288
sardine 120
Sardinia 316
sashimi 121
satellite 281
satellite dish 269
satellite navigation 201
satsuma 126
Saturday 306
Saturn 280
sauce 134, 143, 155
saucepan 69
Saudi Arabia 318
sauna 250
sausage 155, 157
sausages 118
sauté v 67
save v 177, 223
savings 96
savings account 97
savoury 155
saw v 79
saxophone 257
scaffolding 186
scale 121, 256, 294
scales 45, 53, 69, 98, 118,
   166, 212, 293, 310
scallop 121
scalp 39
scalpel 81, 167
scan 48, 52
scanner 106, 176
scarecrow 184
scared 25
scarf 31, 36
schist 288
scholarship 169
school 162, 299
school bag 162
school bus 196
school uniform 162
schoolboy 162
schoolgirl 162
schools 169
science 162, 166
science fiction film 255
scientist 190
scissors 38, 47, 82,188, 276
scoop 68, 149

scooter 205
score 220, 256, 273
score a goal v 223
scoreboard 225
scorpion 295
scotch and water 151
scrabble 272
scramble eggs 157
scrape v 77
scraper 82
screen 59, 63, 97, 176, 255,
   269
screen wash 199
screen wash reservoir 202
screw 80
screwdriver 80
screwdriver bits 80
script 254
scrollbar 177
scrotum 21
scrub v 77
scrum 221
scuba diving 239
sculpting 275
sculptor 191
sea 264, 282
sea bass 120
sea bream 120
sea horse 294
sea lion 290
sea plane 211
seafood 121
seal 290
sealant 83
sealed jar 135
seam 34
seamstress 191
search v 177
seasonal 129
seasons 306
seat 61, 204, 209, 210, 242,
   254
seat back 210
seat belt 198, 211
seat post 206
seating 254
secateurs 89
second 304, 309
second floor 104
second hand 304
second-hand shop 115
section 282
security 212
security bit 80
security guard 189
sedative 109
sedimentary 288
seed 122, 127, 130
seed tray 89
seeded bread 139
seedless 127
seedling 91
seeds 88, 131
seesaw 263
segment 126
self defence 237
self-raising flour 139
self-tanning cream 41

semidetached 58
semi-hard cheese 136
seminal vesicle 21
semi-skimmed milk 136
semi-soft cheese 136
semolina 130
send v 177
send off 223
Senegal 317
sensitive 41
sentence 181
September 306
serve 231
serve v 64, 231
server 176
service included 152
service line 230
service not included 152
service provider 177
service vehicle 212
serving spoon 68
sesame seed 131
sesame seed oil 134
set 178, 230, 254
set v 38
set honey 134
set sail v 217
set square 165
set the alarm v 71
seven 308
seven hundred 308
seventeen 308
seventeenth 309
seventh 309
seventieth 309
seventy 308
sew v 277
sewing basket 276
sewing machine 276
sexually transmitted disease
   20
shade 41
shade plant 87
shallot 125
shallow end 239
shampoo 38
shapes 164
share price 97
shares 97
shark 294
sharp 256
sharpening stone 81
shaving 73
shaving foam 73
shears 89
shed 84
sheep 185
sheep farm 183
sheep's milk 137
sheet 71, 74, 241
shelf 67, 106
shell 129, 137, 265, 293
shelled 129
shelves 66
sherry 145
shiatsu 54
shield 88
shin 12

ship 214
ships 215
shipyard 217
shirt 32
shitake mushrooms 124
shock 47
shocked 25
shoe department 104
shoe shop 114
shoes 34, 37
shoot v 223, 227
shop 298
shop assistant 188
shopping 104
shopping bag 106
shopping centre 104
shops 114
short 32, 321
short sight 51
short wave 179
short-grain 130
shorts 30, 33
shot 151
shotput 234
shoulder 13
shoulder bag 37
shoulder blade 17
shoulder pad 35
shoulder strap 37
shout v 25
shovel 187
shower 72
shower block 266
shower curtain 72
shower door 72
shower gel 73
shower head 72
showjumping 243
shuffle v 273
shutoff valve 61
shutter 58
shutter release 270
shutter-speed dial 270
shuttle bus 197
shuttlecock 231
shy 25
Siberia 313
Sicily 316
side 164
sideline 220
side order 153
side plate 65
side saddle 242
side street 299
sidedeck 240
side-effects 109
sideline 226, 230
Sierra Leone 317
sieve 68, 89
sieve v 91
sift v 138
sigh v 25
sightseeing 260
sign 104
signal 209
signature 96, 98
silencer 203, 204

silk 277
silo 183
silt 85
silver 235, 289
simmer v 67
Singapore 319
singer 191
single 151
single bed 71
single cream 137
single room 100
singles 230
sink 38, 61, 66
sinus 19
siren 94
sirloin steak 119
sister 22
sister-in-law 23
site manager's office 266
sit-up 251
six 308
six hundred 308
sixteen 308
sixteenth 309
sixth 309
sixtieth 309
sixty 308
skate 120, 247, 294
skate v 224
skate wings 120
skateboard 249
skateboarding 249, 263
skein 277
skeleton 17
sketch 275
sketch pad 275
skewer 68
ski 241, 246
ski boot 246
ski jump 247
ski pole 246
ski run 246
ski slope 246
ski suit 246
skier 246
skiing 246
skimmed milk 136
skin 14, 119, 128
skin care 108
skinned 121
skipping 251
skirt 30, 34
skull 17
skydiving 248
skyscraper 299, 300
slalom 247
slate 288
sledding 247
sledgehammer 187
sleeping 74
sleeping bag 267
sleeping compartment 209
sleeping mat 267
sleeping pill 109
sleepsuit 30
sleet 286
sleeve 34
sleeveless 34

slice 119, 139, 140, 230
slice v 67
sliced bread 138
slicer 139
slide 167, 263
slide v 229
sling 46
slip 35
slip road 194
slip-on 37
slippers 31
slope 284
slotted spoon 68
Slovakia 316
Slovenia 316
slow 321
slug 295
small 321
small car 199
small intestine 18
small of back 13
smash 231
smile 25
smoke 95
smoke alarm 95
smoked 118, 121, 143, 159
smoked fish 143
smoking 112
smoking section 152
snack bar 113, 148
snail 295
snake 293
snare drum 257
sneeze 44
snooker 249
snore v 71
snorkel 239
snout 293
snow 287
snowboarding 247
snowmobile 247
snowsuit 30
soak v 130
soap 73, 178
soap dish 73
soccer 222
socket 60, 80
socket wrench 80
socks 33
soda bread 139
soda water 144
sofa 62
sofabed 63
soft 129, 321
soft cheese 136
soft drink 154
soft drinks 144
soft toy 75
software 176
softwood 79
soil 85
solar system 280
solder 79, 80
solder v 79
soldering iron 81
soldier 189
sole 15, 37
solids 164

Soloman Islands 319
soluble 109
solvent 83
Somalia 317
somersault 235
son 22
sonata 256
song 259
son-in-law 22
sorbet 141
sorrel 123
sorting unit 61
soufflé 158
soufflé dish 69
sound boom 179
sound technician 179
soundtrack 255
soup 153, 158
soup bowl 65
soup spoon 65
sour 127
sour cream 137
sourdough bread 139
south 312
South Africa 317
South Korea 318
southern hemisphere 283
Southern Ocean 313
souvenirs 260
sow v 90, 183
soy sauce 135
soya beans 131
space 280
space exploration 281
space shuttle 281
space station 281
space suit 281
spade 88, 265, 273
Spain 316
spanner 80
spare tyre 203
spark plug 203
sparkling 144
sparring 237
sparrow 292
spatula 68, 167
speaker 174, 176, 258, 268
speaker stand 268
spearfishing 245
specials 152
spectators 233
speed boating 241
speed limit 195
speed skating 247
speedboat 214
speedometer 201, 204
spell v 162
sperm 20
sphere 164
spices 132
spicy sausage 142
spider 295
spike v 90
spikes 233
spin 230
spin v 76
spin dryer 76
spinach 123

spine 17
spire 300
spirit level 80, 187
splashback 66
spleen 18
splint 47
splinter 46
split ends 39
split peas 131
spoke 207
sponge 73, 74, 83
sponge cake 140
sponge fingers 141
spool 245
spoon 65
sport fishing 245
sports 105, 220, 236, 248
sports car 198
sports field 168
sports jacket 33
sportsman 191
spotlight 259
sprain 46
spray 109
spray v 91
spray can 311
spray gun 89
spring 71, 307
spring balance 166
spring greens 123
spring onion 125
springboard 235, 238
sprinkler 89
sprinter 234
sprocket 207
square 164, 272, 299
square foot 310
square metre 310
squash 231
squat 251
squid 121, 295
squirrel 290
Sri Lanka 318
St Kitts and Nevis 314
St Lucia 314
St Vincent and the
   Grenadines 314
stabilisers 207
stable 185, 243
stadium 223
staff 175, 256
stage 167, 254
stages 23
stainless steel 79
stair gate 75
staircase 59
stake 90
stake v 91
stalk 122, 297
stalls 254
stamen 297
stamp 98
stamp collecting 273
stamps 112
stance 232
stand 88, 205, 268
stapler 173
staples 173

star 280
star anise 133
starfish 295
starfruit 128
start school v 26
starter 153
starting block 234, 238
starting line 234
state 315
statement 180
stationery 105
statuette 260
steak 121
steam v 67
steam train 208
steamed 159
steeplechase 243
steering wheel 201
stem 111, 112, 297
stencil 83
stenographer 181
step machine 250
stepdaughter 23
stepfather 23
stepladder 82
stepmother 23
stepson 23
stereo 269
sterile 47
stern 240
stethoscope 45
stew 158
stick 224, 249
sticks 133
sticky tape 173
still 144
sting 46, 295
stir v 67
stirrer 150
stirrup 242
stitch 277
stitch selector 276
stitches 52
stock broker 97
stock exchange 97
stockings 35
stocks 97, 110
stomach 18
stomach ache 44
stone 36, 275
stoned fruit 126
stop 269
stop button 197
stopper 166
stopwatch 234
store directory 104
stork 292
storm 287
stout 145
straight 39, 165
straight on 260
straighten v 39
strap 35
strapless 34
stratosphere 286
straw 144, 154
strawberry 127
strawberry milkshake 149

english

english

stream 285
street 298
street corner 298
street light 298
street sign 298
street stall 154
stress 55
stretch 251
stretcher 94
strike 228, 237
string 230, 258
string of pearls 36
strings 256
strip v 82
stroke 44, 233, 239
strokes 231
strong 321
strong flour 139
stub 96
study 63, 162
stuffed 159
stuffed olive 143
stump 225
styles 39, 239, 301
submarine 215
subsoil 91
substitute 223
substitution 223
subtract v 165
suburb 299
succulent 87
suction hose 77
Sudan 317
sugarcane 184
suit 273
sulphur 289
sultana 129
summer 31, 307
summons 180
sumo wrestling 237
Sun 280
sunbathe v 264
sunbed 41
sunblock 108, 265
sunburn 46
Sunday 306
sunflower 184, 297
sunflower oil 134
sunflower seed 131
sunglasses 51, 265
sunhat 30, 265
sunny 286
sunrise 305
sunroof 202
sunscreen 108
sunset 305
sunshine 286
suntan lotion 265
supermarket 106
supersonic jet 211
supplement 55
supply pipe 61
support 187
suppository 109
surf 241
surfboard 241
surfcasting 245
surfer 241

surfing 241
surgeon 48
surgery 45, 48
Suriname 315
surprised 25
sushi 121
suspect 94, 181
suspenders 35
suspension 203, 205
swallow 292
swamp 285
swan 293
Swaziland 317
sweater 33
sweatpants 33
sweatshirt 33
swede 125
Sweden 316
sweep v 77
sweet 124, 127, 155
sweet potato 125
sweet shop 113
sweet spreads 134
sweet trolley 152
sweetcorn 122
sweets 113
swim v 238
swimmer 238
swimming 238
swimming pool 101, 238,
  250
swimsuit 238, 265
swing v 232
swings 263
swiss chard 123
switch 60
Switzerland 316
swivel chair 172
sword 236
swordfish 120, 294
symphony 256
synagogue 300
synchronized swimming 239
synthetic fibre 31
Syria 318
syringe 109, 167
syrup 109
system 176

T
tab 173
table 64, 148
table tennis 231
tablecloth 64
tack v 241, 277
tackle 245
tackle v 220, 223
tackle box 244
tadpole 294
tae-kwon-do 236
tag v 229
tai chi 236
tail 121, 210, 242, 280, 290,
  294
tail light 204
tailbone 17
tailgate 198
tailor 191

tailored 35
tailor's 115
tailor's chalk 276
tailor's dummy 276
tailplane 210
Tajikstan 318
take a bath v 72
take a shower v 72
take notes v 163
take off v 211
take-away 154
talcum powder 73
tall 321
tamarillo 128
tambourine 257
tampon 108
tan 41
tandem 206
tangerine 126
tank 61
Tanzania 317
tap 61, 66
tap water 144
tape dispenser 173
tape measure 80, 276
target 249
target shooting 249
tarmac 187
taro root 124
tarragon 133
Tasmania 319
tattoo 41
tax 96
taxi driver 190
taxi rank 213
tea 144, 149, 184
tea with lemon 149
tea with milk 149
teabag 144
teacher 54, 162, 191
teacup 65
team 220, 229
teapot 65
tear 51
teaspoon 65
teat 75
techniques 79, 159
teddy bear 75
tee 233
teeing ground 232
teenager 23
tee-off v 233
telegram 98
telephone 99, 172
telephone box 99
telescope 281
television series 178
television studio 178
temperature 286
temperature gauge 201
temple 14, 300
ten 308
ten thousand 309
tenant 58
tend v 91
tendon 17
tennis 230
tennis court 230

tennis shoes 231
tenon saw 81
tent 267
tent peg 266
tent pole 266
tenth 309
tequila 145
terminal 212
termite 295
terrace café 148
terraced 58
territory 315
terry nappy 30
test 49
test tube 166
text message 99
textbook 163
Thailand 318
thank you 322
Thanksgiving 27
the day after tomorrow 307
the day before yesterday 307
theatre 254, 299
theme park 262
therapist 55
thermals 267
thermometer 45, 167
thermosphere 286
thermostat 61
thesis 169
thick 321
thigh 12, 119
thimble 276
thin 321
third 309
thirteen 308
thirteenth 309
thirtieth 309
thirty 308
this way up 98
this week 307
thistle 297
thoracic vertebrae 17
thread 276
thread v 277
thread guide 276
thread reel 276
three 308
three hundred 308
three-door 200
three-point line 226
thriller 255
throat 19
throat lozenge 109
throttle 204
through 320
throw 237
throw v 221, 227, 229
throw-in 223, 226
thruster 281
thumb 15
thunder 286
Thursday 306
thyme 133
thyroid gland 18
tibia 17
ticket 209, 213

ticket barrier 209
ticket inspector 209
ticket office 209, 216
tie 32
tiebreak 230
tie-pin 36
tiger 291
tights 35, 251
tile 58, 272
tile v 82
till 106, 150
tiller 240
timber 187
time 234, 304
time out 220
timer 166
times 165, 261
timetable 197, 209, 261
timing 203
tin 289, 311
tinned food 107
tip 36, 122, 246
tissue 108
title 168
titles 23
to 320
toad 294
toast 157
toasted sandwich 149
toaster 66
tobacco 112, 184
today 306
toddler 30
toe 15
toe clip 207
toe strap 207
toenail 15
toffee 113
toggle 31
Togo 317
toilet 72
toilet brush 72
toilet roll 72
toilet seat 72
toiletries 41, 107
toilets 104, 266
toll booth 194
tomato 125, 157
tomato juice 144, 149
tomato sauce 154
tomorrow 306
toner 41
tongs 150, 167
tongue 19, 37, 118
tonic water 144
tonne 310
tool rack 78
toolbar 177
toolbelt 186
toolbox 80
tools 187
tooth 50
toothache 50
toothbrush 72
toothpaste 72
top coat 83
top dress v 90
top tier 141

topaz 288
topiary 87
topping 155
topsoil 85
torch 267
tornado 287
tortoise 293
touch line 221
touchdown 221
tour bus 260
tour guide 260
tourer 205
touring bike 206
tourist 260
tourist attraction 260
tourist bus 197
tourist information 261
tourmaline 288
tournament 233
tow away v 195
tow truck 203
towards 320
towel rail 72
towels 73
tower 300
town 298
town hall 299
townhouse 58
toy 75
toy basket 75
toys 105
track 208, 234
tracksuit 31, 32
tractor 182
traffic 194
traffic jam 195
traffic light 194
traffic policeman 195
trailer 266
train 35, 208
train v 91, 251
train station 208
trainer 37
trainers 31, 251
tram 196, 208
transfer 223
transformer 60
transmission 202
transplant v 91
transport 194
trapezium 164
trapezius 16
trash 177
travel agent 190
travel agent's 114
travel sickness pills 109
traveller's cheque 97
tray 152, 154
tray-table 210
tread 207
tread water v 239
treadmill 250
treble clef 256
tree 86, 296
trekking 243
trellis 84
tremor 283
triangle 164, 257

triceps 16
trifle 141
trim v 39, 90
trimester 52
trimmer 88
Trinidad and Tobago 314
tripod 166, 270, 281
trolley 48, 100, 106, 208, 213
trolley bus 196
trombone 257
tropic of Cancer 283
tropic of Capricorn 283
tropical fruit 128
tropics 283
troposphere 286
trot 243
trough 183
trousers 32, 34
trout 120
trowel 89, 187
truffle 113, 125
trug 88
trumpet 257
truncheon 94
trunk 291, 296
trunks 238
try 221
t-shirt 30, 33
tub 311
tuba 257
tube 311
Tuesday 306
tug boat 215
tulip 111
tumble 235
tumble dryer 76
tumbler 65
tuna 120
tune v 179
tune the radio v 269
tuning peg 258
Tunisia 317
turbocharger 203
turf v 90
Turkey 318
turkey 119, 185, 293
Turkmenistan 318
turmeric 132
turn 238
turn v 79
turn the television off v 269
turn the television on v 269
turnip 124
turpentine 83
turquoise 289
turret 300
turtle 293
tusk 291
tutu 191
tweezers 40, 47, 167
twelfth 309
twelve 308
twentieth 309
twenty 308
twenty minutes 304
twenty thousand 309
twenty-first 309

twenty-one 308
twenty-second 309
twenty-third 309
twenty-two 308
twig 296
twin room 100
twine 89
twins 23
twist ties 89
two 308
two hundred 308
two o'clock 304
two thousand 307
two thousand and one 307
two-door 200
types 199, 205
types of buses 196
types of camera 270
types of farm 183
types of plants 86
types of fishing 245
types of train 208
typhoon 286
tyre 198, 205, 206
tyre lever 207
tyre pressure 203

U
Uganda 317
ugli 126
Ukraine 316
ulna 17
ultrasound 52
ultraviolet rays 286
umbilical cord 52
umbrella 36, 233
umpire 225, 229, 230
uncle 22
unconscious 47
uncooked meat 142
under 320
under par 233
undercoat 83
underexposed 271
undergraduate 169
underground map 209
underground train 209
underpass 194
underwear 32, 35
underwired 35
uniform 94, 189
United Arab Emirates 318
United Kingdom 316
United States of America 314
universe 280
university 299
unleaded 199
unpasteurised 137
unpick v 277
unsalted 137
until 320
up 320
upper circle 254
upset 25
Uranus 280
ureter 21
urethra 20
urinary 19

urology 49
Uruguay 315
usher 255
uterus 20, 52
utility room 76
Uzbekistan 318

V
vacuum cleaner 77, 188
vacuum flask 267
vagina 20
valance 71
valley 284
valve 207
vanilla 132
Vanuatu 319
varnish 79, 83
vas deferens 21
vase 63, 111
Vatican City 316
vault 235, 300
veal 118
vegetable garden 85
vegetable oil 135
vegetable plot 182
vegetables 107, 122, 124
veggie burger 155
veil 35
vein 19
venetian blind 63
Venezuela 315
venison 118
vent 283
ventouse cup 53
Venus 280
verdict 181
vest 33, 35, 251
vet 189
vibraphone 257
vice 78
video game 269
video phone 99
video recorder 269
video tape 269
Viet Nam 318
viewfinder 271
village 299
vine 183
vinegar 135, 142
vineyard 183
vintage 199
viola 256
violin 256
virus 44
visa 213
vision 51
visiting hours 48
visor 205
vitamins 108
v-neck 33
vocal cords 19
vodka 145
vodka and orange 151
voice message 99
volcano 283
volley 231
volleyball 227
voltage 60

volume 165, 179, 269, 311
vomit v 44

W
waders 244
waffles 157
waist 12
waistband 35
waistcoat 33
waiter 148, 152
waiting room 45
waitress 191
wake up v 71
walk 243
walking boot 37
walking boots 267
walkway 212
wall 58, 186, 222
wall light 62
wallet 37
wallpaper 82, 177
wallpaper v 82
wallpaper brush 82
wallpaper paste 82
walnut 129
walnut oil 134
walrus 290
ward 48
wardrobe 70
warehouse 216
warm 286
warm up v 251
warrant 180
wash v 38, 77
washbasin 72
washer 80
washer-dryer 76
washing machine 76
wasp 295
waste disposal 61, 266
waste disposal unit 61
waste pipe 61
wastebasket 172
watch 36
watch television v 269
water 144, 238
water v 90, 183
water bottle 206, 267
water chamber 61
water chestnut 124
water closet 61
water garden 84
water hazard 232
water jet 95
water plant 86
water polo 239
watercolour paints 274
watercress 123
waterfall 285
watering 89
watering can 89
watermelon 127
waterproofs 245, 267
waterskier 241
waterskiing 241
watersports 241
wave 241, 264
wavelength 179

english

wax 41
weak 321
weather 286
weaving 277
website 177
wedding 26, 35
wedding cake 141
wedding dress 35
wedding reception 26
wedge 233
Wednesday 306
weed v 91
weed killer 91
weeds 86
week 306
weekend 306
weekly 307
weigh v 310
weight 166, 244
weight bar 251
weight belt 239
weight training 251
wellington boots 31
west 312
western 255
Western sahara 317
wet 286, 321
wet wipe 75, 108
wetsuit 239
whale 290
wheat 130, 184
wheel 198, 207
wheel nuts 203
wheelbarrow 88
wheelchair 48
wheelchair access 197
whiplash 46
whipped cream 137
whisk 68
whisk v 67
whiskers 290
whisky 145
white 39, 145, 272, 274
white bread 139
white chocolate 113
white coffee 148
white currant 127
white flour 138
white meat 118
white rice 130
white spirit 83
whiting 120
whole 129, 132
whole milk 136
wholegrain 131
wholegrain mustard 135
wholemeal bread 139
wholemeal flour 138
wicket 225
wicket-keeper 225
wide 321
widescreen television 269
width 165
wife 22
wig 39
wild rice 130
willow 296
win v 273

wind 241, 286
windbreak 265
windcheater 33
windlass 214
window 58, 96, 98, 177, 186,
 197, 209, 240
windpipe 18
windscreen 198
windscreen wiper 198
windshield 205
windsurfer 241
windsurfing 241
windy 286
wine 145, 151
wine glass 65
wine list 152
wine vinegar 135
wing 119, 210, 293
wing mirror 198
wings 254
winner 273
winter 31, 307
winter sports 247
wipe v 77
wire 79
wire cutter 80
wire strippers 81
wire wool 81
wires 60
with 320
withdrawal slip 96
without 320
witness 180
wok 69
wolf 290
woman 23
womb 52
women's clothing 34
women's wear 105
wood 79, 233, 275, 285
wood glue 78
wood shavings 78
wooden spoon 68
woodpecker 292
woodstain 79
woodwind 257
woodworking 275
wool 277
work 172
work day 306
workbench 78
workshop 78
worktop 66
world map 312
worm 295
worried 25
wound 46
wrap 155
wrapping 111
wreath 111
wrench 81, 203
wrestling 236
wrinkle 15
wrist 13, 15
wristband 230
writ 180
write v 162

X
x-ray 48
x-ray film 50
x-ray machine 212
x-ray viewer 45

Y
yacht 215, 240
yam 125
yard 310
yawn v 25
year 163, 306
yeast 138
yellow 274
yellow card 223
Yemen 318
yes 322
yesterday 306
yoga 54
yoghurt 137
yolk 137, 157
you're welcome 322
Yugoslavia 316

Z
Zambia 317
zebra 291
zero 308
zest 126
Zimbabwe 317
zinc 289
zip 277
zone 315
zones 283
zoo 262
zoology 169
zoom lens 270

english

謝辞 shaji • acknowledgments

DORLING KINDERSLEY would like to thank Tracey Miles and Christine Lacey for design assistance, Georgina Garner for editorial and administrative help, Sonia Gavira, Polly Boyd, and Cathy Meeus for editorial help, and Claire Bowers for compiling the DK picture credits.

The publisher would like to thank the following for their kind permission to reproduce their photographs:
Abbreviations key:
t=top, b=bottom, r=right, l=left, c=centre

Abode: 62; **Action Plus:** 224bc; **alamy. com:** 154t; A.T. Willett 287bcl; Michael Foyle 184bl; Stock Connection 287bcr; **Allsport/Getty Images:** 238cl; **Alvey and Towers:** 209 acr, 215bcl, 215bcr, 241cr; **Peter Anderson:** 188cbr, 271br. **Anthony Blake Photo Library:** Charlie Stebbings 114cl; John Sims 114tcl; **Andyalte:** 98tl; **apple mac computers:** 268tcr; **Arcaid:** John Edward Linden 301bl; Martine Hamilton Knight, Architects: Chapman Taylor Partners, 213cl; Richard Bryant 301br; **Argos:** 41tcl, 66cbl, 66cl, 66br, 66bcl, 69cl, 70bcl, 71t, 71tl, 269tc, 270tl; **Axiom:** Eitan Simanor 105bcr; Ian Cumming 104; Vicki Couchman 148cr; **Beken Of Cowes Ltd:** 215cbc; **Bosch:** 76tcr, 76tc, 76tcl; **Camera Press:** 27c, 38tr, 256t, 257cr; Barry J. Holmes 148tr; Jane Hanger 159cr; Mary Germanou 259bc; **Corbis:** 78b; Anna Clopet 247tr; Bettmann 181tl, 181tr; Bo Zauders 156t; Bob Rowan 152bl; Bob Winsett 247cbl; Brian Bailey 247br; Carl and Ann Purcell 162l; Chris Rainer 247ctl; ChromoSohm Inc. 179tr; Craig Aurness 215bl; David H.Wells 249cbr; Dennis Marsico 274bl; Dimitri Lundt 236bc; Duomo 211tl; Gail Mooney 277ctcr; George Lepp 248c; Gunter Marx 248cr; Jack Fields 210b; Jack Hollingsworth 231bl; Jacqui Hurst 277ccr; James L. Amos 247bl, 191ctr, 220bcr; Jan Butchofsky 277cbc; Johnathan Blair 243cr; Jon Feingersh 153tr; Jose F. Poblete 191br; Jose Luis Pelaez.Inc 153tc, 175tl; Karl Weatherly 220bl, 247tcr; Kelly Mooney Photography 259tl; Kevin Fleming 259bc; Kevin R. Morris 105tr, 243tl, 243tc; Kim Sayer 249tcr; Lynn Goldsmith 258t; Macduff Everton 231bcl; Mark Gibson 249bl; Mark L. Stephenson 249tcl; Michael Pole 115tr; Michael S. Yamashita 247ctcl; Mike King 247cbl; Neil Rabinowitz 214br; Owen Franken 112t; Pablo Corral 115bc; Paul A. Sounders 169br, 249ctcl;

Paul J. Sutton 224c, 224br; Peter Turnley 105tcr; Phil Schermeister 227b, 248tr; R. W Jones 309; R.W. Jones 175tr; Richard Hutchings 168b; Rick Doyle 241tctr; Robert Holmes 97br, 277ctc; Roger Ressmeyer 169tr; Russ Schleipman 229; Steve Raymer 169tr; The Purcell Team 211ctr; Tim Wright 178; Vince Streano 194t; Wally McNamee 220br, 220bcl, 224bl; Yann Arhus-Bertrand 249tl; **Demetrio Carrasco / Dorling Kindersley (c) Herge / Les Editions Casterman:** 112ccl; **Dixons:** 270cl, 270cr, 270bl, 270bcl, 270bcr, 270ccr; **Education Photos:** John Walmsley 26tl; **Empics Ltd:** Adam Day 236br; Andy Heading 243c; Steve White 249cbc; **Getty Images:** 48bcl, 100t, 114bcr, 154bl, 287tr; 94tr; **Dennis Gilbert:** 106tc; **Hulsta:** 70t; **Ideal Standard Ltd:** 72r; **The Image Bank/ Getty Images:** 58; Johnny Arthur 190tl; Philip Achache 246t; **The Interior Archive:** Henry Wilson, Alfie's Market 114bl; Luke White, Architect: David Mikhail, 59tl; Simon Upton, Architect: Phillippe Starck, St Martins Lane Hotel 100bcr, 100br; **Jason Hawkes Aerial Photography:** 216t; **Dan Johnson:** 26cbl, 35r; **Kos Pictures Source:** 215cbl, 240tc, 240tr; David Williams 216b; **Lebrecht Collection:** Kate Mount 169bc; **MP Visual.com:** Mark Swallow 202t; **NASA:** 280cr, 280cl, 281tl; **P&O Princess Cruises:** 214bl; **P A Photos:** 181br; **The Photographers' Library:** 186bl, 186bc, 186t; **Plain and Simple Kitchens:** 66t; **Powerstock Photolibrary:** 169tl, 256t, 287tc; **Rail Images:** 208c, 208 cbl, 209br; **Red Consultancy:** Odeon cinemas 257br; **Redferns:** 259br; Nigel Crane 259c; **Rex Features:** 106br, 259tr, 259tr, 259bl, 280b; Charles Ommaney 114tcr; J.F.F Whitehead 243cl; Patrick Barth 101tl; Patrick Frilet 189cbl; Scott Wiseman 287bl; **Royalty Free Images:** Getty Images/Eyewire 154bl; **Science & Society Picture Library:** Science Museum 202b; **Skyscan:** 168t, 182c, 298; Quick UK Ltd 212; Sony: 268bc; **Robert Streeter:** 154br; **Neil Sutherland:** 82tr, 83tl, 90t, 118, 188ctr, 196tl, 196tr, 299cl, 299bl; **The Travel Library:** Stuart Black 264t; **Travelex:** 97cl; **Vauxhall:** Technik 198t, 199tl, 199tr, 199cl, 199cr, 199ctcl, 199ctcr, 199tcl, 199tcr, 200; **View Pictures:** Dennis Gilbert, Architects: ACDP Consulting, 106t; Dennis Gilbert, Chris Wilkinson Architects, 209tr; Peter Cook, Architects: Nicholas Crimshaw and partners,

208t; **Betty Walton:** 185br;

Colin Walton: 2, 4, 7, 9, 10, 28, 42, 56, 92, 95c, 99tl, 99tcl, 102, 116, 120t, 138t, 146, 150t, 160, 170, 191tctl, 192, 218, 252, 260br, 260l, 261tr, 261c, 261cl, 271cbl, 271cbr, 271tcl, 278, 287br, 302, 401.

DK PICTURE LIBRARY:
Akhil Bahkshi; Patrick Baldwin; Geoff Brightling; British Museum; John Bulmer; Andrew Butler; Joe Cornish; Brian Cosgrove; Andy Crawford and Kit Hougton; Philip Dowell; Alistair Duncan; Gables; Bob Gathany; Norman Hollands; Kew Gardens; Peter James Kindersley; Vladimir Kozlik; Sam Lloyd; London Northern Bus Company Ltd; Tracy Morgan; David Murray and Jules Selmes; Musée Vivant du Cheval, France; Museum of Broadcast Communications; Museum of Natural History; NASA; National History Museum; Norfolk Rural Life Museum; Stephen Oliver; RNLI; Royal Ballet School; Guy Ryecart; Science Museum; Neil Setchfield; Ross Simms and the Winchcombe Folk Police Museum; Singapore Symphony Orchestra; Smart Museum of Art; Tony Souter; Erik Svensson and Jeppe Wikstrom; Sam Tree of Keygrove Marketing Ltd; Barrie Watts; Alan Williams; Jerry Young.

Additional Photography by Colin Walton.

Colin Walton would like to thank:
A&A News, Uckfield; Abbey Music, Tunbridge Wells; Arena Mens Clothing, Tunbridge Wells; Burrells of Tunbridge Wells; Gary at Di Marco's; Jeremy's Home Store, Tunbridge Wells; Noakes of Tunbridge Wells; Ottakar's, Tunbridge Wells; Selby's of Uckfield; Sevenoaks Sound and Vision; Westfield, Royal Victoria Place, Tunbridge Wells.

All other images are Dorling Kindersley copyright. For further information see www. dkimages.com

日本語 nihongo • english